DINNER
with the
PRESIDENT

★ DINNER ★
— with the —
PRESIDENT

FOOD, POLITICS, and a
HISTORY of BREAKING BREAD
at the WHITE HOUSE

Alex Prud'homme

ALFRED A. KNOPF · New York

2023

THIS IS A BORZOI BOOK
PUBLISHED BY ALFRED A. KNOPF

Copyright © 2023 by Alex Prud'homme

All rights reserved. Published in the United States by Alfred A. Knopf,
a division of Penguin Random House LLC, New York, and distributed in Canada
by Penguin Random House Canada Limited, Toronto.

www.aaknopf.com

Grateful acknowledgment is made to Alfred Music for permission to reprint lyric
excerpt from "The Room Where It Happens" (from the Broadway musical *Hamilton*),
words and music by Lin-Manuel Miranda. Copyright © 2015 by 5000 Broadway Music
(ASCAP). All rights administered by WC Music Corp. All rights reserved.
Reprinted by permission of Alfred Music.

Library of Congress Cataloging-in-Publication Data:
Names: Prud'homme, Alex, author.
Title: Dinner with the president : food, politics, and a history of
breaking bread at the White House / Alex Prud'homme.
Description: First edition. | New York : Alfred A. Knopf, 2023. |
"This is a Borzoi Book published by Alfred A. Knopf." |
Includes bibliographical references and index.
Identifiers: LCCN 2022018067 | ISBN 9781524732219 (hardcover) |
ISBN 9781524732226 (ebook)
Subjects: LCSH: White House (Washington, D.C.)—Miscellanea. |
Presidents—United States—Biography. | Food—Political aspects—
United States. | Food habits—United States.
Classification: LCC E176.1 .P978 2023 | DDC 973.09/9 23/eng/20220—dc07
LC record available at https://lccn.loc.gov/2022018067

Front-of-jacket images: (top) President Kennedy makes a toast at a State
Dinner, 1963. Corbis / Getty Images; (bottom) President Dwight Eisenhower
Inauguration Lunch, 1957. AP Images.
Jacket design by John Gall

Manufactured in the United States of America
First Edition

For Erica C. Prud'homme,
who inspired my love of food and cooking,
and Hector P. Prud'homme,
who inspired my love of history and politics

The kitchen is where we deal with the elements of the universe.
It is where we come to understand our past and ourselves.

—Laura Esquivel

The destiny of nations depends on the manner
in which they nourish themselves.

—Jean Anthelme Brillat-Savarin,
The Physiology of Taste

Nothing is more political than food. Nothing.

—Anthony Bourdain

Contents

Introduction

At the President's Table

Th: Jefferson presents his compliments to The Hon'ble Doct. Mitchell and requests the favour of his company to dinner on wednesday 2y first next at half after three o'clock. or at whatever eater hour the House may rise

The favour of an answer is requested.

I. In the Dining Room Where It Happened
(How the Sausage Gets Made)

It is hard to remain enemies when you've broken bread together.
—New Testament

On the evening of June 20, 1790, Alexander Hamilton and James Madison arrived at a modest house on Maiden Lane in lower Manhattan for a secret dinner. As their host, Thomas Jefferson, ushered the rivals into his drawing room, Hamilton, President George Washington's Treasury secretary, and Madison, a shrewd Virginia congressman, could barely look at each other. Ignoring the tension, Jefferson poured each a glass of Hermitage, a fine white wine the French called *doux et liquoreux* (sweet and liquory). As they settled in, mouthwatering aromas—of capon and chestnuts simmered in cream, root vegetables roasted in olive oil, beef braised in red wine and herbs—suffused the room. In the kitchen, James

Hemings, a slave chef who had trained under some of Paris's finest cooks, was conjuring a sumptuous meal designed to open the antagonists' minds and lull them into a state of amenable pliability.

Jefferson was Washington's secretary of state, a former ambassador to France, and a skilled host who understood how to use food and drink to build political consensus. In most societies the dining table is considered a neutral place where conversations can be had, grievances aired, laughter shared, and alliances built outside the usual conventions. It is a strategy as old as mankind. "Breaking bread" is an ancient phrase that refers to the primal activity of humans eating food with others. Everyone must eat to survive, after all, and social dining helps to define us as human beings; we seem to *need* to converse over food, even when we disagree with each other.

The stakes could not have been higher that night in New York. Washington's presidency was just a year old, and American democracy was more hopeful experiment than fully functioning political system. Many special interest groups were vying to shape the structure of government. The quarrel between Hamilton—a Federalist aligned with northern states—and Madison—a Virginia slaveholder who personified southern Democratic-Republicans—revolved around "two of the most irritating questions that ever can be raised," Hamilton said: how to pay off America's Revolutionary War debts and where to build a new federal city. These arguments seem obscure today but were so divisive in 1790 that the Republic was tipping toward an existential crisis.

Jefferson was quietly aligned with Madison, a fellow Democratic-Republican from Virginia, but he was also a pragmatist who feared the men's rift could lead to "a dissolution of our union at this incipient stage [which] I should deem . . . the most unfortunate of all consequences."

This was not hyperbole. The day before, he had spotted the usually sharp Hamilton lingering in front of Washington's house on Broadway looking "sombre, haggard, and dejected beyond description." The Treasury secretary confided that he was about to tender his resignation. Taken aback, Jefferson asked Hamilton to pause and "dine with me" before taking such a rash step.

"I thought it impossible," Jefferson wrote, "that reasonable men, consulting together coolly, could fail, by mutual sacrifice of opinion, to form a compromise which was to save the union." Affecting a carefree air, Jefferson meticulously planned the evening. (The only record of this dinner comes from his notes, which were likely written with an eye to posterity.

This account is based on a reconstruction by the historian Charles A. Cerami.)

As Hamilton and Madison polished off their glasses of Hermitage, Jefferson ushered them into the dining room, where they encountered their first surprise: the offer to sit wherever they pleased rather than at assigned seats, as traditional British etiquette dictated. Further, they were seated at a round rather than rectangular table, to avoid any implied hierarchy. These details were part of Jefferson's effort to construct a more egalitarian, "American" code of conduct. Finally, in place of human waiters the food was served by "dumbwaiters," a set of squat rectangular shelves next to each diner, which held the meal's four courses. (As the men finished each plate, they placed their dirty dishes on the dumbwaiter and retrieved the next course.) Imported from France, the dumbwaiters were the latest in gastrotechnology, and a symbol of Jefferson's worldliness. The devices made "the attendance of servants entirely unnecessary," explained the pundit Margaret Bayard Smith. "When he . . . wished to enjoy a free and unrestricted flow of conversation . . . [Jefferson used dumbwaiters] believing . . . that much of the domestic and even public discord was produced by the mutilated and misconstructed repetition of free conversation . . . by these mute but not inattentive listeners."

The dinner likely began with a green salad dressed with wine jelly, an inventive combination of Madeira, milk, lemon juice, sugar, and gelatin. Jefferson was a renowned gardener who ate an unusually vegetable-forward diet for his day. He was also a knowledgeable oenophile with a famous cellar. With the salad, he poured a Carbonnieux, a white Bordeaux. As they ate, the men chatted about many things—farming, architecture, Virginia, France (though not of the Revolution, which they disagreed on)—but left aside the burning questions that had brought them together that evening.

Hemings's second course was capon stuffed with Virginia ham, chestnut puree, artichoke bottoms, and truffles simmered in chicken stock, white wine, and cream, napped with a reduction of calvados, the fiery apple brandy of Normandy. Here Jefferson likely poured a Montepulciano, a robust Italian red wine that counterpointed the dish's rich, layered flavors. The third course was *boeuf à la mode,* a luxuriant, deeply flavored beef roast braised in wine, brandy, tomatoes, and aromatic herbs. This slow-cooked amalgam of proteins, collagens, vegetables, and alcohol was designed to further ease Hamilton and Madison into an open frame of mind. For insurance, Jefferson poured a bottle of Chambertin, a dark, complex Grand Cru Burgundy known as "the King of Wines."

After a palate cleanser of meringues and macaroons, the next surprise was dessert: vanilla ice cream encased in a warm puff-pastry crust. Ice cream was a rare delicacy at the time, and this pièce de résistance—akin to a modern baked Alaska—gave the startling impression that the cold confection had just been removed from a hot oven. It was Jefferson's signature dessert, one he reserved for special occasions. Hemings had mastered the recipe in Paris, and even the reticent Madison beamed when he took a bite. Jefferson paired the dessert with a *champagne non-mousseux,* an unusual cloudy champagne without bubbles. (A wine Jefferson had introduced to President Washington, which helped solidify their friendship despite their differences.)

As dinner concluded it was time to get down to political horse-trading. Hamilton and Madison's disagreement had become an overheated, emotional public argument, but at heart it was a cold calculus about money and power.

The first question they addressed was the "assumption" of the nation's debt. Washington needed a sound financial system to borrow from Europe and pay off America's $25 million in war loans. Without it, his new country risked financial collapse. But Hamilton and Madison disagreed on how to structure such a system. Hamilton favored a centralized government that would impose taxes and "assume" (absorb) the costs of war into the national debt, which would make America an attractive investment; the states would then pay into a federal debt repayment plan. Madison favored decentralized governance, with no federal taxation, and feared Hamilton's approach—"a bitter pill to Virginia and other states that had already paid most of their wartime debt"—would turn America into a monarchy.

Neither man would budge at first. But the longer they steeped in Jefferson's exquisite food, drink, and cajolery, far from the usual political pressures, the closer the rivals edged toward compromise. Hamilton wondered if adjusting the debt assessment downward might mollify southern states. That would be a step in the right direction, Madison replied. But his constituents would need something more in return—such as a new federal city in a southern state.

This raised the evening's second trick question: where to site the permanent capital of the United States. While the Constitution mandated the building of a new federal city, it did not specify its location. New

York was the temporary seat of government, and some favored keeping it there, but others, hungry for the prestige conferred by hosting the capital, had suggested sixteen other sites dotting the map from Philadelphia to Charlottesville. The debate over this question had escalated to the point of no return.

Over snifters of Jefferson's brandy, Hamilton and Madison agreed to take a step back. Acknowledging the rhetoric had grown so heated that further public debate was meaningless, they agreed to hammer together a deal in private. By the end of the night, Hamilton had consented to move the capital from New York to Philadelphia for ten years, while a new federal city was established on a "southern" site. In return, Madison would allow Hamilton to assume $35 million of state debts into the national debt, making the federal government the chief taxation authority and establishing America's credit in Europe. When Hamilton agreed to revise the debt balance, saving Virginia $13 million (a key fact that Jefferson omitted from his account), Madison promised to deliver the necessary votes. Over the summer congressmen on both sides switched their positions and passed the Funding Act (the assumption of states' debts) and the Residence Act (the new permanent capital).

Known as the Dinner Table Bargain, the agreement was a coup for all three participants, but especially Jefferson. With toothsome food and wine, and a deft juggling of egos and political calculations, he had helped save the Union and, not incidentally, enhanced his own standing.

When word of "the great compromise" leaked out, it was hailed as a watershed moment in the nation's evolution. Though Jefferson would gripe the deal was "unjust," and was "acquiesced in merely from a fear of disunion," others were more sanguine. "There is no single state paper in the history of the U.S., with the exception of the Emancipation Proclamation, which was of such immense importance and produced such wide and far-reaching results," noted Senator Henry Cabot Lodge.

The Dinner Table Bargain continues to reverberate today. Questions about state's rights, the role of the federal government, and backroom political machinations have not gone away. But in 2020, the coronavirus revealed there is strength in working together and weakness in disunion. Jefferson's 1790 dinner and its lessons have gained new cultural cachet thanks to Lin-Manuel Miranda's 2015 musical, *Hamilton,* which memorialized Jefferson's gastro-political feat from the perspective of a jealous Aaron Burr, who was not invited. In the song "The Room Where It Happens," Burr raps, in part,

Now Madison and Jefferson are merciless
Well, hate the sin love the sinner

. . .

But decisions are happening over dinner
Two Virginians and an immigrant walk into a room
Diametrically opposed
Foes
They emerge with a compromise,
Having open doors that were previously closed
Bros
The immigrant emerges with unprecedented financial power
A system he can shape however he wants
The Virginians emerge with the nation's capital
And here's the pièce de résistance
No one else was in the room where it happened
The room where it happened
The room where it happened

. . .

No one really knows how the game is played
The art of the trade
How the sausage gets made
We just assume that it happens
But no one else is in the room where it happens

. . .

Click boom! Then it happened.

II. *Eating at the White House*

You can't even consider the history of the White House
without realizing that the common denominator is the dinner table.
—William Seale, *The President's House*

Like any other house, the White House runs on food. But no other building represents the presidency, or is subject to as much scrutiny, as 1600 Pennsylvania Avenue. It is at once a home, a busy office, a social hub, a decorative arts museum, the only residence of a national leader that invites the public inside, a "fortress disguised as a home" Michelle Obama said, and, as Jackie Kennedy put it, "an emblem of the American Republic." In short, the Executive Mansion is the most powerful house in the world. And so it follows that the meals and food policies created there are among the most influential in history.

In the same vein, the president is both a symbol of the nation and a flesh-and-blood human being, and his food choices bridge those disparate roles. What he eats determines his health and sets an example for the nation. How his food is prepared, by whom, and the context of his meals semaphore his priorities. His policies and the way he pulls governmental levers influence the flow of goods and services to millions of Americans and to billions of people around the world. His messaging about food touches on everything from personal taste to global nutrition, politics, economics, science, and war—not to mention race, class, gender, money, religion, history, culture, and many other things.

Hardly frivolous, a meal at the White House is never simply a meal: it is a forum for politics and entertainment on the highest level. One of the main duties of the president and First Lady—sometimes referred to as the First Host and Hostess—is to welcome guests into their home. They do this nearly every day, in ways large and small. These affairs are an integral and important, if little noticed, tool of government.

Food is sustenance and metaphor, and who has a seat at the table, and who does not, matters. While the pardon of a Thanksgiving turkey or a visit from a school group requires minimal work, an inauguration or state dinner can take months of planning, cost millions of taxpayers' dollars, and significantly impact an administration. Canny leaders such as the two Roosevelts and Dwight D. Eisenhower understood that their choice of guests, food, and entertainment can influence and amplify their agenda. Less savvy men, such as Andrew Johnson, Warren Harding, and Gerald Ford, have discovered that a single drunken speech, poor choice of guests, or terrible food can undermine their legacy. There is another aspect of White House life that people rarely consider but can be revealing: the intimate gatherings of the First Family behind the scenes. How presidential couples have balanced, or failed to balance, their public and private lives is often more fraught than it appears, and can have high political stakes. I didn't know any of this when I stumbled over the idea for this book, almost by chance.

IT WAS A HOT, humid, blindingly bright Thursday in August 2016 when I made my way through a side door, past security checkpoints, and into the White House. I had been invited to discuss the role of freshwater in the twenty-first century, the subject of my book *The Ripple Effect,* with mid-level staff. Before my meeting, a friend who worked in the Obama administration invited me to join him for lunch.

We met in the White House Mess (often called the Navy Mess), a low-ceilinged, wood-paneled restaurant on the ground floor of the West Wing, adjacent to the Situation Room. It is essentially a small cafeteria, albeit the most unusual cafeteria in the universe. The walls are decorated with paintings of men-o'-war, and the galley is manned by navy stewards—a holdover from the days of presidential yachts (the last of which, the *Sequoia,* was sold by Jimmy Carter in 1977). My friend ordered the lunch special—jambalaya, a fragrant stew of garlic, tomatoes, peppers, okra, andouille, shrimp, and strong seasoning that smelled enticing. I am normally an adventurous eater and would have joined him, but worried that my larynx wouldn't survive the Cajun spice bath, I ordered a more timid Caesar salad. As we finished, my friend offered to guide me on a quick tour of the mansion.

Like many Americans, I had visited the capital plenty of times but had never gotten around to taking a White House tour, and I jumped at the chance. It was a stroke of luck.

THE WHITE HOUSE, also known as the People's House, is a familiar image, but walking through the building can be disorienting. It is a large space divided into many smaller ones. The building stands 168 feet long, 152 feet wide, and 70 feet high (on the south side, where it is built into a gently sloping hill), with an internal volume of 55,000 square feet stacked in six floors that encompass 132 rooms—including 16 family or guest rooms, 35 bathrooms, 1 main kitchen, 1 pastry kitchen, and 1 family kitchen in the president's private quarters. The building sits on 18.7 acres of heavily manicured and defended property in the middle of the urban sprawl that is twenty-first-century Washington, D.C.

On the day of my visit, the Obamas were vacationing on Martha's Vineyard, and the normally buzzing mansion was hushed and shadowy. There were no public tours under way. Many of the lights were dimmed and rugs were rolled up. As we traversed hallways, our footsteps echoed off its solid wood, marble, and plaster surfaces. On the State Floor (the first floor), we crossed the white-and-pink marble Entrance Hall, where Jefferson had displayed animal pelts collected by Lewis and Clark, and Andrew Jackson had showcased a giant, malodorous cheese that was

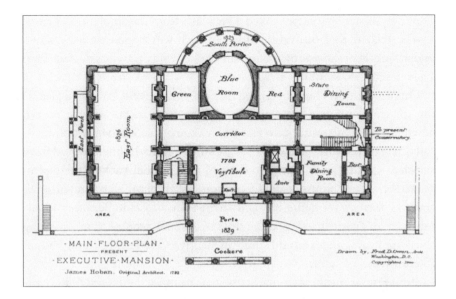

devastated by a ravenous mob. We walked through the East Room, where Abigail Adams hung her laundry to dry and where the body of Abraham Lincoln and six other presidents had lain in state. In the cream and red-hued China Room Room, cabinets displayed rows of elegant White House porcelain, the "state service," whose symbolic patterns have been chosen by First Ladies for more than two centuries. (Chipped and broken pieces are destroyed, and were once thrown into the Potomac River, to keep the collection sacrosanct and out of the hands of souvenir hunters.)

In the West Wing, I peeked into the Oval Office, which is more impressive in person than in photographs. Through a door adjacent to the Resolute desk, I could see the President's Dining Room, a private retreat where chief executives have huddled with advisers, heads of state, or family since William Howard Taft (at some 350 pounds, our heaviest leader) built "the Oval." Down a hallway is the State Dining Room, where Ulysses S. Grant liked to shoot bread balls at his children and hosted America's first state dinner for a foreign leader in 1874.

The Obama White House had a reputation as a foodie kind of place. The president was raised in Hawaii and Indonesia, had a taste for challenging dishes, and was known to slip out on dates with his wife to trendy restaurants. Michelle Obama had planted an eleven-hundred-square-foot vegetable garden on the South Lawn in 2009, which played at least two roles: it provided fresh produce for her family and charities, and it was a political statement about the importance of healthy eating in a time of obesity, a stance that provoked a backlash from corporate food giants. It was striking that the White House, which was largely built by slaves and where generations of slaves had cooked, was now home to a First Lady descended from slaves.

On the Ground Floor, I glanced into the Executive Kitchen—a gleaming and well-equipped but surprisingly tight space, just twenty-seven and a half feet long by twenty-two feet wide. The cooks and their assistants—Filipina, Black, white—dressed in toques and starched whites, moved from stainless-steel sink to counter to stove in a silent, focused choreography.

As the White House unfolded around us, the bronze busts and portraits of former residents brought them to life as complex individuals rather than as idealized, godlike figures. I could picture them roaming those hallways, and I would discover nearly every one of them had an interesting food story.

Presidential meals often had personal meaning, and sometimes contained coded political messages. James Garfield and Dwight Eisenhower liked bowls of squirrel soup. William Howard Taft had a taste for possum. Zachary Taylor died after eating cherries and drinking cold milk. Woodrow Wilson had chronic indigestion and consumed dubious elixirs, yet he and Herbert Hoover saved millions of lives with innovative food policies. The gourmand Theodore Roosevelt and his gourmet cousin Franklin D. Roosevelt led the nation over bison steaks and terrapin soups. (A gourmand is someone who eats and drinks to wretched excess. A gourmet is a connoisseur of fine dining.) JFK liked clam chowder, LBJ favored chili, Richard Nixon ate cottage cheese almost every day, and George W. Bush liked ballpark hot dogs.

The presidents' food choices reflected the state of the nation. Yet Americans no longer eat many of those things, and a dish considered the very height of sophistication in one era can seem dull, quaint, or repulsive in another. I came to think of presidential menus as something like tree rings: their ingredients, recipes, and techniques are mini histories of how the country has evolved over time.

After the tour I stood alone in a hallway for a minute, when the enormity of the building's history struck me with an almost palpable force. It seemed to reverberate from deep inside the thick walls and solid parquet floors and gave me a jolt. I wasn't the only one who has felt this way, it turns out: Harry Truman swore the place was haunted, and a guard told me that some visitors are so overwhelmed by the building they become physically sick or pass out.

∙ ∙ ∙

AT THE TIME, I had recently finished writing *The French Chef in America,* a book about how Julia Child became our first celebrity television cook and helped launch the American gastronomic revolution of the 1960s and 1970s. While piecing the story together, I discovered that Julia had visited the White House numerous times, made TV documentaries about two significant dinners there, and was an outspoken promoter of the Executive Kitchen.

Julia's husband, Paul Child, was the twin brother of my grandfather Charles Child, and I grew up listening to their stories around the dinner table. Between 1948 and 1961, Paul served as a cultural attaché to American embassies in France, Germany, and Norway, and Julia was a diplomatic spouse. She studied French cookery in Paris and coauthored *Mastering the Art of French Cooking,* the seminal recipe book published in 1961 (and still in print). In 1963, Julia appeared on public television in *The French Chef* and within four years had won her first Emmy and a Peabody, and appeared on the cover of *Time* magazine.

It was then, in 1967, that Julia and Paul approached President Lyndon

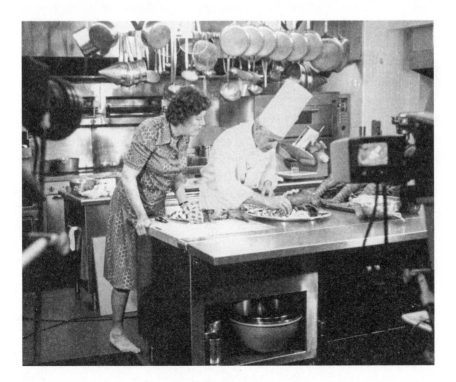

B. Johnson with a novel idea: to film a behind-the-scenes look at a White House dinner, and to explain why the time and effort to produce such a meal is worth it—"to show a side of the People's House that most of the People have never seen," the Childs explained, and to educate the public about "diplomatic life . . . [and] the tremendous importance that [a state dinner] plays in our international affairs."

As gastrophiles and former diplomats, Julia and Paul were uniquely suited to the job. No one had thought to televise a state dinner before, and Johnson—bedeviled by the Vietnam War, the Cold War, racial strife, protesting feminists, angry environmentalists, and untamable rock 'n' rollers—had largely retreated from public view. But if anyone could sweet-talk the mercurial LBJ, it was Julia. "She could charm a polecat," Paul liked to say. Sensing a chance for positive media attention, the Johnsons granted Julia access to a state dinner for the prime minister of Japan.

In preparing for their documentary, the Childs accumulated piles of research, and as I read through it fifty years later, I was reminded that a state dinner has several functions: it honors a visiting head of state, is an assertion of power and an extension of influence for both host and guest, and celebrates the culmination of knotty diplomatic negotiations with a cathartic release. It is also a showcase for the skills of the White House cooks and the best of American ingredients.

In November 1967, the Childs and a small crew from WGBH in Boston spent three days at the White House, filming in black and white (this was before the wide use of video or color television). Their cameras panned over the mansion's facade, wandered through its rooms, and zoomed in for close-ups of the kitchen at work. As the spry, sharp-featured executive chef, Henry Haller, explained his quenelles (poached fish dumplings), the six-foot-two-inch Julia craned over him to coo at his lobster tails and inhale the aromas wafting from his pots.

On the night of November 14, the Japanese prime minister, Eisaku Satō, and his wife stepped from their limousine into the flicker of the paparazzi's flashing cameras. A stream of happy, excited guests—Vice President Hubert Humphrey, cabinet members, military brass, financiers and industrialists, ambassadors, the actors Kirk Douglas and Ida Lupino, the St. Louis pitcher Bob Gibson—dressed in sleek tuxedos and glittering gowns surged into the White House.

On a signal from the maître d', a platoon of waiters bore Haller's banquet into the crowded State Dining Room and the Blue Room. The meal began with a seafood vol-au-vent (lobster, bay scallops, shrimp, and quenelles in puff pastry, napped with a *sauce américaine*); moved on to a sautéed noisette (fillet) of lamb, with mushrooms and asparagus; artichoke bottoms and a *sauce Choron;* and concluded with a green salad, and cheese with grapes. Each course was paired with a small-batch American wine. For dessert, the pastry chef Ferdinand Louvat created a Bavarian cream mousse with fresh strawberries.

"This is an absolutely delicious dinner" for 190 people, Julia narrated the film. "If I could do it for six people, I'd be proud indeed." And Paul reported in *The Economist,* "Many Americans who dislike President Johnson half-believe that dinner at the White House is limited to such gustatory curiosities as *Pedernales Chili* and *enchiladas.* Alas for prejudice! The truth is that official food at the White House is delectable."

After dinner, Tony Bennett ripped off his jacket and crooned hits in the East Room as the audience cheered. "They really seem relaxed, friendly, and happy together," Julia noted of the president and the prime minister. "And that's the point of this whole affair."

When the documentary, *White House Red Carpet,* aired as a TV special in April 1968, it was hailed as a groundbreaking event. The telecast drew a large audience, provided the first intimate glimpse of the First Kitchen at work, humanized diplomacy, and demonstrated the public's hunger for White House coverage.

Julia took note. And nine years later, she participated in a second telecast about the presidential mansion, as part of a team covering the American bicentennial. For the extra-special occasion, held on July 7, 1976, President and Mrs. Gerald R. Ford invited Queen Elizabeth and Prince Philip to a white-tie soiree, held under a tent stretched over the Rose Garden. (It was not technically a state dinner because monarchs are not heads of state.) Inside, a temporary floor with rugs had been laid on the grass, air-conditioning was installed, and Japanese paper lanterns were hung from the ceiling, setting an elegant mood.

Every minute of the evening had been tightly choreographed—from the queen and prince boarding a limousine at 8:02 p.m., to their dinner at 8:18. But at five o'clock a raging wind blasted off the Potomac, lightning crackled, and a deluge soaked the guests and turned the lawn into a mud pit. Eventually, the storm passed, the celebrants regrouped and some changed clothes, and the party carried on.

Haller's menu—one of "the most memorable" of his career, he'd say—began with New England lobster with a sauce rémoulade (a green mayonnaise, made with lemon, mustard, gherkins, capers, tarragon, and chervil), then moved on to a stuffed saddle of New Hampshire veal, with Arkansas rice croquettes, blanched broccoli in a Mornay sauce (an enhanced hollandaise), a salad of fresh Maryland vegetables, and a selection of Trappist cheeses. For dessert, the pastry chef Heinz Bender created a Georgia peach custard spiked with brandy and served in fluted vanilla bombes. It was all paired with a selection of excellent, small-batch American wines.

Despite the fabulous meal, Queen Elizabeth gave a stiff speech, Bob Hope's jokes fell flat, and Julia deemed the Captain & Tennille's saccharine warbling of "Muskrat Love" as "not very queenly." Nevertheless, she was thrilled to participate in a "real *event*" at the White House with the queen (one of the few celebrities Julia was actually impressed with).

Inspired by these visits, Julia began to champion the role of presidential dining, which "is responsible for the nation's gastronomic image." At a time when the White House was viewed with suspicion, she recognized the practical and symbolic importance of the meals served there, and felt it was her patriotic duty to publicize them. Encouraging First Families to take food as seriously as French leaders do, Julia urged them to maintain high culinary standards, spotlight regional cuisines, and champion "the good in American cooking."

As I toured the White House in 2016, Julia's visits there simmered in the back of my mind, and it occurred to me that it would be instructive and entertaining to re-create her documentaries for a modern audience. It was not a well-formed thought, but in retrospect I see that my long-standing interest in history, politics, and food came together in that instant. This book had been launched without my knowledge.

About two years later I circled back and sketched out a narrative history of the American presidency viewed through the lens of food. I envisioned a cook's tour, a look at our leaders and their appetites—and thus a glimpse of their inner selves—and the interplay between the food of politics and the politics of food.

III. Why Food Matters

As of this writing, America has had forty-six presidents, from George Washington to Joseph R. Biden. Every one of them has a food story, but I decided it would be impractical, and not very interesting, to catalog each one of them. Instead, I focused on the most compelling anecdotes and chose twenty-six chief executives to represent the whole. This left much on the cutting-room floor but allowed me to explore the way one man's personal tastes can impact major food policies and the fortunes of a particular ingredient, or company, or an entire industry, and to examine food as a political (and politicized) issue, and why it matters.

To take one example, the story of Ronald Reagan's jelly beans is not simply about his love of a cute candy. It speaks to how he weaned himself from tobacco, judged people's character, and deflected scrutiny. It limns the role of the sugar industry and food marketing. And it demonstrates how food can be a powerful communications tool. Reagan's jelly beans sent a message to voters: "I like the same food you do, so vote for me." But when he gobbled jelly beans and labeled ketchup a "vegetable" while defunding school lunches, it sent a message to children that real vegetables are not as important as sugary substitutes, and he faced a backlash. At the White House, every choice, every bite, has consequences.

To keep things simple, I have arranged the narrative chronologically and divided it into three sections: Part I, "The Eighteenth and Nineteenth Centuries: Setting the Table"; Part II, "The Twentieth Century: Feast and Famine"; and Part III, "The Twenty-First Century: Which American Cooking Is Most American?" Though the book travels straight through time, its structure was dictated by what material was available and germane. Part I represents only a quarter of the book, for instance, because there is only so much information about early presidents, and at points I leapfrog forward and back—jumping from, say, James Madison (who left the White House in 1817) to Abraham Lincoln (who began his tenure in 1861), then doubling back to Zachary Taylor (who served only a year, from 1849 to 1850)—to explain an idea or era.

As I dug into this rich material, certain themes popped out: how Indigenous and slave cooking influenced the American diet; the underappreciated role of First Ladies in both the domestic and the political spheres of the White House; the way Washington, D.C., evolved from a scrubby backwater into a gleaming metropolis, to name a few. And I was intrigued by the notion of presidential hunger—for food, of course, but also for the other trappings of office, such as attention, power, wealth, and carnal pleasure. As Abraham Lincoln said at the first glimmers of his presidential ambition, "the taste *is* in my mouth a little."

Every era witnessed large societal trends, which inevitably affected our leaders' palates and policies. Consider, for example, America's love of Chinese food. The first group of Chinese immigrants arrived in California from Canton in 1815, lured by the gold rush, and established restaurants in San Francisco. Though the Chinese Exclusion Act of 1882 was harshly discriminatory, those cooks adapted to the American palate with sweet and fried foods and flourished with ersatz dishes like chop suey. The lifting of immigration quotas in 1965, and Richard Nixon's visit to Beijing in 1972, led to a surge in Chinese restaurants in the States—there are some forty thousand now—and an appreciation for subtler or spicier regional fare. In spite of their disparate backgrounds, many—perhaps most—U.S. presidents enjoyed Chinese food, even those with the most parochial tastes, like Calvin Coolidge and Nixon.

At the Library of Congress and the Smithsonian's National Museum of American History, I found a seemingly inexhaustible trove of information about our commanders in chief. To understand what made our leaders tick, I visited half a dozen presidential homes—from Monticello (in Virginia) to Hyde Park (in New York) and the Coolidge Homestead (in Vermont). For insight into what it is like to work in the White House, I spoke to former cooks and staff members. And to understand why food is such a powerful human connector, the political aspects of eating in groups, and the historical role of feasting, I consulted academics. I also made the foods our chief executives liked, from Washington's striped bass grilled on a cedar plank to Lincoln's gingerbread men, Eisenhower's two-day soup, and Jimmy Carter's grits and eggs; I mixed FDR's reverse martini, and used a kit to home-brew Obama's honey ale with my son (it was tasty). To cap it off, I hosted a "Presidential Dinner," with dishes cooked by a former executive chef, and a guest list that included former White House staff, journalists, food experts, and historians.

As I pieced together this gastronomic political history, I wondered what the narrative arc from George Washington to Joe Biden tells us about our presidents and the evolution of American cookery, the nation, and ourselves.

PART I

The Eighteenth and Nineteenth Centuries

Setting the Table

As the colonists established themselves in the New World in the seventeenth century, much of their cooking was based on local ingredients prepared with English recipes. But as Americans won their independence in the eighteenth century, distinct regional cuisines emerged among New England Puritans, Pennsylvania Quakers, Virginia planters, and western frontiersmen. Transoceanic trade routes, undergirded by slavery, made imported tea, sugar, spices, and rum into household staples. An identifiably American diet—an amalgam of indigenous foods, European tools and techniques, African vegetables and spices, and splashes of frontier inspiration—emerged. In the late eighteenth and early nineteenth centuries, the Industrial Revolution increased the efficiency of food production, which led to the mass marketing of foods, the exploitation of workers and the environment, and a burgeoning middle class.

— 1 —

GEORGE WASHINGTON

The First Kitchen

AMERICA'S FOUNDING PRESIDENT
April 30, 1789–March 4, 1797

★

I. No Bread, No Soldier!

An army marches on its stomach.

—attributed to Napoleon Bonaparte

On Christmas night of 1777, General George Washington huddled over a wavering candle in a small stone house in Valley Forge, Pennsylvania. He was cold and hungry. As his officers sipped water and grumbled about the lack of alcohol, the general spooned a slurry of mutton, cabbage, and potatoes into his tender mouth. A battered spoon was his only eating implement. In the chaotic retreat from the well-fed, well-armed redcoats at the Battle of Brandywine in September, the general had lost his treasured camp chest, a handsome wooden box outfitted with a cookstove, pots, platters, plates, bottles, glasses, and a full set of silverware.

To add injury to insult, he found eating painful. Washington was forty-five years old and had lost all but one of his teeth, a bicuspid, the consequence of cracking walnuts in his mouth as a boy, he said, but also due to genetics, poor dental hygiene, and the teeth-grinding stress of war. To compensate, he wore a set of serious dentures. Fashioned from bits of lead and steel with gold springs, and a base of hippopotamus tusk inlaid with cow and human teeth (nine of which he bought from slaves), they seem more of a torture device than an aid to mastication. The apparatus rubbed Washington's gums sore and pushed his lower lip out, which gave him a hissing lisp. He avoided giving long speeches and preferred soft foods, such as pickled tripe. The ivory dentures were stained brown by the dark Madeira wine he favored, which led to the false assumption that Washington's choppers were made of wood. When people stared at his mouth, the hero of the American Revolution grew self-conscious and kept his lips clamped shut.

Valley Forge was a rolling upland twenty miles, or a day's horseback ride, from British-occupied Philadelphia. On paper, it appeared to be an excellent strategic winter redoubt—protected by high ridges, surrounded by deep woods, with plenty of freshwater—that blocked the redcoats from piercing the American heartland. Though not as snowy and cold as some years, in the winter of 1777 Valley Forge was an icebound cul-de-sac, "a dreary kind of place," Washington confided to his diary. And it lacked one essential: food.

When Washington's fourteen thousand men, five hundred women and children, and untold numbers of slaves and pack animals arrived in the snowy Pennsylvania valley, it was as if a teeming, grimy city had suddenly been dropped onto the pristine landscape. The Continental army was a grand name for the rough collection of farmers, shopkeepers, sailors, and other nonprofessional fighters who had volunteered from the thirteen colonies and Europe. Nearly every one of them was shivering, disease-ridden, and slowly starving to death.

The quartermaster reported that he had just twenty-five barrels of flour and a bit of salt pork left. Soldiers went for days without food or water and subsisted on whatever they could scrounge—mushrooms, crab apples, tubers, a bit of rice flavored with a tablespoon of vinegar. They hunted, fished, and foraged as much as possible, but quickly depleted the valley's larder. When one volunteer found half of a small pumpkin on the ground, he "devoured it with as keen an appetite as I should a pie," he wrote. When the women made soup, it was "full of burnt leaves and dirt, sickish enough to make a Hector spew," a visitor wrote. For much of that winter the troops subsisted on "fire cakes"—patties of flour and water with a dash of salt, if they could find it, formed into sticky cakes, smeared over stones, and baked in glowing embers. The result was a dense, soot-blackened biscuit that looked like a hockey puck and tasted like oyster crackers mixed with ash.

Learning of the Continental army's plight, the governor of Connecticut sent three hundred head of cattle to Valley Forge. The troops slaughtered the bovines and ravenously consumed every bit of sinew, fat, and gristle in five days of nonstop consumption. Still, they remained famished.

To add to their misery, many soldiers lacked blankets or warm clothes and were dressed in rags or thin shirts. Washington calculated that a third of them had no shoes, and those who did often had their toes sticking out, leaving bloody streaks in the snow. Some men were "literally naked," General Steuben noted. While the general's honor guard lived in rudimentary wooden huts with small fireplaces, most of the camp's tenants wintered in canvas tents that flapped in the sharp wind. Some suffered frostbite; others had legs or feet amputated. Open latrines and decaying horse carcasses emitted a putrid stench and incubated bacteria. Thirty percent of the army suffered pneumonia, typhus, scurvy, dysentery, and other diseases. The revolutionaries grew so weak they could barely engage the redcoats flitting through the woods nearby.

By the end of the winter of 1777, two thousand men had perished at Valley Forge. Morale was dissolving. Three hundred officers quit, convinced the revolution was lost. Public support for the uprising waned. The Pennsylvania legislature had fled Philadelphia to hole up in Lancaster. Imploring the Continental Congress for resources, Washington wrote that without food his men would "starve, dissolve, or disperse"—adding ominously that "three or four days [of] bad weather would prove our destruction."

"Happily, the real condition of [the Continental army] was not well understood" by the British, noted John Marshall, a future chief justice. "The characteristic attention of [Washington] to the lives and comfort of his troops saved" the American experiment.

The general took drastic steps to maintain discipline and morale—flogging soldiers caught stealing food, forbidding card games and gambling, and staging competitions for the best hut design. Reviewing his troops, he appeared resolute and promised that spring would bring new supplies and victory. But in private he despaired. Pacing the crepuscular encampment at night, Washington could hear the men cursing his name and swearing, "No bread, no soldier!"

George Washington could be a hard, fierce man. He stood six feet two inches tall (at a time when the average height was five feet seven inches) and was a lithe horseman and dancer equipped with a sharp intelligence and a ramrod will. A keen hunter at home in Virginia, he once chased a single fox across fields, through woods, and over hills for seven grueling hours until he finally caught and killed the exhausted creature; on another day, he killed five Mallards and five bald eagles. Such unrelenting focus made him an excellent military commander who forged a nation under extreme conditions. But in the winter of 1777 the hunter had become the quarry.

As Washington slurped his stew on Christmas night, he knew his stand at Valley Forge could prove a, or perhaps *the*, decisive moment in the revolution, one that would seal the fate of the would-be democracy.

Not long after that moment of reckoning he made a curious discovery. Contrary to everything the general had been told, there was plenty of meat, grain, and vegetables nearby. But it was hidden. Local farmers and shopkeepers had kept their stores from the rebels and sold them to the redcoats instead. King George III paid better than Washington did, in pounds sterling, a far more robust note than the Continental currency. Enraged, Washington declared that the profiteers' "avarice and thirst for gain must plunge everything . . . in one common ruin."

He sent a thousand men out to snatch cattle, pigs, horses, sheep, poultry, and grain stores, to sabotage mills—to "forage the country naked!," in the words of General Nathanael Greene—and selectively punished a few of the worst offenders in public, as a warning. It had the desired effect. Soon, the army's storehouses were filled with bushels of potatoes, parsnips, carrots, onions, and cabbage, along with nineteen dozen eggs, fifty pounds of butter, thirty-eight pounds of veal, twenty-eight chickens, six bushels of apples, and two barrels of beer. To the starving troops it was a nearly unimaginable bounty.

As their strength returned in the spring, the general grew philosophical about his neighbors' cupidity. "Instead of being blinded by political fervor, Washington recognized that fallible human beings couldn't always live up to the high standards he set for them," notes the historian Ron Chernow. "He believed that many Americans had expected a speedy end to the conflict and, when the first flush of patriotism faded, were governed by self-interest."

Today Valley Forge is an undulating green National Historical Park that spreads over thirty-five hundred acres surrounded by banal tract housing, big-box malls, and chain restaurants. To get there, you drive west from Philadelphia on I-76, a traffic-choked expressway that follows the contours of the Schuylkill River, drop down to North Gulph Road, past the beige Valley Forge Casino, then take a left on a winding road that eventually deposits you at stop 5 on the Encampment Tour trail in Valley Forge Park.

There, nestled in a grassy bowl, is the stout stone house with pale yellow shutters that served as Washington's headquarters for six months, from December 1777 to June 1778. Built by Isaac Potts, a Quaker who ran a gristmill, the humble structure served as Washington's Pentagon, Situation Room, bunkhouse, and mess hall. It was the place where he met with key allies—the French Marquis de Lafayette, the Prussian General Steuben, Quartermaster Nathanael Greene—to plot strategy and tactics.

The house is built around the kitchen, an open rectangular room with a wide fireplace that contains a small bread oven and a metal crane from which iron pots hung over the fire. Nearby stands a worktable with a few bowls, and a tall wooden cabinet holding plates and crockery. In that space Washington's slave cooks, Hannah and Isaac, stretched meager rations to feed up to thirty people three times a day. The house grew so crowded that Washington built a wooden dining room on the back side. Every night, the general, his wife, Martha, and about twenty-five others crammed into the stone house to sleep. As I walked through it, I imagined Washington and his commanders nestled in the short beds on the second and third floors while everyone else was packed together on the ground floor's hardwood like so many snoring sardines.

In the spring of 1778, warm fragrant breezes blew the winter chill out of the valley. When the reinvigorated Continental army spied an early run of shad surging up the Schuylkill, they waded into the river to attack the flashing shoals with shovels, pitchforks, buckets, and tree branches, capturing as many as possible for a feast. It seemed a providential sign that their fortunes were taking a turn for the better.

On May 6, Washington and fifteen hundred men and women sat at tables laden with pickled cucumber and cabbage, roast chicken, veal pie, planked shad, parsnips, potato pie, carrot pudding and apples in crust, watercress salad, and plates of nuts. (Washington never kicked his obsession for black walnuts and hazelnuts.) The general granted each soldier a gill, or quarter pint, of rum or whiskey. He extolled their "uncomplaining patience during the scarcity of provisions" and said they had "won the admiration of the world, the love of their country, and the gratitude of posterity!"

The party lasted until five o'clock, when Washington consented to play rounders (also called wickets), an early version of baseball, with the troops. As he rode away that evening, the soldiers twirled their hats in the air, cheering, "Long live George Washington!" By which they meant: long live the United States of America.

WE HUMANS ARE social creatures, and for as long as we have gathered, food has played a political role. In ancient Rome and Greece, meals were used to create and reinforce personal, regional, and national identities. They were also harbingers of change: the wretched excesses of imperial Roman banquets foretold the collapse of the empire. In early America, settlers combined traditional European recipes with indigenous foods to produce a new kind of cuisine that ultimately helped forge a national identity and spur their uprising: "One might say that the whole revolutionary enterprise unfolded in a series of conversations . . . taking place at dinner tables," wrote the historian Catherine Allgor.

The economics of food, most notably the British taxation of tea, provoked the Boston Tea Party in 1773, the spark that lit the revolutionary fuse. Food was a potential weapon: in June 1776, Americans sympathetic to the British planned to assassinate Washington by poisoning a dish of his favorite Long Island peas; alerted, the general had the plotters arrested, and hanged one of them "as a warning." Meals were often an integral part of funereal mourning during the war and, of course, victory celebrations.

In September 1783, Great Britain signed the Treaty of Paris, which officially brought the American Revolution to an end. George Washington's scruffy volunteers had sent the most powerful military force in the world packing. With that, Americans laughed, danced, cheered, and sang in a full-throated, cathartic release. The unaccustomed plenitude of food and drink represented a victory in its own right and renewed a sense of hope, prosperity, and grace in daily life.

Even the stoic general was not immune to the emotion of the moment. Exhausted and relieved, Washington lodged at Fraunces Tavern, a four-story brick building that still stands at the corner of Broad and Pearl Streets in lower Manhattan. The proprietor, Samuel Fraunces, was a mixed-race West Indian nicknamed Black Sam. An instinctual host with a flair for the dramatic, Fraunces wore silk knee britches and white ruffled shirts and carefully powdered his black hair. He ensured the footmen provided a "bountiful and elegant" table, Washington wrote. "Besides being an excellent cook, he knew how to provide genteel dinners. He gave aid in dressing them, prepared the dessert, made the cakes and did everything appreciatively."

In December 1783, Washington resigned his commission as commander in chief and eagerly returned to Mount Vernon, his sprawling plantation in Virginia. The house and its farms were a personal obsession, a constant work in progress, the place that defined him. But he had visited only once in the past eight years. With tears streaming down his cheeks, the general bade his officers farewell over a splendid dinner at Fraunces Tavern with a menu of more than twenty dishes ranging from crab claws with dill and mustard sauce washed down with Fish House punch, to sorrel soup with sippets (toast), poached striped bass with white wine, beef and kidney pie, roast lamb, smoked country ham, rice ragoo, green beans, watermelon pickles, pear honey, Tipsy Squire tansy pie, whiskey nut balls, chocolate truffles, tobacco, coffee, and many glasses of port.

Admiring his voluntary abdication of power at the height of his success, Americans compared Washington to Cincinnatus—the Roman farmer who was called to war, given absolute power, triumphed in battle, then voluntarily retired to his farm—as a paragon of civic virtue. King George III deemed his foe "the greatest character of the age."

II. A Booke of Cookery

The best glimpse into George Washington's mind and palate can be found at Mount Vernon, near present-day Alexandria, Virginia. The plantation was originally built by his great-grandfather in 1674, and through a series of land purchases, Washington built a 7,600 acre property. Like other Virginia planters, he used a hundred slaves to grow tobacco, which he traded for food, wine, furniture, and farm equipment. After a poor crop left him in debt, Washington diversified into wheat, corn, and many other plants. He also bred horses and kept a thousand head of sheep, cows, and pigs, brewed beer, and became a successful whiskey distiller. Which is one way to say that the Father of Our Country was intimately familiar with the production, sale, and consumption of food and drink.

The main house at Mount Vernon is a tall, handsome structure with red roofs, colonnades, outbuildings, and extensive grounds situated on a bluff overlooking the Potomac River. As was common, the kitchen was housed in its own building, set apart from the main house as a precaution against fire and to mitigate the heat and smell of the hearth; it also physically segregated white owners from their Black slaves. In 1775, Washington expanded the kitchen to include three rooms on the first floor: a larder to hang meats and store and cool food; a scullery to prepare food and wash dishes; and a central workroom, with a brick-lined fireplace equipped with five long spits for roasting, a collection of skillets, pots, and pans, a toaster, pewter ice cream pots, and the like. The cook slept in a loft on the second floor.

The day at Mount Vernon began at five in the morning, when Washington rose to read and correspond. At seven, a slave summoned the household by ringing "the great bell" for a breakfast of tea, coffee, or hot chocolate and a plate of sliced ham or tongue with bread and butter.

One of Washington's favorite things to eat was hoecakes—fried cornmeal patties—also known as johnnycakes, cornpone, spider bread, or bannock. Originally a Native American dish, hoecakes earned their name by being cooked on the blade of a hoe. They became popular with European immigrants and slaves, and the recipe spread from New England to the Deep South. (The poet Joel Barlow celebrated the dish in his 1793 poem "The Hasty Pudding.") Washington might have been fond of hoe-cakes because they were soft on his gums, and he especially enjoyed them "swimming in butter and honey." And who wouldn't?

The main meal of the day was dinner, a late lunch served at the stroke of three in the afternoon. Washington was a stickler for propriety and would sternly rebuke those who were ill-dressed or, especially, late to the table. "The cook is governed by the clock and not by the company," he'd say. His step-grandson, George Washington Parke Custis, recalled, "Precisely at a quarter before three, the industrious farmer returned, dressed, and dined at three o'clock. At this meal he ate heartily, but was not particular in his diet, with the exception of fish [especially baked shad or cod], of which he was excessively fond, partook sparingly of dessert, drank a homemade beverage, and from four to five glasses of Madeira wine. . . . [W]ith old-fashioned courtesy he drank to the health of every person present, and then gave his toast—his only toast—*all our friends*."

Washington was not a big drinker, and when he did imbibe, he usually favored wine or beer over hard beverages. Like many in the Anglicized gentry, he liked to raise a glass to toast the health of his tablemates. Known as "healths," these toasts revealed Washington's dual nature.

During the revolution, the Marquis de Chastellux, the chief liaison between French and American forces, noted that after a camp dinner "apples and a great quantity of nuts were served, which General Washington usually continues eating for two hours, *toasting* and conversing all the time." Later, a light evening supper was served, with more toasts of Madeira or Bordeaux wine. These healths made Chastellux uncomfortable. A diner would hold up his glass and address each person, even if there were twenty or thirty people at the table, intoning, "Sir, will you permit me to drink a glass of wine with you?" before drinking "to their health." Like most Frenchmen and Puritan Americans, Chastellux considered the English custom "an absurd, and truly barbarous practice." He recalled, "The actor in this ridiculous comedy is sometimes ready to die with thirst. . . . The bottle is passed to you, and you must look your enemy in the face, for I can give no other name to the man who exercises such an empire over my will; you wait till he likewise has poured out his wine and taken his glass; you then drink mournfully with him." Eventually, Chastellux discovered the secret to healths: "You have very small glasses, you pour out yourself the quantity of wine you choose . . . and the toast is only a sort of check in the conversation, to remind each individual that he forms part of the company."

Though he had a politician's knack for remembering names and faces,

Washington was bad at small talk and could not land a joke to save himself. One day he mentioned how a gust of wind had swept the toupee off the head of a reverend and sent it spinning into the Potomac. His companions could not guess if he was being humorous or simply reporting an odd fact.

At home, Washington dressed well but simply and greeted his guests with a solemn bow but never a handshake. When Senator William Maclay visited Mount Vernon, he declared it "the most solemn dinner ever I sat at . . . scarce a word said until the [table] cloth was taken away. Then the president . . . with great formality drank to the health of every individual by name round the table. Everybody imitated him, charged glasses, and such a buzz of 'health, sir,' and 'health, madam,' and 'thank-you, sir,' and 'thank-you, madam,' never had I heard before."

The Washingtons welcomed a near-constant stream of visitors to Mount Vernon and "entertained in a very handsome style," a guest recalled. The general demurred, describing his mansion as "a well-restored tavern," and saying, "My manner of living is plain, and I do not mean to be put out by it. A glass of wine and a bit of mutton are always welcome. Those who expect more will be disappointed."

Despite his self-deprecation, Washington's artfully composed table might feature a boiled pork leg at the head and a roasted goose at the foot; the first course could include roast beef, boiled beef, mutton chops, hominy cabbage, potatoes, pickles, fried tripe, and onions. With that done, three servants would clean "the cloth" and lay out a second course of mince pies, fruit tarts, and cheese. The general enjoyed a pint of beer and two or three small glasses of wine, which subtly lightened his mood.

Supper, a light evening meal, was offered at about six thirty. Custis recalled that Washington usually had nothing more than a cup of tea in the evening. He would sip it while leafing through newspapers and reading aloud "passages of peculiar interest, making remarks upon the same." At nine o'clock, the general would retire to bed.

Washington loved the "domestic felicity" of Mount Vernon, but it proved short-lived. Though he did not actively pursue the presidency, he understood the value of socializing with constituents—at weddings and cockfights, in taverns, or at Quaker, Catholic, and Presbyterian services—and enjoyed the attention. "The chief part of my happiness," he wrote in 1755, is "the esteem and notice the country has been pleased to honor me with."

On April 30, 1789, George Washington was inaugurated in New York

City as the Republic's founding president. For months afterward, citizens praised him as "the Hero of the Revolution" at numerous high-spirited parties. On September 14, for instance, he was feted in Philadelphia by the Light Horses, a cavalry corps that had wintered at Valley Forge. That night, fifty-five "gentlemens" celebrated at City Tavern, the framers' unofficial pub near Independence Hall, with lively music, dinner, and forty-five gallons of alcohol—including sixty bottles of claret, fifty-four bottles of Madeira, twenty-two bottles of porter, twelve bottles of beer, eight bottles of cider, and seven large bowls of punch. (The nine musicians imbibed an additional twenty-one bottles of wine.) The tab for the party came to 89 pounds, 4 shillings, and 2 pence—equivalent to about $15,400 in current dollars. Line items in the bill noted broken wineglasses, tumblers, and decanters, along with candles and cigars, though it is unlikely the levelheaded president was responsible for any of the shenanigans.

WHEN THE WASHINGTONS MOVED to Manhattan, the nation's temporary capital, they rented a mansion at 39 Broadway, near current-day Bowling Green. To prepare for official entertaining, they installed a staff of twenty, including seven slaves, and hired Samuel Fraunces as their steward.

The United States was raw, young, and vigorous at that point, but lacked standardized social customs. As a rising tide of friends, pols, curious citizens, and opportunists trooped to his door, Washington found himself overwhelmed and snappish, which left some of his visitors confused. This raised an aspect of nation building that people don't generally consider: the role of table manners (rules of polite behavior and speech), etiquette (a broad code for social conduct), and protocols (approved behavior in governmental and diplomatic settings) in building social cohesion and a common identity. It is easy to dismiss these things as fussy leftovers from the past, but rules of social engagement are practical tools that help people of diverse backgrounds get along.

Some of our rawer citizens did not know how to use a fork, ate with their fingers, and spat at the table, for instance. Others, including President Washington, relied on ornate British norms that dated to the seventeenth century. As newly empowered revolutionaries, most Americans rejected these old-world strictures as antiegalitarian, but they didn't have ready replacements—or, more precisely, they had a confusing mishmash of ideas about how to behave.

President Washington began the long, slow process of creating a more identifiably "American" set of social rules for the New World. One of the first things he did was to insist he be addressed as "Mr. President" rather than "His Highness the President" or "His Excellency," as some die-hard Tories liked to do. When it came to his time and energy, the cabinet ruled that Washington would invite only government officials or people with important business to dinner and would host separate meetings with members of Congress, foreign dignitaries, and the public.

Every Tuesday afternoon, from three to four o'clock, the president held a levee—a political reception (the word derived from the French *lever*, "to rise," or welcome visitors)—for ambassadors and "strangers of distinction." At four o'clock every other Thursday, he hosted a congressional dinner, to which he invited an equal number of northern and southern legislators. And every Friday, Mrs. Washington hosted a public reception in her drawing room. These changes were not universally popular, but they created a new framework for social situations and helped to create a common identity for the nation.

In the meantime, chatelaines like Martha Washington (who also wore dentures, incidentally) transcribed their "receipts" (recipes) into books. The first cookbook printed in America was *The Compleat Housewife,* by E. Smith, in 1742. It consisted of basic instructions for roasting meats over the fire, making pottages (soups or stews) and ketchups (any number of combinations of vinegar, mushrooms or oysters, and spices), baking bread, and making marchpane (marzipan) and cakes. In 1747, Hannah Glasse published *The Art of Cookery* in England, which supplanted traditional dishes—such as meats with fruit, sugar, and spices—with new ones that included exotic spices such as Indian curry, turmeric, ginger, and black pepper and refined pastries, cakes, and ice creams.

Amelia Simmons, author of *American Cookery* in 1796, and Lydia Maria Child, author of *The American Frugal Housewife* of 1832, included distinctly American recipes for turkey with cranberry sauce, baked beans, chowders, soft gingerbreads, Indian pudding, and pumpkin pies. Mary Randolph's 1824 magnum opus, *The Virginia House-Wife,* gives instructions for making barbecued shoat (young pig), fried chicken, okra, sweet potatoes, beaten biscuits, and "Dough Nuts," along with Spanish dishes such as gazpacho, French dishes such as *boeuf à la daube* (beef stew), and no fewer than fourteen recipes using tomatoes—including tomato ketchup, tomato marmalade, and tomato soy. (Randolph was a cousin of Thomas Jefferson's, and her book has continued to influence modern chefs, including James Beard and José Andrés.)

With no refrigeration or modern preservatives at hand, colonial cooks relied on fresh, flavorful ingredients, such as "new layd eggs," thick cream, fresh chicken or trout, carrots and lettuces, apples, and honey from the comb. People experimented with whatever additives were at hand, including ambergris (a sperm whale secretion) or musk from the musk flower.

These are some of the exotic ingredients found in Martha Washington's family cookbook. The original is a sheaf of 531 handwritten recipes, bound together in two sections, *A Booke of Cookery* and *A Booke of Sweatmeats*. (The original is kept at Mount Vernon, but its contents have been reprinted in numerous editions; they were annotated by the food historian Karen Hess in 1981 and are available in print or online.)

Each book opens in 1749—a year before eighteen-year-old Martha Dandridge married her first husband, the wealthy, thirty-eight-year-old plantation owner Daniel Custis (he died in 1757; Martha married George Washington two years later). They run through 1799, when Martha bequeathed the heirlooms to her granddaughter Nelly Custis. *A Booke of Cookery* begins with "How to stew a neck or Loyne of muton," runs through "To boyle Pigeons," "stew Sparrows," "make Pullpeches," "dress whittings codlings or haddocks," "pease porrage of greene pease," and "a dish of mushrumps," and ends with sweets like "a whipt possit" and "pepper cakes yet will keep halfe a year." *A Booke of Sweatmeats* explains ways to clarify sugar syrups, flies through two hundred recipes for fruit and flower preserves, and lands with ninety recipes for medicinal waters, spirits, and powders using herbs, spices, sugar, and treacles ("panacean electuaries").

Though Mrs. Washington knew more about arranging menus and supervising the kitchen than most women of her class, and was especially proud of her smoked ham, she rarely, if ever, took to the stove. It is likely that she read recipes aloud to her illiterate slaves, but it was they who did the cooking.

Among the three hundred and seventeen men, women, and children the Washingtons owned, most of whom Martha brought to the marriage, none were as central to their lives as the head cook. One man in particular remains the object of fascination for his culinary skill and mysterious disappearance.

III. The First First Chef

In December 1790, the Washingtons moved into the Robert Morris house, a rented mansion at Sixth and Market Streets in Philadelphia, America's second temporary capital. The president used the move as an excuse to fire his cook, Rachel Lewis, whose "dirty figure" did not suit his vision for "the principal entertaining rooms of our new habitation."

For unknown reasons Samuel Fraunces's employment ended in 1789, and finding qualified, reliable staff for the Washingtons' new home proved a challenge. The First Couple tried out a French chef and then a Baltimorean cook who could not bake a cake, a fatal flaw in the eyes of the First Lady, who prized baked goods, especially a Great Cake—a white edifice made with forty eggs, five pounds of flour, five pounds of fruit, four pounds of butter, four pounds of sugar, mace, nutmeg, wine, and brandy, and five and a half hours of baking—at Christmastime.

Eager to entertain, President Washington demanded that his slave cook Hercules be brought from Mount Vernon. A compact and dapper man, Hercules (a.k.a. Uncle Harkless) was born in Virginia around 1754, trained under Samuel Fraunces, and became an integral part of the Washington household in Philadelphia.

Fraunces and Lewis notwithstanding, Hercules was the nation's first true First Cook, a job now titled executive chef (an innovation of Jackie Kennedy's). It is only a slight exaggeration to say that the reputation of President Washington, his family, and the United States itself, rested in Hercules's hands.

He consulted with the First Lady on menus and was largely responsible for the planning, shopping, and making of the family's meals. Like a modern pitmaster, he cooked over open flame, which required experience, patience, intuition, and skill. A wizard at flaring and banking fires, Hercules roasted mutton and game on spits and simmered vegetable stews in iron cauldrons. He used an extensive *batterie de cuisine*—copper pots and cast-iron pans, knives, spoons, and whisks—to produce course after delectable course of soups, starches, vegetables, fruits, and desserts.

Though married with children, Hercules was bound to presidential food production nearly twenty-four hours a day. He lived next to the kitchen and rose before dawn to light the fires, bake bread, and prepare breakfast. Mid-morning, he strolled Philadelphia's outdoor markets, shopping for fruits and legumes and arranging for the delivery of fish and meat. In the afternoon he salted meats, monitored the wine and ice supply, and catered late afternoon dinners that included anywhere from two to thirty guests and could stretch for hours. In the evening, Hercules was often called on to fix a quick supper for impromptu guests—a midnight snack of ham, biscuits, and brandy for a weary traveler, say.

In the tradition of chefs immemorial, Hercules appears to have been a dexterous, intelligent, mercurial perfectionist who cared deeply about taste, texture, and flavor—"a capital cook . . . a celebrated *artiste* . . . as highly accomplished a proficient in the culinary art as could be found in the United States," recalled George Washington Parke Custis. Hercules was also an exacting manager, Custis wrote: "Under his iron discipline, wo[e] to his underlings if speck or spot could be discovered on the tables or dressers, or if the utensils did not shine like polished silver. With the luckless wights who had offended in these particulars there was no arrest of punishment, for judgment and execution went hand in hand. . . . His underlings flew in all directions to execute his orders, while he, the great master-spirit, seemed to possess the power of ubiquity, and to be everywhere at the same moment."

This description would suit many top chefs today. And like them, Hercules's gastronomic prowess granted him special privileges. When his wife, Alice, died in 1787, Martha Washington gave the chef three bottles of rum to help "bury his wife." And she gave Hercules and Ona Judge—Martha's favorite slave, who laid out her clothes and plaited her hair—money to attend plays or circuses on their own, an unusual privilege. Like the French chefs working in America, Hercules was allowed to sell slops—extra food, animal skins, tallow, used tea leaves—and keep the proceeds. He made $100 to $200 a year this way, much of which he spent on fine clothing.

Mid-height, with dark brown skin and a face described as "homely," Hercules fashioned himself into a "celebrated dandy" who dressed in silk finery, a waistcoat with a gold watch chain, and a black hat and carried a gold-tipped cane as he strolled through Philadelphia's markets like a celebrity. Yet he was enslaved.

When Hercules requested that his adolescent son, Richmond, join him in Philadelphia as a scullion (kitchen helper), the president hesitated. The City of Brotherly Love was an abolitionist hotbed, where adult slaves who resided in the state for six consecutive months could demand their freedom. Several slaves had attempted to escape Mount Vernon, and a few had succeeded. If he allowed Richmond to join Hercules, Washington worried, then father and son might attempt to escape. Yet in deference to the cook, he brought Richmond to his father.

In May 1796, Ona Judge slipped away from the Washingtons' house in

Philadelphia while they ate dinner. With the help of an abolitionist ship captain, Judge made her way to Portsmouth, New Hampshire. Martha Washington was furious and pushed her husband to recapture her favorite slave. They tracked Judge to Portsmouth, but authorities there cautioned that abducting the runaway could touch off a riot. The president backed down, but was determined to prevent another escape.

To ensure that the all-important Hercules remained in place, Washington resorted to subterfuge. Every time slaves were taken out of Pennsylvania and returned, a six-month clock of enslavement would reset. Using this loophole, the president began to rotate servants between Philadelphia and Mount Vernon. When Hercules discovered the ruse, he was "mortified to the last degree to think that a suspicion could be entertained of his fidelity," a secretary reported.

As his second term neared its end, Washington looked forward to retirement and in November 1796 sent his most valued house slaves—the cook Hercules, the butler Frank Lee, and the waiter Cyrus—to Mount Vernon, where they were kept hard at work to "keep them out of idleness and mischief." By then, the plantation encompassed eight thousand acres, including five farms that housed 316 slaves. In early 1797, Hercules was sent outside to work alongside field slaves digging enough clay for a hundred thousand bricks, spreading manure, and smashing stones into sand. The proud cook was forced to give up his fine silks for rough woolens, his prized kitchen tools for rakes and hammers.

On February 22, 1797, George Washington turned sixty-five and prepared to retire. In Philadelphia, thousands paraded by the presidential mansion, paying tribute to the Father of the Nation. That evening, the guests at his birthday ball were so resplendent that the room "appeared like a grove of moving plumes," a newspaper reported. But as the partygoers sipped punch and whirled in the capital, Hercules slipped away from the plantation and disappeared into the Virginia countryside. Rainy days and snowy nights followed. Travel was arduous, and it took days to reach Alexandria, where he likely boarded a schooner to Baltimore. Incensed again, Martha Washington dispatched slave catchers to find the runaway chef, but his trail had gone cold.

When Louis-Philippe, the future king of France, visited Mount Vernon, he asked Hercules's six-year-old daughter, "Are you deeply upset that you will never see your father again?"

"Oh! Sir, I am very glad," she replied. "He is free now."

In 1801, Hercules was spotted on a Manhattan street, and authorities alerted Mrs. Washington. But she had hired a white woman to cook by then and declined to pursue him. Wherever he landed, it is likely that Hercules lived as a free man and was well compensated to cook for a discerning household.

HERCULES'S SKILL AT COOKING in an open hearth was the result of centuries' worth of human development that stretched back to the moment *Homo sapiens* learned to harness flame and cook meat and vegetables. This was one of mankind's greatest evolutionary leaps, a skill that distinguished humans from other creatures and led to the development of brains that are larger than other primates'.

"We are the only species that controls fire and consumes cooked food on a regular basis," notes Richard Wrangham, an emeritus professor of biological anthropology at Harvard. "It is one thing that makes us unique." His colleague Rachel Carmody, an assistant professor of human evolutionary biology at Harvard, writes that cooking food essentially predigests it—by loosening starch bonds, swelling legumes, unwinding proteins—which allows our enzymes to access calories with less work than if food is raw. In other words, cooking changes food physically and chemically. By softening and breaking down vegetables, starches, and meaty proteins, cooking makes it easier and faster to consume them.

Cooked food often tastes better, and provides more energy (digestible calories), than raw food. And Carmody has found that the gut microbiome reacts differently to cooked versus raw food. Plants that grow in the ground, like potatoes or beets, produce antimicrobial compounds to protect themselves: eating tubers raw is not very tasty, takes time, and is hard work for the body; cooking them breaks down compounds and reduces the "metabolic cost" of eating. Today's "raw food diet" does not provide enough calories for healthy development over the long term; it can lower your body mass index (or weight-to-height ratio) and causes over 50 percent of women to stop menstruating, which hinders reproduction.

"Cooking completely transformed our biology," says Wrangham. "It was an evolutionary change." Though no one knows exactly when this step occurred, he believes it took place sometime between 1.6 and 1.9 million years ago, when *Homo erectus* emerged. (Others disagree, with some saying fire was controlled 40,000 years ago, and others saying it was 400,000 years ago.) Wrangham maintains that cooking caused our mouths and guts to shrink and our brains to grow. Further, it seems that cooking altered man's relationship to time.

While many animals graze on the move, and it takes half a day for a gorilla to digest enough calories, humans can cook and eat a meal in about an hour. This gave early hominids the time to develop language, define gender roles—men hunted, women foraged and cooked—and create social groups that evolved into complex societies. "Fires draw people together," Wrangham explains. The Latin root of "fireplace" is "focus," and "if you do not participate in the group, you will be excluded." In other words, cooking helped define us as human beings. "We are the people of fire."

IV. The President's House

In 1791, George Washington and the French engineer Pierre L'Enfant searched for a site for the nation's permanent capital city. Their solution was a compromise, achieved with the help of Jefferson's Dinner Table Bargain: a sixty-five-acre plat of land on the north bank of the Potomac River donated by Maryland and Virginia. (Despite persistent rumors that the city was built in a swamp, only 2 percent of the city's area is considered swampy.) To avoid further turf wars between North and South, the municipality was designated a "federal city," meaning it was not controlled by any one state. The commissioners in charge of the capital named it Washington, in honor of the president, and added "District of Columbia," the feminine form of "Columbus," a poetic name for the United States.

The Irish architect James Hoban designed the President's House as a grand Georgian mansion in the Palladian style, which he likely based on the neoclassical Leinster House in Dublin. On October 13, 1792, Washington laid the mansion's cornerstone, and keenly followed the framing, bricklaying, and sandstone masonry work, much of which was done by immigrant craftsmen and free or enslaved Black laborers. But George Washington never set foot inside the cherished building.

In December 1799, he toured Mount Vernon in chilly rain and snow and returned to the house just before his three o'clock dinner. Though cold and soaked, he insisted on eating at the stroke of 3:00. The next day he had a sore throat, but again tramped through snow. His throat grew raw and constricted, and doctors applied a blister of cantharides—a.k.a. Spanish fly, a mixture of ground beetles—to his neck, to draw out the inflammation. It didn't work. They asked him to inhale a vinegar-water steam, but he choked. And when they fed him a molasses-butter-vinegar paste, he gagged. That concoction was the last thing the Father of the

Nation consumed. He died of acute laryngitis on December 14, at age sixty-seven.

In many ways, Washington's food and entertaining choices helped define his presidency. He was a farmer who led a revolution sparked by dinner table conversations; he saved the revolution by providing enough food to sustain his army in the winter of 1777; he helped forge a national identity by consuming a hybrid American cuisine and establishing social codes that reflected egalitarian ideals. He also relied on slaves as cooks and plantation workers, perpetuating a system that contradicted the ideals that he and the nation stood for. In the end, George Washington seemed to accept the good and bad of the table he had set for the nation with equanimity. As he passed away, he muttered, "'Tis well."

2

JOHN ADAMS

The First Host

THE SECOND PRESIDENT
March 4, 1797–March 4, 1801

★

I. "The Great Castle"

In 1796, Vice President John Adams was elected America's second president, its sole Federalist leader, and the only commander in chief who was a devotee of codfish cakes and potatoes. Though he had been exposed to more refined fare while serving as commissioner to France, minister (ambassador) to the Dutch Republic, and minister to Great Britain, Adams was descended from flinty Massachusetts Puritans who survived on foods from the rocky soil and wavy coast of New England, where winters were severe, the growing season short, and frugality a paramount virtue. Though a strong believer in temperance, he began every morning with a gill (a half cup) of hard cider and a handful of Baptist cakes—dough fried in bacon fat, also known as holy pokes or huffjuffs—for his health.

Adams was a sharp contrast to his predecessor. If George Washington was a southern man of action—a wealthy planter, hunter, and general who enjoyed large parties—John Adams was at heart a frugal Yankee intellectual: a not-well-off attorney, diplomat, writer, and small-scale New England farmer who preferred modest get-togethers or quiet reading at home. His wife, Abigail, felt the same way. But politics is, by definition, a social undertaking, and the Adamses could not escape the citizens' desire to be officially entertained.

Adams complained that the vice presidency was not demanding enough—"the most insignificant office that ever the invention of man contrived," he griped, and "not quite adapted to my character . . . too inactive, and mechanical." Money, on the other hand, was a constant worry. When the Adamses followed President Washington from New York to Philadelphia, they rented a mansion they could barely afford where they were expected to host regular receptions and cover the food and beverage costs. It fell to Mrs. Adams to receive the public for several hours nearly every day. Dutifully plying her visitors—who included any well-dressed citizen who arrived at her door—with lemonade and ice cream, Abigail used the opportunity to discover what was on the public's mind and divine the inner workings of Congress. This was valuable political information, but the Adamses resented the expense and lost time incurred by constant socializing. It was largely due to Abigail's careful management of the crops and rental properties on their farm in Quincy, Massachusetts, that the Adams family remained solvent.

A related challenge was the management of household staff. While the Adamses were firm believers in liberty for all, did not own slaves, and hired both white and free Black workers as cooks, valets, coachmen, and maids, the prevalence of cheap alcohol made staffing a challenge. Adams found "the most scandalous Drunkenness and Disorder among the servants that I ever heard of," while Abigail complained that she had hired and fired seven cooks in eighteen months, "not a virtuous woman amongst them all; the most of them drunkards."

Adams narrowly won the tightly contested election of 1796 and assumed the presidency the following March. His main opponent, Thomas Jefferson, was named his vice president. They had been close friends in Paris, but now their contrasting personal styles, conflicting ambitions, and opposing politics strained the relationship. While Jefferson was a talented and enthusiastic socializer, the largest party Adams hosted in Philadelphia was a "drawing room service" when a hundred people gathered to mourn George Washington's death. But that changed when Adams moved south, to the new federal capital of Washington, D.C., where a small, competitive social scene was bubbling up.

ON NOVEMBER 1, 1800, President John Adams arrived at the brand-new President's House—which some insisted on calling the President's Palace—after a bumpy, nineteen-day carriage trek from Philadelphia. In spite of eight years of construction, at a cost of $232,372, the mansion remained a work in progress.

Thanks to the hobgoblins of spiking costs and a lack of stone and skilled labor, the architect James Hoban had been forced to scale back his design and eliminate a planned third floor. The result was a stolid building 168 feet long and 85 feet wide, with pale gray sandstone walls rising 45 feet high, two rows of eleven windows, and no wings or outbuildings. It was the biggest building in the country and impressive in parts.

Adams found the north door framed by four Ionic columns and a graceful stone transom decorated with garlands, roses, acorns, and ribbons carved by Scottish stonemasons. But the front steps were only half-built. Inside, carpenters' tools and wood shavings littered the unfinished mahogany floors. The Grand Staircase was just an idea. The rooms were cold and damp, despite the blazes set in all thirty-nine fireplaces, in an attempt to dry the still-curing walls, which were coated in plaster mixed with odoriferous hog hair, horsehair, and the beer in the wallpaper paste (a foodstuff baked into the People's House). There was no running water, few lamps, and even fewer servants. The toilet was an outhouse. The grounds were little more than a muddy field with a small kitchen garden surrounded by scrub brush, shanties, and abandoned kilns.

Mrs. Adams would dub the President's House "the great castle," partially in jest and partially in tribute. It was unfinished because the city itself remained a work in progress, explained Thomas Claxton, a congressional doorman who helped the president move in. With new government employees and others streaming into town from all over, there was such a demand for goods and laborers that supply chains were hopelessly bollixed. "Even the most trifling articles" had to be brought from great distances, Claxton wrote, while items from abroad took months to arrive.

Nevertheless, on his second night in residence Adams penned a letter to Abigail about the building's potent symbolism:

> I pray Heaven to bestow the best of Blessings on this House and all that shall hereafter inhabit it. May none but honest and wise Men ever rule under this roof.

Moved by these words, Franklin Delano Roosevelt, America's thirty-second president, would have Adams's prayer inscribed on the State Dining Room fireplace in gold letters, where it remains a beacon today.

ADAMS WAS LONELY in the giant house, and he was not much of an interior decorator. He wrote Abigail plaintive letters, beseeching her to join him in Washington City, as it was known. But she hesitated. She had settled into a rhythm between Philadelphia and the farm in Quincy, suffered ill health, and worried about her daughter's failing marriage. With the election of 1800 looming, there was no guarantee John would win a second term. Further, the "roads" leading to the capital were essentially footpaths, which made travel by coach arduous.

Mrs. Adams shipped the president some of the furnishings they had collected abroad—tables, sofas, chairs, carpets, lamps, silver, china, and glassware—but the "castle" in Washington was so large that the First Couple's contributions decorated just a few rooms. To help, Congress bequeathed the house a set of furniture bought for the Washingtons, and Claxton purchased new cabinetry, carpets, and other decorations to make the place semi-habitable. Most of the walls remained bare, though Congress allotted $800 to commission Gilbert Stuart to paint his famous full-length portrait of George Washington, which still hangs in the President's House.

As they wrote back and forth, the Adamses found they missed each other. And in the wet winter of 1799, Abigail uprooted herself and traveled south. With her arrival, the seat of government began to transform into a warmer, more social place, and the tradition of First Families turning the Executive Mansion into a temporary home was inaugurated.

Abigail Adams did not have a college education, but she was a sharp-minded autodidact and the first American woman presented at the British court. While John was known as a brilliant if vain and stubborn politician, Abigail was judged the superior writer. Her letters are full of wit, gossip, political analysis, and broadsides about the imperative of equality for women and slaves. "If we mean to have Heroes, Statesmen and Philosophers," she railed, "we should have learned women."

Dismayed by the shambolic state of the President's House, Mrs. Adams rolled up her sleeves and did her best to make the gloomy space presentable. She stuck candles "here and there for light"; chopped firewood to keep the chill at bay; cooked, and oversaw cooks, in the large kitchen hearth in the basement; washed dishes and clothes in a tub; and hung laundry on a line strung across the large, half-built parlor that is now the East Room. Settling in, she eventually managed to hire a combination of free and enslaved Black cooks, maids, and workers to help run the house.

Then, with a thrifty eye on her husband's $25,000 salary, and writing caustic letters to her two sisters about the tedium of life in the sticks, Abigail began to host official visitors. Duty-bound to host lunches for gentlemen, drawing rooms for ladies, and weekly "great dinners" for congressmen and "their appendages," the First Lady was soon entertaining up to fifteen groups a day. "I dread it," she complained. The frugal Adamses were astonished by the opulent, leisurely parties hosted by their wealthy southern colleagues, many of whom—such as Jefferson and Madison—had been raised on bounteous meals from plantations cultivated by slaves. Praising a dinner hosted by Chief Justice Benjamin Chew, the heir to a Maryland estate, President Adams marveled at the offerings with a note of puritanical guilt: "Turtle and every other thing, flummery, jellies, sweetmeats of twenty sorts, trifles . . . with a dessert of fruits, raisins, almonds, pears, peaches . . . Parmesan cheese, punch, wine, porter, beer . . . A most sinful feast again! Everything which could delight the eye or allure the taste."

When they entertained, the Adamses served plain New England fare: a first course of, say, Indian pudding (a porridge made from cornmeal, a.k.a. "Indian" flour), sweetened with molasses (a by-product of distilling sugar into rum, and an important element of the slavers' "triangle trade") and smoothed by butter; followed by a second course of veal, neck of mutton, bacon, and vegetables. Gourmet cuisine it was not, but it was hearty and the best they could do. "As we are here," Abigail wrote, "we cannot avoid the trouble or the expense."

The First Lady noticed that the citizens of Washington City expected her to host an official opening reception at the People's House. But she wasn't settled yet, and refused to be pressured into it. Slowed by ill health (she might have had malaria), worried about her son's alcoholism and her husband's disputes with Hamilton and Jefferson, Abigail understood that a housewarming party for the new mansion would be closely watched and that she and her husband would be judged by it. She stalled, restocked her tea service—pieces of which had been broken or stolen en route to Washington—and waited for construction to be finished, or finished enough, before hosting a celebration worthy of the President's House.

II. *The First Party*

If we take a step back, the citizens' hunger for a presidential housewarming can be seen as an evolutionary imperative. We primates are social creatures "biologically engineered for human interaction," says Robin Dunbar, an emeritus professor of evolutionary psychology at Oxford University. Like cooking with fire, learning to eat together amicably was a key milestone in human social development. Group meals provided physical, social, and spiritual nutrition and kept early humans from warring against each other over scarce resources. But there is something even deeper at work when we share a communal table. Eating alone can be enjoyable, but consistent isolation can lead to anxiety, depression, and numerous health problems. Epidemiological studies in Britain have found that loneliness is second only to smoking as a risk for cancer or heart disease, and the anxiety of isolation during the COVID pandemic seems to back that up. Eating with others has the opposite effect: it conjures feelings of happiness and security, builds trust and social networks, and reduces stress.

"We simply don't know why" this is the case, said Dunbar. But "eating socially really *is* good for you. It's amazing." His theory is that eating, drinking, and conversing around a table trigger the endorphin system, which humans find deeply satisfying. Endorphins are naturally occurring opioids chemically related to morphine and are part of the brain's pain-management system. In primates, endorphins are released by grooming—cuddling, patting, and the slow stroking of hairy skin. The release of endorphins produces a high, which encourages us to get along with each other and repeat the behavior. But humans don't have enough time or patience to groom everyone all the time. As it turns out, eating and drinking in a group stimulate the human neural system "even better than social grooming," Dunbar says. In other words, a dinner party can give many people an endorphin rush at the same time, which enhances bonding in a friendly feedback loop.

This is a defining human trait: even our closest primate relatives— chimpanzees, bonobos, gorillas—don't eat together the way we do. And the larger a social group is, the better its chances of survival become. Almost inevitably, small cooking circles expanded into large feasts, which took on their own rituals and meanings, and enhanced the building of societies (more on this later).

As culinary studies have boomed recently, social anthropologists have put a name to this activity: "commensality," a term borrowed from biology, which means "sharing the table." In a broad sense, commensality refers to expanding the communal table, both literally, by adding chairs and place settings, and figuratively, by inviting people of all kinds to join a meal. Jesus was said to have dined with everyone from the Pharisees to tax collectors and prostitutes. In Homeric legends, Odysseus knew that failing to share food and a seat at the table could insult the gods, who sometimes disguised themselves as hungry travelers.

I have come to think of people with a knack for entertaining—such as Thomas Jefferson and Dolley Madison—as "commensalists." And though the details have shifted over time, the human impulse to eat and drink together remains eternal.

THE ADAMSES DIDN'T CARE much about fine food, brilliant social events, or, apparently, inviting the public into the Executive Mansion, but many of their Washington neighbors did. A lot. They practically demanded the First Couple host a housewarming for the building that represented their status and the nation. Finally, on New Year's Day 1801, the cerebral administrator and his pragmatic wife capitulated to human desire. And so it was—as sometimes happens in the history of White House entertaining—that a miscast character was thrust into a critical role at a watershed moment. John Adams, the president who didn't care for parties, hosted one of the most significant parties in American history: the opening of the People's House to the people.

The short, plump, balding president—nicknamed His Rotundity—welcomed guests dressed in velvet and lace, and stood docilely beside his wife. With a subversive twinkle in her eye Abigail Adams, who was married to one of America's most outspoken antimonarchists, received her guests from a throne-like chair, looking for all the world like a queen. Rather than a full meal, they served platters of desserts—cakes and tarts, syllabub (a traditional English dessert that combines heavy cream with sherry, brandy, sugar, and nutmeg), floating islands (a rich boiled custard topped with meringue, an Adams favorite), curds, creams, jellies, trifles, sweetmeats, fruits, and bucket loads of tea, coffee, wine, and punch.

It was a grand party, a roaring success that inaugurated entertaining at the White House and marked the dawn of a new century. It also proved to be the Adamses' first and last big social event in Washington, D.C.

In the bitterly fought election of 1800, Thomas Jefferson unseated Adams and barely defeated Aaron Burr to become the nation's third president. "The Revolution of 1800" destroyed what was left of the Adams-Jefferson friendship, signaled the end of the Federalist Party, and heralded the rise of the Democratic-Republicans. The election also demonstrated that America was capable of a peaceful transfer of power, which was no sure thing. Adding to Adams's misery, Abigail had fled north to Quincy, and their alcoholic son Charles had died by the time the votes were tallied.

Avoiding Jefferson's inauguration, John Adams slipped out of Washington in the predawn hours of March 4, 1801, and made his way home. From the seclusion of his Massachusetts farm, he observed his successor's pyrotechnic entertaining in Washington with a mix of disdain, confusion, and perhaps a tinge of regret at missed opportunities. "I held levees once a week that all my time might not be wasted by idle visits," Adams wrote. "Jefferson's whole eight years was a levee. I dined a large company once or twice a week. Jefferson dined a dozen every day."

3

THOMAS JEFFERSON

America's Founding Epicure

THE THIRD PRESIDENT
March 4, 1801–March 4, 1809

★

I. A Great Variety of Jimcracks, Vegetables,
Ice Cream, and Wine

On the afternoon of March 4, 1801, Thomas Jefferson walked two hundred steps from Conrad and McMunn's, his humble boarding-house, to the Capitol in Washington, D.C. Dressed plainly, he took the presidential oath and delivered an inaugural speech in a voice so low that people had to lean in to hear him. "We are all Republicans, we are all Fed-eralists," he said, and promised "equal and exact justice to all men." Then he walked past an ornate presidential coach to Conrad and McMunn's, threaded his way through the dining room, and sat among thirty anony-mous men at "the lowest and coldest seat," far from the fire. Jefferson's inaugural dinner was the antithesis of today's extravagant spectacles. It was also a shrewd bit of political theater.

Standing six feet two and a half inches tall, with chiseled features, bright eyes, and reddish hair swept back, the fifty-seven-year-old Jeffer-son was a trim man with expansive appetites—for ideas, power, commen-sality, and pleasure. An aristocrat by birth, he was a bohemian by nature, a Janus-like man who presented different versions of himself depending on the circumstances. Jefferson combined gracious southern noblesse oblige with a republican sense of inclusion; he was a wealthy plantation owner and sophisticated global citizen who dressed casually and bucked monarchial etiquette; he was the primary author of the Declaration of Independence and an eloquent foe of slavery who owned six hundred men, women, and children. He was one of our most charismatic, com-plex, and confounding presidents, a flawed genius, and a key figure in the evolution of American cookery.

Thomas Jefferson was "our most illustrious epicure, in fact, our only epicurean president," the food historian Karen Hess wrote. That assertion will be disputed by fans of Grant, FDR, Eisenhower, the Kennedys, Car-ters, Reagans, and Obamas, among others, but there is no doubt that our third president set a new standard for the quality of food, wine, and con-versation that has rarely, if ever, been matched at the President's House.

The mansion remained unfinished when Jefferson, a Democratic-Republican, moved in. He mocked the building as a Federalist boondoggle "big enough for two emperors, one pope, and the grand lama." But he had a keen appreciation for the role that food and entertaining could play in his presidency, and in truth was eager to turn his new home into center stage for Washington's social-political whirligig.

The nation was struggling with an $83 million debt, a public divided over slavery and the French Revolution (he was in favor of it; the Federalists were not), and a rising concern that the United States would tear itself apart. To mend these rifts, Jefferson launched a gastronomic charm offensive—hosting a series of lunches and dinners to meet his colleagues, lower the rhetorical heat, broker détente, and have fun. But first he had to upgrade the facilities and hire a competent staff.

AN INVETERATE ARCHITECTURAL TINKERER, Jefferson bought an iron stove for the kitchen, built a wine cellar/icehouse, replaced candles with oil lamps, installed a bell system to call servants, and replaced the backyard privy with two indoor water closets. Washington City remained a small town with a dearth of skilled labor. With effort, he recruited a butler, a valet-porter, a housekeeper, and three Irish coachmen and would later add a scullion, footmen, a washerwoman, and a stable boy—a group he called his Washington "family."

But he could not find a decent maître d'hôtel—the all-important combination of butler, household manager, and social secretary—or a competent chef. Fretting that he was having "as great [a] difficulty in composing my household as I shall probably find in composing an administration," Jefferson wrote to Philippe de Létombe, the French envoy to Philadelphia: "You know the importance of a good *maître d'hotel* . . . and the impossibility of finding one among the natives of our country. . . . Honesty and skill in making the dessert are indispensable qualifications, that he should be good humoured and of a steady, discreet disposition is also important."

Létombe recommended Étienne Lemaire, a Frenchman who, for $30 a month, agreed to prepare menus, shop, oversee the kitchen staff, and recommend wines. Lemaire was "a very smart man . . . well educated, and as much of a gentleman in appearance as any man," judged Edmund Bacon, the overseer at Monticello, Jefferson's Virginia plantation. Others were less impressed. One of the president's granddaughters described the maître d' as "a portly well-mannered [man] . . . of whose honesty his master had a higher opinion than the world at large, and who I fancy made a small fortune in his employ."

Shopping in the Georgetown market, Lemaire recorded his purchases in a daybook, which reveals Jefferson's tastes, the array of goods, and the cost of groceries in the first decade of the nineteenth century. There were squirrel and rabbit for ragouts. Perch from Tiber Creek ("caught" by firing a shotgun into their midst), sturgeon from the Potomac, oysters and shad plucked from Chesapeake Bay. Avians of every description: guinea fowl; domestic and wild turkeys; a brace of pheasant; half a dozen partridge; a dozen wild pigeons; and squab to be roasted in a flaky crust for breakfast. Best of all was canvasback duck, "the king of ducks," a brown-headed, white-backed waterfowl that feeds on *Vallisneria,* or wild celery, along the Potomac River, which imparted a subtle flavor to its meat. (So prized were canvasbacks that they were nearly wiped out in the early twentieth century.)

Though the president ate red meat sparingly, Lemaire procured venison, suckling pig, and sides of beef for guests, along with teas, spices, cheese, crackers, preserves, hickory nuts, strawberries, watermelons, pineapples, oranges, and Cuban chocolates. Dairymen delivered milk and cream (nine cents a quart), butter (thirty cents a pound), and eggs (thirty cents a dozen) to the front door. And a baker delivered a dozen fresh loaves of bread a day (twelve and a half cents each).

Eventually, Jefferson secured Honoré Julien, a skilled French cuisinier who had cooked for the Washingtons in Philadelphia. For $25 a month, he manned two fireplaces in the vaulted kitchen in the basement beneath the Executive Mansion's entryway. Wielding long-handled skillets, manipulating roasts impaled on spits and cranes suspending heavy pots of vegetable stew, and shuffling breads and pastries in and out of a small bread oven, Julien filled his hot grotto with the aromas of sizzling butter and onions, fried guinea fowl, and the acidic snap of vinegar on lettuce.

Jefferson's diet was unusual in that carnivorous era, when most Americans subsisted on gluttonous helpings of meat and potatoes. Many ate steak at both breakfast and lunch, the main meals of the day, and gave "short shrift . . . to fresh fruits and vegetables," noted the historian Harvey Levenstein in *Revolution at the Table,* his study of early American eating. It was a habit that "made constipation the national curse." Americans consumed "piles of indigestible matter," Charles Dickens observed, and James Fenimore Cooper, author of *The Last of the Mohicans,* wrote in 1833 that Americans were "the grossest feeders of any civilized nation ever known . . . [whose diet was] heavy, coarse, and indigestible."

By contrast, Jefferson considered "animal food" (meat) a "condiment for the vegetables which constitute my principal diet" rather than an "aliment." Not a strict vegetarian in the modern sense, he maintained what is now called a vegetable-forward diet—heaping his plate with lettuce and cooked vegetables, accented with small portions of fish or fowl and occasional helpings of red meat. Jefferson "ate heartily, and much vegetable food," his grandson Thomas J. Randolph recalled. He preferred "French cookery because it made the meats more tender." And guests enthused over the "handsome," "neat and plentiful" meals, at which the president liked to serve his guests by himself.

One of Jefferson's greatest pleasures was to offer a sumptuous repast of, say, grilled shad roe, roasted turkey, new potatoes, green beans, corn bread, tomato salad, and ice cream to a group of friends, and linger late over imported wines and scintillating talk about science, architecture, history, and politics. "Never before had such dinners been given in the President's House, nor such a variety of the finest and most costly wines," a guest recalled.

"What he did eat he wanted to be very choice," noted Edmund Bacon. "He dined at four o'clock, and they generally sat and talked until night. It used to worry me to sit so long; and I finally . . . went off and left them."

IN DECEMBER 1801, the 150 members of the Seventh Congress arrived in Washington for their first session. Most of the men were single, there were no theaters and few taverns, and the congressmen slept in dank bunkhouses. Aware of their isolation, Jefferson and his daughters Patsy and Polly began hosting three congressional dinners a week. A meticulous documenter, the president noted that every legislator was invited at least once, with Federalists and Republicans invited on alternate afternoons, and he would mix in philosophers, diplomats, Georgetown swells, even a Cherokee chief, to keep things interesting. Jefferson hosted these dinners in what is now the Green Room (a parlor for receptions today), and larger events were held in a public dining room. The president insisted on meaningful conversation over partisan bickering.

Not everyone understood what they were served at Jefferson's table. One congressman noted that the menu included "rice soup, round of beef, turkey, mutton, ham, loin of veal, cutlet mutton, fried eggs, fried beef . . . and a pie called macaroni which appeared to be a rich crust filled with the strillions of onions, or shallots, which I took it to be, tasted very strong, and not agreeable. Mr. [Meriwether] Lewis told me there was none in it; it was an Italian dish, and what appeared like onions was made of flour and butter [pasta], with a particularly strong liquor [sauce] mixed with them . . . ice cream very good, crust wholly dried, crumbled into thin flakes: a dish somewhat like pudding—inside white as milk or curd, very porous and light, covered with cream sauce—very fine. Many other jimcracks, a great variety of fruit, plenty of wine and good."

Ice cream was Jefferson's signature dessert. Julien used French "freising moulds," and on big occasions, such as the Fourth of July, would purchase hundreds of eggs and hire men to hand crank ice cream makers so the public could share in the cold delights. Though he was not the first to introduce ice cream to America, the recipe for vanilla ice cream that Jefferson brought from Paris is considered the first of its kind handwritten by an American. That, and nine other recipes he copied in France, survive. They range from a method for preserving haricots verts (green beans) to instructions for *nouilly à macaroni* (pasta dough), wine jellies (salad dressing), and *biscuit de Savoye* (a light sponge cake). Lemaire's surviving recipes include instructions for pancakes, *boeuf à la mode,* and breast of mutton.

Jefferson's granddaughter Virginia J. Trist would later compile these and other Jeffersonian favorites into a Monticello cookbook, updated in 1976 as *Thomas Jefferson's Cook Book.*

There were at least two broad objectives to his largesse. Jefferson used meals to "cultivate personal intercourse with the members of the legislature that we may know one another and have opportunities of little explanations of circumstances, which, not understood might produce jealousies & suspicions," he wrote. "I depend much on the members for the local information." But an English visitor discerned a subtler rationale: "Neither could he [anywhere else] have had the members of the legislature so dependent upon him . . . his house . . . being in fact almost necessary to them unless they chose to live like bears, brutalized and stupefied."

A natural commensalist, Jefferson understood what might be called the power of feasting. Historically, "feasts" were large symbolic events designed to foster political and economic alliances, display wealth and prestige, and incur social debts. "Traditional feasts were entertainment with ulterior motives," writes Brian Hayden, an archaeologist and professor emeritus at Simon Fraser University in British Columbia. "Feasts helped to transform egalitarian hunters and gatherers into the kinds of societies that laid the foundation for early states and even industrial empires. They created hierarchies and inequalities, the advantaged and the disadvantaged. . . . Political power . . . was partly based upon debts incurred through feasts."

Hayden believes that feasting was a catalyst for the domestication of plants and animals. It is a big claim, but he says "the evidence is pretty clear" that feasting predates agricultural and meat surpluses, which are prerequisites for the development of civilizations.

To host a feast, a leader needed to have surplus food—and not just any food, but delicious, nutritious food available on demand. Wild game was not always at hand, and its fat content was only about 3 percent of the protein. But domesticated animals can be butchered anytime, and their meat has a fat content of 20 to 30 percent. Feasting, Hayden argues, helped to develop ranching and farming.

Feasting was also an effective way to broker marriages, conduct business, and negotiate treaties. The Incas and Sumerians used feasts to "make the empire go 'round," Hayden said, and the Egyptians used banquets to attract workers: "If you want to build the pyramids, feed them and they will come." Further, a successful feast sends a message that a society is thriving, thanks to the host's leadership.

On the other side of the equation, a guest who accepts an invitation to a feast embarks on an implied alliance: by incurring a debt of food and entertainment, the guest is expected to support the host in social or political ways and to reciprocate with similar or better gifts. "Feasts tend to be competitive because the underlying motive . . . is to secure advantageous relationships via debts (for marriage, defence or economic endeavours)," Hayden writes. "Once embroiled in the debt system, it is almost impossible to extricate oneself, and failing to reciprocate . . . often [resulted in] murder and warfare."

He surmises that feasting emerged among European hunter-gatherers during the Upper Paleolithic, some thirty thousand years ago, and became common in the Mesolithic era, about fifteen thousand years ago. And where would humans be without feasts? "We would still be hunters and gatherers," Hayden said with a chuckle.

TO THE DISMAY of traditionalists, Jefferson used the semiotics of dress and etiquette to shape a more egalitarian social system in Washington. He dressed for dinner in a dark jacket, scarlet embroidered waistcoat, twill corduroy breeches, and comfortable satin shoes. It was his version of casual chic, a sartorial indicator of his priorities. "It was the object of Mr. Jefferson to preserve, in every trifle, that simplicity which he deemed the most appropriate characteristic of a republic," a visitor wrote. "He wisely judged that . . . example was better than precept, and set about new-ordering the manners of the city." Jefferson canceled the formal levees of his predecessors and converted the mansion's large party space—today's State Dining Room—into a library and office. He issued his own dinner invitations, shook his guests' hands instead of bowing stiffly, rode his horse without an attendant, and insisted on being addressed as "Mr. Jefferson" instead of "Mr. President."

In a symbolic rejection of hierarchy, Jefferson sat dinner guests at oval or round tables, with neither a head nor a foot, which proved "a great influence on the conversational powers," observed his friend Margaret Bayard Smith, the political commentator. Inspired by *pêle-mêle,* the French principle of equality, Jefferson abjured seating by rank in favor of "pell-mell" seating, where guests sat next to whomever they liked.

"When brought together in society, all are perfectly equal, whether foreign or domestic, titled or untitled, in or out of office," Jefferson wrote in an 1804 Memorandum on Official Etiquette. "It would have been better . . . in a new country to have excluded etiquette altogether."

These changes infuriated certain visitors, sometimes intentionally. The first time the British minister (ambassador) and his wife, Mr. and Mrs. Anthony Merry, dined at the President's House, Jefferson greeted them in a pair of battered carpet slippers. When the dinner bell rang, he offered his arm to the woman next to him, Dolley Madison (who occasionally volunteered as the widowed Jefferson's cohost), rather than to Mrs. Merry, as British etiquette dictated. Dolley's husband, Secretary of State James Madison, escorted the woman nearest to him, and other cabinet members followed suit. The Merrys were deeply offended. When Jefferson repeated this insurrection on another evening, Mrs. Merry unleashed her wrath on Mrs. Madison. If she was going to insult his friend, Jefferson snapped, "she will have to eat her soup at home."

Though it seems laughable now, the "Merry Affair" temporarily threatened diplomatic relations with the British Crown. The minister and his wife declined further invitations, which suited the president just fine. He invited all sorts of Americans into the People's House, with sometimes unexpected results.

On New Year's Day 1802, for example, a delegation from a Baptist church from Massachusetts gave Jefferson a 1,235-pound cheese—"the greatest cheese in America for the greatest man in America"—drawn by six horses, as a tribute. It was crafted by free Black farmers from the milk of nine hundred cows, became a national sensation, and inspired poetry, newspaper accounts, and the first use of "mammoth" as an adjective (prompted by the discovery of mammoth bones). Jefferson insisted on paying $200 for the cheese, 50 percent above market price.

The giant cheese was a foretaste of years of presidential food gifts—salmon, turkeys, possum, jelly beans, broccoli, pretzels—that donors made out of goodwill, patriotic fervor, or opportunism. The tradition continued until the September 11, 2001, terrorist attacks, when fears of food poisoning put a permanent end to it. Though people continue to send food to the White House, it is destroyed.

UPON HIRING LEMAIRE as maître d', Jefferson declared, "While I wish to have every thing good in it's [sic] kind, and handsome in stile, I am a great enemy to waste and useless extravagance, and see them with real pain." If that was true, then he must have suffered every day, for he was permanently in arrears.

By outward appearances, the president was a wealthy plantation owner with an annual salary of $25,000 (equivalent to about $500,000 today). In fact, he was saddled by heavy debts and survived on credit. Like John Adams, Jefferson was chagrined to discover that he was required to furnish the mansion, pay for servants, groceries, and clothing, maintain the stable, and the like. Unlike Adams, one of Jefferson's biggest expenses was food.

He spent about $50 a day on provisions (about $1,000 today) and more than $16,500 on wine during his presidency (about $330,000 today). Much of this cost was due to imported delicacies: the manifest for an 1806 shipment from Bordeaux, for instance, included almonds, tarragon vinegar, Maille mustard, anchovies, Parmesan cheese, bologna, seedless raisins, figs and prunes, olives, and olive oil. These were hardly necessities, and, Lemaire observed, "Mr. Jefferson's salary did not support him while he was president."

A compulsive cataloger, Jefferson recorded nearly every financial transaction he made—from the fifty cents he gave to a grandson, to the $30 he paid the Marine Band, to the thousands of dollars he spent on his farms. But Jefferson's fastidious bookkeeping hardly slowed his spendthriftery. "Let the price be what it has to be," he airily told a wine merchant, and the man surely took him at his word. Jefferson's heedless consumption was amusing, but ultimately came at a tragic price, one that rubs much of the shine from his sparkling reputation.

II. *Grief, Appetite, and France*

On New Year's Day 1772, Thomas Jefferson married Martha Wayles Skelton, his twenty-three-year-old third cousin. She was well educated, a dancer and harpsichordist, and a widow described as "vivacious," "impulsive," and "beautiful," with large hazel eyes and luxuriant auburn hair. Arriving at Monticello in a snowstorm, the newlyweds toasted each other with a bottle of wine and "song and merriment and laughter." When Martha's father, John Wayles, died, she inherited eleven thousand acres of prime Virginia farmland, 135 slaves, and a mountain of debt—all of which she passed on to Jefferson.

He recalled their married life as "ten years of unchequered happiness." Martha managed the kitchen at Monticello "with cookery book in hand," and read recipes aloud to the enslaved cook Ursula. Martha suffered poor health, in part due to her nine pregnancies which resulted in six children, though only Martha and Mary (called Patsy and Polly) survived. Her last pregnancy was especially difficult, and in 1782 Martha died at thirty-three, shortly after giving birth to a daughter who died of whooping cough.

As she faded, Martha asked her husband to promise he would never remarry because she could not imagine another woman raising her children. Jefferson agreed. After her funeral he was bereft. "A single event wiped away all my plans and left me a blank which I had not the spirits to fill up," he wrote to a friend. He burned their love letters, shut himself in his room for days, rode his horse alone for hours, and remained inconsolable for weeks.

Appetite can be a barometer of mental health, and today the relationship between food and grief is a burgeoning field of study. Couples often court over food and drink, bond while cooking and eating together, and associate important memories with specific dishes, ingredients, or places. Losing a partner is disorienting, and the absence of someone you ate with can make even simple things like turning on the stove hard to bear. Some widowers (now used as a gender-neutral term, like "cook") turn to food for solace and overeat to compensate for their loss. Others lose weight, because shopping and cooking remind them of their missing partner, or their own mortality.

In almost every culture, family and friends bring food to console those who are grieving, a human impulse that helps ease widowers back into the rhythms of life. Such was the case with Jefferson. By October 1782, he began "emerging from the stupor of mind which had rendered me as dead to the world as [she] was whose . . . loss occasioned it."

Renewed, Jefferson threw himself into socializing and politicking. In 1783 he was elected as the Virginia representative to the Congress of the Confederation, the precursor to today's Congress. A year later, he was dispatched to Paris to help the minister to France, Benjamin Franklin, and minister to the U.K. and the Netherlands, John Adams, negotiate treaties. France was the ultimate glamorous posting for an eighteenth-century up-and-comer. But some believe that Jefferson was sent abroad at least in part to distract him from what his daughter Patsy called "violent burst[s] of grief."

JEFFERSON ARRIVED in Paris in August 1784, having just turned forty-one, and settled at the Hôtel de Langeac, a town house on the corner of the Champs-Élysées and the Rue de Berri. The following year Franklin returned to Pennsylvania, and Jefferson succeeded him as minister to France. The diplomatic post represented both an escape from his past and an adventure that would rocket him into the future. "Behold me at length on the vaunted scene of Europe!" he wrote to a friend. "You are perhaps curious to know how this new scene has struck a savage from the mountains of America. Were I to proceed to tell you how much I enjoy their architecture, painting, sculpture, music, I should want words."

And then there was the cuisine.

In Paris, Jefferson clambered and spelunked his way through meals that were high, low, and in-between. Every Tuesday he attended court dinners hosted by King Louis XVI, where he sampled multicourse banquets—replete with unctuous roasts and rich, buttery sauces, rare champagnes, and breathtaking desserts—and observed how the nobility used entertaining as a means of political persuasion. In his off-hours, Jefferson poked around the city's outdoor food markets, eager to sample unfamiliar mushrooms, garlic, snails, wild boar, and lemon puddings. It is possible he ate at Mathurin Roze de Chantoiseau's consommé shop, which opened in the 1760s and is considered the first true restaurant, or the Grande Taverne de Londres, which opened around 1782 as the city's first luxury eatery. (The word "restaurant" derives from the French *restaurer,* or "to provide food for," or "to restore to a former state.")

Jefferson chewed his way through France, Italy, and Spain—tasting Alpine cheeses, Norman brandy, Mediterranean olive oils, rich cassoulets, fantastical cakes, marzipan, and chocolate bonbons. He observed chefs in action, sketched a macaroni-making machine, and educated himself about wines and the *terroirs* that defined them. In Italy, he found a strain of rice so prized that its export was forbidden upon pain of death. Undeterred, he smuggled pocketfuls of the rice home. Worried that the supply would not be enough to cultivate a useful crop, he paid a muleteer to "run a couple of sacks across the Appenines to Genoa," where it was shipped to Monticello.

So rapturous was Jefferson about his Parisian meals that Patrick Henry—the Founding Father who declared, "Give me liberty or give me death!"—denounced him as a turncoat, thundering, "He has abjured his native victuals in favor of French cuisine." But Henry was misinformed. Even amid the splendors of Europe, Jefferson wrote with a note of hometown pride that there was "no apple here to compare to our Newtown pippin" (a dessert apple). He had a barrel of the apples and seventy-five tree grafts shipped to Paris. Also Virginia hams, which he judged "better than any to be had" in Europe, along with cranberries and pecans. He grew "Indian corn" and requested his Virginia farmhands send watermelon, cantaloupe, and sweet potato seeds for his Parisian garden.

WITH AN EYE on the future, Jefferson ensured he would continue to eat deliciously back home by importing his slave cook, James Hemings, to Paris "for the particular purpose of learning French cookery." Hemings was only nineteen, but had distinguished himself as a trusted attendant in Virginia, and was trained to cook in the "English" style, over a hearth—which required physical labor, a creative bent, and enough science to roast meats, stew greens, and bake bread—in Monticello's small brick kitchen.

Embarking for Paris in July 1784, Jefferson and Hemings traveled from Charlottesville to Boston, sailed to London aboard the *Ceres,* then to the port of Le Havre, and on to Paris by coach. Shortly after arriving, Jefferson enrolled his young Black cook in a series of *stages* (apprenticeships) with accomplished French chefs. Hemings began his tutorial with the chef Combeaux, the caterer hired to cook for Jefferson, and two years later learned the exacting discipline of French pastry with a female chef. In 1777, Jefferson arranged for Hemings to cook at the Château de Chantilly, the country estate of the Prince de Condé north of Paris, where the food was said to be even better than that served at the Versailles Palace.

Something of a chameleon, Hemings adapted to French customs and developed a taste for fine wine and cheese. He learned to make specialties like foie gras (duck or goose liver), *pommes frites* (French fries), crème brûlée (custard topped by caramelized sugar), ice cream (which was probably invented in Iran around 500 BC and popularized in France in the seventeenth century), whipped cream, and meringues.

Slavery was illegal in France, and Jefferson paid Hemings 24 livres— about $4—a month, which was comparable to white servants' pay. Hemings used his wages to hire a French tutor, which made his command of the kitchen and daily life easier, and eventually he spoke the language more fluently than his master.

When he completed his culinary training in 1787, at age twenty-one, Hemings was made *chef de cuisine* (head chef) at the Hôtel de Langeac. There, he was privy to diplomatic conferences and cooked for statesmen, scientists, aristocrats, and artists. He began to find a cooking style of his own, combining French and American elements that delighted his patron: chestnut puree with calvados sauce, for instance; or capon stuffed with Virginia ham; or "snow eggs," his version of *îles flottantes* (floating islands)—poached meringues set adrift in a pool of crème anglaise.

A moody perfectionist with much on his mind, Hemings began to drink to excess, which irked his employer. While Jefferson adored wine, he drank it in moderation and disliked hard liquor. Hemings's bibulousness wasn't their only point of tension.

AT THE TIME, Paris was home to more than half a million people— nearly the population of Virginia—including a thousand free Black residents. Slavery was frowned on, and Jefferson's good friend Lafayette pleaded with him to give up "this Wide Blot On American . . . Civilisation." Yet Jefferson refused to address the matter. He was not alone, of course: it would take another seventy-eight years, the Civil War, and the Thirteenth Amendment to end slavery in America. But Jefferson's reluctance stemmed as much from his complicated domestic arrangement as from his wish to maintain the status quo.

In 1787, Jefferson had his eight-year-old daughter, Polly, and his fourteen-year-old slave Sally Hemings, one of James's younger sisters, brought to Paris. Polly and her older sister, Patsy, were enrolled in boarding school, and Sally Hemings was trained as their maid, for which she was paid 12 livres—about $2—a month.

Under the Freedom Principle in French law, Sally and James Hemings could have petitioned the court for "manumission," or freedom. But for reasons unknown—perhaps because the Hemingses were young and lived under Jefferson's wing or because he had made promises to keep their family intact in return for their continued service—they never did. Nor did Jefferson offer to set them free.

His views on slavery were a contradictory mix, ranging from bright hope to principled resistance, willful ignorance, and bleak cynicism. Slaves had built the President's House and Monticello. Black farmers and cooks nourished Jefferson and his family. Jefferson wrote "all men are created equal" into the Declaration of Independence. He railed against slavery as a "moral and political depravity"; pushed for the education of slaves; worked with, and arguably befriended, a number of the men he owned; allowed at least one slave to buy his freedom, and others to escape; and eventually set seven men free. Yet Jefferson accumulated so much debt that his heirs broke up slave families and sold a hundred and thirty people to satisfy his creditors. This cruel denouement was not something the humanistic side of Jefferson would have found joy in, yet his fecklessness made it inevitable, as he must have known it would.

In Paris, Jefferson's voracious appetites began to blur. He socialized with successful men and flirted with beautiful women—most famously, Maria Cosway, a musician who was inconveniently married. And with time, he began to treat his teenage slave Sally Hemings as more than a maid. Rumors that they had a sexual relationship began circulating in 1802, when James Callender, a political rival, accused Jefferson of keeping, "as his concubine, one of his own slaves . . . SALLY" in a Virginia newspaper.

Jefferson neither confirmed nor denied the rumor, and it mostly lay fallow. When it cropped up, the story was often cast in a romantic light, implying that *she* had tempted *him*. In a spate of 2017 media reports, Sally Hemings was described as Jefferson's "mistress," implying that she was an equal participant in the relationship. "Not a victim but an agent of change?" people wondered on Twitter. This interpretation strains credulity. By law, masters owned the bodies of slaves, who had no legal recourse. And bits of evidence supported the accusation: Jefferson was at

Monticello when Sally became pregnant; her children were fair-skinned and shared names of his family members; and he granted them freedom, though he never freed Sally.

In 1998, a Y-chromosome haplotype DNA analysis published in the journal *Nature* confirmed that Sally Hemings had six children by Thomas Jefferson. Though some of his white descendants insist the president's brother Randolph sired Sally's children, the Thomas Jefferson Foundation affirmed in 2019 that "the issue is a settled historical matter."

In a further kink to the twisted family knot, Martha Jefferson's father, John Wayles, had fathered the mixed-race Sally and James Hemings. In other words, Thomas Jefferson's wife and his slave Sally were half sisters; James was Martha's half brother. Jefferson's children by Sally were three-quarters white but treated as Black. This conundrum boggles the modern mind, but it was not unheard of at the time. And Jefferson's miscegenation helps explain the evolution of American cuisine.

A few of Jefferson's mixed-race descendants are proud to be related to him. But other observers condemn him as a sexual predator who treated Sally Hemings as a possession rather than a human being, one that he used—or consumed—as he wished. The writer Britni Danielle charged that Sally Hemings "wasn't Jefferson's mistress; she was his property. And he raped her." Curiously, the word "rape" is linked to appetite by the Latin root *rapere*—to take by force—which also forms the basis of "ravenous" and "rapacity," words usually associated with hunger.

Food and sex have been linked since Eve bit into the apple. Both are intimate, emotional, stimulating experiences; they ensure survival and give pleasure, but are difficult to control. This presents a dilemma: strong appetites demand satisfaction and can overwhelm reason. Thomas Jefferson was the first president to be accused of sexual scandal but hardly the last.

In Paris, meanwhile, the French Revolution was on the boil. After dining on pâté and frogs' legs with King Louis XVI, Jefferson passed malnourished common folk seething over a punitive salt tax. When grain crops failed, spiking the price of bread from 50 to 88 percent of their income, the mob turned violent. On July 14, 1789, Jefferson witnessed the storming of the Bastille. In 1793, the revolutionaries guillotined Louis XVI and his wife, Marie Antoinette.

Jefferson privately supported the uprising, but as a canny diplomat he stayed in touch with the court. They urged him to calm the masses, but he invited Lafayette, who was advising the communards, to eat and discuss the ideas that would become his "Declarations of the Rights of

Man and of the Citizen," a founding document of western European democracy. In August, Jefferson offered his apartment to members of the National Assembly for a strategy session over dinner. Though he provided the food and space, the American hung back to observe their talk as "a silent witness."

IN SEPTEMBER, the violence in Paris flared alarmingly, and Jefferson packed his entourage and sailed home. He brought a few souvenirs from his five years abroad: eighty-six crates filled with silver, porcelain, furniture, wallpaper, books, and art and comestibles ranging from Parmesan cheese to anchovies, olive oil, vinegar, mustard, almonds, raisins, nectarines, and a mere 680 bottles of French and Italian wine.

Settling at Monticello, Jefferson framed his wine importation as an act of resistance, declaring, "The taste of [America was] artificially created by our long restraint under the English government to the strong wines of Portugal and Spain." Early in his drinking career, Jefferson had enjoyed the heavy, sweet, alcoholic wines like port and sherry favored by the aristocracy. But during the American Revolution he befriended Hessian prisoners (mercenaries fighting for Britain), who offered bottles of German wine that better suited his tastes. Living in Europe, Jefferson grew enamored of lighter French, Italian, and Spanish varietals and came to think of wine as an integral part of a meal, a flavor enhancer and digestive aid rather than purely an inebriant.

Jefferson waxed poetic about his favorites. Italian Nebbiolo was "about as sweet as the silky Madeira, as astringent on the palate as Bordeaux, and as brisk as Champagne," he observed. Pining for sherry, he wrote, "If I should fail in the means of getting it, it will be a privation which I shall feel sensibly once a day."

He sipped his wine from a small glass: "a perfectly sober . . . three or four glasses at dinner, and not a drop any other time," he wrote. This was confirmed by a slave named Isaac who said he had never seen Jefferson "disguised in drink."

As a legislator, he pushed for lower tariffs on lighter vintages to encourage their popularity in America. "The delicacy and innocence of these wines will change the habit from the coarse and inebriating kinds," he wrote. "It is much to the comfort and temperance of society to encourage them." But his quixotic crusade was ahead of its time, and failed.

·   ·   ·

IN MARCH 1790, President Washington named Jefferson the nation's first secretary of state. The promotion delayed his return to France—permanently it turned out—and Jefferson moved to New York. He and James Hemings arrived in March, and three months later hosted Hamilton and Madison for the Dinner Table Bargain (detailed in the introduction). While Jefferson's social choreography that night helped secure the nation's future, the dinner was also a triumph for its cook.

James Hemings was proving indispensable to Jefferson's political fortunes, and in December 1790 the two moved to Philadelphia. There, the chef was paid $7 a month, the same wages paid to non-slaves, and was granted wide latitude to shop in the city's markets. He cooked for the president, cabinet members, congressmen, and European dignitaries. It was a fractious period, though, and by 1793 Jefferson had tired of public life. He retired to Monticello and invited Hemings to join him. But the chef balked at returning to a slave state and at age twenty-eight petitioned for manumission.

Reluctantly, Jefferson agreed, but on one condition: that Hemings train a replacement cook: "Having been at great expence [sic] in having James Hemings taught the art of cookery, desiring to befriend him, and to require from him as little in return as possible, I hereby do promise and declare, that if the said James should go with me to Monticello . . . and shall there continue until he shall have taught such person [to cook] . . . he shall thereupon be made free."

Over the next two years, Hemings trained his younger brother Peter as his replacement in the Monticello kitchen. And on February 5, 1796, Jefferson discharged James Hemings "of all duties and claims of servitude."

Suddenly the world was his oyster. James was a free man, a talented cook, and literate and bilingual and had $30 burning a hole in his britches. In the spirit of young men everywhere, he hit the road. He might have returned to France, where many of his former acquaintances had been killed or driven away.

Returning to the States, he found work as a cook in Philadelphia. When Jefferson ran into Hemings on the street, he was dismayed to find that James "is not given up to drink. . . . He tells me his next trip will be to Spain. I am afraid his journeys will end in the moon. I have endeavored to persuade him to stay where he is, and lay up money."

Jefferson's advice to save money was a "delicious irony," notes the historian Annette Gordon-Reed, as was his disapproval of Hemings's peripatetic travels. In any event, Hemings moved to Baltimore, where he cooked in a tavern. After winning the presidency in 1800, Jefferson offered to hire Hemings as his chef, but the men could not agree on terms. Gordon-Reed speculates that the president refused to acknowledge Hemings as fully free, while the equally prideful Hemings refused to bend to his former master. Further, it is likely he had deeply mixed feelings about his sister Sally and her children.

Skilled, intelligent, and troubled, James Hemings did not fit into the world as it was. He was not accepted as fully Black or white, it seems, and his sexuality might have been fluid. After drinking so "freely" that he was "delirious for some days," a friend reported, Hemings committed suicide in Baltimore at age thirty-six. It was, Jefferson observed, "a tragical end."

III. Monticello

The past is never dead. It's not even past.
—William Faulkner, *Requiem for a Nun*

Jefferson was a born plantsman. "There is not a sprig of grass that springs uninteresting to me. . . . Agriculture is our wisest pursuit, because it will in the end contribute most to real wealth, good morals & happiness."

When he turned twenty-one, Jefferson inherited a five-thousand-acre plantation in the rolling green hills outside Charlottesville, Virginia. The holdings comprised the home farm at Monticello ("Little Mountain" in Italian), along with three "quarter farms" nearby—Tufton to the east, Lego to the north, and Shadwell (where he was raised)—and forty slaves. And soon he began transforming the property into a physical manifestation of his many interests.

His primary crop was tobacco until the 1790s, when he switched to rye and wheat. But Jefferson's true passion was his one-thousand-foot-long vegetable garden, planted in terraced beds on the protected, southeastern side of Monticello.

Over sixty years of farming, he would cultivate 330 varieties of eighty-nine species of herbs, fruits, and vegetables, many of which were new to this country. He planted Italian broccoli and squash; figs from France; peppers from Mexico; beans and salsify collected by Lewis and Clark; cauliflower, rutabaga, artichokes, peanuts, and sea kale. Jefferson did not introduce tomatoes to North America, but he had eaten "tomatas" in Europe and became one of the first Virginians to grow them; his daughters used them in gumbo or pickled them. He tended a plot of asparagus for twenty-two years, planted fifteen varieties of English peas, and competed with his neighbors to bring them to market first. A salad lover, he planted lettuces every week to keep up with the demands of his hungry table.

In 1802, Jefferson brought the fifteen-year-old slave Edith "Edy" Hern to the President's House to train under the chef Honoré Julien. She worked there for seven years, preparing "extremely elegant [meals] cooked rather in the French style," he noted, and was paid $2 a month. In 1806, Jefferson added Edy's sister-in-law, Frances "Franny" Gillette Hern, to help, and she too proved a dab hand in the kitchen. Three years later Jefferson retired to Monticello, naming Edith and Frances his household cooks. This displaced Peter Hemings, but he trained as a beer brewer, an experiment that proved an "entire success."

A product of the Enlightenment, Jefferson organized his garden into twenty-four squares, arranged according to which part of the plant was harvested: fruits (beans and tomatoes), roots (carrots and beets), or leaves (cabbage and lettuce). He indulged in "ornamental farming"— interspersing green, white, and purple broccoli, multicolored runner beans, and pink-blossomed cherry trees. He kept livestock and bees and conducted agricultural experiments, which he chronicled in his *Garden Book* from 1766 to 1824.

Some of Jefferson's experiments fared better than others. Convinced that Monticello's climate was equal to "the best wine countries," he planted old-world *Vitis vinifera* grapes and new-world varieties like the *Vitis labrusca,* or fox grape. But his vines were planted incorrectly, or succumbed to the root louse phylloxera, and did not survive. His crops rarely turned a profit, and his neighbors considered him the worst farmer in Virginia. But Jefferson didn't seem to care, and he treated the plantation as a large-scale agricultural laboratory, which it still is.

ON A SHIMMERING, humid morning in September 2019, I attended the thirteenth edition of the Heritage Harvest Festival, a celebration of Monticello's gastronomic and horticultural legacy. There, the present seemed to collide with the past.

Some two thousand people of all colors and creeds milled around the domed mansion, listened to historians under white tents, and sampled food trucks near Mulberry Row—the gravel drive once lined with workshops and shacks for slaves and farmworkers. A Jefferson reenactor in a white wig held forth on the West Lawn, a scene so beautiful it was almost possible to forget that was where Jefferson's heirs auctioned off slaves in 1826 to cover his debts. One of those auctioned was Peter Hemings, who was bought by a nephew and set free.

Four hundred thousand people tour Monticello annually, and many of them are hungry. In 2011, Alice Waters—the food activist, chef, and organic impresario at Chez Panisse restaurant in Berkeley, California— paid a visit, saying, "It's through food that Jefferson built community, explored biodiversity and expressed generosity." He was "our first edible educator."

But at the café Waters suffered "a shock." There was no stove or fresh food available, just salty potato chips, sweet drinks, and plastic-wrapped sandwiches. "It was . . . *unfortunate*," Waters said. "I really couldn't believe it. *Here,* in this special place, junk food had taken over." She set out to change "everything," to better reflect the legacy of our founding epicure. The space was reinvented as the Farm Table café, which includes a full kitchen and a Jeffersonian menu of seasonal vegetables, local sausage, and macaroni and cheese. Eighty percent of its food is grown locally, 35 percent of which comes from Tufton Farm. The changes were a leap forward, though food prices rose and plastic cutlery and potato chips were still in evidence. "It's a great improvement," Waters said diplomatically. "But the farms here could provide enough food for the whole café and more; *that* should be the goal." She was looking to the future, but the past lingered in the dappled shadows.

IN 1809, Jefferson replaced the small brick kitchen used by the Hemings brothers with a much larger one in a new south wing. The space was equipped with sixty copper pots, a wide hearth, and a state-of-the-art "stew stove"—a twenty-eight-foot-long brick counter with eight adjustable cast-iron grates that held pots for stewing and pans for frying. It was a marvel of culinary technology. Fueled by charcoal, it allowed cooks to precisely control the heat in making French-influenced dishes such as *bouilli* (boiled meat) with *sauce hachée* (a rich tomato sauce). Yet, the only time Jefferson entered his magnificent kitchen was to wind the clock, the slave Isaac Granger Jefferson wryly noted.

It was the most modern kitchen in America and it turned Monticello into a machine for entertaining. Take, for instance, the tall set of shelves that rotated plates of food from a corridor into the dining room, where they were placed on dumbwaiters, containing "everything necessary for the progress of dinner from beginning to end," without the need for eavesdropping servants. Directly below the dining room Jefferson built a 220-square-foot wine cave, packed with bottles from France, Italy, Spain, Portugal, Germany, and Hungary, and secured by a thick, iron-strapped, double-locked door. Two slim, pulley-operated wine elevators, cleverly hidden behind panels on either side of the fireplace, lifted two bottles apiece from the cellar to the imbibers above.

In 1967, the original, small brick kitchen was converted into a tourists' bathroom. Why this was considered a good idea has not been explained, but starting in the 1990s the Thomas Jefferson Foundation acknowledged the importance of the slaves who were the engine of the plantation. In 2017 the original hearth was excavated, revealing ashes from its last cooking fires two centuries ago. The reopening attracted media attention and set off soul-searching, particularly among Jefferson's descendants.

"I was a big admirer of Jefferson because of his authorship of the Declaration of Independence, but my dad never discussed our connection," said Gayle Jessup White, a community engagement officer at Monticello. "I didn't learn that I was related until I was thirteen. And it was all oral history." She is descended from Thomas Jefferson on her father's side and Peter Hemings through her mother's line. "As a kid, I held my connection to Jefferson up with pride," White said. But she was shocked to discover she was descended from his slaves, too. "It is a matter that simply exists," she said. "I accept it as it is."

Standing in the original kitchen, White says, "I feel the weight of history." When the hearth was exposed, she dropped to her knees and rubbed the floor's red clay on her arms. "It was virgin earth, and my ancestors had stood on that ground," she said with a tremor. "It was the closest I've ever been to them physically." Thomas Jefferson stood in that little room, and the Hemings brothers spent countless hours cooking there. "I represent those who never had voices of their own," White said. The original kitchen is "the most sacred ground on this plantation," and its exhumation "gives the enslaved the humanity that they've been robbed of."

The combination of Jefferson's vision and resources with the skill of the Hemings brothers, the Herns, and other slave chefs resulted in a distinctly Virginia cuisine. Blending French technique with ingredients from the States, Europe, and Africa, and their own creative flights, they created a fusion cookery of a high order. As their knowledge was passed down, "Jefferson's Table" circulated through the nation's bloodstream and helped to define American taste. It still does.

4

JAMES MADISON

To Jemmy's Health,
and Dolley's Remorseless Equanimity

THE FOURTH PRESIDENT
March 4, 1809–March 4, 1817

★

I. Mrs. Madison's Snuff and Squeezes

James "Jemmy" Madison was the "Father of the Constitution," a political philosopher, and America's fourth president, but he cared little about the food on his plate or the political value of entertaining. His wife, Dolley Madison, on the other hand, was a consummate hostess, social activist, romantic matchmaker, and political fixer extraordinaire who essentially created the role of First Lady as we know it today.

"Poor Jemmy! He is but a withered little apple-John," cackled Washington Irving, the diplomat and author of "Rip Van Winkle." But "Dolley" (as everyone called her) was "a sunny little Quakeress," Irving enthused, "a fine, portly, buxom dame—who has a smile & pleasant word for every body."

She was an unlikely "Mrs. Presidentress," as First Ladies were called. Born Dolley Payne, she was raised a strict Quaker in Virginia, married a lawyer, and had two sons in Philadelphia. Then, in a blink, she lost her husband, a son, her mother-in-law, and her father-in-law to the yellow fever epidemic of 1793. The brutal loss helps explain why Dolley was so attuned to maintaining harmony: having witnessed how short and capricious life can be, she wanted to welcome, entertain, and fill the belly of every person she met.

Dolley and "the great little Madison," as she called him, were introduced by Aaron Burr in 1794. Jemmy was a small, thin man with an outsized intellect who appeared taciturn in public but revealed a sharp wit in private. Seventeen years older than Dolley, he was wealthy, unmarried, childless, an Episcopalian, and a distinguished congressman from Virginia. Dolley was a plump woman with pale white skin, rouged cheeks, blue eyes, and curly black hair and, despite being a poor single mother, possessed an irrepressible energy and unerring social instinct. After a whirlwind romance the Madisons married, and Dolley became the mistress of Montpelier, the Madison family plantation just down the road from Jefferson's Monticello. (Madison doted on Dolley's aptly named son Payne, who repaid him by squandering the family fortune.) The tobacco farm, blacksmith shop, store, and brandy distillery at Montpelier relied on nearly a hundred slaves, a fact that troubled Madison—who was responsible for much of the Bill of Rights—but did not overly concern Dolley.

Though rough around the edges when she arrived in Washington in 1800, she learned social niceties on the job, as it were. Her husband was Jefferson's secretary of state, and Mrs. Madison insisted on renting a large home on F Street suitable for entertaining. She befriended the wives of congressmen and the Spanish and French ambassadors and regularly hosted dinner parties for forty or more guests. In the meantime, she worked with the architect Benjamin Latrobe to help the president decorate the Executive Mansion and often pinch-hit as a hostess at his parties.

Dolley was a gifted conversationalist with a knack for remembering names and faces, and disarmed critics with her personal warmth. Though she claimed to be uninterested in politics ("men's work"), she quietly pushed her husband's legislation, and was so adept at backroom patronage that she staffed many positions in the growing federal bureaucracy. Frequently, her social grace paid bountiful political dividends. When Thomas Jefferson snubbed the British ambassador, Anthony Merry, in 1803, for instance—by escorting Mrs. Madison to the dinner table instead of Mrs. Merry, which deeply offended the British—Dolley unsnarled the diplomatic tangle by befriending Elizabeth Merry and hosting the British couple for dinner at her F Street home.

At a time when women were expected to hang back and play a subordinate role, Mrs. Madison gleefully chucked her drab Quaker outfits and strode into the limelight sheathed in pink satin dresses and red velvet gowns, glittering turbans, and regal headdresses festooned with bird of paradise feathers, the better for her admirers to spot her in a crowd. "The accomplished Mrs. Madison . . . presides, it is said, better than any other woman can in the country," noted the Maine Republican James C. Jewett. And a friend noted that Washingtonians could not resist Dolley's "conciliatory disposition . . . her frank and gracious manners, [and] frequented her evening circle and sat at her husband's table."

WHEN THE MADISONS MOVED into the Executive Mansion in 1809, Dolley took presidential entertaining to new peaks. As if presiding over a tribal watering hole, she encouraged people of all stripes to mingle, eat, and converse at the Madison White House.

Starting on March 30, 1809, and lasting through the end of Madison's second term in 1817, Dolley hosted "drawing rooms" (a less Eurocentric-sounding term than Washington and Adams's "levees") every Wednesday night. To ensure a large and diverse crowd, she published invitations in newspapers, welcomed both men and women, and included everyone from carriage drivers and barbers to students, foreign dignitaries, socialites, businessmen, and legislators. She understood that the dining room was "a stage from which to convey an image of power, cultivate political loyalties, and project dignity and authority," wrote the historian Edith Mayo.

Like Jefferson, Dolley was an adept stage manager who employed a veteran French steward, Jean-Pierre ("French John") Sioussat, and a dozen servants and slaves who served dinners prepared in Jefferson's now familiar Anglo-French-Virginia style and bottle after bottle of enviable European wine, procured with Jefferson's help.

While Jemmy sat in the middle of a long table, where he could converse and avoid "the trouble of serving guests, drinking wine, etc.," observed the society columnist Sarah Seaton, Dolley sat herself amid cabinet members and took command of the food, drink, and table talk. She liked to carve the ham or turkey to start, then had a second course of fruits, nuts, and desserts delivered to the table. She often showcased special or regional dishes—especially southern ones, such as ham croquettes, corn and lard "oysters," "fairy butter" (hard-boiled eggs mixed with sugar, butter, and orange-flower water), chicken and okra soup, and crab omelets with eggplant and tomatoes—that would surprise her guests. Dolley had a sweet tooth and was fond of apricot or pink peppermint ice cream for dessert.

After dinner, the president would retreat to a corner to murmur with his Democratic-Republican cronies. Dolley would serve a Yard of Flannel punch (ale, rum, eggs, ginger, sugar), pass snacks, make introductions, and ask young women to play the piano or dance "figures" for the crowd. Then she would sweep her guests off for rounds of parlor games and dancing.

So popular, and politically necessary, did these evenings become that her guests referred to them as "Mrs. Madison's Wednesday nights," or, due to the hot crush of bodies, "squeezes."

Attending a squeeze in 1811, Washington Irving was dazzled by the "collection of great and little men, of ugly old women, and beautiful young ones," and felt as if he had "emerged from dirt and darkness into the blazing splendor of Mrs. Madison's Drawing room." And when a group of Federalists refused to attend a squeeze out of pique, Dolley responded by packing her drawing room with so many of their rivals that it "alarm'd [the Federalists] into a return," she noted triumphantly.

When the political rhetoric blew too hot, Dolley cooled things down with her secret weapon: a pinch of snuff. The tobacco from her silver snuffbox had "a magic influence" on combatants, friends would say, chuckling. One evening the fiery Kentucky congressman Henry Clay defied President Madison, and Dolley took him aside to offer him a snort of tobacco. It was, Margaret Bayard Smith wrote, a "perfect security from hostility."

"Everybody loves Mrs. Madison," Clay said, relenting his opposition.

"That's because Mrs. Madison loves everybody," Dolley sweetly replied.

IN SPITE OF her outsized persona, Dolley Madison maintained a studied neutrality and was a cipher in public. "By her deportment in her own house, you cannot discover who is her husband's friends or foes," Congressman Jonathan Roberts of Pennsylvania said. And a woman from New York observed, "There is something very fascinating about her—yet I do not think it possible to know what her real opinions are; she is all things to all men."

Dolley's social strategy was perfectly calibrated for an era when the idea of bipartisanship was rare and President Madison had few levers to control a sharply divided House—a body some historians have described as "the worst Congress ever dealt a president." Bloody-knuckled electioneering, scandalous innuendo, duels, and the occasional political murder were routine, though recompense was not. When the Madisons' enemies falsely accused him of offering to trade sex with Dolley for votes, he had no meaningful way to defend himself or his wife's honor. But Mrs. Madison played a long game, as poker players say. As an outsider, she understood that small gestures can have a great impact. Smiling and welcoming even the most venal critics into her home Wednesday after Wednesday, she wore them down with unflappable kindness.

At times, it seemed as if Dolley Madison were the glue that held the Republic together—with smiles, a bite of ice cream, a pinch of snuff, and an iron will. She was hailed by Daniel Webster as "the only permanent power in Washington."

Writing of Mrs. Madison's social prowess, the historian Catherine Allgor observed, "The superior food, the lovely setting, and the refined behavior allowed people to feel open, relaxed, and included. The power of dining, of course, went both ways. Even the most backward rube understood this, as when one southern representative responded to a dinner invitation from James Madison: 'I won't dine with you because you won't dine with me.' For foreign diplomats in Washington, the dinner table was their office, and they spent plenty of money in the primitive city on dinner parties, leaving guest lists and tactical memoranda for their successors. . . . [T]he social atmosphere successfully masked the high political stakes."

The cumulative effect of Dolley's "remorseless equanimity," as a friend described her social tact (and tactics), was to assert Jemmy's leadership, bolster the constitutionally weak Office of the President, and solidify the role of the Executive Mansion as the nucleus of All That Mattered in Washington, D.C. In the process, she helped define the role of First Lady as we currently understand it, though that title did not yet exist.

II. "Mrs. Presidentress"

At the time, the chief executive's wife was known as "the President's Lady," "Mrs. President," or "Mrs. Presidentress." Her duties were not clearly stated but seemed obvious: to be a supportive spouse and official hostess who directed the kitchen and orchestrated presidential entertaining. That role has more or less endured, at least in the public imagination. But the reality is more complicated. In fact, First Ladies have always played a political role, overtly or covertly, and they have always used food and drink to further their husbands' agendas.

The role of Mrs. President is not a job, exactly. It is not a paid position or an elected one. It comes with no official duties. Yet it is a high-profile, full-time occupation laden with symbolic importance. The position has evolved steadily and quietly, for the most part, with occasional breakthrough moments—Eleanor Roosevelt's social activism, Jackie Kennedy's gastronomic revolution—that make news. Today, First Ladyhood encompasses political duties and social causes, along with the raising of children, the planting of gardens, and socializing on a grand and intimate scale. The position comes with a full-time staff with offices in the East Wing of the White House, and it has become increasingly politicized and scrutinized.

Some women—such as Martha Washington, Mamie Eisenhower, Nancy Reagan, and Hillary Rodham Clinton—enjoyed the role, with caveats. Others—such as Barbara Bush and Michelle Obama—had decidedly mixed feelings about it. And a few—such as Margaret Taylor, Bess Truman, and Melania Trump—shied away from, or outright resented, the role of First Lady. Dolley Madison loved being "Mrs. President" and became the most famous hostess in America. Yet she is best remembered for a dinner that was never served.

ON AUGUST 24, 1814, thousands of British troops were advancing on Washington, D.C., during the War of 1812. Two days earlier, James Madison had left the President's House to take charge of his army in Virginia. Assuming he would return victorious, Dolley prepared a celebratory dinner. The slave Paul Jennings described it as an opulent meal. "I set the table myself, and brought up the ale, cider, and wine, and placed them in the coolers," he wrote. (Others recall the details differently.) But when the redcoats marched through the city largely uncontested, Mrs. Madison instructed two servants to spirit away the red velvet drapes from the Oval Room, a copy of the Declaration of Independence, the blue-and-gold Lowestoft china, and Gilbert Stuart's portrait of George Washington from the State Dining Room. As evening set, she fled.

Entering the abandoned President's House, the British found "a bountiful dinner spread for forty guests," an English correspondent wrote, and "several kinds of wine in handsome cut glass decanters." Details of the menu have been lost, but the officers sampled the Madisons' food and drank an ironic toast with the president's wine—"to 'Jemmy's health'"—then smashed all of the mansion's windows and burned the white building down to a charred shell.

Madison was blamed for the debacle, and his opponents called for his impeachment. But with several dizzying military victories, including General Andrew Jackson's rout of the British at New Orleans, and a hastily sketched-out peace treaty, the administration was rescued. Jubilant once again, Dolley hosted a rowdy victory party at their temporary residence, the John Tayloe House (known as the Octagon House, for its shape, and still extant). "No one . . . who beheld the radiance of joy which lighted up [Dolley's] countenance [could doubt that] all uncertainty was at an end," reported the *National Intelligencer*.

Though the truce with England was less secure than Dolley made it appear, her good cheer helped persuade Congress not to move the capital back to Philadelphia, as some called for. She had every wineglass filled for a toast and invited the servants to eat and celebrate late into the night. It took some of the revelers two days to recover. But with that shrewd bit of commensality, Dolley Madison convinced Americans they had won a second war of independence against the king of England.

=5=

ABRAHAM LINCOLN

Corn, Gingerbread, and Thanksgiving

THE SIXTEENTH PRESIDENT
March 4, 1861–April 15, 1865

★

I. Premonitions

After two days of unremitting rain, Pennsylvania Avenue had become a swamp. Undeterred, thousands of spectators forded the muck to crowd around the East Portico of the Capitol, eager to hear their president speak. It was Saturday, March 4, 1865, and Abraham Lincoln was celebrating his second inauguration. There was a mixed sense of hope, commemoration, and danger in the breeze. But as Lincoln stepped to the podium, the clouds parted, and the Capitol dome soaring behind him— a symbol of all that the nation had bloodied itself over in the past four years—was brilliantly lit by the sun. It seemed an omen. The Civil War was winding down, and the North was on the cusp of victory; a month later, Robert E. Lee would surrender to Ulysses S. Grant at Appomattox. Yet the president had lost his appetite.

Standing about six feet four inches tall, Lincoln was the tallest president. At the start of his administration, in 1861, he had weighed a robust 180 pounds; now, four years later, his body had been whittled down to 150 pounds. His face was thin and lined with worry, his coarse black hair was disheveled, his brow was permanently furrowed, his gray eyes were sunk in their sockets. Lincoln was fifty-six but looked seventy.

The Civil War was the most lethal conflict in American history, killing some 800,000 people and nearly cleaving the nation in two. Its brutal unrelentingness had consumed him. Lincoln suffered from insomnia, poor circulation, constipation, and a brooding malaise. He wandered the streets of Washington alone at night armed with just a stick, or ghosted through the halls of the Executive Mansion in the wee hours. Sometimes he'd collapse on a couch. One day Lincoln couldn't get out of bed, and Horace Greeley, the editor of the *New-York Tribune,* declared the president "seemed unlikely to live."

Lincoln managed to soldier on, but hardly noticed what was on his plate and sometimes forgot to eat. When he did remember, he nibbled distractedly on a cracker or piece of cheese, maybe an apple. Breakfast was one egg and one cup of black coffee. Lunch was a biscuit, a piece of fruit, and a glass of milk. His spartan diet seemed to mirror the nation's ennui. For dinner, his wife, Mary Todd Lincoln, would arrange ample meals featuring his favorite foods—such as chicken fricassee (small pieces of chicken seasoned with nutmeg and mace, then fried), black-berry pie, and other dishes that reminded him of his childhood on the Kentucky frontier—or her favorites, such as foie gras, or tongue in aspic, or truffle-stuffed turkey breast.

Lincoln did not want a civil war and had tried to avoid it through diplomacy and appeasement. But on April 12, 1861, Confederate troops attacked Fort Sumter, which guarded the harbor at Charleston, South Carolina. After a thirty-four-hour bombardment (no one was killed), the Union troops surrendered. Lincoln had been in office for just over a month. "Both parties deprecated the war," he somberly intoned, "but one of them would make war rather than let the Nation survive, and the other would accept war rather than let it perish."

Lincoln narrowly avoided several assassination attempts—including the time someone shot a bullet through his "eight-dollar plug-hat"—and with morbid humor he kept a file of death threats he'd received that he labeled "Assassinations." One night, he dreamed that someone was crying in the White House. He went in search of the bereaved and in the East Room discovered a catafalque bearing a corpse lying in state. An honor guard stood by, and a line of mourners paid their respects.

"Who died?" Lincoln asked.

"The president," a dream figure replied. "He was assassinated."

The dreaming Lincoln shrugged. He was a fatalist who reasoned that if someone was determined to kill him, there was little he could do to stop them.

In his second inaugural address that cloudy-sunny afternoon in 1865, Lincoln urged his countrymen to embrace compassion and solidarity over vindictiveness. Noting that slavery was "somehow the cause of the war," he paraphrased Matthew 7:1, saying, "Let us judge not, that we be not judged . . . With malice toward none, with charity for all, with firm-ness in the right as God gives us to see the right, let us strive on to finish the work we are in, to bind up the nation's wounds."

Then it was time for Americans to breathe a collective sigh of relief and to celebrate. Aware that all eyes were on them, President and Mrs. Lincoln tried to mask their weariness by hosting "a great public recep-tion" at the White House that evening. Hundreds of people attended, and the crowd's energy bordered on manic. William H. Crook, one of Lin-coln's bodyguards, recalled,

The White House looked as if a regiment of rebel troops had been quartered there—with permission to forage. The crowds were enormous, and there were some rough people present. A fever of vandalism seemed to seize them. . . . [T]he damage created . . . was something monstrous. . . . A great piece of red brocade, a yard square almost, was cut from the window-hangings of the East Room, and another piece, not quite so large, from the curtain in the Green Room. Besides this, flowers from the floral design in the lace curtains were cut out. . . . Some arrests were made, after the reception, of persons concerned in the disgraceful business. These things distressed the President greatly. I can hardly understand why, when he was so calm about things usually, these acts of rowdyism should have impressed him so painfully. It was the senseless violence of it that puzzled him. "Why should they do it?" he said to me. "How can they?"

Two days later, on March 6, the Lincolns hosted their second inaugural ball. It was held in the U.S. Patent Office Building (now the National Portrait Gallery and the Smithsonian American Art Museum). During the Civil War the building's vast central hall was used as a hospital for soldiers injured at the Battles of Manassas, Antietam, and Fredericksburg. Walt Whitman had worked there as a medical orderly, and at the inaugural ball he noted, "I could not help thinking, what a different scene" was on display. The hall, once "fill'd with a crowded mass of the worst wounded of the war," had been transformed by "beautiful women, perfumes, the violins' sweetness, the polka and the waltz."

Four thousand revelers strolled into the reception room, which was draped with large American flags, and a dais was set with blue and gold sofas for the First Couple. A military band played background music until 10:00 p.m., when the band struck up vigorous waltzes, Virginia reels, and quadrilles. Alcohol flowed. People began to bow, curtsy, and wheel faster and faster. At eleven o'clock, President and Mrs. Lincoln arrived to strains of "Hail to the Chief" and took their seats on the dais. He wore a plain black suit and white kid gloves. She dressed in a white silk gown with a lace shawl, a headdress of white jasmine and purple violets. "Mr. Lincoln was evidently trying to throw off care for the time, but with rather ill success and looked very old," *The New York Times* reported. "Yet he seemed pleased and gratified, as he was greeted by the people."

Everything went smoothly, until the stroke of midnight, when the doors to the large "supper room" were thrown open. The hall was decorated with sugar models of the U.S. Capitol, Fort Sumter, and Admiral David Farragut aboard the USS *Hartford*. They were spectacular examples of the confectioners' art, but as the room warmed, the sugar Capitol began to soften and melt. As the drunk, ravenous crowd surged inside, they eyed a nearly miraculous sight: a 250-foot-long table heaped with exquisitely prepared food—from oyster stew to courses of beef, veal, poultry, game, pâtés, smoked meats, salads, cakes and tarts, jellies and creams, ice cream, fruit ices, dessert, coffee, and chocolates.

Next to that was an even bigger table that held twice as many sweet pastries as savory entrées. (What we now call dessert was called pastry: desserts were light, post-dinner snacks such as nuts, grapes, and raisins.) The sweets were the work of the confectioner G. A. Balzer and, *The New York Times* recorded, included

> ornamental pyramids—nougat, orange, caramel—with fancy cream candy, coconut, macaroon, chocolate; tree cakes—cakes and tarts, almond, sponge; belle alliance, dame blanche, macaroon tart, *tarte a la Nelson*—tarte *a la Orleans*, tarte *a la Portugaise*, tarte *a Vienne*, pound cake, sponge cake, lady cake, fancy small cakes; jellies and creams— calf's foot and wine jelly, Charlotte *Russe*, Charlotte *a la vanilla; blanc mange, crême Napolitaine, crême a la* Nelson, *crême* Chateaubriand, *crême a la* Smyrna, *crême a la* Nasselrode, *bombe a la* vanilla, ice cream with vanilla, lemon white coffee, chocolate, burnt almond, maraschino, fruit ices, strawberry, orange, lemon; dessert—grapes, almonds, raisins, etc., coffee and chocolate.

Eyeing the trove wolfishly, the guests assaulted the beautifully arranged platters. "The onset of the crowd upon the tables was frightful," a reporter from *The Washington Evening Star* wrote. Glasses smashed on the floor as people carried away entire legs of lamb and grabbed handfuls of ice cream. People "could be seen snatching whole *pates,* chickens, legs of veal, halves of turkies [*sic*], ornamental pyramids, etc., from the tables and bearing them aloft over the heads of the shuddering crowd," the *Star* continued. "The floor of the supper room was soon sticky, pasty and oily with wasted confections, mashed cake, and debris of fowl and meat."

The *Times* recoiled: "In less than an hour the table was a wreck . . . positively frightful to behold." Several inebriates passed out. Others reveled through the night and stumbled out into the cool air just as dawn lit the city's muddy streets.

The Lincolns gamely remained at the party until 1:30 a.m., and one can imagine they found the debauchery bewildering and sad. Ruminating on the "fever of vandalism," Crook intuited the crowd had "some premonition that there would not be much more of Mr. Lincoln's administration [and it] made them lawless. They wanted to get mementos while they could."

II. *"The Taste* Is *in My Mouth a Little"*

Tall, rawboned, and thoughtful, Abe Lincoln was raised on the Kentucky and Indiana frontiers, where his diet included possum stew and squirrel dip and he developed a lifelong love of raw honey from the comb. His stepmother, Sally Lincoln, observed, "Abe was a moderate eater and I now have no remembrance of his special dish: he sat down and ate what was set before him, making no complaint." A lawyer friend, Leonard Swett, wrote, "I never . . . heard him complain of a hard bed or a bad meal."

This has been the popular view of Lincoln the eater: as a passive, disinterested consumer who viewed food as "fuel for the furnace" rather than as an aesthetic experience worth savoring. But that portrait is only partly accurate. Like much about Lincoln, the truth is more nuanced and situational. For him, food represented a source of strength and work, but was also associated with love and tragedy.

When times were good, Lincoln was an enthusiastic omnivore. His first food memory was of eating corn cakes for breakfast, a dish that remained a favorite. Growing up, his cousin John Hanks remembered, "Abraham was a good and hearty eater—loved good eating." As an adult, Lincoln often mentioned his favorite treats—raw honey and corn bread, vanilla almond cake, potatoes, fruit, lemon pie. While campaigning for office, he collected the recipes of dishes he'd enjoyed at boardinghouses. As a young married lawyer in Springfield, Illinois, he milked Old Bob, the family cow, helped Mary with the grocery shopping, carefully chose cuts of meat, and happily donned a blue apron to cook dinner for their three boys. Even at the White House, Crook recalled, "Mr. Lincoln . . . never lost his tastes for things that a growing farmer's boy would like. He was particularly fond of bacon."

Lincoln was born in 1809 and raised with his sister, Sally, on a large farm in central Kentucky. He learned to husband farm animals and hunt and fish. His mother, Nancy, was said to be a good cook, but there is scant evidence of what she set on the table. The "domestic books" of that era included recipes for venison, rabbit, squirrel, pheasant, turkey, quail, woodchuck, and bear. Nancy and Sally kept a vegetable garden and foraged for berries, cherries, and nuts. Lincoln's father, Thomas, farmed corn and wheat.

Despite Kentucky's bounty, life on the frontier was capricious. Lincoln's brother, Tommy Jr., lived just three days. And there were freak weather events, such as "the year without summer," when a snap frost in July 1816 killed the Lincolns' crops. In search of more hospitable climes, Thomas bought eighty acres of land, for less than $3 an acre, in southern Indiana. He cleared part of the heavily wooded lot and built a lean-to. "Here I grew up," Lincoln wrote of Indiana. It was "a wild region, with many bears and other wild animals still in the woods." At night, he would lie in bed listening to panthers scream.

When he turned seven, Abraham was given an ax and put to work clearing fields and building a house and barn. Over the next fourteen years, the Lincolns acquired a cow, horses, sheep, hogs, oxen, and chickens. Nancy kept a vegetable garden and maintained a small orchard.

Apples were a useful fruit. The Lincolns would eat them fresh off the tree or stew, bake, and juice them. They fried thin slices of pale green apples that ripen in June. They cut red apples into rounds and dried them for winter snacks. They chopped piles of apples and heated them in large iron kettles outdoors, to produce sweet apple butter and tangy applesauce. The local cask maker would distill apple juice into applejack brandy, a favorite holiday treat for the adults.

Corn is a work- and water-intensive crop, but it was a staple food in the Lincoln household. The Indiana soil was rich, and their cornstalks grew astoundingly high. Young Abe took their kernels to be ground into cornmeal. Corn provided food for people, cows, pigs, and horses; with the help of a backyard still, corn was transformed into whiskey, which could be bartered for goods or sold for cash. Yet corn was often scorned as forage fit only for animals. In 1842, Henry Andrews lamented in the *Union Agriculturist,* the leading farm journal of the day, "There is no grain grown in the U.S. of more value as to its general usefulness for both man and beast than the Indian corn, and yet with what contempt it is treated by many when it is occasionally placed on our tables in the form of bread. How many . . . exclaim against corn bread or its usefulness any farther than for [live]stock. I think the cause of dislike is more from the want of knowledge [of] how to prepare it for the table, than anything else."

Young Abe Lincoln didn't need convincing: he was a near corn-oholic.

He inhaled corn cakes, corn bread, cornmeal mush, hominy, and especially corn dodgers. He liked to joke that he could "eat corn cakes twice as fast as anyone could make them," and they remained his favorite breakfast and Sunday supper at the President's House.

Corn dodgers are small oval-shaped treats, about two inches long, made from coarse stone-ground cornmeal fried in butter or bacon drippings. Cooked right, they have a crisp crust and a soft, deeply corn-flavored interior. Corn dodgers were Lincoln's equivalent to Proust's madeleines—a mnemonic touchstone recalling his young days on the frontier. Lincoln's cousin Dennis Hanks recalled that by age twelve "Abe . . . [would] put a book inside his shirt an' fill his pants pockets with corn dodgers an' go off to plow or hoe. When noon came he'd set under a tree an' read an' eat."

It was an agrarian idyll, but in the summer of 1818 a suffocating heat and humidity descended, killing much of the vegetation. Snakeroot, a harmless-looking white flower, spread wildly. It was toxic, and the cows that grazed on snakeroot lapsed into a coma and died; people who drank milk from an infected cow could likewise fall into a coma and die of "milk sickness." Nancy's uncle and his wife succumbed, leaving the Lincolns to care for their son, Dennis Hanks. Then Nancy was stricken and died, and a year later Thomas Lincoln married Sarah "Sally" Bush Johnston, a widowed mother of three. The reconstituted Lincoln family now included six children. They managed, but in January 1828 Abe's sister Sally died in childbirth and was buried with her baby boy in her arms.

In 1831, at age twenty-two, Lincoln and some friends set out into the world. Moving to New Salem, Illinois, he worked as a day laborer and filled out to a muscular 220 pounds. Then he moved to Springfield, where he studied law and became interested in politics. One of the "Long Nine," a group of sequoia-height lawyers, Lincoln helped persuade legislators to move the state capital from Vandalia to Springfield.

On the evening of November 4, his senior law partner, John Todd Stuart, brought Lincoln to a party in Springfield, where he was introduced to Mary Todd. She was twenty-three, stood five feet three inches tall, and had piercing blue eyes, thick cheeks, a blunt nose and lips, and dark hair parted in the middle. With a quick temper and a generous laugh, she was raised in a comfortable brick mansion staffed by slaves in Lexington, Kentucky. She was schooled in the social graces, spoke French, and dreamed of living in the President's Mansion.

When they were introduced, the gangly Lincoln bowed his head and said, gravely, "Miss Todd, I wish to dance with you in the worst way." She agreed, and they took a few stiff turns around the floor. Later, Mary assured her sisters that Lincoln did, indeed, dance "in the worst way."

He was thirty-three, an angular, not well-educated, laconic, indebted country boy who had been raised on squirrel stew. She was a well-educated, outspoken southern belle who was the daughter of a powerful businessman and was raised on pâté, roasted venison, delicate lettuces, and pastries. Her sisters did not approve of the "plebeian" Lincoln, but Mary found Abraham charming and patient, with a gentle manner, a dry wit, and a keen mind.

Though women could not vote, the Todds were encouraged by their father to be politically informed. Mary and Abe bonded over Shakespeare and a shared history of lost mothers (hers died when she was six). But it might have been Mary's love of baking that sealed the deal. She bought eleven pounds of sugar every two weeks, but when she was on a tear, she'd use as much as ten pounds of sugar a week. It was probably her White Cake, aptly known as Courting Cake, that did the trick. The recipe had been handed down through the Todd family, and Mary put her own spin on it. Lincoln considered the simple burnt sugar (some say it was almond) confection "the best cake" he'd ever eaten.

Their courtship suffered bumps, and Mary's sisters tried to talk her out of marriage. Elizabeth claimed she did not have time to bake a wedding cake and would serve gingerbread and beer instead. That would be just fine for her "plebeian" fiancé, Mary snapped. In the end a delicious cake was baked, and the interior was still warm when the newlyweds sliced it open.

When the Lincolns' first son, Robert, was born in 1843, they purchased a house in Springfield, where they lived for seventeen years. They had three more boys, but only Robert outlived his mother. Years later, when Mary Todd Lincoln suffered bouts of grief and rage, Lincoln stood true: "My wife is as handsome as when she was a girl, and I . . . fell in love with her; and what is more, I have never fallen out."

Mary Todd Lincoln hired women, or relied on relatives and neighbors, for housework, and trained herself to cook. While she is usually depicted wearing genteel ruffles and lace, Mrs. Lincoln sweated over her dinners and left her recipe books, stove, and a revealing pile of garbage as evidence. In 1846, Mrs. Lincoln bought Eliza Leslie's best-selling *Directions for Cookery, in Its Various Branches,* which provided instructions for both open-hearth and stovetop cookery. And details of the Lincolns' domestic life were revealed in the 1980s when archaeologists excavated the grounds of their Springfield house (the only home they owned). They found pottery shards, bottles, eggshells, and bones from sirloin steaks, lamb, mutton, pigs' feet, squirrel, mourning dove, and especially turkey. The Lincolns were of the generation that transitioned from cooking over fire in a hearth to the more compact and efficient iron stove, one of which—a Royal Oak #9, with a four-burner cooktop, a firebox, and a metal warming shelf—they bought in 1860.

As a young lawyer in Springfield, Lincoln became a leader of the Whig Party, a state legislator, and a U.S. congressman from Illinois. Mocked as a hick and misfit—"the original gorilla"—Lincoln developed a thick skin and deflected criticism with dry humor. He practiced law for several years but was so rankled by the pro-slavery Kansas-Nebraska Act that he returned to politics in 1854 to become a leader of the new Republican Party. When his friend Lyman Trumbull asked if Lincoln might seek the presidency, Abe replied, "The taste *is* in my mouth a little."

Soon, he was off campaigning. In stump speeches and debates, Lincoln used plain language and homespun stories to depict himself as a compassionate, straight-talking man of the people. Food was a constant theme. His humble tastes reflected the mood of the electorate and led to some of his most memorable and politically effective aphorisms. One of his favorite yarns was the parable of "the Hoosier and the Gingerbread Men." It began when his parents moved from Kentucky to Indiana in December 1816, he recalled:

> Once in a while my mother used to get some sorghum and ginger and make some gingerbread. It wasn't often and it was our biggest treat. One day I smelled the gingerbread and came into the house to get my share while it was hot. My mother had baked me three gingerbread men. I took them under a hickory tree to eat them. There was a family that lived near us that was a little poorer than we were and their boy came along as I sat down.
>
> "Abe," he said, "gimme a man?"
>
> I gave him one. He crammed it in his mouth in two bites and looked at me while I was biting the legs from my first one.
>
> "Abe," he said, "gimme that other'n."
>
> I wanted it myself, but I gave it to him and as it followed the first I said to him, "You seem to like gingerbread."
>
> "Abe," he said, "I don't suppose there's anybody on this earth like

gingerbread better'n I do." He drew a long breath before he added, "and I don't suppose there's anybody on this earth gets less'n I do."

Lincoln used the gingerbread story to disarm his critics and bond with audiences of humble stock. As he liked to remind them, he was not raised with "the pleasures of life."

His most famous use of the anecdote occurred on August 21, 1858, in his first encounter with the Democratic senator Stephen A. Douglas. As usual in their seven famous debates, the central issue that day was slavery. The men verbally sparred before an audience of thousands in Ottawa, Illinois, for three hours—with Douglas framing Lincoln as an abolitionist, while Lincoln accused Douglas of whipping up fear to divide the Republicans and perpetuate slavery.

Douglas began by heaping praise on Lincoln's achievements to the point of mockery, then falsely accused his rival of setting "the states at war." Rather than counterattack, Lincoln appeared surprised that the eminent senator would so misinterpret his views. With a knowing wink to the crowd, Lincoln declared, "I am not very accustomed to flattery and it came the sweeter to me. I was rather like the Hoosier with the gingerbread, when he said he reckoned he loved it better any other man, and got less of it."

This gambit delighted the audience and positioned Lincoln as an honest, trusting country boy pitted against a cynical city slicker. And it wasn't the last time Lincoln used food imagery to skewer his rival.

In October 1858, during their sixth debate, Lincoln mocked Douglas's "Freeport Doctrine," which held that settlers of new territories could ignore the U.S. Supreme Court's *Dred Scott* decision (ruling that slaves could not be citizens and that states could not ban slavery) by not enforcing slave owners' rights. It was Douglas's attempt to appease both pro- and antislavery factions. Lincoln derided such convoluted logic as a "species of humbuggery" that was akin to "the homeopathic soup that was made by boiling the shadow of a pigeon that had been starved to death."

And so, with the help of gingerbread men and shadowy pigeon soup, Lincoln helped split the Democratic Party and set himself on course to become the nation's sixteenth president and its first Republican chief executive. Mary went to sleep early on the night of November 6, 1860, convinced that he would win. But they had not even left Springfield when, on December 20, South Carolina seceded from the Union, quickly followed by Mississippi, Florida, Alabama, Georgia, Louisiana, and Texas.

III. Abe's Dinner, Mary's Grief

En route to Washington in February 1861, Allan Pinkerton, head of the Union Intelligence Service, discovered a pro-slavery plot to assassinate the president-elect. He hustled the Lincolns aboard a heavily guarded railway carriage and secreted them into the capital in the middle of the night. For the next ten days, they lodged in the luxe Parlor No. 6 at Willard's Hotel, a few blocks from the White House.

On March 4, Lincoln stood below the East Portico of the Capitol, his chin sprouting the first hairs of his famous beard (he was the first president with facial hair other than sideburns). In his monumental first inaugural address he attempted to assuage the large crowd and preserve the Union, saying, "I have no purpose . . . to interfere with the institution of slavery in the States where it exists. . . . We are not enemies, but friends. . . . The mystic chords of memory, stretching from every battlefield and patriot grave to every living heart and hearthstone all over this broad land, will yet swell the chorus of the Union, when again touched, as surely they will be, by the better angels of our nature."

Afterward, the Lincolns repaired to Willard's Hotel for an inaugural luncheon. As furniture was put into storage, the hotel was "furling all sails for the storm," the president recalled, and everyone sensed the nation teetering on the edge of civil war. Yet he was in a celebratory mood and personally chose the menu: mock turtle soup (real turtle was expensive, and mock turtle soup was made with ground beef, celery, carrots, onions, tomatoes, herbs, and a calf's head, whose simmered face meat, tongue, and brains added a deep, layered flavor); corned beef and cabbage; parsleyed potatoes; blackberry pie; and coffee, his beverage of choice.

After lunch, the Lincolns moved into the Executive Mansion, just vacated by James Buchanan, widely considered one of the worst presidents in history. A wealthy Pennsylvania Dutchman, Buchanan was a gourmand fond of duck and sauerkraut who kept an arbor of muscadine grapes for grape pie. He was America's only bachelor president, and employed Cornelia Mitchell, a well-educated, free Black chef, who prepared everything from corn pone to terrapin soup and lobster.

Buchanan invited his orphaned niece, Harriet Lane, a blonde woman with violet eyes, to live at the President's House and play the role of presidential hostess. But they viewed socializing less as a form of pleasure than as a political duty to be approached systematically. Buchanan reinstituted formal European etiquette and hosted soigné banquets catered by the French chef Charles Gautier, who became famous for his oysters, roasted partridge, soufflés, and the like. Washingtonians were wowed by the spectacle, if not by its ringmasters.

Buchanan badly underestimated the divisiveness of slavery, which split his Democratic Party and handed the election to Lincoln, failed to counteract the financial panic of 1857, and was blind to corruption in his administration. Even so, his enviably "correct" social record seemed to trigger Mary Todd Lincoln's insecurities, and she approached her social duties with a mix of dread and pluckiness.

MUCH OF WASHINGTON SOCIETY sided with the South and snubbed Mrs. Lincoln as an unsophisticated naïf allied with the North. Others condemned her as a Confederate spy when it was revealed that one of her brothers fought and died for the South, against her wishes. Determined to prove herself worthy of their respect, Mary spent lavishly on silk brocade dresses and elegant shoes from New York and Paris, though, to Lincoln's dismay, she did not always keep her thrifty husband apprised of her spending. The federal government granted her $20,000 (equivalent to some $620,000 today) to renovate the Executive Mansion with handsome new furniture, wallpaper, carpeting, and a seven-hundred-piece set of Bohemian cut glassware for her table.

Thus armed and outfitted, Mary Todd Lincoln steeled herself for her first presidential levee in December 1861. Convinced that her "smiling guests [would] pull her to pieces," she wore a demure wreath of flowers in her hair and a broad silk dress. She served an unostentatious "Gallo-American" menu with wine at tables decorated with vases of flowers. To Mary's intense relief, the guests were pleasant and well behaved, and the party went off just as planned. Then Mrs. Lincoln hosted a small dinner for Prince Napoleon of France, and the newspapers hailed her "exquisite taste" and "practical good sense . . . equal to her . . . charming manners."

Emboldened, Mary raised the stakes by inviting eight hundred guests to an elaborate dinner in February 1862. Though she was criticized by abolitionists and secessionists alike for entertaining during the Civil War, she was praised for her social judgment. Rather than invite people from all social strata, which could lead to a "horrible jam," Frank Leslie's Weekly wrote, Mrs. Lincoln had invited "respectable people . . . distinguished, beautiful, brilliant people."

She spruced up her dining room with elaborate decorations—a model steam frigate, a Chinese pagoda, the goddess of Liberty above a replica fountain, sugary mermaids, and more. The Marine Band played spunky tunes (though no dancing was allowed), and the crowd's thirst was slaked by champagne punch served in a ten-gallon punch bowl.

The Lincolns consumed alcohol sparingly. The president occasionally had a glass of champagne or wine but eschewed hard liquor and mostly drank coffee. One of Mary's brothers had a weakness for whiskey, which no doubt encouraged her abstinence, and she was a devotee of Sarah Josepha Hale, author of *The Good Housekeeper,* who banned alcohol from her recipes with stern admonitions: "Never make any preparation of which alcohol forms a part for family use!" Even so, the First Couple were constantly given bottles of fine wine and liquor by admirers. With a frontiersman's hatred of waste, Lincoln had the bottles sent to military hospitals around Washington for medicinal purposes.

Mary's fabulous 1862 dinner was cooked by the New York caterer Maillard, and included course after course of pâté, canvasback duck, beef fillet, ham, venison, terrapin (turtle), chicken, pheasant, sandwiches, jellies, cakes, bonbons, ices, and fruits. It was praised by *The New York Herald* as "one of the finest displays of gastronomic art ever seen in this country." Yet it was a prelude to heartbreak.

MARY TODD LINCOLN WAS a softer target than her husband and was denounced for any number of perceived transgressions. When the Lincolns served alcohol at diplomatic receptions, where it was expected, for instance, temperance groups accused her of outrageous "leniency." But that was just a warm-up for truly venomous attacks.

In February 1862, Jefferson Davis was named president of the Confederacy, and Willie and Tad Lincoln, the president's third and fourth sons, contracted typhoid fever. They were probably sickened by drinking Washington's water, drawn from the contaminated Potomac River. From the day they arrived at the President's House, the boys had been a loud, mischievous presence—exploring the basement, interrupting meetings, galloping ponies across the lawn, and wrestling on the floor with their indulgent father. Tad eventually recovered from the sickness, but Willie, "his mother's favorite child," grew steadily weaker.

When the Lincolns hosted a large official dinner, Mary found herself torn between her social-political duties and her maternal impulse. Dressed in a white silk dress, she attempted welcoming smiles and small talk, and served a sumptuous meal—a dozen savory dishes, ranging from foie gras to truffles and chateaubriand, and a dozen desserts, including chocolate Bavarians to orange glacé and "Fancy Cakes"—then bolted upstairs to Willie's sickroom. Sitting with him, she could hear the "rich notes of the Marine Band . . . in soft, subdued murmurs, like the wild, faint sobbing of far-off spirits," recalled her Black seamstress and confidante, Elizabeth Keckly. Days later, eleven-year-old Willie died.

"My poor boy. He was too good for this earth," President Lincoln said, weeping. "It is hard, hard to have him die." Mrs. Lincoln took to her bed for three weeks and was so psychologically unmoored that she could not bear to attend Willie's funeral. Coldhearted critics tut-tutted that Willie's death was "a judgment of God upon the Lincolns for sponsoring frivolities" at the President's House. Some deemed Mary's heartache "excessive" and not as "genuine" as the grief of mothers whose sons had died in battle.

IV. Thanksgiving

In January 1863, Lincoln freed every slave in Confederate-held territory with the Emancipation Proclamation. The spring and summer brought Union victories at the Battles of Gettysburg and Vicksburg, with huge losses to both sides. In August the president welcomed Frederick Douglass to the White House, which eventually helped spur the Thirteenth Amendment abolishing slavery. On November 19, the president gave his magisterial, 272-word Gettysburg Address to a crowd of fifteen thousand Pennsylvanians. America, he said, was "conceived in Liberty, and dedicated to the proposition that all men are created equal"; the government was "of the people, by the people, for the people." It was against this backdrop that Lincoln proclaimed that a national "Day of Thanksgiving" would be celebrated on the final Thursday of November.

At the time, the only national holidays celebrated were Washington's Birthday and Independence Day. While northern states had celebrated the fall harvest with feasts in November, December, or January, and George Washington promoted the idea as a national holiday, the idea never had much of a pulse. It was largely due to Sarah Josepha Hale, a widow, the editor of *Godey's Lady's Book,* and reputedly the author of "Mary Had a Little Lamb," that Thanksgiving became one of America's defining celebrations. She campaigned for seventeen years to establish the national feast, writing editorials in *Godey's* (America's most popular magazine in the nineteenth century) and letters to Presidents Taylor,

Fillmore, Pierce, and Buchanan, all of whom ignored her. Southerners resented the "repugnant" idea of Thanksgiving as an attempt to force Yankee values on the South, rob workers of a day's wages, and encourage loutish drunkenness. Governor Henry Wise of Virginia rejected "this theatrical claptrap of Thanksgiving," which he associated with antislavery politics.

Hale wasn't entirely alone in extolling a meal based on indigenous ingredients from the Northeast, such as roasted turkey, squash with molasses, and cranberry sauce. Recipes for pumpkin pie began to sprout in popular cookbooks. And local Thanksgiving celebrations were held in twenty-nine states by the 1850s. But when Hale finally connected with President Lincoln after the Civil War, it came at an opportune moment.

Reflecting on his troops' 1863 victory at Gettysburg "in the lamentable civil strife," the president agreed that "a day of Thanksgiving and Praise to our beneficent Father" was a good start to national reconciliation: "It has seemed to me fit and proper that [God's works] should be solemnly, reverently and gratefully acknowledged as with one heart and voice by the whole American people." Citizens, he proclaimed, should "implore of the Almighty Hand to heal the wounds of the nation and to restore it as soon as may be consistent with the Divine purposes to the full enjoyment of peace, harmony, tranquility and Union."

Thanksgiving has been celebrated in various ways ever since and slowly gained acceptance. In 1870, President Ulysses S. Grant signed the Holidays Act, which made Thanksgiving a federal holiday, and later it became a paid holiday for federal workers. Some continued to resist: Texas refused to declare Thanksgiving a holiday into the 1880s. But cooks from other states across the South began to make the holiday their own— baking sweet potato pie with bourbon and pecans instead of pumpkin pie, for instance.

Thanksgiving has long marked a time when presidents were gifted turkeys by patriots, supporters, and opportunists, and lately presidents have courted approval by "pardoning" their birds from death. The tradition allegedly stemmed from a story about Tad Lincoln, who in 1863 asked his father to grant clemency to a Christmas turkey he'd named Jack, and the president did. In the 1870s, the Rhode Island farmer Horace Vose began shipping plump gobblers to the White House, which became a much-publicized tradition. After Vose's death, others leaped at the chance to present their birds to First Families. In 1925 a Vermont Girl Scout troop sent the Coolidges a turkey, and the following year Mississippi supporters sent a live raccoon for the presidential plate. Instead of eating her, the Coolidges adopted her, named her Rebecca, and gave her free rein of the White House—to the public's delight and the housekeepers' dismay.

In 1947 representatives of the turkey industry, angered by President Truman's calls for "poultryless Thursdays" during the war, presented him with the first "official" White House turkey. Claims that Truman was the first modern president to pardon a turkey are disputed, and he and President Eisenhower both happily ate several turkeys at their Thanksgivings. But President Kennedy said of his gift turkey, "Let's keep him going," and informally pardoned the bird in a Rose Garden ceremony on November 19, 1963. (He was assassinated three days later.) Later, the Nixons, Carters, and Reagans sent their presidential turkeys to live on petting farms or in a zoo, which is now standard practice. In 1989, George H. W. Bush granted the first official pardon of a turkey: while animal rights activists protested nearby, he declared, "Not this guy . . . Let me assure you, and this fine tom turkey, that he will not end up on anyone's dinner table . . . he's granted a presidential pardon as of right now."

Confusingly, Thanksgiving was celebrated on various dates in November (which in some years has five Thursdays) until FDR signed a joint resolution declaring that as of 1942 the fourth Thursday in November is the federal Thanksgiving Day. Today, that holiday may be the most popular celebration of the year. Schoolchildren make construction-paper turkeys, dress up as Pilgrims and Native Americans, and hold mini feasts in their classrooms. Adults eat and drink and watch football on TV. To some, like our family, it is a food-and-friends-focused celebration, largely devoid of religious and consumerist overtones. To many others, it is a time to pray and shop for Black Friday deals in the lead-up to the December holidays. The patriotic message of Thanksgiving is that all citizens deserve a day of fellowship, food, and tolerant communion, and the holiday has become a symbol of our better nature. Yet that narrative is a myth.

According to legend, the "first Thanksgiving" in America was a harvest celebration held by the Pilgrims at Plymouth Plantation in the fall of 1621. They had come to America seeking religious freedom, but, lost in a brutal, "empty" wilderness, half of the Pilgrims died of sickness and starvation. Over the following summer the settlers connected with the Wampanoag tribe, who taught the Englishmen how to grow and cook corn, hunt turkey and deer, and dig for clams. The colony was revived, and the two peoples celebrated with a three-day feast, serving fifty-three Pilgrims and ninety Native Americans. It's an uplifting vision, but records show the Wampanoags brought five deer and does not mention turkey; the menu likely included pumpkin, cornmeal, and cranberries, but not sweet potatoes (which had not yet arrived in North America from South and Central America) or pie. Further, the "first" Thanksgiving meal between Native Americans and Europeans may have taken place in Florida in 1565, or Texas in 1598, or Maine in 1607.

European settlers had celebrated fall harvests with feasts for years, and, as David Silverman of George Washington University has demonstrated, adventurers had been in contact with the Wampanoags since 1524, when they began capturing and enslaving Indigenous people. (At least two tribal members had been to Europe, he contends, and could speak English and interpret with the Pilgrims.) In 1616, the Wampanoag were devastated by "the Great Dying," a European epidemic. When the rival Narragansett began encroaching, the Wampanoag allied themselves with the settlers to defend their territory. But relations between the Native Americans and the Pilgrims soured over time, and modern Wampanoag consider Thanksgiving "a national day of mourning."

In retaliation for an alleged murder of an Englishman, settlers burned a village and killed some five hundred tribal members in 1637. William Bradford, the governor of Plymouth, wrote that for "the next 100 years, every Thanksgiving Day ordained by a Governor was in honor of the bloody victory, thanking God that the battle had been won." In King Philip's War of 1675–76, colonists massacred or enslaved some 50 percent of New England Natives, and Native raids killed about 30 percent of the English population. Afterward, settlers celebrated with a day of "thanksgiving." These bloody encounters foreshadowed years of conflict between Indigenous tribes and European colonists. In pursuit of Manifest Destiny, the U.S. government sanctioned at least fifteen hundred attacks on Natives and the usurpation of their property.

Like the truth about Washington's cherry tree (he didn't really chop down a cherry tree and say, "I cannot tell a lie") or Jefferson's inconsistent views on "liberty and justice for all" (mandatory for white people, not for slaves), the truth about Thanksgiving is a more complicated story than the myth allows.

Nor was Thanksgiving always built around a feast. For years, the Pilgrims and their descendants insisted on prayer and fasting on Thanksgiving Day, not gorging on Jurassic-sized turkey legs. That began to change in 1769, when New Englanders, concerned they were losing cultural hegemony, saw an opportunity to boost tourism. They floated the notion that the Pilgrims were America's original settlers, and they ate the corn and turkey that are indigenous to the region.

In 1841, as Frederick Douglass pushed for abolition and riots flared in Boston over financial worries, the Reverend Alexander Young described "the first Thanksgiving, the great festival of New England," in his *Chronicles of the Pilgrim Fathers of the Colony of Plymouth*. Young presented a beguiling, easily digested tale of interracial harmony, one that avoided any mention of murder, rape, slavery, and property theft by Pilgrims. The myth steadily gained adherents, and with Lincoln's endorsement Thanksgiving took on a life of its own.

Later, the celebration served as a convenient political tool and way to cohere the polyglot nation. In the late nineteenth century, the Indian Wars were winding down, and people wanted to include Native Americans in the national story. At the same time, white Protestants were unsettled by the arrival of Catholics and Jews from Europe. Anxiety about new immigrants helped solidify the myth of Natives and Pilgrims peaceably sharing food, knowledge, and land. It allowed Americans to be proud of the country's origins and provided a set of instructions on how to behave in the New World. Not surprisingly, the joy of communal feasting gradually overtook the burdens of prayer and fasting as the holiday's main event.

Today Thanksgiving marks an important, emotionally powerful, increasingly secular moment when Americans of all stripes agree to pause and gather to break bread. The Thanksgiving myth has largely succeeded. The holiday is a distinctly American celebration, one that provides a common menu and a lingua franca that—more than any other festivity—identifies all citizens as brothers and sisters, at least for a day. In its best iterations, we pile our plates high with "all the fixin's"—turkey, stuffing, mashed potatoes, gravy, Brussels sprouts, cranberry sauce, salad, and so on and on. Some choose to serve nontraditional dishes, such as sweet potatoes with marshmallows, iceberg lettuce, or Jell-O "salad." Others experiment with tofu turkey or "Indian lasagna" and the like. But America is tolerant on this point: whatever floats your boat.

Many associate Thanksgiving with the bright pixels of TV football, zeppelin-sized Baby Yoda balloons at the Macy's Thanksgiving Day Parade, and the commercial mayhem of Black Friday. It is an officially sanctioned day of gluttony, and we Americans love it. In its best iterations, it is a cheerful celebration of food, family, community, and thankfulness that helps bind us together like no other holiday. But we should not forget its origins.

V. Last Supper at the "Whited Sepulcure"

When sorrows come, they come not single spies. But in battalions.
—William Shakespeare, *Hamlet*

On Good Friday, April 14, 1865, Abraham Lincoln was called for dinner. He and Mary were due at Ford's Theatre for a production of *Our American Cousin*. But the president was reading a "humorous book" aloud to friends, and each time he was called "he promised to go, but would continue reading," recalled Illinois's governor Richard Oglesby. "Finally, he got a sort of peremptory order that he must come to dinner at once."

Dinner was quick, if not simple. No menu remains, but some have suggested Lincoln ate real turtle soup, to celebrate his victory over the Confederacy; others say he had mock turtle soup with roasted Virginia fowl and chestnut stuffing, baked yam, and cauliflower with cheese sauce. Then he drained a last cup of coffee and just after 8:00 p.m. dashed to Ford's Theatre.

As the Lincolns settled into the Presidential Box, John Wilkes Booth fired a single shot from his Derringer pistol into the president's head, then jumped to the stage and escaped; he was killed two weeks later. Mary Lincoln was spattered with blood and utterly traumatized. The president's limp body was carried to Petersen's boardinghouse, where an army surgeon, following protocol, poured brandy down Lincoln's throat. He died at 7:22 the next morning. Days later, a catafalque was hammered together in the East Room to display Lincoln's coffin, just as he had dreamed.

"I had an ambition to be Mrs. President, that ambition has been gratified, and now I must step down from the pedestal," wrote Mary, who could not bear to attend Lincoln's funeral. "My poor husband! Had he never been President, he might be living today. Alas! All is over with me!" Of her years at the White House, she wrote, "All the sorrows of my life occurred there & that Whited Sepulcure [*sic*] broke my heart."

6

ULYSSES S. GRANT

The Drunken Tanner, the Military Genius, and the First State Dinner

THE EIGHTEENTH PRESIDENT
March 4, 1869–March 4, 1877

★

I. A Flawed Leader in a Gilded Age

When General Ulysses S. Grant moved into the Executive Mansion in March 1869, he brought along an army quartermaster whose cooking philosophy was built on the unwavering belief that quantity trumps quality. His wife, Julia Grant, wasn't so sure about that. But the quartermaster assured her that "we are living at the absolute pinnacle" as he served up hunks of roast beef, turkey, and more turkey, followed by slices of heavy apple pie scaffolded with thick joists of cheese. Night after night he served this anti-haute cuisine regardless of who was at the table—the president and his family, friends, congressmen, titans of industry, heads of state, diplomats, royalty, everyday citizens, you name it. This suited the Grants just fine, for a time.

Forty-six years old when he took office, Grant was the youngest president to that point. A former general and Civil War hero, he was a political tyro and a mercurial man haunted by contradictions. Born in rural Ohio as Hiram Ulysses Grant (the "S." in his name was a clerical error), he was a quiet, moody boy, so repulsed by the blood at his father's tannery that he was nicknamed Useless. But he found his calling as a soldier at West Point, where he won fame for his daring horsemanship. After graduating, he married Julia Dent, and they had four children—Frederick, Ulysses Jr. (Buck), Ellen (Nellie), and Jesse. In the Mexican-American War, Grant reveled in strategy and tactics and discovered he was "always aching for a fight." Proving himself in battle, he was promoted to full captain. But just as his career was gaining velocity, Grant was quietly pushed out of the army. His occasional binge drinking had come to light. Though it never impeded his abilities, Grant's intoxication caused his superiors to lose faith.

Alcohol would torment Grant for most of his life, and over the next seven years he was lost in civilian purgatory—failing as a farmer and businessman in Missouri, selling firewood on a street corner in St. Louis, and the like. He moved his family to Illinois and was slip sliding toward poverty when the Civil War broke out in 1861, which saved him from himself.

On the battlefield, he proved such a ruthless tactician that Useless Grant was rechristened "Unconditional Surrender Grant." After he defeated the vaunted Confederate general Robert E. Lee at Appomattox on April 9, 1865, the war was effectively over. Phoenixlike, the once-cashiered solider was named the Union army's commanding general.

Grant planned to finish his career in the service, but in 1868 the Republicans were trying to impeach Lincoln's successor, the hapless Andrew Johnson, and were in search of a presidential candidate. Attracted by Grant's martial celebrity, party leaders assured him that he was the one and only man who could heal the divided nation. The general wasn't sure he believed them, but he wasn't sure he didn't. When the Republicans unanimously nominated him as their candidate, he hesitated, then tossed his hat into the ring.

Julia asked if he really wanted to be president, and Grant replied, "No, but I do not see that I have anything to say about it. . . . I suppose if I am nominated, I will be elected." And that's what happened.

On March 4, 1869, Ulysses S. Grant was sworn in as America's eighteenth chief executive in a quick and chilly affair—thanks to a cold front and his refusal to share a carriage with Johnson, who escaped impeachment by a single vote. Speaking in a soft voice at his swearing-in, Grant built on his campaign slogan, "Let Us Have Peace," by calling for improved relations with Native Americans, and for passage of the Fifteenth Amendment, which guaranteed voting rights for Black citizens (it was ratified in 1870). The crowd roared in approval and followed Grant back to the presidential mansion, where he celebrated with a few friends over drinks and cigars.

The new president was a sociable fellow but didn't care for ostentatious ceremony, and preferred small groups to big parties full of grasping strangers. When he told the organizers of the inaugural ball that he wouldn't mind skipping the event, they laughed him off, assuming he was joking. He wasn't.

They threw him a lavish inaugural party in the Cash Room at the Treasury, which was still under construction. It was hot and stuffy inside, and the air was hazy with marble dust. When more than a thousand supporters jammed into the claustrophobic space, several women passed out. Outside, a sharp wind spun into a blizzard, and in the confusion people couldn't find their coats, there were not enough carriages, and many guests had to slog home in the teeth of the storm. The event was such a boondoggle that it raised alarms among Washington's elite: Would the simple Grants from Missouri be capable of entertaining in a style worthy of the presidency? It was a reasonable question.

ULYSSES S. GRANT STOOD an unimposing five feet seven inches tall, weighed 135 pounds, and had a slight paunch, thick dark brown hair and beard, a determined set to his mouth, and expressive blue eyes that flickered from quizzical to stern, sad, bemused, impatient, penetrating, or thoughtful in a blink. Most of the time he was inscrutable and self-deprecating. But his bland exterior harbored a molten interior that burst forth at unexpected times. In those moments he seemed impelled by a surging, unconstrained energy that drove him to succeed and fail in spectacular fashion. "Grant's whole character was a mystery even to himself," observed General William Tecumseh Sherman. He was "a combination of strength and weaknesses not paralleled."

Like other soldier-statesmen—General George Washington, General Andrew Jackson, and General Dwight D. Eisenhower come to mind—Grant preferred simple meat-and-potatoes dinners to fancy banquets. He particularly enjoyed the quartermaster's roast beef, corn grits, wheat bread, and rice pudding. Yet the warrior—whom Confederate soldiers dubbed "the butcher"—recoiled at the sight of blood and disliked meat cooked rare, perhaps due to his love of horses and a lingering disgust of his father's tannery. He enjoyed steak, though insisted it be cooked "practically to charcoal." Mrs. Grant shared her husband's simple tastes, but as they grew accustomed to Washington, their diet became increasingly adventurous. In a way, the evolution of their palates mirrored that of the American public, which became wealthier and more sophisticated after the Civil War.

When the Grants moved into the President's House, they brought an unaffected style and an extended family worthy of a sitcom. Their sons Fred and Buck were off at college, but Nellie and Jesse were boisterous presences, and so was the president. Feeling mischievous, Grant would roll bits of bread into spitballs and cannonade them across the table at his children, eliciting squeals of laughter. He so enjoyed warring with his food that he occasionally forgot who or where he was—once lobbing a bread bullet at the British ambassador's wife, Lady Thornton, who was startled.

In the meantime, Grant's father and father-in-law continued to wage the Civil War inside the presidential mansion. "Colonel" Frederick Dent, a dyed-in-the-wool Jacksonian Democrat and former slaveholding planter from Missouri, lived on the second floor. He liked to sip mint juleps and opine on the joys of slavery, the better to provoke everyone. (Julia's mother had died in 1857.) But Dent's main foil was Jesse Grant, the president's father, a hard-core unionist who slept at hotels in Washington rather than subject himself to "that tribe of Dents." The old leather tanner had an ethical blind spot and frequently attempted to profit from his son's good name. His wife, Hannah, never visited Washington while her son was president, probably thanks to her aversion to Colonel Dent. The War of the Geezers was enhanced by the fact that both were losing their hearing. Once, Grandfather Dent bellowed, "You should take better care of that old gentleman, Julia! He is feeble and deaf as a post, and yet you permit him to wander all over Washington." Grandfather Grant heard this perfectly well and responded by shouting at his grandson Jesse, "I hope I shall not live to become as old and infirm as your Grandfather Dent!"

Julia Dent Grant tolerated the hijinks to a point, but she harbored social ambitions. Like Dolley Madison, she was an outsider in Washington with an unaffected personality who liked to socialize with people of all kinds. And like her fellow midwesterner Mary Todd Lincoln, Julia was initially cowed by the swells but determined to prove herself worthy of First Ladyship.

The fifth of eight children, Julia was raised in relative wealth in St. Louis and knew the social niceties. But she has been described as plump and plain, and was afflicted with strabismus, or crossed eyes, from birth. (Grant "fell in love" with her eyes and forbade her to correct them with surgery, fearing the cure would prove worse than the affliction.) Looking out her window, Mrs. Grant noticed ladies and grandees heading to lunches and teas or throwing luxurious parties in their brilliant mansions. She, too, wanted to entertain in style, strabismus be damned.

Step one was to revamp the President's House. Step two was to upgrade her wardrobe. And step three was to cashier her husband's turkey-slinging quartermaster and replace him with a cook worthy of the First Family. But there was another force in play. Unwittingly, the Grants had arrived in town at a turning point in history.

Ulysses S. Grant took office on March 4, 1869, in the midst of Reconstruction. Two months later, Leland Stanford drove the Golden Spike at Promontory Summit, Utah, to create the first transcontinental railroad. The battered South was struggling to adjust to a reconstituted union and an influx of northern carpetbaggers in search of opportunities, while four million former slaves attempted to invent new lives. Meanwhile, the economies of northern and western states—fueled by government spending and high-speed telegraph and railroad networks—became supercharged. This ushered in the Gilded Age, when a new breed of war profiteers, industrialists, and entrepreneurs gleefully upended the old order and transformed America into a global powerhouse.

Salmon and timber from Maine, grain and coal from the Midwest, and gold and apples from California (named the thirty-first state in 1850) began crisscrossing the nation. Fortunes were made and lost overnight, economic disparities widened, European immigrants arrived in droves, and graft flourished. Amid this free-for-all, Grant's Republican Party was wrenched between the idealism of its unhurried agrarian past and the promise of a bright, speeding, mechanized future. And there were other tectonic shifts under way. With fifty-three thousand citizens on its payroll, the federal government was America's largest employer. A series of constitutional amendments expanded federal power to conscript citizens into the army, tax them, oversee the nation's currency, and manage its ballooning debt.

Yet Washington, D.C., remained a small town, and an undistinguished one at that. It was a "generally dingy and neglected" spot, a visitor noted, with "vast, dreary, uninhabited tracts, destitute of verdure and roamed over by herds of horse cars and hacks." President Grant called it "a most unsightly place." He straightened meandering paths into roads, laid sidewalks, erected streetlights, dug sewers and gas mains, and eventually managed to turn the muddy cow town into what he deemed "one of the most sightly cities in the country."

The Executive Mansion was in a similarly threadbare state. After one look, Julia Grant was so horrified that she refused to move in until it was renovated. The timbers supporting the roof and floors were decayed, and the basement was "damp and unhealthy," noted Grant's secretary Orville Babcock, who served as commissioner of public buildings and grounds. "There is hardly a ceiling which has not cracked," he reported. "One large ceiling fell last year, but fortunately when the room was unoccupied."

While Julia Grant directed the mansion's first major renovation since the British torched it in 1814, her family lodged in a spacious house on I Street. She had expensive new carpets and wallpapers installed; swapped old portraits of George Washington for fresh portraits of her husband on horseback and her children; refurbished the Grand Staircase; and installed a huge, prismatic chandelier in the dining room. The East

Room was done over in the New Grecian style, replete with Corinthian columns, gilded relief work, a Hellenic fresco, and thirty-eight gasolier lights. For the table, Mrs. Grant ordered 587 pieces of china, including scalloped white plates encircled by a Grecian ocher rim, with a gold eagle at the top and a cluster of hosta in the center. Outside, she had vagrants and scrub excised from the South Lawn and replaced them with manicured grass and a reflecting pool that shot geysers into the air.

President Grant was more interested in his new billiard room. He had it paneled with wood and spent hours there smoking cigars and rehashing battles with army buddies. He smoked eighteen to twenty stogies a day, which provided a substitute for booze and an outlet for his impetuous energy. Another outlet was the newly refurbished stables, where Grant kept magnificent trotting horses and a fleet of light buggies. He'd race through Washington's streets at breakneck speeds—once earning a $20 speeding ticket, which he insisted on paying.

WITH THE WHITE HOUSE REFURBISHED, the Grants opened their doors to the people. Taking a page from Dolley Madison, Julia held public receptions every Tuesday afternoon and advertised them in newspapers: "In the Blue Room the President's wife . . . one day in each week of the season, from three to five P.M. . . . receives her critic—the public." People lined up outside or simply walked into the White House at these occasions. At official, invitation-only dinners, Mrs. Grant bucked tradition by inviting the wives of senators and cabinet members to stand in the receiving line. This was considered an honor, and the wives were grateful. Such minor, Dolley-esque social niceties helped the First Lady build powerful alliances and were warmly received by the press, especially the society columnists, who were newly empowered and mostly women. With lavender prose—"The gorgeous costumes of the diplomats and the elegant dresses of the ladies formed a picturesque and animated 'coup d'oeil'" (a French phrase, meaning taking in an entire scene at a glance)—their reports brought the details of the Grants' home improvements, furnishings, and flower displays to vivid life for readers.

Food was in the midst of the politicking, as usual, but what was new was the public's interest in what the president and presidentress ate, with whom, and why. Their dinners were no longer called meals; they were now described as "brilliant" and "elegant" soirees. Guests were not simply listed by name and occupation but swooned over as "ethereal," "ravishing," or "stately." Details of Mrs. Grant's couture were minutely cataloged: "pink grenadine, with flounced over-skirt, hair ornaments of fresh flowers, and diamond necklace"; or "Lyons silk velvet, with high bodice, trimmed with black lace and satin."

President Grant dressed somewhat shambolically, returned social calls when he got around to it, preferred to dine outside the mansion with his pals, and thundered, "I'd rather storm a fort!" than have to attend one more fancy ball.

In the early days of their residency, the Grants kept lunches and dinners economical and straightforward. A military man to the bone, Grant insisted on a strict eating schedule. He'd rise at 7:00 a.m. to read, meet his family for breakfast at 8:30 sharp, work until 3:00 p.m., head to the stables for some high-speed riding, and expect everyone at the dinner table at 5:00 p.m. on the dot. Once the meals were under way, however, his mood lightened.

Used to spartan rations of cucumbers and coffee for breakfast, Grant discovered that steak, bacon, fried apples, Spanish mackerel, and buckwheat or flannel cakes, washed down with gallons of strong black coffee, suited him just fine. The Grants began to relax and socialize more. At dinnertime, they would encourage friends to join them at the last minute and asked the kitchen to keep place settings ready, just in case.

WITH THIS SOCIAL MACHINERY up and running, Julia Grant slipped the final piece of the puzzle into place in late 1869, when she replaced the hash-slinging quartermaster with an accomplished steward named Valentino Melah. He had arrived in the United States in 1834 as an orphan from Messina, Sicily, trained in hotel kitchens in New York and New Orleans, and impressed the Grants with sumptuous dinners at the Stetson House, when they vacationed in Long Branch, New Jersey. As their first year in Washington ended, the Grants poached Melah away to cook at the President's House.

Known as "the Silver Voiced Italian," for his persuasive charm, or "the Professor," for his rigorous cooking, Melah quickly took charge. He insisted on formal dinners and seated guests at an enormous U-shaped table, where he regularly served twenty-nine-course—and occasionally thirty-five-course—dinners, featuring a different wine with every third course.

Melah specialized in Lucullan dishes, such as a smooth "aristocratic stew" (which sounds like an oxymoron) that brought "untold elegance" to the presidential table. One newspaperwoman under Melah's spell described his "ambrosial" bisques and crab soups, trout napped in hollandaise, "luscious" partridge legs, delicate beef fillets, heaps of cucumbers, peas, green beans, potatoes, and salads. To finish his guests off, the steward would bury them under an avalanche of pears and quinces, canned peaches, pastries, nuts, petits fours, fresh fruits, ice cream, coffee, chocolate, and his famous lemon rice pudding—"a pudding as would make our great grandmothers clap their hands with joy," the smitten journalist kvelled.

Grant eventually came around to the charms of Melah's fancy grub and made strategic use of his formal decor. When the steward placed a large, flower-draped mirror on the table as an artistic element, the president angled it *just so,* to hide from guests he did not wish to converse with. But, try as he might, Grant couldn't wiggle out of the official levees he was expected to host for cabinet members, Supreme Court justices, congressmen, diplomats, and other muckety-mucks. Rebelling, he conducted these dinners in his own style. Senators and congressmen were traditionally invited to the President's House by a standard formula: thirty-six members at a time, in alphabetical order. But Grant invited only those he wanted to see and included their wives, which diluted the politics and livened the evenings considerably.

The Grants' first big dinner test came on January 26, 1870, when they welcomed Queen Victoria's third son, Prince Arthur, to a twenty-nine-course banquet in the State Dining Room. While most of Melah's dinners cost $700 to $1,500, not including drinks, the food bill for Prince Arthur was a whopping $2,000 (some $41,500 today). Adding to the cost, the steward served six different wines. One supplier charged him $1,800 (about $37,500 today) for champagne alone, which must have made the tanner's son wince. But Julia Grant was thrilled by Melah's gastronomic productions and unapologetic about their cost. "I have visited many courts," she declared, "and, I am proud to say, I saw none that excelled in brilliancy the receptions of President Grant."

Though he was loath to deny his wife her moment in the sun, Grant did try to economize from time to time. At a New Year's reception for the public in 1873, for instance, he invited guests to enjoy a multitude of snacks but served them coffee rather than more expensive wines, beers, and ciders. But there was likely another motive for Grant's sudden parsimony: the demon of alcohol remained hunched on his shoulder.

. . .

TODAY ALCOHOLISM IS considered a chronic disease and is treated with sympathy, therapy, and multistep programs. But in the nineteenth century, alcoholism was regarded as a moral failing, an "intemperate" act of self-indulgence, a weakness to be shunned and ashamed of.

For politicians, any hint of inebriation could be ruinous, as Andrew Johnson discovered after a single drink. At Lincoln's second inauguration, on March 4, 1865, Vice President Johnson was feeling light-headed and suffered diarrhea, cramps, and dehydration. Determined to attend the swearing-in, he downed a tumbler of whiskey, the standard treatment of the day. When he stood to speak to the Senate, Johnson slurred his words and rambled on about his humble roots. He was clearly inebriated. The audience began to snigger. His enemies demanded his resignation. Johnson refused to step down, and after a few days Lincoln signaled his support: "I have known Andy Johnson for many years; he made a bad slip the other day, but you need not be scared, Andy ain't a drunkard."

But the stain proved indelible. Three years later, after Johnson had succeeded Lincoln as president, the Massachusetts congressman Benjamin Butler led an impeachment hearing and derided Johnson as "a drunken tailor." Johnson escaped ignominy by the skin of his teeth, but Democrats abandoned him in 1868, allowing Grant and the Republicans to sweep into office. When Grant served coffee instead of booze at the New Year's celebration of 1873, he doubtless had the fall of Johnson, and his own haunting past, in mind.

Alcoholism was a strain that ran through the Grant family like a streak of red paint. He put up a stiff resistance by not serving alcohol at home, upending his wineglass at dinner parties, confiding his struggles to pastors and friends, joining temperance unions, and enduring long dry stretches without a drop to drink. But occasionally he would succumb and tumble off the wagon into the mud, sometimes literally.

The worst "sprees," as Grant called his binges, occurred during his army days. Lonely, suffering headaches, and marooned in a remote military post, he grew fidgety. Like his fellows, he would hit the bottle. Though Grant didn't drink as much as other officers, alcohol had an outsized impact on him. "With his peculiar organization a little did the fatal [work] of a great deal," a beef contractor said. "He had very poor brains for drinking."

Grant did not drink for fun. He drank alone, late at night, compulsively, and once he started he could not stop. Alcohol unleashed something tightly coiled inside him. A euphoric high flashed through his nerves, tripping them like circuits, and the reticent soldier would turn garrulous and obstreperous. He slurred his words "foolishly" and was said to have occasionally socked a man in the nose.

During and after the Mexican War in 1846–48, or when stationed in Detroit in the winter of 1849, or when he traveled to Panama in 1852, Grant would drink so much he'd throw up or suffer the delirium tremens—terrifying episodes of sweating, shivering, and hallucinations that can last for days. "Liquor seemed a virulent poison to him, and yet he had a fierce desire for it," recalled Officer Robert Macfeely. "One glass would show on him, and two or three would make him stupid."

Grant's commander, George B. McClellan, found his lapses unforgivable. Even when sober, Grant was presumed guilty and reprimanded when things went innocently awry—such as the day his horse slipped and tossed Grant into the mud, injuring him. It was so unlike the expert horseman to fall that his superiors assumed he was drunk.

In his *Memoirs,* Grant gave no reason for his abrupt resignation from the army in 1854, but he implied that he quit to spend more time with his family. There was some truth to that, because he hadn't seen Julia and the kids in two years. But as the historian Ron Chernow concludes in his fine biography *Grant,* "Overwhelming evidence suggests that Grant resigned from an alcohol problem."

Feeling marooned and blue while stationed at Fort Humboldt, in remote Northern California, Grant later admitted, "I got in a depressed condition and got to drinking." In April 1854, his commanding officer, the courtly despot Robert C. Buchanan, announced that if Grant did not resign, he would face a court-martial. Grant's friends urged him to stand trial and seek exoneration, but he could not face the humiliation of the courtroom. A deal was brokered: the army promoted Grant to full captain, and he resigned his commission.

Such episodes left him guilt stricken and remorseful. He might even have lied to his wife about his addiction, or at least shielded her from the full truth. (Known as dipsomania in Grant's time, alcoholism was not recognized as a disease by the American Medical Association until 1956.) Proud and protective, Julia never addressed his drinking in public, though she must have known about it.

Yet even after he had rehabilitated his career in the Civil War, the slur "drunk" clung to Grant like gum on a shoe. If Andrew Johnson was the "drunken tailor," crowed Benjamin Butler, then Grant was the "drunken tanner." Grant did not take the bait and did his level best to remain sober. In spite of the relentless stress of the presidency and many temptations to imbibe, he willed himself to stay on the wagon for most of his adult life—a feat that was at least as difficult as forcing the Confederate surrender at Appomattox.

II. Dinner with the King of the Sandwich Islands

On March 4, 1873, President Grant celebrated his second inauguration with a ball held in a temporary structure built in Judiciary Square. In contrast to his hot and stuffy first inaugural party, his second lacked heat or insulation. The temperature that day reached sixteen degrees at noon and began dropping from there. Live canaries in cages around the room froze to death. Women were so cold that they kept their beautiful gowns hidden beneath coats. Men vainly attempted to warm up by dancing. Valentino Melah's sumptuous dinner, wines, and elaborate ice cream desserts froze as hard as glacial ice. Instead of eating, the guests guzzled hot coffee and hot chocolate until supplies ran out, then retreated home.

To be fair, such snafus were unusual, and the Grants compensated with a series of fantastic parties. One of their most lauded events was an innovation: the Grants were the first to use a state dinner as a tool of gastro-diplomacy.

At the time, a "state dinner" referred to any large party the First Couple hosted for the cabinet, Congress, judges, military officers, or foreign diplomats. Though smooth operators like Thomas Jefferson and Benjamin Franklin understood the many benefits of breaking bread with foreign powers, they did not invite their counterparts to celebrate diplomatic agreements with a banquet. It was the rough-and-ready Grants who hit on the idea of using a black-tie dinner to celebrate the successful negotiation of agreements with a foreign head of state.

The Grants' first state dinner guest was not a French or British king, Russian czar, African chieftain, or Japanese emperor; rather, it was the king of the Sandwich Islands—a.k.a. Hawaii. On the night of December 12, 1874, the Grants feted David La'amea Kamananakapu Mahinulani Naloiaehuokalani Lumialani Kalakaua at a state dinner that established a template that remains largely intact.

Known as the Merrie Monarch, for his ample belly, broad smile, and love of food and drink, King Kalakaua was the first reigning monarch to visit the United States. But he had come to Washington for more than a good meal. He ruled a sovereign nation of 137 islands that was sinking into a sea of red ink, and he had traveled to America in search of a trade deal.

Sugar was one of the most desirable commodities in the world and, with pineapple, was Hawaii's biggest and most valuable crop. But the United States had blocked Hawaiian sugar imports with stiff tariffs, and Kalakaua sought to sell his sugar duty-free.

Sugarcane is a tall, sturdy grass that was probably domesticated in prehistoric New Guinea. It is believed that the first extraction of sugar from the stem of the plant began in India two thousand years ago. The process spread along trade routes to some ninety countries, and today sugar is the world's largest crop by volume. In the fifteenth century, sugar was considered a rare spice, akin to cinnamon, cumin, or saffron, and it became an expensive luxury in Europe. Doctors prescribed sugar as a cure or used it to mask the sharp flavor of drugs. It became a wildly popular sweetener for tea or hot chocolate, and an essential ingredient for baking and candy making. The Portuguese brought sugar to Brazil in the sixteenth century, the Dutch took sugar to the Caribbean in the seventeenth century, and the English spread its use throughout their empire. By 1750 sugar was the most valuable trading commodity in Europe.

It was a sweet business, literally and metaphorically. But sugar was one leg of the triangle trade, a most bitter enterprise. From the late sixteenth to the early nineteenth century, African slaves were shipped to the Caribbean to harvest sugarcane, which was turned into raw sugar, or its liquid form, molasses; the sugar was shipped to New England and made into rum; the rum—and commodities such as timber, fish, and fur—were shipped to Europe; from there, sugar, rum, tools, and guns were sent to Africa, where they were bartered or sold to acquire more slaves. And the brutal triangle would repeat.

In Hawaii, the first sugar mill was probably established on Lanai island by a Chinese farmer in 1802, and by the 1840s Hawaiian sugar was sent by steamship to California. Demand spiked during the gold rush of 1848–55, and the establishment of California's statehood, and again during the Civil War, which choked off domestic supplies from the South. As whites—many of them descendants of missionaries—changed Hawaiian law, took control of government and business, and displaced Indigenous people in the late nineteenth century, the "big five" sugar plantations began a century of hegemony. This had a ripple effect on the economy, demography, and foodways of Hawaii.

Sugar planters imported workers from China, Japan, Korea, Portugal, Puerto Rico, the Philippines, and Southeast Asia. The immigrants brought their own customs and cookery with them, which amalgamated with Polynesian traditions to create a rich, multicultural Hawaiian food culture. The result is a cuisine of Japanese bento and Portuguese sweet bread, regional dishes such as poke (diced raw fish over rice), Spam musubi (canned meat, rice, and seaweed), and loco moco (hamburger, rice, two fried eggs, and gravy).

In 1874, King Kalakaua led a "Reciprocity Commission"—composed of himself, his (mostly white) advisers, and the (all-white) sugar planters—to Washington, D.C. As he sailed from Honolulu to San Francisco and traveled to Washington along the astonishing new railroad system, the king was welcomed as a celebrity. He was greeted by a full marine battalion in Washington, and an "immense crowd" cheered the king's carriage ride along Pennsylvania Avenue to the Arlington Hotel, where he indulged in hand shaking and autograph signing.

In truth, Kalakaua's celebratory arrival was the end, not the beginning, of his diplomatic negotiations with America. The talks were led by the U.S. secretary of state, Hamilton Fish, and his counterpart, Elisha Hunt Allen, a Massachusetts lawyer who had become a Hawaiian citizen and Kalakaua's minister plenipotentiary to the United States.

Grant favored the sugar deal, and on December 18, 1874, he welcomed King Kalakaua as the first foreign leader to be received in a joint meeting of the House and Senate. (In joint meetings, Congress recesses to welcome a foreign leader. In joint sessions, the bicameral body meets to adopt a resolution or attend a presidential address.)

Four days later, on the night of December 22, the Grants and a roster of dignitaries hosted the king at America's first diplomatic state dinner. Much like today, guests were welcomed to the Executive Mansion by the Marine Band. Julia Grant had decked the State Dining Room and East Room with vibrant flowers, Limoges china, and crystal decanters. Though there were "no young ladies present," the *Washington Evening Star* noted, the display was "brilliant beyond all precedent." The chief justice, the Speaker of the House, and cabinet members and their wives were in attendance. Mrs. Grant sat next to the king, and the president sat facing them.

Details of the evening's menu have been lost, but judging from Valentino Melah's other splendiferous banquets, it is likely the Sandwich Islanders feasted on up to thirty courses—ranging from consommé to trout, squab, beef tenderloin (charred to Grant's taste), and "Sorbet Fantasie." One admirer recalled of a Melahnian vegetable elixir, "No soup, foreign or domestic, has ever been known to equal it. It is said to be a little smoother than peacock's brains, but not quite so exquisitely flavored as a dish of nightingale's tongues."

Kalakaua brought two guards who stood in stone-faced vigil on either side of his chair: the king feared poisoning and would eat only after a third attendant, a royal cupbearer, deemed the food acceptable. It is possible that Melah was offended by this unusual custom, though it would not be the last time an honored guest brought a food taster to a state dinner.

Regardless, both the dinner and the trade negotiations were a success, and the Reciprocity Treaty was ratified in May 1875. It allowed Hawaiian sugar and rice to be imported to the United States duty-free; in exchange, American goods could be exported to Hawaii duty-free. As a result, the value of exports from Hawaii to the United States increased from $1.8 million in 1874 to over $13 million in 1890. The deal gave America exclusive access to Pearl Harbor, a strategically located port on Oahu, a move unpopular with many Sandwich Islanders, who feared it was the first step in a planned annexation of the entire archipelago. (Their fears were realized in 1898, when the islands were made a U.S. territory; Hawaii was named the fiftieth state by President Eisenhower in 1959.)

Since then, the Hawaiian sugar business has vanished—the victim of global competition, rising land values, and a dearth of cheap labor. The last Hawaiian plantation shut down in 2016, after 146 years in operation. Today corn is the new sugar, and Hawaii's top crop is corn seed, which undergirds the production of high-fructose corn syrup (HFCS)— glucose made from the starch of the kernels and transformed into fructose. Since the 1970s, HFCS has largely supplanted sucrose (table sugar) as a sweetener because it is cheaper to produce and easier to use. America has become heavily reliant on the crop, which has serious implications for human and environmental health.

Corn farmers have become the victims of their own success. In the nation's infancy, an overabundance of corn led to cheap whiskey and a rise in alcohol-related health problems. Washington and Jefferson decried the "alcoholic republic," as the historian W. J. Rorabaugh put it, and ignited a debate that would lead to Prohibition in the 1920s. Today, a similar overabundance of corn has led to a plethora of products—the use of HFCS to sweeten soda and fast food, corn-fed beef and chicken, corn ethanol to power vehicles, corn in plastics and even in baby diapers. As Michael Pollan, author of *The Omnivore's Dilemma,* sees it, corn has colonized our minds and bodies; we have become "the people of corn," he writes, and the "Alcoholic Republic" has given way to the "Republic of Fat." The federal government's subsidization of corn has fueled an obesity epidemic, while a corn monoculture is expensive and environmentally harmful and risks mass starvation in the event of a blight (as happened during the Irish potato famine). But I am getting ahead of myself and President Grant here.

III. A Bright and Beautiful Dream

The Grants' most famous celebration was the wedding of their daughter, Nellie, in 1874. It began innocently enough, when the First Couple suggested that their spirited sixteen-year-old daughter join some friends, the Adolph Bories, on a European vacation. Part of Grant's motivation was to keep the impulsive Nellie from straying into a summer romance.

Worried that their cloistered daughter would be homesick, the Grants were surprised to learn that she loved touring Paris and was received by Queen Victoria at Buckingham Palace. On the return voyage, the Bories grew ill, and Nellie wandered the decks in search of adventure. She promptly found it, in one Algernon Charles Frederick Sartoris ("Sar-tress"), a handsome Etonian whose father was a member of Parliament and owned a gorgeous estate in Southampton. His mother was an opera singer who held literary salons featuring Henry James and Charles Dickens.

Nellie fell hard and fast for "Algie." But when she introduced him to her parents, the Grants were unimpressed by the callow twenty-one-year-old. The president stared at him silently, then lamented that his daughter hadn't chosen "an American husband." Desperately uncomfortable, Algie blurted out, "Mr. President, I want to marry your daughter!"

With Nellie's pleading, Grant reluctantly agreed.

On May 21, 1874, 250 guests crowded into the East Room for a wedding covered in granular detail by the press corps. There had not been a wedding at the People's House in thirty years, and Nellie Grant's was only the sixth time that such nuptials had been celebrated since 1820, when Dolley Madison's sister Maria Hester Monroe was betrothed there.

Before a huge crowd, Grant led his only daughter down the aisle with tears streaming down his cheeks. Julia—who, in an attempt at good cheer, had bedecked every surface with fresh roses, potted plants, and vases practically exploding with flowers—kept her eyes averted. Addressing the glowing Nellie, Walt Whitman recited his poem "A Kiss to the Bride," which read in part,

> Dear girl—through me the ancient privilege too,
> For the New World, through me, the old, old wedding greeting:
> O youth and health! O sweet Missouri rose! O bonny bride!
> Yield thy red cheeks, thy lips, to-day,
> Unto a Nation's loving kiss.

After the ceremony, the party adjourned to a sensational breakfast in the State Dining Room. The menu, inscribed in a white satin booklet, featured course after mouthwatering course: soft-shell crab on toast, chicken croquettes with peas, beef tongue in aspic, woodcock and snipe, spring chicken with herbs, fresh strawberries with cream, charlotte russe, Nesselrode pudding, and blancmange. For the grand finale, Chef Melah presented an enormous wedding cake decorated with sugar doves and wedding bells and freshly cut flowers. Circling this confectionary sun was a solar system of smaller cakes, ice creams, ices, punch, coffee, cream, and chocolates. As a memento, each guest was given a small box containing a piece of the cake, tied off with a white bow.

As the newlyweds were showered with $60,000 worth of gifts, President Grant slipped away to weep in private. He would grow even more despondent when Nellie followed Algie to England. They had four children and their marriage predictably collapsed, a victim of his womanizing and drinking. Henry James found "something rather touching and tragic" about "poor little Nellie Grant . . . illiterate, lovely, painted, pathetic and separated from a drunken idiot of a husband . . . in a strange land, quite without friends, ignorant, helpless, vulgar, untidy, unhappy."

LIKE THEIR DAUGHTER, the Grants were touchingly naive when it came to judging character. Grant's administration was besmirched by a near-constant stream of scandals, which dogged him into retirement. At least forty Grant relatives profited directly or indirectly from his presidency, and many of his "friends" enriched themselves through graft, extortion, influence peddling, and kickbacks; a few went to jail, and at least one was murdered by a jealous romantic rival. Most disheartening was the revelation that Grant's trusted secretary, Orville Babcock, played a central role in the Whiskey Ring scandal of 1875.

Facing financial difficulties at the end of his life, Grant suffered from jaw cancer (probably the result of his fifteen-cigar-a-day habit) and died in 1885, at sixty-three—just days after he finished writing his *Memoirs.* The book was published by his friend Mark Twain, who gave Grant an unheard-of 70 percent of net profits. The memoir was widely praised and became a lucrative best seller that earned $450,000 in two years and eased Julia's dotage.

In 1876, Grant decided not to run for a third term—some said because of the Whiskey Ring scandal, though he declared he was "never so happy in my life." Julia, however, was heartbroken. Her eight years at the President's House were "quite the happiest period of my life," she recalled, hitting a note that many First Ladies would repeat. "It was like a bright and beautiful dream. . . . When Congress and society got in session, Washington is a mecca for brains and beauty."

PART II

The Twentieth Century

Feast and Famine

The twentieth century began with the tremendous bounty of the Roosevelt-Taftian age of excess, which gave way to a long stretch of plain eating—an age of gastronomic mediocrity—that lasted from Woodrow Wilson through the Hoover years and the privations of the Great Depression. It wasn't until the jaunty Franklin D. Roosevelt arrived that fine food and drink had another champion in the White House. As waves of immigrants from southern and eastern Europe arrived, new kinds of foods were integrated into the American diet, lunch counters and restaurants flourished, and the advent of freezers, rail networks, and interstate highways greatly expanded markets. After World Wars I and II led to mass starvation in Europe, the green revolution fueled by wartime technology greatly increased global food supplies. Americans had more time and money to spend on travel, dining, reading, and watching television—shifts that fueled a series of gastronomic revolutions in the 1960s, '70s, and '80s. As Eisenhower grilled his own steaks, the Kennedys hired a French chef, Nixon went to China, Carter brokered peace in the Middle East, and Reagan and Bush presided over the end of the Cold War, the food and entertaining at the White House underwent dramatic shifts and became the object of public fascination.

7

THEODORE ROOSEVELT and WILLIAM HOWARD TAFT

Two Bears

ROOSEVELT, THE TWENTY-SIXTH PRESIDENT
September 14, 1901–March 4, 1909

★

I. Coarse Food and Plenty of It

On September 6, 1901, the radical Leon F. Czolgosz shot President William McKinley twice with a .32-caliber pistol in Buffalo, New York. One bullet bounced off a button on his chest, but the other lodged in his abdomen. The doctors couldn't find it. They sewed him up and sent him to recover in his hotel. He seemed to improve, but then his wound turned gangrenous, and on Friday the thirteenth his fever spiked. Three hundred and fifty miles away, Vice President Theodore Roosevelt sat by Lake Tear of the Clouds, near the summit of Mount Marcy, the highest of the Adirondack High Peaks, in upper New York State, eating a sandwich.

The notion that a vice president would disappear into the wilderness without any security or way to communicate is absurd. Even in 1901 it was not the kind of thing most ambitious politicians would do, especially one with a suspect heart. But it was classic Roosevelt: brash, romantic, egocentric, and a bit manic. Alerted by a guide, the vice president scrambled down the rocky trail, made a reckless, thirty-five-mile dash aboard a two-seat buggy through the night, and arrived in Buffalo by train on September 14. By then McKinley was dead, and his assassination would foreshadow the carnage that racked the twentieth century. At 3:30 that afternoon, Theodore Roosevelt was sworn in as the nation's twenty-sixth president. He was forty-two years, ten months, and eighteen days old, America's youngest chief executive yet.

A week later, Roosevelt—known as TR to friends, and Ted or Teedie to his family, but never Teddy (a nickname he loathed)—celebrated his first night in the presidential mansion over dinner with his sisters, Anna "Bamie" Cowles and Corinne Robinson. TR noted it was their father's seventieth birthday, but Theodore "Thee" Roosevelt Sr. had died in 1878, at forty-six, of a gastrointestinal tumor. Nineteen at the time, TR said, "I feel as if I should go mad" with grief. Biographers have posited that his father's early death had a profound psychological impact on Roosevelt. Ted knew Thee only as an idealized paternal figure, rather than as an imperfect man; the trauma of Thee's death might have contributed to

Ted's boyishness (a wish to hold on to a happy, coddled childhood) and drive (a wish to please a missing father; a fatalistic desire to live life to the fullest before he, too, was extinguished). And it seems likely that the nature of Thee's illness—the tumor made it painful to eat, causing him to waste away—contributed to Roosevelt's ferocious appetite.

A week after TR arrived in Washington, his wife, Edith (Edie), and their six children, aged four to sixteen, and a bestiary that included dogs, cats, snakes, a duck, a kangaroo rat, a lizard, a badger, and a one-legged rooster, gusted into the White House. They overflowed its eight bedrooms and two bathrooms, lined the halls with trunks, trampled the gardens, snuck into the attic, and rode a pony through the mansion. It was as if a raucous summer storm had engulfed the musty building with constantly shifting periods of sun, rain, lightning, and rainbows. The family freshened up the old manse and made the president happy.

Theodore Roosevelt was a new kind of leader for a new century, a dynamo whose policies shifted from hard right to moderate left, and he was the first president to make food safety and land conservation priorities. Yet you would have been hard-pressed to predict his trajectory early on.

Born in 1858 to one of Manhattan's wealthiest families, Ted was afflicted with life-threatening asthma, a weak heart, and nearsightedness. Worried he'd be bullied or infected, his parents homeschooled him at their East Twentieth Street mansion. TR maintained, "I am of a very buoyant temper," and at Harvard he stocked his room with books, a tortoise, and lobsters and toughened himself by boxing, rowing, hiking, and swimming. Later, he turned himself into a swashbuckling outdoorsman, soldier, and hunter who was constantly out to prove, and improve, himself. In 1902, he gained the nickname Teddy by refusing to shoot a young, tethered bear in Mississippi (his guide shot the bear instead); the story inspired a Brooklyn couple to make toy teddy bears. Embarrassed by the incident, Roosevelt rejected the diminutive nickname, and preferred to be called "Colonel," after his service in the Spanish-American War, or "Mr. President."

Roosevelt married his first wife, Alice Hathaway Lee, known as Sunny, for her beauty and optimism in 1880, and four years later she gave birth to a daughter, Alice Lee Roosevelt. But on Valentine's Day that year, Sunny succumbed to Bright's disease (kidney failure), and Roosevelt's mother was felled by typhoid fever in the same house on the same day. TR drew an X in his calendar and scrawled, "The light has gone out of my life."

Shut down by grief and rage, he housed baby Alice with his sister Bamie, abruptly quit New York politics, and lit out for the Badlands of North Dakota. There, he bought a ranch and a herd of cows, dressed in buckskin and trained as a cowboy, and shot endangered bison. When most of his herd was wiped out in the winter of 1886, TR returned east and married his second wife, Edith Kermit Carow.

Edie was raised in the same haut-bourgeois milieu as Roosevelt. A quietly determined woman, she had decided to marry Ted early on and patiently bided her time. Friends said she was "as calm and imperturbable as a Buddha," a counterbalance to the impulsive Ted. She was gracious, schooled in the social arts, and like the swan that glides smoothly across a lake while furiously paddling beneath the surface, Mrs. Roosevelt made political socializing look easy—"Like a shuttle, keeping everything in harmony," noted the military aide Archie Butt. Circulating White House parties, the First Lady paid attention to each guest, met with the wives of cabinet members every Tuesday, and ensured the household staff was well dressed and courteous. Edie was also a skilled horsewoman and had sound political instincts and a better head for money than her husband. "Whenever I go against her judgment I regret it," TR noted. They had five children together—Theodore (Ted) III, Kermit, Ethel, Archibald, and Quentin—and Edie raised Alice as her own. (Edie miscarried twice while in the White House, probably due to the stress, she'd say.)

The Roosevelts enjoyed "coarse food and plenty of it," Alice declared. It was a funny line and had the advantage of being somewhat true. But it was also part of the myth that TR wove about his supposedly humble tastes. A typical Rooseveltian repast might open with bouillon and move on to salt cod, chicken in rice, baked beans, fresh rolls, Bavarian cream, preserves, and cake. It was not fancy, but it was tasty and abundant.

The attorney Lloyd Griscom described TR at the table "stoking up prodigiously, as though he were a machine." Roosevelt liked to eat the game he shot, the fish he caught, the greens like fiddlehead ferns that he foraged, and the asparagus he had shipped from his Long Island estate, Sagamore Hill. He enjoyed apples, pears, oranges, pineapples, and peaches, but not prunes, bananas, or avocados (a Mexican berry that was cultivated in Florida, California, and Hawaii). While TR occasionally indulged in gourmet items—such as the oysters, green turtle soup, crab flake Newburg, quail, and bread sauce salad at his forty-second birthday—he claimed he was equally happy with pork and beans, or "just a bowl of milk."

Yet Roosevelt could be as dogmatic about food as he was about the importance of "the Strenuous Life," the title of one of his most famous speeches. At breakfast he would order six, eight, or a dozen eggs, hard-boiled (*not* medium or soft-boiled), with homemade rolls (*not* store bought). Or he'd have a big bowl of hominy dressed with salt and butter—a taste he had acquired from his Georgia-born mother; he wasn't afraid to serve them anytime, even at official functions, though at dinner he insisted grits be swamped with meat gravy.

The Rooseveltian lunch was often a mélange of meats, bread, fruits, and tea (he favored the smoky black Hu-Kwa from China, also a favorite of his cousins Franklin Delano and Eleanor Roosevelt and his enemy the financier J. P. Morgan). At dinner, TR was a devotee of grilled steak, wild game, and fried chicken. "The *only* way to serve fried chicken is with white gravy soaked into the meat," he proclaimed. He had a sweet tooth, and his desserts tended to be lingering explorations of the confectionary arts.

Critics tried to paint Roosevelt as a boozer, and though he looked the part, with his thick body and bluff face, he was not especially fond of alcohol. The legend of his supposed bibulousness can be traced to a gold champagne coupe—a bowl-shaped glass mounted atop a foot-tall stem that held a pint of liquid. He called it "the King of Ultima Thule's scepter," and brandished it at family lunches and state dinners. Some charged that he filled it with whiskey, but TR drank nothing stronger than a spritzer of white wine mixed with sparkling mineral water. When a temperance group accused Roosevelt of being a drunk, he sued them and won. At times, Roosevelt could be charmingly clueless about alcohol. At President McKinley's inaugural lunch, Edie recalled, the vice president "drank two glasses of champagne, thinking it was bad fizzy water. . . . Happily, it took no effect whatever, which speaks volumes either for Ted's head or the President's champagne." In fact, Roosevelt preferred to wash down his meals with black coffee (*without* cream) sweetened with up to seven cubes of sugar. Ted Jr. described his father's mug as "in the nature of a bathtub."

In truth, Roosevelt well understood the political utility of fine dining. He frequently used the table as a forum to commend or interrogate colleagues, float policy trial balloons, and launch into encyclopedic digressions on almost any topic imaginable. A prodigious reader, writer, and talker, he dictated letters by the paragraph, wore out stenographers, and shrewdly spun the press while lathered up in the barber's chair. After meeting TR, one journalist observed, "you had to wring the personality out of your clothes." And the English statesman John Morley observed,

"I have seen two tremendous works of nature in America. One is Niagara Falls and the other is the President."

IT IS A TRUISM that a meal at the White House is unlike a meal anywhere else. The mansion carries enormous symbolic weight, and when a president invites a dignitary to dine with him, it confers mutual acceptance, if not parity, between host and guest. TR barked his shins on this essential fact just weeks into his administration, when he hosted a seemingly simple dinner.

On October 16, 1901—four days before the monthlong mourning period for McKinley ended, and with it a ban on official entertaining—the president heard that Booker T. Washington was in town. Born a slave, Washington had become an acclaimed author and the first leader of the Tuskegee Institute, "one of the most useful, as well as one of the most distinguished, of American citizens of any race," Roosevelt said.

Impulsively, he invited Washington to dinner. TR knew it was unusual to invite a Black man to eat at the White House and had paused before doing so. African Americans had visited 1600 Pennsylvania Avenue before: a crowd of Black people attended Andrew Jackson's crazed inaugural celebration in 1829; Abraham Lincoln signed Sojourner Truth's autograph book, and Mary Todd Lincoln hosted a group of Black women; Rutherford B. Hayes invited Frederick Douglass to headline concerts by Black musicians in the East Room. But no Black leader had shared the president's table as a putative equal. In 1901, the nation was still recovering from the Civil War and Reconstruction, former slaves were finding their way, and lynchings took place. Yet it felt natural to the president to "show some respect to a man whom I cordially esteem as a good citizen."

At eight o'clock that night, Roosevelt, Washington, and Philip B. Stewart, a prominent Colorado businessman, shared a quiet dinner and discussed federal appointments in the south. The next day the Associated Press listed the president's guests, as usual, only this time it ignited a political firestorm. Blacks and liberal whites praised Roosevelt, but many southerners and some northerners gushed hateful vitriol: "The action of President Roosevelt in entertaining that n—— will necessitate our killing a thousand n—— in the South before they will learn their place again," jeered Senator Ben "Pitchfork" Tillman, a South Carolina Democrat. Headlines decried TR as "Coon-Faced" and "A Rank Negrophilist."

It was a harsh rebuke to the freshman president. According to the mores of the day, "'Dining' . . . was really a code word for social equality. And the feeling was [that Roosevelt was] actually inviting [Washington] to woo his daughter," explained Deborah Davis, the author of *Guest of Honor,* a book about the dinner. For the duration of his administration critics would point to that evening as Exhibit A of Roosevelt's blithe arrogance. Even some in his inner circle were dismayed. "The president . . . mentioned the inviting of Booker Washington to a meal at the White House as a mistake," a cabinet member confided. "Not in the action itself, but the effect on the South was injurious and misinterpreted."

TR never invited another Black leader to dine at the White House. And in the racial reckoning of the twenty-first century, Roosevelt's views on race were likened to Manifest Destiny, the belief that white settlers had the right and duty to expand across North America. In 2022, a statue of the president was removed from the American Museum of Natural History (which his family helped found) in New York because it depicted Black and Indigenous people as racially inferior.

But at the time Roosevelt remained defiant. "When I asked Booker T. Washington to dinner I did not devote very much thought to the matter one way or another," he wrote. "I respect him greatly and believe in the work he has done. I have consulted so much with him it seemed to me that it was natural to ask him to dinner to talk over this work, and the very fact that I felt a moment's qualm on inviting him because of his color made me ashamed of myself. . . . As things have turned out, I am very glad that I asked him, for the clamor aroused by the act makes me feel as if the act was necessary."

II. *The White House*

Theodore Roosevelt was the first president to use the mansion's nickname, the White House, as its official description. (The name had been used informally since 1789, when the building's sandstone walls were given a lime-based whitewash to protect them from moisture and cracking.) The building turned a century old in 1901 and was, the Army Corps of Engineers found, "dilapidated," with sagging floors and a basement "coated with mold and infested with vermin." The elevator spat sparks. The State Dining Room seated just sixty people. And the building's Federalist style had been warped into what one visitor called "a cross between Neo-Classic and Mississippi River Boat."

A renovation had been rumored for years. Chester A. Arthur wanted to tear the house down and start over. Benjamin Harrison wanted to expand it into a huge quadrangle. William McKinley planned to add large wings featuring columns and domes. But making any significant changes to the President's House risked public outcry, and those ideas withered.

Enter Edith Roosevelt, who required all the charm, resolve, and guile she could muster to direct a remodeling, one of the most controversial aspects of TR's first term. Edie turned to McKim, Mead & White, America's foremost architects, for advice, and in June 1902 Congress appropriated $475,445 for renovations. To avoid raising hackles, the lead architect, Charles McKim, said he was "restoring" the White House and avoided incendiary words like "modernizing."

James Hoban's original architectural plans had apparently disappeared, and McKim took it upon himself to decide which elements of the structure were "original." He pulled the building apart and recomposed it with a series of bold design choices. In the basement, he stripped layers of soot from the walls and built a modern kitchen, turned the boiler room into the Diplomatic Reception Room, and created a new public entrance in the East Wing. On the first floor he revamped the dining room to accommodate 120 guests. To house thirty staff members, miles of telegraph lines, and hundreds of visitors, McKim created a new West Wing—describing it as "temporary," though its walls were hefty enough to support a second story, which was later added—and repurposed the East Wing into the family quarters. When the Roosevelts returned on November 4, 1902, the public generally applauded the restoration, and TR deemed anyone who dared criticize the First Lady's work "a yahoo."

With their house in order, the Roosevelts began to host official dinners catered by Charles Rauscher, a French chef who worked closely with Edie, drafted inventive menus, and charged $8 to $10 a plate. He was especially busy on holidays, which the First Family celebrated with uninhibited zeal. One Thanksgiving meal included an enormous turkey, a roast pig with an apple in its mouth, mounds of sugared sweet potatoes, spinach, boiled rice, pea soup, lettuce and alligator pear (avocado) salad, champagne, apple and mince pies, and ice cream molded in the shape of quails topped with liquefied brown sugar.

This was hardly simple fare. Yet when a magazine made the mistake of complimenting the president as a "gourmet," Roosevelt fired back with characteristic bravado:

When anyone desires to make a widespread impression that the president and family sit down to a four or five course breakfast, a six or seven course lunch and a ten course dinner, the President feels that a denial is not inappropriate. Instead of a breakfast consisting of oranges, cantaloupes, cereals, eggs, bacon, lamb chops, hot cakes, and waffles, President Roosevelt insists that the regular White House Breakfast consists of hard-boiled eggs, rolls and coffee. . . . President Roosevelt declares that when alone he always contents himself with a bowl of bread and milk. When Ms. Roosevelt or the children are present, the luncheon consists of cold meat, tea, cantaloupe in season, and bread. Instead of a ten-course dinner, the president declares that nine times out of ten a three-course dinner is served, and the other time a two-course dinner.

TR did not bother to mention that he was in the midst of a fierce battle to limit the robber barons' exploitation of workers and resources and was straining to distance himself from any "gourmet" pretensions. This humble refrain is common among food-minded presidents—most recently Barack Obama, a man of sophisticated tastes who downplayed his worldly palate so as not to be labeled an elitist.

In the end, TR wrote to Kermit, "I don't think any family has ever enjoyed the White House more than we have. I was thinking about it just this morning when Mother and I took breakfast on the portico and afterwards walked about the lovely grounds and looked at the stately historic old house. It is a wonderful privilege to have been here . . . and I should regard myself as having a small and mean mind if in the event of defeat I felt soured at not having had more instead of being thankful to have had so much."

III. The Most Consequential Camping Trip in American History

The mountains are calling and I must go. . . .
I only went out for a walk, and finally concluded to stay out
til sundown, for going out, I found, was really going in.
—John Muir

On May 15, 1903, Theodore Roosevelt slept in a grove of sequoias, the tallest trees in the world, in the Sierra Nevada of Northern California. He was on a three-day camping trip in Yosemite Valley, a sylvan gem east of San Francisco, with the naturalist John Muir. Every night they fueled up on a hearty dinner over the campfire and delved into Socratic dialogue about how to preserve land for public use, a subject that was, and remains, a political lightning rod.

With the 1904 election on the horizon, Roosevelt had launched on a fourteen-thousand-mile trip, the Great Loop Tour, aboard his private railcar Elysian. Careful not to call it a campaign swing, he spoke to Republicans and Democrats, attended countless political dinners, gave 265 speeches about the need for "a square deal," and drew large crowds. In public TR thrilled to the hurly-burly of campaigning, but in private he itched to slip away into the wilderness with the legendary Muir.

The two were a contrast in styles. Roosevelt was a stout, bespectacled, mustachioed forty-five-year-old from Manhattan who had outfitted himself with a western costume from Brooks Brothers: a heavy Norfolk coat, baggy breeches, leather puttees and thick-soled boots, a cowboy hat, and a kerchief knotted around his neck. Muir was a spry sixty-six-year-old born in Scotland and raised in Wisconsin, with a long face, lively blue eyes, ginger hair, and a flowing gray beard. He dressed like a hobo banker, in a three-piece wool suit with a gold watch on a chain, boots, a battered felt hat, and a stout walking stick. Known as John of the Mountains, Muir called himself a "poetico-trampo-geologist-bot and ornith-natural, etc!-etc!-etc!" He was a geologist, policy wonk, essayist, president of the Sierra Club, and the leading authority on Yosemite Valley, which he described as "by far the grandest of all the special temples of Nature I was ever permitted to enter."

The public had a keen interest in the "camping president's" trip, but TR wanted to be left alone. On May 15, he, Muir, the guides Charlie Leidig and Archie Leonard, and an army packer arrived at the Mariposa Grove, a stand of massive sequoias. They posed for a photograph with a group of politicians, and then, with a quick "God bless you," Roosevelt waved them away. "Pres. Roosevelt . . . is cut off from communication with the outside world," a wire report sulked. "He is camping in big tree country and will remain secluded."

They established camp near the Grizzly Giant, a sequoia that stands 209 feet tall and is estimated to be three thousand years old. At dusk, Leidig made a campfire, grilled steaks, and fried chicken. The party had been supplied with "the best kind of steaks and young broilers," newspapers reported; they were "cooked over the coals, and they appealed strongly to the president." TR gobbled up his dinner and washed it down with gallons of black coffee. Then, as the fire crackled and orange sparks streaked into the night sky, he and Muir dipped into the questions that had brought them together in the mountains.

TR had read Muir's essays on how to "rough it" and was inspired. While he genuinely looked forward to a "bully" adventure, politics coursed through TR's fibers like sap. Muir knew this, and on the verge of departing for Russia had changed his plans. "An influential man from Washington wants to make a trip to the Sierra with me," he wrote his companions, "and I might be able to do some forest good and talking freely around the campfire."

Both men held that God resided in nature, and both wanted to preserve land for the public good. But how? Muir believed Yosemite—"the sanctum sanctorum of the Sierras"—was under human assault and should be preserved. Roosevelt listened, pushed and pulled at Muir's argument, and likely considered how a shift in land use policy would color his own legacy.

In 1864, President Lincoln created the Yosemite Grant, the first time that land was set aside by the federal government for public use. In 1889, Muir and others persuaded Congress to create Yosemite National Park. But control of the Mariposa Grove and Yosemite Valley remained with the state. California took a laissez-faire approach to stewardship, and by 1903 the valley's bear and mountain lion were threatened by hunters, while ranchers, loggers, and farmers strained the ecosystem. In 1894, President Grover Cleveland had signed a bill protecting Yellowstone, Wyoming's geothermal wonderland, as the first "national park." Roosevelt was contemplating whether to apply similar protections to Yosemite, but his views on the stewardship of nature were mutable.

A proponent of economic growth, TR long believed nature existed to benefit man: conserved lands provided fish and game for sport, clean water for drinking and irrigation, timber and minerals for production. His Reclamation Act of 1902 led to economically beneficial but environmentally destructive irrigation projects in twenty states. But during the Great Loop Tour he was exposed to the desert, the Grand Canyon, and the Pacific coast forests, and came to believe that federal lands needed protection. "Conservation of natural resources is the fundamental problem," Roosevelt said. "Unless we solve that problem it will avail us little to solve all others."

As the guides erected a "shelter half"—a half tent, with just the back side closed to the elements—and arranged a pile of forty blankets for

TR (his gear required four mules to carry), Muir wrapped himself in a piece of cloth and slept on a bed of tree boughs. "We lay in the open, the enormous cinnamon-colored trunks rising about us like the columns of a vaster and more beautiful cathedral than was ever conceived by any human architect," the president rhapsodized.

Rising at dawn, TR and Muir had a quick breakfast, then headed up the trail. Avoiding crowds eager to see "the camping president," they posed for a photo at Glacier Point, a thirty-two-hundred-foot-high edifice backdropped by the spectacular Yosemite Falls, and forged through a blinding snow squall. That night, after a thirty-five-mile trek, the men slept in a rocky hollow a mile above Yosemite Valley. Said to have "the greatest view on earth," the spot was later dubbed Roosevelt Point. Snowflakes fell as Leidig prepared a second round of chicken and steak, and the eco-philosophers bantered into the night, their words flowing back and forth, gushing, entwining, and tangling. On their third night the men camped, ate, and talked in a meadow beneath the magnificent cataract of Bridalveil Fall.

"I stuffed him pretty well regarding the timber thieves . . . and other spoilers of the forest," Muir said. "Camping with the president was a remarkable experience. I fairly fell in love with him." The feeling was mutual. After Roosevelt's return to civilization, *The San Francisco Call* noted, "The crisp mountain air seems to have given him a new lease on life. . . . The president also remarked on the amazing appetite he had and how good everything tasted in the woods. He suggested that [Leidig] should be a famous restaurateur."

Back at the White House, Roosevelt launched an unprecedented initiative to preserve federal lands and redrew the nation's map, which provoked a fight that continues today. Declaring, "The rights of the public to the natural resources outweigh private rights," TR protected Yosemite Valley and the Mariposa Grove. Then he set aside Pelican Island, Florida—where egrets and pelicans were being decimated for feathers to adorn ladies' hats—as the first of fifty-one federal bird sanctuaries. He preserved the Tongass Forest in Alaska, Native American ruins in New Mexico, and elk and bison rangeland in Yellowstone. He founded the U.S. Forest Service and signed the Antiquities Act, which allows presidents to protect forests, mountains, water sources, and public lands (a step toward the creation of the National Park Service in 1916). He created eighteen national monuments, five national parks, and 150 national forests.

In total, Theodore Roosevelt conserved 230 million acres, a tract larger than the state of Texas. It was his most enduring legacy, a feat that labeled him "the Conservationist President." His nightly debates with Muir over fire-licked chicken and steak in Yosemite were hailed as "the most consequential camping trip in American history."

IV. Hitting the Public in the Stomach

> There would be meat stored in great piles in rooms . . .
> and thousands of rats would race about on it. . . .
> [T]he packers would put poisoned bread out for them; they would die,
> and then rats, bread, and meat would go into the hoppers together. . . .
> [T]here were things that went into the sausage in comparison
> with which a poisoned rat was a tidbit.
> —Upton Sinclair, *The Jungle*

One morning in 1906, President Roosevelt was reading Upton Sinclair's novel *The Jungle,* and as he tucked into his eggs, he eyed a sausage link glistening on his plate. With a look of disgust, he picked the sausage up like a dead mouse and tossed it out the window. This account, written by the newspaper humorist Finley Peter Dunne, was apocryphal, though some believed it because it encapsulated the nation's revulsion at Sinclair's disclosures about the Chicago meatpacking industry.

Sinclair was a twenty-seven-year-old "muckraker," as TR derisively labeled the new breed of investigative journalists, who had spent six months undercover in Chicago meat plants and had intended his thinly veiled fiction as a damning critique of capitalism. It was the heyday of the Progressive Era, when American corporations were agglomerating into "trusts" that dominated oil, steel, banking, and tobacco, and the "little man" felt like a cog in a crushing machine. With graphic scenes—of men falling into vats and being rendered into sausage, the butchering of diseased cattle, the use of dyes to disguise rancid ham—*The Jungle* revealed the inner workings of meat production, one of the largest and least regulated businesses in the country.

Sinclair hoped to spotlight the plight of workers, foment a revolution, and turn America toward socialism. But readers focused on the nauseating details of the slaughterhouses run by the Big Four meatpackers—Swift, Armour, Morris, and National Packing—instead. Revolted, the public's appetite for beef, pork, and poultry fell an estimated 50 percent. "I aimed at the public's heart, and by accident I hit it in the stomach," Sinclair wrote, ruefully.

President Roosevelt was a longtime ally of big business who once advocated shooting the leaders of the Populist Party. But in his second term he grew concerned about public health and recognized that the Republican Party's main challenge was to convince voters that "we do stand squarely for the interests of all of the people." Less well known was that TR had a personal connection to the issue of food contamination. When his Rough Riders seized Cuba from the Spanish in 1898, thousands of his troops were sickened by contaminated meat produced in the United States, and several hundred of them died from food poisoning, more than were killed in combat.

The Jungle laid bare the unintended consequences of huge, systemic changes under way in the American food system. As rapid industrialization and urbanization led to a greater use of canned and preserved foods, food producers used shortcuts and corruption to get their way. At the same time, the rise of yellow journalism and advertising-dependent newspapers opened the door for patent medicine hucksters to make false claims about "miracle" elixirs.

Exposés of fruits colored with poisonous red dye, and alcohol distilled with chemical fillers, prompted a second wave of outrage. The "sheer fraud" these snake oil salesmen perpetrated with their "nostrums, salves, appliances, poisons, [and] magic" was "the most wretched and disgraceful evil" encountered by Harvey Wiley, chief chemist of the Agriculture Department. Wiley was an early proponent of "food and drug purity" and pushed for consumer protections. He was effective, but with an ego as grandiose as Roosevelt's, Wiley alienated powerful allies. Yet, despite pushback from industrial food producers and the Speaker of the House, "Uncle Joe" Cannon—an Illinois Republican secretly in league with the meat men—Congress created laws to prevent "the manufacture, sale, or transportation of adulterated or misbranded or poisonous or deleterious foods, drugs or medicines and liquors."

Roosevelt signed the Pure Food and Drug Act and the Federal Meat Inspection Act on June 30, 1906. These were the nation's first laws to make it a crime to mislabel or doctor meat, create new guidelines for food manufacturing, limit additives, require accurate labeling, and impose legal and financial penalties on violators. The Pure Food and Drug Act also took aim at "addictive" or "dangerous" drugs, such as opium, morphine, cannabis, and alcohol. The acts marked the first time the federal government asserted its responsibility for the health and safety of America's foods and drugs.

In 1930, Wiley's Bureau of Chemistry was renamed the Food and Drug

Administration (FDA). By 2019, the FDA had 17,599 employees and an annual budget of $5.7 billion and oversaw some $2.6 trillion worth of food, tobacco, and medical products, including 77 percent of the nation's food supply. Bad actors persist in the food industry, and scandals regularly pop up. The FDA has sometimes struggled to keep pace, but has generally been an effective guardian of public health and is one of the largest, most important, and least understood arms of the federal bureaucracy.

V. William H. Taft: A Gizzard of His Own

The Twenty-Seventh President
March 4, 1909–March 4, 1913

> What he ate did not so much relieve his hunger,
> as keep it immortal in him.
> —Herman Melville, *Moby Dick*

As the election of 1908 hove into view, Theodore Roosevelt was a shoo-in for reelection but decided he'd had enough of the presidency. One evening, he invited Secretary of War William Howard Taft and his wife, Helen (Nellie), to dinner at the White House. Over their meal, TR muttered clairvoyantly, "There is something hanging over his head. . . . At one time it looks like the presidency. Then again it looks like the chief justiceship."

Nellie Taft, a slim, intense woman who had dreamed of living in the White House since visiting as a girl (her father was Rutherford B. Hayes's law partner), perked up: "Make it the presidency."

"Make it the chief justiceship," rumbled her husband, an amiable three-hundred-and-thirty-two-pound legal scholar who aspired to the Supreme Court.

By that point, Roosevelt had transformed himself from an arch capitalist into a defender of workers' rights, a shift that alienated many of his Republican brethren, who considered him a "mad messiah." But TR kept a tight grip on the levers of power and used the dinner to gauge Taft's willingness to continue his antitrust, anti-tariff, pro-conservation agenda. That night, Taft convinced his mentor he would make a worthy successor.

Taft's opponent in 1908 was the fiery Nebraska Democrat William Jennings Bryan, who was making his third bid for the White House. Taft was a genial Ohioan who found the hustle and bustle of stumping "uncomfortable." To inject energy into his run for office his team created "spectacle politics," including free food at campaign stops. It is an age-old tactic that reliably draws crowds, and usually features pancake breakfasts or rubber-chicken dinners. But at one stop things got weird.

When Taft arrived at Fargo, North Dakota, in September, he was greeted by several thousand people who had traveled hundreds of miles to see the candidate in the flesh. A "surging meaningless crowd" escorted him by torchlight to a woodlot, where Taft gave a quick speech and local pols orated before dinner was served in a "natural amphitheater." There, bonfires created "a weird light and smoke effect," papers reported. Taft was a large man with a booming voice, yet it was the spirit of Roosevelt that animated the crowd, as if TR's meaty face, with its pince-nez glasses and bushy mustache, were grinning toothily from the smoke like the Wizard of Oz.

The barbecue feast included ten steer and twenty mules, which symbolized the Democratic Party. Two large black bears fattened on walnuts were also scheduled to become part of the menu, but a debate broke out about the wisdom of roasting animals that symbolized Roosevelt. *The New York Herald* claimed Taft "ate bear meat with as much gusto as any of the thousands of enthusiastics" gorging on the free dinner—the implication being that Taft was happy to feast on TR's largesse. But that account was fanciful. As *The New York Times* wrote, "It would never do to have the candidate eat up the 'real Teddy bear.'" Other papers noted the animals were not eaten but chained under a banner reading, "We Are Real Teddies." The confusion over the bears' fate was emblematic of the challenge of linking Taft to Roosevelt while presenting the candidate as worthy in his own right. Having ridden in on TR's coattails, Taft would find it difficult to dismount.

TAFT WAS INAUGURATED the twenty-seventh president in 1909. He was fifty-one, a rotund man with an expressive bushy mustache, big cheeks, cheerful lidded eyes, and brown hair parted in the middle. While his wife, Helen (Nellie) Herron Taft, was "inexpressibly happy" to become First Lady, the new president was less enthusiastic about the White House, which he'd later call "a prison," and "the loneliest place in the world."

Influenced by Nellie—the first First Lady to smoke cigarettes, ride in an inauguration parade, lobby for safety standards for federal workers, publish her memoirs, and drive a car—Taft expanded the West Wing and built the first Oval Office on the White House's south side. (Franklin D. Roosevelt would further expand the West Wing and move the Oval Office to the building's southeast corner, where it remains.)

Even before he took office there were rumors of tension between Taft and his mentor, Roosevelt, and though Taft assured TR there was not "the slightest difference between us," his views skewed to the right over time. He later described an inauguration eve dinner together as "a funeral," while gossips said Mrs. Roosevelt and Mrs. Taft "gave each other precise courtesy." The military aide Archie Butt disputed that, and said the men had spent a pleasant evening cursing Congress. But the fault lines were real, and spreading.

TAFT STOOD ABOUT six feet tall, and his weight yo-yoed between 270 and 354 pounds, making him the heaviest president in history. He "liked every sort of food with the single exception of eggs," said Elizabeth Jaffray, the Tafts' acerbic Canadian-born housekeeper. "He really had few preferences but just naturally liked food—and lots of it."

The president would begin his day with a "physical culture man" (a personal trainer) followed by a breakfast worthy of a medieval king. His primary nourishment was steak, which he liked cooked medium, sprinkled with salt and pepper, and smeared with butter. "He wanted a thick, juicy twelve-ounce steak nearly every morning," Jaffray recalled, along with two oranges, toast, and a torrent of coffee with buckets of cream and sugar. But he was just as happy to start the day with a pile of waffles or a haunch of venison, or both. On a visit to Savannah, Georgia, he gorged on grapefruit, potted partridge, broiled venison, grilled partridge, waffles with butter and maple syrup, bacon, hominy, hot rolls, more venison, and a pond's worth of coffee.

Taft would often have steak for lunch and dinner, too. If not beef, then he might tackle a menu that progressed from bouillon to smelt with tartar sauce, lamb chops, Bermuda potatoes and green peas, raspberry jelly with whipped cream, bonbons, and more coffee.

His dinner often featured prodigious quantities of seafood, including salmon, terrapin (turtle) soup, or lobster Newburg—a rich dish of lobster, butter, cream, cognac, sherry, eggs, and cayenne pepper popularized by Delmonico's, New York's finest restaurant. One of Taft's favorite repasts was the mussel soup called Billy Bi (or Billy By), a dish created in Paris for the expat American businessman William B. Leeds, known as Billy B. (Some say the patron's surname was Brands or Beebes.) Leeds didn't want his friends to suffer the indignity of wrenching mussels from their shells, so the chef at Chez Maxim's served just the cooking liquor— a luxurious broth made of fish and mussel stock, white wine, heavy cream, butter, onion, celery, and thyme. It's a dish I recommend, albeit with the mussels included with the broth.

BY 1911, President Taft had tipped the scales at 332 pounds, though Jaffray sniped that he "looks as if he actually weighs 400." Concerned, Nellie Taft instructed the president (via Jaffray) to slim down. Hearing his wife's edict, Taft grumbled, "I tell you, it's a sad state of affairs when a man can't even call his gizzard his own." But he agreed to replace his usual twelve-ounce breakfast steak with an eight- or six-ouncer. Though Taft complained about his "terrible sentence," Jaffray wrote, "Somehow, he really didn't take off any great amount of weight."

He suffered from sleep apnea, snoring, and grogginess and was notorious for dozing off at cabinet meetings. "While I was talking to him . . . his head would fall over on his breast and he would go sound asleep," recalled the Indiana senator James Watson. "He would waken and resume the conversation, only to repeat the performance." Nellie dubbed him "Sleeping Beauty."

It wasn't until the early twentieth century that a person's weight was considered an indicator of the vitality and self-discipline desirable in a chief executive. In the 1950s the word "corpulence" was replaced by "obesity" and was identified as a medical problem. Since then, obesity has been traced to poor nutrition and a lack of exercise and associated with heart disease, diabetes, joint problems, and high cholesterol. Taft's struggle resonates today, when obesity is considered a chronic disease that afflicts nearly half the American population.

When he was forty-eight and weighed 314 pounds, Taft wrote to the British diet expert Dr. Nathaniel E. Yorke-Davies, who advised him to lose 70 pounds. To do so, Taft would start his day with a cup of hot water flavored with lemon juice, Gluten biscuits, and a mere six ounces of lean grilled steak. Later, he'd heap his plate with vegetables and snack on stewed prunes. He weighed himself daily, kept a food diary, played golf, and rode horses (apologizing to the animals). He'd send Yorke-Davies weekly updates, including notes on his bowel movements. In April 1905 he weighed 255 pounds—a loss of 59 pounds—no longer suffered from "acidity of the stomach," and felt "excellent," he announced. In fact, Taft had fudged how many pounds he'd shed and confided that he was "pretty continuously hungry."

While campaigning, he packed the weight back on, and ballooned to as much as 354 pounds. A rumor held that Taft was so big that he became stuck in a bathtub. It sounded vaguely plausible but wasn't true, though he did have a custom bathtub installed in the White House. Stretching seven feet, eleven inches long, by forty-one inches wide, it weighed a ton, could fit four regular-sized men, and was said to be the largest tub ever made for an individual.

Like Jack Sprat and his wife, Taft was large and jovial, while Nellie was thin and zealous. She was ahead of her time in many ways, and would have made a fine chief executive herself. The First Lady was more interested in politics than the president was, and silently monitored his meetings then offered advice in private. Channeling her energy, Mrs. Taft landscaped the Washington Mall, and in March 1912 planted 3,020 cherry trees donated by Japan. (In 1965, Japan donated an additional 3,800 trees, which were planted by Lady Bird Johnson.) When it came to household management, Nellie was either an efficiency expert or a holy terror, depending on your perspective. She replaced the male cooks with three Irishwomen and frequently dropped into the kitchen to make "helpful" suggestions. One cook quit in frustration and another left to get married (they were quickly replaced). Nellie had a passion for technology and installed a twelve-foot-long Imperial French Coal Range, a forty-quart Peerless Ice Cream Freezer, and an electric silverware buffer in the kitchen.

To organize menus and cleaning, she dispensed with the traditional male stewards and installed Elizabeth Jaffray as the first White House housekeeper. "I wanted a woman who could relieve me of the supervision of such details as no man, expert steward though he may be, would ever recognize," Nellie explained. "The White House . . . has to be more vigilantly watched [than a normal home]. Dust accumulates in corners; mirrors and picture glasses get dim with dampness; curtains sag . . . floors lose their gloss; rugs turn up at the corners . . . things get out of order generally; and it is a very large house. Kitchen helpers . . . neglect their shining copper pots and pans and kettles . . . they need a woman's guidance and control."

Nellie kept a gimlet eye on her food budget, reducing it to just $868.93

a month by ordering wholesale, nixing pricey or out-of-season goods, and using fresh milk from their cow Pauline Wayne (the last bovine to board at the White House). They paid for state dinners and official functions from Taft's $75,000 salary. But Mrs. Jaffray objected to their "butter by the tub, potatoes by the barrel, fruit and green vegetables by the crate."

Mrs. Taft fulfilled her childhood dream by managing the president's social schedule, and in the winter of 1909–10 she invited eighty people for dinner one night, seventy the next, and hosted a reception for two thousand guests the day after that. She hosted teas, and the president committed to at least four large receptions a year. But just three months into their administration, the First Lady collapsed from a stroke, at forty-seven. Her faced drooped; she suffered aphasia, struggled to speak, and wore a veil. Her family managed to keep her condition secret, and though she recovered she'd never be the same dynamic woman she had been. One evening, Nellie sat alone in a small room adjacent to a roaring state dinner. Elegantly dressed in a new gown and jewelry, she sat at a table set for one, with fine linen, silver, and a floral centerpiece; she ate what her guests ate and listened in on their conversations through a door cracked slightly ajar. It must have been an exquisite torture for someone who had waited a lifetime for that moment.

AFTER STEAK, Taft's favorite dish was roasted possum (or opossum), North America's only marsupial. Possum was a sought-after comestible then, and in 1909 hunters in Texas sent a "large white possum" to the White House by express mail. At a Thanksgiving, Taft paired a twenty-six-pound "monster" possum with a thirty-pound turkey and a fifty-pound mince pie. In Georgia, a waiter lifted the cover from a silver platter to reveal a live, tethered possum; the animal bared its teeth and hissed at Taft, but "it was the reproachful look which left the lasting impression," *The New York Times* reported. When an eighteen-pound "Billy Possum and taters" (sweet potatoes) were served with persimmon beer, the president quickly reduced the dish to "a shattered wreck," a guest recalled. A doctor sitting nearby cautioned that possum was rich, greasy, and unhealthy. "Well, I like possum," Taft replied. "I ate very heartily of it. . . . Not only am I very fond of possum, but that possum is very fond of me."

As an alternative to the Roosevelt-inspired teddy bear, Taft's operatives tried to market a stuffed "Billy Possum" toy. But real possums rifle through garbage and eat ticks, snakes, and the skeletons of dead animals (for calcium). Billy Possum didn't capture the public imagination.

Today the big-eyed, gray-haired, pink-nosed marsupial is no longer a popular menu item, though it remains an apt political metaphor. Possums famously pretend to be dead—playing possum—when threatened. It's an involuntary action, like fainting, in which the animal's eyes close while it emits a foul-smelling odor and foams at the mouth. But eventually the "dead" possum will twitch its ears and come to. Taft played political possum, as it were: at first he followed Roosevelt's lead, but like a possum twitching its ears, the true Taft slowly came to life and wandered off in his own direction.

In a telling moment, TR cautioned Taft not to mention his love of golf in public because it would color him as a privileged man of leisure. "It is just like my tennis," TR said. "I never let a photo of me in tennis costume appear." But Taft argued that golf was "a game for people who are not active. . . . When a man weighs 285 pounds you have got to give him some opportunity to make his . . . muscles move." People in western states condemned Taft's golfing as immoral, but many more applauded his pastime, which inspired a golf boom that doubled the number of players on public courses.

The tennis/golf divide symbolized the ways that Roosevelt and Taft, the somewhat progressive and increasingly conservative wings of the GOP, drifted apart. Roosevelt worried that his protégé's antitrust policy targeted U.S. Steel, a company TR considered a "good trust," and he felt betrayed when Taft fired Gifford Pinchot, TR's head of the U.S. Forest Service. "Yes, Taft carried out TR's policies—carried them out on a shutter," Senator Jonathan Dolliver of Iowa acidly noted.

In 1910, Roosevelt began to openly attack Taft, while Taft claimed his former mentor was "the most dangerous man in American history . . . because of his hold upon the less intelligent voters and the discontented." Two years later, Roosevelt announced he would run for a third term and deemed Taft a "puzzlewit." Taft called him a "honeyfugler," and said, "I have been a man of straw long enough; every man who has blood in his body and who has been misrepresented as I have is forced to fight." To which TR's boosters countered: Taft "has too big a paunch to fight or have much of a punch, while a free-for-all, slap-bang, kick-him-in-the-belly, is just nuts for the chief."

The 1912 Republican convention in Chicago was bedlam. Roosevelt ran as an independent candidate of the Bull Moose Party, comparing himself to a raging bull moose ready for a fight. It was a battle of mutually assured destruction. In the end they both lost to Woodrow Wilson, who became the first Democratic president since Grover Cleveland in 1892.

Roosevelt and Taft did not talk to each other for years. But they managed to reconcile in 1918, at a chance meeting in a Chicago hotel. TR was fifty-nine by then and, at 237 pounds, had swelled to Taftian dimensions. He had less than a year to live. Taft lived until 1930, when he died at age seventy-two of heart failure. At that point, he weighed a relatively feathery 280 pounds and was the only person to have served as both president and chief justice.

VI. *Heart of Darkness*

In 1909, three weeks after Taft's inauguration, Roosevelt embarked on an industrial-scale African safari under the auspices of the Smithsonian Institution, which gave it a zoological gloss. TR and his son Kermit, assisted by three scientists and 250 African porters, gun bearers, and guides, killed 512 large animals and collected 23,151 specimens—which was more than they were allowed. While condemning "game butchery" as "wanton cruelty," Roosevelt defended his killing as scientifically important and called his critics soft in the head. After felling a bull elephant, Roosevelt fondly recalled, "I toasted slices of elephant's heart on a pronged stick before the fire, and found it delicious; for I was hungry, and the night was cold."

Friends like John Muir struggled to reconcile the Roosevelt they admired—the conservationist president—with his amoral doppelgänger, the "boyish" man who rashly shot a neighbor's dog, rushed to kill endangered bison, and culled the docile giraffe he supposedly admired. Like modern tech bros such as Mark Zuckerberg (who ate only the animals he killed himself for a year), TR saw himself as a predator who lived by his wits and the primal code of life and death. Roosevelt's discordant relationship with nature seemed to belong to two different people, and in a way it did. An analysis by the Duke University Medical Center found that 8 percent of presidents showed signs of bipolar disorder, most notably Theodore Roosevelt and Lyndon Johnson.

When faced with the loss of loved ones, some people, like Thomas Jefferson, lose their appetite, while others eat superabundantly. Roosevelt was of the latter persuasion. A sickly child who was despondent over the death of his parents and his first wife, TR grew to five feet ten and bulked up to well over two hundred pounds. Gifford Pinchot observed that TR "ate nearly twice as much as the average man," and the economist Irving Fisher added, "The president is running his machine too hard. . . . [F]riction . . . will probably increase to almost a stopping point." Roosevelt acknowledged that "I eat too much," but that did not slow his consumption.

A fatalist who did not expect to see old age, TR was determined to see his children turn twenty-one. He did, and on January 6, 1919, he died in his sleep, at sixty. Medically speaking, a blood clot had lodged in his lung and stopped his breathing, but you could say that Theodore Roosevelt burned so brightly that he snuffed himself out. Or, more elementally, that he ate himself to death.

8

From WILSON to COOLIDGE and HOOVER

Heartburn, Hard Cheese, and a Hail of Rotten Tomatoes

WOODROW WILSON,
THE TWENTY-EIGHTH PRESIDENT
March 4, 1913–March 4, 1921

★

I. Food Will Win the War

"The science which feeds men is worth at least as much
as the one which teaches how to kill them."
—Jean Brillat-Savarin

Woodrow Wilson was a tall, thin neurasthenic who suffered chronic indigestion, preferred a bland stack of pancakes to lamb chops "done up in pajamas," as he put it, and appeared utterly disinterested in food. Yet, just as the antisocial John Adams was thrust into the role of First Host, so the dyspeptic Wilson was fated to nourish millions of strapped Americans and starving Europeans during and after World War I.

He was inaugurated on March 4, 1913, and managed to antagonize much of Washington in his first day on the job: Wilson broke precedent by not naming his cabinet until his first presidential lunch, insisted his wife, Ellen, precede him into a room, and, perhaps most unforgivably in the eyes of society, canceled the inaugural ball. The latter was allegedly for the sake of austerity, though friends said the Wilsons were private people who held the presidency in such esteem they didn't dare sully it with "ball-gown frivolity."

First Lady Ellen Wilson was a short, plump, melancholic woman and accomplished painter. Unlike her husband, she was an advocate of equal rights for women and Black people. She disliked big parties and preferred to host small receptions to "show that dinners and other social functions at the White House can be both beautiful and simple." That wasn't much of a stretch, for when it came to food and entertaining, simplicity was Wilson's middle name.

Once, Wilson wrote with uncharacteristic ardor about the foods of his native Virginia: "I am very fond of country hams, peach cobblers, butter and buttermilk, fresh eggs, hot biscuits, homemade ice cream and plain white cake." But this was an exception. In general, he was a timid, picky eater for whom a big meal might include clear soup, chicken salad, and strawberry ice cream.

If Roosevelt and Taft lived to eat, Wilson ate simply to live. He managed to host the occasional state dinner, but his menus typically consisted of items you might find at a midsized country club: fillet of sole, fillet of beef, breast of chicken, a few vegetables. Nor had he developed a meaningful food policy when he took office. But that abruptly changed when a globe-shattering crisis seemed to spring from nowhere.

In June 1914, it was inconceivable to the average American that an obscure crime across the Atlantic—the assassination of Archduke Franz Ferdinand, the presumptive heir to the Austro-Hungarian throne, in Sarajevo, Yugoslavia—would ignite the first-ever "world war." The battle would pitch seventy million troops into combat, kill nine million people, erase empires, cause famines, set the stage for the pandemic of 1918 and the Great Depression, and anticipate a second, even more horrific globe-spanning conflagration.

As news of barbaric trench warfare and new killing machines— submarines, tanks, and airplanes—made headlines, Europhiles and hard-liners pushed for American intervention, while isolationists and doves pulled against it. In a symbolic moment, hostilities broke out in the White House kitchen, where—like a scene cut from *Casablanca*—the head cook, Sigrid Nilsson, a pro-German Swede, brawled with her colleagues Olive Caveau of France and Elizabeth Colquist from Ireland, who favored the Allies. The Canadian housekeeper Elizabeth Jaffray broke up the fight and threatened all three combatants with termination unless they shaped up. (A cold truce lasted until 1919, when Nilsson left to get married.)

Food was used as a weapon by both sides. When the British navy blockaded German supply routes, the kaiser's troops seized French and Belgian food stores, which caused mass civilian starvation. Riots broke out, and as the news went from bad to worse Wilson's central nervous system seemed wired directly into the conflict. With every thrust and parry in Europe, he suffered hypertension, heartburn, and constipation in Washington. When his secretary raised diplomatic questions at dinner, Wilson had to excuse himself to recover from a headache and stomach pains. Even minor distractions set him off, such as the staring eyes of a moose hung by Roosevelt in the State Dining Room, which so disturbed Wilson that he had to turn his back in order to digest. (The moose was removed.)

Diagnosed with "excess stomach acid," the president was prescribed powdered medications and a stomach pump to force water into his belly.

They didn't help. Ellen tried to limit Woodrow's workaholic tendencies and encouraged him to relax. But she also suffered ill health and was diagnosed with Bright's disease, a kidney inflammation. On August 1, 1914—just days after the Austro-Hungarian Empire and Germany declared war on Russia—Mrs. Wilson succumbed, at fifty-four. Ellen's death crushed Wilson's spirit. He considered resigning and secretly hoped to be assassinated.

But in March 1915, Wilson literally bumped into Edith Bolling Galt, a wealthy young widow who was visiting the White House. A friend of Wilson's cousin, Galt rounded a corner and ran smack into the American president, whom she barely recognized. Edith was as indifferent to politics as Wilson was to food. Nevertheless, they hit it off and soon began to venture out on dates. Rumors whirled about their romance, which some criticized as "too soon" after Ellen's death. But the impulsive Wilson enjoyed Edith's companionship and began to rely on her for advice, and in December they married.

Meanwhile, Wilson's pacifism was tested when a German U-boat sank the British liner RMS *Lusitania* in May 1915, killing 128 Americans. He ran for reelection in 1916 under noninterventionist slogans like "America First" and "He Kept Us Out of the War," and eked out a win over the Republican Charles Evans Hughes. But then the Zimmermann telegram—in which the kaiser offered to finance a Mexican invasion of America—was published, forcing Wilson's hand. Reluctantly, he asked a joint session of Congress for a declaration of war, and on April 6, 1917, they granted his wish. Fearing the worst, the president wept in private.

THE NATION WITH the biggest army or best weapons is not always guaranteed victory, but the combatant that can best feed its soldiers and citizens has a distinct advantage. Even before committing troops, Wilson declared that "food will win the war" and began shipping rations and matériel to the European Allies. In August 1917, he passed the Food and Fuel Control Act, which gave him the power to regulate the purchase, storage, distribution, and export of provisions. Building on that, he established the U.S. Food Administration and appointed a multimillionaire mining executive named Herbert Hoover to run it. Soon American convoys were shipping tons of American produce and ten thousand Yankee troops across the Atlantic every week. Wilson understood that aid shipments saved millions of lives, built psychological resistance to "the

Hun," and were effective strategic and propaganda tools. But he left the difficult work of creating and implementing those programs to Hoover, a logistics expert with a growing sideline in charity.

In 1914, Herbert Hoover was running a mining business in Europe when he was drafted to lead the Commission for Relief in Belgium. The private group led the evacuation of 120,000 American civilians from Europe and negotiated agreements between the German, British, French, Dutch, and Belgian governments to allow for the shipment of some 5.6 million tons of flour, grain, sugar, and other supplies—most of it donated by the American public—to the Continent. The effort saved 10.5 million lives and averted famine and epidemics in Belgium and northern France. It also launched Hoover's political career, unwittingly if he is to be believed.

"I did not realize it at the moment, but on August 3, 1914 [the day Germany declared war on France], my career was over forever," Hoover said. "I was on the slippery slope of public life." It was a new life built on food.

When America declared war in 1917, Wilson appointed Hoover to lead the Food Administration, whose main task was to persuade Americans to eat less, grow more, and donate their stores to the cause. A canny marketer, Hoover launched a publicity campaign urging civilians to stop snacking, change their diets, harbor resources, and use substitutions— soybeans for meat, molasses for sugar, vegetable shortening for butter, whole wheat "Victory Bread" for white bread, and so on—to provide for the doughboys (a nickname for U.S. infantrymen, many of whom were teenagers and survived on rice-flour cakes baked in campfires, akin to the fire cakes at Valley Forge).

U.S. soldiers were better fed than other nations' troops: at a cost of twenty-six cents per soldier per day—more than $727 million ($15.7 billion today) in total—they were fed basic stews and fresh bread baked in field kitchens just behind the front lines. In an innovation, each soldier carried emergency rations—bread, meat, coffee, and sugar, containing more than three thousand calories—designed to last a week, and kept in tins to preserve them from spoilage, gas attacks, and vermin.

On the home front, Hoover mobilized hundreds of thousands of volunteers, controlled food costs, and organized distribution centers. His name became a verb: to "Hooverize" meant to economize. To make his messages easily digestible, Hoover issued a blizzard of posters, flyers, pamphlets, and advertisements that touted "Wheatless Mondays and Wednesdays," "Meatless Tuesdays," and "Porkless Thursdays and Saturdays." The nutrition experts Houston and Alberta Goudiss wrote that one wheatless meal a day per American family resulted in 90,000,000 extra bushels of wheat for the nation every year; two meatless days a week resulted in 2,200,000 pounds of meat a year. Stoking patriotic fervor, Hoover instructed restaurants, shopkeepers, and manufacturers to replace Germanic food names with more American-sounding monikers: sauerkraut was rebranded "Liberty Cabbage" and frankfurters became "Liberty Sausages." His Clean Plate campaign taught children to recite a pledge: "At table I'll not leave a scrap of food upon my plate. And I'll not eat between meals, but for supper time I'll wait."

Hoover attracted like-minded managers with innovative ideas. The timber baron Charles Lathrop Pack, for instance, organized Victory Gardens (a.k.a. War Gardens), which encouraged Americans to grow their own fruits and vegetables to free up supplies for the troops—or, as Pack put it, "The Seeds of Victory Insure the Fruits of Peace." The program taught families how to grow, cook, and can their own fruits and vegetables. By the end of the war, more than five million Victory Gardens had produced $1.2 billion worth of food. The program catalyzed a generation of politically engaged cooks—most notably Alice Waters of Berkeley's Chez Panisse, who was inspired by her parents' Victory Garden to reinvent the café at Monticello and push Michelle Obama to plant a vegetable garden in the White House lawn.

With resources stretched thin during the war, Americans began to cook more, and more inventively, turning rationed goods into scalloped cabbage, potato bread, bean and tomato stew, and other thrifty dishes. Noting this, Hoover teamed with schools, clergy, and the press to educate citizens about vitamins, calories, proteins, and carbohydrates. As he saw it, smart dietary choices would supply healthy foods to the Yanks overseas and the folks back home. He was right: during the war, the nation consumed less sugar and fat and more fresh vegetables and whole wheat than before the war.

Compliance with these edicts was voluntary and relied on people's patriotism and goodwill. The Wilsons set a frugal example by rationing their meat, wheat, and gasoline, and hired a flock of sheep to maintain the White House lawn. Though the sheep were more interested in nibbling flowers than grass, they were a public relations coup and their "White House wool" raised $52,823 for the Red Cross. But the spirit of collective sacrifice eventually crumbled in the face of human self-interest. While many citizens adhered to meatless and wheatless days, those on the economic margins did not, or could not. When people hoarded food, the result was panic and price gouging. Wheat prices spiked dramatically, from 78 cents per bushel in 1913 to $2.12 a bushel in 1917, when speculators, including European governments, bid up the price on the Chicago Board of Trade. In response, the U.S. Food Administration bought and sold wheat at a fixed price of $2 a bushel. This calmed nerves, temporarily. But in 1918 the administration had to ration sugar: each citizen was limited to eight ounces a week, which raised costs and led to black-market trade. Wilson also imposed strict limits on alcohol, which unintentionally catalyzed the temperance movement that led to Prohibition in 1920.

As America's involvement in the European conflict deepened, Wilson's hypertension soared, his kidneys began to fail, and at times his right arm—already weakened by an 1896 stroke—was temporarily paralyzed. Stoically, or foolishly, Wilson downplayed the seriousness of his condition and blamed it on a "rather hard game of golf."

When a neurologist predicted that Wilson would not survive his first term, the navy doctor Cary Grayson made it a personal mission to improve the president's health. Eschewing the powders and stomach pump, Grayson focused on healthy eating, exercise, and sleep—a standard fitness regime today. To encourage Wilson to spend more time outside, Grayson taught him to play golf. The president became obsessed and played at all hours, sometimes at five o'clock in the morning, and conditions—even in the snow, when he had golf balls painted red. He was not a natural athlete and once took twenty-six strokes to make a single hole. "My right eye is like a horse's. I can see straight out with it but not sideways," he conceded. "As a result, I cannot take a full swing because my nose gets in the way and cuts off my view of the ball." Wilson didn't keep score and summed up his game as "an ineffectual attempt to put an elusive ball into an obscure hole with implements ill-adapted for the purpose."

While some of Dr. Grayson's dietary advice—such as his emphasis on bland but nutritious foods—helped stabilize the presidential stomach, some of his other cures were less palatable. At breakfast, for instance, Grayson insisted the president drink a glass of grape or orange juice with two raw eggs every morning, for strength. While this concoction would certainly jolt Wilson awake, he compared its ingestion to consuming "an unborn thing."

.   .   .

AS IF THE WAR had not put enough strain on his flighty gastric system, Wilson added to his dyspepsia with inept politicking and romantic entanglements. A learned PhD, he could stir crowds with soaring oratory, but his small talk was as weak as his handshake, which felt like "a ten-cent pickled mackerel in brown paper—irresponsive and lifeless," wrote the Kansas newspaperman William Allen White. And Wilson revealed his prejudice when he declared the presidency requires a man "put on his war paint" and "crush" his rivals or those he considered inferior. Most notoriously, the Virginia native praised the Ku Klux Klan and railed about "the intolerable burden of . . . ignorant Negroes," forced capable Black officials out of the government, and segregated federal workers— all decisions that have tarnished his legacy. (In 2020, Princeton removed Wilson's name from its School of Public and International Affairs.)

Though he had an undertaker's mien, Wilson had a romantic streak that swung between Apollonian probity and Dionysian appetite. He hosted the first White House Mother's Day party, had a giddy sense of humor, and was a devoted husband and father. But the same man declared, "No man has ever been a success without having been surrounded by admiring females . . . A pretty girl is my chief pleasure." He confided to Ellen that he did not dare spend a night alone in New York City, for his "imperious passions" might lead him astray. She dismissed this as harmless fantasy, but letters reveal that he likely consummated at least one extramarital affair.

It began over dinner in Bermuda in 1907. Wilson was the fifty-year-old president of Princeton University and had retreated there alone to convalesce from "the blue devils." One night his eye was lured by a tall woman with dark curly hair dressed in a sparkly gold dress. Her name was Mrs. Mary Allen Hulbert Peck, and she was a forty-four-year-old New Yorker who was separated from her husband. In those delicious days in Bermuda, they bantered over tea and dinners. The following winter, Wilson returned to Bermuda and shared more dinners with Peck. He visited her apartment in New York. She visited him in Princeton. "I found him longing to make up as best he might for play long denied," Peck recalled. "That . . . is why he turned to me, who had never lost my zest for the joy of living."

Wilson claimed to have told Ellen the truth about his dalliance and that she "understood . . . [and] has forgiven." But his enemies were less sympathetic. As Wilson campaigned for the White House in 1912, Republican operatives offered Peck thousands of dollars for her story. In a panic, Wilson drafted a statement that read, "I am deeply ashamed and repentant." But the affair was never publicized, in part because Teddy Roosevelt declared, "No evidence could ever make the American people believe that a man like Woodrow Wilson, cast so perfectly as the apothecary's clerk, could ever play Romeo."

I include this melodrama because it is a testament to the bewildering power of appetite, the primal intertwining of food and sex, and the pressures of the White House. Wilson's relationship with Peck did not impact his ability to lead and may have helped him relax though his wives and daughters no doubt had a different perspective. Even the president seemed vexed by his "poor, mixed, inexplicable nature."

WORLD WAR I ENDED on November 11, 1918, leaving many Europeans famished and destitute. In an Armistice Day address, Wilson intoned, "Hunger does not breed reform; it breeds madness." That was true on the global scale, and it would also prove true in his own life. Wilson's poor digestion weakened his constitution and helped him slide into a kind of madness.

After hammering together the Treaty of Versailles—the peace between America, the Allies, and Germany—in 1919, Wilson advocated for a League of Nations to prevent future world wars. But isolationists led by Senator Henry Cabot Lodge blocked him. Without an agreement Wilson predicted, with fateful accuracy, "there will come some time, in the vengeful Providence of God, another war in which not a few hundred thousand men from America will have to die, but as many millions as are necessary."

In Paris, Wilson suffered fevers, labored breathing, and diarrhea, and in April 1919 he was forced to withdraw from the peace talks. He was diagnosed with the Spanish flu—the 1918 influenza that killed some thirty million people—but some experts believe Wilson had a stroke. As he convalesced, the president grew addled and paranoid. He accused the hotel staff of being spies, claimed that someone was stealing his furniture, and terminated long-standing friendships. Yet he was determined to win reelection in 1920. While campaigning in Colorado, Wilson suffered another stroke and then another at the White House. His administration spun the press a load of wishful thinking—"the president is able-minded and able-bodied," spokesmen declared—but he was partially paralyzed, flew into rages, and sometimes babbled incoherently.

The cabinet continued to meet, which gave the impression the government was functioning. But Wilson retreated into a darkened bedroom and subsisted on bread, bouillon, and water for two months. Edith fiercely guarded the door. She met with cabinet members, took their questions inside, and emerged with answers. Were they Wilson's or hers? No one but Edith knew. She "never made a single decision about public affairs," and described herself as a "steward," though others described her as a "regent." Either way, the woman who once ignored politics was now the most powerful First Lady in history.

(Wilson's absence in 1919–20, and the shooting of John F. Kennedy in 1963—which could have left him brain-dead had it not killed him—led to the Twenty-Fifth Amendment in 1967, a procedure to replace an incapacitated president.)

At the hazy end of his second term Wilson suffered one last indignity when the Senate ratified the Eighteenth Amendment, which launched Prohibition. Wilson has been demonized as the movement's author, but in fact he pushed against it. He was a moderate drinker who enjoyed a sip of wine at dinner or a short whiskey by the fire; he believed wine and beer should be legal and that states should regulate hard liquor. In 1919 he vetoed the Volstead Act, an anti-drinking law, but Congress overruled him. And in January 1920, the National Prohibition Act went into effect and endured for thirteen dysfunctional years.

II. Calvin Coolidge: Hard Cheese, Silence, and Quan

Calvin Coolidge, the Thirtieth President
August 2, 1923–March 4, 1929

Woodrow Wilson was replaced by Warren Gamaliel Harding, a Republican Ohio gadabout, devotee of hot dogs, beer, cigars, poker, and young women, whose administration was plagued by trysts and corruption, including the infamous Tea Pot Dome scandal. He is generally considered one of the worst presidents in history. Harding died of heart failure in 1923, leaving the United States in the hands of his temperamental opposite: Vice President Calvin Coolidge, a pale, moody, dry-witted Vermonter. Upon Coolidge's arrival at the White House, Alice Roosevelt Longworth observed, "the atmosphere was as different as a New England front parlor is from a back room in a speakeasy."

Coolidge was raised in Plymouth Notch, Vermont, a hamlet nestled on a green saddle between blue mountains. His family were farmers, and as a boy Calvin (Cal) learned to turn raw milk into Plymouth Cheese, a tasty cheddar-like curd, at his father's cheese factory; it is still made there according to a recipe brought from Europe in the 1600s, and remains tasty.

Cal was one of the most taciturn, eccentric penny-pinchers to ever inhabit the Oval Office. He complained about money incessantly and was known to be "silent in five languages." Most famously, a dinner companion said, "I made a bet today that I could get more than two words out of you." Silent Cal eyed her coolly and replied, "You. Lose." His aptly named wife, Grace, had taught at a school for the deaf, and, the joke went, she "had taught the deaf to hear; now she might be able to teach the mute to speak." She was also a Vermonter, but of the cheerful, unflappable variety. When she baked an apple pie at the White House, Cal dryly observed that the crust could be used to pave a road. Grace took his quips in stride, and charmed the public with her love of baseball, long walks in all kinds of weather, and pet racoon Rebecca (who lived in a tree house on the White House grounds).

"Weaned on a pickle," according to Ms. Longworth, President Coolidge grazed on nuts, was fond of corn muffins and pork-apple-pie (a dessert made of apples, maple sugar, cinnamon, nutmeg, and bits of salt pork), and consumed small amounts of simple wholesome food. He believed that chickens should be raised where they are eaten, and his White House flock had a distinct taste because their coop was built on top of Teddy Roosevelt's former mint garden. Coolidge called every meal "supper," and preferred to eat alone or with Grace and their boys, Calvin Jr. and John. He enjoyed the White House's roast beef so much that he ate it at almost every official dinner, regardless of what his guests were served, and complained that six Virginia hams "seems an awful lot" for a sixty-person dinner. He averred that his "greatest disappointment" as president was that the leftovers from his ham dinner had disappeared.

Cruising on the presidential yacht *Mayflower,* the Coolidges developed an unlikely friendship with the ship's Cantonese steward, Lee Ping-Quan (pronounced "Chew-ah-n"). The president took a shine to Quan's veal curries, which he accessorized with peppers, olives, sweet pickles, onions, eggs, carrots, chestnuts, almonds, lettuce, boiled ham, Bombay duck, American cheese, and chutney. The First Lady enjoyed the steward's chop suey so much she asked for the recipe. As for dessert, the president "preferred my jelly roll best," Quan wrote. "He had a very sweet tooth."

The Coolidges hosted dinner cruises for up to thirty guests aboard the *Mayflower,* evenings that "called for all the skill at Quan's command," the steward recalled. With four cooks and eight waiters to assist him, his dinners featured up to twenty dishes that fused American and Chinese standards—including homemade candy, grapefruit cocktail, consommé, fried soft-shell crabs on corn cakes, roasted capon with cranberry sauce, chicken chop suey with rice, bamboo shoots and tomato salad, and strawberries with whipped cream, almond cookies, and cakes.

Quan considered himself a gastronomic artist and maintained that food plays "an important role in the destiny of man." A successful meal engaged all of the senses, he wrote: music, for instance, "by its pleasing effect on the ears, stimulates appetite," so he arranged for a navy band to play aboard the *Mayflower.* The ultimate goal of a dinner party, Quon believed, was to "promote conviviality":

> The intellectual parts of a dinner, like the seasonings of a salad, must be superlative; and it is for the hostess to blend the guests with deft touch and judgment. . . . It is always well to have at least one witty man or one witty woman at a dinner to lift the conversation out of the ordinary. If there are more, so much the better. . . . Especially if one has the rare faculty of being able to amuse without appearing to do so. It is clear that we dine gregariously not merely to appease hunger and gratify appetite, but to enjoy the pleasures of the table in the most congenial assembly in order to exchange views with our fellows, and to improve our minds by the absorption of the good that comes out of the conversation and good cheer.

III. *Herbert Hoover: America's Food Czar*

Herbert Hoover, the Thirty-First President
March 4, 1929–March 4, 1933

One day in 1927, President Calvin Coolidge surprised everyone, including his wife, Grace, by announcing he would not run for reelection. Seeing an opening, Secretary of Commerce Herbert Hoover launched a pro-business, isolationist, tolerant-of-Prohibition campaign for the office and ultimately defeated the like-minded but anti-Prohibition Democrat Alfred E. Smith. Hoover vowed to put "a chicken in every pot and a car in every garage," adding, "I have no fear for the future of the country. It is bright with hope." And why wouldn't he feel that way in the fall of 1928, when life was full of promise?

Born poor and raised an orphan by relatives in West Branch, Iowa, Hoover trained as an engineer at Stanford and built a sterling career as a mining executive. Specializing in depleted or struggling mines, he extracted copper, gold, silver, zinc, and lead around the world. In the process, he contracted malaria, stumbled into a tiger's den in Burma, built model towns in Siberia, advised the emperor of China, and was caught up in the Boxer Rebellion. Along the way he accrued a $4 million fortune (about $100 million today), and declared, "If a man hasn't made a million by age forty he isn't worth much."

During World War I, President Wilson put Hoover in charge of the U.S. Food Administration and its successor, the American Relief Administration (ARA), which he used as a springboard into a second career as a food Samaritan and a third career as a politician. Applying rigorous business strategies to saving lives, Hoover epitomized a new breed of technocratic humanitarian. He persuaded Congress to appropriate $100 million to the ARA to supply food to blasted, famine-racked Europe, and delivered more than four million tons of goods worth $150 million to children in twenty-one nations, including Germany.

General John J. Pershing called him "the food regulator of the world," and the press lionized him as "America's Food Czar" (a label Hoover dismissed as too showy).

Like Wilson, Hoover believed that his relief work did not just save lives; it opened new markets for American farmers to unload wartime stockpiles and created goodwill in Europe after the Russian Revolution of 1917. He believed Bolshevism would shrivel once the food crisis was solved, and said, "The prime objective of the United States in undertaking the fight against famine in Europe is to save the lives of starving people. The secondary object, however . . . [is] to defeat Anarchy, which is the handmaiden of Hunger."

Millions of Russians faced starvation, but fearful of relying on America, the government resisted Hoover's provisions. "Gentlemen, food is a weapon," the diplomat Maxim Litvinov lectured. But when five to ten million Russians died in the famine of 1921, they had no choice but to ask for help. Within a year, the ARA was feeding eleven million Russians a day. When critics bucked at the program's $60 million cost, Hoover brushed them off: "Twenty million people are starving. Whatever their politics, they shall be fed."

· · ·

THE HOOVERS MOVED INTO the White House in 1929 and spent their first seven months luxuriating on the tail end of the Roaring Twenties. At 7:30 every morning, the president would meet with his "Medicine Ball Cabinet," rain or shine, on the White House lawn, where they would toss a heavy medicine ball back and forth for exercise while discussing policy. In the evening, the president dressed in a formal dinner jacket and ate a seven-course meal—appetizer, soup, fish, meat, salad, dessert, and fruit—in the State Dining Room, even when he was alone.

A famously speedy eater, Hoover grew restless if a meal took too long. With a signal from his wife, Lou, the kitchen would sometimes eliminate a course to quicken the pace. This was part of a sophisticated communications strategy the Hoovers had developed while living abroad. Like the general manager of a baseball team, Lou directed her fifty-eight staff members with hand signals: when she dropped a handkerchief, a team of ushers sprinted into position; when she patted her hair, the butlers served the meal; when she held her hand on her water glass, they scurried to clear the table. And when the Hoovers had something private to discuss, they spoke in Mandarin, which they had learned in China.

The president tried to slow his feeding when company was over, as it increasingly was. Ever the efficient engineer, he hired three full-time secretaries to build interesting guest lists, write invitations, design seating arrangements, and assist Lou with flower and table decorations. Indeed, the Hoovers packed their social schedule so tightly that they dined alone just once a year, on their wedding anniversary, February 10.

The First Couple insisted on serving "the best" foods at official functions, including costly imported or out-of-season delicacies, sometimes catered by guest chefs. For smaller get-togethers they relied on Mary Rattley, an inventive Black chef who worked in the White House private quarters and put her own spin on familiar dishes—oyster soufflé, Maryland caramel tomatoes, vanilla wafers, Virginia ham—and jealously guarded her culinary tricks. When a guest pestered Lou for the recipe to Ms. Rattley's famed cucumber sauce for seafood, the cook vaguely replied, "It calls for lemon juice, cream, and a lot of things which must be right to keep the cream from curdling." Pressed for detail, she said, "Well, just ask her how she thinks a black cow eats green grass and gives white milk." Thereafter, her condiment was dubbed "black cow sauce."

Obsessed with time management, Hoover banned the household

staff from interacting with him, and when he burst out of the elevator, frightened maids would jump into closets to hide. Occasionally, though, Hoover's efficiency backfired. Consider the tale of the headless salmon.

ON APRIL 1, 1912, Karl Anderson, a boatbuilder in Bangor, Maine, caught a beautiful, eleven-pound Atlantic salmon in the Penobscot River. He packed his catch in ice and sent it by train to President Taft, to show "honor and respect." Thus began the annual tradition of a Presidential Salmon that would continue for the next eighty years.

Atlantic salmon was prized as less oily and more delicately flavored than other salmon; it commanded high prices and was known as the King of Fish. The anadromous fish's spring spawn drew thousands of recreational anglers, and every Fourth of July Mainers celebrated with a feast of salmon, peas, and new potatoes, which symbolized their link to the water and land.

Taft was an enthusiastic salmon consumer, but he promoted industries—paper mills, hydroelectric dams, and logging—that decimated the fish. Mills poisoned the water the salmon swam in; dams blocked their migration upstream; loggers destroyed the headwaters where they spawned. As transportation and freezer technology improved, Atlantic salmon were fished commercially and shipped across the country, which further depleted their stocks.

Though Hoover did not have many avocations other than smoking Havana cigars, he was a dedicated fly fisherman: it was a solo sport that allowed the intense president to rhythmically cast in a river for trout (a cousin of the salmon) and "wash one's soul with pure air."

Knowing this, the Maine congressional delegation sent Hoover a Presidential Salmon in the spring of 1931. When the fish arrived, the White House cooks beheaded it and stored the body on ice. But then a Maine congressman appeared, requesting a photo with the president and the salmon for the folks back home. Scrambling, the cooks managed to dig the fish's head out of the garbage and surgically reattach it to its silver body. They posed the Presidential Salmon between Hoover and the congressman, and the triumphant photo ran in all the Maine papers. Legend has it that no one noticed the surgery, and Maine did not vote Democratic for years.

FDR set a record by accepting thirteen salmon from Maine, but the tradition was paused during Eisenhower's presidency, when the Penobscot was polluted by human waste. It resumed when Lyndon Johnson ate Maine salmon steaks poached in wine and herbs. The last Presidential Salmon was delivered in 1992: a nine-and-a-half-pounder caught by a fisherman who hand delivered his catch to President George H. W. Bush in Kennebunkport, Maine. Since then, Atlantic salmon have been declared endangered. In the distant past, runs of 75,000 to 100,000 salmon spawned in the Penobscot. But in 2014 only 248 salmon returned. A restoration effort to decommission dams, restore habitat, and introduce farmed smelt led to a return of 1,426 salmon in 2020, but only 561 a year later. It will take at least seventy-five years, or fifteen generations of Atlantic salmon, for stocks to recover, if they ever do.

ON OCTOBER 29, 1929, seven months after Hoover took office, the stock market crashed, and the good times vaporized. As the nation spiraled into the Great Depression, people gathered in long gray lines in search of food, money, and social services. Hoover had predicted the fiasco as commerce secretary, warning that easy credit and reckless speculation were a recipe for disaster. "The political machinery [is] unable to cope," he prophesied, and "I will be the one to suffer."

As the Depression deepened, Hoover lost thirty-five pounds. Slumped at the table with eyes cast down, he ate mechanically. The staff took bets on how quickly he'd finish a meal—eight minutes flat one night; nine minutes and fifteen seconds the next—before he returned to his office.

By December 1930, America was contending with drought, crop failures, and growing food shortages. Hoover insisted there was "minimum actual suffering," though many citizens were hungry and cold, and blamed him as an out-of-touch plutocrat. The homeless built shanties called Hoovervilles and described their empty pockets turned inside out as "Hoover flags." The president responded by throwing his mind, body, and spirit into reengineering the economy. He created unemployment commissions, propped up banks with the Reconstruction Finance Corporation, invested in infrastructure such as the Hoover Dam, and wore everyone out. "My men are dropping around me," he said with a sigh. "Fighting this Depression is becoming more and more like waging a war. . . . The conditions we have experienced make this office a compound hell."

By the time he began campaigning for reelection in 1931, Hoover's hair had turned white and his hands shook. He was pitted against the charismatic Democratic governor of New York, Franklin Delano Roosevelt. Hoover belittled his opponent as "a gibbering idiot," yet it was he who lost his place in the middle of speeches. Angry crowds attacked "America's Food Czar" with produce: in Detroit, they threw rotten eggs; in Kansas, a hail of rotten tomatoes. When a Girl Scout troop presented Hoover with flowers, he teared up and said to Lou, "I can't go on with it anymore." Roosevelt won all but six states.

FRANKLIN D. ROOSEVELT

The Gourmet's Lament

THE THIRTY-SECOND PRESIDENT
March 4, 1933–April 12, 1945

★

I. A Soup Full of Flattery

One night in February 1941, Franklin D. Roosevelt hosted a crowded reception for military brass in the Blue Room, then slipped upstairs to his oval study on the second floor for a private dinner with Wendell Willkie. Roosevelt had defeated Willkie in the election of November 1940, making him the only president to serve more than two terms. But Willkie was a former Democrat turned popular Republican, and the president admired him. Maybe, FDR thought, he could persuade Willkie to take up a delicate assignment. Roosevelt believed it was time for America to join the Allies in confronting Nazi Germany, but a strong isolationist bloc in Congress refused to back him. The president quietly forged ahead and was in search of a trusted envoy who could liaise with America's allies. Willkie—a lawyer and utility executive from Indiana who had pushed for racial integration at home and intervention in Europe—was his leading candidate. FDR often used meals to take people's measure. But the envoy job was especially challenging and persuading his formal rival to take it on would require a silken hand.

Much like Thomas Jefferson plotting his Dinner Table Bargain with Hamilton and Madison, Roosevelt affected a carefree air while meticulously choreographing his tête-à-tête with Willkie. A gourmet with an instinct for people's hidden motivations, FDR researched what his guests liked to eat, drink, and smoke, then constructed a menu that was more than a simple list of things to eat. It was a meal layered with signs and symbols.

FDR built the Willkie dinner around an exotic dish: terrapin soup—or stew, as the president insisted on calling it—was a delicacy made with the flesh and juices of a diamondback terrapin turtle simmered with butter, cream, tomatoes, vegetables, a mix of spices (thyme, allspice, cloves, cayenne), and a jot of sherry or Worcestershire sauce. It was rich and deeply flavored, and not to everyone's taste. But Roosevelt was betting it would appeal to Willkie on several levels. First, it was a satisfying meal and one of his favorite dishes. More deeply, Willkie, the son of German immigrants who was raised in the Midwest, was a self-made man who aspired to be a player in global politics. By serving him terrapin soup in his private study, decorated with maritime prints and ships' models, FDR was welcoming Willkie into an exclusive club. On yet another level, terrapin soup was a quintessentially American dish, one that dated to Native American tribes and the early colonies: by sipping terrapin soup, Willkie would join the national continuum. In other words, Roosevelt was serving a soup full of flattery.

The diamondback terrapin is native to the Chesapeake Bay, and in the seventeenth century the Abenaki and Delaware introduced it to colonists as *turpen,* or "good tasting turtle." Initially, terrapin was considered so common that it was fed to servants and slaves—so much so that Maryland banned serving it more than three times a week. But the recipe evolved to produce an elegant dark brown medley that counted George Washington, John Adams, and many other presidents as fans. (Dwight Eisenhower was probably the last president to serve the dish at the White House.)

During the nineteenth century, the "white and sweet" terrapin flesh—said to have the texture of lobster or frogs' legs—was served at Delmonico's in Manhattan, considered the finest restaurant of its day. But as the dish gained popularity, the terrapin population dwindled, prices soared, and the soup became the victim of its own success. In response, cheaper green turtles or snapping turtles were substituted. (Snapping turtle flesh is said to taste of six distinct kinds of meat: chicken, beef, shrimp, veal, fish, and goat—or, as one wag put it, "muddy, dirty, mushy and chewy.") By the twentieth century, Heinz sold a canned Real Turtle Soup. And a sweet-sour Mock Turtle Soup—made from boiled head of veal or a mélange of tripe, sweetbreads, and beef tendons—appeared on menus. Campbell's canned version of the mock soup, with a "tempting, distinctive taste so prized by the epicure," was popular in the 1950s. Andy Warhol called it his favorite Campbell's flavor and searched for stray cans after it was discontinued. Efforts to farm terrapin failed, cooks tired of the laborious preparations for the soup, and by the 1980s the public had lost interest in consuming turtles. Though terrapin soup is still served in parts of the South, the dish, like squirrel stew, canvasback duck, or possum—once considered the epitome of sophisticated taste—has largely disappeared from American menus.

For the Willkie dinner to succeed, Roosevelt needed a specialized cook, but that was hard to come by. First Lady Eleanor Roosevelt rarely stepped behind the stove. None of the White House cooks had the requisite skills, nor did their boss, the culinarily challenged housekeeper Henrietta Nesbitt. She feared terrapins as "huge brutes . . . crawl[ing] around in the cellar," and once botched the soup so badly that FDR refused to let her try again. For Willkie, the president borrowed a chef from the private Metropolitan Club, who produced an exquisite broth.

Over bowls of the elixir FDR and Willkie built a personal and political rapport. After dinner, they talked, smoked, and drank whiskey deep into the night. "Great bursts of laughter" could be heard from behind the door, FDR's son Jimmy reported. Soon after that dinner, Willkie departed on a diplomatic mission to England, North Africa, the Soviet Union, and China on Roosevelt's behalf.

TERRAPIN SOUP WAS FDR's lucky soup, and he regularly served it to foreign dignitaries and to luminaries like Will Rogers. Yet it was just the kind of food his wife, Eleanor, did not approve of. She viewed it as an elitist dish and disliked its earthy looks and taste. FDR liked to serve the broth, meat, bones, and flippers in the turtle's shell, and Eleanor never forgot the zoologist who inspected his bowl and hissed, "These are the bones of rats!"

The Roosevelts' opposing views of terrapin were emblematic of their many diverging tastes. During their unmatched, twelve-year residence in the President's House, food played an outsized role and was laden with political, economic, psychological, and emotional weight. For FDR, food was a reminder of home, a bridge to other cultures, a tool of persuasion, a means of exploration, self-expression, and disinhibition. Though he is not often credited as a gourmet on par with Jefferson, I'd say Roosevelt possessed the second most discerning palate of any president. Yet his fine-tuned tastes proved a curse as much as a blessing, and set him apart from his nuclear family.

II. "Plain Foods, Plainly Prepared"

Madame, I only gave you the recipe. I did not teach you how to cook.
—Auguste Escoffier

Unlike most chief executives, Franklin Roosevelt spent a considerable amount of time thinking—obsessing, really—about food and drink. As the large, well-equipped kitchen at Springwood, his family's mansion in

Hyde Park, New York, suggests, his heart skipped a beat when he was served something *interesting*: kippered herring or creamed chipped beef for breakfast; green gumbo, abalone steaks, or chicken in aspic for lunch (which he called dinner); appetizers of caviar and champagne, followed by dinners (suppers) that would challenge most Americans' palates: buffalo tongues, frogs' legs, oyster crabs, and tripe pepper pot. He delighted in the "curious food gifts" that were sent to him from all over the world: ptarmigan from Greenland, teal duck from Egypt, a jar of crayfish and three pounds of smelt in summer; six Scottish pheasants in the winter; whitefish "fresh from Duluth"; a fifty-pound cherry pie.

FDR liked to grind his own coffee (using Filipino green beans, sourced for him by the navy) and brew his own French roast. In 1933 he had repealed Prohibition with the Twenty-First Amendment, and he took great satisfaction in mixing cocktails, serving fine wines, and sipping bourbon. When deprived of thick, juicy steaks during World War II, the president was given to flights of epicurean fancy that could veer into the delirious. He once waxed rhapsodic about a whole, fresh fish baked in mud—"the most delicious thing in the world," he declared—though his children did not believe he'd ever eaten such a creature. It was the idea that he *might*, someday, that excited him.

The Roosevelt children—Anna, James (Jimmy), Franklin, Elliott, Franklin Delano Jr., and John—were hearty eaters, but their palates were more influenced by their mother's tastes than their father's. Eleanor regarded meals as a source of calories rather than as an aesthetic experience, and favored dry whole wheat toast for breakfast, a bowl of almond soup for lunch, and kedgeree—an Anglo-Indian plate of fish, rice, and mashed hard-boiled eggs—for dinner. "Very few things which I eat or drink matter to me a great deal, and it is more or less habit how I happen to take them," she said.

Mrs. Roosevelt was far more interested in food as Food: a philosophical question to be pondered, a dietary conundrum to be dissected, a way to brand herself and her husband's administration for public consumption, and a political statement about female empowerment and scientific rigor. "Mother is a wonderful woman . . . but, as she herself will tell you, she has no appreciation of fine food," Jimmy recalled. "Victuals to her are something to inject into the body as fuel to keep it going, much as a motorist pours gasoline into an auto tank."

Though her cookery was limited to baking popovers and scrambling eggs on a chafing dish, and she was raised with wealth and a household staff, Mrs. Roosevelt empathized with the millions of Americans suffering in the Depression. She recognized that as First Lady she had what her cousin Teddy Roosevelt called a "bully pulpit"—a prominent stage from which to promote a personal/political agenda—and educated herself about cookery and calories in order to set an example for the nation. First she consulted Sheila Hibben, America's foremost gastronome and a proponent of fresh foods and historic recipes. Hibben tipped the Roosevelts off to Martha Washington's crab soup (made with fresh crab, cream, Worcestershire sauce, and sherry) and advised that regional dishes—such as New England johnnycakes, corned beef, potatoes, and Indian pudding—would raise morale and help the nation persevere. "Crisis or no crisis, the tension of the country is better for preoccupation with the *art* of cooking," Hibben declared.

But Mrs. Roosevelt didn't see food as art, and she turned to Cornell University's home-economics department, which had developed a radical new vision for the housewife of the future: by training in chemistry, nutrition, and sanitation, homemakers could supplant the decadent, homey meals of yore with healthy, economical, modern foodstuffs. "The woman who boils potatoes year after year, with no thought of the how or why, is a drudge," said the president of the American Home Economics Association. "But the cook who can compute the calories of heat which a potato of given weight will yield, is no drudge."

Inspired, Eleanor used the White House kitchen as a laboratory and lectern. She extolled simple, thrifty meals as lessons in self-reliance. In her newspaper column, "My Day," she promoted dinners made with rationed goods—such as prune whip, spaghetti topped with boiled carrots, and Milkorno (a dried skim milk and cornmeal food supplement developed at Cornell)—to help stretch limited budgets. This rationalist approach paid little heed to the flavors, colors, textures, or associations—the emotional pleasures of eating—that ignited her husband's senses.

The Roosevelts' divergent tastes practically assured marital tension. To make FDR's discomfort even more acute, the pairing of Mrs. Nesbitt, the bumbling housekeeper who oversaw the Executive Kitchen, with the urbane Franklin D. Roosevelt seems like a dark cosmic joke. It was one authored by the First Lady.

"A LOAF OF BREAD SENT ME" to the Roosevelts, Henrietta Nesbitt recalled. Raised in Duluth, Minnesota, she was taught how to bake strudel and cakes by her Austrian mother. She married Henry Nesbitt, a gentle soul whose attempts to sell whale meat, wooden barrels, and insurance failed in the Depression. In search of work they moved to Hyde Park, New York, about ninety miles from Manhattan, in 1927. There, Mrs. Nesbitt attended the Episcopal church and joined the League of Women Voters, where she met Eleanor Roosevelt, a woman with the "kindest face I've ever seen." Though they hailed from vastly different backgrounds, the two bonded over children and Mrs. Nesbitt's whole wheat bread. She had given a loaf to a neighbor, who passed it on to a friend, who shared a bit with Mrs. Roosevelt, who loved it. "Would you mind making up some extra for us?" Eleanor asked, fatefully.

"Would I!" Mrs. Nesbitt exclaimed.

FDR was in the midst of a New York gubernatorial campaign, and the Hyde Park kitchen could not keep up with the demand for campaign food. Mrs. Nesbitt—as the Roosevelts called her—jumped in, churning out breads, stolen, rolls, coffee cakes, strudels, streusels, fruit pies (pumpkin, cherry, and apple), plum pudding, dark fruit cake, white Scottish fruit cake, and roasted peanuts. Henry Nesbitt did the shopping and helped with slicing, mixing, and packaging. When FDR won in 1928, Eleanor persuaded the Nesbitts, small-town Republicans who believed that "only saloonkeepers are Democrats," to undergo a political awakening. "I was branching out for myself in the thinking line," Mrs. Nesbitt wrote. A devotee of astrology, she believed the astral bodies foretold "the start of the woman's era." While she admired FDR, she was cowed by his intellect. "He seemed on another plane, pure thought it was and over our heads. . . . Still, knowing the way he liked peanuts, I wasn't as awed as I might have been."

In 1932, Roosevelt defeated Herbert Hoover to become America's thirty-second president and inherited a nation in economic chaos. At his inauguration on March 4, 1933, Roosevelt rallied the nation with words that continue to stir: "The only thing we have to fear is fear itself!" In his first hundred days in office, he pushed groundbreaking laws and signed executive orders that led to the New Deal, which helped turn America's fortunes around.

Eleanor took up the mantle of First Ladyship reluctantly. Though the role was considered a great honor, she disliked the pressure and scrutiny that came with it, and only agreed to support Franklin's campaign on the condition that she would control their domestic sphere. An ambitious man with a pragmatic streak, he agreed.

When they moved into the White House in 1933, Mrs. Roosevelt hired

Henrietta Nesbitt as the housekeeper and Henry as a custodian. Eleanor did not care that they had no experience catering meals for hundreds of people on a brightly lit stage. She wanted "someone I know" in the kitchen; self-conscious about her wealth, Eleanor believed that hiring the Nesbitts was a useful and charitable thing to do. It was also a quiet act of rebellion.

Mrs. Nesbitt's duties included many aspects of normal housework, amplified—ensuring the presidential mansion's sixty rooms were immaculate, its hundred-plus windows spotless, its floors waxed, and its silverware shined to a fare-thee-well. One of her most important jobs was to oversee the Executive Kitchen. Touring the space on her first visit, Mrs. Nesbitt spied grime, outdated fixtures, and something skittering in the shadows. "I can't work up any charm for cockroaches," she wrote. "This was the 'first kitchen in America,' and it wasn't even sanitary. . . . The refrigerator was wood inside and bad smelling. Even the electric wiring was old and dangerous. I was afraid to switch things on."

There was "only one solution," Eleanor declared: "We must have a new kitchen."

Public Works Project No. 634 began in the summer of 1935—a complete kitchen renovation overseen by specialists from Westinghouse and General Electric. Once completed, the kitchen gleamed with a sixteen-foot stove, six roasting ovens, a soup kettle, a meat grinder, a massive deep fryer, waffle irons, mixers, a thirty-gallon ice cream freezer, five dishwashers, updated wiring, and dumbwaiters to lift food upstairs to the dining rooms.

FDR was eager to host, and on March 7, 1933, Mrs. Nesbitt (who didn't actually cook) and the kitchen crew served their first White House menu, a simple lunch of stuffed eggs, cold cuts, and salad for the president and a few advisers. It went well. Not long after that she supervised the Roosevelts' first diplomatic dinner—lamb chops, baked potatoes, green peas—for the Polish ambassador. That, too, was a success. And then, like a roller coaster climbing the first incline, then tipping over and barreling down the back side, the White House head cook, Ida Allen, and a rotating cast of eight to twenty assistants, were off on a wild, swooping, gut-wrenching ride.

Mrs. Nesbitt believed that meats should come from the cheaper cuts, such as sweetbreads, beef tongues, brains, and offal, while vegetables should come from cans, potatoes should be mashed, and salads should be molded from gelatin and dotted with marshmallows, nuts, or crushed peppermint candy. Some of her "economy meals" ("the best meals for the least money") descended into tragicomedy—a torrent of noodles with chicken scraps, pig hocks, mysterious casseroles, curried tidbits, croquettes of leftovers, stuffed with this and that, gumbo z'herbes (the "cheapest soup," made with leftover meats and greens), jellied prunes with cheese, and an Echo Emerald "salad" made of lime gelatin, celery, pineapple, pimiento, and vinegar.

"Yes, the commander in chief ate leftovers," Mrs. Nesbitt proudly declared. "Relished them, too."

The kitchen was on constant call, and served "so many meals it all blurred into one long one. I lost track," the housekeeper wrote. A tea for twelve hundred guests was scheduled, then canceled, then reinstated as a tea for forty-two hundred. On another day, the First Couple shook the hands of 1,175 visitors, who consumed seventy-seven pounds of cookies and drank untold gallons of punch in half an hour flat—"a new record!" Eleanor exulted. Mrs. Nesbitt began to see roast turkeys, baked hams, sweet potatoes, fudge, and raspberry puree whirling in her dreams. "I was sick of food," she declared. "So was the president."

FDR complained bitterly about her insistence on "plain foods, plainly prepared," which he said, "would do justice to the Automat." After one bowl of oatmeal too many, he yelled, "My God! Doesn't Mrs. Nesbitt know there are breakfast foods besides oatmeal? It's been served to me morning in and morning out for months and months now and I'm sick and tired of it!" He ripped ads for cornflakes from newspapers as "a gentle reminder." She paid no attention. When FDR said he disliked broccoli, Mrs. Nesbitt, called "Fluffy" behind her back, instructed the cooks to "fix it anyhow. He *should* like it." She believed that he, like "all men," "needed his vegetables." And when Roosevelt requested hot coffee for his guests, she served iced tea instead. "It was better for them," she insisted.

The president's anguish was hardly a secret. After a long stint of liver-with-string-bean dinners, a *New York Times* headline noted, "Same Menu Four Days Palls on Roosevelt." When subjected to another bout of repetitive meals, FDR wrote to Eleanor,

> Do you remember that about a month ago I got sick of chicken because I got it . . . at least six times a week? The chicken situation has definitely improved, but "they" have substituted sweetbreads, and for the past month I have been getting sweetbreads about six times a week. I am

getting to the point where my stomach positively rebels and this does not help my relations with foreign powers. I bit two of them today.

But the First Lady was deaf to his pleas. When the housekeeper and ten cooks produced thirty-two hundred sandwiches for a veterans' party, costing just thirty and a half cents a head, Eleanor nudged Franklin, saying, "You ought to get a manager like Mrs. Nesbitt to run the country. You'd save money."

It was an understatement to say the Roosevelt White House cuisine "did not enjoy a very high reputation," a staff member grumbled. Mrs. Nesbitt's salad "resembled the productions one finds in the flossier type of tea shoppe." Ernest Hemingway described a 1937 dinner there as "the worst I've ever eaten . . . rainwater soup followed by rubber squab, a nice wilted salad and a cake some admirer had sent in. An enthusiastic but unskilled admirer." The journalist Martha Gellhorn (his third wife) "ate three sandwiches in the Newark airport before we flew to Washington. We thought she was crazy at the time but she said the food was always uneatable and everybody ate before they went there to dinner. She has stayed there a lot. Me, I won't be staying there any more."

Curiously, Roosevelt seemed powerless to direct his own diet. Eleanor placated her husband one minute and soothed the housekeeper the next, advising her not to take his "tizzy-wizzies" personally. "When he said 'The vegetables are watery,' and 'I'm sick of liver and beans,' these were figures of speech," Mrs. Nesbitt rationalized. "But the newspapers didn't understand that." After Jimmy wrote damningly about the housekeeper, Eleanor defended her: "The responsibility for what she spent and for what she ordered was [mine] and [mine] alone. . . . Father never told me he wanted to get rid of Mrs. Nesbitt."

It is hard to believe, but apparently true. FDR was no shrinking violet when it came to Congress, industrialists, or Nazis, but he shied from confrontations with his staff—even the valet who fell asleep and stranded the president in his wheelchair. (Roosevelt contracted polio in 1921 and was paralyzed from the waist down.) A charismatic and gregarious public figure, the president was a loner at heart. He was a single child raised by an older, distant father and an overbearing mother, and, Eleanor observed, "it became part of his nature not to talk of intimate matters." And Jimmy recalled, "Pa couldn't even bring himself to insist that Mother fire Mrs. Henrietta Nesbitt . . . who was responsible for serving him the uninspired meals which he disliked so passionately."

After his formidable mother, Sara, died in 1941, FDR transferred her cook Mary Campbell from Hyde Park to the White House, where she made his old favorites in the private kitchen. Outflanked, Mrs. Nesbitt complained that Campbell's dishes were too rich, but conceded that FDR "liked her cooking. . . . Mary was awed neither by ration points nor Presidents."

Roosevelt said, "ostensibly in jest but actually (or so all of us suspect) with a lot of real feeling," Jimmy wrote, that the main reason he ran for a fourth term in 1944 was "'so I can fire Mrs. Nesbitt!'" Tellingly, Jimmy noted, "Everybody was against Mrs. Nesbitt—everybody except Mother." Which raises the question: Why was Mrs. Roosevelt so loyal to the ham-handed housekeeper? Eleanor never answered that question directly. But it seems likely that she used Nesbitt's horrible diet, at least in part, as a shield, or weapon, against her inconstant husband.

THE ROOSEVELTS SHARED a deeply complex marriage. Eleanor admired Franklin's intellect and charisma, but disapproved of his bold pronouncements and quirky humor, was self-conscious about her looks, and did not understand the primal tug of sex (an ordeal to be borne, she told her daughter, Anna). FDR admired her intelligence and calm willfulness, but missed the frisson of romantic excitement.

In September 1918, when he was the assistant secretary of the navy, Eleanor discovered Franklin was carrying on a passionate affair with Lucy Mercer, her former social secretary. It was a bitter betrayal that summoned painful memories of Eleanor's father, Elliott Roosevelt (Theodore's younger brother), who was addicted to drugs, drink, and women and died in a carriage wreck when she was nine. Mercer was an attractive, unmarried woman from a once-wealthy family, a food lover and art appreciator who had a knack for prompting Franklin's fun-loving side. Like Woodrow Wilson, Roosevelt had a deep need for female attention. Mercer's presence was an open secret in the family, and though Anna was prepared to hate her, they became good friends. Alice Roosevelt Longworth opined that her cousin FDR "*deserved* a good time . . . he was married to Eleanor."

The Roosevelts contemplated divorce, but his advisers warned it would end his political career. The navy was famously puritanical, they noted, and the public would be outraged by such libertine behavior. And then there was his mother. When FDR raised the question with Mrs. Sara, she threatened to disinherit him. In the end, they stayed together for the sake of family, politics, money, and the ghost of their youthful love. But from then on, Jimmy recalled, the marriage became "an armed truce that endured until the day he died." Later, Eleanor wrote, "I have the memory of an elephant. I can forgive, but I never forget."

The Roosevelts increasingly ate apart, slept apart, vacationed apart, and worked apart. It is likely that FDR had other romances, and it has been rumored that Eleanor also found extramarital succor. While her papers reveal that she had numerous infatuations—for her bodyguard, a biographer, the journalist Lorena Hickok, the pilot Amelia Earhart— there is scant evidence those relationships tipped into the erotic.

Against this background, Eleanor staunchly promoted Mrs. Nesbitt's dispiriting grub. The choice was so dissonant with FDR's epicurean-ism that it remains a fascination. The historian Barbara Haber believes Mrs. Roosevelt did not intentionally serve bad food, but lacked a dis-cerning palate and wanted to please everyone; Eleanor approved of the housekeeper's menus to exemplify "simple foods that . . . reflected the hard times," and to protect FDR, who suffered from high blood pres-sure, indigestion, bronchitis, and bouts of depression. But the biographer Blanche Wiesen Cook wrote that Nesbitt "was an expression of [Elea-nor's] passive-aggressive behavior . . . a tool of ER's revenge."

III. A Simple Picnic

As he was perusing the newspaper one morning in 1938, a news item caught Roosevelt's attention. King George VI and his wife, Queen Eliza-beth, were planning a goodwill tour of Canada. Left unstated was their real agenda: to drum up resistance to the rise of Nazi Germany. The pres-ident recognized the royal visit to North America as an opportunity. If he could convince his public that Britain deserved support, there was a chance he could build an alliance against the Fascists. But the United States was still emerging from the Depression, and much of the public was in a xenophobic funk. Many resented the British, who they believed had dragooned America into World War I and never repaid their debts. Worried about Hitler, and determined to rebuild the alliance with Brit-ain, FDR hatched a plan.

"I think it would be an excellent thing for Anglo-American relations if you could visit the United States," he wrote to the king. "It occurs to me . . . that you both might like three or four days of very simple country life at Hyde Park—with no formal entertainments and an opportunity to get a bit of rest and relaxation."

George replied, "I can assure you that the pleasure . . . would be greatly enhanced by the thought that it was contributing in any way to the cordiality of relations between our two countries."

Thus began a risky dance between the two nations. If Roosevelt's gambit backfired, the U.S.-U.K. alliance would sour further, entrench American isolationists, and give Hitler a pass to invade western Europe. But if he succeeded, he might shift the balance of geopolitical power. It wouldn't be easy. No reigning British monarch had ever set foot on U.S. soil. And Roosevelt knew that to win over the American public, he had to present the king and queen as something other than pretentious royals who feasted on roast beef and goblets of claret. Instead, he would have to present them as a likable couple that everyday Americans could relate to. His plan called for a bit of culinary stagecraft.

Hoping to display the Windsors' "essential democracy," the president plotted moments of pomp and relaxation, including, FDR insisted, a "simple picnic" at Hyde Park, as everyone called Springwood, the Roosevelt mansion overlooking the Hudson River in upstate New York.

The king and queen arrived in Washington, D.C., in June 1939 and were greeted by a large, curious crowd. The Roosevelts hosted them at a formal dinner at the White House. After a visit to Mount Vernon, where the great-great-great-grandson of King George III paid his respects at the tomb of George Washington, the Roosevelts and Windsors drank tea on the South Lawn. Then the two couples attended the 1939 World's Fair in New York and proceeded to Hyde Park. And it was there, on June 11, that FDR staged his coup de théâtre.

To the public's delight, the president's picnic was an all-American hot-dog-and-beer cookout. The only objector to the menu was Mrs. Sara, who declared that hot dogs were not suitable for royalty. Uncharacteristically, her son ignored her.

The press was barred as 150 guests—including earls, bishops, equerries, and ladies-in-waiting along with Roosevelt's friends, staff, and neighbors—made their way to Top Cottage, his fieldstone retreat near Springwood. The king and queen sat on folding chairs on the small porch. The hot dogs were served on silver trays, but everyone, including the Windsors, ate them from paper plates. The king eyed the hot dog and said, "What should I do?," recalled James Roosevelt. "Put it in your mouth and keep chewing until you finish it," FDR quipped.

More refined lunchables were also provided—Virginia ham, roasted turkey, cranberry jelly, a green salad, strawberry shortcake, orange and lime soda, hot or iced coffee, and iced tea—but only Mrs. Sara stuck to the refined fare.

The king enjoyed his hot dog so much that he had a second and washed it down with a cold beer, like a regular human. *The New York Times* was so gobsmacked that it ran a front-page story with the headline "King Tries Hot Dog and Asks for More: And He Drinks Beer with Them."

The Windsors thoroughly enjoyed their visit, and though FDR played it down as nothing more than a weekend jaunt, he and King George had managed to discuss weighty matters of state in private. The king reported to London that Roosevelt promised to defend British convoys and sink German U-boats, and "wait for the consequences," and pledged to remind American and Brazilian farmers that the U.K. was one of their best customers.

Roosevelt's Hot Dog Summit helped shift Americans' resentment of Britain to a warm embrace, and just in time. Three months later, German troops blitzkrieged Poland. The United States began to ship supplies to Europe in 1940, and a year later FDR sent troops into combat. The lunch at Hyde Park would be hailed as "the picnic that won the war."

IV. The Stomach Governs the World

On Sunday, December 7, 1941, Mrs. Nesbitt noted in her diary, "One p.m. small lunch, about thirty-four, in State Dining Room." Thirty-four guests were no challenge for her crew of eight cooks and helpers. They routinely made breakfast for thirty hungry politicians, lunch for eighteen hundred ladies with discerning tastes, a garden party for five hundred veterans, and a dinner for a thousand finicky diplomats. Mrs. Nesbitt was delighted to pour tea for the queen of England and shop for Madame Chiang Kai-shek. "Do I sound cocky?" she wrote. "I was."

But as she left for work, her son Buck, a naval officer, shouted, "Did you hear?" Mrs. Nesbitt stopped and turned, and the globe seemed to wobble on its axis. The U.S. fleet at Pearl Harbor had been attacked by Japanese bombers. Ships were sinking. Americans were dying. Within days, the Axis—Japan, Germany, and Italy—had declared war on the United States.

The mood was electric at the White House. The mansion's windows were painted black, and air raid shelters were dug into the lawn. The surrounding streets were blocked off and bristled with armed Secret Service men. The First Lady helped organize a defense of the Pacific coast. Men were overheard plotting to nab FDR "by the elevator." A butcher who had supplied the White House was sacked because he was born in Germany. The kitchen staff locked their milk and food supplies, did background checks on vendors, and used an unmarked truck to pick up groceries. "Too much was going on. Too fast," Mrs. Nesbitt wrote. "'Hush-hush,' 'Confidential,' 'V.I.P.'"

On December 22, just days after the surprise attack in Hawaii, FDR told Eleanor, "We will be having some guests tonight." It was just before Christmas and he had declared war; it was hardly an opportune moment for visitors. The guests would require a room big enough to hang maps in, the president continued, and "see to it that we have good champagne and brandy in the house and plenty of whiskey." When she asked who the guest was, he said the man's identity was so sensitive he could not tell even her.

A black limousine roared up the White House driveway, and out stepped Winston Churchill, the prime minister of Great Britain. Eleanor was stunned. She had never met the great man, and traveling transatlantic was an extremely risky gambit. England had fended off the Germans in the Battle of Britain, and Churchill had maintained morale with galvanizing oratory—"We shall fight on the beaches, we shall fight on the landing grounds, we shall fight in the fields and in the streets, we shall fight in the hills; we shall never surrender!" But his pleas for aid had fallen on deaf ears in the United States.

The Pearl Harbor attack killed 2,403 Americans, sank four battleships and eight other vessels, and flipped public opinion in favor of war. But Churchill feared the United States would send troops to the Pacific, leaving Britain to fend for itself. Determined to persuade Roosevelt to pursue a "Europe First" strategy, the prime minister knew his best chance was to risk an in-person visit.

It didn't hurt that FDR enjoyed good food, fine drink, and talk as much as he did. Both men were armed with charm, erudition, and wiliness. They had met once, in a secret rendezvous off Newfoundland, in August 1941 (Roosevelt had said he was "going fishing"). They bonded over cocktails, witty banter, and an elaborate feast of caviar from Joseph Stalin, smoked salmon, roasted grouse from Scotland, and, in a nod to British naval tradition and Roosevelt's taste, turtle soup. Their talks eventually bore fruit in the Atlantic Charter, a framework for world peace that paved the way for the United Nations.

To cross the Atlantic, Churchill hazarded U-boats and a tumultuous gale, but he arrived safely at the White House in a double-breasted peacoat, with a walking stick topped by a flashlight for use in London blackouts. He "looked poor-colored and hungry," Mrs. Nesbitt observed. "They had pared to the bone over there."

Roosevelt invited seventeen guests for dinner—including the British ambassador, generals, advisers, Eleanor, and a few friends. Churchill was fond of champagne, but FDR insisted on mixing sturdy cocktails and was especially proud of his "reverse martini" (see the Recipe section, page 389).

Working with the caterer (and future White House chef) François Rysavy, Mrs. Nesbitt and the kitchen crew managed to pull together a broiled chicken dinner. The war-deprived British gratefully consumed every morsel and washed it down with bottles of wine. At the end of the meal, Roosevelt raised a flute of champagne and toasted "to the Common Cause!"

He invited the prime minister to bunk at the White House. The strategically minded Churchill secured a bedroom across the hall from Harry Hopkins, Roosevelt's adviser, and commandeered an office next to the president's. The prime minister lived on "tummy time" and would sleep most of the morning, then rise to eat and drink prodigiously in the afternoon and work through the night. He suffered "indy"—indigestion—and when visited by the "black dog" of depression, he'd self-medicate with "a hot bath, cold champagne, new peas, and old brandy." Hearing this, Adolf Hitler called him a "superannuated drunkard supported by Jewish gold."

On his first day in Washington, Churchill posed with FDR for photographs: Roosevelt jauntily tilted his Camel cigarette wedged into a cigarette holder up at an angle, and Churchill puffed the enormous cigar that seemed permanently affixed to a corner of his mouth. Both understood the power of such images and made sure they were spread far and wide to project strength and unity, troll Hitler, and fortify British and American resolve.

That night they shared a simple dinner of noodle soup; roast beef; stuffed potatoes and broccoli; orange and watercress salad; Bavarian cream pie; and coffee. Afterward, the two leaders stayed up until two o'clock in the morning. Fueled by brandy and tobacco, they fleshed out a plan to send American troops to Europe and delved into what Eleanor described as their passions for "new people, new places, new things"— politics, literature, religion, and other "new experiences in life."

Such wide-ranging banter was Churchill's métier. He liked to position wineglasses and decanters like chess pieces to demonstrate how the Battle of Bull Run was fought. "It was a thrilling experience," an observer recalled. "He got worked up . . . making barking noises in imitation of gunfire and blowing cigar smoke across the battle scene in imitation of gun smoke."

Delighted, Roosevelt said with a chuckle, "It is fun to be in the same century with you."

But Eleanor, like Churchill's wife, Clementine, did not approve of these late, alcohol-fired nights. "Mother would fume and go in and out of the room making hints about bed," Elliott Roosevelt reported. "Still Churchill would sit there." They looked like "two little boys playing soldier," Eleanor recalled. "They seemed to be having a wonderful time—too wonderful, in fact. It made me a little sad somehow."

On December 26, 1941, Churchill addressed a joint session of Congress with a rousing call—"Now we are the masters of our fate!"—and raised two fingers in the V-for-victory sign. The applause was thunderous. That evening, he suffered a heart attack. After a short recuperation, and several more dinners with Roosevelt, Churchill risked the return to London aboard a lumbering flying boat, an easy target for German fighters. As the Boeing lofted above the clouds, the prime minister dozed off and Lord Beaverbrook confided to the pilot, "If we lose Churchill, we lose the war."

ALL CONCERNED, with the possible exception of the First Lady, deemed the prime minister's visit a coup. He and FDR deepened their alliance and set the stage for summit meetings between the Big Three—Roosevelt, Churchill, and Joseph Stalin—on the fate of Europe. The wild card was Stalin. Churchill considered the Soviet a "hardboiled egg of a man." But the Nazis were a common enemy and immediate threat.

When they first met, in 1942, Stalin had plied Churchill with caviar, sturgeon, and vodka in Moscow at a time when his people were starving. Impervious to the Briton's charm, the Soviet demanded that the United States and Britain attack German troops in France to relieve pressure on the eastern front. When Churchill said the Allies were planning an attack in North Africa, the conversation ground to a halt. The prime minister stood to leave, but Stalin invited him to stay for "a drink." Churchill accepted. Glasses of Crimean champagne led to a snack of radishes and then to a feast of chicken, beef, mutton, fish, "enough to feed thirty people." Over food, the conversation turned productive, and Stalin seemed open to sending his troops to the Pacific theater. Four hours later, he offered a delicacy: the head of a roast suckling pig. Churchill, who had once raised pigs and was fond of them, declined. Stalin, he wrote, "tackled it with relish. With a knife he cleaned out the head, putting [the brains] into his mouth with his knife. He then cut pieces of flesh from the cheeks of the pig and ate them with his fingers." After six hours of eating, drinking, and talking, Churchill stumbled back to his villa at 3:15 in the morning, feeling "definitely encouraged," he told Roosevelt.

Nineteen forty-two swept by, as the battles at Corregidor, Dunkirk, and North Africa unfolded in a kaleidoscopic rush. Nothing tasted right to the president. His staff scoured Washington for delectable oddments—musk ox, ptarmigan, quail, pheasant, fresh brook trout—in a vain attempt to distract him from the turmoil. But nothing seemed to placate the presidential stomach.

In 1943, Mrs. Nesbitt wrestled with strict rationing, like "every other housekeeper in the land." Government bureaucrats categorized the White House akin to a tugboat, allotting the Roosevelts just two months of food stamps. But the bean counters' calculations for meat, sugar, coffee, and canned goods were based on the First Couple's lightest months of entertaining, which greatly underestimated their needs. The Roosevelts sacrificed favorites, such as roast beef and butter, and stretched their provisions to feed their guests—four presidents, one prime minister, various celebrities, and their entourages. Mrs. Nesbitt seemed to exult in the wartime thrift as a necessary corrective for the nation's gluttony. "I thought smaller meals a fine idea, sending people away from the table satisfied but not stuffed," she wrote, "and I don't think we'll ever go back to those teeming dinner tables of our mother's day." The Roosevelts, she claimed, preferred simple meals, and rationing was "no problem at all."

On June 6, 1944, Allied troops streamed across the English Channel in the D-day invasion of Normandy. It was an event the entire world had been anticipating, but that evening Roosevelt cursed, "Damn it, I don't want beef!"

"Then what do you want?" Eleanor asked, soothingly.

"I want steak!" he thundered.

Mrs. Nesbitt noted in her diary that the president "looked thin and worn, but his mind was acute—too fast-working. . . . [H]e was worn out waiting for the rest of us to catch up. His meals were all he had to vent his irritation and worry on." Even the implacable Eleanor "looked harassed . . . [and] people tired her who never had before. There was a limit even for Mrs. Roosevelt."

THE BIG THREE SUMMITS WERE held in Tehran, Yalta, and Potsdam, and each was structured around a series of meals that revealed the leaders' temperaments, their nations' aspirations, and the shifting global order. The first was held in Tehran, Iran, in November 1943. Roosevelt opened with a steak and baked potato dinner. On the second night, Stalin hosted, and he and FDR poked Churchill with ill-tempered barbs. The prime minister sensed that the power dynamic was changing, and the Big Three was morphing into the Big Two.

On November 30, Churchill hosted a party for his sixty-ninth birthday. Promising "a never-to-be forgotten" event, he got his wish. Things began badly, when Stalin refused to shake the prime minister's hand and declined Roosevelt's cocktail. At dinner, the marshal had to ask which piece of cutlery to use. The menu included Persian soup, boiled salmon from the Caspian Sea, turkey, and a cheese soufflé. Copious amounts of French and Iranian wine were poured, and Churchill was presented with a cake decorated with sixty-nine candles in a V shape.

As the evening wound down, a fabulous "Persian Lantern Ice" dessert arrived. It was an ice cream confection set on top of an ice block on which a candle burned inside a perforated metal tube. When it arrived, the lamp melted the ice and caused the metal tube to list. The waiter wobbled, and watched in horror as the pile of ice cream inexorably slopped over the head of the Russian interpreter, Pavlov, who was in the midst of translating Stalin's speech. It was a shockingly funny yet terrifying moment, and the room went dead silent. "Ice cream was oozing out of his hair, his ears, his shirt and even his shoes," a British diplomat said. Fearful for his life, Pavlov carried on translating Stalin's words, until towels were brought to wipe him down. With the ice literally broken, the mood lightened and the Big Three agreed to cooperate on troop movements and the postwar order in Europe.

Tehran was considered a diplomatic triumph for Winston Churchill, but when it came to gastro-politics the prime minister left a haunting legacy. He understood the power of food and was not afraid to use it— playing the charming epicure who brokered agreements over fine wine one minute and the coldly calculating strategist who used starvation as a weapon the next. In Afghanistan, he burned crops to quell restive

Pashtun tribes. In Kenya, he forced Indigenous people off the fertile highlands to make way for British farmers. And in India, he and Lord Cherwell—Frederick Alexander Lindemann, a scientist with a Malthusian bent—destroyed rice stocks to deny sustenance to advancing Japanese troops. As a result, about three million people starved to death in the Bengal famine of 1943. FDR must have known about the prime minister's unsparing policy, but turned a blind eye. Some consider Churchill a hero. Others have deemed him "a war criminal." The best one can say is that he was both.

Food has been used as a weapon of war since the Greek siege of Troy three thousand years ago. Roman legions salted the earth to render it infertile. During the American Civil War, Confederate soldiers poisoned wells with dead animals and the Union General William Tecumseh Sherman conducted a scorched-earth campaign across the South. The drive to acquire and deny calories was a defining factor of World War II, as it was in World War I. In both cases, one of America's decisive advantages was the ability to produce butter as well as guns. Hitler said Germany had lost World War I in large part because of the Allied food blockade, and one reason he invaded the Soviet Union was to plunder grain fields, which, according to his "Hunger Plan," would feed his countrymen while starving his enemies. Some four million Soviets starved to death in German camps. A million German POWs were starved in Soviet camps. When the Japanese seized Vietnamese rice, one to two million people died of hunger. The brutal lesson, Churchill said, was "the stomach governs the world."

ON JANUARY 20, 1945, Franklin D. Roosevelt was inaugurated to an unprecedented fourth term. Two weeks later, the second Big Three meeting was convened in Yalta, on the Black Sea. As Roosevelt, Churchill, and Stalin debated how to apportion postwar Germany, FDR's face was drawn and dark semicircles drooped beneath his eyes. He looked "tired to the point of an inhuman loneliness. . . . [T]he whole world seemed [to be] pulling him down," Mrs. Nesbitt wrote.

In March, American planes bombed Tokyo and Berlin into cauldrons of flaming dust, and the end of the war was in sight. After a long weekend with Eleanor in Hyde Park, FDR departed for a vacation at his "southern White House," in Warm Springs, Georgia. There, he soaked his polio-racked body in eighty-eight degree thermal baths, which improved his spirits and allowed him to move his right leg a bit. Then, on April 12, the president suffered a cerebral hemorrhage and died at sixty-three.

Despite the shock, "all went smoothly as clockwork" at the White House, Mrs. Nesbitt noted. What she failed to mention was that two of FDR's female admirers, Lucy Mercer and Daisy Suckley, were with him in Georgia. In a black veil, Eleanor accompanied her husband's body to Washington on a funeral train as thousands of citizens paid tribute along the tracks. FDR's body lay in state in the East Room of the White House and was buried at Hyde Park. (Roosevelt's death just eighty-two days into his fourth term spurred the Twenty-Second Amendment in 1951, limiting presidents to two terms.)

En route from Hyde Park to Warm Springs, Roosevelt had stopped in Washington for his last dinner at the White House. He ordered his lucky meal, terrapin soup. "A man came in from one of the hotels and cooked it in cream and in the shell, just as he liked it," Mrs. Nesbitt wrote. "I was pleased that we had terrapin, and that it turned out just right."

HARRY S. TRUMAN

Bourbon, Berlin, and the Comforts of Fried Chicken

THE THIRTY-THIRD PRESIDENT
April 12, 1945–January 20, 1953

★

I. The Haunted House

O n April 12, 1945, Harry S. Truman was tucking into a bourbon and water in the Senate Cloakroom when he was interrupted by a phone call. It was Roosevelt's press secretary, who asked Truman to join him as "quickly and quietly" as possible at the White House. "Jesus Christ and General Jackson," the vice president cussed as he sprinted over. There, his suspicions were confirmed: FDR was dead. Now Harry Truman—son of a mule trader, a failed haberdasher, and a small-town Democrat from Independence, Missouri—was the most powerful man in the world.

Finding Eleanor Roosevelt in her sitting room, he asked, "Is there anything I can do for you?" She looked him in the eye, and replied, "Is there anything we can do for *you*? For you are the one in trouble now."

Truman hastily withdrew and canceled his weekly poker game. "I guess the party's off," he said to his pals.

As VP Truman had only met with FDR twice, and now he would preside during some of the most harrowing and eventful years of the twentieth century. "Being President is like riding a tiger," he said. "You have to keep riding or be swallowed."

On May 8, 1945, he celebrated his sixty-first birthday, spent his first full day in the White House, and learned the Germans had signed an unconditional surrender. In July, he represented the United States at the final Big Three summit in Potsdam, Germany, and debated thorny questions about the future of Europe. Then, on August 6, the B-29 bomber *Enola Gay* released the uranium-235 atomic bomb Little Boy over Hiroshima, Japan, incinerating the city. Three days later, Americans dropped the plutonium-cored bomb Fat Man on Nagasaki, and Stalin sent a million Russian soldiers into Manchuria. On August 14, Japan surrendered.

World War II, the most destructive conflagration in history, was finally over.

In Washington, half a million people "celebrated the winning of the war with a screaming, drinking, paper-tearing, free-kissing demonstration which combined all the features of New Years' Eve and Mardi

Gras," *Yank* magazine reported. "Every girl was fair game, and rank was no obstacle. . . . The number of bottles which were passed freely among strangers would have startled anyone."

PRESIDENT TRUMAN FOUND HIMSELF in "a dizzy whirl" but looked forward to the challenge. His wife, Bess, however, confided, "I just dread moving" into the White House. They had met in sixth grade in Independence, Missouri, married in 1919, and had a daughter, Margaret. Bess coveted the anonymity that allowed her to drive her own car and shop for her own food. Suddenly thrust into First Ladyhood, she disliked being compared to Eleanor Roosevelt and had zero interest in the limelight. But the press clamored for information, demanding to know if she'd host parties and what she would wear.

"I'm not the one elected. I have nothing to say to the public," she said. "Tell 'em it's none of their damn business." The message went out: "Mrs. Truman hasn't quite made up her mind yet."

Bess had a cool, skeptical temperament that counterbalanced Harry's folksy charm and quick temper. She was a wise political counselor and played a vital, if largely unacknowledged, role in his career. "Although it went unsuspected by nearly everybody . . . Bess Truman entered into nearly every decision the president made," the chief usher, J. B. West, wrote. "She probably had more influence on political decisions than Mrs. Roosevelt had on social issues." He appreciated Mrs. Truman's "dry, laconic, incisive and very funny wit. . . . If you weren't looking for one raised eyebrow, one downturned corner of her mouth, you might miss the joke entirely."

The staff wagered on whether Bess was calm ("she's wearing one gun this morning") or moody ("both guns smoking"). And it didn't take her long to collide with Henrietta Nesbitt. A good home cook who was fond of soft, warm biscuits, Bess objected to the hard, cold rolls she was served. When the housekeeper assured her the biscuits were home baked, Bess tartly replied, "I believe I know the difference." It took President Truman's personal intervention to ensure that his wife's biscuit recipe was used by the White House kitchen.

Mrs. Nesbitt—whom Margaret Truman called "the Roosevelts' tyrannical housekeeper"—continued to serve a farrago of tongue, rutabagas, canned stringed beans, and other thrifty menu items that annoyed the Trumans. When Mrs. Nesbitt served Brussels sprouts, the president pushed them aside. When she served them again, she said, "This is how Mrs. Roosevelt did things." Bess's ire finally boiled over the day she asked for a stick of butter to take to a potluck. "Oh, no, we can't let any of our butter go," wailed Mrs. Nesbitt. "We've used up almost all of this month's ration stamps." Bess turned to Harry and said, "It's time to find a new housekeeper."

The way Mrs. Nesbitt told it, she loyally stuck to her post "until the Trumans got settled," before deciding to move on. Others said she was fired for insolence.

Mary Sharpe, an assistant housekeeper, took her place. The First Lady approved of Sharpe's cleanliness almost as much as her wit. One Thanksgiving, Bess announced she wanted to celebrate with a quiet family gathering and "a good traditional menu." When the press inundated her with dopey questions—"what is Mrs. Truman's recipe for stuffing?"; "does the President like light or dark meat?"—Bess deputized Sharpe to answer for her. In asking how the presidential turkey would be dispatched, a journalist noted, "In some countries they pour whiskey down the turkey's throat to make it tender." Not missing a beat, Sharpe replied, "We pour whiskey down the guests' throats, and they just *think* the turkey is tender!" Bess roared with approval.

A SPRY FIVE FEET SEVEN, Harry Truman identified as "a meat and potatoes man." He kept a high-protein, low-calorie diet, consumed "no butter, no sugar, no sweets" and used a rigorous exercise regime to stay one step ahead of the tiger. "A man in my position has a public duty to keep himself in good condition," he declared. "You can't be mentally fit unless you're physically fit."

He rose at 5:30 every morning and took a brisk two-mile walk. Then he swam laps in the White House pool (installed by FDR), proceeded to the rowing and exercise machines, took a sauna, and then dived back into the pool. Finally, he'd administer himself a one-ounce shot of bourbon, a treatment that men of his generation considered a good way to "get the engine going."

Bess Truman never fully accommodated herself to life in the White House fishbowl. She had opposed Harry becoming president, and felt "superfluous" when he didn't consult her on the atomic bombing of Hiroshima. She harbored a "smoldering anger," Margaret wrote, which resulted in an "emotional separation." Every June, Bess would flee home to Missouri, with her mother and her mother's Black cook, Vietta Garr (both of whom lived in the White House). After Margaret graduated from college in 1946, she joined Bess in Independence. This left Harry alone in Washington for weeks. Never tempted by other women, he found himself rattling around the mansion. "Never so lonesome in my life," he scribbled on New Year's Day 1947 like a mopey teenager.

Truman kept an informal style, but the tradition-bound staff insisted that dinner be served by two tuxedo-clad butlers. Harry played along, but was amused by the ritual:

> Had dinner by myself tonight. . . . A butler came in very formally and said, "Mr. President, dinner is served." . . . Barnett in tails and white tie pulls out my chair, pushes me up to the table. John in tails and white tie brings me a fruit cup. Barnett takes away the empty cup. John brings me a plate, Barnett brings me a tenderloin. John brings me aspara-gus, Barnett brings me carrots and beets. I have to eat alone and in silence in a candlelit room. I ring. Barnett takes the plates and the but-ter plates. John comes in with a napkin and silver crumb tray—there are no crumbs but John has to brush them off the table anyway. Barnett brings me a plate with a finger bowl and doily and John puts a glass saucer and a little bowl on the plate. Barnett brings me some chocolate custard. John brings me a demitasse (at home a little cup of coffee— about two good gulps) and my dinner is over. I take a hand bath in the finger bowl and go back to work. What a life!

At night, the old house creaked and groaned, and the clocks whirred and chimed. No porters or Secret Service men were posted then, and Truman swore he heard ghosts knocking on the door, roaming the cor-ridors, and rummaging through his belongings. "Damn place is haunted sure as shootin'," he wrote to Bess.

True or not, the Executive Mansion was something of a haunted house. Once again it had suffered from benign neglect, as many of the structure's load-bearing walls had been removed in stopgap renovations over the years. The structure had become a rickety firetrap, "staying up from force of habit only," Truman was informed. One day in 1947, the president was taking a bath on the second floor, where the floor "sagged and moved like a ship at sea," he noted. Directly below him, Bess was hosting a tea for the Daughters of the American Revolution in the Blue Room. When she noticed a large chandelier wavering, the ladies scattered, and the presi-dent joked that they had almost witnessed him dropping through the ceiling, as naked as a baby. A few months later, Margaret's piano sunk a hole through the floor of the First Family's private quarters.

Before Truman could undertake a renovation, though, he had an election to worry about. In November 1948, the underdog Truman surprised the nation—especially the *Chicago Tribune* editors who ran the headline "Dewey Defeats Truman"—by defeating Thomas Dewey, the Republican governor of New York, in one of the greatest electoral upsets in American history.

With that essential business out of the way, Truman turned his attention to saving the Executive Mansion. The building was in such bad shape, he was told, that the most expedient approach was to simply build a new White House. But Truman, a self-described American history buff and "architectural nut," rejected the idea in favor of carefully removing everything from the building's interior, excavating the basement, pouring a new concrete foundation, erecting a new "skyscraper-strength" skeleton of steel beams, and reinforcing the original sandstone walls. The job took nearly two years and cost some $5.7 million (nearly $53 million today).

When the First Family moved into the revamped White House on March 27, 1952, the building looked almost identical to the original, but was in fact larger, stronger, and more efficient—as if someone had built "a modern office inside a deserted castle," in the words of John Hersey. The 62 rooms, fourteen baths, and one elevator in 1949 had been expanded to 132 rooms, twenty baths (with showers), five elevators, twenty-nine fireplaces, and two new subbasement service areas, including a bomb shelter. The family quarters in the Executive Residence included 54 rooms and sixteen baths. On the ground floor, the kitchen was outfitted with new appliances; on the second floor, Truman controversially added a balcony behind the portico (purists worried that it disrupted the classical lines of the south facade); the third floor was expanded and a new solarium replaced an old one, affording sweeping views over memorials, the Potomac River, and the Virginia hills. It was the most complete renovation of the White House, which remains essentially the same today.

MOST HISTORIANS AGREE the Cold War began in the spring of 1947, with the announcement of the Truman Doctrine to curb Soviet expansionism. Europe remained a shambles. Millions of people had been displaced or killed, and the landscape was wrecked. Food—the lack of it, the difficulty of transporting it, and the growing need for it—was an emergency.

Echoing Wilson and Hoover, Truman asked Americans to voluntarily ration their meals in order to send food to the Allies. Founding the Citizens Food Committee, he aimed to send 100 million bushels of American grain to Europe and brought back Meatless Tuesdays and Eggless Thursdays, restricted beer and alcohol production (which require grain), and distributed recipes for dishes such as baked canned salmon topped with crushed potato chips. In solidarity, the First Couple canceled all state dinners for the 1947–48 season. But once again, an idealistic food conservation program broke down in the face of human nature and was quietly shelved.

It was then, in June 1948, that Soviet troops blockaded Berlin, which lay a hundred miles inside their occupied zone in Germany. West Berlin had only enough food to last thirty-six days and was defended by just a few thousand Allied troops. With some 1.5 million soldiers around the city, the Soviets threatened to attack. The United States hinted it would retaliate with atomic bombs. In truth, neither side wanted to start a third world war. But to prevent a crisis, five thousand tons of food would need to reach the city every day. All ground routes were sealed off, and it seemed nearly impossible. But flight paths were clear.

Truman launched Operation Vittles, in which unarmed American and British cargo planes began to fly staples such as milk, flour, baking powder, salt, medicines, coal—and twenty-one tons of candy for children—into West Berlin. Soon, flights were landing there every thirty seconds to deliver 5,000 to 8,000 tons of cargo a day. By the time the Soviet blockade lifted in May 1949, some 278,000 flights had delivered more than 2.3 million tons of food and coal. Dubbed the Berlin Airlift, the operation was one of the West's most significant humanitarian efforts, and propaganda coups, of the Cold War.

II. Comfort Food

At 9:20 on Saturday evening, June 24, 1950, Harry S. Truman was at home in Missouri when 90,000 North Korean troops crossed the 38th parallel in a surprise invasion of South Korea. Fearing World War III, the president rushed back to Washington the next day, for an emergency meeting. It was four o'clock Sunday afternoon when he called to alert the White House staff he was inbound and asked for cocktails and dinner to be served to his war cabinet at Blair House (the president's guest house, where the Trumans were living during the White House renovation).

Most of the staff had scattered for the weekend. Rushing around

Washington in a cab, the chief butler, Alonzo Fields, bought supplies and implored the D.C. police to help round up his cooks and assistants. As the president and thirteen advisers had drinks in the Blair House garden, Fields busied himself making canapés and the staff began to trickle in. By 8:15 they had produced a meal of Truman's favorite comfort food: fried chicken breast served with currant jelly and cream gravy; shoestring potatoes; buttered asparagus; scalloped tomatoes; hot biscuits; and vanilla ice cream with chocolate sauce. In that tense moment, recalled Secretary of State Dean Acheson, the food was "especially excellent." After dinner, Truman and his advisers huddled over drinks at a long mahogany table, mapping out a strategy for the Korean War.

CONTEMPLATING HIS PROSPECTS for the 1952 election, Truman benched himself. Bess wanted to return to Missouri, and Harry found that riding the presidential tiger was exhausting. Scouring a list of potential successors, his eye alighted on General Dwight D. "Ike" Eisenhower. Though Ike was a Republican, the idea wasn't totally crazy. In June 1945, Truman had dispatched his executive plane, a Douglas VC-54C Skymaster he called the *Sacred Cow,* to pluck General Eisenhower from Germany and bring him to Washington. The five-star general was given a hero's welcome. Just off the front lines, the bald, gap-toothed warrior nodded—stiffly at first and then with growing ease—at the crowd's thunderous applause.

At a raucous lunch, 1,100 Washingtonians squeezed into the Statler Hotel, where Ike feasted on baked chicken, sipped a Coca-Cola, and enjoyed two giant cakes topped by ice sculptures—one of a bald eagle, the other of a four-engine bomber. That night Truman and Ike dined at the White House and bonded over their midwestern roots in Missouri and Kansas. Truman knew what the general would be hankering for: a home-cooked meal. The dinner was overseen by Bess and Vietta Garr and featured a cornucopia of down-home foods, including corn on the cob, perhaps a country ham, and Ozark apple pudding. Harry and Ike dug in like two farmhands at a "simple and homey . . . community supper in Missouri," said an aide.

In 1950, Truman named Eisenhower the commander of NATO forces and two years later urged the general to run as a Democrat. But Ike remained a Republican and defeated the Democratic governor of Illinois, Adlai E. Stevenson. Tensions flared between Truman and Eisenhower, and at Ike's inauguration the two got into a spat over protocol:

what sort of hat to wear (Truman favored a top hat; Eisenhower insisted on a homburg); where they should officially greet, inside or outside the White House; who would sit where on their drive to the Capitol. The goodwill they had created over sweet Ozark apple pudding had soured, irreparably.

= 11 =

DWIGHT D. EISENHOWER

The President Who Cooked

I. Squirrel Stew and Two Day Soup

C'est la soupe qui fait le soldat (the soup makes the soldier).
—Napoleon Bonaparte

Dwight David Eisenhower was not a gourmet, and did not care for rich sauces or fine wine, but he was the most accomplished presidential cook. Nicknamed Ike, he was born in Texas in 1890 and raised in Kansas and was the last president born in the nineteenth century. He was the third of seven boys: his father, David, worked at a creamery, and his mother, Ida, was a committed pacifist who insisted that her sons learn to cook, wash, sew, and read history. Ike enjoyed the process of turning raw ingredients into a satisfying meal. "Cooking gave me a creative feeling," he'd say.

On a small patch of land in Abilene, young Ike grew corn and cucumbers and sold hot tamales to neighbors. When his brother Milton had scarlet fever, Ike was deputized as the family cook while Ida nursed his brother. "I don't think the family lived too well during those two weeks," he recalled, "but I learned something about the preparation of simple dishes." With his mother's tutoring, he mastered vegetable soup, roast chicken, grilled steak, boiled potatoes, and baked apple pie.

An enthusiastic hunter and fisherman, Ike was mentored in woodland cookery by Bob Davis, an illiterate outdoorsman. On camping trips with friends, Ike was in charge of the grub: once, their supplies ran so low that he and a friend shot and skinned three squirrels; adding their meat to leftover potatoes and beans, Ike stretched the ingredients into a stew. The future politician slyly called it "crow stew," which sounded less appetizing than squirrel, and persuaded his mates to eat bread instead; the stew was left to Ike and his coconspirator.

Ike recalled the squirrel stew as a valuable lesson: a good cook with limited but tasty ingredients could whip up a decent meal. In the army, he learned the opposite lesson: cooks with decent ingredients but little skill usually produced terrible meals. As an officer, Eisenhower drilled his soldiers on the importance of a balanced diet, nutritious food, and aesthetic presentation. "Food is part of a soldier's pay, and it is my determination to see that none of his pay is going to be counterfeit," he declared.

In October 1915, Eisenhower was a twenty-five-year-old second lieutenant stationed in San Antonio, where he met Marie Geneva "Mamie" Doud. She was the spirited, eighteen-year-old daughter of a wealthy Colorado family. She was raised with a cook and maid and had a monthly $100 stipend from her father, a meatpacking executive. Ike and Mamie courted over Mexican dinners and married the following July. Moving into a bug-infested, two-bedroom apartment with no electricity, Mamie explained that while she knew how to make fudge, "I was never permitted in the kitchen when I was a young girl. . . . I was a cooking school dropout."

Ike happily volunteered for KP and liked to say, "I've been a mess sergeant since the day I got married. . . . The only way I could get the family away from a diet of steak and potatoes was to make a hobby of cooking. . . . I enjoy it a lot."

In 1917 Mamie gave birth to a son, Doud Dwight "Ikky" Eisenhower. The boy was a delight, but when he died of scarlet fever at age three, the Eisenhowers' marriage was strained nearly to the breaking point. Happily, Mamie gave birth to a second son, John, in 1922. Ike spent World War I teaching tank warfare and, after stints in Panama and the Philippines, was promoted to colonel, and kept cooking and eating. He didn't care for "hifalutin' gourmet stuff," recalled his orderly, John Moaney, but produced decent chops, steak, grilled fish, and fried chicken.

In 1942, Eisenhower was promoted to lieutenant general and put in charge of all American forces in Europe. While in London planning the invasion of North Africa, he grew disenchanted with English breakfasts of kippers, cold oatmeal, and weak coffee. Moaney invited his boss into the soldiers' mess, where infantrymen feasted on eggs, bacon, and strong coffee—rare delicacies in war-strapped Britain. Ike could not have been happier.

In 1943, FDR promoted Eisenhower to supreme commander of the Allied Expeditionary Force in western Europe. The job put him in charge of nearly three million Allied troops and the invasion of Normandy on D-day. The move brought Ike into close contact with Winston Churchill. One day, the prime minister requested a lunch of hot dogs and baked beans. Referencing FDR's 1939 hot dog "picnic that won the war," Churchill declared Ike's hot dogs "a delicacy fit for a king, which is why His Majesty enjoyed them so much himself." But it was Eisenhower's baked beans—in which he replaced the usual tomato or ketchup base with a slow-cooked molasses, salt pork, and onion sauce that produced a resoundingly deep, rich flavor—that everyone remembered.

In 1944, Eisenhower was promoted to five-star general of the army, a rare accolade. Mindful of Napoleon's dictum that "an army runs on its stomach," the general kept his troops' fitness up by supplying them with reasonably tasty, calorie-packed meals. As the Allies pushed the Germans inland from the French coast, they subsisted on K rations— a packet of dehydrated food (meat, beverage, candy) that could be quickly reconstituted—and C rations, a slimmer package of food carried by troops in combat. Following right behind the front line, General Eisenhower liked to snug his lunch rations next to his jeep's engine; once the food was heated, he would eat it off the hood, as if it were a picnic table.

After the war, Ike pictured himself living on a farm and teaching history. But in 1948, Columbia University persuaded him to move to New York City and serve as its thirteenth president. It was not an expected career move for a five-star general who lacked a college education but Ike quickly adapted, and made news. When the Eisenhowers arrived on campus, they were asked to contribute a recipe to a cookbook, *What's Cooking at Columbia.* Expecting a short note from Mrs. Eisenhower, the student editors were thrilled to receive Ike's lengthy, hand-typed recipe for "Two Day Vegetable Soup," a dish he had been cooking since childhood. With a base of homemade chicken and beef stock, a plethora of vegetables ("Your vegetables should not all be dumped in at once.... Your effort must be to have them nicely cooked but not mushy, at about the same time," he wrote), pearled barley, and "a small handful" of diced meat, the soup required hours of slow and patient simmering to get just right. With a culinarian's touch, the general recommended a peppery-flavored garnish: "In the springtime when nasturtiums are green and tender, you can take a few nasturtium stems, cut them up in small pieces, boil them . . . and add them to your soup."

Eisenhower's "Two Day Vegetable Soup" caused a sensation. Newspapers across the country reprinted the recipe and soon markets were deluged with requests for nasturtium stems, an item most people had never considered food before. Ike marveled that a simple recipe learned from his mother garnered more attention than any other statement he made as the president of an Ivy League university.

II. Ike's Hidden Weapon

At his inauguration in 1953, Eisenhower was sixty-two and Mamie was fifty-six. The White House was their thirty-sixth residence and the first home they would live in for longer than a year since 1916. "At last I have a job where I can stay home nights," Ike said, "and, by golly, I'm going to stay home."

From the start, Eisenhower used a series of "knife and fork" meetings to introduce himself to Congress and educate himself about the customs of Washington. Between February and May 1953, he wined and dined 527 senators and representatives (just 4 congressmen did not attend). The lessons he drew from these seemingly simple meetings were, in fact, profound: a relaxed, intimate conversation over a meal with the president made people feel good about him, and themselves, and provided an excellent source of information.

Eisenhower's congressional dinners were such a success that in June 1953 he began hosting a series of private stag dinners at the White House, to take the pulse of the nation. Each event featured fifteen men from broadly different backgrounds—CEOs from eastern cities, ranchers from western rangelands, scientists from midwestern laboratories, engineers from the Southeast, religious leaders from the Southwest, and soldiers, educators, journalists, artists, and friends from all over. So eager was the president to connect that he hosted a stag dinner nearly every week. Guest lists were drawn up far in advance and seating was carefully arranged so that a fiery union leader, say, was not seated next to an arch capitalist.

On stag nights Ike kept the format uniform and the pace quick. At 7:30 a line of black limousines disgorged their tuxedo-clad passengers at the White House door, where the president greeted each guest. At 8:00, they filed into the State Dining Room and sat for dinner. The president often based his menus on food sent by constituents—steak from Texas, salmon from Alaska, turkeys from Pennsylvania, and the like. Conversation began with light banter, but Ike expected everyone to add something meaningful and grew irritated when the conversation lagged. (Some nervous attendees researched Eisenhowerian topics ahead of time.) Businessmen addressed trade and taxes; cattlemen opined on calves and cows; athletes and army friends focused on golf, fishing, and war stories.

Once word got out about the president's "secret dinners," people wanted to be in on the action. But the coveted invitations could not be bought, which made them only more desirable. Those who believed they should be invited took umbrage when they were not. Celebrities clamored to be included, and sometimes they were. And when a group of Republican women objected to being excluded, the president invited them to a series of breakfasts. By April 1955, Eisenhower had hosted more than seven hundred guests at forty-nine events.

At these meals, he floated trial balloons about education and foreign aid, or tested theories about civil rights and inflation, but more often he sat back and listened. This was a management technique he'd honed during the war. The general would ask his staff to present solutions to strategic questions: as each made their case, he'd listen, synthesize their arguments, and make his own decision. In this way, he learned to value others' input and to trust his own instincts, his gut.

Eisenhower was a good listener. "In conversation he is not a fencer, and he's never flippant or casual," one guest noted. Another said, "He can go on with a flow of conversation all evening long." Ike was amused to discover that good food and drink loosened lips: many guests revealed personal views at odds with their public statements. Intrigued, reporters made much ado about Ike's "hidden weapon . . . presidential charm and food." The stag dinners, they wrote, provided him with a way to build political consensus and spin journalists. That was generally accurate, though the secret weapon occasionally backfired.

When the names of Ike's guests were published, it caused a stir because it revealed whom he trusted and whom he didn't. When he decreed his guest lists private, that set off a counter-backlash because many who dined with the president wanted others to know they had. "Why travel thousands of miles to eat at the White House if you can't talk about it?" they wondered. Further, it left diners feeling "uncomfortably stuffed with both food and secrets."

The stag nights usually ended by 11:00 p.m., by which point, *U.S. News & World Report* noted,

Those who have put money and work into political campaigns go away feeling that they have had a hand in shaping national policies. The President of the United States has asked their opinions. Financiers get the feeling that they are a part of the Government. Businessmen glimpse policies in the making. Farm and labor leaders get a chance to speak their minds. Educators tell their problems to the president in person. Editors, publishers, commentators get a sense of being on the inside of news in the making. . . . All of them can go home and tell their friends: "I told Ike . . ." And some of them did. Or, more often it is: "The President told me . . ." And it may be that he did. . . . This is tending to give them a personal interest in keeping Mr. Eisenhower in the White House. It helps them forget the money they spent and the work they did to put him there. It softens the blow when they learn that the job or the law that they wanted does not fit into his program. It puts them in a good mood to go out and work for his election again.

III. Mrs. Ike and the Rise of TV Dinners

Unlike Eleanor Roosevelt or Bess Truman, Mamie Eisenhower loved being First Lady. Having followed her husband around the world, "Mrs. Ike" could entertain in style and was unfazed by foreign leaders or the intricacies of protocol. And like Dolley Madison, she loved to organize a party and wear fancy clothes. At the inaugural balls thrown on the night of her husband's 1953 swearing-in, Mamie wore a pink gown that glistened with two thousand faceted rhinestones, pink silk shoes, and long pink gloves. Pink was her signature color, and she applied it to everything from toilet seat covers to the ribbons adorning White House lamb chops. In private, the First Lady suffered numerous ailments, including a heart murmur and inner-ear trouble. She disliked athletics and was sensitive to heat and cold. She would sometimes sleep until noon or spend an entire day in bed, her "big pink office."

Mrs. Eisenhower was happy to portray herself as an exemplar of the traditional 1950s housewife—with the notable exception of cooking—calling it "the best career that life has to offer a woman." She frequently hosted women's lunches, offering light fare such as open-faced sandwiches, tomato pudding, caramel-frosted cake, and cookies, with grape punch, coffee, or tea. And she was thrifty, turning leftovers into dinner salads or the "one-dish wonders"—turkey hash, tuna casseroles, ground meat dishes—then in vogue. Used to running households around the world, the First Lady took command of the Executive Mansion, holding daily conferences with the maître d', who oversaw the butlers; the chief usher, who oversaw social planning; and the housekeeper, who was responsible for maintaining the building.

Mamie raised staff eyebrows when she ordered a double bed, so that she and Ike could sleep together (as the Roosevelts and Trumans had not), and was, "gay, breezy, open," recalled assistant chief usher J. B. West. But she had "a spine of steel" and knew "exactly what she wanted." Upon spying Ike's lunch menu one day, Mamie snapped, "What's this?" When the cook sheepishly replied that the president had approved the menu, she said, "I run everything in my house. In the future all menus are to be approved by me and not by anybody else."

The White House was in excellent shape thanks to the Truman renovation, but Mrs. Eisenhower wanted to stamp it with her own decorating preferences. She "loved quality . . . rich silks and brocades, and the best china and sterling silver money could buy," her granddaughter recalled. A devotee of antiques, Mamie dreamed of replacing the Trumans' reproduction furniture with original pieces. And while she could accept donations from citizens—a mahogany sofa here, a bronze bust of Lincoln there—she was limited by budget, politics, and laws. Mamie was "terribly disappointed that she couldn't transform the entire mansion," recalled J. B. West.

Her true passion was for "beautiful tableware." Mamie ordered service plates with the presidential seal and a gold coin border from Castleton, a manufacturer in Pennsylvania. And she used donations to complete a project started by First Lady Caroline Harrison to have samples of each administration's china. (Five administrations are not included in the White House collection because they did not commission their own patterns.)

With her "china closet in order," an observer wrote, Mrs. Eisenhower highlighted the role of First Ladies, and her "activism . . . was portrayed as an extension of her role as a woman and wife, thereby allowing American women to identify with her." In this way, Mamie Eisenhower set the table, as it were, for Jackie Kennedy's more celebrated refurbishing.

Ike understood that his wife's bright smile, pink dresses, and home decorating made her a relatable "everywoman" and political asset. Yet their relationship had been stressed over the years—first by the death of Ikky, then by the turbulence of army life and World War II. In Europe, General Eisenhower's personal driver and secretary was a raven-haired former model named Kay Summersby, whom Ike called "Irish" (she was born in County Cork). They were close. The question is, how close? Ike scribbled notes such as "How about lunch, tea & dinner today?" One of those events might have indicated innocent fun, but three meals in one day seemed to indicate something more. Some historians have disputed the notion of an Eisenhower-Summersby romance. But General Omar Bradley said the rumors were "quite accurate," and Harry Truman said Ike wanted to marry Summersby. In a 1976 memoir, *Past Forgetting: My*

Love Affair with Dwight D. Eisenhower, she wrote, "I suppose inevitably, we found ourselves in each other's arms in an unrestrained embrace. . . . It was as if we were frantic, and we were."

But that was the past. In Washington, Ike was a model of decorum, and Mamie endeared herself to the public by throwing euphoric holiday parties. In 1953, she revived the White House Easter Egg Roll, which had been suspended since the Truman renovation. For St. Patrick's Day, she donned a green brocade dress and hosted an Irish lunch in the Green Room. For Halloween, she decorated the State Dining Room with black cats, Indian corn, and glowing jack-o'-lanterns, in what the press called "the most interesting party ever given in the dignified setting." At Christmas, she celebrated with a delirium of wreaths, poinsettias, gift boxes, candies, and twenty-seven decorated trees throughout the mansion.

AS PRESIDENT, Eisenhower retained his military discipline. He was up at 6:00 a.m. and ate breakfast at 7:00, lunch at 1:00, and dinner at 7:00. The First Couple liked steaks provided by a rancher friend in Kansas, and the president's hunting provided game birds for Eisenhower's quail hash. His fishing trips brought fresh trout, which he rolled in cornmeal and fried in bacon fat. Mamie steered the cooks into her file of homey recipes—baked seafood casserole, fluffy turnips, Danish tomatoes, devil's food cake with seven-minute frosting, deep-dish apple pie, baked caramel custard. With such economy, she was proud to say, they kept their food budget to $100 a month.

The Eisenhowers liked a predinner nip and a glass or two of wine with their meal; he liked to sip scotch afterward. But tradition dictated protocol in the White House. On their first night there, the butler served the president a glass of whiskey and then delivered the First Lady's drink. Taken aback, Ike said, "Look, in my house the ladies are served first." The next evening, and the one after that, the same thing happened. "It finally dawned on me," he wrote. "These boys are teaching me how to be president."

Mamie liked Scrabble and canasta, while Ike preferred bridge, which he'd play for hours on Saturdays in a foursome. He didn't care if his tablemates were Democrats or Republicans, as long as they liked to bet and eat takeout. They would start on a weekend afternoon, break for a takeout dinner, then continue into the night. Like Calvin Coolidge, and many other presidents, the Eisenhowers were especially fond of Chinese food.

Beginning in the 1930s, Ike frequented Washington's Sun Chop Suey Restaurant, where he ordered egg rolls, chicken chow mein, fried rice, egg foo yong, roast pork, Chinese vegetables, and almond cookies.

Television was emerging as an exciting new medium, and Ike, Mamie, and her mother liked to eat dinner while watching the evening news. Swanson frozen TV dinners were all the rage, and while "gossips say [the First Family's trays] contained frozen TV dinners," the food historian Poppy Cannon wrote, that seems unlikely. Instead, the Eisenhowers probably ate simple dinners of Salisbury steak, mashed potatoes, and salad, made in the White House kitchen and served on china set on collapsible tables, as the Reagans later did. Ike preferred Westerns, while Mamie was a devotee of soap operas, quiz shows, and comedies—especially *As the World Turns, You Bet Your Life,* and *I Love Lucy.* To accommodate their tastes, the Eisenhowers had "his" and "hers" TV sets in the family quarters. When Jackie Kennedy moved in, she noticed two holes in the wall. "What are those portholes for?" she asked. The usher explained that Mr. and Mrs. Ike liked to sit next to each other and watch different shows on their respective sets.

Truman made the first televised White House address, in October 1947—to announce the ill-fated Citizens Food Committee—but Eisenhower was America's first real TV president. Noticing that public attention was shifting from newspapers and radio to television, his advisers converted the old kitchen in the White House basement into a media center. The space was wired for radio broadcasting and TV cameras; a rug and silk curtains softened the light and sound. The Resolute desk—given to President Rutherford B. Hayes by Queen Victoria in 1880—was stationed in front of a fireplace and bracketed by flags, to provide a commanding stage.

In January 1955, Eisenhower appeared in the first televised press conference from the White House, which the Big Three networks aired in black and white. The public knew his clipped voice from the radio, but now they could see the commander in chief's lively eyes, gap-toothed grin, and erect bearing while he discussed "Communist China," unveiled his budget, and deflected "loaded questions" about his policies. Though he shifted about, didn't look into the camera, and rushed his words, the event brought the president directly into people's homes in a new way. And with coaching from the actor Robert Montgomery, Ike eventually became comfortable in front of the camera.

He evolved in other ways, too. Over time, the five-star warrior seemed to channel his mother's pacifism by raging against "this damnable thing of war," Soviet expansionism, and the French war in Indochina (Vietnam). He endorsed Atoms for Peace, which pushed for the peaceful use of nuclear power. In his televised farewell speech to the nation on January 17, 1961, Eisenhower warned against an arms race and, in a phrase he coined, "the military-industrial complex."

IV. The Farm, and a Weapon Mightier Than Arms and Bombs

Eisenhower was proud of his rural roots, and his interest in food and agriculture was both politically expedient and deeply personal. "You know, farming looks mighty easy when your plow is a pencil, and you're a thousand miles from the corn field," he'd say. In 1950, he fulfilled a dream by purchasing a 189-acre farm near the Gettysburg battlefield in Pennsylvania. Equipped with a barn, a tractor, a putting green, and a staff to raise his Eisenhower Farm Black Angus cattle and vegetables (which he froze and proudly brought to the White House), the Gettysburg retreat was a place for Ike to unwind and entertain.

Having lived in every kind of home, "except an igloo," Mamie decorated the farmhouse—the only home they owned—with collections of silverware and figurines, pink drapes, army-green tiles, and chairs monogrammed "Commander in Chief" and "First Lady." The kitchen featured the latest gizmos, including two stoves, a plate warmer, a refrigerator with a chilled water dispenser, a dishwasher, a Veg-O-Matic, bright green linoleum counters, and a red plastic cake stand. (The Eisenhowers deeded the house to the National Park Service, and the kitchen remains a time capsule.) Using his position in ways now considered unethical, the president shipped wine from France to the farm duty-free, stocked his liquor cabinet with bottles confiscated by the General Services Administration, and outfitted the property with $300,000 worth of equipment and home furnishings donated by friends with political interests.

Dolores Moaney (wife of Ike's aide, John Moaney) cooked homey dinners at the farm. They were often served on the porch, and guests included politicians, industrialists, and other leaders. In much the way Jefferson and FDR operated, Eisenhower used these quiet meals to "take the measure of the man."

But more often than not Ike cooked for family and friends at the farm, where he served homemade chicken-noodle soup, old-fashioned beef stew (made with pepper and paprika), summer succotash, and Mamie's

Million Dollar Fudge. When prime ministers or former generals visited, he would tour them around the battlefield and discuss strategy and tactics. Then he'd prepare one of his famous barbecues: each steak was three or four inches thick; he'd liberally season them with salt, black pepper, and garlic powder, then nestle them directly into the red-hot embers, which produces a delicacy that is charred on the outside and pink on the inside, and known as Eisenhower Steak.

IKE'S GASTRONOMIC ZEAL naturally informed his presidential food policy. A disciple of General George C. Marshall—the architect of the Marshall Plan, who warned that "hunger and insecurity are the worst enemies of peace"—Eisenhower signed the Agricultural Trade Development and Assistance Act, better known as Food for Peace, in 1954. It was an outgrowth of Senator Hubert Humphrey's report "Food and Fiber as a Force for Freedom," which, like Hoover's post–World War I food program, argued that aiding distressed nations provided both humanitarian assistance and a powerful foreign policy lever. (America has shipped food abroad since 1812, when James Madison sent aid to earthquake-racked Venezuela.)

To Ike, Food for Peace was a way to spread American "soft power" and to dispose of surplus grain accumulated during the war. In 1954, the United States shipped 3.4 million tons of food, mostly to Europe; by 1956, it had shipped 14 million tons. Today, America remains the world's largest supplier of food aid, sending some 10 million tons of food worth $1.5 billion abroad annually. As of this writing, Food for Peace has operated for almost seventy years and has fed over three billion people in 150 countries.

At the 1959 World Agricultural Fair in New Delhi, India, Eisenhower described America's effort to end world hunger as a "genuinely noble war." He described "food, family, friendship, and freedom" as weapons "mightier than arms and bombs; mightier than machines and money; mightier than any empire that ruled the past or threatens the future."

V. The Question

Presidential cooks are often anonymous, but many of them—starting with George Washington's slave Hercules—led adventurous lives worthy of Hollywood. The Eisenhowers' cook François Rysavy, for instance, was born in Czechoslovakia and orphaned at four years old during World War I. His aunt adopted him and taught him to make pastry, but when she too was killed, Rysavy was orphaned a second time. He apprenticed in a bakery and learned to cook savory dishes at restaurants and hotels across Europe and North Africa, before moving to the United States. Settling in Washington, Rysavy freelanced in FDR's White House kitchen, and in January 1955 he was named the Eisenhowers' head chef (the title executive chef was created by Jackie Kennedy in 1961).

Rysavy brought an unusual global repertoire that included dishes such as Moroccan brandied lobster, Viennese veal cutlet, chicken Lafayette, mushrooms Provençal, cheddar cheese mousse, and rum fruit savarin. In researching historical recipes, the chef tried his hand at Washington's chicken fricassee, bouquet of garden vegetables à la John Adams, Jefferson's filled pannequaiques (pancakes), and Andrew Jackson's burnt cream. Rysavy was dismayed that Eisenhower, who had lived in France during the war, never developed a taste for wine and disliked classical dishes made with butter and cream.

Like the general-presidents who preceded him, Ike was a prodigious carnivore. He preferred steak cooked rare, three minutes to a side, and like President Taft sometimes ate a four-ounce steak for breakfast, a six-ounce hamburger for lunch, and an eight-ounce steak for dinner. Yet Ike remained trim, was not especially fond of sweets, and was not a midnight snacker. His physicians provided little dietary oversight, and the president seemed to think he was indestructible.

In 1955, Eisenhower led a global summit in Switzerland focused on easing Cold War tensions. Afterward, he and Mamie took a vacation in Denver. On a Friday in September, Ike fixed himself a hearty breakfast of dark coffee, sausage, bacon, and cornmeal pancakes (using his own blend of meal), which he fried in bacon grease. The food tasted especially good in the crisp, high air of the Rockies. But as the day wore on, it sat uncomfortably in the presidential stomach.

On Saturday, he played golf and gobbled down a hamburger with a double slice of raw Bermuda onion. Again, Eisenhower suffered indigestion. Feeling queasy, he spent the afternoon painting landscapes. For dinner he had leg of lamb with pan-roasted potatoes, then played billiards and went to bed. At 2:30 in the morning the president thrashed about and complained of stomach pains. Mamie gave him milk of magnesia and called the White House physician, who diagnosed a heart attack. When he injected the president with morphine, to relieve the symptoms, Ike's blood pressure dropped, his pulse rate spiked, and he went into shock. "Shaken," the doctor asked Mamie to wrap herself around Ike, to calm him. She did, and he drifted into a deep sleep.

The next day, Eisenhower was taken to Fitzsimons Army Hospital, where aides told the press that the president had suffered "digestive upset . . . twenty-four-hour stuff." Later, Ike's condition was updated to a "mild coronary thrombosis." Then the word "mild" disappeared from the narrative. By Monday, news of the president's condition had spread around the world and the stock market had lost $14 billion.

Ike was a physically active, mentally sharp, sixty-four-year-old, but he had a quick temper and smoked up to four packs of cigarettes a day. Doctors ordered him to rest quietly for seven weeks. Such forced time off went against every instinct in the president's body, but he had little choice. The heart attack, "my first serious illness," he said, left him feeling depleted. In typical fashion, he embarked on a goal of "total rehabilitation." He "ordered" himself to take midday naps—"I rather resent the inconvenience"—and to stop smoking. But reducing his weight from 178 to 172 pounds on his five-foot-ten-inch frame proved "no small item for a man with my love of food."

The president returned to the White House in November 1955 and suffered through a "lite" diet. His day began with decaffeinated coffee, soy toast, and stewed prunes. At 11:00 a.m., he had a dish of yogurt or cottage cheese with shredded carrots. Lunch was a cup of vegetable soup, three rye crackers, a small salad, and a glass of water. Dinner might include a cup of turkey soup (145 calories), three Ry-Krisp crackers (60 calories), six trimmed short ribs (195 calories), a medium baked potato (100 calories), one cup of string beans (30 calories), and a sliced pear (65 calories), for a total of 595 calories.

Ike's light diet was as trying for Rysavy as it was for the president. Preparing a small, lean piece of steak, the chef furtively spread a micro-layer of butter across the top "to give it better color," he explained plaintively. "It was so juiceless." Ike spotted the glistening fat and decreed that further steak buttering was forbidden.

Most important, the doctors lectured, Eisenhower must keep his temper in check. It was not the big problems that upset him, but "the little silly annoyances" that spiked his blood pressure. He should avoid "irritation, frustration, anxiety, fear, and, above all, anger."

With a snort, Ike replied, "Just what do you think the Presidency *is*?"

Eisenhower convalesced at his Gettysburg farm. It was a calm, green spot, but the very things that made it restorative also made it isolating and boring. Like Gulliver hamstrung by Lilliputians, he struggled against his limitations: he simply could not "eat slowly," he found, and he woke up early, ready to "attack the future." But as he began to decompress into a routine of walks, swinging a golf club, and light office work, his spirits lifted.

It was then that he was confronted by an existential question: With the election of 1956 approaching, would he—*could* he—run for a second term? It was the Question on everyone's mind. Republican leaders urged him to declare his reelection campaign. His doctors warned against it. The Democrats questioned his ability to lead. Were younger Republicans ready and able to fill his seat?

EISENHOWER WAS NOT close to his vice president, Richard M. Nixon. Nixon had been chosen to bridge a party divide: while Ike was a famous general and moderate Republican whose policies blurred into Democratic terrain, Nixon was a striving, forty-two-year-old conservative from Orange County, California. The two had little in common and rarely socialized.

Returning to the White House in January 1956, Eisenhower convened a dozen advisers to address the Question over dinner. Because of its sensitive nature, the guest list was kept secret. Only Eisenhower and his secretary, Ann C. Whitman, were privy to the list. It included four from the cabinet: John Foster Dulles, George M. Humphrey, Herbert Brownell, and Arthur E. Summerfield. Five of the president's staff: Sherman Adams, James C. Hagerty, Jerry Persons, Howard Pyle, and Thomas Stephens. And three advisers: Henry Cabot Lodge II, Leonard Hall, and Ike's brother Dr. Milton Eisenhower.

It was a shock, then, when the guest list was leaked to the press. Reporters bayed for more detail: Why was Eisenhower hosting a secret dinner? Was it a campaign meeting, a farewell, or something else? Why were some insiders invited but others not?

The president was irate. He trusted Whitman implicitly, and could not fathom how the newspapers got hold of his guest list. Racking his brain, he dimly recalled a meeting with Nixon in December. Ike had shown the vice president the guest list and explained that he would not be invited because he didn't want Nixon to feel "embarrassed" by frank discussion of other possible running mates. In a flash of insight, Ike realized that the only plausible leaker was Nixon, who, in a fit of pique, tried to derail a meal he was not invited to.

Eisenhower rescheduled the dinner for Friday, January 13. Undeterred by superstition, he and his thirteen guests had a jovial discussion over the meal, before the tone turned serious. "Should I run again?" Ike asked. The Question led to a spirited if lopsided discussion. The most obvious reason *not* to run was his fragile heart, and Milton argued that if his brother retired, he would still be a valuable elder statesman. But everyone else believed Ike was "the only man" who could check the party's hard-right wing and defeat the Democrats. Ike kept his thoughts to himself and bade his counselors good night at 11:15.

Over cocktails, John Foster Dulles told Eisenhower he was the most respected leader in the world and was therefore "required" to serve a second term. "I suspect that Foster's estimate . . . is substantially correct," Eisenhower wrote in his diary. Ike, the historian Stephen Ambrose observed, "had come to think of himself as 'indispensable.' "

Mamie pledged to support her husband's decision, whatever it was. But she was not ready to depart the White House just yet, and warned that "idleness" for a man of Ike's temperament "would be fatal."

The question of a running mate remained a dilemma. Nixon was the logical choice, but Ike didn't trust him. Yet the alternatives were even less promising, and out of pragmatism he stood by his vice. When aides suggested that the First Couple invite Pat and Richard Nixon to Gettysburg as a gesture of reconciliation, Mamie balked: "What on earth would we talk about? We don't have anything in common. She doesn't play bridge!"

Nixon, meanwhile, nursed a dark resentment. "General Eisenhower never asked me to see the upstairs of the White House," he stewed. "It was years before he asked me inside the house at Gettysburg."

On February 29, 1956, Ike declared he would run again.

VI. The Big Chill

On June 7, 1956, President Eisenhower enjoyed a Waldorf salad dinner at the White House, suffered cramps and vomiting, and was rushed to Walter Reed Army Medical Center. He was diagnosed with ileitis, a painful inflammation of the small intestine. "What a bellyache!" the president griped. After surgery at Walter Reed, he returned to campaigning with the slogan "I Like Ike."

This time, Rysavy was instructed to make the president's meals virtually fat-free. The chef "suffered" but did his best. Anticipating the light nouvelle cuisine of the 1970s, Rysavy substituted ingredients: rather than pour melted butter over cooked beans, he used chicken bouillon in vegetable stock to add moisture and flavor. He stopped frying food. He did not butter the steak. Ike complimented the chef, but asked him to add a bit of lean ham to his vegetables, to bump up the flavor.

In November 1956, Eisenhower defeated Adlai Stevenson by an even larger margin than he had four years earlier. Ike celebrated his second inaugural on a Sunday with a small, private affair in the East Room. That night, David Eisenhower and Julie Nixon, both eight years old, met at the dinner of creamed chicken, rice, and peas; they would marry a dozen years later. A well-attended swearing-in and parade was held on Monday, and in a vigorous display Ike stood the entire time. But questions about his health continued to dog him.

A year later, the president was confined to bed by "a chill," which was in fact a mild stroke, forcing him to miss a state dinner for King Mohammed V of Morocco. Ike recovered and in September 1959 greeted the Soviet leader, Nikita Khrushchev, his wife, and their children. It was the first visit by a Soviet premier to the United States. At the state dinner in his honor, Khrushchev brought a food taster, and Mamie sat her guests at a large, E-shaped table for a feast of cold curried soup, roast turkey with cranberry sauce, sweet potatoes, and green salad. The Soviets reciprocated with dinner at their embassy: caviar and fish fillets (served with vodka); stuffed partridge (more vodka); a choice of perch soup or Ukrainian borscht (wine); flounder in champagne sauce and Caucasian shashlik—a meat and vegetable kebab—with asparagus (more wine); baked Alaska, macaroons, and fresh fruits (champagne).

After a tour of the United States, the premier returned to the U.S.S.R. convinced he had formed a personal bond with the president. But then the good vibrations popped like a soap bubble. On May 1, 1960, the Soviets shot down an American U-2 spy plane and captured its pilot, Francis Gary Powers. Eisenhower was angry and humiliated. Once again, U.S.–Soviet relations slid backward into a cold war.

THE CHEF FRANÇOIS RYSAVY RETIRED in 1957 and was replaced by Pedro Udo, a U.S. Navy cook from the Philippines. Ike liked Udo because he could bang together a meal competently and quickly, and Mamie liked him because he had a flair for cake decoration. But not everyone was a fan. When representatives of the incoming Kennedy administration inspected the kitchen in 1960, they noted that it was in the basement and the food "must be plenty cold" by the time it reached the First Family on the second floor. They described Udo's state dinner as "nothing short of *awful*." Mrs. Kennedy was already hatching plans to revolutionize the food and entertaining at the People's House, and clearly Udo wouldn't do.

Eisenhower was the first president limited to two terms by the Twenty-Second Amendment, but that hardly dampened his incorrigible cooking. In the First Family's kitchen, he flipped pancakes and basted chickens with homemade barbecue sauce on an electric rotisserie. On the third floor, he grilled meats in the glass-walled solarium, which filled with greasy smoke because it was ventilated only by a window. He set a charcoal grill on the White House roof and used it to roast corncobs in their husks. The press couldn't get enough of the cooking president and his homespun nostrums—"I find that self-rising flour makes my baking much easier," he'd say, like a TV housewife hawking Pillsbury. And when it came to pancakes, he'd observe, "I mix my batter at night and let it stand until morning." Asked about Eisenhower's obsession, a press aide sighed and said, "You can't stop the president from cooking."

— 12 —

JOHN F. KENNEDY

Camelot and Clam Chowder

THE THIRTY-FIFTH PRESIDENT
January 20, 1961–November 22, 1963

★

I. A Delicious Evening

What a thing to be in the Mouth of Fame.
—John Keats

The food is marvelous, the wines are delicious, there are cigarettes on the table, people are laughing, *laughing out loud,* telling stories, jokes, enjoying themselves, glad to be there." This is how the conductor Leonard Bernstein recalled the night of November 13, 1961, when President John F. Kennedy and First Lady Jacqueline B. Kennedy hosted Luis Muñoz Marín, the governor of Puerto Rico, at an "artist party" at the White House. "When the moment comes for you to greet the President and the First Lady, two ravishing people appear in the doorway who couldn't be more charming if they tried," Bernstein continued. "It was like a different world, utterly like a different planet."

He was describing one of the many extraordinary evenings the Kennedys hosted during their administration, which lasted two years and 306 days. They were a golden couple who ushered in a period of youthful, cosmopolitan vigor not seen at 1600 Pennsylvania Avenue since the Franklin and Teddy Roosevelts lived there.

The "Kennedy Style" was partly a reflection of the early 1960s—a jazzy answer to the nation's yearning for something new, polychromatic, and exciting after the gray deprivations of two world wars, the Depression, the Cold War, and Korea. But the zing of their parties was as much the result of design as it was the beneficiary of timing.

JFK was the front man: witty, rich, movie-star handsome, strategic thinking, and, at forty-three, the youngest elected president ever. Standing beside him was Jackie: a demure, elegant, quietly willful thirty-one-year-old with an unerring instinct for the drama, power, and sheer fun of entertaining at one of the greatest venues on earth. A Francophile, Mrs. Kennedy modeled her soirees on the court of Louis XIV—where the Sun King used a heady blend of politics, food, and culture to assert himself as Europe's leading seventeenth-century monarch—and Madame de Récamier, who ran a Parisian salon where politicians mingled with artists in the early nineteenth century. Jackie conjured a sense of magic, transforming the White House into a "showcase for great American art and artists." It was a form of seduction, and revolution, which not coincidentally burnished the family name, enabled the president's agenda, and redefined the role of First Lady.

Fine dining was central to her vision, and the Kennedys proved to be the greatest presidential epicures since Thomas Jefferson. (FDR would have qualified, but for Mrs. Nesbitt's gloomy fodder.) "Perhaps more than any other President and First Lady in history, John and Jacqueline Kennedy cared about food," wrote Letitia Baldrige, Jackie's social secretary. "They wanted to offer their guests great cuisine and *tous les plaisirs de la table*" (all of the pleasures of the table).

The November 1961 artists dinner began with "very good drinks" and "ashtrays everywhere just inviting you to poison yourself with cigarettes," Bernstein recalled. As 155 guests overflowed the State Dining Room to fill the Blue and Green Rooms, the air was electric. Some of America's leading musicians—Aaron Copland, Gian Carlo Menotti, the conductor Leopold Stokowski—mingled with government officials, diplomats, artists, industrialists, and wealthy patrons. A special, unnamed artist was scheduled to perform after dinner, and everyone buzzed with guesses about who it might be.

The Kennedys' accomplished French cook, René Verdon—whom Jackie had anointed the first "executive chef"—had prepared an exquisite banquet: sole mousse, paired with a smooth Chardonnay; fillet of beef Montfermeil (filets mignons served with a rich sauce of carrots, cauliflower, broccoli, asparagus, zucchini, and snow peas that had simmered for an entire day to concentrate the flavors), paired with a deep Cabernet Sauvignon; a pheasant breast galantine stuffed with herbs, bacon, and a mirepoix of carrots, celery, and shallots; a green salad with beets, asparagus, and watercress; and a dessert of champagne sorbet with chocolate truffles, fruit tarts, and madeleines.

After dinner, the crowd surged into the East Room. The lights dimmed, a hush fell, and then the mysterious guest emerged into the spotlight. The crowd audibly gasped once they recognized him: Pablo Casals, the reclusive, eighty-four-year-old Spanish maestro revered as "perhaps the greatest cellist who ever lived." He had not played at the White House since 1904, when he entertained Teddy Roosevelt. Initially, Casals had declined the Kennedys' invitation, claiming he didn't like to perform after eating. In truth, he resented America's support for the Spanish dictator Francisco Franco in the 1930s. But Jackie solved the impasse with a neat trick: rather than name Casals the guest of honor, the Kennedys hosted a state dinner for Governor Muñoz Marín of Puerto Rico, where Casals lived. This allowed the cellist to call his White House appearance a private rather than public recital.

Playing solo, he began with Mendelssohn's Trio No. 1 in D Minor, op. 49, then segued into pieces by Schumann and Couperin. The audience was transfixed for a solid hour. *The New York Times*'s music critic hailed it as a command performance: "The moment Senor Casals drew his bow across the strings, it was with the power and authority he always has had." Moved by the applause, Casals added a folk song from his native Catalonia, "The Song of the Birds," as a tip of the hat to his hosts. It was, said Mrs. Kennedy, "an unbelievable dream."

Bernstein was nearly overcome: "I've never seen so many happy artists in my life. It was a joy to watch it. And the feeling of hospitality, of warmth, of welcome, the taste with which everything was done. The goodness of everything; it was just *good*."

Much had changed since Bernstein was last in that room, a year earlier. In April 1960, he and his orchestra performed at a lugubrious state dinner hosted by the Eisenhowers for the president of Colombia. There were no cigarettes, cocktails, or bonhomie that night. "The food was bad, and the wine was bad," Bernstein recalled. The atmosphere "was very stiff. . . . Dinner was at a huge horseshoe shaped table at which seventy-five people or so were seated so that nobody could ever really talk to anybody. . . . By the time I got to play I was a wreck. And by the time I finished playing I was more of a wreck."

The day after the Kennedy party, Bernstein and his wife, Felicia, were packing to return to New York, when they received "a very secret little message" asking if they would be available for an intimate dinner at the White House. The conductor had pressing obligations and hardly knew JFK. But this was a once-in-a-lifetime opportunity. Changing plans, the Bernsteins joined the Kennedys and the Bradens—Joan was a close friend of Jackie's, and Tom was a former CIA agent and the author of *Eight Is Enough,* which spawned the TV series—for dinner in the small dining room on the mansion's second floor.

"You dine on Abraham Lincoln's china with Madison's spoons," Bernstein marveled. "The furniture is very beautiful. Everything in it is presidential and old."

Later, the group retired to the Oval Room (the president's drawing room, not the office), where JFK presided from his rocking chair, smoking cigars and chatting "in great high spirits," Bernstein said. "It became the sort of place that you were most happy to be in the world." The couples laughed and traded gossip and jokes, as if time stretched to infinity. "It was all so familiar and familial," Bernstein recalled. "I couldn't tell you *one* thing we talked about the whole night; it was just so delicious."

While it was an exceptional evening for the Bernsteins, such moments were a regular feature of the Kennedy years. They were a welcome diversion from race riots and Cold War missiles, and, as Jackie saw it, serving good food in a congenial setting was simply good politics. "The French know this," she said in a lilting voice, which camouflaged her incisive intelligence. "If you put busy men in an attractive atmosphere where the surroundings are comfortable, the food is good, you relax, you unwind, there's some stimulating conversation. . . . [It's] part of the art of living in Washington."

As the clock reached 1:00 a.m., Bernstein grew anxious for the president, who usually left social gatherings by 10:00. "Don't worry about it," Jackie said, shrugging. "If he wants to stay up, let him stay up. He hasn't done this in ages."

When Bernstein gave this account to the journalist Nelson Aldrich Jr. as part of an oral history, he savored those intimate hours in the Kennedys' inner sanctum even more than the remarkable dinner with Casals. "It was really divine, and I suppose the quality about it that made it so specially touching was the suddenness, the unexpectedness, the improvised quality of the evening. We were so delighted to have been picked . . . to stay on and have dinner privately. It was really like . . . being touched by a hand from beyond, chosen for that wonderful moment."

Two years later, almost to the day, JFK was assassinated in Dallas. In an instant, the bright radiance of the Kennedy Style was reduced to the subdued, elegiac flicker of the "eternal flame" at his grave site in Arlington National Cemetery.

Speaking to the political historian Theodore H. White, Jackie said she was "ashamed" that she was unable to pinpoint a grand historical allusion to her husband's presidency. Instead, she found herself "obsessed" with a song from the Broadway musical *Camelot,* written by Frederick Loewe and Alan Jay Lerner, a college friend of Jack's. Before going to sleep, she said, Kennedy would often listen to the cast album. His favorite lines came at the end of the record:

Don't let it be forgot
That once there was a spot
For one brief shining moment that was known as Camelot.

White published a tribute in *Life,* "For President Kennedy: An Epilogue," that established Camelot as a metaphor that has defined JFK's presidency ever since.

"We never really knew how different life was then until it was over," Bernstein mused. "The murder in Dallas was . . . the worst experience of my life. . . . For thinking people and working artists, I had the feeling that at that moment everybody became aware of how excited and happy they had been. . . . I don't think . . . we all realized to what an extent America had a new image and a new promise for the artist until he was killed. Then it dawned on us like a very bleak dawn. And I must say it's never been the same since. . . . I can't get over it. I don't think anybody can."

II. *Jack and Jackie*

One night in May 1951, the journalist Charles Bartlett and his wife, Martha, invited their friend Jack Kennedy, a six-foot tall, 150 pound, thirty-three-year-old bachelor congressman from Massachusetts, to dinner. It was a small party for eight guests at their brick row house in Georgetown. As they progressed from cocktails to chicken casserole to a game of charades, Jack was intrigued by a dark-haired, sloe-eyed twenty-one-year-old named Jacqueline Bouvier. "Jackie," as her friends called her, was raised in Manhattan, Long Island, and Virginia. The daughter of a socialite mother and the dissolute Wall Street banker "Black Jack" Bouvier, Jackie was Debutante of the Year in 1947 and schooled at Miss Porter's, Vassar, in Paris, and at George Washington University, where she earned a degree in French literature. In 1951, she was working as an inquiring photographer for the Washington *Times Herald,* when the Bartletts invited her to dinner.

Like Jack, Jackie was raised Catholic and had a mischievous sense of humor. He was smitten. "I've never met anyone like her," he told a friend. The feeling was mutual. In September 1953, the Kennedys were married in Newport, Rhode Island. A reception for twelve hundred was held at Hammersmith Farm, the estate of Jackie's stepfather, Hugh D. Auchincloss. News of the wedding hit the front page of *The New York Times.*

What the newlyweds didn't know was that the Bartlett dinner was a setup engineered by Jack's father, Joseph "Joe" Kennedy, to put Jacqueline Bouvier in his son's line of sight. It was a "honey trap," as spies say. A Midas-like businessman and ambassador to England, Joe Kennedy had a tentacular reach and big plans for his second-born son. (His oldest, Joseph Jr., had been killed in World War II.) He felt it was time for Jack to grow up, get married, and kick his political career into high gear. As usual, Joe Kennedy got his way.

After defeating Richard M. Nixon by just 112,803 votes, the narrowest margin in the twentieth century, John F. Kennedy was sworn in on January 20, 1961. At home, racial strife was spilling into street violence. In Europe, the Cold War deepened as the Soviet premier, Nikita Khrushchev, built the Berlin Wall.

The day before JFK's inauguration a nor'easter ripped through Washington, dropped the temperature to twenty degrees, and buried the city in eight inches of snow. But the National Guard, the sanitation department, and seventeen hundred Boy Scouts shoveled the streets clear, and the celebrations that night sizzled. Frank Sinatra headlined a preinaugural ball—featuring the comic Milton Berle, actors Sidney Poitier and Ethel Merman and Laurence Olivier, the musicians Harry Belafonte and Ella Fitzgerald, and Gene Kelly doing an Irish jig—which raised some $2 million dollars to retire Kennedy's campaign costs. They rocked until 1:30 in the morning, when Jackie went to bed and Jack slipped off to a second ball, hosted by his father. Kennedy didn't sleep until 3:30. Nevertheless, he was red-cheeked and energetic at his inauguration the next day.

John F. Kennedy was the first chief executive born in the twentieth century, and when he replaced the seventy-year-old Eisenhower—the oldest president in history at that point—the symbolism was clear: JFK was the embodiment of a new era. He gave one of the shortest (thirteen minutes) and most eloquent inauguration speeches ever. Emphasizing the need for collective sacrifice and action, he intoned in his distinctive Brahmin brogue: "And so, my fellow Americans, ask not what your country can do for you; ask what you can do for your country."

Late that night, still high on adrenaline, Kennedy arrived at the home of the journalist Joseph Alsop, who offered him a glass of champagne and a bowl of terrapin soup. JFK "took the wine but needed no more than a glance to reject what had formerly been the greatest delicacy of the United States," Alsop recalled. "It hardly mattered. I soon observed that what he really wanted was one last cup of unadulterated admiration, and the people crowded around gave him that cup freely, filled to the brim."

•   •   •

WASTING NO TIME, the Kennedys hosted their first official party on January 29, a dinner for cabinet members, congressmen, appointees, fundraisers, and a few journalists. When the social secretary, Letitia Baldrige—who had been a friend of Jackie's at Miss Porter's, a girl's boarding school in Connecticut—asked what kind of beverages to serve, the Usher's Office informed her that the Eisenhowers served one bowl of fruit punch and one bowl of mildly spiked punch at their parties. If this was a warning from the Old Guard, the tyros ignored it.

Though he was not a big drinker, President Kennedy told the social secretary, "I want a good party." With that, Baldrige ordered plenty of "quality liquor," circulated waiters with trays of mixed drinks, and had the Marine Band play Cole Porter tunes. "The party was a smash," she noted with satisfaction. But when the Woman's Christian Temperance Union heard that booze was served, protests erupted across the country. "Liquor in the White House!" gasped headlines.

Kennedy was furious. "What did you do to me?" he thundered. "Isn't this job difficult enough without you alienating an entire section of America?" Baldrige felt she'd had her "timbers shivered." The Kennedys reverted to an Eisenhowerian drinks program for a while, and when they quietly resumed serving cocktails, no one noticed. A year and many parties later, JFK thanked Baldrige for the smashing cabinet party, saying it was "the greatest thing that's ever been done for White House entertaining."

The First Lady, meanwhile, had set an ambitious goal: to make the Executive Mansion a magnet for the most interesting and powerful people in the world. To do so, she would need to overhaul the building's decor and reconceive it as a backdrop—a stage set, really—for a new kind of presidential entertaining. It helped that she had an eye, connections, and money.

Guided by a vision of the White House as a showcase for the best of American culture and the locus of global power, Mrs. Kennedy used a palette of bold primary colors—yellow, red, blue—to update the rooms, decorated them with fine nineteenth-century antiques, and hung them with museum-quality paintings. She created the new position of White House curator, hired leading architects and designers, established a private fundraising group to solicit art, antiques, and donations from the public, and courted the media. "Everything in the White House must have a reason for being there. It would be sacrilege to 'redecorate' it—a word I hate," Jackie said. "It must be restored . . . that is a question of scholarship."

Though she could be shy, Jackie made sure her work was publicized. In February 1962, she led a television crew on a tour through the refurbished People's House. The resulting TV documentary (which aired on CBS and NBC, and later on ABC) garnered eighty million viewers, earned Jackie an honorary Emmy Award, and made her beloved by the American public. She had put the Kennedy White House on the pop-cultural-political map in a new way.

To brighten the lugubrious State Dining Room, the First Lady had the dark green walls repainted in two tones of white, to highlight its craftsmanship. She replaced Mamie Eisenhower's large U- or E-shaped tables with small round tables, which nearly doubled the number of guests while making conversation more intimate. To speed things up, reduce food waste, and leave more time for mingling and entertainment after state dinners, she reduced the traditional five-course meals to four courses (fish or soup, entrée, salad and cheese, dessert). And she swapped the large urns of flowers that had once blocked views with smaller, more natural flower arrangements inspired by Flemish still lifes, "the opposite of what you'd find in a funeral home," she slyly noted.

To complete her vision, Mrs. Kennedy went in search of a chef worthy of the President's House. Her first choice was Bui Van Han, the Tonkinese chef at the French embassy in London. Said to be one of the world's greatest, if least known, gastronomes, Bui produced refined fare such as *côtelettes de pigeon à l'espagnole* and *paupiette de sole à la Richelieu*. Much to the relief of the French ambassador, Bui declined the offer.

Undaunted, Mrs. Kennedy consulted her father-in-law, who knew his way around America's finest restaurants. One of his favorites was La Caravelle, a temple of haute cuisine in New York. Named after the tri-masted vessels Christopher Columbus sailed to the New World, the restaurant was in the Shoreham Hotel on West Fifty-Fifth Street. There, the chef Roger Fessaguet, who had worked at Le Pavillon, Manhattan's original French restaurant, used roast duck and pike quenelles to lure such luminaries as Salvador Dalí, Walter Cronkite, and Marlene Dietrich. JFK's favorite dishes there were the vichyssoise (a cold creamy leek and potato soup) and the chicken in champagne sauce, which he'd order to take out and reheat on the family plane as he campaigned across the country.

As legend has it, Fessaguet suggested she hire one of his kitchen lieutenants. But according to someone who was there, this narrative is only partly correct. "I worked at Le Pavillon and Fessaguet recommended me to the Kennedys," Jacques Pépin, the cookbook author and TV chef, told me. Before moving to the States, Pépin worked as the personal chef for President Charles de Gaulle at the Élysée Palace. "But in France the president's chef is not treated as anything special," he said, laughing. "He's at the bottom of the social scale. It's a lot of hard work and no recognition."

Pépin was honored by the Kennedys' offer, but he and the chef Pierre Franey had already been hired by Howard Johnson Sr., founder of the eponymous chain of roadside eateries. "I liked John Kennedy," Pépin said, "but I didn't want to move to Washington. And I didn't realize *at all* the potential of the job." He declined Mrs. Kennedy's offer, with "no regrets," and recommended his roommate, a chef at the Essex House hotel named René Verdon.

Solidly built, with a round face, a rim of dark hair under a white toque, cheerful eyes, and a gap-toothed smile, Verdon was a French chef from central casting. He agreed to join the Kennedys and spent two weeks at La Caravelle learning their favorite dishes. On April 5, 1961, Verdon served a lunch for the British prime minister, Harold Macmillan, and sixteen guests at the White House. The menu included trout in Chablis and *sauce Vincent;* beef au jus; artichoke bottoms *Beaucaire;* and a dessert of meringue shells filled with chocolate and raspberries that he called *désir d'Avril* (April Desire). The meal was a hit.

"There's nothing like French cooking to promote good Anglo-American relations," Craig Claiborne wrote in *The New York Times.* Verdon was hired at a salary of $10,000 a year plus room and board. It marked a turning point in American food history, the dawn of a gilded age of White House cookery.

Verdon was hardworking, detail oriented, and even-tempered. He used seasonal food, grew vegetables on the roof, planted herbs in the East Garden, and hired the skilled pastry chef Ferdinand Louvat. "I cooked everything fresh," Verdon said. "If the ingredients are superb, then the cooking can be, and must be, simple." This was the kind of White House food Mrs. Kennedy had dreamed of, and soon *la Maison Blanche* gained a reputation for serving some of the finest meals in town, or anywhere.

JACKIE KENNEDY WAS in sync with a subtle shift in the zeitgeist. Just as she hired Verdon, Americans were beginning to spend more time and money at restaurants, travel abroad, buy cookware, and try new recipes at home. TV stations across the country aired cooking shows—from a housewife demonstrating "how to make average food appetizing" in Kentucky to the British restaurateur Dione Lucas demonstrating French technique in New York.

In October 1961, Alfred A. Knopf published *Mastering the Art of French Cooking* by Julia Child and her French friends Simone "Simca" Beck and Louisette Bertholle. The cookbook sold well, and by 1963 Mrs. Child was hosting *The French Chef* on WGBH, Boston's public television station. At a time when Big Food hawked time-saving meals in a can, Jell-O salads, and Sanka to "harried housewives" who allegedly did not like to cook, Julia's message was counterintuitive: "Nothing is too much trouble if it turns out the way it should. Good results require that one take time and care." She struck a nerve. "Julia," as everyone called her, was the first celebrity TV cook to break into the mainstream. She appeared on the cover of *Time* in 1966, won her first Emmy that same year, and helped launch the American Food Revolution.

Julia beamed into people's kitchens to demystify recipes and to explain what shallots were and how to sharpen a knife, drink wine, eat cheese, "cook fearlessly," and, above all, "have fun!" This was as much a life philosophy as it was an approach to cooking, and the message empowered millions, particularly women. Looking back, Julia noted, "I was lucky the Kennedys were in the White House and Jackie hired French chef René Verdon. Suddenly everyone was interested in French cuisine."

One of Verdon's sous-chefs was a man named Julius Spessot. A native of Istria, Italy, Spessot "had an eighth-grade education. No money, no nothing," his widow, Luisa, told me. But he could cook. Spessot had learned to carve elaborate ice sculptures on an Italian ocean liner, and in 1954 he jumped ship in New York and eventually landed at the Essex House, where he worked for René Verdon. When the Kennedys hired Verdon in 1961, he brought Spessot along.

Spessot assisted Verdon at large banquets and cooked in the Kennedys' private quarters, delighting JFK with his pasta with lobster sauce. "Julius, you made my day!" Kennedy said, beaming. The president was equally enamored of his rich *zuppa inglese,* or "English soup," a dessert inspired by trifle: layers of sponge cake and custard topped with fruit and whipped cream. "Don't you dare make that again," Jackie warned, "he liked it *too* much. People don't want a pig as president."

Yet the glamorous job at the White House was a hardship. Spessot earned $5,700 in 1961 and $8,100 in 1962—paid by checks, Luisa said, that were issued by Joe Kennedy, whose $1 billion fortune underwrote JFK's $10 million trust fund (about $60 million today). While JFK used his $50,000 government expense account for official entertaining, and donated his $100,000 salary to charity, he paid for private entertaining out of his (or his father's) pocket. The Spessots were not so lucky.

"I tried to save, but we were poor and living in a tiny apartment in Virginia," Luisa recalled. One compensation was the fruits, vegetables, and meat that purveyors gifted Julius. "He'd come home with all these bags of food, and sometimes cash," Luisa said, laughing. "It wasn't much, maybe $50 a week, but it was a big help." The pastry chef Ferdinand Louvat gave Spessot "bags of goodies"—leftover cakes, cookies, and ice cream, Luisa said. The White House was a good experience, she added. "If they had paid more, we would have stayed. But we couldn't do it." Julius quit in 1963 and built an airline catering company in New York. He died in 2003, and his three children became middle-class professionals. His was a classic immigrant tale, and in that the Spessots had more in common with the Kennedys than they realized.

IT WAS FOOD—a *lack* of food—that uprooted both of JFK's great-grandfathers from Ireland and sent them to the New World in search of something to eat. After the potato famine of 1840, Thomas Fitzgerald, from County Limerick, and Patrick Kennedy, of County Wexford, landed in Boston. They flourished in business and politics and were fierce rivals. In a courtship worthy of *Romeo and Juliet,* their grandchildren Rose Fitzgerald and Joe Kennedy married against their wishes.

Rose and Joe raised their nine children in Bronxville, New York, and in Brookline and Hyannis Port, Massachusetts, and fed them hearty New England standards: cod, chowder, baked beans, corn muffins, hot dogs, ice cream. Jack was handsome, athletic, slim, beset by a bad back, and not especially interested in food. His "tastes are distressingly normal—plain food—children's food—good food," Jackie wrote. "He likes anything."

For breakfast JFK stuck to a routine of orange juice, boiled or poached eggs, bacon, toast with marmalade, and coffee with milk. At lunch he was known as a "soup, sandwich and fruit" man. At dinner he favored lamb chops, steak, chicken, or turkey and mashed potatoes. Joe Kennedy sometimes flew fresh crabmeat from Joe's Stone Crab in Miami to the White House aboard his plane. For dessert Jack liked chocolate, or the exotically flavored ice creams from Louis Sherry, on whose board Joe sat.

President Kennedy's favorite meal was a bowl of Boston clam chowder. In his recipe, René Verdon used two pounds of littleneck clams, potatoes, butter, milk, salt pork, onions, and whipping cream. It made a rich and delicious brew. At a meeting with the Canadian prime minister, Lester B. Pearson, JFK served bowls of the chowder for lunch. Pearson enjoyed it so much he asked for the recipe. On the second day, the two again ordered chowder. And when they ordered it again on the third day, Verdon was amazed. "I would like to think [the chowder] played a small part in enhancing U.S./Canada relations," Baldrige wrote.

JACKIE KENNEDY "was no less attentive [to family meals] than for a state dinner," Verdon noted. "She preferred simple meals prepared with the freshest seasonal ingredients." She took her breakfast—orange juice, toast with honey, and coffee with skim milk—on a tray in bed, where she would read the paper and play with her children, Caroline and John. Her lunch was a cup of broth and a slim sandwich, though she sometimes indulged in a grilled cheese. Her favorite dinner was cold poached salmon, followed by lamb with potatoes, string beans, and ice cream.

Jackie kept her weight at exactly 120 pounds. Like many women of her era, she smoked cigarettes, usually filtered L&Ms, which curbed her appetite. If she gained two extra pounds, she would fast for a day, increase her exercise time, and resort to a fruit-only diet.

Kennedy was attuned to the optics of his presidency. He nixed Verdon's use of French on his menus and highlighted popular California wines from Inglenook, Almaden, and Wente Brothers at public functions. But at private dinners he poured distinguished first-growth Bordeaux from France, including Château Margaux or Château Haut-Brion.

III. *Jackie Kennedy's Soft Power*

> *To entertain is to give of oneself. It's a kindness.*
> —Letitia Baldrige, *In the Kennedy Style*

Jacqueline Kennedy felt at home in France. Her father's family, the Bouviers, originated in Provence (the family name translates as "cowherds," betraying humble roots). She studied in Paris during college and spoke the language beautifully. As a girl, she had strolled down the long, refractive Hall of Mirrors in the Versailles Palace and wondered what it would have been like in the court of the Sun King. She came close to finding out.

June 1, 1961, was the last day of a quick diplomatic visit to France. President Kennedy was there to persuade President Charles de Gaulle not to develop nuclear weapons and to rely on the United States against the Soviets. It did not go well. De Gaulle was leery of American meddling and determined to restore French pride after the losses of World War II, the Suez crisis, and Indochina (Vietnam). But even the "irritating . . . vain . . . impossible to please" de Gaulle (as JFK's advisers called him) was not immune to the charms of the American First Lady.

Jacqueline Kennedy embodied what is now called soft power, the eye-dazzling, emotionally connective aspect of American culture associated with Hollywood, rock 'n' roll, bold visual arts, theater, and literature (if not yet food and wine). It is a form of seductive propaganda that can be as persuasive as military "hard power." De Gaulle was awed by her knowledge of French history, and his public was thrilled by her chic ensembles, especially her pillbox hats. Kennedy deadpanned, "I am the man who accompanied Jacqueline Kennedy to Paris, and I have enjoyed it."

On their last night, the Kennedys were feted in the Hall of Mirrors at Versailles, which had been transformed into an eighteenth-century performance space. A long rectangular table draped in white lace was illuminated by tall white tapers that were reflected by the mirrors, gleaming silver, and sparkling crystal. Waiters materialized from behind painted screens that hid ovens, coolers, and staging tables. The sublime six-course dinner was paired with three beautiful wines and a champagne. Afterward, musicians dressed in period costume led the group by candlelight down a darkened hallway to a jewel-like theater, where, on a stage lit by torches, dancers performed a ballet originally commissioned by Louis XV.

The evening "was magic," recalled Letitia Baldrige. "The whole thing was a logistical miracle, carried off with . . . style and panache." Jackie agreed. Back in Washington, she wondered if she could conjure a similarly magical night.

It so happened that General Ayub Khan, the president of Pakistan, was scheduled for a state dinner on July 11. Pakistan was an important ally, but relations with America had grown frosty. And JFK, still smarting from the Bay of Pigs fiasco in April, needed a diplomatic win.

Jackie knew just the spot for her coup de théâtre: Mount Vernon, George Washington's Virginia plantation. It was appropriate, she said, because Khan was a former general who would appreciate the historical allusion to Washington. The fact that a state dinner had never been held outside the White House didn't bother her. Nor did it matter that Mount Vernon was remote, had last hosted an official function in 1926, and had minimal electricity, kitchen facilities, and restrooms. And when the Pakistanis worried that it would be seen as a snub that their dinner was not being held at the White House, the State Department scrambled to convince them that Mount Vernon was a special site that would generate even more favorable press.

The dinner was just a month away, which left barely enough time to design a menu, curate the guest list, send invitations, arrange entertainment, and take care of all the details of such an ambitious undertaking. While her staff worried about the "insurmountable" problems, Jackie saw "possibilities." She had "a total mastery of detail—endless, endless detail," the chief usher, J. B. West, said.

To accommodate 132 guests, a large blue-and-yellow tent was erected on the lawn, and chairs, tables, linens, and staff were trucked to the property. Jackie wanted Verdon to pay homage to Martha Washington's food, but his dishes had to be cooked at the White House, transported to Mount Vernon, and reheated. Further, Khan was Muslim and did not consume pork or alcohol.

The chef welcomed the challenge. But as the minutes ticked down to party time, the mood tightened. Portable toilets set in a thicket of poison ivy were moved, as were hulking army trucks that blocked the tent. Mosquitoes held "their own state dinner" on the sweaty workmen, Baldrige wrote, and were sprayed with insecticide. But when a breeze wafted the poisonous gas toward Verdon's food, he threatened to quit and return to France. The staff teetered on the edge of nervous collapse.

At such moments, Mrs. Kennedy smiled and in "a quiet little phrase of iron," Baldrige recalled, insisted, "Of *course* it can be done."

Then the flotilla arrived. President Kennedy had captained the patrol-torpedo boat PT-109 during World War II and suggested transporting guests to Mount Vernon by water. Two presidential yachts, a navy yacht, and a PT boat (equipped with sweaters and headscarves, to keep bodies warm and hairdos in place) sailed from Washington down the Potomac to George Washington's pier. It added to the magic of the evening.

While General Khan and his daughter, Begum Nasim Akhtar Aurang-zeb, drank nonalcoholic orange drinks, the Americans sipped bourbon mint juleps from silver cups, as Washington had done. An army unit dressed in Continental army uniforms reenacted a 1776 military drill with fife, drums, and the firing of muskets. Just before the eight o'clock dinner, Kennedy walked Khan through the garden, alone, to discuss two top secret operations. The CIA had been flying U-2 spy planes from Pakistan over China to monitor its nuclear weapons program; the agency was also parachuting trained insurgents and weapons into Tibet. But when Kennedy gave India, Pakistan's blood enemy, $1 billion in aid, Khan was furious and suspended the Tibetan airdrops. That night at Mount Vernon, JFK's charm and Jackie's spectacular mise-en-scène convinced Khan to resume the Tibetan flights. (The CIA's operations helped spur China's invasion of India in 1962, and the geopolitical chess match in Asia that continues today.)

The Kennedy men wore tuxedos, General Khan wore a white dinner jacket with black tuxedo pants, and his daughter wore a white satin sari. Jackie dressed in a sleeveless gown of white organza and lace with a chartreuse silk sash, designed by Oleg Cassini. "As they walked with their escorts across the lawn from the veranda, the women looked from a distance like pale butterflies. A light breeze fluttered the pastel organza, chiffon, and lace of their dresses," Baldrige wrote. "Candlelight flashed off diamond earrings and necklaces, and glimmered on the crystal goblets and vermeil flatware. Even a group of fireflies appeared to add their special glow."

Under the tent, Verdon's dinner included crabmeat and avocado mimosa, followed by *poulet chasseur* (chicken breasts in a tomato mushroom sauce) and *couronne de riz Clamart* (rice baked with vegetables and Parmesan cheese); dessert was *framboises à la crème chantilly* (raspberries topped with sugar and whipped cream) and *petits fours secs* (palmier cookies dipped in melted chocolate). Raising a flute of Moët & Chandon Impérial Brut champagne, Kennedy toasted Khan as the George Washington of Pakistan. After dinner, the group followed a path lit by pungent citronella (anti-mosquito) candles to a forest grove. There, musicians from the National Symphony Orchestra played Morton Gould, Mozart, Debussy, and Gershwin.

It was a flawless, unprecedented, and so far unrepeated evening.

"Jackie wanted to do Versailles in America," said Oleg Cassini. "No one suspected then, not even the president, that . . . there was nobody to touch Jackie using style as a political tool."

THE KENNEDYS' MOST CELEBRATED White House party was held on April 29, 1962, which Letitia Baldrige referred to as the "Brains Dinner."

Hearing this, Verdon was horrified. *"Non, non, Mademoiselle,* we are not serving brains for dinner!" he objected. The social secretary laughed and assured the chef that the Kennedys had *invited* "brains" and were not planning to *eat* them.

The brains in question were forty-nine Nobel Prize winners—an extraordinary group that included Robert Frost, Linus Pauling, Pearl Buck, Katherine Anne Porter, John Dos Passos, J. Robert Oppenheimer, James Baldwin, and John Glenn. Hardly the frazzled academics the staff had imagined, the brains proved to be a sophisticated, thirsty, high-spirited group.

As the Marine Band played "Hail to the Chief," the Kennedys descended the Grand Staircase to the Entrance Hall. Tan from a Palm Beach vacation, "Jack and Jackie actually *shimmered,*" observed the novelist William Styron. "You would have had to be abnormal, perhaps psychotic, to be immune to their dumbfounding appeal. . . . [A] number of the guests . . . appeared so affected by the glamour that their eyes took on a goofy, catatonic gaze."

Verdon created a seafood mousse appetizer decorated with morel mushrooms and lobster that he called *La Couronne de l'Élu Victoria* (Crowns of Victory), to honor the laureates. That was followed by beef Wellington (beef tenderloin encased in puff pastry and named after the Duke of Wellington, who defeated Napoleon at Waterloo), served with *duxelles* (shallots, mushrooms, and foie gras) and a rich Madeira sauce; *pommes de terre chipp* (handmade potato chips); *fonds d'artichauts favorite* (artichokes in a cream sauce with truffles); and a dessert of *bombe caribienne* (Tahitian vanilla ice cream mixed with pineapple, rum, coconut milk, and cinnamon).

Then an air force band strummed lively tunes and herded the guests toward the East Room for the night's entertainment. But the chemist Linus Pauling started to waltz across the floor, and soon all the brains were whirling around. When they were finally seated, the actor Fredric March read from an unpublished novel by Ernest Hemingway, whose widow, Mary Hemingway, was in the room. Then he read a speech by General George C. Marshall, who had won a Nobel for the Marshall Plan; his widow was also there. With impeccable timing, JFK quipped, "I think this is the most extraordinary collection of talent, of human knowledge, that has ever been gathered together at the White House—with the possible exception of when Thomas Jefferson dined alone." The laureates roared, and Kennedy's words passed into legend.

Two weeks later, the Kennedys' trip to Paris paid spectacular dividends in Washington when the First Lady orchestrated a dinner in honor of André Malraux, the French minister of cultural affairs and her "intellectual crush." As he toured her through the Impressionist paintings in Paris, they shared a naughty sense of humor. "What did you do before you married Jack Kennedy?" Malraux asked. *"J'ai été pucelle"* (I was a little virgin), she replied.

The guest list for the Malraux party included painters like Franz Kline and Mark Rothko; writers like Saul Bellow and Tennessee Williams; the film director Elia Kazan, the actress Julie Harris, and the choreographer George Balanchine. But the star was Charles Lindbergh, the first man to fly transatlantic solo from New York to Paris aboard the *Spirit of St. Louis,* in 1927. After the murder of their son and criticism of his pro-Fascist views, Lindbergh and his wife, Anne Morrow Lindbergh, had retreated into seclusion. But JFK wondered, "Where are the . . . really great Americans, like Charles Lindbergh?" When the pilot was traced to an unlisted phone number, he was gratified by the invitation. And when he appeared at the White House, guests wept at seeing their childhood hero in the flesh.

At dinner, Malraux whispered to Jackie that he had persuaded France to lend the *Mona Lisa* to the United States. Leonardo's masterpiece had not left the Louvre in four hundred years and was priceless, but de Gaulle recognized the controversial loan as a chance to mend fences with America, and the deal was done.

It was almost undone when Soviet nuclear missiles were discovered in Cuba. After a tense standoff, a détente was secretly brokered over meals in Washington: the terms were proposed at a lunch of escargots at the Occidental restaurant on Pennsylvania Avenue; agreed to with cups of black coffee at the Statler Coffee Shop; and finalized over a Chinese dinner at the back of the Yenching Palace on Connecticut Avenue. As a result, Khrushchev agreed to remove his missiles from Cuba and Kennedy withdrew U.S. missiles from Turkey.

With nuclear Armageddon averted, the *Mona Lisa* was unveiled at the National Gallery on January 8, 1963. "Mona Mania" drew more than a million visitors and delivered a publicity bonanza for the White House.

The event heralded a golden interlude, observed the historian Arthur M. Schlesinger Jr., during which the nation was inspired by the First Lady to become a better version of itself. "The things people had once held against her—the unconventional beauty, the un-American elegance, the taste for French clothes and French food—were suddenly no longer liabilities but assets," he wrote. Jackie "represented . . . a suggestion that America was not to be trapped forever in the bourgeois ideal," but could reach for "a dream of civilization and beauty."

IV. The Hell of a Glittering World

Jacqueline Kennedy rarely discussed her marriage in public, but she was perceptive about its benefits and traps. In a 1953 letter to her confidant, the Catholic priest Father Joseph Leonard, she wrote, "Maybe I'm just dazzled and picture myself in a glittering world of crowned heads and Men of Destiny—and not just a sad little housewife. . . . That world can be very glamorous from the outside—but if you're in it—and you're lonely—it could be a Hell."

Though she is considered America's most elegant, sphinxlike First Lady, Jacqueline Kennedy was at heart a bookish introvert. She enjoyed the White House, but occasionally shirked her duties to spend time reading, riding horses, playing tennis, traveling, or shopping. (Her mother-in-law, Rose Kennedy, or Second Lady, Lady Bird Johnson, would substitute as JFK's hostess.) The real sphinx in the marriage was JFK.

Charles Bartlett, who introduced the Kennedys, was struck by the way Jack used his great charm to pull people into his orbit, only to keep them at a distance, revealing just parts of himself. "No one ever knew John Kennedy," Bartlett said, "not all of him." Jackie knew him best, and she was painfully aware of his infidelities.

His liaisons spanned the gamut from the nineteen-year-old White House intern Mimi Beardsley to married friends like Mary Pinchot Meyer, gauzy celebrities like Marilyn Monroe, and shadier sirens like Judith Campbell Exner, the mistress of the mafia boss Sam Giancana. Jack was "like my father in a way—loves the chase and is bored with the conquest—and once married needs proof he's still attractive, so flirts with other women and resents you," Jackie confided. "I saw how that nearly killed Mummy."

JFK liked to celebrate his birthday with splash-out parties—most famously in 1962, when he turned forty-five and Marilyn Monroe suggestively purred, "Happy biiiirthday, Mis-terr Pres-i-dennt," at a fundraiser in Madison Square Garden. There was no subtext: her sex appeal was on full display, as was his.

A year later, on May 29, 1963, Jackie arranged for a birthday dinner cruise aboard the presidential yacht *Sequoia*. A couple dozen friends and family members—including Bobby and Ethel Kennedy, Sargent and Eunice Shriver, the English actor David Niven, the Rat Packer Peter Lawford and his wife, Patricia Kennedy, and the Bradlees—were aboard. It had been a rough week: Kennedy had threatened to send troops to integrate the University of Alabama, angering the right; then he refused to withdraw from Vietnam, angering the left. He needed to unwind.

At eight o'clock the *Sequoia* cruised down the Potomac. After cocktails on the fantail, dinner was served in the saloon—crabmeat *ravigote,* noodle casserole, asparagus hollandaise, roast fillet of beef, and a dessert called *bombe président sauce chocolat,* washed down with bottles of 1955 Dom Pérignon. A three-piece band played for guests in "festive yachting clothes," who roasted JFK with gifts, such as a pair of boxing gloves for battling Congress.

The night turned sultry, with thunder, lightning, and rain, and soon everyone was soaked. While he was horsing around, Ted Kennedy's pant leg was ripped off, leaving him with "white underpants on the port side flashing," Niven reported. The band picked up the tempo, and soon "they were doing the twist, the cha-cha, and everything in between," recalled the Secret Service agent Clint Hill. "It was wild. I don't think I had ever seen the president and Mrs. Kennedy having more fun. Nobody wanted the night to end." Despite the presence of his wife and one of his mistresses (Mary Meyer), Kennedy pursued Tony Bradlee, wife of his friend Ben Bradlee, of *Newsweek* and the future editor of *The Washington Post.* "It was a pretty strenuous attack . . . his hands wandered," Tony recalled. She felt "kind of flattered, but appalled, too." The next day, the Kennedys and Bradlees helicoptered to Camp David for an afternoon of golf and swimming. They pretended nothing had happened, and life went on.

BUT SOMETHING *HAD* CHANGED. That summer of 1963 the Kennedys' marriage seemed to reach an equilibrium. Jackie found their union was "never more intense and more complete," Schlesinger wrote. "It turned out to be the time of the greatest happiness."

She was pregnant with a boy, Patrick Bouvier Kennedy. But he was born prematurely, and when he died, Jack wept and draped himself over the small coffin. Overcome, Jackie fled to Greece to join her sister Lee aboard Aristotle Onassis's yacht. After a two-week retreat, she returned Stateside, to the tumultuous summer of 1963. Americans were demanding tax cuts. The Vietnam War was escalating. And on August 28, Martin Luther King Jr. delivered his "I Have a Dream" speech.

Just before Thanksgiving, the Kennedys boarded Air Force One for a campaign swing through Texas. On November 22, JFK had his usual breakfast—two boiled eggs, toast with marmalade, orange juice, coffee— and gave a speech in Fort Worth. Then he and Jackie flew to Dallas, where they climbed aboard a Lincoln convertible with Governor and Mrs. John Connally. At 12:30 the motorcade drove slowly toward a rally, surrounded by cheering crowds. Nellie Connally beamed and said, "Mr. President, you can't say Dallas doesn't love you."

"No, you certainly can't," Kennedy replied.

As the limousine came abreast of the Texas School Book Depository, Jackie, dressed in a pink coat and matching pillbox hat, and Jack, dressed in a gray suit, smiled brightly and waved.

= 13 =

LYNDON B. JOHNSON

How Barbecue Led to Diplomacy
and Chili Led to Civil Rights

THE THIRTY-SIXTH PRESIDENT
November 22, 1963–January 20, 1969

★

I. At the Ranch: Rare, Medium, and Well-Done Policy

Ninety-eight minutes after President Kennedy was shot by Lee Harvey Oswald, Vice President Lyndon B. Johnson was sworn in as his replacement aboard Air Force One in Dallas. Addressing a joint session of Congress five days later, Johnson intoned, "An assassin's bullet has thrust upon me the awesome burden of the presidency." And then he began to stitch together some of the most meaningful legislation of the twentieth century, much of which revolved around nutrition and race, two subjects that have been tightly braided throughout American history.

The United States emerged from World War II as something new: the first "superpower." But the stark reality was that by 1962 fifty million Americans, more than a quarter of the population, were hungry and impoverished, according to the social activist Michael Harrington. Even by the U.S. government's conservative estimate, thirty-four million Americans lived beneath the poverty line, three-quarters of whom were children or senior citizens. For Johnson, the issue was personal: he was raised in a house where there was sometimes no food, and his parents had to rely on neighbors for dinner, which was stressful and humiliating. In his first State of the Union address, LBJ called for an "unconditional war on poverty" by the federal government, and committed to finishing the work started by FDR's New Deal and Truman's Fair Deal. "No single weapon or strategy will suffice, but we shall not rest until that war is won. . . . The richest nation on Earth can afford to win it. We cannot afford to lose it."

Many in Congress disagreed with his goals and methods, but Johnson pleaded, cajoled, wheedled, and bullied his colleagues into supporting much of his agenda. One of his most effective tools was food, barbecue in particular.

In 1951, LBJ and his wife, Claudia Alta "Lady Bird" Johnson, bought a ranch house in the central Texas hill country, where he was raised. They called it the Stonewall ranch, but everyone else called it the LBJ Ranch or the Texas White House. While working as a Democratic congressman, Johnson frequently brought politicians, donors, staff, and foreign diplomats from Washington to Texas and seduced them with visions of the cowboy life. On a typical visit, the lanky, loquacious Johnson would tour his guests around the property on horseback. They would pass slowly beneath oaks and across pastures, soaking in a landscape most had seen only in Hollywood Westerns. Back at the house, Johnson would treat them to a down-home Texas barbecue. Softening his targets up with sticky ribs, molasses-sweetened beans, thick hunks of corn bread, salad, coffee, and "plenty of beer," LBJ would begin to home in on the real purpose of the visit. As he speechified about the importance of civil rights legislation, wondered about keeping American troops in Vietnam, or considered the question of school lunch, he would ask for favors, or poke his finger into chests to make a point, or explode into red-faced shouting to get his way. Often, he succeeded.

When Johnson progressed from the House to the Senate, his cookouts grew bigger and more elaborate, as did the ranch itself. Lady Bird, who used her inheritance to build a successful radio and TV business, expanded the property with guest suites, a swimming pool, a radio tower, and an airstrip for small jets. When Johnson ran against John F. Kennedy for the Democratic presidential nomination in 1959, he hosted a large barbecue at the ranch for the Mexican president, Adolfo López Mateos. Though Johnson lost the primary, his barbecue was a howling success. A year later Kennedy named Johnson his running mate, and they narrowly defeated Richard Nixon and Henry Cabot Lodge, to capture the White House.

They were an odd couple. While Kennedy epitomized suave, moneyed, northeastern sophistication, Johnson cultivated an image as a plainspoken, dirt-under-the-nails Texas rancher. The image was based on truth, but LBJ heightened and romanticized his biography, which played into notions primed by Louis L'Amour novels and Marlboro cigarette ads (which debuted in 1954) that nearly everyone found irresistible, particularly Europeans.

In April 1961, Vice President Johnson hosted a ranch barbecue for West Germany's chancellor, Konrad Adenauer, who cherished the Wild West myth and knew that many German families had settled central Texas. That meal, observed the LBJ biographer Hal K. Rothman, "began a universalization of the ranch, its transformation from a place of continental iconography to one of international symbolic meaning." The American West, as well as "its barbecues, beans, and chuck wagons, had a cross-cultural resonance that allowed even those raised in other parts of the world to participate in an American myth made universal by popular fiction and the movies. Foreigners could see their preconceived vision of the 'real America' in the vistas, settings, entertainment, and libations of the LBJ ranch."

The Kennedys understood the magnetic pull of this myth and planned a triumphant barbecue finale at Johnson's ranch at the end of their campaign swing through Texas in November 1963. Instead, JFK was assassinated the day before the dinner, and LBJ was thrust into leadership.

A month later, the West German chancellor, Ludwig Erhard, was due in Washington for a series of meetings about the Berlin Wall. Still adjusting to "the tornado of activity," Lady Bird and LBJ had retreated to the ranch for a quiet Christmas. They invited Erhard to join them, and he accepted with delight.

On December 29, the American and German delegates accomplished seven hours of meetings—in which they discussed the defense of western Europe, and tariffs on poultry and grain—an hour of prayer at church, a joint communiqué, and President Johnson's first diplomatic dinner. The next day, LBJ hosted the first presidential barbecue in history. It was a chilly afternoon, so the three hundred guests ate in the Stonewall High School gym, which had been given "the look and feel of a chuck wagon dinner," with hay bales, red lanterns, saddles, lassos, and red-checked tablecloths. The legendary Fort Worth pitmaster Walter Jetton was hired to serve "beans (pinto beans, always), delicious barbecued spareribs, cole slaw, followed by fried apricot pies with lots of hot coffee. And plenty of beer," Lady Bird wrote in her diary. Jetton's coffee was said to be so strong that "it will float a .44" caliber pistol.

As the delegates ate from paper plates, they were serenaded by a mariachi band, and the Texas comedian Richard "Cactus" Pryor apologized for not providing barbecued sauerkraut. The Germans laughed and helped themselves to more ribs. After lunch, Johnson presented Erhard's delegation with Stetson hats, while the chancellor gave the president a fine bottle of sweet white German wine, a 1959 Piesporter Goldtröpfchen Feinste Auslese. To prove he could go from lowbrow to high, LBJ brought out Van Cliburn, the piano prodigy, who was raised in Texas.

The meeting went smoothly, and the menu led to colorful reportage. LBJ "left time for relaxation as well as pomp, to nurse friendships as well as alliances, and to dig into tender Texas steaks as well as tough affairs of state," *The New York Times* reported. "Rare, medium and well-done foreign policy" was served: the setting was rare; the American stance on disputed issues was moderate, and the answers to diplomatic questions were well prepared.

Johnson quelled Erhard's concerns about American intentions in Europe, while the Germans agreed they would not negotiate with the Soviets independently, as France had done; both emphasized military and economic cooperation. Just a few years after World War II, the former enemies displayed "the smoothest relationship within the Western alliance," the *Times* marveled.

In describing LBJ's modus operandi that weekend, W. D. Taylor of the *New York Herald Tribune* coined the phrase "barbecue diplomacy," a moniker the president embraced. The combination of food and place had proven so effective at breaking barriers and building comity that LBJ repeated the pattern again and again. In the five years he was in office, he visited his ranch seventy-four times and spent 490 days—about 25 percent of his presidency—in Texas.

PRESIDENT JOHNSON USED his bully pulpit to push for enhanced civil rights, voting rights, public education, environmental protection, health insurance, and nutritional programs that would collectively add up to a "great society." He imagined a nation "where no child will go unfed, and no youngster will go unschooled. . . . The Great Society rests on abundance and liberty for all." One of the Great Society's signature programs was Head Start, which, in its early incarnation, provided education, medical aid, and meals to poor children. With an emphasis on nutrition, Head Start elicited food metaphors—the most evocative of which equated the American economy to a pie that could be sliced into many pieces.

The columnist Walter Lippmann wrote, "A generation ago it would have been taken for granted that a war on poverty meant taking money away from the haves and turning it over to the have nots. . . . But in this generation a revolutionary idea has taken hold. The size of the pie can be increased by intention, by organized fiscal policy and then a whole society, not just one part of it, will grow richer." And the historian Joshua Zeitz wrote, "The architects of the Great Society were convinced that the means to a just society was not cutting the pie into smaller slices so that everyone would enjoy an equal share, but baking a larger pie."

The Great Society was controversial, and its tenets continue to be a flash point today. In 1983, President Ronald Reagan denounced LBJ's program for inculcating "the central political error of our time": the belief that federal assistance was the primary vehicle for social change. "Government is not the solution to our problem," Reagan asserted, "government *is* the problem." Congress disagreed and blocked the dismantling of Head Start. As I write this, millions of Americans have turned to the government for help during the COVID-19 pandemic, and the ideological war of words continues.

Food was also integral to Johnson's groundbreaking civil rights legislation. Though he was a white rural Texan who was initially reluctant to tackle race, LBJ had a personal connection to the issue. Her name was Zephyr Wright. She was the Johnson family's Black cook, whose life experience, and recipes, influenced American history.

II. Mrs. Wright's Chili

In 1942, Lady Bird Johnson hired Zephyr Wright as a cook and maid and her husband, Sammy Wright, as a driver. The Wrights worked for the Johnsons for twenty-seven years—first at the ranch and then in Washington—and became part of their extended family. Mrs. Wright specialized in traditional southern food: homemade spoon bread, fried chicken, steak, shrimp curry, hash, brownies, and homemade ice cream with cooked custard and fruit. She could whip up a chocolate soufflé, one of LBJ's favorites, and was revered for Sunday breakfast feasts that included deer sausage, cured bacon, popovers, grits, scrambled eggs, homemade peach preserves, and coffee.

But Mrs. Wright's most celebrated recipe was for chili, the second most famous Texas food after ribs. The First Lady might have undersold the chili when she declared it was "almost as popular as the government pamphlet on the care and feeding of children." And she received so many requests for the recipe that she handed out xeroxed copies, or mailed postcards inscribed with the directions, to people across the country. Journalists referred to the dish as "Lady Bird Johnson's Pedernales River Chili," after the watercourse flowing past the ranch, but it was Zephyr Wright's creation.

Like barbecue, chili is a near-mythical concoction with as many "original" or "correct" recipes as there are cooks. Partisans tend to advocate for their version dogmatically. Mrs. Wright's recipe is a straightforward, no-frills mix of coarsely ground meat, onion, tomatoes, salt, cumin seed, oregano, chili powder, garlic cloves, and hot water.

LBJ's colleagues enjoyed Mrs. Wright's food so much they struggled to argue with him while eating it, which proved a political asset. But Johnson liked it a little too much. His taste for her dishes, along with midnight snacks, root beer, and Cutty Sark with soda, led him to steadily gain weight. (He'd suffered a heart attack in 1955.) He announced he was going on a diet, but complained about the small helpings and low-calorie foods he was fed. Mrs. Wright was soft-spoken but no pushover, and one night she left a note under his plate: "You have been my boss. . . . Now I am going to be your boss. . . . Eat what I put in front of you and don't ask for any more and don't complain." LBJ ruefully showed the note to a group of senators, saying, "When I feel the arrogance of power, Zephyr will take it out of me."

In this quiet but forceful way, Mrs. Wright led Johnson to a valuable political insight.

While he was a congressman, the Wrights followed LBJ back and forth between Washington and Texas. But many gas stations, hotels, and restaurants refused to provide them with basic services because of their race. Mrs. Wright was indignant. In 1948, Johnson was elected to the Senate, and one day he asked her to drive from Washington to Austin to join him at a celebration. "Senator, I'm not going to do it," she replied. A heavy silence hung between them. "When Sammy and I drive to Texas and I have to go to the bathroom, like Lady Bird or the girls, I am not allowed to go to the bathroom. I have to find a bush and squat. When it comes time to eat, we can't go to restaurants. We have to eat out of a brown bag. And at night Sammy sleeps in the front of the car with the steering wheel around his neck while I sleep in the back. We are not going to do it again."

Johnson placed his napkin on the table and walked out of the room. Mrs. Wright did not know what to make of that. But on July 2, 1964, he signed the landmark Civil Rights Act into law. The president had invited Mrs. Wright to attend the ceremony in the Green Room, and after signing the bill he handed her the pen, saying, "You deserve this more than anybody else."

III. Verdon and Haller

Politics, barbecue, and chili were commingled in the 1964 presidential election, when LBJ campaigned against the Republican Arizona senator Barry Goldwater. So important was Texas food to his image that LBJ hired Walter Jetton to cater barbecue fundraisers across the country and persuaded Esther Coopersmith (the wife of a Washington, D.C., real estate mogul and campaign contributor) to serve as his national coordinator of barbecues. "Mrs. Coopersmith . . . is given credit for having turned barbecue into a symbol of the Johnson campaign—a symbol that experts . . . have compared favorably to the 1952 hole in Adlai Stevenson's shoe," Brendan Gill wrote in *The New Yorker.*

At a crowded rally staged by the Young Citizens for Johnson in New York City, the jocular, 240-pound Jetton brought trucks equipped with ovens, refrigerators, and barbecue grills to feed them. Playing his role to the hilt, Jetton wore a large cowboy hat, an aquamarine shirt, a black shoestring tie, trifocals, and a white apron smudged with barbecue sauce. He served the Young Citizens a thousand pounds of pork ribs, a thousand pounds of beef brisket, five hundred chickens, two thousand ears of corn, and three thousand fried apple pies, along with untold quantities of beans, salad, biscuits, coffee, soft drinks, and beer.

"The President loves sourdough biscuits, but if he has one favorite dish, I reckon it's barbecued ribs," the pitmaster drawled. "The President likes things just so—he don't want no fooling around—and if you do things the way he wants them, why, he's very complimentary and easy to get along with."

In October, a month before the election, the Johnson-Goldwater donnybrook reached a "fever pitch," declared the *Gentry Serenader,* but "there is one issue on which the nominees might find common agreement. They both like chili." The paper noted that "violently dedicated partisans can be comforted by the knowledge that although both men like" the dish, each favored his own recipe. LBJ preferred Mrs. Wright's Pedernales version: a black chili poured over breast of chicken. While Goldwater favored a "cowboy style," in which cheeseburgers placed on open-faced toast "swam" in a pool of red chili con carne made with chili beans, mushrooms, sugar, vinegar, paprika, cayenne, and chili powder.

In November, Johnson and Hubert Humphrey triumphed over Goldwater and William E. Miller, winning 61 percent of the popular vote, the largest margin of victory in a presidential election to that point. It is possible that Mrs. Wright's chili tipped the scales.

WHEN THE JOHNSONS MOVED into the White House, they retained the Kennedys' French chef, René Verdon, to cook for official functions and relied on Zephyr Wright for family meals. But it surprised no one when, at the end of 1965, Verdon resigned. He had chafed at the Johnsons' tastes, which he described as "more South" than the Kennedys', their insistence that he use canned and frozen vegetables instead of fresh ones, and that they had instructed Verdon to prepare a cold garbanzo bean puree—a dish that was "already bad hot," the chef snorted. It didn't help matters when Mrs. Johnson hired Mary Kaltman, formerly of the Driskill Hotel in Austin, as a "menu coordinator" to supervise the French chef. Verdon quit "in a Gallic huff," *Time* reported. In a parting shot, he famously quipped, "You can eat at home what you want, but you do not serve barbecued spareribs at a banquet with the ladies in white gloves!" (To which a young Bill Moyers, LBJ's press secretary, replied that Verdon's "reputation as a chef far exceeds the pleasures he delivered to the table.")

To some White House watchers, Verdon's departure marked the end of a gilded period. "Onlookers have speculated as to what marks the end of the Kennedy era," *The Washington Post* lamented. "The resignation that truly signals the end of the Kennedy era is that of Chef Rene Verdon." (He went on to write books and cook at Le Trianon, a highly regarded restaurant in San Francisco.)

IN FEBRUARY 1966, Lady Bird hired Verdon's replacement: a forty-three-year-old, sharp-featured, preternaturally calm Swiss cook named Henry Haller. Trained in classical French cuisine, Haller had worked in Montreal, in Phoenix, and at the Hampshire House in New York. LBJ enjoyed Haller's food there, and Lady Bird brought him to Washington.

Haller's first six months were probationary, and while his family remained in New York, he moved into a small room on the White House's third floor. From there, he oversaw three kitchens: the main kitchen on the ground floor; the family kitchen (Zephyr Wright's domain) on the second floor; and a sous-kitchen in the subbasement. Like FDR and JFK, Johnson would impulsively invite congressmen or diplomats to work over meals at the White House. A stolid sort, Haller was unfazed. When the king of Saudi Arabia insisted on bringing a royal food taster and four briefcases packed with his own victuals, Haller shrugged. And when it came to LBJ's cowboy cuisine, Haller said, "I'm here in this country longer than the President's previous chef, and I've learned to be flexible." His mantra about the First Family was, "Whatever they want, that's what they're going to get."

Impressed, the Johnsons hired Haller as executive chef, and he moved with his family into a house in the Virginia suburbs. His workday lasted from 6:00 a.m. to midnight, and though he was initially paid $10,000 a year—far less than what he could have earned at a top restaurant in New York—he said "there is no better job" than cooking for the president. Aside from government lunches and state dinners, Haller catered many special events, most notably the weddings of the two Johnson daughters. (Luci Baines Johnson married Patrick Nugent in August 1966, and celebrated with a reception at the White House. Lynda Bird Johnson wed Chuck Robb in the East Room in December 1967.)

In 1968, Lyndon Johnson began campaigning for reelection. But when the Tet Offensive resulted in more than 100,000 South Vietnamese and American casualties, U.S. support for the war waned and LBJ fared poorly in the New Hampshire primary. In a surprise, he withdrew from the race, and the Republican challenger Richard Nixon grabbed the brass ring.

RICHARD M. NIXON
and GERALD R. FORD

The Unlikeliest Gastro-diplomat
and the Instant President

RICHARD NIXON:
THE THIRTY-SEVENTH PRESIDENT
January 20, 1969–August 9, 1974

☆

I. *"Just a Bowl of Cottage Cheese"*

After years of wandering the political wilderness, Richard Milhous Nixon defeated Vice President Hubert Humphrey in the fraught campaign of 1968. In the run-up to the election Martin Luther King Jr. and Robert F. Kennedy were assassinated, and the country was racked by furies. Though the Oval Office would prove as narcotic to Nixon as the One Ring was to Gollum in *The Lord of the Rings,* he began his administration on a gracious, optimistic note, saying, "The greatest honor history can bestow is the title of peacemaker."

After the ceremony the Nixons moved into the White House. The executive chef, Henry Haller, was ready for them. The kitchen staff had spent two weeks researching the Californians' diet and laid in so many supplies that Haller joked, "I think we could open a grocery store in the pantry. We've tried to find out everything they like."

As she prepared for the parties that evening, Patricia "Pat" Nixon ordered four steaks—for the president, their daughters, Tricia and Julie, and Julie's husband, David Eisenhower (Ike's grandson). President Nixon liked his steak lightly seasoned and cooked medium rare, while the others preferred theirs braised in a light sauce of herbs, garlic, and shallots. Nixon thanked Haller in person, while his son-in-law declared the dinner as good as that at any French restaurant. Haller beamed. The kitchen was off to a perfect start with the new First Family.

In the meantime, Mrs. Nixon asked for "just a bowl of cottage cheese." It was a simple request, but it was as if she had tossed a bucket of gravel into the smoothly whirring gears of Haller's Swiss food production machine, causing them to seize and shower sparks. *Cottage cheese?!* Frantically searching the refrigerators, the chef realized there was not a single "spoonful of cottage cheese in the house. . . . No one had alerted" him about the Nixons' devotion to the diet food.

Cottage cheese is a mild, loose curd mixed with whey, low in fat and calories, but high in protein, which makes it a popular snack. As healthy eating gained adherents in the 1960s and 1970s, cottage cheese came to symbolize California cuisine and was a leitmotif in the Nixons' San Clemente household. But it was not yet a staple in Washington. On the night of the inauguration many stores were closed, and the streets of Washington were clogged with celebrants. But an intrepid staffer commandeered a White House limousine, scoured supermarkets, and triumphantly returned with a container of the precious curds.

"After that night," Haller vowed, "cottage cheese was always on hand."

Pat was not the only curd-loving Nixon. "I eat cottage cheese until it runs out of my ears," the president said, with only slight exaggeration. Every week, Chief of Staff H. R. "Bob" Haldeman had a fresh batch of Nixon's favorite cottage cheese flown in from the Knudsen dairy in Los Angeles. And nearly every day the president ate a dollop for lunch. He'd plop it on a pale-yellow ring of canned pineapple, occasionally dress it up with a Ry-Krisp cracker or, when he felt daring, a squirt of ketchup. "Ketchup disguises almost anything," Nixon said, in what might have been a Freudian slip.

Richard Nixon did not savor his food, care about its textures and flavors, linger over dessert, or enjoy a communal table. For him, eating was a means to stay alive and a trial. "Unless I have a guest, I eat breakfast alone in five minutes, never have guests for lunch—I do that in five minutes, too," he said. Dining with his family, he rushed through his meal and spoke in monosyllables. "Dick eats everything but he likes meatloaf" best, Pat said. He disliked dinner parties and seemed incapable of small talk, an odd trait for a career politician. "I am an introvert in an extrovert's profession," he acknowledged.

Yet, in retrospect, the meals Nixon ate, the banquets he attended, and the food policies he championed helped define his legacy and era, and—like Woodrow Wilson, another food-phobe—he forged nutrition programs with lasting impact.

BORN IN 1913, and raised with four brothers in Yorba Linda, California, Nixon was a poor athlete but a good student who excelled at debate. His parents were devout Quakers. Frank Nixon had a sixth-grade education, had failed as a lemon farmer, and ran a grocery store/gas station in Whittier. Hannah Milhous Nixon named four of her five boys after English kings: Richard was inspired by Richard the Lionheart. The Nixons struggled through the Depression, and two of their sons died of tuberculosis. But the family was hardworking and survived on California's bountiful meat, vegetables, and fruits.

Hannah recalled Richard as a fastidious boy who channeled his adolescent energy into mashing potatoes. He was "the best potato masher you could wish for," she said. Unlike his brothers, who crushed the spuds to smithereens with an up-and-down motion, Richard used a whipping motion that smoothed the potatoes so that his batch was the only one without lumps. For Nixon, mashing seemed a form of therapy. "Even in these days when I am visiting Richard and Pat in Washington, he will take over the potato mashing," his mother said. "He actually enjoys it."

As a young man Nixon worked hard, carefully positioned himself, and took advantage of lucky breaks. He served in the U.S. Naval Reserve during World War II and made enough by gambling on poker to finance his early political career. In 1946, he was elected to the House, in 1950 to the Senate. To appeal to his Southern California base, he positioned himself as an unyielding anti-Communist conservative and would growl in private, "If you can't lie, you'll never go anywhere."

In 1952, Eisenhower named Nixon, who was thirty-nine, his vice president. Though he served as veep for eight years, Nixon alienated the general. First, when Nixon was accused of accepting illegal campaign gifts in 1952 (he barely salvaged his career with the Checkers speech, in which he declared his innocence and refused to give up Checkers, the family dog who was one of the illicit gifts), then by leaking the guest list to Ike's secret dinner in 1956. Their lack of chemistry grew farcical when Ike attempted to teach Nixon to cast for trout. "After hooking a limb the first three times, I caught his shirt on my fourth try," Nixon recalled. "The lesson ended abruptly." When asked about the vice president's contributions to his administration, Eisenhower grunted, "If you give me a week, I might think of one."

Nixon had no choice but to row his own boat into the election of 1960. Public interest was so intense that minor incidents seemed to reflect larger meaning, and concerns about food safety reflected the unease of the era. Take Nixon's choice of a dinner condiment in November 1959, which resulted in an odd front-page headline in *The Washington Post*: "Vice President Has Cranberries in Wisconsin."

In the weeks before Thanksgiving 1959, Arthur Flemming, the secretary of health, education, and welfare, announced that "some" cranberries had been contaminated by a weed killer that caused "cancer in rats," and to be safe, he advised people not to buy the tart red berries. The announcement scared the public and jolted the $50 million cranberry industry. Restaurants struck the berries from their menus, grocers emptied their shelves, and consumers threw cranberries into the garbage.

Mamie Eisenhower announced that she would serve applesauce with her turkey.

Farmers and cranberry lovers were outraged. To demonstrate a common touch, Nixon ate not one but four helpings of cranberry sauce at a political dinner. "I see no reason for hysteria," he declared. "I am certain [Flemming] is working rapidly to separate those comparatively few contaminated berries, and I . . . expect to eat traditional cranberries with my family on Thanksgiving Day." Not to be outdone, his rival, the Democratic senator John F. Kennedy, drank two glasses of cranberry juice and joked, "If we both pass away, I feel I shall have performed a great public service by taking the Vice President with me."

The Food and Drug Administration had detected the herbicide in cranberries, and it fell to the agency to test tons of the fruit as quickly as possible. The FDA dedicated a quarter of its staff to sample trainloads of cranberries. Meanwhile, newspapers published recipes for substitutes, such as lingonberries, spiced cherries, and pickled pear. Just before Thanksgiving, the government announced it had verified seven million pounds of cranberries and created a label "to tell the housewife whether she's buying tested, taint-free cranberries." Newspapers printed a recipe for "Mrs. Flemming's Cranberry Ring"—a package of lemon Jell-O mixed with a quart of cranberries—for Thanksgiving. Yet cranberry sales dropped 70 percent below average for Thanksgiving and 50 percent below average for Christmas. By January 1960, the Ocean Spray cooperative had laid off a third of its workforce, and cranberry growers reported $20 million in losses.

The great cranberry scare of 1959 heralded a new public concern about food safety, which anticipated later fears about tainted grapes, spinach, cookie dough, deli meats, burgers, and other staples of the American diet. The cranberry case also marked the beginning of a new kind of consumer activism, led by women, who were largely responsible for preparing the nation's meals. In response, a Virginia housewife named Ruth Desmond established the Federation of Homemakers to address "deep concerns" about the chemical treatment of vegetables and meat and the lack of food industry oversight. The federation grew into an effective consumer watchdog that later testified against General Mills and spurred investigations into the ingredients of baby food and peanut butter.

GASTRONOMICALLY SPEAKING, the Nixons—California "waist watchers" who insisted on light meals, small portions, little sugar, and no snacks—were the opposite of their predecessors, the barbecue-, chili-, beer-, soda-, and whiskey-inhaling Johnsons.

Pat Nixon stood just five feet six inches tall, kept her weight at 110 pounds, and looked so frail that her husband forbade photos of her in a bathing suit. Dick Nixon was proud to have maintained his "marriage weight" of 175 pounds, kept slim to look good on television, and wore a suit and tie for every meal, even when dining alone. (He also wore a suit and dress shoes at the beach.) A child of the Depression, his controlled diet verged on mania, as if any hint of corporeal indulgence led to feelings of guilt.

Nixon usually began his day with a bowl of wheat germ, a bit of fruit, a glass of OJ, and a cup of coffee, sometimes with nondairy creamer. The First Lady also ate simple breakfasts, but had a weakness for Haller's blueberry muffins. The president's lunch was the ubiquitous cottage cheese and/or an occasional green salad, sometimes with a piece of banana bread. He hydrated with a glass of ice water or milk. Family dinners followed the same pattern: no appetizer but for the occasional baked grapefruit or clams on the half shell; an entrée of red or white meat, with a baked potato or pasta, and vegetables or a salad. The Nixons were particularly fond of chicken—baked or broiled, in a pot pie, cordon bleu, with mushroom crepes, divan, in a sauce supreme, or à la king. They also liked a boiled dinner of cabbage and corned beef, and "ethnic dishes" such as spaghetti and meatballs, a Spanish omelet, or beef enchiladas with refried beans.

Nixon was not a frequent or adept drinker. But he was a California native and oenophile who collected fine bottles from estates such as Château Lafite Rothschild and Château Haut-Brion, and Dom Pérignon champagne. He was notorious for his covetousness. As the story goes, Nixon would serve bottles of $6 wine to guests and keep a $30 bottle of Château Margaux for himself—wrapping the bottle in a towel, or pouring the wine from a decanter, to obscure its label.

The Nixons reserved dessert for special occasions. When they indulged, they gravitated to classic sponge cake, Boston cream pie, or napoleons. The president enjoyed baked Alaska, a meringue and sponge cake edifice that envelops an ice cream core—his favorite flavors were vanilla and pistachio paired with raspberry sorbet—and set alight (which reminded Chef Haller of the White House illuminated by floodlights, a Nixon innovation).

Tricia and Julie shared their parents' plain tastes. One night, Tricia asked Haller for a hot dog. He didn't have any but remembered the vending machine in the West Wing. Using the loose change in his pocket, he bought a hot dog from the machine, reheated it, and served it to Tricia. She deemed it the best she'd ever tasted.

GIVEN NIXON'S DISINTEREST in food, it was paradoxical that he convened the first and so far only White House Conference on Food, Nutrition, and Health. Though he never fully articulated his motivation, it is likely the initiative was driven by a mixture of political pressure, scientific consensus, business opportunism, and perhaps the memory of his own Depression-era privations.

In 1967, Americans were shocked to learn that malnutrition and chronic hunger were pressing issues in the wealthiest nation in the world. That year, the NAACP attorney Marian Wright brought a group of senators including Robert F. Kennedy to the Mississippi delta, where they met impoverished Black children with open sores and bloated bellies, a sign of malnutrition. When RFK publicized the racially tinged issue, Mississippi's governor, Paul B. Johnson Jr., dismissed "Socialist-minded senators" from the North, adding, "All the Negroes I've seen around here are so fat they shine." The *Jackson Daily News* argued that studies claiming fifty-four thousand Mississippians were dangerously hungry simply couldn't be true: "Who would stand idly by and permit starvation when there is so much plenty in the land?"

Their responses revealed misconceptions about federal food policies and what famine can do to the human body. The media latched on to the story, and in 1968 CBS aired "Hunger in America," an exposé that showed malnutrition was a far greater problem than many knew, especially in rural areas. Further reports prompted corporate chieftains such as the president of Quaker Oats, Robert Stuart, to push for federal intervention. "The nation cannot live with its conscience if the [hunger] problems are not solved," Walter Cronkite intoned.

The public was moved, farmers saw an opportunity to sell surplus commodities, and Nixon was goaded into action. In December 1969, he convened the White House conference on nutrition and asked three thousand experts to study the matter. On Christmas Eve, Dr. Jean Mayer delivered a report that included eighteen hundred recommendations. Vowing to "put an end to hunger in America for all time," Nixon followed 1,650 of them. He authorized feeding programs for women and children, expanded the food stamp program, improved the labeling of ingredients, and nearly doubled school lunch initiatives to cover some 6.6 million students.

These changes dramatically improved nutrition in the 1970s, but in the 1980s the Reagan administration whittled Nixon's programs down, and when the fiftieth anniversary of the Conference on Food, Nutrition, and Health was celebrated in 2019, Donald Trump didn't bother to mention it.

II. Chopstick Diplomacy

Unlike presidents Kennedy and Johnson, Richard Nixon disdained official meals, and he held diplomatic dinners in extra-special contempt. After hosting his first state dinner, for Canada's Pierre Trudeau in 1969, he analyzed the evening "as if it had been a major military battle," Chief of Staff Bob Haldeman recalled. The president's main grievance was that official meals took too long. Like a fidgety child, he complained "about the ineffable boredom of state dinners," Henry Kissinger said. He "cajoled and threatened to speed up the serving of White House meals in order to reduce the time he had to spend in small talk with his visitors."

The fastest state dinner Nixon ever managed, "the world record for White House dinners, so to speak . . . was an hour and twenty minutes," Kissinger wrote, "even under the merciless prodding of Haldeman." In an effort to lower the record, Nixon suggested cutting the soup course. "Men don't really like soup," he alleged. Suspecting there was more to the story, Haldeman asked Manolo Sanchez, Nixon's valet, "Was there anything wrong with the President's suit after that dinner?" Sanchez nodded and said, "Yes, he spilled the soup down his vest." That was the last time soup was served at a Nixon state dinner.

When the president visited Italy in September 1970, his "obsession," as Kissinger put it, was "unintentionally let loose . . . and caused unending discomfiture." Between morning meetings about NATO and a visit to the Vatican in the afternoon, Nixon was treated to lunch in the Quirinale Palace, overlooking the Eternal City. Most Italians consider a lengthy midday meal a birthright, but the lunch for Nixon was over in just fifty-five minutes, a standard that the president "never permitted the White House staff to forget," Kissinger lamented. "Alas, like many Roman achievements, it proved impossible to emulate" in America.

Against this backdrop, it was a quintessential Nixonian contradiction that the greatest triumph of his presidency would revolve around a diplomatic dinner featuring an exotic cuisine, unfamiliar eating implements, and toasts with potent liquor in a place he loathed. Nixon was heading to Communist China.

ONE AFTERNOON IN FEBRUARY 1972, Jack Davies got a call in his office at the Schramsberg Vineyards, in Napa Valley, California. A man on the other end ordered fifteen cases of Davies's 1969 Blanc de Blancs, a sparkling white wine. The vineyard produced only five thousand bottles of the wine every year, which were aged in caves dug into a hillside by nineteenth-century Chinese laborers. Though not widely known, the Schramsberg Blanc de Blancs was coveted by aficionados, and Nixon had served the delicate, lemony-flavored vintage at his inauguration.

The man on the phone ordered 180 bottles, enough to serve three hundred people. They retailed at $6.49 apiece, and the $1,300 order was "extraordinary," recalls Davies's son, Hugh, who now runs Schramsberg. When Jack Davies asked whom the large order was for, the caller declined to answer or identify himself. He did say, however, that if the winery delivered twelve cases to Travis Air Force Base, a government jet would pick them up. With a shrug, the winemaker packed his International Harvester Scout with cases of Blanc de Blancs and drove an hour to Travis. He delivered the wine, then returned to work.

On February 24 a neighbor called, saying, "Jack, turn on your TV!" When he did, Barbara Walters was standing in Tiananmen Square with a bottle of his Blanc de Blancs. She said something like "This is the blank-de-blank wine from California that will be served at Premier Zhou Enlai's banquet," in her distinctive nasal voice. Davies was stunned.

"We had no idea where our wine went," Hugh says, laughing. "And that's how we found out it landed in Beijing with President Nixon."

Nixon had flown there on Air Force One—renamed the *Spirit of '76* for the visit—to attend a landmark diplomatic tour of the People's Republic of China (PRC). Diplomatic relations had soured in 1949, when Mao Zedong's Communists took control of mainland China, and worsened during the Korean War. The "Nixon in China" trip was the culmination of years of advance work and part of a grand overture intended to open the Middle Kingdom to the world after twenty-two years of miserable isolation. As at the Big Three meetings at the end of World War II, food and drink played a central role in Nixon's Sino-American rapprochement of the 1970s. Over a series of banquets, meetings, and carefully staged

BILL OF FARE

OF THE

Presidential Inauguration Ball

IN THE

CITY OF WASHINGTON, D. C.,

On the 6th of March 1865.

Oyster Stews ....
Terrapin " ....
Oysters, pickled ....

BEEF.

Roast Beef ....
Filet de Beef ....
Beef à-la-mode ....
Beef à l'anglais ....

VEAL.

Leg of Veal ....
Fricandeau ....
Veal Malakoff ....

POULTRY.

Roast Turkey ....
Boned " ....
Roast Chicken ....
Grouse, boned and roast ....

GAME.

Pheasant ....
Quail ....
Venison ....

PATETES.

Patête of Duck en gelée ......
Patête de fois gras ....

SMOKED.

Ham ....
Tongue en gelée ....
    do   plain ....

SALADES.

Chicken ....
Lobster ....

Ornamental Pyramides.

Nougate ....
Orange ....
Caramel with Fancy Cream Candy
Cocoanut ....
Macaroon ....

Croquant ....
Chocolate ....
Tree Cakes ....

CAKES AND TARTS.

Almond Sponge............
Belle Alliance ....
Dame Blanche ....
Macaroon Tart............
Tart à la Nelson ....
Tarte à l'Orleans ....
    do   à la Portugaise ....
    do   à la Vienne..........
Pound Cake..............
Sponge Cake ....
Lady Cake ....
Fancy small Cakes..........

JELLIES AND CREAMS.

Calfsfoot and Wine Jelly .....
Charlotte à la Russe.........
    do   do   Vanilla ....
Blanc Mangue ....
Crème Neapolitane ....
    do   à la Nelson..........
    do   Chateaubriand ......
    do   à la Smyrna.........
    do   do Nesselrode.......
Bombe à la Vanilla ....

ICE CREAM.

Vanilla ....
Lemon ....
White Coffee ....
Chocolate ....
Burnt Almonds ....
Maraschino ....

FRUIT ICES.

Strawberry................
Orange ....
Lemon ....

DESSERT.

Grapes, Almonds, Raisins, &c.

Coffee and Chocolate.

Furnished by **G. A. BALZER**, CONFECTIONER,
Cor. 9th & D Sts., Washington, D. C.

The menu for Abraham Lincoln's ill-fated second inaugural ball,
at the Patent Office Building, March 6, 1865

The general's camp chest

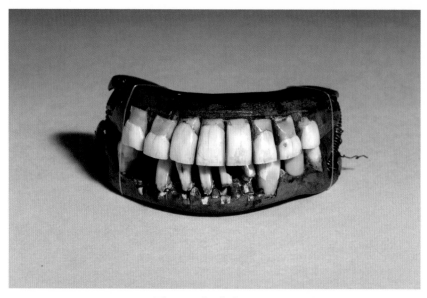

The president's dentures

Thomas Jefferson's sketch of a "maccaroni" machine, with pasta-making instructions, c. 1787

The "King Mob" at Andrew Jackson's inauguration party on March 4, 1829, grew so rowdy that the White House staff used a potent punch to lure his admirers outside before they crushed him. (For a version of this punch, see Recipes, p. 383.)

Circa 1891, with President Benjamin Harrison's
cook, Dolly Johnson

Circa 1909, Theodore Roosevelt's kitchen

1948, the Harry S. Truman kitchen

2009, Michelle Obama with chef Cristeta Comerford
and pastry chef Bill Yosses

Teddy Roosevelt's "shocking" dinner with Booker T. Washington,
October 16, 1901

Franklin D. Roosevelt served hot dogs and beer to the Windsors
at "the picnic that won the war," June 11, 1939

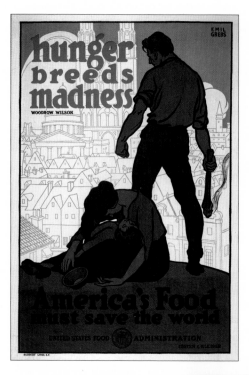

A poster from World War I

A poster from World War II

Mrs. Henrietta Nesbitt, c. 1940

Chef René Verdon (third from left), with Julius Spessot (to his right), and assistant cooks, c. 1962

Pastry chef Roland Mesnier, Nancy Reagan, and chef Henry Haller, July 30, 1982

Walter Scheib with Hillary Rodham Clinton, 1994

John F. Kennedy stays cool
aboard his yacht, the *Honey Fitz*,
September 7, 1963

The Kennedys' "Brains Dinner" for Nobel laureates,
with novelist Pearl Buck and poet Robert Frost, April 29, 1962

Luci B. Johnson and Patrick Nugent cut their wedding cake, August 6, 1966

Richard M. Nixon's last presidential lunch: cottage cheese on a pineapple ring,
with a glass of milk, August 8, 1974

Ron and Nancy enjoy a TV dinner, November 6, 1981

A magical night: Mrs. Reagan arranged for Princess Diana to dance with the sinuous
Saturday Night Fever star John Travolta at a White House gala, November 9, 1985

The Easter Egg Roll has been one of the most popular White House events since Lucy Hayes inaugurated the tradition in 1878

Easter 1958

Easter 2018

Dolley Madison helped to invent the role
of "Mrs. Presidentress."

Laura Bush introduces the annual gingerbread White House, December 3, 2001

A bipartisan congressional lunch in the President's Dining Room, May 16, 2012

The president ate *bun cha* noodles with the TV star
Anthony Bourdain in Hanoi, Vietnam, May 23, 2016

James K. Polk pattern, c. 1849

On April 14, 1865, Abraham Lincoln
sipped his last cup of coffee
from this cup.

A Rutherford B. Hayes oyster plate, 1877

The Reagans' elegant, controversial service, 1982

HOLIDAY DINNER

Sweet Delicata Squash Bisque with Vermouth
Crispy Blossom Fritter

LANDMARK CHARDONNAY "Overlook" 2003

Cajun Beef Filets
Parmesan Grits
Steamed Asparagus

SHAFER CABERNET Hillside Select 1997

Garden Salad with Cheese Croutons

Roasted Praline Pecan Ice Cream Cake
Butter Rum Sauce

SCHRAMSBERG "J. Schram" 1999

The White House
Friday, December 16, 2005

A menu for a George W. Bush holiday dinner
was signed by guests, December 16, 2005

Waiters at a state dinner for Canadian Prime Minister Justin Trudeau,
March 10, 2016

The Reagans hosted a banquet for Prince Charles and Lady Diana
in the State Dining Room, November 9, 1985

tourist excursions, Chinese and American leaders brokered a détente and posed for photo ops that flashed around the world.

In fact, Nixon's overture was rooted in the dank soil of Machiavellian electioneering. With the 1972 campaign under way, he wanted to burnish his diplomatic credentials, isolate the Soviets, and pry China's enormous market open for U.S. business. But "the silent majority" of Middle Americans who had put him in office were leery of the Communist "reds." The administration used this mistrust to its advantage by repeating the phrase "Only Nixon could go to China"—meaning that only an uncompromising leader could broker peace with a despised enemy. In the end, Nixon's overture ranked among the seminal geopolitical coups of the twentieth century, one he described, immodestly but accurately, as "the week that changed the world."

If Nixon's tour of China represented a historic opportunity, it also contained pitfalls. His negotiations with Premier Zhou Enlai would include knotty questions about Taiwan and China's sponsorship of North Vietnam, and neither side forgot that their armies had clashed in Korea a dozen years earlier. But China's relations with neighboring Russia had soured (they fought a border skirmish in 1969), and Chairman Mao understood that one way to reestablish ties with the West was to break bread together—or, as the Chinese put it, "If you eat the things of others, you will find it difficult to raise your hand against them."

Noting that banquets play an outsized role in Chinese culture, Nixon's advisers wrote, "The Chinese take great pride in their food. . . . They react with much pleasure to compliments about the truly remarkable variety of tastes, textures and aromas of Chinese cuisine." The diplomat Winston Lord, who was married to the Chinese novelist Bette Bao Lord, coached Nixon on what he might be served—from dog meat to sea cucumber, bear paw, or bird's nest soup. "Banquet food served in [the PRC] is to the 'Chinese food' served in restaurants in the U.S. as Beef Wellington is to a cafeteria hamburger," a memo read. "Fortunately, one's taste buds are a more reliable guide to the excellence of these delicacies than one's imagination. Most Westerners are surprised to find . . . that they like them very much."

The State Department tutored Nixon on the importance of "face," or maintaining dignity at the table, and warned, "You should not be offended at the noisy downing of soups, or even at burping after a meal." (Burping is considered a compliment to the host.) But they advised against false praise—saying that "a particular dish is 'good' or 'interesting' when in fact you do not like it, as your hosts, in an effort to please, may serve you extra portions to your embarrassment."

Nixon spent weeks studying Chinese history, politics, and culture, with an emphasis on eating. One of his biggest challenges was chopsticks. He was not dexterous, but in practicing with ivory, wood, and silver chopsticks, he trained himself to pluck wood chips, marbles, and mothballs from plates. Eventually, he could hold a cashew without bobbling it. This was no trivial matter. His ability to use chopsticks adroitly could seal a deal with the Middle Kingdom and would prove more important to American public opinion than his groundbreaking statesmanship.

Another concern was that aside from ersatz chop suey or sweet-and-sour chicken, Nixon didn't eat much "Asian" food. When Henry Kissinger took a reconnaissance trip to Beijing in 1971, he was served "Dragon, Tiger, Phoenix" stew, an amalgam of snake, cat, and chicken. And when Deputy National Security Adviser Alexander Haig visited in 1972, he was served tiny deep-fried sparrows. "It was very crunchy, but not bad," an aide said. Nixon's aides worried that complex, flavorful Chinese dishes would prove challenging to the impatient, cottage cheese–loving president and could lead to a diplomatic faux pas.

Equally eager to put on a good show, Beijing asked, "What is President Nixon's favorite Chinese food?" Chief of Staff Bob Haldeman, a former J. Walter Thompson adman, understood China's real question: What did Nixon want the American public to *see* him eat?

Haldeman's job was to portray the stiff, awkward president as an effective leader by staging photos with Nixon standing beside Chairman Mao Tse-tung, striding atop the Great Wall, and eating Peking duck in a palace while his Democratic challenger, George McGovern, gnawed stale doughnuts in freezing Iowa. (Haldeman didn't mention that the *Spirit of '76* was packed with hamburger, steak, lobster, bean and bacon soup, white bread, ketchup, cherry pie, ice cream, scotch, champagne, and wine—just in case.) Taking this into account, the chief of staff replied, "The President will eat anything served to him."

THE *SPIRIT OF '76* touched down in Beijing on February 21, 1972. It was 11:32 a.m. local time and 10:32 p.m. in the States: prime time. For the first time, every moment of a diplomatic visit would be transmitted into millions of American homes via satellite link. Though he loathed the press, and they him, Nixon had brought a hundred journalists and had rehearsed looking into the camera, smiling, engaging in lively banter, keeping his sweat in check, and projecting self-assuredness to the folks back home.

Nixon's weeklong visit would take him from Beijing to Hangzhou and Shanghai. On his first day, Nixon met with Chairman Mao, unaware that the chairman was ailing. (This would be their only meeting.) Born a peasant, Mao had a gruff humor and laid out China's policies in a brief, casual-seeming way. Only later did the Americans realize how disarmingly effective he had been. That evening, the more polished and long-winded premier, Zhou Enlai, hosted a banquet for six hundred people in the Great Hall of the People, a palatial space abutting Tiananmen Square. Under bright television lights and enormous flags, the president and the premier sat at a large ring-shaped table in the main dining hall. The dinner lasted for four hours, all of which was televised live.

"We had our first taste of food and, Ed, you know what? It tasted like Chinese food!" Barbara Walters reported. "It's just better than the Chinese food we get in our country."

A white tablecloth was decorated by a centerpiece of low greenery highlighted by orange kumquats. Twenty places were set, each with chopsticks personalized with the guest's name, along with knives and forks, plates, and three glasses: for orange juice, wine, and Maotai— a brand of *baijiu,* the potent spirit distilled from sorghum and rice that was a Politburo favorite.

At Chinese banquets toasts with cups of Maotai, and hearty shouts of *"ganbei!"* (or "dry your cup!"), are a virtually required form of welcome. But with an alcohol content well over 50 percent, Maotai had a reputation as "pure gasoline." This was a grave challenge for Nixon. When it came to hard liquor, he was "much more susceptible" to inebriation than most people, warned the domestic affairs adviser John Ehrlichman. If Nixon was tired, just one drink could knock him "galley west," Ehrlichman said; when well rested, "about two and a half drinks will do it." Alexander Haig was so concerned that he cabled, "UNDER NO REPEAT NO CIRCUMSTANCES SHOULD THE PRESIDENT ACTUALLY DRINK FROM HIS GLASS IN RESPONSE TO BANQUET TOASTS."

At the opening banquet Zhou rose to toast Chinese-American friendship. Nixon responded with compliments to the chefs and quoted Chairman Mao, saying the two nations should "seize the day, seize the hour."

Each time Premier Zhou raised his glass of Maotai, all eyes and cameras shifted to Nixon. Though he took very small sips, and visibly winced as he swallowed the firewater, Nixon kept pace with Zhou, drink for drink. It was a test of fortitude, and to the intense relief of his staff Nixon passed.

Meanwhile, platters of food came whizzing into the banquet hall, nine courses in all, a gourmet feast reserved for very special guests. First, the cold hors d'oeuvres—salted chicken, "vegetarian ham" (tofu), sliced cucumber and tomatoes, crisp silver carp, duck with pineapple, Cantonese salted meat sausage, and three colored eggs (including preserved, "thousand-year" eggs, an acquired taste with a sulfurous aroma that caused a *Today* show host to look physically revolted). To put the Westerners at ease, plates of bread and butter were incongruously spread around the table. The meal continued with delicacies such as a consommé with spongy bamboo shoots and egg whites; shredded shark's fin; fried and stewed prawns; dark, woody mushrooms with mustard greens; steamed chicken with coconut; cold almond junket, pastries, and melon with tangerines for dessert.

A few items were lost in translation, such as the beverage labeled "boiled water (cold)." And there were moments of levity, such as when the CBS anchorman Walter Cronkite squeezed his chopsticks and accidentally squirted an olive onto the next table. But there were no major missteps, and Nixon and Zhou got acquainted as two human beings and not simply as government proxies. Both sides considered the banquet a success.

Some American observers critiqued the dinner as too simple, not understanding the political context. The official menu released to the Chinese public (and written in Taiwan) was kept deliberately brief: after the austerity of the Cultural Revolution, Chairman Mao did not dare highlight a luxe cornucopia prepared for foreigners. But the actual meal drew from classical Chinese cuisine—sophisticated dishes that relied on restrained flavors and subtle mouthfeel rather than bright sauces and pungent spices. "The food is vastly more interesting and delicate than the kind of mixture you tend to get in the United States," *The New York Times* reported. The shark's fin and almond junket, for instance, were examples of "bland" dishes coveted by Chinese diners with refined palates.

Like his gambling in the navy, Nixon's bet on "chopstick diplomacy" paid off handsomely. The two nations issued their first joint communiqué in February 1972, which signaled the end of two decades of hostilities and the beginning of a new era of diplomacy. While government representatives conducted sometimes contentious negotiations in private, it was the image of Nixon wielding a duck gizzard with chopsticks that helped convince American voters that he was worthy of reelection. "Here is a tremendous picture: the President of the United States with chopsticks!" ABC's Harry Reasoner marveled. *The New York Times* reported that "some images were simply beyond words or still photographs," such as the sight of the president "carefully wielding chopsticks." Nixon's foray to China scored the highest public recognition of any event in the history of the Gallup poll to that point.

One of the great ironies of the trip was that the timorous, taste-challenged president exposed American palates to a cuisine built on multilayered sauces, exotic ingredients, and occasionally pyrotechnic spices from the other side of the globe. In the aftermath, Chinese food became all the rage back home. Though it had been in vogue in the United States a century earlier, when gourmet Cantonese cookery flowered in 1880s New York (some claim it was first popularized in 1860s San Francisco), Nixon's trip inspired Americans to abandon the bland, gooey fare at chop suey joints to try more challenging Sichuan or Hunan cooking and sip Maotai.

Nixon did not explore authentic Chinese cuisine further, but as the heights of 1972 tilted into the depths of 1973, he found solace in the pupu platters and cocktails at an ersatz tiki bar a stone's throw from the White House.

III. The Comfort of Mai Tais and Corned Beef Hash

President Nixon was not shy about eating and drinking in public and enjoyed going to fine restaurants with friends like Bebe Rebozo, a Cuban American millionaire, to eat duck à l'orange or beef Stroganoff. But his "favorite" venue was Trader Vic's, the pseudo Polynesian-Chinese-themed pub that drew tourists and college kids like flies to honey.

One evening in October 1973—when the Watergate hearings were under way and Vice President Spiro Agnew was being excoriated for bribery and tax evasion—Pat, Julie, and Tricia Nixon decided to walk across Lafayette Square to dine at the Trader Vic's in the Statler Hilton. Passing between large faux tiki heads at the door, they proceeded into a dim basement decorated with Oceanian paraphernalia—spears, carved masks, clamshell lights, Japanese fishing buoys, and bamboo. Sipping the bar's famous rum cocktail, the mai tai (the name supposedly means "out of this world" in Tahitian), they perused the menu, which included pork in sweet-and-sour sauce, barbecued beef, fried rice, and rum raisin ice cream with pralines.

The brainchild of "Trader" Victor Bergeron in Oakland, California, in 1944, the mai tai is a deep yellow potion composed of aged dark rum, fresh lime juice, orange curaçao, and the almond syrup orgeat. It was one of many cocktails—including the Samoan fog cutter ("a potent vaseful" of rums, fruits, and liqueurs, the menu promised), the suffering bastard ("a forthright blend of rums, lime and liqueurs"), and the scorpion bowl ("a festive concoction" of rums, fruit juices, and brandy, bedecked with a flower)—that graced the Gauguin-inspired menus illustrated with topless islanders and a rum-soaked seafarer. Between the 1950s and the 1980s, Bergeron franchised twenty-seven Trader Vic's, from Honolulu to Atlanta, Dubai, and Munich. The outpost in the Plaza Hotel in Manhattan was a beloved fixture from 1958 until 1993, when the building's owner, the brash real estate developer Donald J. Trump, deemed it "tacky." Recalling that franchise's closing, Nixon lamented, "My entire family was very sorry."

In its heyday, the Trader Vic's in Washington was a clubhouse for Nixon confidants like Agnew and Attorney General John Mitchell (later imprisoned for his role in Watergate). The columnist Diana McLellan recalled "seeing Julie Eisenhower breast-feeding her baby and drinking a mai tai in one corner while Democratic mayors were debating marijuana laws in another."

On October 3, 1973, a month before Nixon declared, "I am not a crook" as the Watergate investigators closed in, he and Pat joined Julie and some friends at Trader Vic's. "We decided, 'Why not be young again and go along,'" Pat recalled. Under the circumstances, it's easy to understand the appeal of the bar's mind-boggling drinks and decor. The president sipped a mai tai and Pat had a Jack Daniel's. They ordered platters of Americanized "Asian" food—egg rolls, crab Rangoon, lobster Cantonese, pressed almond duck, beef and tomatoes, sweet-and-sour pork, fried rice, snow peas, and "royal tropical fruits" for dessert. The dim subterranean bar was a fantasy, and it provided a momentary sense of innocence and escape for the embattled president. For an hour and a half, people lined up to talk to him, while he hugged a waitress, signed autographs, and posed with the Saudi ambassador and his son. Nixon was so distracted that he forgot to pay the check; the restaurant billed the White House.

AS HIS PRESIDENCY STAGGERED, Nixon turned to a different kind of comfort food: a dish he reserved for special occasions, one that held a mysterious, Rosebud-like significance for him, as if it were too special for daily consumption and could be eaten only at moments of great celebration or stress.

Amid daily revelations about Watergate in November 1973, seventy-five worried Republicans attended a White House breakfast. They pressed Nixon on the "childish" burglars and his firing of the special prosecutor Archibald Cox. The president claimed he knew nothing about the scandal and pleaded to his allies, "I need your help." But it was too late. In a private meeting with GOP supporters on August 8, 1974, Nixon tearily acknowledged he had lost their support and would step down, becoming the only president to resign from office. Then he tripped over a chair and nearly crashed to the ground. Recomposing himself, Nixon delivered the message to the nation on live television and radio: "I shall resign the Presidency at noon tomorrow."

At six o'clock the next morning, Henry Haller arrived at the White House to discover Nixon, dressed in pajamas, standing in the private kitchen. Instead of his usual wheat germ and coffee, he ordered one last presidential breakfast: corned beef hash topped by a poached egg—the dish that held special significance for him. He sat alone at a table in the Lincoln Sitting Room and savored every bite. Once he had cleaned his plate, Chief of Staff Alexander Haig laid down a letter with a single typed sentence: "I hereby resign the Office of President of the United States."

Nixon picked up a pen and signed his name.

AT 12:03 P.M. ON AUGUST 9, 1974, Gerald Ford was hastily sworn in as the nation's thirty-eighth president by Chief Justice Warren Burger, making him the only man to serve as both vice president and president without being elected by the Electoral College.

"Our long national nightmare is over," he declared wishfully. Nixon did not watch the swearing-in, and as the two couples walked toward Marine One, Ford made awkward small talk: "Drop us a line if you get the chance. Let us know how you're doing." Nixon scoffed at Ford's sentimentality. As the Nixons clattered away in a helicopter, Ford assured his wife, Betty, "We can do it."

The Nixons transferred to Air Force One and winged across the country to San Clemente. They were the only passengers aboard. Observing rows of seats usually filled by the press, Nixon muttered, "Well, it certainly smells better back here." Somewhere high above Jefferson City,

Missouri, Dick and Pat poured themselves martinis, then retreated to separate compartments to sip their numbing drinks and stare out the window as the nation slipped away beneath them.

IV. Gerald Ford: The Instant President

The Thirty-Eighth President
August 9, 1974–January 20, 1977

The turnover on August 9 happened so quickly that the Fords did not have time to pack for the White House, and after the inauguration they returned to their split-level ranch house in Alexandria, Virginia, where they celebrated over lasagna. The next morning President Ford, dressed in short baby-blue pajamas, walked out to pick up the morning paper, and was startled when a clutch of reporters began firing questions at him. He waved sheepishly, then went inside to fix a breakfast of orange juice, melon, an English muffin with margarine and jam, and tea.

"You are what you eat," Haller observed. Gerald Ford, like his food, was "unpretentious, honest, wholesome, hearty, and all-American." In the wake of the dark melodrama surrounding Nixon, the chef wrote, America was "prepared to trade political pomp and glory for public confidence and stability."

A genial, modest man, Jerry Ford had an unorthodox rise to the top of the political heap. In October 1973, the Michigan Republican was minority leader of the House who aspired to nothing more than becoming Speaker. But the GOP was in disarray, and he was considered a safe candidate to replace the convicted Spiro Agnew as vice president.

"I happen to be the nation's first instant Vice President," Ford told the Grocery Manufacturers of America. Adding that he preferred instant coffee and instant oatmeal to the genuine articles, he said, "I only hope that I prove to be as pure, as digestible, and as appetizing to the consumers who did not have a chance to shop around for other brands of Vice President when I was put on the market."

Ten days after his swearing-in, the Fords and two of their four children moved into the President's House. That evening they celebrated with prime rib, new potatoes with parsley, green beans, salad, and ice cream. The basic, hearty dinner was typical of the Fords' "Michigan gourmet" diet.

Ford did not cringe at socializing the way Nixon did, but he did enjoy quiet meals at "home" in the mansion. Ford maintained that "eating and sleeping are a waste of time," and his lunch, like his predecessor's, often consisted of a ball of cottage cheese slathered in A.1. Sauce, a slice of raw onion, and a bite of ice cream. Betty favored leftovers or soup with homemade "toasting" bread. Dinner favorites included midwestern classics like tuna casserole, stuffed cabbage, spareribs with sauerkraut, hamburgers topped with bacon, liver, and onions, or lobster foo yong (a "Chinese" egg and lobster dish) with a salad or cooked vegetables. While the Fords did not eat a lot of sweets, the First Lady liked to serve chocolate angel food cake, which was light and sweet but not high in fat, for dessert. The president's favorite food, she said, was butter pecan ice cream.

To celebrate their first White House Christmas, the Fords hosted a congressional ball for a thousand guests. In a new spirit of openness, it was a nonpartisan event and the first party for the entire Congress in six years. Many of the legislators had never attended a formal White House party before, and were agog. The State Floor was transformed into a holiday wonderland, with a large crèche in the East Room, an enormous buffet and a gingerbread house in the State Dining Room, and a Christmas tree in the North Hall. In a toast, the dieting President Ford observed, "That big Michigan Christmas tree and I have a lot in common. Neither of us expected to be in the White House a little while ago. Both of us were a little green. Both of us have been put on a pedestal and—I will add this as a postscript—both of us have been trimmed a little."

. . .

PRESIDENTIAL MEALS SAY something about their eaters, their era, and what it means to be American. The details of each dish—the ingredients, where they were sourced, who prepared them and how, the way they were presented, to whom, when, and why—send a powerful message about the president's values and the state of the nation. And the public pays attention.

In 1976, Ford, who was prone to gaffes, invited ridicule by biting into a tamale still wrapped in its corn husk on a visit to San Antonio. His faux pas seemed to mirror the country's post-Nixon stumbling. Trying to quell the fallout from the "Great Tamale Incident," Mayor Lila Cockrell said, "The president didn't know any better. . . . [H]e didn't get a briefing on the eating of tamales." But when Ford shed fifteen pounds at the White House, people clamored for details about his diet, and magazines reprinted Haller's low-calorie menus. The president got a kick out of that. But not everyone was pleased by the example set by the Instant President.

Julia Child, a diet skeptic who was attuned to both the symbolic and practical roles of presidential food, scoffed at Ford as a *tête de lard* ("fathead") who lacked the wit to recognize that what he ate represented something far more important than his own looks. Similarly, when the Fords hosted the Windsors at the 1976 bicentennial celebration, Julia was thrilled to attend, but resented the tacky entertainment, the amateurish telecast, and, most of all, her inability to taste the wine or comment on Henry Haller's cooking for a large audience eager to hear about it. Ford, it seemed, did not fully grasp the significance of the moment, his role in it, or the broader importance of food and entertaining. He had a good time and danced with Queen Elizabeth that night; but a more savvy president, like Jefferson, FDR, or Kennedy, would have seized the opportunity to spread "the good news about good food at the White House," as Julia put it—and reaped the political dividends.

With the arrival of Jimmy and Rosalynn Carter in 1977, Julia was optimistic that they would "do something about improving" the fare at the People's House, and promote regional dishes. She advised Mrs. Carter to look deep into her larder, consider its symbolic importance, and promote "the good in American cooking."

JIMMY CARTER

In Search of Grits and Peace

I. Southern Food and Hospitality

As the election of 1976 heated up, voters perused a lengthy slate of candidates, most of whom came from northern or western states. When the former Georgia governor James Earl "Jimmy" Carter tossed his hat in the ring, his name recognition was at 2 percent. A thumbnail sketch defined him as a southern Democrat with a broad toothy smile, a full head of sandy-silver hair, and a taste for grits. But that was about it. The press described him as "mysterious," but his flinty mother, Lillian Carter, had another take: "Jimmy isn't mysterious. I would say he is original and stubborn."

A vote for Carter was seen as a leap of faith. But in truth, he understood politics better than many people gave him credit for. He knew that his outsiderness was an asset and that optics were important. Carter was a peanut farmer and the son of a peanut farmer, and his devotion to southern food was integral to his pitch. When he hosted a "down-home lunch" in Georgia, the menu included fried chicken, baked cheese grits, turnip greens, candied apples, corn bread, and biscuits. It was the kind of familiar yet exotic menu that set him apart in the public imagination.

"Jimmy," as everyone called him, and his wife, Rosalynn, liked to cook together—as they did much else, including discussing politics and policy. Their table in the small town of Plains, Georgia, featured southern staples: catfish, biscuits, wild rice, country ham with redeye gravy (ham drippings mixed with coffee), and homemade peach ice cream. They liked Brunswick stew (a vegetable mélange traditionally made with squirrel or rabbit, though the Carters used chicken) or "a mess of greens"—collard, mustard, or turnip greens, boiled with salt pork—and poured their pot likker (leftover cooking liquid) on corn bread. They made Hoppin' John (black-eyed peas with rice flavored by bacon or salted pork) and "Red and White" (red beans and white rice); they turned eggplant, zucchini, yellow-neck squashes, turnips, and tomatoes into casseroles.

Like Eisenhower, Carter grew up fishing for bream and bass, shooting quail and duck with a 16-gauge shotgun, growing vegetables in his garden, and cooking. Jimmy was not a gourmet, but enjoyed making a good meal and was, for my money, the second-best presidential cook after Ike. Rosalynn made Sally Lunn (a light tea cake served hot with butter) and local specialties such as the "Plains Special"—a molded ring of cheddar cheese mixed with a pound of grated nuts, onion, mayonnaise, and a sprinkle of pepper, served with crackers and her own strawberry preserves. Theirs was "the kind of cooking . . . to which [those] who strayed away from the simple ways of our forebears' prepared food are now returning," she said.

These homey dishes added color, texture, and dimension to Carter's biography as a navy submarine officer and small-towner made good. In the end America took a chance on him, and he beat Ford by a slim margin—50.1 percent to 48 percent of the vote. The couple from Plains were the first residents of the Executive Mansion from the Deep South since Woodrow Wilson, who hailed from Virginia, or, some said, Zachary Taylor, who was born in Virginia and raised in Kentucky.

ON THEIR FIRST MORNING in the White House, in January 1977, the Carters ordered eggs and grits for breakfast. Grits, the cornmeal staple of southern states, was a dish that the family served at any meal. Nine-year-old Amy Carter reported that "Daddy makes grits . . . then breaks a couple of eggs into it and adds some cheese, and it's yummy." Grits are made from hulled corn kernels that have been washed and boiled into hominy, a word that originated with the Algonquin word *tack-hummin,* or "ground corn" (and might have also derived from the Old English *grytt,* or "coarse meal"). There are two grades of hominy: coarsely ground grits, and finely ground cornmeal, called *polenta* in Italy and Latin America. Their preparation is simple, requiring just cornmeal, water, salt, and plenty of stirring. In southern kitchens they are served hot with melted butter, fried golden brown, or baked with vegetables or cheese. Italian *polenta* is generally not a breakfast food; it is served later in the day with olive oil or tomato sauce and Parmesan cheese.

"While New Englanders gasped and Midwesterners gagged, Southerners smiled with knowing satisfaction" at the Carters' grits, the chef Henry Haller recalled. In time, "distinguished visitors really expected to be served grits, and most were pleasantly surprised to discover they actually liked the taste."

"That sounds mighty good to me," Julia Child said. She was thrilled that the Carters would bring "authentic Southern" cooking to Washington. And why stop there? she wondered. Why not showcase dishes from Cajun Louisiana, Yankee New England, the Florida Keys, the midwestern corn belt, the desert Southwest, California, Alaska, Hawaii, Puerto Rico, or Guam? The new First Family should spread the gospel of American regional cuisine far and wide, Julia urged. And she wrote, "Whatever our new First Lady does to make White House entertaining more American, let her vigorously publicize it."

Rosalynn Carter didn't need encouragement to ballyhoo southern hospitality, for it was a subject she had given a good deal of thought to. In the February 1977 issue of *McCall's*—which hit newsstands just as she moved into 1600 Pennsylvania Avenue—the First Lady introduced herself to the nation like this:

> Each family that occupies the White House brings something of its own region to Washington. Despite the protocol and continuity in style that is tradition, there are differences in flavor of entertaining. What Jimmy and I hope to bring to the White House is a bit of that elusive pleasure we call Southern hospitality: We enjoy having people in and we know that we can help them feel welcome, whatever the occasion.

Mrs. Carter believed the point of entertaining was human contact, the sharing of sustenance, and a generosity of spirit that would inspire reciprocal acts of kindness—or commensality, if you will—in a positive feedback loop. She made clear this was the essence of her church teaching and *real* southern hospitality, as opposed to the advertised or Hollywoodized version of "southernness."

In 1953, Jimmy Carter inherited his father's peanut farm in Americus, Georgia. The next year the region faced a drought and the farm made just $187. But Jimmy was patient—or "stubborn," as his mother said—and by 1970 had become a prosperous agribusinessman. Rosalynn grew up three miles away and was three years younger than he. The daughter of a farmer-mechanic, she helped her mother cook, sew, and take care of her three siblings when her father died. As newlyweds, the Carters did their own shopping, cooking, and cleaning; "Jimmy cooked as much as I did," she said. When you read Mrs. Carter closely, you discern her pride in her heritage and a warning not to condescend:

> There probably are still people who think of Southern hospitality in terms of magnolias and leisure, grand balls and crinoline, and a house

full of servants. I guess there was something like that in the South once upon a time. But never, I assure you, for most of us. My life was not like that. My mother's life was not like that. And I don't think that lavish entertaining is what Southern hospitality is all about. To me, what it is, and always has been, is simply a genuinely warm welcome to anyone who drops in. . . . My mother, Jimmy's mother, and I have always worked, and we never had household help. In this respect, Southern women are just like women everywhere else, trying to balance off the demands of a job against the real pleasures of having a home and sharing it with friends.

The Carters didn't mind when hungry friends or relatives dropped by uninvited, and they were not embarrassed to return the favor. "If there's any secret to hospitality, maybe it's just that everything doesn't have to be perfect," Rosalynn wrote. "The house might not be perfectly straight and the children aren't going to be perfectly neat. The only thing you can do is just relax and make everyone else more comfortable. . . . Jimmy used to say to me, 'Just do your best and the rest will take care of itself.' That's especially good advice."

It was a generous and relatable sentiment, but one that did not always translate easily to Washington, D.C., where some people approached their entertaining, like their politics, as a blood sport. "The press had painted us as country farm people who would bring gingham and square dances to the White House. We did. Sometimes. But we also brought a parade of America's greatest classical talent and some of the most elegant events."

In this way, the Carters began their tenure with a surge of goodwill: they were honest, well intentioned, and effective. At first. But over time, it became clear they were not all that interested in adapting to Washington's ways, and eventually the District dismissed them as starchy, pious, stingy, and parochial. The end of the Carter administration was seeded in its beginnings.

II. Soft Cardigans, Burned Cookies, and Willie on the Roof

The First Lady liked to cook at home in Plains, but in moving to busy Washington, she was thrilled to have a staff who would shop and prepare meals for her family and friends, many of whom were eager to spend a night at the White House. But her generosity wasn't cheap. While Henry Haller and his four kitchen assistants were government employees, the president is required to pay for the food and drink he, his family, and private guests consume. (State dinners are paid for by taxpayers.) When Mrs. Carter was presented with a $600 food bill for their first ten days of residency in January 1977, she suffered sticker shock. From then on, she insisted the staff buy the cheapest brands of food and use leftovers whenever possible.

She cut the number of White House calligraphers in half, sent xeroxed invitations to a picnic, and once asked her music teacher to perform as the after-dinner entertainment. To further reduce costs, the Carters sold the presidential yacht, *Sequoia,* and greatly reduced the number of televisions, radios, and newspapers and magazines in the White House.

Unlike the suit-wearing Nixon, Carter often dressed in a folksy plaid shirt, jeans, work boots, and a loose cardigan—made famous on his televised "Fireside Chats." And he didn't welcome guests with trumpets and flourishes, but would drawl, "Hi! C'mon in!" Social ceremony "does not appeal to me," he explained. "I'm no better than anyone else, and . . . I don't think we need to put on the trappings of a monarchy in a nation like our own."

The Carters had four children. While one or more of their three grown sons—John William (Jack), James Earl (Chip), Donnel Jeffrey (Jeff)—occasionally stayed over at the White House, only Amy, the Carters' youngest, grew up there. She wore glasses, attended public school, and raised eyebrows by reading a book at a state dinner for Canada's Pierre Trudeau. For her twelfth birthday, the French-born executive pastry chef Roland Mesnier, whom the First Lady hired in 1979, baked a cake decorated with marzipan versions of some of her favorite possessions: her cat Misty Malarky; a piano; a violin; and a pair of roller skates.

Amy loved her skates, but they occasionally landed her in trouble. Some worried her scooting would damage the mansion's hardwood floors, and they could be a distraction. After a day at public school, the First Daughter liked to bake sugar cookies in the family kitchen. Mesnier would send ingredients from his pastry kitchen—butter, sugar, flour, baking powder, an egg—so Amy could mix them herself. She'd cut out the cookies and set them in the oven, and while they baked, she'd start roller-skating. When smoke poured forth and a burning smell filled the halls, Secret Service agents would scramble. Finding the burned cookies, they opened windows for a clearing breeze. Crestfallen, Amy would say, "There was a small accident." (Mesnier kept extra cookies on hand that she could take to school.)

Another person who pushed the boundaries of propriety at the White House was the "outlaw" country musician Willie Nelson, a good friend of the Carters'. One night in 1980, Willie joined them for dinner and played a concert on the South Lawn. Later, Willie and "a friend inside the White House" crept out of the third-floor solarium to take in the sights "with a beer in one hand and a fat Austin Torpedo in the other," *Rolling Stone* reported. Later, the insider was identified as Chip, the Carters' middle son. "Could have been [him], yeah," Willie said. "It seemed like the thing to do. . . . [W]hy not, you know? . . . [The president] knew me and he knew Chip so, you know, there wasn't much we could do to embarrass him."

WHEN IT CAME to official entertaining, President Carter drew praise and criticism for his economizing and simplifying. He wore off-the-rack suits and cut the color guard and the playing of "Hail to the Chief." He occasionally deputized Vice President and Mrs. Mondale, or Carter family members, to stand in for him at dinners.

Moreover, the Carters were light drinkers. The president was fonder of coffee, tea, or milk than alcohol, but was not averse to the occasional beer, scotch, or margarita in the private quarters. But to his wife's mind, hard liquor was "unnecessary" at official functions, and not serving it "saved money." As Georgia's First Lady, Rosalynn served only domestic wine or vermouth with cassis at receptions, beer at picnics, and wine at formal dinners. "I don't know how I would have managed to squeeze out money for hard liquor," she explained. She continued this habit in Washington, probably due to a combination of personal taste, religious belief, and life experience. (Jimmy's brother, Billy, was an alcoholic who made headlines with intemperate statements, business failures, and the loud promotion of his Billy Beer.) When critics labeled her "Rosé Rosalynn," she bristled: "They make me sound like a real prude. I'm not a prude!" Besides, she pointed out, the Carter state dinners cost taxpayers a mere $4.50 per serving.

Such economy was deliberate, said Mary Finch Hoyt, Mrs. Carter's press secretary. The "Man from Plains" wanted to set a low-key tone yet retain the "policy, protocol, the whole image of an Administration that leaves a definite imprint on history."

.   .   .

ROSALYNN CARTER WAS a thoughtful, self-sufficient woman who never fully adapted to White House life, with its helpmeets, limits, expectations, and scrutiny. "Official entertaining can't replace the kind of entertaining I love to do in my home," she said. "It can never be truly spontaneous. It is done to support a policy, to forge alliances with other countries and to create good will." Her husband generally agreed, but there was one notable exception to that rule, a singular moment when presidential food and spontaneity helped create the conditions for a remarkable diplomatic breakthrough.

III. The Impossible

It was at breakfast on the morning of July 20, 1978, that Jimmy Carter decided once and for all to tackle an issue that had bothered him for years: the blood feud between Israel and its Arab neighbors. Jews and Muslims had been killing each other for centuries, and practically everyone warned that it would be "impossible" to resolve the conflict. But Carter was a willful optimist who believed that under the right circumstances he could bring the Israeli prime minister, Menachem Begin, and the Egyptian president, Anwar Sadat, together to negotiate a truce. "First Egyptian-Jewish peace since time of Jeremiah," Carter scribbled to himself.

He had decided that "peace in the Middle East would be one of his most important responsibilities," Rosalynn wrote. "He was convinced that an end to war in that region was vital to the peace of the world."

His advisers worried that a failed peace talk could destroy his administration or haunt his reelection bid. But the more people doubted him, the more Carter dug in. "I slowly became hardened against them, and as stubborn as at any other time I can remember," he recalled.

Carter knew the negotiations required a special kind of meeting place. "It was necessary we be completely isolated from the press so that neither Begin nor Sadat nor their representatives would feel constrained . . . to explain what they were doing," he wrote. When he and a team decamped to Camp David, the remote presidential retreat on Maryland's Catoctin Mountain, to discuss the plan, he was struck by how tranquil the 125-acre compound was. No president had brokered peace between foreign leaders on U.S. soil before, but, Carter mused, "It's so beautiful here. I don't believe anybody could stay in this place, close to nature, peaceful and isolated . . . and still carry a grudge. . . . If I could get Sadat and Begin both here together, we could work out some of the problems between them."

The camp was built by FDR, who called it Shangri-La; it was rechristened Camp David by Eisenhower, after his father and grandson. The grounds include rustic cabins with trails, tennis, golf, fishing, books, movies, games, and excellent food prepared by navy stewards. Less well known is that burrowed deep beneath the pastoral camp is a bunker, Orange One, fortified against nuclear attack. Some considered Camp David a gilded cage because it is so remote and heavily guarded. But practically speaking, it was just a thirty-five-minute helicopter ride from the White House. Carter invited the combatants to a peace summit there, and to the surprise of many both the Israelis and the Egyptians accepted.

On September 5, 1978, the three—Begin, an Orthodox Jew; Sadat, a pious Muslim; and Carter, a devout Baptist—went into the mountains of Maryland to forge peace in the Holy Land. Feeling bullish, the president predicted it would take a week, tops, to achieve his goal. "Compromises will be mandatory," he said. "Without them, no progress can be expected." Sadat was tall, trim, and urbane, with a bald pate rimmed by dark hair, a mustache, thin lips, and almond-shaped eyes in an oval face. Begin was shorter and more rectilinear in shape, with thick dark-rimmed glasses, a slash of a mouth, and a serious look in his eye.

Both had strong personalities. "Whereas Begin has a tendency toward literalism and an obsession with detail, Sadat is often imprecise with words and has little patience for precision and for real negotiating," Carter's brief read. "In this situation, the danger of genuine misunderstanding, followed by feelings of betrayal and recrimination, is very great."

On Tuesday, September 5, Carter surprised his guests by welcoming the Israeli and Egyptian delegates dressed in faded blue jeans and an open-necked shirt. Sadat was a stylish dresser who favored beige leisure suits and black turtlenecks; he took a brisk walk around the camp every morning. Begin almost always wore a gray jacket and tie: in poor health, he took slow walks with his wife, Aliza. Camp David's rustic cabins are named after trees: the Carters stayed in Aspen; Sadat was in Dogwood; and the Begins were housed in Birch. They were a hundred yards away from each other, and Carter hoped the proximity would encourage chance encounters and friendly talk.

Each side had a large entourage of delegates who were billeted in nearby cabins, while the American advisers were relegated to a military barracks. The challenge of feeding more than a hundred people with different diets and religious strictures was "complicated," Mrs. Carter recalled. After lengthy discussions about food security, the parties agreed that cooking for the three leaders would be done in the Carters' kitchen in Aspen lodge and served in their residences.

Sadat was a heart attack survivor who maintained a low-sodium diet: he brought a personal chef to provide boiled meat and vegetables. As devout Muslims, the Egyptian delegation drank water or fruit juice, and Sadat was partial to mint tea sweetened by honey. To conform to kosher dietary laws, the Israelis brought a mashgiach, or food supervisor, who ensured that nonkosher ingredients—such as shellfish, lard, or gelatin— did not touch the food. In a section of the Aspen kitchen reserved for the Israelis, a rabbi passed a blowtorch over the stoves, worktables, and pots; tableware, floors, and walls were scrubbed clean. With that, "we marveled at the ease with which Sadat's chef, our regular stewards, and the kosher cooks shared the same kitchen," Mrs. Carter wrote. "We had a lot of laughs about the food."

As the talks got under way, Sadat and Begin avoided each other, warily, while Carter shuttled between them. Begin declared that Israel would not give back any territory captured in the 1967 war. Expecting this, Carter nodded patiently and met with Sadat, who began with a similar hard line—that Israel must return the captured territory and pay for its use. But then he slipped the president a list of concessions he was prepared to make.

Emboldened, Carter brought the two leaders together for a conversation on the Aspen patio. It didn't go well. Sadat demanded that Israel withdraw from the West Bank and Gaza, relinquish East Jerusalem, and allow a Palestinian nation. Glaring at his enemy, Begin responded with a few words, harshly delivered: "Sinai settlements must stay!"

"Security yes! Land no!" Sadat shouted back.

Acrimony polluted the air like smoke from a grease fire. A weary Carter told his team, "It was mean. They were brutal with each other, personal." The two men were so incompatible, he realized, that "any subject deteriorated into an unproductive argument."

This arrangement left many of the Egyptian, Israeli, and American officials with a lot of nervous energy but not much to do. When not preparing documents for their leaders, the delegates shot pool, drove golf carts, watched 58 movies, and ate. A lot. The delegates' meals were prepared by U.S. Navy stewards in the large staff canteen at Laurel. The food was delicious, but the Israeli and Egyptian visitors sat at opposite ends of the dining room, and "the atmosphere remained oppressive and tense," an Israeli recalled.

Carter resorted to "proximity talks," in which Begin and Sadat would be in the same area but not talk directly, while the Americans shuffled proposals back and forth and the delegates worked through the details. There were more meetings and more confrontations, and Carter worried that his historic opportunity was slipping away. "There must be a way" to peace, he insisted. "There must be."

Rosalynn had an idea. Hosting a reception for the delegates, she arranged for platters of food to be displayed in different rooms—cheese fondue here, strawberries dipped in chocolate there, drinks on the patio—"hoping people would circulate instead of staying in small cliques," she said. The bored, hungry Israelis and Egyptians followed the cookie crumbs, as it were, and were soon chatting with each other. The American pies, cakes, and mousses were so popular that the delegates were "gaining too much weight. But the desserts were too good to pass up," the First Lady noted. "For months afterward the participants complained about the ten extra pounds they'd put on at Camp David." In a more serious vein, she wondered, if the delegates could "talk peacefully" and enjoy cookies together, "why couldn't their leaders?"

On Friday, President Carter spent hours with Sadat and Begin and persuaded them to agree in principle to a peace proposal. It was an important step forward. That evening, the movie theater was converted into a banquet hall for Shabbat (rest) eve, the traditional Jewish Sabbath dinner. The day's tension seemed to evaporate as the Carters joined the Israeli delegation in eating, singing, and laughter, because, as Begin said, "the Bible says you cannot serve God with sadness."

Then it was back to negotiating, with meetings running from sunup to sundown, and sometimes until 3:45 in the morning. On the Israeli side, Begin proved less flexible than his deputies. On the Egyptian side, Sadat proved more flexible than his advisers. The negotiations bogged down, and a frustrated Sadat packed his bags for Egypt. Carter warned that if he left, it would end their diplomatic gains, their personal friendship, and probably his presidency. Reluctantly, the Egyptian unpacked his bags. In gratitude, Carter requested "a little more wheat and corn" for Egypt, which Congress approved. The two relaxed by watching Muhammad Ali defeat Leon Spinks to reclaim the world heavyweight boxing championship. Then the Baptist and Muslim presidents called the Muslim American boxer to congratulate him.

Time was running out. In the tense stalemate, Begin and Sadat avoided each other and lost their appetites. Neither would budge on the question of Israeli settlements in the Sinai and on the West Bank. On the penultimate night, Mrs. Carter sent a platter of cheese and crackers into Begin and Carter. At midnight they broke up their meeting, and Carter wolfed down the pepper steak that had been made hours earlier, and collapsed into bed.

In the final minutes of the summit's final day, Sunday, September 17, a draft peace agreement was initialed by Carter, Begin, and Sadat. Against all security precautions, the three leaders flew in the same helicopter to the White House, and a crowd cheered as they touched down on the South Lawn. When they signed the accords in the East Room, everyone there had tears in their eyes. Henry Haller cobbled together enough food to feed two hundred—a few leftovers from a brunch, pecan and strawberry tarts from a concert, and some extra carrot cakes from the fridge. It wasn't a perfect banquet, but it would do.

The president looked dazed. The weary Israeli held up a glass of wine. The frazzled Egyptian held a glass of orange juice. They toasted to achieving the impossible. "History was indeed made that night," Rosalynn wrote.

After thirteen days of intense bargaining in the mountains and months of follow-up, the Camp David Accords led to a formal peace treaty between Israel and Egypt. It was signed at the White House on March 26, 1979. That night, the Carters hosted a celebratory Peace Treaty Dinner for 1,340 people, the largest sit-down meal in White House history to that point. Under an enormous yellow tent and six smaller orange tents on the South Lawn, 280 waiters served 134 tables "with militaristic precision," Haller fondly recalled. The dinner began with Columbia River salmon in aspic and moved on to roasted sirloin steaks with green beans, carrots, and mushrooms, and ended with a hazelnut and chocolate Gianduja mousse. (A hundred and ten kosher meals were served to the Jewish guests.) After dinner, an Egyptian rock band, an Israeli duo, and the American soprano Leontyne Price performed, and the party stretched till midnight.

As Carter smiled and shook hands, Sadat thanked the president, saying, "I think that he worked harder than our forefathers did in Egypt building the pyramids."

The treaty was built on diligence, compromise, and the connections made over food. It dared the world to hope that a lasting peace in the Middle East was in hand. And remarkably it was. Sadat and Begin were awarded the 1978 Nobel Peace Prize; in 2002, Carter was awarded a Nobel for his human rights work. Jihadis assassinated Sadat in Cairo in 1981, Begin grew embittered and reclusive, and bloody conflicts continue to flare between Israelis and Palestinians; yet the truce between Egypt and Israel has held since 1978.

"The impossible had been made possible," Rosalynn Carter wrote. "A miracle? Yes . . . it was a miracle."

IV. Trigger

Initially, observers cheered the end of Nixon's "imperial presidency" and the arrival of the Carters as a breath of fresh air. But as time went on, those cheers turned to sniping about the Carters' low-budget informality, which made them—and therefore the nation—appear cheap, naive, and not to be taken seriously.

Perception informs reality, but some of the carping was unfair. The Carters were frugal, but they did not stint on official entertaining, and hosted nearly a hundred presidents, prime ministers, kings, and Pope John Paul II at "glittering" dinners. The food served by chef Henry Haller at these events was no worse than his much lauded meals for the Johnsons, Nixons, Fords, and later the Reagans. To build rapport with their guests, the Carters chose thoughtful personal gifts or events—presenting German chancellor Helmut Schmidt and his wife pots of crepe myrtle, a small purple flower they loved; arranging for Egyptian president Anwar Sadat, who was "hooked" on American Westerns, to be serenaded by the Statler Brothers, a gospel and country music group; and ensuring that Japanese prime minister Masayoshi Ohira was feted at an outdoor barbecue while Bobby Short played jazz standards. Occasionally, things didn't go exactly as planned—such as the night when the Carters descended the Grand Staircase for a state dinner preceeded by Amy's cat, Misty Malarky Ying Yang.

But the Carters made no major social mistakes, and it seemed gratuitous when the press "pigeonholed [Carter] as a hick peanut farmer who knew nothing about fine food," recalled pastry chef Roland Mesnier. "This was completely untrue, as I knew very well."

Though Carter had achieved notable policy successes—the establishment of the Departments of Energy and Education, the SALT II talks, the Camp David Accords—he was denounced for pardoning Vietnam draft dodgers, and presiding during the 1979 energy crisis, debilitating unemployment and inflation, the Three Mile Island nuclear accident, and the Soviet invasion of Afghanistan. Praised early on for his calm resolve, Carter was increasingly portrayed as weak, pettifogging, and indecisive. Then came the killing blow.

On November 4, 1979, a group of Muslim students stormed the U.S. embassy in Tehran, taking fifty-two Americans hostage for 444 days. It was the longest hostage crisis in American history, and it gripped the world's attention. In characteristic fashion, Carter threw himself into negotiations with Ayatollah Khomeini, camped out in the Oval Office, and survived on stale sandwiches. As the Iranians used the hostages as a bargaining chip, Carter ordered a covert rescue mission, Operation Eagle Claw. Landing in Iran's Great Salt Desert, American special forces encountered a dust storm and unexpected civilians. When they aborted the mission, a helicopter crashed into a transport plane, which exploded in a bright fireball, and killed eight Americans and an Iranian. It was a debacle.

In the election of 1980, Carter ran neck and neck with his Republican challenger, Ronald Reagan, while negotiating with Iran. Pressure mounted on the president to show decisiveness and bomb Tehran. But Carter, a deeply moral man, didn't want to risk killing the hostages. The ayatollah did not release the Americans, and Reagan won 50.7 percent of the vote to Carter's 41 percent. "There's no doubt about it," Carter said. "Had the hostages been released . . . I would've been reelected." And if he had bombed Tehran, Rosalynn added, he would have won.

As the moving men packed lamps and books and rugs, the Carters hosted a "final supper" at the White House. Haller served southern specialties in the private dining room to just a dozen guests, mostly family and friends. Almost everyone was teary. Between courses, a thirteenth guest arrived: Willie Nelson, carrying his battered guitar "Trigger," named after Roy Rogers's horse. And in his high, scratchy voice, Willie sang the Carters out with a bittersweet rendition of "Georgia on My Mind."

RONALD REAGAN

Jelly Beans, Weight Loss, and Glasnost

THE FORTIETH PRESIDENT
January 20, 1981–January 20, 1989

✦

I. A New Beginning

When Ronald Reagan celebrated his inauguration in the Capitol on January 20, 1981, each table was decorated with a vase of California roses, in honor of his adopted home state, and each guest was given a silver-plated box filled with multicolored jelly beans, his signature snack. The marbled Statuary Hall echoed with loud talk and clinking tableware as guests dug into chicken piquante, rice pilaf, and fresh asparagus. At 2:15, an aide leaned down to whisper into Reagan's ear. The just-minted president smiled, stood up, and said, "With thanks to Almighty God, I have been given [the kind of] tag line . . . everyone wants. . . . Some 30 minutes ago, the . . . planes bearing our prisoners left Iranian airspace and they're now free."

The crowd erupted. Reagan couldn't have scripted a better launch to his administration if it had been authored by Frank Capra.

At that moment, Jimmy Carter, the man who had strained nearly to the breaking point to win the hostages' release, was driving to the airport. He was utterly drained. When the limousine's phone rang, Vice President Walter Mondale answered. It was the news from Tehran: after 444 days, the fifty-two hostages had been freed. The two men stared at each other with tears streaming down their cheeks. They were relieved, but could not help wondering what might have been. Politics can be a brutal arena, and the hostages' release would forever be associated with Ronald Reagan, not Jimmy Carter.

At sixty-nine years and 348 days, Reagan was the oldest newly elected president in history at that point. At his inauguration, he, like Jack Kennedy, wore a formal morning suit: gray jacket, vest, and striped pants. Nancy Reagan wore a $3,000 raspberry-red dress and coat by Adolfo, with a matching hat reminiscent of the famous pillbox worn by Jackie Kennedy. Though they denied it, the Reagans were striving for the kind of effortless glamour not seen at the White House since Camelot.

Reagan's inaugural was the biggest and, at $16 million, the most expensive in history by then. (By contrast, Carter's "'people's' inauguration" in 1977 cost just $3.5 million.) With a huge parade, laser light shows, fireworks, and dozens of performances around town, it ushered in a pro-business, antigovernment, anti-Soviet era and sent a clear, brash message: times had changed. Gone were Carter's soft sweater-vests, failed hostage rescue, and earnest moralizing; Rosalynn's small-town friends and molded cheese rings; Amy's roller skates and burned cookies; White House staffers "in bare feet" (so a National Security Council member claimed); and outlaw guests smoking weed on the roof. In came "Queen Nancy" Reagan, who insisted on pressed suits and ties, crisp skirts and shiny high heels, Hollywood players and haute cuisine.

The Reagans' inaugural guests included a dozen wealthy, conservative friends who called themselves "the Kitchen Cabinet." (The term originated with Andrew Jackson's intimate circle, a group of unofficial advisers who clashed with his official staff, the "Parlor Cabinet.") Reagan's Kitchen Cabinet—including the department store heir Alfred Bloomingdale, the auto dealer Holmes Tuttle, the steel magnate Earle Jorgensen, the oilman William Wilson, and the Colorado beer magnate Joseph Coors—had supported him as he hopscotched from the presidency of the Screen Actors Guild to the California governor's mansion and into the White House. Their wives, who called themselves "the Group," had been Nancy's close friends since the 1950s. The Group appeared at Reagan's inaugural dressed in matching sable coats and blond bouffants.

"Some folks are jokingly calling it a coronation," one Reaganite said. It didn't seem like a joke to critics, who singled out Nancy's wardrobe—including a $10,000 Galanos gown and diamond earrings worth $480,000 loaned by Harry Winston—as particularly cringeworthy at a time of national belt-tightening. The cost of her handbag alone was equivalent to more than a year's worth of food stamps for an entire family, the press calculated. It was the kind of critique Mrs. Reagan would court, and resent, over the next eight years.

For the kitchen staff, the fortieth president was a mystery. A West Coaster who was virtually unknown in Washington, Reagan was said to be a man of simple tastes who hated tomatoes and liver but loved steak, Mexican food, and sweet desserts. As for Mrs. Reagan, she was a five-foot-four-inch-tall, 110-pound woman known as "the Iron Butterfly" for her ferocious drive, eye for detail, and instinct for political stagecraft.

The chef Henry Haller took Nancy's perfectionist tinkering—with the food, china, and flower arrangements—in stride. But the pastry chef Roland Mesnier was "scared shitless" and thought he might be fired when a Reaganite glared at the raspberry puree smeared on his chef's whites. "No one knew what to expect," he recalled.

Privately, Mrs. Reagan felt the same way about "permanent Washington" and its notoriously tight-knit tribes—those listed in the city's Green Book social registry, or the "cave dwellers," whose roots extended back to the founding of the capital.

With greater insecurities and sharper political instincts than Rosalynn Carter, the new First Lady set out to woo the Establishment. A former actress, Nancy bought the right costumes, learned proper manners, studied diction, and hired Mabel "Muffie" Brandon Cabot, a bluestocking Democrat from Boston, as her social secretary. When Nancy cried, "I don't want to be Rosalynn Carter!" Cabot coolly replied, "Mrs. Reagan, you don't have a chance in hell of being Rosalynn Carter." Nancy also hired Letitia Baldrige, Jackie Kennedy's first social secretary, to coach her on the finer points of White House entertaining. Mrs. Reagan "wanted to have people consider her a woman of great taste and knowledge," Baldrige recalled. "She wanted everything to be perfect. If there was a mistake on the table—the way the silverware was put down, for example—that would upset her terribly."

From the start of her husband's administration, Nancy made a point of reaching across the aisle, which was part of a "social strategy" mapped out by Deputy Chief of Staff Michael Deaver. First, she introduced herself to the mostly left-leaning crowd of socialites, bureaucrats, lobbyists, lawyers, journalists, and diplomats at the venerable F Street Club. Then she engineered a reception for Reagan deep in enemy territory, at the home of Katharine Graham, chairman of the Washington Post Company and publisher of its titular newspaper. A committed liberal, Graham introduced the Reagans to power brokers such as Henry Kissinger, Ben Bradlee, Vernon Jordan, George Will, and Alan Greenspan. True believers on both sides of the aisle were scandalized. The Democratic superlawyer Clark Clifford dismissed Reagan as "an amiable dunce," while traditional Republicans chafed at Nancy's parvenu social ambitions. But in retrospect, Deaver said, the First Lady's networking proved "a very smart thing."

HAVING NAVIGATED HOLLYWOOD and Sacramento, Mrs. Reagan understood the power of political entertaining, even—or especially—when it came to private events. In the language of protocol, a *private* White House party is one the First Family hosts for friends and donors. Journalists are usually excluded. Taxpayers are not billed for the wine, food, or extra staff. In return, government officials do not have much say in the food, guest list, entertainers, or other details. Private parties tend to be looser and livelier and go later than official dinners, and invitations to these soirees are highly prized.

On February 6, 1981, three weeks after Reagan took office, the First Lady staged her first White House party: a private, "surprise" black-tie dinner dance to celebrate the president's seventieth birthday. The guests included Hollywood friends such as Frank Sinatra, Cary Grant, Elizabeth Taylor, Gregory Peck, Charlton Heston, and Jimmy Stewart. These were the Reagans' people, and their faces would appear at almost every White House party over the next eight years. They feasted on lobster *en Bellevue* with sauce rémoulade, stuffed veal with a wine sauce, and plenty of California red. Roland Mesnier baked an enormous birthday cake accompanied by ten satellite cakes, each ringed by seven lit candles, representing the president's seven decades. The cost of the lavish spread was not disclosed, and the Kitchen Cabinet picked up the tab. With that first party under her belt, Mrs. Reagan was eager to tackle a bigger, riskier objective: her first state dinner.

Twenty days after President Reagan's birthday, a crowd of citizens braved the chill to wave little Union Jack flags by the South Lawn, where the First Couple greeted Prime Minister Margaret Thatcher and her husband, Denis, a retired oil company executive. The two leaders were officially meeting to reaffirm the "special relationship" between the United States and the U.K.; unofficially, they were getting to know each other. Reagan, a former lifeguard from Illinois, welcomed Thatcher, the daughter of a Lincolnshire grocer, in a style befitting royalty—with a trill of heraldic trumpets, a color guard, and a nineteen-gun salute. It was the kind of pageantry Washington hadn't seen in years and that Carter had disdained as "monarchical." But the contrast was the point. When Carter hosted Thatcher in 1979, their lack of chemistry was glaringly obvious, but Reagan and Thatcher sipped from the same cup.

When they first met, at the House of Commons in 1975, Thatcher pointed to her head and told a colleague Reagan had "nothing there." But after her first state visit in 1981, the two became "ideological twins," she said. "This is the century when we have had the biggest battle of ideas in history. Between totalitarianism and freedom. Coercion versus liberty. Ron Reagan was a passionate warrior in this battle. I was also a warrior. So we had both sides of the Atlantic covered. And we won."

The prime minister endured a tarantella of meetings, visits with Congress, and photo ops. With her lips pressed together quizzically, she observed Reagan the gracious host—"the relaxed, almost lazy generalist who charmed everyone," noted her biographer Charles Moore. By contrast, Thatcher was a "hyperactive, zealous, intensely knowledgeable leader, who injected energy into all her doings but also displayed what Reagan considered to be the elegance of a typical, gracious English lady."

Nancy Reagan, meanwhile, worried over every detail of her first state dinner, grimly insisting it "*has* to be fun." She understood how splendid food and drink can amplify diplomatic goodwill and further the president's agenda—or, as she said, "You can get a lot of business done at these dinners."

The men dressed in sleek tuxedos, and the women wore sparkling sequined dresses with the wide shoulder pads then in fashion. Mrs. Reagan was sheathed in a slim gown with a flower print that projected a chic Hollywood glamour. Mrs. Thatcher, "the Iron Lady," swept her cropped brown hair back into a helmet and wore a black dress and black velvet jacket, which projected the image of a powerful cold warrior. In truth, Britain was struggling economically and beset by the Irish Troubles, racism, and violent protests over social inequality. Mrs. Thatcher had a lot riding on the dinner, too. ("How did I do?" she earnestly asked a White House staffer after a speech at another event. The staffer was touched to see that the Iron Lady was "human after all.")

In the Diplomatic Room, guests were greeted by waiters with trays of cocktails, another luxury the Carters had banished. The State Dining Room was decorated with baskets of red and blue anemones, and just ninety-four guests had been invited. Haller prepared a classic Anglo-American feast: supremes of pompano in champagne; roasted racks of lamb with sweet mint sauce; and soft hearts of lettuce with creamy wedges of Brie. President Reagan showcased sparkling wines from California. For dessert, Mesnier served crowd-pleasing, richly flavored Grand Marnier soufflés.

The dinner went off without a hitch and helped re-cement the special relationship between the United States and the U.K. "Oh, the anemones on the green moiré tablecloths! It was magical," recalled Social Secretary Muffie Brandon. "The Reagans had such ease as hosts. . . . There was a sense of a new beginning—which was the slogan of the Reagan campaign."

·   ·   ·

A MONTH LATER the Reagans toured Ford's Theatre. When he looked up at the box where Abraham Lincoln was assassinated, the president felt "a curious sensation" that it was "still possible for someone who had enough determination to get close enough . . . to shoot" him.

On March 30, Reagan attended a luncheon with AFL-CIO leaders at the Washington Hilton. When he emerged into the parking lot at 2:27 p.m., John W. Hinckley Jr.—a twenty-five-year-old Texan who believed that by killing the president he would impress the actress Jodie Foster—fired a .22-caliber pistol in Reagan's direction. One of his bullets ricocheted off a limousine and lodged three inches from Reagan's heart. Another bullet hit Press Secretary James Brady, a Secret Service agent, and a policeman. The president coughed up blood and was rushed away.

"Honey, I forgot to duck," Ron joked at the hospital. Nancy was not amused.

Vice President Bush hastily returned from Texas to assume control, and Reagan grew listless with a 103-degree fever.

Nancy attempted to feed him, but he wasn't hungry. Frantic, she called Ann Allman, a Czech woman who worked as their housekeeper in Los Angeles and was a creative home cook. Allman made batches of Reagan's favorite soups—split pea, and hamburger soup made with beef broth, lean ground beef, fresh tomatoes, and hominy—which friends brought from L.A. to Washington. Nancy placed a television set and a bowl of hamburger soup in front of her husband. "I thought if he watched the news, as we often did over dinner . . . I could get some food into him," she said. "Ronnie didn't eat much . . . but at least he tried."

On April 28, Reagan addressed a joint session of Congress and used their post-shooting goodwill to relaunch his Economic Recovery Program, which reduced federal spending and income taxes while increasing the military budget by $26 billion. The plan had been mocked by Democrats as hocus-pocus "Reaganomics." But Congress passed the budget, and Reagan declared it "the greatest political win in half a century." His approval ratings soared to 59 percent. In truth, he was still recovering, so he and Nancy slipped away to their little ranch house in California, the one place where they could be their true selves.

II. To the Rancho, and the Stars

They called the property Rancho del Cielo, meaning "the Ranch in the Sky," or "Heavenly Ranch," in Spanish. You get there by driving into the mountains above Santa Barbara—high chaparral country of oak, syca-more, and sun-browned grass in the Santa Ynez Mountains. At the top of a rugged, seven-mile driveway the Reagans' house sat in a meadow twenty-four hundred feet above sea level. Up there in the empyrean it was hot during the day and chilly at night. To the west, the Pacific spread wide and sparkling. To the east lay gnarled vineyards, rolling horse farms, and purple lavender fields. The rancho "cast a spell over us," Reagan wrote. "If it isn't heaven itself, it probably has the same zip code."

They spent three hundred days there during his administration. The house was a simple one-story, roughly twelve-hundred-square-foot, whitewashed adobe structure with five modest rooms, a faux-brick vinyl floor, aluminum windows, a red tile roof, and no central heating. The living room held brown sofas, an orange Naugahyde chair, cowboy paint-ings, and mounted jackalope heads. A minibar featured green Mexican goblets and pewter mugs. In the kitchen, jars of onion flakes sat next to an electric range painted in a 1970s hue called Harvest Gold.

Up there, the Reagans' routine was synced to the diurnal rhythms: up at 8:00 a.m. for breakfast and paperwork; a horseback ride at 10:00; lunch at noon; and outside work between 1:00 and 5:00 p.m. As night fell, they tucked into enchiladas, chile rellenos, tacos, refried beans, and guaca-mole, usually cooked by Ann Allman.

Every Thanksgiving, the extended Reagan family gathered at the ran-cho under Nancy's strict rules: guests arrived at 5:00 p.m.; dinner was served at 6:00; there would be no political talk or football watching, but plenty of Irish blessings, meandering reminiscences, and bad jokes. All-man invariably prepared a feast of turkey, sweet potatoes, Monkey Bread (a soft, sticky pastry baked with cinnamon sugar, so-called because it is torn apart and eaten with the fingers), mincemeat pie, and persimmon pudding.

"Nancy didn't cook," said her stepson, Michael. "Nancy? We didn't let her boil water!"

The president insisted on carving the bird with an electric knife, though he sliced a finger one year. After dessert and coffee, everyone was ushered out at 8:00, no lingering allowed.

The Santa Ynez hills are known for excellent Pinot Noirs (made famous by the movie *Sideways*). Noting that his father had been the governor of the biggest wine-producing state in the nation, Michael Reagan said, "He got a lot of people drinking red wine." White House wines had been relatively uninspired since the Kennedy days, and Reagan hired the Sacramento oenologist David Berkley to advise him on which vintages could play a dual role: acknowledging a White House guest in a special way while pairing well with Chef Haller's food. Berkley replaced traditional, sharp Chenin Blancs with smoother Chardonnays, and encouraged the use of bold Zinfandels and Merlots for the first time.

AS HE RECUPERATED from the assassination attempt, Reagan joked that the next time he spoke at the Hilton, he'd be sure to "wear my oldest suit." He often used humor to deflect fear and discomfort, though friends said he was more rattled by the shooting than he would admit. Nancy, meanwhile, was a "world-class worrier" who feared chaos and disorder.

After Ron's shooting, she dropped from a featherweight 114 pounds to a nearly skeletal 104 pounds; her dress size fell from a 6 to a 4 to a 2. Her cheeks and eye sockets grew hollow, despite thick applications of makeup and her attempts at a smile. She found herself tearing up at awkward moments.

Some worried that Nancy had cancer. Others speculated that she suffered from anorexia nervosa, a complex mental and eating disorder that causes people to stop eating to lose weight. Anorexia is commonly associated with stress and questions of control. As *Psychology Today* explains, "The sufferer attempts to take control of her life by exerting control over one section of her life, her diet and thereby her body, and illness develops when that exertion of control turns into its opposite, the state of being controlled by a pathological compulsion to control."

Nancy denied she was starving herself. She was busy, she explained—traveling fifty-seven thousand miles a year, exercising on a stationary bike, and worrying about Ronnie. "People believe that when one occupies this position life is all roses and glamour," she said. "How I wish I was one of those people who never lets anything show on her face. Everything shows on mine. . . . I eat. I always have but, no matter what I do, I lose [weight]. This has happened to me before. But I'm trying. I love cookies and I have them by my bed. Truly, there's nothing physically the matter and I plan to keep nibbling cookies until I'm my normal size 6 again."

In fact, Mrs. Reagan was brooding about "the presidential (or Tecumseh) curse"—the notion that a commander in chief had died in office roughly every twenty years. JFK was shot eighteen years earlier, in 1963. A superstitious person, Nancy turned to the San Francisco–based astrologer Joan Quigley, who said that she could have predicted Hinckley's attack: "it was very obvious" from Reagan's chart. As Nancy secretly consulted Quigley on a regular basis, the astrologer created color-coded calendars alerting her to "dangerous days," and Nancy altered the president's schedule accordingly. In 1988, the former chief of staff Don Regan, who had clashed with Mrs. Reagan, revealed "the most closely guarded domestic secret of the Reagan White House": the president's schedule was based on the stars and was "cleared in advance with a woman in San Francisco."

Quigley exulted in her new status. "Not since the days of the Roman emperors, and never in the history of the United States presidency, has an astrologer played such a significant role in the nation's affairs," she said. Mrs. Reagan was humiliated, but wrote, "No First Lady need make apologies for looking out for her husband's personal welfare. . . . Nobody was hurt by it—except, possibly, me."

III. Jelly Bellys and TV Dinners

In 1962, Ronald Reagan left the Democratic Party and recast himself as a conservative Republican. Four years later he was elected governor of California. On election night, the Reagans celebrated with veal stew and fresh coconut cake, a lucky meal they would repeat on special occasions. Otherwise, Reagan's food tastes were shaped by his midwestern roots. He gravitated to homey fare, such as meat loaf with mashed potatoes, beef and kidney pie, pizza, and anything sweet, especially jelly beans.

He had been a pipe smoker who appeared in Chesterfield cigarette ads, but quit smoking when he ran for governor. To combat his cravings, he substituted jelly beans for tobacco. The candies became his signature accessory, and—just as barbecue defined LBJ or peanuts defined Carter—they helped identify Reagan in the public mind as a relatable, fun-loving sort.

His favorite jelly beans were made by the Herman Goelitz Candy Company in Oakland. In 1965, Goelitz introduced a mini jelly bean in which the entire bean is flavored (in standard beans, only the shell is flavored, and the center is made of sweet jelly). In 1976, Goelitz introduced "gourmet" candies called Jelly Bellys, which were a quarter the size of regular beans, cost three times as much ($4 a pound), and came in thirty-six flavors including green apple, root beer, very cherry, grape, and Reagan's favorite, licorice. When he won the presidency in 1980, Jelly Bellys caught the nation's attention. "Addicts vow" that the candies are "to the ordinary jelly bean what *foie gras* is to liverwurst," *Time* wrote. Their flavors were so nuanced that "the beans should be eaten one at a time, not by the vulgar handful. How else to appreciate the richness of the coffee mocha, the tang of the pina colada, the bouquet of the strawberry daiquiri?" Thanks to Reagan, Goelitz became a "worldwide company overnight," its CEO crowed, and sales doubled to $16 million a year. In 1981, the company shipped three and a half tons of red (very cherry), white (coconut), and blue (blueberry) beans to Reagan's inauguration, during which forty million jelly beans were consumed. The White House placed a standing order of 720 bags of jelly beans a month. Some fans crafted jelly-bean portraits of Reagan, and when he died in 2004, people left Jelly Bellys at his grave site.

In the Oval Office, Reagan kept a crystal jar filled with Jelly Bellys on his desk. He'd snack on them, dole them out to visitors, and use them to gauge people's essential nature. "You can tell a lot about a fella's character by whether he picks out all of one color or just grabs a handful," he said.

WHAT WAS Reagan's essential character? Jelly beans were one way to divert personal questions; humor was another. When asked how he remained so youthful looking, Reagan quipped, "I keep riding younger and younger horses." With his folksy charm, he made people feel that "you were the most important person in the room," Michael Deaver said.

Yet Reagan was essentially unknowable. He used "a preternatural affability" to "maintain . . . his privacy," wrote the columnist George Will. "He was a very complex, private man and not the 'hail fellow well met' that he appeared to be."

Nancy was more clearly defined. Her parents divorced acrimoniously; she graduated from Smith and worked as an actress. Becoming First Lady was the "role of a lifetime," every headline declared. Though she assiduously prepared for the role, it was one she never fully inhabited. "You don't just move into the White House, you must learn to live there," she recalled. "Life in the mansion is different."

Dressing in signature red ensembles, inviting Mother Teresa to tea, working for antidrug and pro-education charities, she hoped to build respect. But Nancy's hunger for approval was so palpable that, like Mary

Todd Lincoln, she could be off-putting. Critics faulted her for borrowing gowns from Bill Blass and not returning them, for lavishly redecorating the President's House (with funds provided by her friends), and for "the gaze"—the adoring, unblinking stare she directed at her husband with big, doe-like eyes. "Ronnie says I should just forget" the critics, Nancy wrote. "But I can't. . . . Everything I did or said . . . was instantly open to criticism. . . . My clothes. My friends . . . The way I looked at my husband! My entire life was suddenly fair game."

A famously picky eater, she made a breakfast from vitamin pills, orange juice, and a health shake. For lunch, she espoused a lo-cal diet of fruits, steamed vegetables, or California-style salads: avocado slices with orange sections; watercress and alfalfa sprouts; Riverside salad, with radicchio, watercress, and grapefruit in a tangy dressing. She liked chicken pot pie, and fish—especially salmon mousse, broiled trout with kiwi, or swordfish Véronique (baked swordfish napped with lemon butter). At dinner parties she would serve paella Valenciana, a combination of chicken and fish over rice.

When Nancy was at home, President Reagan's breakfast consisted of bran cereal with skim milk, melon or grapefruit, and decaf coffee. Once a week, she would allow him eggs—scrambled, poached, or soft-boiled—with whole wheat toast or a muffin. Lunch was a bowl of soup in the Oval Office: navy or black bean, Scotch broth with barley, or lentil with diced hot dogs. Like the Eisenhowers, the Reagans liked to plop into soft chairs and eat dinner while watching the evening news. Their "TV dinners" became famous, but they weren't frozen TV dinners in flimsy aluminum trays: they were full meals on porcelain plates served on folding tables. (The Reagans often watched the evening news, and liked mainstream entertainments like *The Carol Burnett Show* and *The Waltons.* The president's favorite sitcom was *Family Ties,* whose main character was a Reaganite Republican raised by ex-hippies.)

The minute Nancy left town, Ron would revert to bachelor fare: a thick steak cooked well done, gooey macaroni and cheese, and rich chocolate mousse for dessert. Those items were banned by the First Lady, and the latter was a virtual state secret. "We would have been shot if she ever found out!" Mesnier recalled.

While Henry Haller diplomatically noted that the First Lady was "a sophisticated diner. She has an artist's eye for visual appeal," Mesnier considered Nancy "a tough character" who routinely "had a problem with" his desserts. She "never made effusive compliments. It was high praise indeed to hear that everything was fine," he wrote. When he once added a bit of chocolate to a fruit plate, the First Lady scalded him: "I am the only person who decides what is to be served at White House dinners, Roland. Not you or anyone else . . . no chocolate!"

Yet there were times when the stern "taskmistress" revealed a surprising sense of humor. One day Mesnier made a hazelnut yule log with chocolate bark and marzipan squirrels and nuts. Displaying the dish to Nancy and her stepdaughter, Maureen, he said in a thick French accent, "Here we see a squirrel eating his nuts." The ladies burst out laughing. Embarrassed, Mesnier said, "I had no idea that in English the word 'nuts' is . . . slang for 'testicles.'"

THE PERSONAL AND POLITICAL SPHERES of White House life were separated by a very thin membrane, and occasionally it burst. Such was the case in September 1981, when President Reagan proposed cutting $1.46 billion from the school lunch program, the oldest federal feeding program in the country. Pitched as a way to reduce "waste" by the Agriculture Department, the cuts would shrink the amount of food in school lunches, lower nutrition standards, and reduce the number of poor children eligible for free food. The plan reduced vitamin requirements and slimmed six-ounce containers of milk to four ounces, but most notoriously it deemed sweet ketchup and relish "vegetables."

"Ketchup Is a Vegetable?," headlines jeered. Not only did the administration have "egg on its face, but ketchup too."

The proposal set off a firestorm as critics noted that the money taken from kids' lunchrooms was about the same as the $1.44 billion spent on five executive dining rooms at the Pentagon, while Reagan kept federal tobacco subsidies in place. One irate food service director said, "That our young people are not as important as keeping the price of cigarettes down is absolutely criminal." Reeling, the president claimed he wasn't aware of the details of his plan and shelved the cutbacks.

By a quirk of fate, the day Reagan announced he was shrinking public school lunches, his wife announced that she had acquired a new set of bone china for the State Dining Room: 4,732 plates, service plates, dessert plates, coffee cups, and saucers—enough to set a formal state dinner for 220 people—at a cost of $209,508. The White House china is produced by Lenox, an American porcelain company that has done the job since Woodrow Wilson ordered 1,700 pieces of tableware in 1918. The Reagan pattern nodded to the Wilson plates, which featured a gold presidential seal—the presidential arms—set on a creamy white background encircled by rings of deep blue and gold. The Reagan pattern used the same design elements but replaced the blue with a band of scarlet red, Mrs. Reagan's signature color, with gold filigree. The pattern was elegant—but too much so, for those angered by cuts to school lunches.

The new china was long overdue, Mrs. Reagan argued, because the White House had not bought a complete set of china since Bess Truman ordered a green-and-gold set in 1951, and so many plates had been broken over the years that there were not enough pieces in a single pattern for a large dinner party. (Most place settings include twelve to nineteen pieces, from a finger bowl to plates, soup bowls, and a coffee cup.) The Reagans were hosting many more guests than their predecessors—75,761 people dined at the mansion in their first term alone, while the Carters hosted just 47,797 over four years—and the mismatched table service embarrassed the First Lady. Further, the new china was underwritten by private funds, a detail overlooked in the brouhaha. Mrs. Reagan had a point, but like Marie Antoinette allegedly declaring "Let them eat cake" while poor Frenchmen starved, her purchase of fancy china while her husband slashed children's meals "was a symbol of my supposed extravagance," Nancy ruefully admitted. "The timing . . . was unfortunate."

IV. Dinner, Dancing with Di, and Nuclear Diplomacy

Food may not be the answer to world peace, but it's a start.
—Anthony Bourdain

Over their eight years in the White House, the Reagans held more official dinners than any other First Couple. They hosted seven kings and three queens, seventy-seven prime ministers, forty-five foreign ministers, thirteen princes, and a sheik at numerous banquets and fifty-two state dinners (or fifty-four, depending on your definition of a state dinner). This feat was just shy of LBJ's record fifty-five state dinners, but quadruple the number hosted by George W. Bush or Barack Obama. "It was a vital part of our roles as President and First Lady," Mrs. Reagan said. "And it was a duty that we enjoyed immensely."

Their wining and dining worked to project power, abundance, and connections on a global scale and, on a personal level, showed the Reagans could compete in Washington. Hovering in the background were the ghosts of the Kennedy parties, the casual elegance and sheer fun of which the Reagans' almost never matched. Almost.

In November 1984, Ronald Reagan declared it was "Morning in America" and with help from a superheated economy defeated Walter Mondale to win a second term. The following July, the president was diagnosed with colon cancer. After he recovered, he and the First Lady were in need of a pick-me-up. A party, perhaps—but not just any party, a *royal* party.

In May 1981, the Reagans had hosted a black-tie dinner for Charles, the thirty-two-year-old Prince of Wales and heir to the British Crown. He was engaged to the vivacious Lady Diana Spencer, a dozen years his junior. After a spring feast of roasted saddle of lamb in mint sauce, Reagan gave the prince some advice on marriage. "The step you are about to take is really a very serious step," he said. "But your sense of humor will carry you through." Charles was not known for his humor. But Lady Di was adored as "the People's Princess," for her coltish looks and outspoken support of AIDS patients and land-mine victims. Only nineteen, she proved a jujitsu master at publicity, alternately flirting with and running away from the paparazzi, which made her all the more desirable.

In 1985, Charles and Diana toured America, culminating in a White House gala on November 9. Mrs. Reagan and her social secretary, Gahl Hodges Burt, brainstormed over how best to harness the Windsor charisma to the Reagan presidency. They consulted with Buckingham Palace and spent months planning: aside from the usual splendid food and entertainment, they learned, the princess would enjoy an after-dinner dance. But the burning question was, who would make a dazzling dance partner for Di? After some head-scratching, they hit on an inspired choice. Arrangements were made.

On the night of November 9, Prince Charles was dashing in a tuxedo with a red carnation in his lapel, but Princess Diana looked stunning as she glided into the White House in a floor-length midnight-blue velvet gown, a diamond-encrusted choker, her thick blond hair cropped stylishly short, her cheeks flushed, her smile bright, her eyes sparkling.

"Nothing short of absolute perfection would do" for Mrs. Reagan, Mesnier recalled. He and Haller were ordered to provide "the finest dinner anyone had ever seen." The meal began with a fennel-infused lobster mousse and proceeded to a glazed chicken entrée and a profusion of side dishes. For "a distinctly feminine" dessert, Mesnier prepared white chocolate baskets filled with sorbet "peaches," inside of which was a dark chocolate "pit"; the arrangement was framed by hundreds of handmade sugar flowers.

After dinner the crowd swept into the Entrance Hall, where the marble floor is laid in a pink-and-white checkerboard pattern. The Marine Band tuned up, and Reagan asked Lady Diana to dance. Prince Charles squired the First Lady. At midnight, the party was humming along when Mrs. Reagan nudged a man in the shadows. As he stepped into the light, the crowd gasped: it was the actor John Travolta, famed for his sinuous moves in *Saturday Night Fever*.

He gamely asked the president if he could cut in. Reagan smiled as Nancy swept him away. With a bow, the actor addressed the princess: "Would you care to dance?" She dipped her head "in that Lady Diana way," Travolta recalled, and "we were off for fifteen minutes." The audience cheered, while photographers madly snapped, and the band pounded out the disco beat of "Stayin' Alive." The two beautiful people shimmied and whirled across the checkerboard floor as if time were suspended.

Later, Diana would famously struggle with depression, would attempt suicide, and was in the grip of bulimia nervosa. (Like anorexia, bulimia is a mental illness and eating disorder that can lead to death. Superficially, they are opposites: an anorexic believes she is in control of her eating and her life; a bulimic believes she is not in control; in reality, neither sufferer is in control.) But that night with Travolta, Di became "the people's princess."

Nancy Reagan beamed. She had finally pulled off a night worthy of Jackie Kennedy—one that fused Ronald Reagan with British royalty, Hollywood celebrity, diplomacy, and domestic politics in one supernova moment. The photographs of Di and Travolta would help define the 1980s, and the evening was hailed as the most famous state dinner of modern times (though technically a state dinner is held in honor of a head of state, which the royals were not).

Mrs. Reagan managed to enjoy herself, and her social coup paid political dividends. It even warmed up the eastern Establishment. "They thought, 'Those Californians, they don't know anything,'" said Betsy Bloomingdale. "But the Reagans surprised them. Everything was so beautifully done. After a while, the old guard in Washington had to admit that they turned out to be pretty good."

IF THE DANCE PARTY for Charles and Diana represented the peak of the Reagans' social display, then their state dinner for Mikhail and Raisa

Gorbachev two years later would prove their most significant diplomatic meal.

In his first term Reagan derided the Soviet Union as "the Evil Empire" and led the biggest peacetime military buildup in history. When he deployed Pershing II missiles in Europe and announced the Strategic Defense Initiative—a putative space-based missile shield nicknamed Star Wars—fears of nuclear conflagration leaped. But in his second term, Reagan the hawk transformed into a closet dove.

"Don't you get it?" he said to friends. "I'm doing this so I can get the Soviets to the table."

In June 1987, Reagan stood at the Berlin Wall and theatrically declared, "Mr. Gorbachev, tear down this wall!" Six months later, the fifty-six-year-old Gorbachev accepted the seventy-six-year-old Reagan's invitation to arms reduction talks in Washington. They would cap their meetings with the first state dinner for a Soviet leader since Khrushchev dined with Eisenhower in 1959. But it was not the first time Reagan and Gorbachev had broken bread together, and—much like Nixon's gastrodiplomatic détente with China—the Russian state dinner was the result of years of careful advance work.

In 1985, Reagan and Gorbachev held a series of private dinners, got to know each other, and developed a rapport. Years later, the Russia specialist Jack Matlock recalled that "including private dinners [in the diplomatic process] was built on the idea that these two leaders must not only respect each other but also like each other to accomplish [peace]. It was also a signal to the bureaucracy that it was okay to be friends with the other side. . . . It helped reduce tensions, ultimately. Being friendly . . . does not achieve everything, but it becomes a lot harder to achieve your common goal if you're not being friendly."

On the afternoon of December 8, 1987, Reagan and Gorbachev signed the Intermediate-Range Nuclear Forces (INF) Treaty, which eliminated all Pershing II missiles in Europe. That night the Gorbachevs stepped out of a Soviet ZIL limousine and were escorted into the White House by the First Couple. President Reagan wore a tuxedo, and Mrs. Reagan wore a beaded black gown with flowers running up the sleeves. The Soviet leader dressed in a three-piece navy suit (to blunt criticism of bourgeois excess) while Raisa Gorbachev, who had been mocked as a "Gucci comrade" for shopping in Paris, wore a two-piece black brocade gown with a skirt that swished around her ankles.

Meanwhile, Henry Haller—who, after serving five administrations, was the longest-serving executive chef yet—retired to write a cookbook-memoir. In September, he was replaced by Jon Hill, who had cooked in restaurants from Florida to Hawaii, and was the first American-born executive chef. (After just four months on the job, and a handful of state dinners, including the Gorbachev banquet, Hill "quit," becoming the shortest-tenured White House chef in history; according to "unconfirmed reports," Mrs. Reagan considered his food "sub-par." In January 1998, he was replaced by the German-born Hans Raffert, who had cooked at 1600 Pennsylvania Avenue since 1969, and was best known for the charming White House gingerbread models he built every Christmas.)

For the Gorbachevs, Hill devised a menu that featured American ingredients with a Russian spirit: salmon from the Columbia River (where many Russians had settled) with lobster medallions in a caviar sauce; roasted veal loin with wild mushrooms in champagne sauce; zucchini boats loaded with vegetables; a green salad with crushed walnuts and Brie. The meal was paired with fine vintages from California. Mesnier's dessert was an homage to some of Russia's favorite flavors: tea sorbet in honey ice cream, served on a large oval platter with fresh raspberries. After dinner the leaders toasted to peace, and the pianist Van Cliburn, the first American to win the Tchaikovsky Competition, in 1958, played Schubert, Rachmaninoff, and Brahms in the East Room. Then, on the spur of the moment, he added the soulful "Moscow Nights," which the Russian delegation softly sang along to. With that, Gorbachev wrapped the pianist in a bear hug, and promised, "Winter is on the wane."

= 17 =

GEORGE H. W. BUSH

The Yin and Yang of Broccoli

THE FORTY-FIRST PRESIDENT

January 20, 1989–January 20, 1993

★

I. The WASP Diet

George Herbert Walker Bush was the scion of an American dynasty descended from *Mayflower* Pilgrims that included bankers, politicians, athletes, and entertainers. He spent eight years as Reagan's vice president and in 1988 was elected president. Yet in spite of his cosmopolitan résumé he had plain tastes. He was raised in Greenwich, Connecticut, and his palate was determined by the DNA of his tribe: white Anglo-Saxon Protestants. Reinventing himself as a Texas petroleum executive in 1948, Bush regarded food as a form of refined fuel rather than as a health aid, artistic expression, or other airy-fairy notion, as he might have put it.

"The principal lesson of WASP cookery . . . is that life is to be endured, not enjoyed," wrote *The Washington Post*'s Jonathan Yardley. "The essence of WASP cookery—talk about oxymorons!—is undercooked meat accompanied by overcooked vegetables. . . . I hate broccoli, but once a week I take a deep breath and eat it . . . and no doubt will continue to do so after they deposit me in the great broccoli patch in the sky."

INDEED, PRESIDENT BUSH MADE headlines with a famous Yardley-like diatribe. "I do not like broccoli. And I haven't liked it since I was a little kid and my mother made me eat it. And I'm President of the United States, and I'm not going to eat any more broccoli!" he wailed. Though he would laugh it off as a joke, Bush's jeremiad sounded more like a heartfelt cri de coeur against a grave injustice, one he had nursed over a lifetime. But he might have misjudged, for even trivial gripes about food from a president can have large economic and political repercussions.

Not only did Bush send a message to children that vegetables are not important, but outraged broccoli farmers sent ten tons of their crop to Washington, D.C., in March 1990. The press took note and needled the White House about the protest. Bush tried to defuse the situation with humor: "Now, look. . . . There are truckloads of broccoli at this very minute descending on Washington. My family is divided. For the broccoli vote out there: Barbara loves broccoli. . . . So she can go out and meet the caravan of broccoli."

"You're darn right I do," said Mrs. Bush. "I love broccoli." When the shipment arrived, she added, "We're going to have broccoli soup, broccoli main dish, broccoli salad, and broccoli ice cream."

But when the Bushes hosted a state dinner for the Polish prime minister, Tadeusz Mazowiecki, a few days later, not a single green floret appeared. Sensing hypocrisy, the media railed about "Broccoli-Gate" and asked where the ten-ton shipment had gone. The White House said it had donated the veggies to homeless shelters. Broccoli-Gate mystified the Poles, who had never heard of the crunchy green crucifer.

Almost as famous as his distaste for Cruciferae was Bush's fondness for snacks. He liked beef jerky, popcorn, Butterfingers, Blue Bell vanilla ice cream (which he had flown to Washington from Houston), and, most famously, pork rinds. Like Reagan's love of jelly beans, Bush's affinity for pork rinds generated headlines and charmed his political base. But Bush's snack seemed less genuine than Reagan's. This gets to a larger point: the way presidents talk about food can be unintentionally revealing. While he might have actually enjoyed the crunchy, greasy pork rinds, Bush's constant mention of them, and his ostentatious splashing of Tabasco sauce on them, appeared to be a calculated appeal to working-class southern voters. And while he liked to be photographed fishing, Bush never ate his catch, or as Barbara put it, "he's no fan of slimy white fish." This led to a perception that he was fishing for show. (He released his catch or gave them to his Secret Service agents.)

Such tropes were part of a broader effort to portray George H. W. Bush, a thin-lipped graduate of Phillips Academy and Yale, as a Regular Guy. The effort yielded spotty results and occasionally backfired—most jarringly in 1992 when Bush bought a gallon of milk at a supermarket and declared himself "amazed" by the checkout scanner. The incident revealed that he had not shopped for himself in years, which did not impress voters. Bush's lack of what he called "the vision thing"—an inspiring agenda tied to an emotional bond with constituents—doomed his reelection in 1992.

Barbara Bush, meanwhile, had endeared herself to Texas voters by making a big pot of spaghetti with tomato sauce and serving it on paper plates. Though she didn't love to cook, Mrs. Bush was a mother of six who could produce a competent batch of food when she had to. Her repertoire included Yankee classics like New England clam chowder and mushroom quiche, along with Texas-themed snacks like "Mexican Mound" (a ziggurat of nachos), "Zuni Stew" (pinto beans piled with vegetables, chiles, and Muenster cheese), barbecued chicken, lemon bars, pralines, and—most popularly—chocolate chip cookies (the recipe for which was printed in *Parade* magazine and widely distributed).

When eating alone, the Bushes would, in true WASP fashion, occasionally have bowls of cereal for dinner—Wheat Puffs for the First Lady, Life for the president. In Texas they adapted to the local diet of barbecue and white bread or broiled steak and potatoes. In Washington they kept to a simple diet of tomato bisque, salad, or Chinese food prepared by their personal chef, the Filipino navy steward Ariel De Guzman.

Much like the patrician, ascetic-seeming Woodrow Wilson, the lean and nerdy George H. W. Bush had unexpected carnal appetites. He was perceived as a genial, grandfatherly man who spoke in a circumlocutory patois ("it's no exaggeration to say the undecideds could go one way or another"), presided over the collapse of the Soviet Union and a peaceful end to the Cold War, and guided the first U.S. invasion of Iraq. But the same man was a Nixon loyalist, was implicated in the Iran-contra scandal, and used race-baiting ads to demonize his Democratic rival Michael Dukakis.

When it came to his personal life, Bush was equal parts heroic and ungallant. In 1953, his marriage was severely tested by the death of their three-year-old daughter, Robin, from leukemia, after which George helped Barbara cope. But his long-running affair with Jennifer Fitzgerald, who worked for Bush in various capacities in the 1970s and 1980s, drove Barbara to depression and suicidal thoughts, according to the biography *The Matriarch,* based on Mrs. Bush's diaries. (It was published in 2019 after both Bushes had died.) Even so, the Bushes stayed married for seventy-three years, making theirs the second-longest presidential marriage in history, after the Carters.

IN THE BACK of the public mind lurks the fear that the president could be poisoned. When Zachary Taylor died on a hot day in 1850, at age sixty-five, many suspected "Old Rough and Ready" had been fed cherries or cucumbers and iced milk laced with arsenic by pro-slavery enemies. Conspiracy theories about his death festered for years. But when his body was exhumed in 1991, no sign of the poison was found. Instead, it appears he died of a "combination of official scandals, Washington heat, and doctors," Samuel Eliot Morison wrote in *The Oxford History of the American People.*

President Taylor likely came down with acute gastroenteritis acquired from Washington's open sewers, which swarmed with flies. He probably could have survived, Morison notes, but the capital physician and a quack from Baltimore "drugged him with ipecac, calomel, opium, and quinine . . . and bled and blistered him too. On July 9 he gave up the ghost."

This story was revived in January 1992, when President Bush was on a state visit to Japan. At a banquet hosted by Prime Minister Kiichi Miyazawa, Bush suddenly threw up, lurched off his chair, and passed out. As word spread from Tokyo to the United States, CNN received a call from a man who identified himself as Bush's physician. At 6:45 the next morning, a CNN anchorman began to report the "tragic" news that the president had died, when a supervisor yelled, "Stop!" The anchor halted mid-sentence, then reported, accurately, that the president had suffered a stomach flu. Like the charlatan who treated President Taylor, Bush's "doctor" was revealed to be a seventy-one-year-old prank caller from Idaho. Though mortified, Bush recovered the next day. "The President is human," his press secretary, Marlin Fitzwater, explained. "He gets sick."

THE BUSHES LIKED to entertain, and they hosted twenty-five state dinners between 1989 and 1992. These meals were prepared by the formidable executive chef Pierre Chambrin. He was almost a caricature of a French chef of the Escoffier school: a big, acerbic man who smoked cigarettes, went out of his way to not suffer fools, and lavished great care on rich, classic dishes such as lobster in aspic, steak in béarnaise sauce, fresh green salads, and elaborate cheese courses.

In May 1991 the Bushes welcomed Queen Elizabeth and Prince Philip to an official dinner—the first U.S. visit for the royals since they had attended Gerald Ford's bicentennial celebration in 1976. Chambrin prepared a luscious dinner that included Maine lobster (a nod to the Bush family compound in Kennebunkport, Maine), cucumber mousse with aurora (creamy tomato) sauce, crown roast of lamb (a nod to the royals), *dauphine* potatoes, vegetable bouquets, a watercress and endive salad, and wedges of chèvre and St. André cheese. In a similar vein, Roland Mesnier's dessert was a ten-inch-high, dark chocolate "carriage" filled with a pistachio marquise (mousse), packed with a load of fresh raspberries, and placed on an Olde London Town street paved with marzipan cobblestones.

It was the kind of meal that fit the occasion and its participants perfectly. But it was also an exercise in nostalgia, a look back to a quickly fading past. The end of the twentieth century was nigh, and the dawn of the twenty-first century was in sight. New times required new leaders, a new set of priorities, and a new approach to food at the White House.

PART III

The Twenty-First Century

Which American Cooking Is Most American?

As the millennium turned, the American diet reflected the shifts and divisions in our politics. At first the nation was led by Bill Clinton, a baby boomer whose diet effloresced from fatty red meat indulgences to lighter, healthier steamed fish and vegetables, and ultimately tapered into veganism. His regime was followed by the more predictable, Texas-themed George W. Bush diet, the gastronomically adventurous Obamas, the retrograde meals of Trump and Biden, and hints of a polyglot future in the cooking of Kamala Harris. In the first two decades of the twenty-first century, meanwhile, the public's attention drifted from legacy print and television media to the internet and mobile phones, which accelerated and amplified political messaging and people's interest in food (and "food porn"). Cooking became trendy in new ways: powered by the speed of communication and the flood of information, the public's tastes simultaneously broadened and fractured into specialties and subspecialties. Faced with declining fish stocks and crop yields, deforestation, declining freshwater supplies, and pollution, food manufacturers began to experiment with fake ("beyond") meat, printed foods, insects, and genetically modified crops to feed a growing population on a quickly warming planet. The politics of food became increasingly acute, first in a tug-of-war between big (industrial) and small (local, organic) food businesses, and again when climate change, the coronavirus, and Russia's invasion of Ukraine revealed structural weaknesses in the nation's—and world's—food systems. So far, the twenty-first century has been a confusing time in the food of politics and the politics of food.

WILLIAM J. CLINTON

Torn Between Renunciation and Appetite

THE FORTY-SECOND PRESIDENT
January 20, 1993–January 20, 2001

★

I. In Search of a New Kind of Eating

In 1992, Bill Clinton ran his presidential campaign on the slogan "For People, for a Change." At his first dinner as president—a banquet for governors held in January 1993—he and his wife, Hillary Rodham Clinton, made two big changes to the status quo: they asked guests to smoke outside (to advocate for healthy living and to preserve the mansion's antique furnishings), and they invited outside chefs to advise on the White House menu. Both initiatives are common now, but were considered unusual, even radical, at the time.

Before the dinner, the social secretary, Ann Stock, consulted with the incumbent executive chef, Pierre Chambrin, as usual, but she also solicited ideas from three well-known restaurant cooks: Anne Rosenzweig of Arcadia and Larry Forgione of An American Place, in New York, and John Snedden of Rocklands Barbeque and Grilling Company in Washington. "We're trying to get a kitchen cabinet . . . who will advise us about new menus," Mrs. Clinton explained. "It will keep us up to date about what a lot of American chefs are doing. . . . Asking people for their advice, whether it's about policy or food, is a way to give even more people a feeling of inclusion. And you get good ideas."

She seemed to be indicating that larger change was on the way. The resulting menu was a sophisticated mix of all-American ingredients: smoked shrimp with mango horseradish chutney; roasted beef tenderloin with baby vegetables in a zucchini basket; Yukon gold potatoes with Vidalia onions; a salad of winter greens with hazelnut dressing and goat cheese. The wines hailed from Virginia, California, and Oregon. Mesnier's dessert was an apple sherbet terrine with applejack mousse and hot cider sauce.

The dinner was hailed by guests, but the kitchen crew felt slighted. "I can't say I'm very pleased," growled Chambrin, the epitome of an old-school chef. "It's always difficult with something new."

Relations with him deteriorated from there. He was annoyed when the Clintons began to invite colleagues—up to fifty at a time—for dinner on short notice (a habit of many First Couples). Adding to the strain, the president was a talker who habitually arrived late, which made serving hot, tasty food a challenge. In response, Chambrin staged a slowdown, declaring the Clintons "will have to learn to wait" for their food. The pastry chef Roland Mesnier reminded his countryman that the First Family was "not hard to please," but "you do have to *please*. If you can't do that, you don't belong" at the President's House.

Then Mrs. Clinton, who worried about her husband's genetically weak heart and years of unwise eating, invited outside diet consultants to coach him. The biggest name was Dr. Dean Ornish, a celebrity cardiologist and director of the Preventive Medicine Research Institute, in California. Ornish advised Clinton to eat more fruits and vegetables, keep dietary fat at 10 percent of calories, and replace burgers and fries with stir-fried vegetables with tofu or salmon. "The president did like unhealthy foods," Ornish said, but the soy burgers he put on the menu "were delicious and nutritious."

When Chambrin scorned the outsiders and their edicts, his obstinacy did not go unnoticed. "Pierre is incapable of doing low fat. He truly doesn't understand and isn't willing to be taught," an anonymous Clintonite said. "His desk is covered with cookbooks, but they are all in French and they are all by dead people."

In March 1994, the White House announced that Chambrin and three assistant cooks had resigned. The chef was paid an unprecedented $37,026 settlement. He landed a job at the St. Louis Club and years later would gripe, "Hillary Clinton don't know nothing about food. . . . She was *une personne* political. She did it because it was popular at the time."

With Chambrin gone, the Clintons cut back their entertaining to give themselves time to figure out what kind of food they wanted to serve, what messages it should send, and which chef could bring their vision to life. They aspired to showcase innovative cookery that fused local ingredients with global flavors, classical technique, and the latest in dietary science. "The big issue about health is so paramount," the First Lady said.

"The Clintons, a minority choice, were elected to offer 'change.' So the cuisine, too, must change," opined the London *Independent*. "Maybe the Clintons will at last define what US cuisine is. Or which American cooking is most American. That would be no mean achievement."

⋅   ⋅   ⋅

WITTINGLY OR NOT, the Clintons had scratched an old itch. For years, people have debated just what "American cuisine" is, or if it actually exists. In the 1820s, a British visitor lamented Americans' habit of scarfing down dinner in twenty minutes flat, without apparent joy or conversation. Fifty years later, Russia's grand duke Alexis opined that America had no discernible cuisine. In the 1930s, the wine importer André Simon wrote "An American Tragedy," an essay that lamented American diners' obsession with speed, sugar, and shows (singing waiters and the like). But it wasn't only the Europeans. During the Clinton administration, the American anthropologist Sidney Mintz defined cuisine as a cultural phenomenon that citizens discuss and have opinions about: because the United States did not have that tradition, he maintained, it did not have a proper cuisine. Noting that the nation's favorite entrées in 1994 began with pizza and ham sandwiches, moved through hot dogs and hamburgers, and ended with spaghetti, Mintz sniffed, "I don't think anyone wants to call that array a cuisine."

These views raised howls of protest from those who pointed to regional specialties—Louisiana gumbo, Florida key lime pie, apple pie ("as American as . . .")—and eclectic mixes of immigrant foods—hamburger chow mein, say, or pizza topped with pineapple and ham—as evidence that we have an identifiable cuisine that does not fall into traditional categories. The protests continue today. In 2019's *American Cuisine: And How It Got This Way,* the Yale historian Paul Freedman wrote that food in the United States is characterized by regionalism, standardization, and variety. It "is recognizably different from that of the rest of the world. It has a distinctive set of tastes that can be called American cuisine."

The Clintons didn't set out to define American cooking per se, but they did lead the nation in a new gustatory direction suited to the fast-approaching millennium. Viewed one way, they were leading by example from the top; seen from a different angle, they were merely following the herd of baby boomers toward lighter, healthier menus. The changes the Clintons wrought at the White House were evolutionary rather than revolutionary, but in the culture at large food became an important part of the national conversation and a bigger business than ever during their tenure.

Americans' interest in modern cooking as pleasurable, or at least something more than fuel, was seeded in the 1960s by the adventurous, Eurocentric recipes of Julia Child, James Beard, and Graham Kerr (the "Galloping Gourmet"), and the food writing of Craig Claiborne and

M.F.K. Fisher, among others. It blossomed in the 1970s, with the arrival of lighter, healthier nouvelle cuisine, along with bottled water and quiche, from France; looser immigration laws that brought new kinds of Asian and Central American foods; and, as more women joined the workforce, changing dining habits. The healthy eating trend flowered in the 1980s, with the arrival of kiwi fruit, sushi, and the California cookery popularized by inventive chefs like Wolfgang Puck, Deborah Madison, Judy Rodgers, Jeremiah Tower, and Jonathan Waxman.

In the 1990s, a broad swath of the American public had the time, money, and interest to contemplate food and how it relates to human and environmental health. On television, cooking became a form of entertainment and chefs became stars. Recipes multiplied in newspapers, magazines, and books. Cookware stores bloomed out of muddy fields. Restaurants embraced new types of fusion cuisines. Farmers, academics, and activists promoted locally grown and organic food and raised pointed questions about Big Agriculture's sustainability. The Clintons rode that wave of gastronomic interest and pushed it further.

One spur to this phenomenon was Food Network, which debuted in 1993, the same year the Clintons took office. With a relatively small, $10 million budget, Food Network showcased cooks with a flair for performing—Emeril Lagasse, Sara Moulton, Jacques Pépin, Marcus Samuelsson, Ming Tsai, Mario Batali, David Rosengarten—and grew into a slick, 24-7-365 infotainment juggernaut that changed media, restaurants, and food production. With an assist from the publishing business, Food Network created the "celebrity chef" phenomenon. They were a small group of mostly white, mostly male cooks who—unlike the pale, overworked, and underpaid kitchen trolls of yore—were CEOs, lifestyle gurus, entrepreneurs, real estate tycoons, and media moguls.

As the internet began connecting people in an entirely new way in the mid-1990s, food blogs, zines, podcasts, radio shows, apps, and even food video games proliferated. This new media "flattened" gastronomy and turned highbrow cuisine into middlebrow pop culture. Suddenly everybody thought they could cook, or at least post and editorialize about what they were eating.

If you were to point to the moment when the new politics of food was publicly asserted, you could trace it to December 9, 1992, when Alice Waters, the leader of the "delicious revolution" in Berkeley, wrote a letter to President-elect Clinton and Vice President–elect Al Gore Jr., urging them to model a diet of "seasonal, pure foods [and] health."

The three were baby boomers: Waters was forty-eight, Clinton was forty-six, and Gore was forty-four. She spoke their language and appealed to their youthful populism, but she also called them to action. Waters (who would reimagine the café at Monticello in 2018, as I mention in the introduction) demanded the White House abandon the rich, elaborate foods in vogue since the Kennedy administration and replace them with healthful plates heaped with fresh lettuces, fruit, multigrains, and light sauces, prepared in a global fusion style—the kind of food she served at Chez Panisse.

Americans, she warned, "are set in their addictions to salt and sugar and fat. I have to believe you can change people's minds. An example has to be set at the top."

Waters's letter—cosigned by four hundred well-known cooks, who called themselves Chefs Helping to Enhance Food Safety (CHEFS)—was a combination of flattery and provocation: unless the Clintons updated the White House cuisine, she implied, they risked being seriously out of step with modern America. And she sounded another important theme: the inherently *political* nature of the presidential diet, a subject long overlooked, or pointedly ignored, at the mansion.

Politics always simmers just below the surface of any talk about food, but the attitude of most First Families was, "Good food is nice, but it's not as important as government," which ignores the fact that dining is a powerful, primal tool for consensus building, persuasion, and message-signaling. For their part, White House chefs had always taken a stoic line: "We are cooks, not politicians, and any talk about food policy is above our pay grade." Waters was having none of it. She stressed that not all meals are equal, that food production and environmental quality are essential to human health, and that White House chefs should play a more public role. To some, this was a call to action; to others, near heresy.

Diminutive and soft-spoken, with an oval face and dirty blond hair cropped stylishly short, Waters was hard to ignore. She had just been anointed the first female "Best Chef in America" with a James Beard Award and had a stellar lefty résumé. In 1967, she joined the Free Speech Movement at UC Berkeley and cooked for Vietnam War protesters. Then she ate her way through Paris and Provence. When she opened Chez Panisse in 1971, Waters and her troupe of lettuce worshippers (she washed each leaf individually, it was said, and served only "perfect" peaches) opposed pesticides and preached the value of organic gardens.

Waters's gospel spread, and her hippie ethos—she dressed in vintage clothing and ran her restaurant as a freewheeling collective—made her a media darling. Praised as a crusader, she declared, "We chefs . . . believe that good food, pure and wholesome, should be not just a privilege for the few, but a right for everyone. Good food nourishes not just the body, but the entire community. . . . [A] discriminating quest for fish and meat of quality would herald the need to care for our waters, pastures and areas surrounding them."

While the Clintons were impressed by Waters's passion, others thought she was overstepping. A Bush insider snickered, "Tree huggers in the White House kitchen? *Quelle horreur!*" Accused of elitism, Waters doubled down, declaring, "Just seeing what Clinton eats is pretty distressing. McDonald's and Cokes. It's a terrible image." This inflamed Defenders of the Common Man, who wondered why "the food police" would not allow Clinton to "tear into a burger without having Alice Waters tear into him? . . . It's time for the culinary busybodies to get out of his kitchen."

Finally, Waters seemed to suggest it was high time to appoint an American chef to lead the Executive Kitchen. This set off more hand-wringing. The nouvelle cuisine master Paul Bocuse declared that nationalism was important to French gastronomy and that it was ridiculous not to have an American cook in the White House. But the Swiss-born Henry Haller disagreed, saying, "I would be a hypocrite" to say a chef's nationality was more important than his ability.

Contrite, Waters said her letter "wouldn't have received such attention . . . if it had been correctly interpreted." Yet she had touched a nerve. "A decision about the White House chef is not something [we] have been able to focus on," the new administration said. But Hillary Clinton stirred the pot by calling Waters "a breakthrough figure. . . . I think what she says makes a lot of sense."

The good news, lost in the hot air and flashing cleavers, was that many ordinary Americans suddenly cared about who was cooking what in the Executive Mansion and why. That was new.

THE CLINTONS SPENT six months interviewing chefs across the country, but ultimately found their man across the street. Patrick Clark was a thirty-nine-year-old Black chef who weighed three hundred pounds, sported a dramatic mustache, and ran the kitchen at the Hay-Adams Hotel, which overlooked the White House. The only Black chef of his stature at the time, Clark trained in France with the innovative Michel

Guérard, made his name at Odeon—the Manhattan two-star bistro made famous by Jay McInerney's 1984 roman à cocaine, *Bright Lights, Big City*—and was named one of the James Beard Foundation's "Best Chefs."

The Clintons were so pleased by Clark's Moroccan barbecued salmon and his smoked-and-seared venison loin that they offered him the job of executive chef. He declined, explaining, "I have five kids and five college tuitions." The starting salary for a White House chef was between $50,000 and $70,000. The Hay-Adams paid Clark a princely $170,000 a year, and he would later find security in a $500,000 annual salary at the 850-seat tourist palace Tavern on the Green in New York. (He cooked almost until the moment he died of congestive heart failure in 1998, at forty-two.)

The Clintons started their search again. Their quest captured the public imagination, and within days the White House had received four thousand applications. Asked repeatedly when they would resume hosting, Hillary replied, "We're not going to entertain until we have the chef I want." Her inadvertent use of the pronoun "I" was telling, for she and Bill had very different ideas about food.

II. The People's Palate

William Jefferson Clinton was raised in Hope, Arkansas, on a steady diet of grilled steak, chicken enchiladas, French fries, pies, cakes, and other foods loaded with salt, sugar, and fat. As a teen, he was an overweight saxophonist—"a fat band boy," as he put it. As the governor of Arkansas, he patronized nearly every restaurant in Little Rock—grazing on barbecued pork at Sims Bar-B-Que, jalapeño cheeseburgers at Doe's Eat Place, enchiladas loaded with smooth melt cheese at Juanita's, and the like.

In 1991, when the six-foot-two, forty-five-year-old Democrat campaigned for the White House, his cravings for fast food became the stuff of legend. In New Hampshire, he inhaled almost a dozen doughnuts before an aide whisked the box away. He frequently pressed the flesh and scarfed burgers at McDonald's, a habit memorialized by a *Saturday Night Live* sketch showing Clinton (Phil Hartman) "going jogging," which meant ambling into the Golden Arches to distract patrons while helping himself to their fries. Fueled by cheap calories, Clinton's weight ballooned to 230 pounds. This turned some voters off, but his struggle with "the battle of the bulge" made him relatable to many others.

The candidate's populist tastes represented "the kind of diet most people his age and older grew up eating: heavy on the meat, dessert at every meal and tiny amounts of vegetables, the tinier the better," *The New York Times* reported.

An armchair psychologist might say that Clinton gorged on unhealthy comfort foods as compensation for the turmoil of his childhood. Bill Clinton was born William Jefferson Blythe III. His father was a traveling salesman who died in a car crash before Bill's birth. Clinton's mother, Virginia, married four times (she married one man twice), and at fifteen Bill took the surname of his stepfather, Roger Clinton Sr., a car dealer and abusive alcoholic gambler. Shortly after Bill was born, Virginia left for nursing school and lodged him with her parents. In the racially tense South, they were a tolerant white couple who ran a grocery and were willing to do business with anyone. In this way, Bill Clinton was schooled in the vagaries of love, betrayal, and compassion from the start.

He coped by becoming a gifted talker, copious eater, and alleged serial philanderer. As rumors about an affair with Gennifer Flowers and charges of sexual harassment dogged him, Clinton's inability to restrain his lust for fried chicken and cinnamon rolls was all too easily equated with his weakness for women who were not his wife. In both cases, Hillary came to his defense.

Speaking about his diet, she said, "An occasional trip to a fast-food restaurant is not the worst of all possible sins. The good news is my husband loves to eat and enjoys it. The bad news is he loves to eat, even when things are not always right for him."

Food was a constant theme on the campaign trail, where Hillary was often an effective surrogate for Bill. Taunting President Bush, she'd say, "Let's put broccoli in the White House again!" But when asked about her career as a corporate lawyer, she snapped, "I suppose I could have stayed home and baked cookies and had teas, but what I decided to do was to fulfill my profession." It was a political misstep. Intending to explain her life choices, she had insulted stay-at-home women and was labeled a "radical feminist."

The First Lady apologized profusely and spent years trying to reshape her image from a sharp-elbowed lawyer to a traditional spouse and mother. Her hairdos and wardrobe seemed to change weekly, and when *Family Circle* asked Mrs. Clinton and Barbara Bush to participate in a chocolate chip cookie bake-off in 1992, she obliged (and won). When Hillary ran for the Oval Office in 2016, however, she resurrected the line about "baking cookies" as a badge of honor.

Political optics aside, Mrs. Clinton was genuinely interested in tasty, salubrious food and underwent a culinary awakening in Georgia. While her husband was gorging on gooey burritos, she insisted, "We are trying to move toward healthy, fresh American food" at home, meaning grilled skinless chicken breast rather than deep-fried chicken wings. "We do a lot of vegetables and a lot of fiber and a lot of fruit," she said.

Raised in the Chicago suburbs, Hillary Rodham (she kept her maiden name until 1982, when she added "Clinton" to assuage Arkansas voters) was a gifted academic who said, "I'm a lousy cook, but I make pretty good soft scrambled eggs." She could also whip up a decent tossed salad and was fond of spicy curry, but—admitting to being "periodically undisciplined about what I eat"—was not above the occasional olive burger, made from six ounces of ground sirloin topped with chopped pimento-stuffed green olives (now called the Hillary burger).

She collected bottles of hot sauce and shared a weakness for ice cream and chocolate with her daughter, Chelsea, sweet treats that Bill was tragically allergic to. His dessert abstinence became "one of the serious issues of our marriage," Hillary said, laughing. "Chelsea and I love chocolate. One of our favorite things is rich, rich, rich chocolate cake with thick chocolate icing." That was a sentiment that many voters could get behind.

Mrs. Clinton's tastes were a sign that she had "a stylish palate," observed the food writer Mimi Sheraton. "How can anyone not admire a woman who, like so many of us, is torn between renunciation and appetite, with a weakness for the hot and spicy and the cool and sweet, and who surely represents the people's palate?"

In the 1992 election, Bill Clinton defeated George H. W. Bush and the billionaire independent Ross Perot, becoming the nation's third-youngest (forty-six) chief executive after Theodore Roosevelt (forty-two) and John F. Kennedy (forty-three). And with a dawning insight that you are, in fact, what you eat, Clinton strove to adopt a cleaner, healthier diet with help from a new chef.

III. Scheib and the Casa Blanca Gang

On March 5, 1994, *The New York Times* ran a story headlined "High Calories (and Chef!) Out at White House" about Pierre Chambrin's unceremonious departure. On a flight, Jean Scheib read the article and nudged her husband, Walter: "You should apply for that job."

He shrugged. They were returning from his mother's funeral, and he was depressed. His mother had been a devotee of Julia Child's and had raised him in Bethesda, Maryland, on dishes like beef tongue, bouillabaisse, and paella. While other kids were out playing baseball, Walter would dice onions, cook, and watch Graham Kerr on *The Galloping Gourmet.* He trained at the Culinary Institute of America in Hyde Park, New York, did *stages* in France, and worked in kitchens across the United States. By 1993, Scheib—a tall, dark-haired, pink-cheeked, bespectacled thirty-nine-year-old—was the executive chef at the Greenbrier, a luxury hotel set on eleven thousand acres in the Allegheny Mountains. (Hidden beneath its grounds was a Cold War bunker to shelter Congress in the event of a nuclear attack.) In the hotel's state-of-the-art kitchen, Scheib's staff of two hundred honed a sophisticated "contemporary American" style that integrated local, seasonal ingredients with Asian and Mediterranean flavors and European technique.

Still immersed in grief, Scheib was distracted, so Jean sent his résumé in without telling him. He was invited to audition for Mrs. Clinton, and arrived in the White House kitchen, which he was shocked to discover was a cramped space filled with obsolete tools and painted an odd shade of blue. The gas ranges, broiler, griddle, and counters dated to the 1970s and were woefully underpowered. It was "a backward-looking spectacle that recalled the American attitude toward food as fuel," he recalled. He whipped up a lunch sourced from local green markets: poached lobster tails lacquered with a ginger sauce; roast rack of lamb; a spicy curried sweet potato mousse; and a spring lettuce salad. The First Lady and her advisers—known collectively as Hillaryland—were smitten.

"The money might not be as good as you're used to," said the chief usher Gary Walters, "but if you get the job, you'll be part of living history."

Scheib was hired on April 1, 1994, making him the nation's sixth executive chef—only the second American after Jon Hill—since Jackie Kennedy created the position in 1961. His appointment "marks another milestone in the evolution of America's rapidly changing dining habits," observed *Nation's Restaurant News.* "When the White House sends such an unmistakably clear message about diet, there is ample reason to believe that the politics of food and health are more and more in the country's collective thoughts. And we can only speculate that this will lead to even more changes in the future."

Scheib arrived at the White House just as political typhoons were beginning to churn. Clinton had lowered taxes on the poor and raised them on the rich, signed the Brady bill gun law, and backed the North

American Free Trade Agreement. Conflicts had broken out in Somalia, Bosnia, and Ireland. Diplomats worried about the nuclear ambitions of North Korea, Pakistan, and Iraq. Mrs. Clinton was chairing a task force to build a national health-care system. Meanwhile, accusations were made about Clinton's alleged affairs, the death of Deputy White House Counsel Vince Foster, and the Whitewater real estate scandal.

Scheib led a full-time staff of five he called "the Casa Blanca Gang"— two assistant cooks, a steward, and two staff cooks—and a part-time crew of twenty assistants who pitched in for big events. He quickly learned that the president liked a grab-and-go breakfast from the Navy Mess, while Hillary started her day with fresh grapefruit juice, blueberries, and Quaker oatmeal. Fourteen-year-old Chelsea grazed on whatever was at hand. At lunch, the president was an omnivore, but was happiest with a pizza and salad. The First Lady didn't like frisée lettuce, but enjoyed his Chilean sea bass or tartine of grilled eggplant. The Clintons' favorite dish was crab cakes, which they served at lunch, dinner, or watch parties for University of Arkansas football games, and they served fifteen to twenty thousand mini crab cakes every Christmas.

The chef grew frustrated by the White House's dysfunctional supply chain. "If you wanted a ripe tomato, you should have written 'ripe' on the requisition form," a bureaucrat said, after Scheib rejected a box of hard, tasteless pink orbs. It took him two years to find good suppliers, replace the kitchen's antique appliances with high-speed ovens and new storage cabinets. But his biggest challenge was to improve the president's diet.

Scheib typed up weekly menus that were low in red meat, fat, and carbohydrates, and high in fruits, vegetables, and whole grains. Hillary— who had a commanding presence but seemed far more relaxed and sympathetic in person than the character she played on TV, Scheib noted—penciled queries in the margins: "Walter, could you please calculate calories?" or "What is jicama salad?"

With input from nutritionists, they crafted heart-healthy meal plans, but lest the "Clinton diet" become a gossipy distraction, they were kept private. For the record, a typical menu included half a grapefruit, shredded wheat with skim milk, and oatmeal toast for breakfast; Boston lettuce and watercress salad with a side of bagel chips and hummus for lunch; and navy bean soup, broiled arctic char with an orange tarragon sauce, and multigrain rice for dinner. Together, the First Lady and the executive chef promoted contemporary American cuisine in a new way. They didn't lead a revolution, exactly, but their efforts led to a significant evolution in White House cookery and influenced the way citizens thought about what they ate.

SETTLING IN, the Clintons began to host weekly themed receptions—an Eastern Shore cookout, say, or a New Orleans jazz celebration, or a congressional luau—for two hundred to four hundred guests at a time. The South Lawn became a favorite party venue, though hot grills, wind, rain, and unexpected drop-ins proved a challenge. When the Olympic torch arrived during a congressional picnic in June 1996, the skies suddenly opened, forcing Speaker of the House Newt Gingrich to hide beneath a picnic table. And just before Clinton honored twenty-eight hundred AmeriCorps volunteers at a picnic, a light plane crashed on the South Lawn; the area was cordoned off as a "crime scene," and the crowd was herded inside for an impromptu Big Mac feast.

The Clinton administration grew increasingly fractious, and as political tensions mounted outside the White House, personal relations grew strained in its back corridors. Sixteen hundred Pennsylvania Avenue is staffed by ambitious people whose egos occasionally clashed. This was true in the kitchen, where hostilities flared between Scheib and Roland Mesnier. It began with a squabble over ingredients: when Scheib used orange sections in a salad, he forgot to mention it; Mesnier used oranges in his dessert that day and denounced the chef for repeating one of "his" ingredients, which is considered a faux pas. To avoid further duplication, the two, who shared a small office but rarely spoke, left notes for each other.

"Mrs. Clinton presided over a minor revolution. . . . [Scheib] made a great many changes, far too soon, with the result that many . . . staff members were furious," Mesnier wrote in his memoir. Scheib countered that the pastry chef was simply jealous. "I was stealing his spotlight," he wrote in his memoir. Less credibly, he added, "I did nothing to promote myself. If anything, I shied away from such attention."

Yet the pressure was relentless, and the two had no choice but to work in sync, if not together. In the stretch between Thanksgiving and Christmas the Clintons hosted functions almost every day. Scheib began cooking at 6:30 a.m. and worked until early the next morning. As the Clintons added guests, he streamlined procedures to feed up to fifteen hundred people at a time. Perversely, once the kitchen raised its game, Hillary added another thousand mouths to feed. "We were there . . . to bring

Mrs. Clinton's almost magical notion of what White House entertaining should be to life," Scheib wrote like a good soldier.

For the 1993 Christmas parties, Mesnier baked twenty chocolate logs and two thousand petits fours in a day. Feeling burned out, he bought a house in rural Virginia and contemplated retirement. But then he was dragooned back to the White House to whip together lemon tartlets, a carrot cake, and a gingerbread house. Before she let him go home, Hillary had one more special request: to prepare a treasured family recipe. As she thrust a scrap of paper into his hand, he blinked uncomprehendingly at the ingredients, then bent to his mixing bowls like Dr. Frankenstein in his lab, making the Coca-Cola-flavored jelly with black glacéed cherries she had requested. It was "an atrocious concoction," he wrote, "but I bowed to family tradition."

IN 1994, Scheib oversaw the construction of a small vegetable garden on the White House roof. The grounds crew planted four varieties of tomatoes and two kinds of peppers, squashes, and cucumbers in ten-gallon planters, along with rows of herbs, including basil, thyme, mint, and chives. Up there, the vegetables were too high for insects, and no pesticides were required. (The roof already had a flower garden in a greenhouse. And the First Lady's Garden was an ornamental herb garden growing on the mansion's east side.) Scheib used the vegetables for the Clintons' meals, and he sourced other produce from local farmers and food co-ops. Their identities were not publicized, for security reasons, and if a grower's name leaked, they were dropped from the list.

Finding his footing, Scheib cooked most of the Clintons' twenty-nine state dinners. Each menu included three standard elements, he said: the best American ingredients; a culinary nod to the honored guest's home cuisine; and interesting flavors that would appeal to different palates. Usually served, eaten, and cleared in about ninety minutes, state dinners "are not Escoffier," Scheib said (referring to the legendary French chef Auguste Escoffier). "You can spin it any way you want," but a state dinner is "still a banquet. How you serve 240 people and have them not think it's another rubber-chicken-circuit dinner, that's the job."

His first state dinner was held in June 1994, in honor of the emperor Akihito and the empress Michiko of Japan. The meal served as a capstone to diplomatic talks with America's most trusted Asian ally and as a display of the Clintons' new approach to food, wine, and service. It began with an appetizer of quail with corn custard and a tomato-cumin sauce. The entrée—arctic char with lobster sausage, mushroom risotto, braised fennel, and a vegetable ragout—was a nod to Japan's love of seafood. Char is a cousin to salmon, with beautiful orange flesh and a subtle taste; popular today, it was little known at the time. The meal featured two other unusual twists. The char was served with Pinot Noir, a light- to medium-bodied red wine, in contrast to the usual pairing of fish with white wine. And the dinner was served "American style," meaning the food was plated in the kitchen, which the cooks preferred, rather than the conventional "French style," in which waiters held platters from which guests helped themselves, which can be slow and awkward.

With the Japanese emperor successfully fed, Scheib was ecstatic. "I get to do every day what most chefs get to do once or twice in their life if they're lucky," he enthused. "People will have to pry me out of here with a crowbar."

IN SEPTEMBER 1994, Boris Yeltsin, the president of the Russian Federation, joined Clinton for talks about eastern Europe. The two were burly, sociable men, and their meeting was dubbed "the Bill and Boris show." The state dinner paid homage to Russia with a vodka-marinated salmon with cucumber salad and kasha pilaf. But then things went sideways. Yeltsin downed glass after glass of wine and grew increasingly boisterous. Worried, the butlers substituted water. But when the Yale Russian Chorus began to sing, Yeltsin rushed the stage to conduct with sweeping arm movements. After safely depositing him at Blair House, the official guesthouse, his hosts breathed a sigh of relief.

Early the next morning, U.S. Secret Service agents discovered the Russian president weaving unsteadily down Pennsylvania Avenue dressed in nothing but underwear. He "wanted a taxi to go out for pizza," Clinton recalled. Eventually, Yeltsin "got his pizza" and was coaxed back to bed. But the next night he eluded his security detail again, and crept down to the Blair House basement. A guard mistook Yeltsin for an inebriated burglar, and the situation grew tense when U.S. and Russian agents converged. After a standoff, Yeltsin was repatriated to his room.

This made for an amusing anecdote, but it had at least two serious consequences. On a personal level, Yeltsin was an alcoholic whose addiction impaired his ability to lead and worsened his health. (He died of a heart attack in 2007.) On a global level, Yeltsin's antics seemed a metaphor for Russia's loss of direction and prestige. One critic was the former KGB agent Vladimir Putin, who began his rise to power with a vow to restore Russian pride.

A week after the Yeltsin tragicomedy the Clintons hosted Nelson Mandela, the winner of the 1993 Nobel Peace Prize. He was that rare figure: an individual who seemed to embody a race, a nation, and the aspirations of billions of people around the world. Mandela had caused a sensation in 1990, when he was a guest of the Bushes'. Now the Clintons welcomed him back as the first Black president of South Africa. He was greeted by one of the largest crowds ever seen at the White House. Cannons boomed a twenty-one-gun salute, and Mandela spoke movingly of his struggle to end apartheid. "That victory is your victory," he told the crowd.

The Mandela state dinner on October 4, 1994, was one of the most significant White House events of the twentieth century. The challenge was to make it inclusive and respectful of protocol and to spice it with a dash of the old Kennedy magic. The Clintons aimed to conjure a nimbus of personalities, decor, symbolism, energies, food, wine, and music into a spectacular experience that fizzed in the mind long after the last plates were cleared. The scrum for tickets was intense, but the Clintons made sure to invite famous Black Americans, such as Maya Angelou, Jesse Jackson, Harry Belafonte, David Dinkins, and the ethereal singer Whitney Houston, who performed that night.

The meal was served in the East Room, where President Johnson had signed the Civil Rights Act of 1964, with overflow tables in the Green Room. Mrs. Clinton used the Roosevelt china in the East Room and the Johnson and Reagan patterns in the Green Room. (The Clinton china, which depicts the White House's north facade in gold, would not be commissioned until 2000, when it was used to celebrate the mansion's two hundredth anniversary.)

Scheib's kitchen catered 220 dinners that night, 20 percent more than usual. Most of the Casa Blanca crew were Black, and the mood in the kitchen was a mix of nerves, pride, and euphoria. The Clintons had invited Patrick Clark—the Black chef who declined their job offer—and his wife as guests. The chef accepted, and his white sous-chef Donnie Masterton cooked one of their signature dishes: sautéed halibut with a wasabi-sesame crust in a carrot juice broth. Scheib and his team cooked everything else, including layered late-summer vegetables with lemongrass and red curry, which combined South African ingredients, Southeast Asian seasoning, and European technique, in a hat tip to Cape Malay cuisine. "No visiting head of state inspired as much excitement," Scheib recalled of Mandela. "It was an honor."

IMPRESSED BY SUCH MEALS, Chelsea Clinton asked for cooking lessons. Born in Little Rock, Arkansas, in 1980, she came of age in the governor's mansion and used food to define herself from early on. One day in 1991, the sixth grader was given two articles to read in school: one about the harmful effects of red meat on the human body, and the other about the way cattle are mistreated at slaughterhouses. At dinner that night, she announced she was giving up red meat. Her parents agreed, and two years later were surprised again when Chelsea announced she would become a full-blown vegetarian. They moved into the White House in 1993, when Chelsea was twelve. She spent more time in the Executive Kitchen than her parents did and was keen to learn how to transform raw ingredients into artfully composed meals. Furthermore, it was one of the few places the First Daughter could hang out like a regular person.

By the summer of 1997, Chelsea was seventeen and had been accepted to Stanford University. As a parting gift, Scheib taught her and a friend how to shop for vegetables, care for knives and pans, and make soups, salads, vegetable stocks, and vinaigrettes. The girls learned to substitute tofu (soybean curd) and tempeh (bricks of fermented soybeans) for meat, and to make vegetable risotto, buckwheat linguine with lentils, baba ghanoush, black bean enchiladas, and the like. At the end of the course, Chelsea donned a chef's toque and accepted a certificate from "The White House Culinary Program."

IV. Pressure Cooker

Bill Clinton's second term from 1997 to 2001 brought the nation into the twenty-first century and was more fraught than his first. Nineteen ninety-eight was a particularly uncomfortable year. On August 7, attacks on the U.S. embassies in Kenya and Tanzania killed 224 people, including 12 Americans. Then the independent counsel Kenneth Starr launched an investigation into the Clintons' alleged improprieties in Arkansas— including the Paula Jones sexual harassment case, which revealed the president's affair with the twenty-two-year-old White House intern Monica Lewinsky, which began when she delivered pizza to him. That culminated in his impeachment and eventual acquittal.

A dank gloom enveloped the President's House, and the Clintons reduced their torrential socializing to a trickle. Chelsea turned eighteen in 1998 and suffered "psychic damage" from the controversies, said Carl Sferrazza Anthony, a historian and friend of hers. "When you're a bright young person . . . and you're hearing what people are saying about your dad, it's going to affect you."

Again, Chelsea turned to the kitchen for solace, this time to learn how to bake. Roland Mesnier taught Chelsea and a friend how to grease a pie mold, make fresh ice cream, and shape marzipan paste into rose leaves. Though her flowers "bore a striking resemblance to cabbages," she was determined to surprise her parents with their favorite desserts. After dinner, the waiters presented Chelsea's handiwork: a mocha gâteau with marzipan roses for Hillary, and a cherry pie for Bill. Insulated from political vitriol for a night, the three dug in, alone together.

AFTER THE CLINTONS LEFT the White House in 2001, Clinton continued to be dogged by high cholesterol, a "bent and ugly" coronary artery, and rumors of sexual impropriety. "Because of your genetics, moderate changes in diet and lifestyle aren't enough," admonished Dr. Ornish. But "more intensive changes . . . [can] reverse" heart disease. Clinton underwent a quadruple bypass in 2004, and six years later he transformed himself into America's first president to become a vegan. (Once she had children, meanwhile, Chelsea reverted to eating meat.)

Replacing meat, eggs, dairy, and oil with snow peas, garlic hummus, spiced quinoa, and shredded beets, Clinton spoke out on the dangers of obesity, promoted exercise, and pushed for better nutrition policies. Sounding a lot like his onetime gadfly Alice Waters, he blamed "the way we consume food and what we consume" for soaring costs and a dysfunctional health-care system. Clinton lost twenty pounds and looked healthier. But, as was often the case with the former president, the story didn't end there neatly.

Confusion set in when he mentioned that he ate an omelet or a piece of salmon once a week, which to purists meant he wasn't a true vegan. And his message was further muddled when he consulted Dr. Mark Hyman, whose belief that "fat does not make you fat or sick" was the opposite of Dean Ornish's "low-fat" mantra. Recent studies about whether eating fat leads to heart disease have been inconclusive. But the two experts agree that restricting sugar and refined carbohydrates while eating a whole food, vegetable-forward diet reduces weight and aids cardiac health.

As a politician, Bill Clinton had an uncanny ability to channel the public's appetites, instincts, and contradictions. As an eater, now in his seventies, he continues to embody the nation's vacillation between renunciation and appetite, our uncertainty about who or what to believe. A centrist, not an absolutist, he has chosen a middle path in the hope of having it all.

— 19 —

GEORGE W. BUSH

T-Ball, Freedom Fries,
and a Changing of the Guard

THE FORTY-THIRD PRESIDENT
January 20, 2001–January 20, 2009

⋆

I. Unlearning the Lessons

George W. Bush, the oldest son of President George H. W. Bush, was as picky an eater as his father was but in a different way. He did not care for soup, salad, or "any green food," though he did eat broccoli. Nor did he care for "wet fish," by which he meant poached, steamed, or boiled swimmers of any kind. He had a taste for ballpark hot dogs or a grilled cheese sandwich made with white bread and Kraft Singles. And he liked to snack on pretzels or homemade Chex Mix. Acceptable dinner items included grilled beef tenderloin, firm-fleshed fish that had been fried, grilled, broiled, seared, or stir-fried, and anything Tex-Mex.

His wife, Laura Welch Bush, liked food that was "generous, flavorful, and identifiable." That meant steel-cut oatmeal for breakfast and enchiladas, poached salmon, tomato aspic, and other classics later in the day. She had no time for fusion cooking ("too highbrow"), finely diced vegetables ("you can't tell one from the other"), aged balsamic vinegar reductions ("pretentious"), or foods arranged in sculptural structures ("piled on top of each other")—that is, the kind of food the Clintons liked to eat and that Walter Scheib liked to cook. In contrast to her predecessor's questing palate, Mrs. Bush's "taste was defined and set," Scheib wrote. She "wanted . . . country club food—conservative, traditional American fare."

Laura favored light lunches of, say, grilled salmon with an endive and watercress salad. The president liked a PB and J or a BLT sandwich with a side of Lay's potato chips. For dinner, the First Couple liked chicken pot pie or chicken with vegetables on buttermilk biscuits. It was the kind of food Scheib could make in his sleep. "Food wasn't much of a priority," he lamented. Their "disdain for the Washington social scene was so well documented . . . [that I] knew that entertaining wouldn't be" important in the George W. Bush White House.

Scheib considered his collaboration with the Clintons a "historic" leap forward, but now felt lost. "I'm not going to lie: When [they] left the White House, a piece of me went with them." But in the next breath, he reminded himself that his "singular objective" was the First Family's happiness: "You have to check your politics and ego at the door." If Mrs. Bush wanted to serve fried catfish and hominy casserole instead of Scheib's barbecued duck with root vegetable coleslaw on jalapeño corn bread, so it was. "By definition she was right," he reminded himself.

LIKE BILL CLINTON and Donald Trump, George Walker Bush was born in the summer of 1946. Raised in hot and dusty Midland, Texas, W. (pronounced "dubyuh"), as he called himself, was educated on the green campuses of Andover and Yale, then earned an MBA at Harvard Business School. (He is the only president with an MBA.) In 1977, he met Laura Welch at a backyard barbecue. He was a hotheaded partyer; she was a devout teacher and librarian. They married and settled in Midland. In 1981 they had twin girls, Barbara (named after his mother) and Jenna (named after her mother).

In those days W. was a charming rake who never quite lived up to his potential. Known as "the Bombastic Bushkin," he was partial to "the four Bs—beer, bourbon, and B&B." Though not a clinical alcoholic, he was the kind of social drinker who did not stop once he started. Bush was close to his mother, Barbara, but had a complicated relationship with his father, the then–vice president, George H. W. Bush. Once, a buzzed W. smashed his car into a neighbor's garbage can, then challenged Bush Sr. to a "mano a mano" fistfight. "Alcohol," W. admitted, made him "say foolish things."

When W. turned forty years old in 1986, he swore off booze and embraced the church. He credits his wife: "She is just a very calm and loving person who reminded me in a mature and sobering way that going to a party and . . . [drinking] four bourbons on the rocks [was] not all that smart." With the help of the reverend Billy Graham, W. reengaged with his faith and attended Laura's Methodist church. "If you become more spiritual, you begin to realize the effect of alcohol is over-consuming because it begins to drown the spirit," he said. "If you change your heart, you can change your behavior."

A well-timed sale of his struggling oil company, Spectrum 7, that year netted W. more than $300,000. He parlayed that into a share in the Texas Rangers baseball team, which eventually garnered him a $15 million fortune. With lifetime financial security in place, he joined his father's presidential campaign and began to plot his own career in politics. By the time of his Texas gubernatorial run in 1994, W. went to bed early, ran an eight-minute mile, and was rigidly punctual. Routine seemed a way to control his berserker impulses.

After defeating Al Gore in the disputed election of 2000, Bush Jr. was sworn into office in January 2001. He gave himself a new nickname, 43, to distinguish himself from his father, the forty-first president, called 41.

In Midland, W. was known for wearing scuffed loafers and a robe. But for a Texas-themed inaugural party in Washington he donned a tuxedo, shiny cowboy boots, and a white felt cowboy hat. Some sniggered at the costume, but others embraced it as a sign that a cocky, Reaganesque posse was back in town. The point was underlined when Bush served two and a half tons of beef brisket and twenty thousand pounds of shrimp that night.

W.'s efforts to portray himself as an easygoing Regular Joe were more successful than his father's. Bush 43 seemed an affable guy's guy, "the kind you could have a beer with" (his teetotaling notwithstanding), many said. One way he enhanced this image was through baseball. While many presidents have used America's pastime as a sign of their regularness, few have identified themselves with the game as closely as Bush. President Washington played rounders, an early version of baseball at Valley Forge, while Teddy Roosevelt, Taft, Wilson, Truman, Eisenhower, and Kennedy were photographed at ball games, usually eating hot dogs. But as an owner of a major-league team, and the first Little Leaguer in the White House, Bush 43 trumped them all.

Sandlot-themed meals became a signature of 43's administration. The first took place on February 7, when he hosted a dinner for legends of the game such as Cal Ripken Jr., Joe Torre, Don Baylor, Billy Beane, and Tom Glavine. That morning, a man brandishing a gun at the White House was shot in the leg by Secret Service agents, but the baseball dinner went ahead. Held in the Old Family Dining Room, on the mansion's first floor, it was one of Scheib's first official meals for the Bushes. He cooked a hearty "male menu" of pan-seared sea bass with saffron risotto and caponata sauce. The guests ate it up, then autographed baseballs for the president, who added them to his collection of more than 250 signed balls.

A month later, Bush hosted lunch for Hall of Famers like Yogi Berra, Johnny Bench, and Sandy Koufax, along with the baseball commissioner, Bud Selig, in the State Dining Room. It started well, when Bush paid homage to Berra's malaprops ("Ninety percent of this game is half mental") while poking fun at his own tortured syntax ("They misunderestimated me"), saying some think Berra "might be my speechwriter." But when the first course—crisp shrimp and roasted artichokes with fennel and wild sorrel soup—arrived, the president barked, "What's this? Something that washed up on the shore?"

The room fell silent. Panicking, the butlers quickly cleared the plates away. The Hall of Famers were baffled, and the kitchen was horrified when the untouched food suddenly flooded back. Scheib realized that the green soup and sautéed pink shrimp—a menu he had planned with Mrs. Bush—looked "wet" and represented everything 43 couldn't stomach. The Casa Blanca Gang scrambled to cook porterhouse veal steaks with garlic polenta, fiddlehead ferns with spring vegetables, and a wild mushroom sauce. The plates were eaten clean, but Scheib was left a nervous wreck.

On May 6, Bush invited two teams of kids to play T-ball on the White House lawn. As the Junior Red Sox faced off against the Junior Rockies, every child had a chance to hit, there were no outs, and everyone won. It was a feel-good moment, except for one important detail: the kitchen had prepared a ballpark menu of grilled hot dogs and the president made it clear that "ball park dogs are *steamed,* not grilled." Nevertheless, the event was repeated—with steamed hot dogs—that summer, until the innocent fun was cut short.

II. Food as an Anchor, and Farce

On September 5, 2001, the Bushes hosted their first state dinner. The guests of honor were old friends, the Mexican president, Vicente Fox, and his wife, and while there were many Texans and Bush donors there, the only celebrity was Clint Eastwood. The menus were decorated with the American flag crossed over the Mexican flag: printed electronically, they were hand-painted by White House calligraphers, and were the first to use both Spanish and English. Scheib created a bicultural menu, which opened with Maryland crab, chorizo pozole, and vegetables; an entrée of pepita-crusted bison—"the perfect metaphor," Scheib said, because bison range from southwestern states into Mexico and back; and a red and gold tomato salad. The assistant usher Dan Shanks, a former restaurant sommelier, served the California Chardonnay Mi Sueño (My Dream) with the crab. Roland Mesnier created a mango and coconut ice cream dome with peaches, a red chili pepper sauce, and a tequila sabayon for dessert. President Bush toasted the Foxes with a glass of 7UP, while President Fox referred to his host as Jorge and told rambling stories. It was a night of bonhomie and cross-cultural friendship.

Six days later, Walter Scheib was preparing peppered beef tenderloin for a western-themed congressional picnic. Mesnier was decorating watermelons with cattle horns. It was a gorgeous blue-sky day, with the late summer heat tempered by a cool breeze.

"Well, that's two," a worried usher said.

Scheib stared at the television in disbelief. The World Trade Center towers in New York spewed flame and dank clouds of smoke. Other hijacked planes were said to be heading for Washington. Walkie-talkies crackled and people yelled, "Get out of here!" Hundreds of tourists and military personnel streamed out of the White House and a burly emergency response team armed with machine guns encircled the grounds. At 9:37 a.m., a jet accelerated overhead, and after a percussive *thump!* smoke rose in the distance. It was American Airlines Flight 77, which had been hijacked and flown into the Pentagon, killing almost two hundred people.

The streets were gridlocked. Cell phone networks crashed. A prayer circle formed. A woman stumbled toward the White House, zombie-like, until a guard pointed a shotgun at her and shouted, "Halt!" She kept coming, and he said, "Goddamit lady . . . I'm going to have to shoot you." She turned and melted into the crowd.

In the White House kitchen, Scheib sent his sous-chefs John Moeller and Cristeta "Cris" Comerford home. But the grounds were crawling with police and Secret Service, and they were hungry. So, he fired his grills and began to cook. Food for a thousand picnic guests was stored in mobile refrigerators on the driveway, and as butlers hauled provisions inside, the chef sizzled the tenderloins, then sliced and plated them as fast as he could. Dan Shanks dressed bowls of salad. Soon, a dozen security personnel lined up. Then 50 more, then 150. The skeleton crew sweated in the grease and smoke and worked robotically. By the evening of September 11, they had served eight hundred meals.

For weeks after the attacks, White House employees drifted through the hallways with blank faces. Even President Bush blinked back tears. Then someone mailed letters containing anthrax to senators and media outlets. Worried, Scheib kept a watchful eye on his car mirror, gauging if he was being followed. He reminded his wife and boys, "Don't talk to anyone whom you don't know about what I do. If [they] ask, just say I work for the Park Service."

Roland Mesnier suffered "extreme anxiety" after 9/11. "So many dead!" he mourned, causing him to become "far more cautious."

The chief usher, Gary Walters, offered the staff psychological counseling, but Mesnier and Scheib declined to participate: the former had
lived in Paris during periods of unrest and trusted his own wits; the latter
considered therapy "a waste of time." But months later, Scheib realized
he was edgy, and perhaps suffering from post-traumatic stress disorder,
which smoldered inside him like buried ordnance. "I didn't realize . . .
how life-altering the experience" of the terrorist attack was, he conceded.

All White House social events were canceled, though the president
held working lunches with world leaders to coordinate the War on Terror. Adapting to the mood, Scheib kept his menus simple: a single course
with a side, such as garlic-rosemary chicken on polenta with asparagus,
or fillets of beef with a bean salad. "We could have served [them] ham
sandwiches," he recalled, "and they would've continued on with their
work without a word."

Before 9/11 it would have been very difficult to poison the First Family, and afterward it was virtually impossible. For years, people had sent
unsolicited cheeses, salmon, brownies, and other goodies to the president, and the chefs frequently sampled them. No longer. After 9/11 every
homemade pie, commercial bottle of Florida orange juice, promotional
jug of Vermont maple syrup, or Alaskan king crab leg was destroyed.

A new protocol created a firewall around the procurement, delivery,
storage, and preparation of meals. The cooks were barred from shopping
in markets and had to order food by fax. The list of approved grocers
dropped from thirty-five to ten. When Scheib needed unusual ingredients, vendors would order them from third parties who had no clue their
food was destined for the president's kitchen. Part-time cooks and waiters were subjected to extensive background checks.

Overnight, Scheib noticed, Americans began to eat differently: "Right
after 9/11 . . . the food changed from being very eclectic and very forward-
thinking, to going back into very safe food. Your mother's table, if you
will. . . . [T]he country was very confused . . . and . . . wanted to grab
onto an anchor, and in this case, that was food." (This ethos may have
spurred the locavore and Slow Food movements, he speculated.)

Not surprisingly, the attack prompted a surge of patriotic fervor.
As always, food was intertwined with politics, sometimes to a farcical
degree. Consider the battle over French fries. Long popular in Europe,
deep-fried potato sticks became a hit in America in 1802, when Thomas
Jefferson enjoyed "potatoes served in the French manner," and by 2003
fries were a ubiquitous snack. But when France opposed Bush's invasion

of Iraq, the Republican representatives Bob Ney of Ohio and Walter B. Jones of North Carolina demanded that the French toast and French fries served in congressional cafeterias be renamed "Freedom toast" and "Freedom fries." It was a jingoistic stunt, and a hat tip to Hoover's rebranding frankfurters "hot dogs" in World War I. Ney declared it was "a small but symbolic effort to show strong displeasure . . . with our so-called ally." The French embassy huffed that it was focused on the "very serious issues of war" and not "on potatoes."

The food fight was too delicious to ignore, and Freedom fries became a staple for satire. "In France, American cheese is now referred to as 'Idiot Cheese,'" Tina Fey announced on *Saturday Night Live.* In 2005, the cook Anthony Bourdain launched a food and travel show called *No Reservations.* In the pilot episode, "Why the French Don't Suck," he gloried in Parisian cuisine in a pointed riposte to Freedom fries. After Ney was imprisoned for corruption in 2007 Congress quietly reverted to using the name French fries on its menus. Asked about the scuffle, Jones said, "I wish it had never happened."

III. The Case of the Errant Pretzel

As the initial shock of 9/11 wore off in the winter of 2001, the Bushes began to host small receptions and parties. While the Clintons invited glossy celebrities and important dignitaries for conversations about Big Ideas and led midnight raids on the fridge, the Bushes invited Texas friends and donors and hit the hay by 10:00 p.m.

At first glance, Clinton and Bush seemed to be polar opposites who had swapped identities. Clinton was raised poor by a single mother in Arkansas, aspired to a rococo, Kennedyesque lifestyle, and summered on salt-breezed Martha's Vineyard among the "white-wine swillers," as W. put it. Bush 43 was a Yankee blueblood raised amid Texas oil wealth who affected a down-home persona; though his parents summered on the Maine coast, he retreated to an air-conditioned ranch in Crawford, Texas. The political messaging was stark. But upon closer inspection, the two presidents were not so different.

"There was no red-state food and no blue-state food," Scheib said. Meals were the "only time [presidents] can be just normal . . . a husband, a father, a friend. So our goal was really to give them a home to come to." The menus at the Clinton and Bush White Houses "didn't delineate along party lines, but [they did] delineate very closely along gender lines," the chef continued. He would "cook to the taste and the style of the First Lady. And then the President, if he was wise, he'd go along with it. The President runs the world, but the First Lady runs the house."

Like many of their predecessors, Clinton and Bush would eat light, healthy meals with their wives, but the minute Hillary and Laura left town, the men would indulge in meaty feasts. Clinton's guilty pleasure was a twenty-four-ounce porterhouse steak with béarnaise sauce and a side of fried onion rings. Bush also liked a thick steak, or huevos rancheros for brunch, and bags of Lay's potato chips. Both men were fans of barbecue, though they split along regional lines: Clinton's Arkansas barbecue was slow-cooked pork swimming in sauce and pulled apart; Bush's Texas 'cue was dry-rubbed beef brisket that was grilled, sliced, and served with sauce on the side. There are few subjects that get eaters more agitated than barbecue, with partisans insisting their version is the "real" one.

"You might be considered a presidential assassin the way you cooked for these guys," the TV journalist Chris Cuomo ribbed Scheib. "Well, I tell you, the first ladies didn't care for it when they heard about it," the chef replied.

Mrs. Clinton and Mrs. Bush also shared tastes. Both were hot sauce aficionados: Hillary amassed sixty varieties in a cupboard called "the hot sauce zone." Though Laura tended to use just one type of hot sauce at a time—her favorite was Yucatan Sunshine Habanero Pepper Sauce—she applied it to nearly everything she ate. More surprisingly, both women favored organic vegetables. While this was an obvious choice for Mrs. Clinton, a devotee of Alice Waters's, Mrs. Bush's insistence on organics was less expected in light of her country-club tastes and the president's ties to corporate interests.

Organic food was synonymous with lefty, elitist, anticorporate politics, something the Republican Party avoided like kryptonite. Mike Johanns, Bush's secretary of agriculture, was a corn ethanol booster (a controversial, heavily subsidized crop); Johanns's chief of staff was the former chief lobbyist for the beef industry; and the head of Bush's FDA came from the National Food Processors Association, a food trade group. In other words, organic food didn't fit W's image.

Mrs. Bush did not publicly disclose her preference for organics, but Scheib revealed that she had relied on them since living in the Texas governor's mansion. The first Whole Foods Market (originally called Safer Way, a spoof on Safeway supermarkets) was founded in Austin, which has a vibrant food scene. "Mrs. Bush was adamant about organic foods," Scheib said. "It goes counter to her perceived personality, but it was never important to her that the information be released." And President Bush never addressed the disconnect between his family's food choices and his administration's food policies.

The Bushes liked other "elitist" foods, too, especially the handmade pretzels from the Hammond Pretzel Bakery, in Lancaster, Pennsylvania. But then one almost got the best of the president.

AT 5:35 P.M. ON SUNDAY, January 13, 2002, W. was munching a Hammond pretzel and watching the Miami Dolphins play the Baltimore Ravens in a football playoff game. The Secret Service had granted him a rare moment of privacy, and he was alone with his dogs, Barney and Spot. Laura was in another room, when a chunk of pretzel lodged in the presidential throat, triggering a "vasovagal syncope"—a sudden drop in heart rate—causing him to black out. Bush tumbled off the couch and hit the floor, bruising his cheek and bloodying his lip. Lying unconscious, he coughed, which dislodged the biscuit, and he came to.

Bush 43's collapse-by-pretzel was reminiscent of Bush 41's fainting episode almost exactly a decade earlier in Japan. Normally, such an accident would be ignored, but this was the American president after 9/11, when the nation felt vulnerable. "I hit the deck," Bush said with a chuckle. "The dogs were looking at me a little funny. . . . If my mother is listening, mother, I should have listened to you: always chew your pretzels before you swallow." Reporters glommed on to the story "like . . . mustard on pretzels," *The Washington Post* punned. And Press Secretary Ari Fleischer said, "You're not going to get us to cough up" details of the incident.

In fact, Hammond pretzels had been introduced to the White House by the sous-chef John Moeller, who hailed from Lancaster. After Bush's near asphyxiation, Moeller almost suffered his own syncope, and worried, "Am I going to be working here tomorrow?"

He kept his job, though the pretzel incident underscored a more "volatile" tone. When he joined the staff in 1992, public interest in presidential food was minimal. A decade later that had changed, and the press jumped at any whiff of gossip in the First Kitchen. This added a new edge, and cooks could be terminated for something as minor as recommending the wrong snack. (I spoke to a part-time cook who said she was fired after making a joke about Hillary Clinton.)

Even as the Bushes' socializing gained momentum in 2002, Scheib found his role "drastically reduced" and repetitive. When Mrs. Bush decided she liked his pea soup with mint, for instance, she asked for it again and again, and the chef worried she'd tire of the dish. She did not tire of the dish. After Bush won reelection in 2004, the First Couple's food orders grew plainer and plainer. "My work had ceased being fun," Scheib recalled. "I hadn't been truly tested in about four years. We had a routine, our menus were routine, and executing them was routine."

Things hit a culinary nadir at a congressional picnic in June 2004, when the Bushes served ready-made spareribs, turkey, dirty rice, and other prepackaged rations. Reduced to "oven technician," Scheib had no role in creating the menu, a job taken over by the food service giant KC Masterpiece, whose founder, Dr. Rich Davis, was a Bush donor. Roland Mesnier was pressed to serve an amateurish pound cake with strawberries and whipped cream. It was dispiriting and an example of the bland corporatization of White House food.

"I was . . . one part private chef and one part chef of a midsize suburban restaurant," Scheib recalled, acidly.

Just before Christmas of 2003, Mesnier had tendered his resignation. After twenty-five years, he was tired, and noticed that his fine motor skills and creativity were waning. He had written a book and, unlike his brother, a pâtissier in France who had worked himself to death without taking a break, he looked forward to enjoying life. Mrs. Bush graciously accepted the news, but W. worked him over: "What's your book called, *How to Kill a President with Calories*? . . . What if your book flops? . . . Why leave? There's no point. . . . Reconsider your decision. You understand? . . . Think about it."

At the summer solstice, Mesnier served a special dessert at the annual lunch for Senate wives—a dome of pistachio cake coated in a rich marquise (a chocolate mousse–like confection) sculpted into the shape of a dress worn by an elegant woman of the French ancien régime, whose head and torso were rendered in blown sugar. It was a fitting, spectacular grand finale, and on July 30 he handed in his security badge and left the White House.

Mesnier had hoped his assistant pastry chef, Susan Morrison, would succeed him. He and the Bushes were impressed by her talent and work ethic. But the top job was grueling, and, he wrote, Morrison declined the promotion because she felt she lacked "the strength" for it. She remained as an assistant, and after a "bake-off" between three candidates, the

Bushes chose Thaddeus DuBois as the new executive pastry chef. DuBois was a bespectacled, round-faced Los Angeleno. The Bushes offered him $120,000 a year—significantly less than he was making at an Atlantic City, New Jersey, hotel—but the White House has a gravitational pull on relatively young, unknown chefs. DuBois lasted two years.

In March 2006, Mrs. Bush decided that he was not a good fit and per-suaded Mesnier to rejoin the kitchen, temporarily. He agreed, and the spring and summer sped by. But as December loomed—it is the pastry kitchen's busiest month, with a relentless schedule of holiday parties that require weeks of work to prepare thousands of cookies, pies, cakes, and a gingerbread White House—Mesnier felt the old pangs return. He needed to find a skilled pastry chef who was capable under pressure and could succeed him, stat.

Leafing through *Food Arts* magazine, Mrs. Bush and her social sec-retary, Lea Berman, admired photos of desserts made by a New York pastry chef named Bill Yosses and invited him to apply for the job. "I never imagined I'd get *that* call," Yosses, an old friend of mine, said. "It was such an honor, but of course I knew it was a long shot." A native of Toledo, Ohio, he was raised on beef Stroganoff and Mamie Eisenhower's cheesecake. Earning a master's in French literature at Rutgers Univer-sity led him to France, where he did a *stage* at the three-star Moulin de Mougins restaurant and discovered the art, challenge, and sugar high of refined patisserie in the 1980s. Captivated by the big white plates deco-rated with dime-sized desserts and colorful swirls of sauce made famous by nouvelle cuisine, Yosses fell in love with "the precision of pastry," but adds, "I love the aesthetics more. I'm proudly superficial—I like pretty pictures!—plus I love a good dessert."

Settling in New York, Yosses helmed the pastry station in some of the trendiest, most sanity-challenging restaurants, including the Polo, Mon-trachet, and Bouley. He was working at Tavern on the Green when the White House called.

One afternoon in the fall of 2006, Yosses auditioned his pastries for Laura Bush and her staff. "I wanted the job, and put everything I could into the presentation," he said. After tempting the Bush twins, Jenna and Barbara, with platters of canapés, petits fours, and fruit *panna cottas,* he unveiled his secret weapon: double chocolate cookies. Every crumb dis-appeared within seconds, and all that remained was the sound of smack-ing lips. The twins gave Yosses a secret thumbs-up, and he "sighed in gratitude" when he was hired the next day.

Yosses is a slim, bald sprite with glasses, a mischievous grin, and a sharp wit leavened by a warm intelligence. He is a history buff who has taught food science at Harvard. He's also gay and married, which did not bother the conservative Bushes. "I felt welcomed," he said.

The December holidays were upon them, and only half joking Yosses said, "Eighty percent of the White House pastry job is dealing with Christmas." He was put right to work making confections for a rush of breakfasts, lunches, teas, and banquets for the cabinet, Congress, religious leaders, and on and on.

In explaining her approach to hostessing, Laura Bush expected a high degree of professionalism, but added, "I don't want the White House to feel like a hotel. I want people to feel like they are in a home. It's a special treat to come here, and everybody remembers it."

LEA BERMAN, Mrs. Bush's social secretary, had previously worked the same job for Lynne Cheney and was married to the sugar lobbyist and Bush fundraiser Wayne Berman. Scheib described Lea Berman as a coldhearted, stiletto-heeled socialite who lived in a thirteen-thousand-square-foot mansion on Embassy Row, as if she was a Lady Macbeth dressed in Versace. They clashed the moment they met.

When Berman suggested he make food like Marco Pierre White, the enfant terrible of British dining known for braised pigs' trotters, Scheib thought, "I'm not sure [the PB-and-J-loving Bush] is going to be big on that." When she suggested he cook dishes from *Martha Stewart Living*, wrote "Yuk" on his menu, or declared, "Your vegetables . . . are always overcooked," he fumed. "I [am] fairly certain I wouldn't have made it this far . . . if I didn't know how to cook vegetables."

It was Christmas 2004, the season of good cheer, that proved Scheib's undoing. When the Texas interior designer Ken Blasingame arrived to decorate the White House, he and Berman squabbled over how many tulips should decorate a platter of food: he wanted just one; she wanted a dozen; the kitchen crew was caught in the cross fire. "You're scaring the kids," Scheib blurted out. Berman glared at him, and Scheib sensed that, "right then and there, she stopped paying attention to me."

(As I will explain later, I had a different experience with Berman.)

In late January 2005 the Bushes hosted a wedding party at the White House for the son of a friend. It was a joyous affair, a reminder that the mansion was a private home. The dinner—wild mushroom soup, rack of lamb with tomato and corn custard, and a salad with Roquefort-walnut dressing—was given high marks. At the end of the night, Laura Bush called out to the kitchen, "Guys, that was just about perfect!" Those were the last words Scheib heard from her.

On February 2, the chief usher, Gary Walters, said, "The First Lady has decided that she's going to go in a different direction." Scheib understood he was being let go. He told himself it was for the best, that he had become stuck "in denial [about] an unhealthy relationship," and that it was time to move on. Still, the rejection stung.

One of the unspoken rules of the White House is that when someone is pushed out, they are expected to respond maturely and self-deprecatingly. Scheib did not subscribe to this fiction. He was angry and hurt. When someone leaked word of his dismissal to *The Washington Post,* the media demanded to know why and who was responsible. A Bush press secretary incorrectly said the chef was "already gone," and Scheib blew a gasket. "I was fired," he told *The New York Times.* "We've been trying to find a way to satisfy the first lady's stylistic requirements, and it has been difficult. Basically, I was not successful in my attempt. The failure is a loss. And I hate to lose because I am super competitive."

With that, his bridges were burned. Scheib was told not to return to the White House and that Mrs. Bush would not write him a job recommendation. Reflecting on his eleven years as executive chef, he said the job meant "being the most famous anonymous person you'll ever meet. . . . It was a great period . . . but I live my life in the windshield and not in the rearview mirror."

He went on to write a book, win on *Iron Chef* in 2006, and regale audiences with tales from his years in the Executive Kitchen. But the loss pained Scheib in the way that one-term presidents struggle with electoral losses. No experience can match life at the President's House. He missed the camaraderie, the pressure, the thrill of being at the center of things. He called the experience of working on "the biggest stage" an "honor and privilege," and, "a narcotic."

Walter Scheib suffered a difficult withdrawal. His marriage ended; he moved to Florida, then to Taos, New Mexico. On June 13, 2015, Scheib went for a hike above Taos Ski Valley and disappeared. Police and aircraft searched the steep trail but found nothing; when a rainstorm lashed the mountains, the search was suspended. A week later, troops with rescue dogs discovered Scheib's body hidden by dense vegetation in a drainage ditch. He was sixty-one years old and in good shape, and the autopsy revealed he had drowned in the desert.

His death was national news, and rumors swirled. Some believed he had been murdered, while others said it was suicide. Under the headline "Dark Mysteries Behind Clinton Chef's Drowning," the *National Enquirer* alleged without proof that Scheib had been privy to nefarious activities among the Clintons—"intimate secrets that threaten to derail Hillary's presidential run," the tabloid hyperventilated. Taos locals had a simpler explanation: Scheib had hiked a challenging trail, it began to rain while he was in a steep canyon, and a flash flood swept him away. It was an all-too-common occurrence, especially for those who were ill-prepared or had lost their way.

IV. The Seventh Executive Chef

After Scheib was fired, Laura Bush and Lea Berman conducted a wide-ranging search for his replacement. In the meantime, the sous-chef John Moeller was named acting executive chef. With his Filipina colleague, Cristeta Comerford, he prepared everything from huevos rancheros for the president's brunch to oysters and spinach au gratin for the First Lady's Shakespeare-themed lunch. The kitchen worked smoothly. Moeller kept his head down and hoped his promotion would be permanent.

Hundreds of chefs applied for the job. As usual, it was difficult to attract top talent: the salary of $80,000 to $100,000 a year with no overtime was well under what a chef could make at a successful restaurant, and opportunities in television or book and endorsement deals were not allowed. But it wasn't just a question of money. The kitchen was small, the full-time staff of five was scant, the hours were long, and it was no state secret that the job could be mundane at times.

The East Wing office conducted dozens of interviews with cooks across the country and whittled the list down to a handful of prospects. Alice Waters didn't offer advice this time. "I look for an open door" to such conversations, she told me; "the door was not open" with the Bushes. The search took on a political charge when Women Chefs and Restaurateurs—which represents two thousand culinary professionals—demanded the White House hire a female chef. "Throughout our history women have been at the helm of feeding American families," the group declared. "Now is the time to have a woman . . . feeding America's first family."

In June, two of the finalists—Chris Ward of the Mercury Grill in Dallas, and Richard Hamilton of the Spiced Pear in Newport, Rhode Island (both male)—were invited to audition for Mrs. Bush. She was looking for "sophisticated restaurant food" and said barbecue and Tex-Mex would not be a priority, Hamilton reported. Her staff "wanted to be wowed." In midsummer the job was quietly offered to Patrick O'Connell, who had earned two Michelin stars at the Inn at Little Washington, in the Blue Ridge Mountains. But like Patrick Clark in 1994, O'Connell declined the offer, presumably for the usual reasons.

On August 14, 2005, Laura Bush made a momentous if not entirely surprising announcement: the nation's seventh executive chef would be Moeller's sous-chef Cris Comerford. "I am delighted," the First Lady said. "Her passion for cooking can be tasted in every bite of her delicious creations."

A naturalized American citizen born in the Philippines, Cristeta Gomez Pasia Comerford was the first female, the first ethnic minority, and the first cook hired from within the kitchen ranks to be anointed executive chef. Comerford was forty-two years old, a short, solidly built woman with broad cheeks, full lips, a laser look in her dark eyes, and a good fit. She had cooked at the White House for a decade, was universally liked, made the kind of food the Bushes enjoyed, and was an exemplar of the American dream.

The tenth of eleven children, Comerford was born in a working-class neighborhood of Manila. Her father was a school principal; her mother, Erlinda, was a dressmaker who read culinary textbooks for fun, but cooked by instinct rather than from recipes. She raised her children on Filipino cuisine—an amalgam of Chinese, Japanese, and Spanish traditions, with the odd American ingredient, such as Spam (introduced by U.S. troops during World War II) thrown in, reflecting the nation's history.

Known as Cris in the kitchen, and Teta to her siblings, Comerford was focused and "so driven. So ambitious," one of her sisters said. She studied food technology but quit school at twenty-three to join an older brother in the Filipino community in Morton Grove, a Chicago suburb. There, she found a job as a "salad girl" at a Sheraton near O'Hare International Airport. After stints at a Chicago hotel and French restaurants in Washington, she polished her credentials as a *chef tournant* (revolving chef) at Le Ciel, in Vienna, Austria.

Walter Scheib recruited Comerford as a part-timer in the White House in 1995, then hired her full time. She was steeped in classical French technique but mostly cooked American or ethnic dishes. She impressed Laura Bush by whipping up a BLT lunch for the president at midday and a dazzling state dinner that night—chilled asparagus soup with lemon cream, and pan-roasted halibut and basmati rice in honor of the Indian prime minister Manmohan Singh. That "little family dinner," as Bush called it, was the first state dinner of his second term and only the fifth of his presidency. It memorialized a controversial Indo-American nuclear energy deal and won Comerford the job as top chef.

John Moeller was disappointed, but bore no grudge against his friend Cris. A few months later he quit, opened a catering company, and wrote a cookbook-memoir. "After thirteen years," he explained, "I figured it might be a good segue to just move on and start to do my own thing."

In hiring Cris Comerford, the Bushes had once again subverted their profile as rigid traditionalists. Even Alice Waters cheered the decision: "I'm glad it's a woman," she said. "That . . . makes a beautiful statement." Women Chefs and Restaurateurs applauded the Bushes for sending "a message around the world. Women make up more than 50 percent of food service workers, but hold less than 4 percent of the top jobs. And this is the top job."

20

BARACK OBAMA

The President with the Global Palate

THE FORTY-FOURTH PRESIDENT
January 20, 2009–January 20, 2017

★

I. Know Where Your Food Comes From

B orn in Honolulu in 1961, Barack Obama was the son of a Kenyan father "black as pitch" and a mother from Kansas "white as milk," he wrote. He was raised in Hawaii until 1967, when his mother, the anthropologist Stanley Ann Dunham, took her six-year-old son to live on the outskirts of Jakarta, Indonesia. She had remarried by then, to Lolo Soetoro, an Indonesian geographer. On his first day in Jakarta, Obama watched a Soetoro relative decapitate a chicken for dinner. When Dunham wondered if Barry was too young to witness the killing, Soetoro shrugged and said, "The boy should know where his dinner is coming from."

That night Obama dined on the stewed chicken with rice and a sweet fruit dessert. As he lay in bed, he recalled, "I listened to the crickets chirp under the moonlight and remembered the last twitch of life that I'd witnessed. . . . I could barely believe my good fortune."

Over the next four years, Obama learned to eat Indonesian staples such as green chili peppers with rice, *nasi goreng* (fried rice), *bakso* (meatballs), *sambal tempe* (fermented soybean cake with chili sauce), and sweet mango and rambutan. He also sampled decidedly non-American fare, such as roasted grasshoppers ("crunchy"), dog meat ("tough"), and snake ("tougher"). In Soetoro's worldview—informed by "a brand of Islam that could make room for the more ancient animist and Hindu faiths," Obama wrote—a man took on the powers inherent to the things he ate. "He promised . . . he would bring home a piece of tiger meat to share. That's how things were, one long adventure, the bounty of a young boy's life."

The boy's Indonesian bounty would have political consequences years later. When he squared off against Mitt Romney in the 2012 presidential race, Republicans charged that Obama was heartless because he had eaten dog meat. Democrats replied that Romney was even more heartless because he had placed the family dog, Seamus, in a crate on the roof of his car and drove on the highway at speed. Such are the brickbats of American political theater.

More to the point, Obama was an adventurous eater from the start, one who learned that food connects people across time, space, and cultures and contains meaning beyond sustenance. He continued his gastronomic education when he attended Occidental College (freshman and sophomore years) in Los Angeles, Columbia University (junior and senior years) in New York City, and Harvard Law School in Cambridge, Massachusetts. Postgraduation, he worked as a community organizer and attorney in Chicago. Each of these places is food mad in its own way, and by the time he entered the White House, at forty-seven, Barack Obama had the most globally informed palate of any president in history (with the possible exception of Herbert Hoover).

IN 2008, George W. Bush was clunking toward the end of his war-torn presidency and was tethered to controversial Big Food companies like Monsanto and Cargill at a time when experts were ringing alarms about climate change and the global food crisis. Stumping for the presidency, Obama aligned himself with the opposition. He spoke the language of the food movement—a loose network of health, environmental, social-justice, and animal-welfare champions—who were animated not only by how their meals tasted but by who supplied their ingredients, where, and how their practices impacted health, the community, the environment, and the world. His stance built support and opposition in equal measure.

The Illinois senator was labeled a "foodie" by people on both sides of the aisle. What is a foodie? The term is just a new, slangier word for gourmet—that is, someone who takes eating, drinking, cooking, and knowledge about food seriously—but with overuse the term has become a signifier for a twee, entitled attitude about eating. Obama never applied the label to himself and tried to distance himself from it, emphasizing instead how his single mother relied on food stamps to feed him as a child in Hawaii. But occasionally his innate epicuriosity slipped out, like a cat scooting out the door.

In July 2007, candidate Obama stood between corn and soybean fields in Adel, Iowa, trying to build a connection to rural voters. In Chicago "the main livestock is squirrels," he joked, before noting that crop prices were falling. "Anybody gone into Whole Foods lately and see what they charge for arugula? I mean, they're charging *a lot of money* for this stuff." The audience didn't react. In fact, there were zero Whole Foods in Iowa, and arugula was perceived as an elitist lettuce. The press jumped on Obama's "gaffe" that "outed him as a foodie."

Arugula-gate, as the incident was inevitably called, was one of several moments where Obama's tastes were used to characterize him as an out-of-touch limousine liberal, an "insufferable foodie." When he ordered a burger with Dijon mustard, the Fox personality Sean Hannity jabbed him as "President Poupon"—a reference to the aristocratic dandy in a 1981 TV ad for Grey Poupon mustard (more bitingly, *poupon* is French for "little baby").

As Obama campaigned in the Democratic primary on the themes of "Hope and Change," he proved himself a gifted politician, but his slogan also opened him to being mocked as a softheaded naïf. "How's that Hope-y, Change-y thing going?" taunted Sarah Palin, John McCain's Republican running mate. This duality would extend to Obama's broader food policies over the next eight years.

He was hailed as "the Food President," the "First Eater," and the "First Foodie," among other snappy sobriquets. He earned his foodie stripes in the 1990s, when he was an Illinois state senator who was just as interested in restaurant menus as he was in his constituents' issues. In Chicago he would scarf down steak and eggs at Valois Restaurant, soul food at MacArthur's, or Italian at Spiaggia. When he and his wife, Michelle, were in the mood for something adventurous—lobster and scallops with tomatillo corn sauce and tamales, say—they would schedule a date at Rick Bayless's fine Mexican restaurant Topolobampo and sit in back, next to the kitchen.

Campaigning for the White House in 2008, Obama pledged to raise federal assistance to organic farms, label genetically modified foods, and regulate pollution from enormous pork and poultry CAFOs (concentrated animal feeding operations) and declared that imported foods would be marked with their country of origin, because, he said—echoing his stepfather—"Americans should know where their food comes from." In an interview with *Time,* Obama distilled a *New York Times Magazine* article by Michael Pollan, the gardener and best-selling author of *The Omnivore's Dilemma,* about the food industry's large, complex, not always benevolent footprint:

> Our entire agricultural system is built on cheap oil. As a consequence, our agricultural sector actually is contributing more greenhouse gases than our transportation sector. And in the meantime, it's creating monocultures that are vulnerable to national security threats, are now vulnerable to sky-high food prices or crashes in food prices, huge

swings in commodity prices, and are partly responsible for the explosion in our healthcare costs because they're contributing to type 2 diabetes, stroke and heart disease, obesity, all the things that are driving our huge explosion in healthcare costs. That's just one sector of the economy.

When Obama handily won the election in November, foodies were ecstatic. They envisioned an ecologically conscientious, healthy, profitable, delicious future. A "second food revolution" was nigh, cheered Ruth Reichl, the editor of *Gourmet* magazine (a venerable title that would fold in 2009). "People are so interested in a massive change in food and agriculture that they are dining out on hope now. That is like the main ingredient," observed Eddie Gehman Kohan, a Los Angeles pastry chef who, on election night, launched *Obama Foodorama,* a blog that would catalog every possible connection between the president and what he ate over the next eight years.

But not everyone agreed the American food system was broken, and even before he took office, entrenched "realists" pushed back against the Obama "idealists." The loose federation of food industrialists that Pollan calls Big Food—a $1.5 trillion industry that encompasses Big Ag (corn and soybean growers), Big Meat (animal growers and processors), supermarkets, and fast-food companies—brusquely reminded the new president that they, not he, held the keys to the kingdom. These companies compete in the marketplace, but when threatened by a common enemy, they join forces, deploy lobbyists, and lean on congressional allies to stall or block limits on their production of cheap, processed foodstuffs.

The first elbow was thrown by Senator Charles "Chuck" Grassley of Iowa—"the Senior Senator from Corn," Pollan dubbed him—who thundered that an urban Democrat had no business blaming rural farmers for the nation's pollution and obesity. A spokesman for Obama backpedaled, saying the president had only "paraphrased" Pollan's *Times* article.

Grassley's early jab was a warning that the foodies' bubbly vision of a gastronomic nirvana was bound to be punctured by Washington's realpolitik. And it was clear that food was just one front in a broader "culture war" that pitted young progressives against an entrenched Old Guard, personified by the Senate minority leader, Mitch McConnell, who vowed to make Obama "a one-term president."

While those troops were massing in the background, a firefight broke out in the foreground. Worried that the Food President–elect had yet to name an administrator of the U.S. Department of Agriculture (USDA), Alice Waters wrote a letter to Obama in December 2008, imploring him to pick a USDA administrator who would favor sustainable, organic food production over Big Food. "Our nation is at a critical juncture," she wrote. "Our next Secretary of Agriculture will play [a central role] in revitalizing our rural economies, protecting our food supply and our environment . . . and creating a sustainable renewable energy future."

The letter, cosigned by eighty-eight food world celebrities, called for "policies that place conservation, soil health, animal welfare and worker's rights . . . near the top of their agenda"—the kind of jeremiad that made Waters famous and occasionally effective. "Alice is a utopian," one of the signers told me, half admiringly. "I rolled my eyes and signed it. She will decide to do something 'impossible'—and, well, you can't turn her down. It doesn't always work, but we wouldn't have made so much progress without her."

The stakes were high. "USDA administrator" is a bland bureaucratic title for one of the most fascinating and contested jobs in Washington. Though most Americans are only vaguely aware of the Agriculture Department, it is an enormous agency that oversees "forestry, farming and food." Created by Abraham Lincoln in 1862, and granted cabinet status in 1889, it now encompasses a bank with some $220 billion in assets, a staff of 100,000, a squadron of firefighting aircraft, a climate change office, and a headquarters on the National Mall with an experimental farm, a shooting range, a photo archive, and a rooftop apiary to study bee colonies, among other things.

A small percentage of USDA's budget—about $146 billion in 2021 ($18 billion less than in 2016)—supported farming programs and rural communities. But nearly 80 percent of the agency's resources are directed to the research, support, and protection of the nation's food supplies. USDA finances free school lunches and mediates conflicts between animals and humans ("animal welfare"). It inspects the meat Americans eat—including nine billion birds a year—and oversees 193 million acres of national grasslands and forest. It runs the Food Safety and Inspection Service, the Agricultural Research Service, and the Food and Nutrition Service. In short, USDA is in charge of America's nutrition, and as a result it is a political hot potato.

Liberals have long complained that USDA is too close to conservative politicians and their Big Food donors, such as George W. Bush's agriculture secretary Edward Schafer, who supported industrial-scale farming in his home state of North Dakota. Alice Waters suggested six candidates for the cabinet post, and others threw their hat in the ring. But Obama ultimately made a pragmatic if not inspiring choice by naming Tom Vilsack, a former governor of Iowa.

The president praised Vilsack for making corn-based ethanol "an agricultural economy of the future that not only grows the food we eat, but the energy we use." Michael Pollan bristled at this, noting that Vilsack never mentioned the word "food" or "eaters," but spoke for "farmers, ranchers . . . [and] agribusiness as usual." Pollan advocated renaming USDA the "Department of Food" and focusing it on "the catastrophic American diet," on the needs of eaters, and on the diversification of farming practices to accommodate climate change, energy independence, and health-care reform.

Undeterred, Alice Waters wrote Obama a second letter. This time, she and her cosigners—Ruth Reichl and Danny Meyer, the New York restaurateur and founder of Shake Shack—volunteered as a Kitchen Cabinet, to provide ideas and contacts and serve as a sounding board. They urged the White House to promote healthy eating, elevate the quality of its food, and redefine the role of executive chef: "The purity and wholesomeness of the Obama movement must be accompanied by a parallel effort in food at the most visible and symbolic place in America—the White House."

Republican skeptics, such as James Thurber of American University, scoffed that the letter writers didn't "have a central, core message. . . . What policy are they trying to change?" To which Reichl replied, "We want to change it all! Who doesn't think obesity is a problem or pesticides is a problem and social justice for farm workers is a problem—these are all things that need to be changed and many feel that the opportunity is finally in sight."

The Kitchen Cabinet letter struck many as well intentioned but tone-deaf. Bloggers scolded Waters for "gastronomical correctness," and Anthony Bourdain, the bad-boy host of *No Reservations,* deemed her "Pol Pot in a muumuu." There's something "very Khmer Rouge about Alice Waters that has become unrealistic," he said. "We're in the middle of a recession . . . [it's not] like we're all going to start buying expensive organic food."

The good news was that there *was* an argument, one that had progressed a good deal since the Clinton-Bush days and extended far beyond the Beltway. "When I started writing about food in this country, nobody seemed to care," Reichl said. "It's very exciting that people now care" to become emotionally invested in food at the White House.

"Nothing is more political than food," Bourdain asserted. "Who gets to eat, who doesn't, why we eat, what we eat, where those dishes originated and under what circumstances, what ingredients are acceptable to people. . . . [T]here is nothing more political than food. Nothing."

II. Breaking Ground

To a greater degree than in most administrations, the Obama White House's food policies were an outgrowth of the First Family's personal struggles and choices. From a distance, Barack and Michelle appeared to lead charmed lives, yet both had lost a parent, Michelle suffered a miscarriage (their daughters, Malia and Sasha, were conceived with in vitro fertilization), and the strain of their careers had sent them to marriage counseling. Under those circumstances, questions about what they ate, and where, took on an outsized importance.

In Chicago, the Obamas reserved Friday nights for dates at Zinfandel, an eclectic restaurant: Michelle would arrive punctually and settle in with a glass of wine; eventually Barack would thread his way through the crowd, kiss her, and sit down to a plate of comfort food. "We ordered the same thing pretty much every Friday—pot roast, Brussels sprouts, and mashed potatoes—and when it came, we ate every bite," she recalled. "I remember those nights with a deep fondness now. . . . That was a golden time for us."

In 2005, Barack was sworn in as a freshman Democratic senator from Illinois and began to commute to Washington, D.C. This left Michelle, a vice president at a hospital, alone with Sasha and Malia. Pressed for time, the girls and their mother ate a lot of sugary cereals, salty snacks, fatty hamburgers, take-out food, soft drinks, and ice cream.

On February 10, 2007, Barack Obama stood in front of the state capitol in Springfield—where Lincoln delivered his "House Divided" speech in 1858—to announce he was running for president. As he stumped across the country, Hillary Rodham Clinton led the Democratic primary by thirty points and Rudy Giuliani and Mitt Romney vied for the Republican ticket. Mrs. Obama recoiled from the combat and compromise of politics, yet she was an effective proxy for her husband and was sucked into campaigning. This left her with even less time to monitor the girls' diets. "Convenience had become the single most important factor,"

Michelle recalled. "I packed the girls' lunch boxes with Lunchables and Capri Suns. Weekends usually meant a trip to the McDonald's drive-through. . . . None of this . . . was out of the ordinary, or even all that terrible in isolation. Too much of it, though, was a real problem."

In the spring of 2007, their pediatrician noticed that Malia was at risk for high blood pressure and type 2 diabetes. Or, as Barack bluntly put it, "Malia was getting a little chubby." She was not alone. Childhood obesity was becoming epidemic: nearly a third of American children were overweight or obese, and working-class Blacks were especially prone to poor nutrition. Obesity raises the chance for heart disease, diabetes, joint problems, high cholesterol, and sleep apnea. "Clearly," Michelle said, "something had to change."

At that point she met a freelance cook named Sam Kass. He was a white twenty-six-year-old former University of Chicago baseball player with a shaved head and a pocketful of corny jokes. He learned to cook in restaurants and was a convert to the health and taste benefits of fresh vegetables, whole grains, and lean proteins. Mrs. Obama was intrigued, but she worried that hiring a personal chef was "a little bougie," yet, she reasoned, "no one else could run my programs at the hospital. No one else could campaign as Barack Obama's wife. No one could fill in as Malia and Sasha's mother at bedtime. But maybe Sam Kass could cook some dinners for us."

Kass prepared hand-cut fettucine enrobed in a velvety sauce of sweet peas, basil, lemon zest, and a sprinkling of Parmesan cheese. It was a fresh, tasty spring dinner. But Sasha and Malia thought of "pasta" as spaghetti with meatballs and were unimpressed by the "fancy pea-sauce." Nonetheless, their mother hired Kass to cook and make dinners she could freeze. There was just one obstacle: Mr. Obama. "It didn't fit with his . . . community-organizer frugality, nor the image he wanted to promote as a presidential candidate," Michelle recalled. When he balked, she gave him a choice: "Either you can hire Sam to make sure the girls are getting good, healthy food and I will campaign for you. Or I will stay home and do the cooking." Kass was hired.

As he got to know the Obamas, Kass noticed "they both love really good food. *Her* tastes are quite adventurous. *He* takes a different kind of joy [in eating]. He really likes good food, but he plays it cool and doesn't get too exercised. He doesn't like fancy stuff. But if it's really good, solid, clean, he'll take good pleasure from that."

Kass enlisted the Obama girls to help him root "fake food" out of the pantry, and replace it with fruits, nuts, and vegetables in clear containers. "We eat what we see," he reasoned. (Big Food knows this, too. One study showed that moving soda from the middle of a supermarket aisle to the end, increased sales by 50 percent.) As Sasha and Malia swept through the kitchen, they grabbed an apple instead of a salty or sugary snack. But, acknowledging that everyone needs a treat, Kass put homemade cookies on the top of the cabinet—accessible, but hard to reach.

While Michelle was a devotee of bacon and French fries, her husband was that rare breed: an ardent gourmet who was a picky, disciplined eater. He did not care for most fried or battered foods, mayonnaise, cake, or sweet muffins. He drank orange juice or green tea in the morning, organic tea during the day, and beer at night. He liked spinach and broccoli, but not asparagus and beets. At times, his food fixation seemed to border on the obsessive. *The New York Times* reported that he snacked on exactly seven almonds—"not six, not eight, always seven almonds," Kass told the paper. Soon, "seven almonds" became a meme. "This seems weird," friends said. But the truth, Obama explained, was that gullible journalists had taken Kass's joke at face value, adding that he might be willing to eat "ten or eleven" almonds.

TUESDAY, NOVEMBER 4, 2008, was the first U.S. presidential election since 1952 in which neither party's nominee was an incumbent president or vice president. Obama and Joe Biden handily defeated McCain and Palin. The following January, 1.8 million people gathered in Washington— one of the largest crowds in the District's history—as Chief Justice John Roberts swore in Barack Hussein Obama as the nation's first mixed-race chief executive.

The night before the inauguration, Dan Barber, the chef at New York's Blue Hill restaurants, cooked a meal for the soon-to-be First Couple and a few friends in Washington. They debated which food issues Obama should prioritize, how to sell his agenda to the public, and what he could accomplish in four years. When the conversation turned to reforming the food system, the president challenged the table, saying, "Show me a movement."

He meant that given his limited political capital, he would not pursue ambitious change unless he had the votes. Mindful of the nation's fatigue with Beltway gridlock and the mistakes of Clinton's first term, Obama did not believe he could overhaul the production and distribution of food, but, he noted, incremental changes could eventually shift the balance of power.

At the end of the night, Barack looked at Michelle and said maybe "*you* can talk about these issues. It'll be a hell of a lot more effective than me." He wasn't entirely wrong about that.

THE FOLLOWING DAY, Obama celebrated his inauguration with a lunch inspired by the bicentenary of Lincoln's birth: a seafood stew (sourced from Maine) topped by puff pastry; duck breast (from Indiana) with cherry chutney; roast pheasant (from Wisconsin) with wild rice stuffing; molasses whipped sweet potatoes; and a medley of winter vegetables. Dessert was apple cinnamon sponge cake and sweet cream glacé, made by Bill Yosses. The lunch was paired with American wines and served on replicas of Lincoln's White House china.

After lunch, the First Family moved into the White House. It was a routine but momentous occasion, due to their race.

While Barack was held up as a shining example of American multiculturalism, Michelle Obama's ancestry reflected a more typical African American experience—from slavery in the South to the Great Migration north and middle-class life in Chicago. She and her brother were raised in a nine-hundred-square-foot apartment "with no privacy," largely by their mother, Marian Robinson, a former executive secretary. (Her father, Fraser Robinson III, died of multiple sclerosis in 1991, when Michelle was twenty-seven.) The Robinsons had an extended family, and someone was always cooking. They ate well, but it wasn't fancy—iceberg lettuce, broccoli, peas, spaghetti and meatballs, lemon chicken, and the like. "We had to eat all of it," or go without, Michelle recalled. The family ate together at the kitchen table, a tradition the Obamas continued at the White House—including Mrs. Robinson, who moved in to help raise her granddaughters.

Being married to the president of the United States is a challenge in ordinary circumstances, but to be the first Black First Lady was a mindblowing experience. Slaves had helped build the President's House, and Michelle Robinson Obama's great-great-grandfather Jim Robinson was a slave at Friendfield, a South Carolina rice plantation, where he is buried in an unmarked grave. Her parents had never discussed him, and she only learned of him while campaigning nearby.

As known foodies, it was rumored that the Obamas would anoint a new executive chef. The usually gastro-oblivious tabloids hollered an announcement was "hotly awaited." Alice Waters said the ideal candidate would be "a person with integrity and devotion" who would champion "seasonal, ripe, delicious food." Though she didn't mention Cristeta Comerford by name, Waters said she wanted to "redefine" the position, and seemed to question the chef's "devotion" to "seasonal, delicious food." Ruth Reichl added that a "name" chef would have a bigger impact on American food than a cabinet appointment like Tom Vilsack.

Some interpreted this as a call to replace Comerford with a celebrity TV chef who could reach the masses and raise the profile of White House cookery. Three candidates who fit that description—Art Smith, Oprah Winfrey's personal chef; Daniel Young, the basketball star Carmelo Anthony's cook; and Rick Bayless, the Obamas' favorite Mexican chef in Chicago—were floated.

But Michelle kept her own counsel and decided Comerford would remain: "She brings such incredible talent . . . and came very highly regarded from the Bush family. She is also the mom of a young daughter, and I appreciate our shared perspective on the importance of healthy eating and healthy families."

Mrs. Obama was just getting started. Two months to the day after the inauguration, on March 20, 2009—the first day of spring—she announced she would turn an eleven-hundred-square-foot plot on the South Lawn into a vegetable garden. It would be the first proper White House garden since Eleanor Roosevelt planted a Victory Garden during World War II. As the cameras clicked, Tom Vilsack, Sam Kass, the pastry chef Bill Yosses, and a White House horticulturist helped Michelle break ground on an L-shaped bed near the tennis courts.

The White House Kitchen Garden—better known as "Michelle's Garden"—was planted on a highly visible site in a historic landscape, and it played at least two important roles. Though she had never gardened before, Mrs. Obama said it would provide fresh, homegrown ingredients for her family and official entertainments. The message to the public was clear: the self-described "mom in chief" ate healthy foods, and you should too. Further, she was going to share her bounty with food banks and educate children about obesity, diet, and exercise. Kids "will begin to educate their families, and that will, in turn, begin to educate our communities," she said.

The garden would also be seen as an extension of Obama's food policies, which were proving controversial. That made Michelle nervous. But getting attention was the point, she realized. "I wanted this garden to be more than just a plot of land growing vegetables on the White House lawn," she wrote. "I wanted it to . . . begin a conversation about the food we eat, the lives we lead, and how all of that affects our children."

Planting the White House garden was a modestly revolutionary act, and it had a long history. In 1800, John Adams seeded the mansion's scrubby lawn with vegetables. Thomas Jefferson added fruit trees and flowers. John Quincy Adams planted ornamental trees in 1825, and a decade later Andrew Jackson built an orangery for tropical fruit. A large greenhouse was added (later replaced by the West Wing). During the Progressive Era of 1890–1920, the school garden movement lured children out of tenements and taught them to grow their own food.

During the world wars, Wilson and Roosevelt encouraged millions of Americans to turn their yards, porches, and window boxes into vegetable plots. Originally called "War Gardens," they were renamed more optimistically "Victory Gardens" and were a roaring success. Franklin Roosevelt, however, opposed his wife's plan for a garden and told Eleanor, "The yard is full of rocks." She ignored him and used eleven-year-old Diana Hopkins—the cute daughter of FDR's adviser Harry Hopkins—as the poster child for her project. Noting that "children can grow things . . . in a very small space," she gave Diana a two-foot-by-two-foot plot in the lawn to tend carrots, beans, tomatoes, and cabbage.

By May 1943, Victory Gardens were producing 40 percent of the nation's vegetables, and Eleanor's charm offensive was so effective that FDR had to eat his words. "I hope that every American who possibly can will grow a victory garden this year," he told the public. "We found . . . that even the small gardens helped. The total harvest . . . made the difference between scarcity and abundance."

Though the farm-raised presidents Truman and Eisenhower did not plant White House gardens, the chef René Verdon grew tomatoes on the Kennedys' and Johnsons' roof in the 1960s. But for those who were serious about farming, the White House's 18.7-acre lawn beckoned. Activists believe that gardening has both physical and psychological benefits and wondered, what better way to inspire a conversation about taste and nutrition than for the First Family to grow vegetables on land owned by the people?

In 1991, Michael Pollan called on George H. W. Bush—who deemed himself "the environmental president"—to abolish the South Lawn and replant it. Observing that lawns unite the nation in an unending carpet of green turfgrass, Pollan cautioned that they require intensive use of water, energy, fertilizers, pesticides, and mowing—an "unsupportable environmental price tag." His opposition was less chemical than metaphysical. "The lawn is a symbol of everything that is wrong with our relationship to the land," he wrote, and a better use of the presidential greens would be as a meadow, wetland, orchard, or vegetable garden. "The White House has enough land to become self-sufficient in food—a model of Jeffersonian independence and thrift. . . . [It could] supply food [to the] poor. Depending on which party is in power, a few elephants or donkeys should be maintained for . . . fertilization."

Pollan's suggestion fell on deaf ears. But Walter Scheib grew veggies on the roof during the Clinton and Bush 43 years. And in 2008, Alice Waters—who had been pushing for a White House garden since the Clinton era—and other gardeners urged the Obamas to plant a much bigger and more visible plot.

When Mrs. Obama and a group of fifth graders dug their spades into the South Lawn in March 2009, cameras clicked as they sowed seeds from fifty-five vegetable varieties in raised beds fertilized by compost, Chesapeake crab meal, lime, and greensand. The plantings included lettuces—arugula (naturally), red leaf, butterhead, galactic, green oak leaf, red romaine—radishes, peas, carrots, spinach, kale, chard, collard greens, and rhubarb. There were no beets, in deference to the president's taste, but there were ten kinds of herbs, from Thai basil to anise hyssop. For spice, hot peppers, tomatillos, cilantro, and fish peppers—an African American heirloom from the mid-nineteenth century used in fish dishes. Two beds were planted with seeds from Monticello, including sea kale, Savoy cabbage, prickly-seeded spinach, and tennis ball lettuce. Berries were planted for Yosses's desserts, and two beehives were built to provide honey. Pest control was managed by ladybugs and praying mantises.

It would be easy to tell when the produce was ready, Kass said, because the Obamas "will be able to taste it." (In addition to cooking and gardening for the First Family, Kass took on an increasingly active political role: in 2010 he was named senior policy adviser for healthy food initiatives, and three years later was promoted to senior policy adviser for nutrition policy.)

Photos of the First Lady flashing her toned biceps while harvesting greens went viral, and the garden was praised by Windsor Castle. It produced a thousand pounds of food annually and inspired families, schools, communities, businesses, houses of worship, and even military bases to seed their own plots.

Such efforts had "phenomenal symbolic value," observed Marion Nestle, an emeritus professor of nutrition and food studies at New York University. "It sends the message, without anybody having to make speeches about it, that growing gardens is a fun and useful thing to do."

But not to everyone. Big Ag saw Michelle's garden as a threat. Though her vegetables were not certified organic (a process that takes three years), and she did not refer to them as such, the press erroneously did. That antagonized the American Council on Science and Health—a euphemistically named chemical industry group—which warned that organic farming would result in "famine."

IN THE MEANTIME, President Obama was focused on the big issues of American food policy, a notoriously difficult and highly partisan arena. The administration scored a few early wins—banning the sale of junk food in schools, mandating that fast-food restaurants include nutritional details on their menus, and replacing the confusing "food pyramid" diet guideline with MyPlate, a simple circle divided into quarters of protein, vegetables, grains, and fruits. But these were mere skirmishes in a preamble to the Battle with Big Food.

By 2010 the four biggest meatpacking companies controlled 84 percent of the market, and small ranchers and farmers complained they were little more than modern sharecroppers. In response, Obama initiated an antitrust investigation of cattle, dairy, poultry, and seed companies, in the most comprehensive prosecution of the food industry since Teddy Roosevelt curbed the Beef Trust in 1905. Secretary Vilsack promised to "make sure the playing field is level," and ordered GIPSA (the Grain Inspection, Packers, and Stockyards Administration)—a USDA agency with antitrust oversight—to draft new rules on anticompetitive behavior.

Furious, Big Meat responded with a $9 million lobbying juggernaut, a figure that did not include political contributions to congressmen on agriculture committees. Conagra and Tyson raised such a stink over the new GIPSA rules that Vilsack was forced to postpone them. Then Big Food claimed Obama wanted to raise food prices and kill jobs, while the Republican-controlled House cut GIPSA's funding. Once the dust settled, agribusiness had won and the president's antitrust initiatives were dead.

Obama was labeled risk averse and ineffectual by friend and foe. Though his $956 billion farm bill in 2014 broke partisan gridlock, he was attacked by the left for cutting $8 billion from the SNAP food stamp program and for allowing companies like Monsanto to hide the details of their GMOs (genetically modified organisms). The most stinging rebuke of the Food President was that his victories were more symbolic than tangible, and his defeats broke the movement's spirit. "Barack Obama sold out the kale crowd," *The New Republic* charged. He "overpromised reforms, underestimated the strength of his opposition, and flinched from real fights."

The First Lady, meanwhile, was making better progress. She chose issues that appealed to everyday Americans, such as the 2010 "Let's Move!" campaign to combat childhood obesity. Worried about "the crisis of inactivity" among kids, Mrs. Obama enlisted celebrities like Beyoncé Knowles and Ellen DeGeneres to sing, dance, and spread the word that working out was healthy and fun. Michelle also spearheaded the Healthy, Hunger-Free Kids Act, which raised nutritional standards for school lunches. She urged Walmart to lower fruit and vegetable costs by $1 billion a year and persuaded soda makers to list calories on their cans.

In a tough speech to the Grocery Manufacturers Association—a trade group that represents brands such as General Mills, Nestlé, and Pepsi—the Harvard Law School grad said, "We need you all to step it up . . . not just to tweak around the edges, but to entirely rethink the products you are offering. . . . While decreasing fat is certainly a good thing, replacing it with sugar and salt isn't. . . . This isn't about finding creative ways to market products as healthy. As you know, it's about producing products that actually *are* healthy."

When Big Food companies dragged their feet, and their lobbyists gummed up reform efforts, the First Lady shifted the focus of Let's Move! from improving nutrition to encouraging exercise. Her supporters were taken aback: it seemed she had retreated from the war against salt, sugar, and fat. But the hard political reality was that the Tea Party revolt of 2010 had labeled the administration "anti-business" and cost the Democrats control of Congress. Even so, Michelle's ideas remained popular, and she kept working with scientists, legislators, and educators. That doggedness won over some critics, such as Kelly Brownell, a Duke University obesity researcher, who said "attention to the issue has really helped push the [health] discussion forward."

With the benefit of time, the Obamas deserve credit for highlighting healthy eating as a subject worth talking about and even fighting over. The president managed to earmark $1 billion for regional food projects, almost double the number of farmers markets (from 4,685 to 8,669 nationwide), empower regulators, ban unhealthy trans fats, and modernize nutritional labeling. And a $50 billion alternative economy—what Pollan calls "Little Food"—sprang up. Though small compared with Big Food, these entrepreneurs exemplified a new, fast-moving marketplace that industrial giants were slow to adapt to and unable to limit.

"I've seen a shift," Obama said. "People . . . are becoming interested in where their food comes from. Towns . . . that didn't have regular access to fresh fruits and vegetables are getting them. Farmers and ranchers are tapping new markets and keeping more money in their pockets." These were the incremental changes he foresaw over dinner with Dan Barber in January 2009, when he correctly predicted that Michelle would have a better chance of success with targeted initiatives than he would with major policy shifts.

In retrospect, the chef Rick Bayless observed, "the importance of Michelle's garden cannot be overstated. Everyone said she shouldn't do it, or couldn't do it, and she did it. She planted it anyway. It had a huge effect, and that spoke louder than pretty much everything else the Obamas did." Pausing a beat, he added in a wistful tone, "Look, they were trying to change the direction of a huge ship. It was heading in one direction, and they *were* able to change it, a little bit, in another direction. But just a bit."

III. *A Little Less Afraid of the Unknown*

The camera panned down a sleepy, rainy street in Hanoi, Vietnam, when the scene suddenly churned with activity. U.S. Secret Service agents parted a crowd, the soundtrack pumped James Brown's "Boss," and out stepped Barack Obama, beaming and loose. As a cheering crowd gathered, the president said, "Hey—how you doin', guys?"

Anthony Bourdain, dressed in jeans and desert boots, led him to a roadside diner called Bun Cha Huong Lien. It was a warm night in May 2015, and they were there to eat *bun cha*—noodles and pork—as if they were two regular guys out on the town. Inside, the lanky president and the hipster TV presenter sat on blue plastic stools, loading bowls with rice noodles, strips of grilled pork belly, and juicy pork patties. Demonstrating how to lubricate the noodles with a *nuoc mam* broth—vinegar, sugar, and fermented fish sauce—Bourdain said, "Slurping is totally acceptable. . . . Get ready to enjoy the awesomeness."

"This is outstanding," enthused Obama, unfazed by hot chili peppers.

The White House adviser Ben Rhodes had prepped Bourdain, saying the president's "philosophy isn't that different from yours. If people would just sit down and eat together, and understand something about each other, maybe they could figure things out."

Obama's *bun cha* dinner, which cost a grand total of $6 ("I picked up the check," his host tweeted), would appear in *Anthony Bourdain: Parts Unknown* in 2016 and became one of the White House's most successful bits of social outreach. The Vietnamese ambassador to the United States was more excited by the show than by any of the agreements he had brokered over trade and human rights.

As they swigged beer "like two dads and Southeast Asia enthusiasts," Obama recalled one of his favorite childhood dinners: grilled carp with bitter rice along a highway in Indonesia. "It was the simplest meal possible," he reminisced, "and nothing tasted so good."

Off camera, Bourdain wondered if his friendship with the rocker Ted Nugent—"who has said many, many deeply offensive . . . things" about Obama—was acceptable. "Of course," replied the president. Those who "disagree with us" are exactly the kinds of "people we *should* be talking to." Noting that John Kerry and John McCain made peace with their former Vietnamese enemies, presumably over food, he added, "You don't make peace with your friends. You make peace with your enemies. . . . Progress is not a straight line. There are going to be moments . . . where things are terrible. But, having said all that, I think things are gonna work out."

After Bourdain's death in 2018, Obama tweeted, "[Tony] taught us about food—but more importantly, about its ability to bring us together. To make us a little less afraid of the unknown."

21

DONALD TRUMP

The Food Fighter

THE FORTY-FIFTH PRESIDENT

January 20, 2017–January 20, 2021

★

I. Gut Instinct

You are what you eat.
—Victor Lindlahr

Donald J. Trump understood the politics of the dinner table better than any president since the Kennedys wowed Nobel laureates with haute cuisine and Lyndon Johnson seduced diplomats with Texas barbecue. But Trump took a different tack than his predecessors. He presented a lurid fast-food "banquet" in the White House, ate fine steaks broiled to a crisp and doused in ketchup, and eschewed vegetables other than the shredded iceberg lettuce in his taco bowls. He did not drink alcohol, but ordered up to a dozen Diet Cokes a day with the push of a button on the Resolute Desk. He used meals to brag, pressure, beg, humiliate, wallow in self-pity, and at least once hurtle cruise missiles at Syria while scarfing down chocolate cake. For him the table was an arena, and he liked to hold court.

This habit was on display in 2002, when Trump, a developer/reality TV star at the time, invited Chris Christie, then the U.S. attorney for New Jersey, to Jean-Georges, the four-star French restaurant in the Trump International Hotel & Tower in Manhattan. When a waiter approached, Trump peremptorily ordered seared sea scallops and the roasted loin of lamb for his guest. To the unknowing, this might seem a generous gesture. It was not. "I'm allergic to scallops," Christie later revealed. And "I've always hated lamb." For Trump, the meal was a gleefully bullying display of dominance.

A similar scenario played out in January 2017, when Trump invited the FBI director, James Comey, to a private dinner shortly after moving into the White House. As they ate, the president pressured the G-man to pledge his "loyalty." The FBI was in the midst of a criminal investigation of Russian meddling in the election, and Comey, shocked, pledged his "honesty" but not his fealty to the president. "The demand was like Sammy the Bull's Cosa Nostra induction ceremony—with Trump, in the role of the family boss, asking me if I had what it takes to be a 'made man,'" Comey recalled.

Within days, Trump superannuated Comey and bragged to Russian officials, "I just fired the head of the FBI. He was crazy, a real nut job. I faced great pressure because of Russia."

WHERE DOES SOMEONE learn table manners befitting King Henry VIII?

Donald Trump acquired his at his parents' four-thousand-square-foot brick McMansion that dominates a hilltop in Queens, New York. As you passed through a library with no books, you descended into a basement bar decorated with "wooden Indians"—carved figures used to advertise tobacco in the nineteenth century, now considered a racist stereotype. The bar was outfitted with stools and dusty glasses but not a drop of alcohol. The patriarch, Fred Trump, didn't drink. Nor did he have hobbies, enjoy food, or socialize much. He was consumed by the accumulation of wealth and equated kindness with weakness.

His wife, Mary Anne Trump, was a self-dramatizing woman who styled her orange-tinted hair in an elaborate coiffure. She suffered years of ill health and was an insomniac who wandered the halls "at all hours like a soundless wraith," wrote her granddaughter, Mary Trump, the daughter of the Trumps' oldest son, Freddy Trump Jr., and now a clinical psychologist. Mary Anne was "emotionally and physically absent," she wrote, and the Trump children "were essentially motherless."

Given these baroque surroundings, it is not surprising that dining was a fraught subject for the family. In elementary school, Donald lobbed hunks of birthday cake at other kids, and he once annoyed his older brother so much that Freddy dumped a bowl of mashed potatoes on Donald's head.

Their dinners usually featured red meat and a starch, with few greens or fruits. One of Donald's favorite things to eat was "my mother's meat loaf," a dish that represented more than homely comfort food: it seemed to hold totemic powers for him and to represent an idyllic, all-American upbringing he never had. (Nixon and Reagan were also meat-loaf-loving presidents.) The family recipe was a standard mix of ground beef, bread crumbs, two eggs, garlic, onion, and peppers, which the maid who did their cooking slathered in tomato sauce and baked at 350 degrees. In Trump's hands, the humble hamburger log became a tool of self-promotion—he noted that on the menu at Mar-a-Lago was "Mrs. Trump's Meatloaf," "the best meatloaf in America," and pretended to make meat loaf with Martha Stewart on television—and a weapon.

In February 2017, he invited Chris Christie for lunch at the White House. Shortly after the election, Trump had abruptly fired Christie as the head of his transition team and replaced him with Vice President Mike Pence (a move said to have been orchestrated by Jared Kushner, Trump's son-in-law, after Christie sent his father, Charles Kushner, to jail in a sordid tax evasion case). Nevertheless, Christie remained eager to play a role in the new administration, and, as he recalled on a sports radio show, Trump said to their tablemates, " 'There's the menu, you guys order whatever you want.' And then he says, 'Chris, you and I are going to have the meatloaf.' "

"We're going to have the *meatloaf*?" Christie replied, nonplussed.

"I'm telling you, the meatloaf is fabulous," Trump said.

"It's emasculating" to have someone tell you what to eat, the show's host interjected.

"No it's not," Christie snapped. But it was, as Trump made clear when he did not offer Christie a meaningful job or a shred of self-dignity. (Eventually, he put Christie in charge of a bipartisan opioid commission.)

Mary Anne Trump did not like the kitchen, ate little, and hardly said a word at the table. Fred Sr. liked everyone to be well dressed and well mannered and taught his children that "the person with the power (no matter how arbitrarily that power was conferred or attained) got to decide what was right and wrong," wrote Mary Trump.

Her grandfather systematically "dismantled" her father, Freddy, who chose to work as a TWA pilot rather than in the family real estate business. His career, marriage, and life dissolved in a haze of booze and tobacco smoke, and he died at forty-two from a heart attack. Freddy would have made "an amazing peacemaker if he didn't have the problem, because everybody loved him," Donald said. "He's like the opposite of me." Watching his brother suffer, Trump avoided cigarettes or even "a drop" of alcohol and molded himself into the kind of preening tough guy his father admired.

ABOARD HIS CAMPAIGN PLANE, *Trump Force One*, the candidate's "four major food groups" were McDonald's, Kentucky Fried Chicken, pizza, and Diet Coke, according to the campaign manager Corey Lewandowski. The press dubbed Trump "the Fast Food President," a moniker he happily embraced. "I think fast food's good," he told CNN's Anderson Cooper. "I like cleanliness, and I think you're better off going to [Wendy's] than maybe someplace that you have no idea where the food's coming from."

He appears to have a lust- and/or fear-based relationship to food, much like his relationship to women, and would go for long periods without eating, then gorge on steak, gallons of Diet Coke, and wedges of cake. He'd daintily eat pizza and fried chicken with a knife and fork, so as not to sully his hands, and avoided pizza crust or hamburger buns, to "keep the weight down at least as good as possible," but had no problem scarfing down two large scoops of ice cream while offering guests just one scoop.

Lewandowski claimed Trump did not eat burger buns and had the stamina of an Olympian: "He would go and work 14 or 16 or 18 hours a day and not eat because he was so focused like a professional athlete."

Nutritionists and foodies were aghast at Trump's unhealthy, proudly unrefined diet. His standard order at the Golden Arches was two Big Macs, two Filet-O-Fish sandwiches, and a chocolate milkshake—estimated by dieticians to be a 2,630-calorie bomb. His foods were larded with sugar, salt, and fat, which can lead to obesity, heart stress, diabetes, and cancers. Poor diet is reportedly the leading cause of poor health in the United States now, resulting in half a million deaths per year.

When Trump took the presidential oath in January 2017, he was seventy years and 220 days old, eclipsing Reagan as the oldest president in history to that point. He ate fitfully, flew into rages, and tweeted at all hours of the night. He stood six feet three, or six two, or maybe six one, depending on your source, and weighed either 239 pounds or 243 pounds (which qualified him as obese). His personal physician, Harold Bornstein, called him "the healthiest individual ever elected to the presidency," but refused to disclose Trump's medical records and later admitted that the president had dictated that assessment.

Yet Trump's philistine diet was an essential part of his appeal. His oldest son, Don Jr., extolled his father as a "blue-collar billionaire," saying, "He is able to talk to those people. He's not talking *at* them. He's talking *with* them."

Trump had a shrewd insight—or, as he put it, "I have a gut, and my gut tells me more sometimes than anybody else's brain can ever tell me." What his gut told him was that we live in a visual era, and food is an important aspect of image making. Just as Reagan used jelly beans to connect with his voters, so Trump posed for photographs with pizza, fried chicken, and taco bowls ("I love the Hispanics!" he tweeted), which conveyed a political message to his base: "I like the same food you do, so vote for me." And, say what you will, it was highly effective.

On January 14, 2019, at a White House "banquet" for the Clemson University Tigers, who had won the NCAA football championship, "President McDonald Trump"—as Borat (Sacha Baron Cohen) called him—conjured up an impossible-looking sight. Dressed in his usual white shirt, extra-long red tie, and black jacket, Trump stood before a groaning table of fast food—ziggurats of McDonald's Quarter Pounders; stacks of Filet-O-Fish sandwiches; chicken wraps from Wendy's; fries from Burger King; pizzas from Domino's; hundreds of packets of ketchup and sauces—in the State Dining Room, as if it were a state dinner, or a satire of one.

Giving the spectacle a truculent, anarchic edge, the greasy burgers were plopped on sterling silver trays, wilting fries sagged in paper cups embossed with the presidential seal, McNugget sauce pods were stuffed in antique silver gravy boats, plastic salad bowls teetered on venerable tureens, and the spread was framed by golden candelabra holding tall white tapers.

It was an image never seen before: a hungry child's fever dream, a grotesque affront to Washington traditionalists of both parties, a calculated middle finger to the "global elites." The tableau was designed for the cameras, and was so outrageous that it went viral, was seared into the collective mind, and stirred disbelief around the world.

With hardly a nod to the Clemson footballers, Trump posed before the burger banquet with a portrait of Abraham Lincoln over his shoulder—an image designed to connect him to a populist America of fast food, football, and Honest Abe. When Trump said he had paid $5,500 for the meal (it actually cost $2,911.44, *The Washington Post* calculated), the subtext was clear: he expected to be repaid with adulation and support. "We went out and we ordered American fast food, paid for by me," he declared. "If it's American, I like it. . . . Lots of hamburgers, lots of pizza . . . Many, many French fries—all of our favorite foods."

The reason Trump had paid for the banquet was that he had instigated a government shutdown, which furloughed thousands of federal workers, including the kitchen crew and waitstaff. Observers wondered why he hadn't catered the banquet from the Trump International Hotel, down the street, but they missed the point: it wasn't about the food, or the Clemson players (trained athletes who seemed nonplussed by the unhealthy meal, and who said, "Our nutritionist must be having a fit"); it was about Donald Trump.

A Twitter user mocked him for turning "the White House into a White Castle." And *The Atlantic* called the banquet "a little bit P. T. Barnum, a little bit Hieronymus Bosch, a little bit *Beauty and the Beast,* had 'Be Our Guest' been staged by Willy Wonka and also set in the apocalypse."

But it was a trap. Trump's allies declared that any critique of the banquet was "elitist," while *Quartz* magazine tut-tutted, "The media comes across as a pack of mean girls by obsessing over Trump's fast food bonanza. . . . [U]ltimately, they got played by his mastery of spectacle." The critics' howls just elevated Trump's image and amplified his message: "I like the same food you do, so vote for me."

The president had divined something primordial: we humans are wired to feel kinship with people who like to eat the same things we do. Ayelet Fishbach, a professor of behavioral science and marketing at the University of Chicago, has found that when people see others wearing similar clothes, they don't feel a special bond, but when they see others eating foods they enjoy, they infer that "people who eat similar foods are probably friends." We "don't use other cues in the same way as food," she told the *Gastropod* podcast. "If I see you eating the food that I'm eating, I think that, oh, we have something in common." The reasons behind this are mysterious, but are probably a holdover from a time when hunting and gathering was a tribal effort.

II. *The Meaning of Burned Steak and Ketchup*

The only vegetable Donald Trump admitted to liking was iceberg lettuce. He had it sliced thin on top of his burger or shredded in his taco bowl. Best of all, he liked a wedge salad, a classic retro dish from the *Mad Men* era, made with a head of iceberg cut into quarters and slathered with a blue cheese dressing, bacon, tomatoes, and chives. It complements a steak nicely. Not coincidentally, steak was perhaps Trump's favorite food.

In Washington, a city with a vibrant food scene, the only restaurant he ate at was BLT Prime by David Burke, the steak house in Trump's hotel. His standard order was a dry-aged New York strip that cost $54, cooked very well done, and drowned in ketchup. When aficionados learned that he had his beautiful cut so seared into charcoal that it "rocked on the plate," as Trump's butler Anthony Senecal put it, they cursed him as a vulgarian.

How well a steak is cooked is a deeply personal choice, and Trump's preference was revealing. The more meat is cooked, the more the juices, texture, and flavor are eliminated: too little cooking, and a steak is nearly indigestible; too much, and it becomes as leathery as the boot Charlie Chaplin gnawed on in *The Gold Rush.* The sweet spot is somewhere in between. "Steaks with even a little bit of red in them are better than steaks without," opined the food writer Helen Rosner. "This is a fact, a chemical and physical truth, the result of an alchemy of fat and protein and salt . . . and the way our bodies connect the chemicals of taste to the chemicals of pleasure." In Trump's desiccated protein, Rosner discerned "an aversion to risk, which is at its core an unwillingness to trust the validity and goodwill of any experience beyond the limited sphere of one's own. It is . . . a confession of a certain timidity, a defensiveness, an insecurity . . . a choice to . . . reject the very premise that expertise outside his person can have value. A person who won't eat his steak any doneness but well is a person who won't entertain the notion that there could be a better way."

Making matters infinitely worse for the purists, Trump drowned his steak in ketchup, in an effort to return some of the juicy flavor that had been cooked out of it. Nick Solares, a "professional carnivore," declared that ketchup should never touch a good piece of meat: "Why on earth would someone choose to cover up such a carefully crafted . . . prime beef with such a sweet, overpowering condiment?"

Ketchup is the nation's favorite sauce, a "quintessentially American" foodstuff, explained Amy Bentley, a food historian at New York University. It is prized as quick, tasty, affordable, consistent, and clean—all attributes that appealed to Donald Trump. The condiment originated in China as *ke-tsiap* or *ke-tchup,* a fermented fish sauce that was carried around the world by seventeenth-century British sailors. A version of the sauce—which mixed tomatoes with vinegar, sugar, shallots, anchovies, and spices—gained popularity in nineteenth-century America, where it jazzed up bland stews and inferior cuts of meat. By the early twentieth century, the H. J. Heinz Company had devised a formula that balanced salty, sour, and umami notes. The secret to Heinz's success is how sweet the recipe is: the modern version contains four grams of sweetener (usually high-fructose corn syrup) per tablespoon, which is a lot. Ketchup pairs beguilingly with proteins and starches, and soon Heinz was selling five million bottles a year. With mass production, the red goo evolved into a "class leveler," Bentley said, that 97 percent of Americans slather on everything from chicken fingers to clam strips, scrambled eggs, and even salad. Today, ten billion ounces of ketchup are sold every year, and it has leaked into Swedish, Japanese, and French cuisine.

Ketchup remained a leitmotif throughout Donald Trump's presidency, but after he left office it occasionally haunted him. During a June 2022 House committee hearing about the January 6, 2021, riot at the Capitol Building, the former White House aide Cassidy Hutchinson testified that on several occasions she'd witnessed Trump throw dishes, or "flip the tablecloth to let all the contents of the table go onto the floor." Most graphically, she recounted the day the president—in a fit of rage at Attorney General Bill Barr, who had dismissed Trump's false claims of election fraud—had "thrown his lunch against the wall" in the dining room next to the Oval Office. "There was ketchup dripping down the wall," she said. "And there's a shattered porcelain plate on the floor." It was an alarming moment, one that recalled the cake-throwing tantrums of Trump as an elementary schoolboy.

DONALD TRUMP'S DIET might have been popular, but it wasn't healthy. His pattern of abstinence followed by gorging on fast food stimulated a cycle of instant satisfaction (a high) followed by a plunge in blood sugar levels (a low), which triggers lethargy and craving for more.

Food scientists have capitalized on the fact that humans are wired to seek energy-rich substances to fill our bellies with. They have engineered junk foods to hit the "bliss point," the perfect combination of sweet, salty, fatty flavors that our lizard brains crave. When empty calories are processed into sugary additives such as high-fructose corn syrup, they enhance the flavor of food, but they also release dopamine, the "feel good" hormone. One tablespoon of HFCS contains fifty-three calories, 14.4 grams of carbohydrates, and 5 grams of sugar. Even seemingly healthy products—such as pasta sauce or light beer—contain as many artificial sweeteners as rich desserts.

In a 2013 study, researchers found that sugar and salt are addictive in lab rats. "Salt is extremely addictive, just as much as sugar," Nia Rennix, a clinical nutritionist, found. "The manufacturers . . . continue to add salt to foods because they want you to continue to purchase" their products. The more salt ingested, the more water your body retains, and the higher your blood pressure gets. And the more of it you ingest, the more you crave it. This strains the heart, brain, and arteries.

In 2020, just one in five American adults was "metabolically healthy," according to a report issued on the fiftieth anniversary of Nixon's 1969 Conference on Food, Nutrition, and Health. Poor metabolic health impairs immunity and underlies type 2 diabetes, cardiovascular disease, and obesity-related cancers. As a result, said Dr. Dariush Mozaffarian, of Tufts University, "only 12 percent of Americans are without high blood pressure, high cholesterol, diabetes or pre-diabetes."

Why is this important? Because the president of the United States is the most powerful man in the world and his words and actions have tremendous consequences. When Trump modeled unhealthy eating, people followed suit. A 2018 survey of 1,050 adults concluded that his fast-food diet increased the likelihood that Americans—both Republicans and Democrats—would order Whoppers. People who pay more attention to media coverage of President Trump's diet are more likely to view fast food as a "socially acceptable meal option" and are more likely to intend to eat fast food, said the study's author, Jessica Gall Myrick, an associate professor of media studies at Pennsylvania State University. Republicans were nearly twice as likely to "report positive attitudes toward fast food than are Democrats," she found. The data suggested that "there could be harm caused to public health by encouraging many Americans to eat fast food."

When COVID-19 swept the globe in 2020, the nation's underlying health problems made millions of Americans extra vulnerable to the pandemic—perhaps even President Trump, who contracted the virus in October 2020.

FIRST LADY MELANIA TRUMP, meanwhile, kept to the light, healthy diet she had relied on since working as a fashion model in Slovenia. She began her day with a green smoothie—"my every day delicious & healthy breakfast"—which included blueberries, apples, celery, carrots, and spinach blended with apple and orange juice, fat-free yogurt, olive oil, flax seeds, vitamin D, and omega-3 supplements. A Sausage McMuffin it was not.

The First Lady was not a fan of diets, saying, "I just like to eat healthy because I feel better and have more energy." She even had the common sense to add, "It's good to indulge cravings and your taste once in a while, as long as you balance those things with healthy foods." (Many nutritionists agree that occasional treats help dissuade people from unhealthy binging.) For her that meant the odd piece of dark chocolate—which, in moderation, can reduce stress and improve heart health—or a small helping of ice cream. She was not above the occasional Whataburger, or sip of Diet Coke, though she insisted it be served in a glass bottle (Coca-

Cola claims it tastes better that way). Melania's words and eating habits were a counterbalance, of sorts, to her husband's.

Though she did not mention her predecessor by name, Melania tacitly acknowledged the popularity of Michelle Obama's garden by posing with Swiss chard, peas, and a group of children there. "I'm a big believer in eating healthy because it reflects your mind and your body," Mrs. Trump said. "Eat a lot of vegetables and fruits so you grow up healthy."

Her husband joked he would turn the garden into a putting green, but didn't, in part because the Obamas had reinforced it with stone, steel, and cement and secured $2.5 million in funding from the Burpee home-gardening company to ensure it was maintained by the National Park Service.

III. Le Bromance and Mateship

When Donald Trump arrived in Washington, he dismissed the city as a "swamp," called the Executive Mansion "a dump," and began a search to replace Cristeta Comerford as executive chef. David Burke and about a dozen other big-shot cooks were asked, but none of them were available. The search fizzled. "I don't know a chef in their right mind who would cook in this White House," quipped Dan Barber, the chef at Blue Hill, voicing what many of his colleagues were thinking.

The Trumps rarely acknowledged Comerford in the way the Bushes and Obamas had. On one tragicomic occasion the president asked her to re-create a McDonald's Quarter Pounder with cheese and a baked apple pie. When her attempt "couldn't match the satisfaction" of a real McBurger, an insider said, Trump dispatched his body man, the former New York cop Keith Schiller, to fetch the genuine articles from a franchise on K Street. Many chefs in Comerford's position would have quit in disgust, as René Verdon had done when LBJ insisted he make garbanzo bean puree. But Comerford stayed. I was not allowed to speak to her, and mutual acquaintances said she remained on the job because she was devoted to the White House, was nonpartisan, and had a family to provide for.

Though he kept up a steady pace of modest congressional lunches and the like, Trump hosted only two state dinners in four years. He didn't care for the formality, and complained, "We should be eating a hamburger on a conference table. We should make better deals with China and others and forget the state dinners."

Even so, he occasionally entertained guests in his own peculiar way. When he hosted China's president, Xi Jinping, for lunch at his Mar-a-Lago estate in 2017, for instance, the menu paid no heed to the guest nation, as is customary. Instead, lunch was a classic Trumpian surf and turf: pan-seared Dover sole followed by dry-aged prime New York strip steak. As they ate dessert—"the most beautiful piece of chocolate cake that you've ever seen"—the president opened a laptop full of state secrets in front of the Chinese leader and with the push of a button launched fifty-nine Tomahawk cruise missiles into Syria (which he misidentified as Iraq). Afterward, Trump seemed more impressed by Xi's clean plate than by the destruction he had wrought. "It was a full day. . . . We're almost finished, and . . . what does he do? Finish his dessert and go home," Trump said admiringly.

Eventually, he agreed to host a couple of state dinners, probably with cajoling from the First Lady, the National Security Council (which is responsible for recommending honorees), the State Department, and donors who wanted to be invited to a White House dinner. The first one, in April 2018, honored Emmanuel Macron, the president of France. Comerford's menu included seasonal specialties and a gracious nod to our oldest ally—young lettuces with a goat cheese gâteau; rack of lamb with jambalaya, Carolina Gold rice, and a burned-onion soubise (sauce); and a nectarine tart with ice cream for dessert. The dinner was served on china with the George W. Bush and Clinton patterns.

Connoisseurs wondered if Trump would serve bottles from the Trump Winery, in Virginia. (The teetotaling president had bought the former Kluge estate out of foreclosure for $6.2 million in 2011 and put his son Eric in charge.) But Macron was served an American Chardonnay made with French grapes and aged in French oak, and a Pinot Noir grown "with French soul, Oregon soil." To gastro-detectives, such thoughtful touches indicated the menu was dotted by Melania's fingerprints.

The meeting was hailed as "le bromance," but when Trump called NATO "obsolete," imposed 25 percent tariffs on European wine, and joked that he would send "some nice ISIS fighters" to France, Macron confronted the president on live television, and le bromance was *fini*.

Trump's second state dinner, held in September 2019, was for the Australian prime minister, Scott Morrison—a pro-coal, anti-immigration conservative who was happy to smile silently as Trump ranted about the "Russia hoax." Their negotiators discussed America's trade war with China and Pacific Rim security, and the menu—ravioli, Dover sole, squash blossoms, apple tart—was standard, if light, Trump fare. Melania, it seems, had taken the night off. The two leaders toasted to "a hundred years of mateship, and a hundred more." (The event was not technically a state dinner, because the prime minister led the Australian government, not the state itself.)

Trump's third state dinner was slated for April 2020, for Spain's King Felipe VI, but he was spared the ordeal when the COVID-19 virus canceled the royals' visit, the White House Easter Egg Roll (for the first time since 1948–52), and most other White House events.

IV. The Wisdom of the Table

In mid-January 2020, an American man in his thirties flew from Wuhan, China, to Seattle, Washington, carrying what is believed to be the first identified case of the COVID-19 virus in the United States. (There is some evidence that the first case arrived earlier.) The virus rapidly spread across the country and cascaded into the worst global pandemic in a century.

The history and mechanisms of the coronavirus remain murky. Some have posited that the virus leaked from a state virology lab, though China denies it, and epidemiologists are increasingly convinced that it originated in food: specifically, at a marketplace in Wuhan, a city of eleven million in central-eastern China. In a musty "wet market," live animals—including bats, snakes, civets, pangolins, dogs, birds, and other creatures destined to be turned into meals—were caged tail by jowl. It was a perfect vector point for disease. The prevailing theory is that in November 2019 COVID-19 jumped from bats or pangolins to humans somewhere near Wuhan and began to multiply.

As the pandemic spread and sickened or killed people, it exposed just how vulnerable the global food system was. Supply chains were ruptured, stores and restaurants were closed, and millions of people went hungry. In the United States, the virus revealed that a handful of large companies had taken control of food production, cut costs, and reduced government oversight. The result was catastrophic.

By late April 2020, nearly sixty-five hundred workers at meat processing plants had been infected, and at least twenty had died, while more than a hundred government meat inspectors were stricken. Dairy farmers had no choice but to tip spoiling milk into their fields, while poultry and hog farmers were forced to sell or kill off their livestock to avoid overcrowded pens. Farming is uncertain in the best of times, but cutting food stores and herds added exponential stress. "It tore me up enough, even though I tried to block it out," the Minnesota farmer Todd Selvik said, after euthanizing five hundred healthy pigs. "It really kind of just messes with you."

Big Meat companies such as Smithfield Foods, Tyson Foods, Cargill, and National Beef Packing began to shutter plants. Alarmed, Trump designated meat processing part of the nation's "critical infrastructure" and invoked the Defense Production Act to force them to remain open. This put a spotlight on the fact that most employees of those plants were migrants or immigrants.

It was an open secret that Trump—who suggested digging moats filled with alligators or building a Great Wall on the Mexican border to deter immigrants—relied on undocumented workers at his properties. When this was publicized in 2019, the Trump Organization fired dozens of employees. But at the Trump Winery undocumented harvesters were kept on through the fall—working sixty-hour weeks picking grapes at night so the sun wouldn't shrink them—then let go before the 2020 election. Trump "waits until the fields are tended, grapes picked, wine made," said the immigration lawyer Anibal Romero. Then "discards [the workers] like a used paper bag. Happy New Year—you're fired."

RESTAURANTS WERE PARTICULARLY hard-hit by the pandemic. A report by the Pew Research Center found that in 2008 undocumented workers made up at least 10 percent of the hospitality industry and 13 percent of the agricultural industry. In 2008, the Pew Hispanic Center reported that more than 20 percent of restaurant cooks were undocumented. Based on anecdotal evidence, those numbers seem conservative. But as armed and amped Immigration and Customs Enforcement agents swept in to cart workers away, restaurateurs faced a Hobson's choice: either fire their undocumented staff or face government prosecution.

The COVID crisis and Trump's harsh policies led to soul-searching in the food community: What, people wondered, is the role of a restaurant in the twenty-first century?

Humans are social animals who strongly respond to the communal aspects of dining out. Since the opening of Mathurin Roze de Chantoiseau's Paris consommé shop in the 1760s, people have gathered in restaurants for sustenance and succor. They provide food and fellowship, and that communality breeds shared values that ultimately strengthen the democracy.

All of that was upended in the summer of 2018, when Trump's rhetoric grew hateful and occasionally boomeranged against his deputies. When Kirstjen Nielsen, secretary of the Department of Homeland Security, ate at a Mexican restaurant in Washington, she was heckled by people shouting, "Do you hear the babies crying? . . . How can you enjoy a Mexican dinner as you're deporting and imprisoning tens of thousands of people?!" Nielsen was driven out of the restaurant, and later her job.

Most controversially, Trump's spokesperson Sarah Huckabee Sanders was asked to leave the Red Hen, a farm-to-table restaurant in rural Virginia, in June 2018. The co-owner Stephanie Wilkinson felt it was "the moment in our democracy when people have to make uncomfortable . . . decisions to uphold their morals." Several of her staff identified as LGBT and felt stung by Trump's ban of transgender military troops and the Supreme Court's ruling that a Christian baker did not have to work for a gay couple. Wilkinson politely asked Sanders to leave the restaurant; she did so, and her group was not charged for their food. But then pro-LGBTQ supporters and armed Trumpists squared off in front of the Red Hen. The president tweeted the restaurant was "filthy" (he had never been there), while the Democratic representative Maxine Waters encouraged people to tell Trumpers "they're not welcome." Right-wing activists posted Wilkinson's home address online, saying, "Go after her children."

The politics of food and the food of politics had collided.

The case ignited an argument over civility. By denying Sanders a seat, some asked, wasn't Wilkinson a hypocrite? What if a Christian restaurateur asked the LGBTQ spokesperson for a Democratic president to leave his establishment—what then? There were no easy answers. *The Washington Post* editorialized that the Trumpers "should be allowed to eat dinner in peace. Those who are insisting that we are in a special moment justifying incivility should think . . . how many Americans might find their own special moment. . . . Down that road lies a world in which only the most zealous sign up for public service." *Eater* countered, "How can a space be open and welcoming to all if it invites people who are the antithesis of those values?"

The New Yorker's Adam Gopnik opined, "Nothing is more fundamental to human relations than deciding who has a place at the table—and nothing is more essential to our idea of humanism than expanding that table. . . . [But] [t]he Trump Administration is . . . all about an assault on civility." Because Sanders chose to amplify Trump's message, she deserved to be barred: "You cannot spit in the plates and then demand your dinner. The best way to receive civility at night is to not assault it all day long. It's the simple wisdom of the table."

V. Something Most Presidents Have Grasped

One day in November 2019, I had tea with Lea Berman, George W. Bush's social secretary. She was a staunch Republican, but candid about her distaste for the man who had taken over the GOP. With long, sculpted dirty-blond hair, deep blue eyes, and an open face, she struck me as someone quite different from the harridan-in-Versace depicted by the chef Walter Scheib. A shy girl raised on an isolated grape farm in Ohio, Berman had learned to deflect criticism and to mollify those who disagreed with her in Washington. After leaving government, she coauthored *Treating People Well,* a book about "the power of civility," with Jeremy Bernard, the Obamas' openly gay social secretary. "The personal smooths the professional," they said. "Getting to know each other" and "attentive listening" help persuade "people to do what we want them to do."

I was alert to Berman's charm but found her sensible. The ability to "disagree agreeably" is essential to the smooth functioning of Washington, she said. "Bad behavior is contagious. But it is empowering to be polite and civil. When leaders get to know each other . . . it opens better communications, makes you feel differently about yourself, makes life much less stressful. It's actually in your self-interest to treat people well. It's glaringly obvious, and it's something most presidents have grasped."

But not Donald Trump, whose three rules of conduct, she said, were "when you're right, you fight; controversy elevates the message; and never apologize."

When I asked about the mood in Washington, Berman sighed, and said, "I've never seen the fury expressed so openly before. It has really shocked me."

A former party planner and food blogger, Berman now runs an animal rescue foundation. She found Trump's boorishness "offensive" and offered this illustration: when Laura Bush arranged for presidential historians to tour the Lincoln Bedroom, they were so moved it nearly brought them to tears. But such hospitality would "never occur to Donald Trump." Instead, when he toured plutocrats through the Lincoln Bedroom, he pointed to a copy of the Gettysburg Address and a rug donated by Ronald Reagan, saying, "Have you ever seen luxury like this?"

Another thing that rankled Berman was that Trump was "just not interested" in participating in the White House Correspondents' Dinner, the Kennedy Center Honors, and other hallowed Washington rituals. When it came to entertaining, she noted, Trump was equally obtuse. "People tend to forget that it's very intimidating to visit the White House, particularly for foreign visitors. Part of making it a good experience is to put them at ease so you can be more successful in your negotiations. Make them feel positive so they go home thinking, 'This is my friend.' But that's all been lost."

When I asked if traditional Republicans felt betrayed by Trump, Berman's eyes flashed sharply as she said, "He's a radical. He stands for everything we are not. We almost hate him more than the Democrats do." Pensively sipping her tea, she added, "People feel demoralized. There's a whole group who don't go out anymore. I'm one of them. We get invited to the White House, but I just . . . *can't.*"

As we prepared to leave, Berman sadly said, "When you visit President Trump's White House, he gives you fast-food burgers . . . which is most unfortunate." Then, in a rising voice, she added, "But there's also a White House tradition of *civility.* It was developed over many years. By people from both sides of the aisle. It is important to them, and for continuity at the White House. It's *important.* And when he leaves, it will return again."

— 22 —

JOSEPH R. BIDEN

We Finish as a Family

THE FORTY-SIXTH PRESIDENT
January 20, 2021–Present

★

I. Food Is Love

Joseph Robinette Biden was sworn in as the forty-sixth president at noon on January 20, 2021, but with half a million Americans dead from the COVID pandemic, and National Guard troops on alert after the violent siege of the Capitol by Trump supporters on January 6, the inaugural committee radically scaled back the celebration. The inaugural luncheon—a staple since the late nineteenth century that has evolved into a lavish, three-course meal accompanied by music in the Capitol's Statuary Hall—was canceled. As was the inaugural ball that evening, for the first time since 1949. And in a last flouting of tradition, the Trumps refused to attend the inauguration (joining the small club of presidents—John Adams in 1801, John Quincy Adams in 1829, and Andrew Johnson in 1869—who snubbed their successors). Yet continuity was maintained, and the transfer of power proceeded smoothly.

Biden was sworn in on the west side of the Capitol, as presidents had been for forty years. He gave an inaugural address that welcomed Vice President Kamala Harris as the first mixed-race woman elected to national office. He promised a period of "renewal and resolve" and pledged to be a "president for all Americans." That night, Tom Hanks hosted a celebration at the Lincoln Memorial, where Bruce Springsteen sang "Land of Hope and Dreams," followed by a musical tribute by the kind of A-list performers Trump had failed to attract. It was a presidential transition unlike any other, and the prospect of a return to normalcy glittered on the horizon.

First Lady Dr. Jill Biden echoed that reassurance by wearing an ocean-blue dress, with a matching coat and COVID face mask, to the inauguration—an ensemble that signified "trust, confidence, and stability," explained the designer Alexandra O'Neill. That night, the Bidens ate a quiet family dinner with their grandchildren at the White House. They did not publicize what the chef Cris Comerford prepared, but it was no doubt good, nutritious, simple fare.

One reason Biden was considered a safe choice in perilous times was that people felt they knew him. "Everybody knows Joe," they said. He was friendly with players across the political spectrum and understood that lawmakers accomplished more when they broke bread together than when they didn't. A moderate consensus builder by nature, Biden was seventy-eight, eclipsing Trump as the oldest man ever elected commander in chief. He had worked in Washington for forty-four years and knew how the gears spun. Having served as Barack Obama's vice president, he knew how the White House functioned. And he had a better sense of the District's geography and mores, its history and social rituals, its languages and meals, than any other president.

If food is a form of language and taste is an expression of identity, then Joe Biden's middlebrow palate neatly encapsulated his Average Joe persona. "He's pretty much a basic eater," his wife said, underscoring the nation's relief at trading the spectacle of Trump's fast-food binges and midnight rage-tweets for Biden's "boring, white-bread" politics.

Like Harry Truman, Biden kept himself trim and fit and dressed in natty suits. Like George W. Bush, he lunched on peanut butter and jelly sandwiches. Like Clinton and Trump, he squeezed ketchup on his burgers. Like many people, Biden hankered for angel hair pasta with red sauce, only more so: he was contractually guaranteed the dish at campaign stops. And for dessert? Biden was an ice cream fanatic, with a special fondness for chocolate chip.

Almost every president since Thomas Jefferson has enjoyed ice cream (with the notable exception of Bill Clinton, who was allergic to it), and the forty-sixth president's rallying cry—"My name is Joe Biden, and I love ice cream"—was hailed as "the most Joe Biden quote of all time."

When Trump accused him of using performance-enhancing drugs for a debate, Biden chuckled and said that "ice cream" was his "performance enhancer." While campaigning, he dropped in on Dairy Queens across the country, and he made a star of the Jeni's Splendid Ice Cream chain, where his standard order was a double scoop of chocolate chip in a waffle cone. When he won the election, the artisanal ice creamery returned the favor. Just as the Herman Goelitz Candy Company made red, white, and blue jelly beans for Ronald Reagan, Jeni's created a new flavor for Biden's inauguration—White House Chocolate Chip, made of chocolate flakes and pieces of chocolate-covered waffle cone in vanilla ice cream—in 2021.

· · ·

JOE COULD BOIL PASTA and heat sauce from a jar, but he was not a cook. When he offered to help in the kitchen, Jill shooed him away. "It's my turf," she explained. "I like doing it by myself."

She was an accomplished cook who had been raised eating well in Pennsylvania and New Jersey, where Sundays meant separate family dinners with two sets of grandparents who didn't get along. Her mother's parents kept an immaculate house and lawn, canned their own peaches, pickles, and applesauce, and served platters of roast beef, mashed potatoes with gravy, green beans, and cake. Her father's parents, the Italian side, kept a funkier house redolent of basil, oregano, fresh tomatoes, and garlic. They taught her to love homemade pasta, tomato sauce and meatballs, Italian wedding soup, good Italian bread, and braciole (stuffed rolled steak simmered in tomato sauce).

"I love to cook," Mrs. Biden said. For her, food was a way to communicate, decompress from her job as an English teacher at a community college (she was the first First Lady to hold a paying job outside the White House), and be creative; like Cris Comerford's mother, Mrs. Biden liked to cook by instinct rather than from recipes.

Previously divorced, Jill married Joe Biden in 1977. While other pols were slapping backs over cocktails in Washington, Joe faithfully returned home to Wilmington, Delaware, by Amtrak train in time for dinner with his family. Food was "an important way of establishing my relationship with" his sons, Beau and Hunter, who had lost their mother and sister in a car crash, Jill said. She raised the boys as her own and had a daughter, Ashley, with Biden.

"Because they were such great eaters and so appreciative, I baked and cooked all the time," Jill recalled. "It's always fun to turn on a little music, have a glass of wine and cook."

She liked healthy meals with plenty of fruits and vegetables and was known for her fried egg sandwiches and chicken Parmesan. Though Joe was a teetotaler (his family had a history of alcoholism), Jill indulged in the occasional martini and declared, "I love French fries!" Her mantra was "food is security and love."

LIKE OBAMA, President Biden came under pressure to "fix the American food system" even before he took office. Though Alice Waters sat this dance out—fed up with national politics, she focused on local issues, such as her Edible Schoolyard Project, "where the doors are open"—

Biden faced a blizzard of demands: that he prioritize climate change, strengthen GMO labeling, support Black farmers, prioritize healthy school meals, improve rules for organic livestock, and support agricultural e-commerce, among other things.

Issues like these had been shunted aside in the previous four years, and before he could launch any major new food initiatives, Biden had to right the ship of state and set it on a new course. There were many examples, but to pick one, consider the U.S. Department of Agriculture, which had gone from being on *Forbes*'s list of best employers to a husk of its former self under the Trump administration. Though it had a $153 billion annual budget and twenty-nine agencies, many of the department's employees had been fired or quit, billions of dollars had been cut from programs, and morale was decimated.

Trump's agriculture secretary, Sonny Perdue, considered Big Ag his "customers," and said, "Our mission is to provide our . . . producers with what they need, when they need it." He was hardly a tough regulator. As American food growers were whiplashed by trade wars with China and Europe, Perdue provided them with $46 billion in aid, far more than any previous farm subsidy. At the same time, he tried to limit SNAP food stamp benefits and pooh-poohed worries about climate change.

Most notoriously, Perdue relocated the department's biggest scientific research agencies—the National Institute of Food and Agriculture and the Economic Research Service—from Washington to Kansas City, Missouri, in 2019. The move was ostensibly "to bring research closer to agriculture" and save $300 million. But critics deemed the move "ridiculous" and politically motivated. Indeed, 64 percent of USDA's top researchers left their jobs, a brain drain that set urgent COVID research back. And rather than save money, the move to Kansas City cost the government between $83 million and $182 million, depending on the metrics. (Trump also relocated the Bureau of Land Management, which oversees 247.3 million acres of federal lands, from Washington to Colorado, with similar results.) The Union of Concerned Scientists called the relocation "a blatant attack on science," and a former employee lamented, "It's had its intended effect. People have left, morale is low. The agency will take a long time to recover from the damage."

Faced with multiple food crises, Biden turned to Tom Vilsack, Obama's USDA secretary, to lead the department once again. The number of hungry Americans had risen from thirty-four million in 2019 to more than fifty million in 2020, and Biden gambled that even if his pick remained controversial, the public hankered for an experienced hand guiding the nation's food supply. Vilsack rushed to vaccinate his employees and turn the department from a climate change denier into a leading investigator and prioritized research on food and health issues. With strong Republican resistance and the looming midterm elections, it was a race against time.

ASSISTING VILSACK and Biden was an experienced politician and cook: Vice President Kamala Harris. The first woman, and Black and Southeast Asian person, to hold such a powerful office, she represented a paradigm shift. If Biden was a reliable white Democrat of the old school, then Harris embodied the young, dynamic, multicultural new school—the face of future America. Combined, the two represented a Democratic "dream ticket," politicos said.

Born in Oakland, California, in 1964, Harris was the daughter of Shyamala Gopalan, a cancer researcher born in Madras (now Chennai), India, and Donald J. Harris, a Stanford economics professor born in Jamaica. Following her high school years in French-speaking Montreal, Harris spent her formative years in foodie cities—Washington, D.C., at Howard University, and San Francisco, at the University of California Law School.

After school she served as the San Francisco district attorney (2004–11) and the California attorney general (2011–17), before returning to Washington as a U.S. senator from California (2017–21). She was a rising Democratic star who voted to impeach Donald Trump for obstruction of justice and abuse of power.

In 2014, Harris married the white Jewish entertainment lawyer Doug Emhoff. Much like Jill Biden, Harris used family dinners as a way to bond with her stepchildren, Ella and Cole Emhoff. While "the Doug" cooked on Wednesdays and Saturdays, Harris reserved Sundays for herself. "It's a tradition I really care about, just having a really good home-cooked meal on a Sunday," she said.

Harris was raised in a household where the transmutation of ingredients into a delicious meal was considered a nearly magical event. As a child, she would hear her mother banging pots and smell her sizzling Indian spices, and "kind of like someone in a trance, I would walk into the kitchen to see all this incredible stuff happening," she said. Noticing her daughter's wide eyes, Gopalan said, "Kamala, you clearly like to eat good food. You better learn how to cook." And so she did, taught by her mother and a neighbor.

As a prosecutor Harris gained a reputation for aggressive questioning, but as she campaigned in the 2020 Democratic primary—under the slogan "Kamala Harris, for the People"—she took pains to humanize herself. Food was an important part of her pitch. One of the "little specialties" Harris mastered in the third grade was scrambled eggs topped with cheese cut into a smiley face, she said. It was the kind of story she told on the campaign trail, hinting that beneath her sometimes stern exterior, Harris had a more relatable, impish side.

Wearing jeans, Converse sneakers, and a Howard University sweatshirt, she baked cookies (shades of Hillary Clinton) with a seventeen-year-old fan and cooked dinner with a family in Iowa. Indeed, Harris used the kitchen to blend the personal and professional spheres of her life in a way that was unprecedented in presidential campaigning.

Like Trump, she posted images of herself with food and her lively videos that often went viral, though her diet was far more eclectic than his. She cooked masala dosas with the comedienne Mindy Kaling, discussed turkey brining with the State Department's Nick Schmit, laughed with the chef Tom Colicchio about Emhoff's "onion-cutting goggles," and tutored the vegan New Jersey senator, Cory Booker, on carrot-chopping knife skills. Most celebrated was the video in which Harris schooled the Democratic senator Mark Warner of Virginia on proper tuna-melt technique. He didn't drain his can of tuna, used heaps of mayo, and microwaved his sandwich, she said, deeming his effort "a hot mess." (Though the point of his video was to encourage people to wash their hands during the pandemic.) Harris demonstrated how to do it right: drain the tuna, dress it with a mix of Dijon mustard, parsley, and lemon juice, add crisp lettuce, top with two slices of cheddar cheese, coat the outside of the bread with more mayonnaise, and toast the sandwich in a skillet until golden brown.

These small, bright moments gave Harris an air of "authenticity," which consultants believe is the coin of the realm in modern politics. It worked. She was seen as not just a consumer of food but a knowledgeable cook who knew her way around a grocery store or farmers market. She was not considered an elitist but a savvy policy wonk who pushed supermarket chains to give workers hazard pay during COVID.

It helped that the public tenor had changed since Obama was castigated for "Arugula-gate": when Harris was criticized for wearing a "creased apron"—which supposedly indicated her cooking was a staged photo op—the attack was laughed away. While campaigning, she employed the age-old tactic of eating in restaurants around the country, talking to their chefs, and listening to their customers' concerns. When possible, she ate handmade meals and remembered their creators.

Recalling the "magic" cilantro rice she had at a small restaurant in Reno, Nevada, Harris said she worried about the cook during the pandemic. "It weighs on me, as it should on all of us. . . . What's happening [to] our small businesses, and in particular our restaurants? Those restaurants in your neighborhood where they know what you like to eat, or they might just sit down with you for a minute to talk? [They] are hurting like you can't believe."

This was smart politics, of course, but Harris's consistent focus on food and cooks appeared genuine rather than purely opportunistic. In 2019, before COVID hit, she said, "People aren't just suffering, they're hungry," and noted that up to 40 percent of college students were food insecure—a number that reached 70 percent at some historically Black colleges and universities. Then there were older people without access to nutritious food, or parents who couldn't feed their children, to worry about. "It's breaking my heart," Harris said. "This issue is not getting enough attention. People are starving in America right now." In response, she launched legislation to support cafés, bodegas, and other small businesses—the places that define neighborhoods—with grants up to $250,000. And she worked with José Andrés, the celebrity chef and founder of World Central Kitchen, to make federal dollars available to cover state-restaurant partnerships in times of crisis.

As the presidential race slogged through 2020, Harris would take a break in her home kitchen refuge. While stuck on conference calls, she'd make a pot of beans (starting with dried, not canned, beans) or cook double batches of Indian or Jamaican dishes to stock the fridge. As any seasoned cook does, Harris considered craft and thrift equally important. Her roast chicken, for instance, took two days to prepare and resulted in three meals. After inserting garlic, lemon zest, and herbs under the skin, she salted and peppered the bird and let it dry out in the fridge for a day; then she rubbed it with butter and olive oil, slow roasted it at 325 degrees for a couple of hours, and turned the drippings into gravy. The result was dinner, while leftovers became chicken salad, and the carcass was boiled with carrots and celery to make a rich soup stock.

Cooking, Harris said, is "a gift that you can give people. That's how I came to it."

. . .

THE STARK CONTRAST OF Joe Biden and Kamala Harris to Donald Trump and Mike Pence was illustrated by their widely different approaches to entertaining. Democrats and many Republicans had been mystified when Trump kept to himself and a small cadre of loyalists at the White House, the Trump International Hotel, or the golf course. Pence was a cipher who refused to eat dinner alone with a woman other than his wife, and emulated Trump by posing with a bucket of Kentucky Fried Chicken.

Though Joe Biden was not an inveterate entertainer in the way the Reagans or Clintons were, he considered socializing part of the job and partook of Washington's traditions. As second couple, he and Jill had hosted an annual "beach party" for journalists at the vice president's house at the Naval Observatory, featuring Super Soaker fights, bouncy castles, and plenty of food and drink.

Biden's inauguration in 2021 brought the sense that a fever had broken in Washington. As the Trump supernova seemed to sputter and COVID vaccines became available, the Establishment dared hope the new administration would "make schmoozing great again," as a *Washington Post* headline wistfully put it. The District's "buffalo"—the bipartisan elite—couldn't wait to return to the Kennedy Center, charity events, museum fundraisers, embassy galas, and the White House—perhaps even at state dinners.

As the nation struggled to recover from COVID anxiety, financial setbacks, and hunger pangs, people dared hope that Biden and Harris would turn the fraught debate over food production and supply into a meaningful discussion and change. When talking about the pasta sauce Jill simmered, the ice cream Joe ordered, or the jerk chicken that Kamala made for Doug, the administration linked their food choices to hard-hit regions of the country, which in turn spotlighted the people who made and served food (including immigrants), and furthered discussions about health, sustainability, and the existential threat of climate change.

The hope was that this approach would lead to discussions and even arguments, which was not necessarily a bad thing when it came to the staff of life. Though great divisions over race, religion, guns, governance, and the like continued to split the nation, the dream inside the Beltway was that people of all stripes would once again be able to "disagree agreeably," as the social secretaries Lea Berman and Jeremy Bernard phrase it.

Or, as Jill Biden's Italian grandfather, Dominic Jacobs (né Giacoppa), liked to say, "*Finire a tarallucci e vino*"—or "to finish with tarallucci and wine" (tarallucci are little cookies). In other words, the First Lady said, "No matter our differences or our arguments during dinner, we finish as a family. All's well that ends well—or at least, I think you're dead wrong, but let's put it aside so we can enjoy the pleasures of life together."

CONCLUSION

Eating Together

✦

I. *My White House Dinner*

Food must be "not only good to eat, but also good to think."
—Claude Lévi-Strauss

This book was partly inspired by the behind-the-scenes television documentaries Julia Child made of important White House dinners in 1967 and 1976. She took viewers into the back halls of the mansion and revealed the tremendous amount of planning, cleaning, cooking, and communication required to pull off diplomatic visits by foreign leaders. As I researched those stories, it occurred to me that it would be instructive and entertaining to re-create her work by attending a state dinner, documenting what it takes to execute such an event, interview key players, maybe even meet the First Couple and the guest of honor.

It was not to be. My numerous queries to the Trump administration went unanswered, except for a terse email from the chief usher, Timothy Harleth (a former rooms manager at the Trump International Hotel), who wrote, "Unfortunately, we're not able to facilitate the request. However, I appreciate greatly the work you are doing." It sounded as if he hadn't bothered to read my query.

Boxed out of the People's House, unable to wangle an invitation to a state dinner, denied access to the Trumps and the chef Cris Comerford, I set out to do the next best thing: I would host my own White House dinner. I wanted to see, smell, and taste presidential food, meet people who had worked in the mansion, dine in a historically appropriate location, and get a sense of what a state dinner is like, more or less. It was a tall order. But I got lucky. People agreed to cook, attend, and cut me deals, and the pieces fell into place.

The chef John Moeller agreed to prepare a four-course dinner based on those he had cooked in the White House from 1992 to 2005, during the George H. W. Bush, Bill Clinton, and George W. Bush administrations. He had served as the executive chef in the interregnum between Walter Scheib and Cris Comerford and had supplied Bush 43's notorious pretzel snack. Each of the dishes Moeller and I agreed on was seasonal and alluded to a historical moment. I invited ten guests, all people who had worked at the White House, or had covered it, or were historians or food experts. They included four men and six women who represented both sides of the aisle and the apolitical middle ground.

On Presidents' Day, February 17, 2020, we gathered at the DACOR Bacon House. A storied home built in 1825 by an industrialist, the mansion is situated on a corner of F Street at Eighteenth, just west of the White House. Over the years, the Bacon House had temporarily housed eight presidents, including Lincoln and Monroe, and a handful of Supreme Court justices. It now functions as a private club for Diplomatic and Consular Officers, Retired (DACOR). They had a full kitchen and dining room and were graciously accommodating. In the spirit of Jefferson and FDR, I carefully planned "my White House dinner," but, as frequently happens at actual state dinners, the evening took some unexpected turns.

AT SEVEN O'CLOCK that night, we gathered around a large table arranged in a horseshoe shape—a nod to traditional White House seating plans used before the Kennedy administration, which made it easy for the ten of us to interact. Echoing Jefferson's rejection of monarchial protocol, I asked people to sit in his "pell-mell" style, wherever they wished. As in his day, some of my guests enjoyed that laissez-faire approach, while others seemed less enthused.

After canapés and wine, Moeller started our dinner with mushroom soup. This was not the cylindrical, gray glop your grandmother would shake out of a can. No, his presidential version was an ambrosial broth made from five kinds of wild mushrooms—morel, king oyster, shiitake, cremini, and beech—foraged by Amish farmers in Pennsylvania.

We chose the soup in homage to George Washington and his starving troops who foraged mushrooms at Valley Forge in the winter of 1777. John Moeller, a robust midsized man with sandy hair, glasses, and a bushy mustache, learned to forage mushrooms while training to cook in Dijon, France. "I get emotional about them," he said. "Mushrooms are one of my favorite things to work with." Adding the diced mushrooms to a base of leeks, chicken broth, minced garlic, and fresh thyme, he used an immersion blender to whiz the medley together into a silky mycological elixir with a hint of earthy nuttiness. The soup was so smooth and tasty it was hard to believe it was dairy-free.

Spooning the soup, Roxanne Roberts, a style reporter at *The Washington Post,* wondered about food safety: "Aren't some mushrooms dangerous? Do people worry about" poisoning the president?

The chef explained how the White House carefully procures ingredients, and said, "It would be almost impossible to poison the president." The sharp-witted food writer Corby Kummer wondered if presidents still use food tasters, as he had seen Reagan do at a G7 summit in Venice.

"No, we didn't use tasters," said Lloyd Hand, who had been Lyndon Johnson's chief of protocol. And James (Skip) Allen, a White House usher for five presidents between the Carter and the George W. Bush administrations, agreed: "Never. We trusted John Moeller."

"I was the last person to taste the food," the chef confirmed.

As wineglasses clinked, I mentioned that the White House struck me as an extraordinary building that represents different things to different people, and where food acts as a bridge between the personal and the professional aspects of life. "What does it mean to you?" I asked the table.

"The White House is the opening shot of every movie about American power and politics," said Roberts, who has covered Washington social events for years and remains impressed by the building's symbolism. "Even though people live and work there, for the vast majority it's a symbol—a symbol of American exceptionalism and power and democracy."

Others noted that the building is a physical representation of the nation: the *idea* of the United States. "It's a very special place," said Skip Allen. "It's the office of a head of state [where important decisions are made], but then the public sees the First Lady in the hallway [and recognizes that] it is her home. It happens all the time."

Nodding, Betty Monkman, the White House curator from 1967 to 2002, said, "The Clintons and Bushes used to say they 'lived above the store.' People freaked out when they saw the First Family walking through." For the Clintons, she added, "it was the first time they lived near where they worked, so Chelsea could walk into the Oval Office to see her dad after school, or the president could be home for dinner," and watch a movie in the screening room afterward.

Ann Stock—a Clinton social secretary and an assistant secretary of state for the Obamas—noted that when citizens enter the President's House, "their whole manner changes. We watched it happen time and time again. They come in and see the portraits of the presidents and First Ladies, and [it hits them]: 'Oh. My. God. I'm in the *White House!*' When the head of Boeing came to dinner, he almost started crying. He said, 'If only my parents could see me now.'"

I understood the feeling. Stock's description reminded me of my first visit to the mansion in 2016, when I was zapped by an unexpected jolt of emotion, or recognition, or some other feeling that is hard to name.

The White House remained an abstraction to most Americans until the early twentieth century, but once people could see the building's interior in stereographs—three-dimensional photographs—it became real and gripped the public imagination. "Even if they were by themselves, a thousand miles away, they could take an interest in the president's domestic life, which often revolved around the table," said Theresa McCulla, a food historian at the Smithsonian's National Museum of American History.

"For those of us who worked there every day, it was a place to come to work. The thrill was gone after a while," Monkman said. What she found interesting was how the look and tone of the house shifted with each administration. "As the personalities change, the house reflects the [families] who live there," she said, from the way the rooms and grounds look, to the faces and clothes in the hallways and the food served.

WITH THAT, Moeller introduced the second course, a gorgeous entrée of roasted organic salmon (from Scotland) set atop sunchoke puree, local spinach, fingerling potatoes, baby carrots, turnips, and Brussels sprouts, with a pinch of truffle salt. The chef described the thick, nutrient-dense orange fillets as "a salmon filet mignon," and he topped them with a thin, pleasantly tangy horseradish crust "to accent the flavors of the season."

We chose this dish because the history of food gifts to presidents—from Hoover's headless salmon to Jefferson's giant cheese and Taft's possum, and all the beers, pies, and other edible presents—made for amusing history. Plus, the dish was delicious, and though Moeller had served it to heads of state, it is not too difficult to replicate at home.

While food is an important component of state dinners, it isn't the central focus, my guests reminded me: diplomacy is. But a banquet like Ulysses S. Grant's for King Kalakaua of the Sandwich Islands is the capstone to important negotiations, and Jimmy Carter's dinner for Begin and Sadat after signing the Camp David Accords was a moment of personal and historical bonding.

A meal at the White House is a "status feast," in the ancient sense. As a political and diplomatic tool, it provides a high-visibility platform from which the American president and his guest can present their narratives to domestic and global audiences. An invitation to dine with the president is rare and confers status on his guest: it sends a message to the world that the guest nation is to be reckoned with; and it sends a similar message inward, to the guest's domestic audience.

At any given time, there is "a waiting list of twenty to thirty" world leaders eager for an invitation, Lloyd Hand said.

"Oh, yes, the best thing about a state dinner is the invitation," Roxanne Roberts said, jumping in. "It indicates that the people who are selected for it are about to be part of something that is historic, and exclusive, and *American*. It's the epitome of what it means to be part of the American dream."

"A state dinner is a celebration, an honor, and a kind of political gift," said Ann Stock.

"But who *had* the honor, and who *didn't*, plays out in these geopolitical puzzles," observed Hand. "It's fascinating."

Such an invite can be deeply meaningful to the guest, he said, recalling the night President Johnson invited President Maurice Yaméogo of the small African nation of Upper Volta (now Burkina Faso) to dinner. When the six-foot-three LBJ said in an offhand way to the much shorter Yaméogo, "Be sure to give your country my regards," Hand said, Yaméogo replied with a wry smile: "Mr. President, maybe you don't understand, but four out of five children in my country died of smallpox until pharmaceutical drugs were made available—by *you*. And now we don't lose more than one out of 100,000. So if I didn't give your regards to my country, the women would rise up and denounce me."

With that, Johnson took a shine to Yaméogo, who liked to quote Abraham Lincoln and had written the Upper Voltan constitution. The president piled the group into a limousine and drove to the Lincoln Memorial at midnight. As Yaméogo stared at his hero, a tear ran down his cheek. The experience has vividly stuck with Hand all these years, and he said, "The impact of a visit to the White House is almost immeasurable for visitors like Yaméogo."

More recently, my tablemates pointed out, the Ukrainian president Volodymyr Zelensky "was desperate" for an invitation to dine with Donald Trump. With his border under pressure from Russian troops, Zelensky was hoping that a state dinner at the White House would send a powerful message to Vladimir Putin. But when Trump refused, the Ukrainian felt "humiliated" that his putative ally did not respond in his time of need. In a phone call, Trump seemed to condition U.S. aid to Ukraine on Zelensky's providing dirt on Joe Biden's son Hunter. (That conversation was at the core of Trump's first impeachment, for abuse of power and obstruction of Congress; he was acquitted.)

If a state dinner is such a useful tool, I wondered, then why did Trump host just two of them?

"Well, it depends on the priorities of the president and his people—if he listens to them," Hand said diplomatically.

"He doesn't value the tool!" an exasperated guest said. "It makes no sense!"

Thinking about the politics of food, and the cliché of red-meat conservatives and leafy-green liberals, I shifted the conversation: "Is there a difference between 'Republican' and 'Democratic' food?" After some spirited palaver, the table's consensus was: "No. Food choices are individual and don't follow party lines." I was surprised by that at first, but as I thought about the nearly universal love of steak, ice cream, and Chinese food among First Couples, it made sense. So much for preconceptions.

OUR THIRD COURSE WAS a palate-cleansing winter green salad with a wedge of Amish sheep cheese. It was February, so the greens were a seasonal choice and a nod to Thomas Jefferson's vegetable fixation. I had planned to use that course to launch into a discussion about the future of food, climate change, and race, but I made a strategic error.

Noticing the wedge of cheese, I mentioned the famous White House gift cheeses—the 1,235-pound wheel given to Thomas Jefferson by Massachusetts Baptists, and the 1,400-pound, odoriferous *fromage* made by New York dairymen for Andrew Jackson that was consumed by a crush of admirers who nearly wrecked the White House, not to mention Obama's Big Block of Cheese days, which paid tribute to those early gifts. That diverted us into raucous stories about populist leaders and misbehaving guests at the White House.

Corby Kummer raised the specter of Trump's burger banquet, and the table grew momentarily subdued as we contemplated the image of congealed burgers in the State Dining Room. Luckily, someone recalled the destruction wrought by Jackson's cheese mob, which lifted our spirits and got everyone talking about ill-mannered guests.

It turns out that when people are invited to dine at the White House, they often become overexcited and do things they regret. "They steal stuff. Oh, man, you have no idea how many things they pinch," Moeller said. "Weird."

For years guests pilfered White House matchbooks or cigarette holders. With those no longer in use, people nick other items small enough to slip into a pocket or purse—silverware, napkins, saltcellars. Many people have taken a silver spoon from the White House, felt guilty, and returned it in a plain box with no return address. "That happens all the time," Moeller said, chuckling.

Betty Monkman revealed that when the waiters retrieve plates from the table, they often count the silverware—one, two, three—at each place setting. If a piece is missing, the waiter will say something like "I think we might have dropped a fork. I'm going to take these plates to the kitchen, and when I come back, we'll take a look." The culprit usually scrambles to remove the purloined sterling silver fork from her purse. "When the waiter reappears, the guest declares, 'Oh, look, it's on the floor!'" Monkman said, laughing knowingly.

"When people's emotions are heightened, they can turn volatile," Ann Stock said. "They behave like schoolchildren on a field trip." When alcohol is involved—especially when it is the White House holiday eggnog ("the best eggnog in the world," my guests vouched)—things can get messy. Overzealous revelers have been known to throw up into potted plants, or a Christmas-tree stand, or pass out on the marble staircase.

The biggest problem is that visitors become so entranced by the mansion they refuse to let go of the president's hand on a receiving line, or insist on a photo with the First Lady, or simply won't leave. In such cases, the socials—the mansion's "beat cops," Lea Berman calls them—employ the "chicken walk," a polite but insistent ushering of obstinate guests toward the door. And when a visitor whines, "Could you *possibly* have seated me *further* away from the president?" the social's job is to smile and remind them, "You are eating dinner at the White House. There are no bad seats here."

MOELLER'S DESSERT WAS a dark, warm, flourless chocolate torte with an almond *tuile,* raspberry sauce, a dusting of white confectioner's sugar, and a sprinkling of blueberries and strawberries. George Washington drank hot chocolate for breakfast, Ulysses S. Grant served a chocolate dessert to King Kalakaua, and Donald Trump ate chocolate cake with the Chinese president, Xi Jinping.

Moeller had served this particular chocolate bomb at numerous state dinners, and it tasted just right: rich and gooey and sweet, with a slightly bitter aftertaste, a palate-lightening zip from the raspberry coulis, and a cool juicy crunch from the berries. The tortes disappeared in an instant, an attribute that came in handy at state dinners, when time is of the essence.

From the kitchen's perspective, a state dinner is "a sprint," Moeller explained. The challenge is to serve from ninety to two hundred people a full meal, from appetizers to dessert, in an hour and a half. But, he said, "we want to showcase the best dishes we can and make the president and First Lady look good."

In preparation, he would consult the State Department about the guest's dietary preferences, medical issues, and religious considerations, then construct a menu based on what was in season. Though dozens of people attend the White House feasts, "we really designed the menu for just four people"—the American First Couple and their guests of honor. The food should nod to the visitors' nation—with an ingredient, flavor, cooking technique, or color combination—look interesting, and taste "pleasant" but not too challenging. "You don't want to serve a sour pickle, or a lot of garlic, which could be offensive," Moeller said.

State dinners are multisensory experiences, the veteran partygoers explained, and they can overwhelm one's ability to process. People spend a lot of time looking at the room decor, talking to their tablemates, or eavesdropping on others. "Food gets a short shrift, historically," Roxanne Roberts said. "After people go to a state dinner, they tell stories about what they saw and who they talked to, but not necessarily about the perfectly cooked meal."

This is one reason why guests sign each other's menus at the end of a meal, as souvenirs to remind themselves, "Oh, *that's* what I ate last night, and *that's* whom I sat next to."

"But are those nights numbered?" I wondered. For years, critics have complained that state dinners are a form of Kabuki—an obscure anachronism that has outlived its usefulness in the internet age. The time, expense, and pomp required to present such an elaborate meal seems out of step with modern ways, the complaint goes. Every few years, a headline wonders if the state dinner is "going the way of the dodo," as *The Christian Science Monitor* did.

I put it to the table: "Is the Kabuki worth something, or has the state dinner become an empty gesture?"

"A state dinner is *never* an empty gesture!" Ann Stock exclaimed. "It's an important political act. It is an *honor*."

"Naaah, they aren't gonna disappear," Moeller said. "Cool stuff happens. The world leaders meet in person, break bread, get to know each other—you can't do *that* in a tweet."

"Anyone who says the state dinner is not important has been to so many it doesn't matter anymore," Roxanne Roberts added. "Or they don't understand anything about the history, tradition, and symbols of our country."

"Or they weren't on the guest list!" Kummer chimed in.

"Okay," I said, "so will state dinners continue to be relevant in the twenty-first century?"

"Yes!" the table agreed. And then, full of presidential food and talk, we signed each other's menus and bade one another good night.

AFTER OUR GUESTS LEFT, Moeller, his wife, Suryati, and I digested the evening over glasses of Pinot Noir. What we had created was not a state dinner *exactly,* but it was as close as we could get without being invited to the White House. The conversation had been stimulating, and as we exhaled in a state of happy fatigue we toasted the dinner, our guests, and "the presidents—all of them, good and bad," for they had brought us together. As we talked past midnight, it gave us a chance to get to know each other, deconstruct the meal, and consider what we might do differently if we ever try such an ambitious party again. It was leisurely and natural, the kind of moment I came to miss terribly just weeks later.

II. At the President's Table, and Ours

Looking back on that night is bittersweet. Our White House dinner took place on February 17, 2020, when, unbeknownst to us, and most Americans, the coronavirus was snaking across the country. It is believed that COVID-19 claimed its first U.S. victim on February 6 and took a second life on the seventeenth, the day of our dinner; those fatalities weren't detected until later, and a third person died on the twenty-ninth. (None of our dining companions were sickened that night, luckily.) As the virus bloomed into a poisonous global pandemic, everyone who could retreated into a cocoon, with compounding feelings of isolation and dread.

By the fall of 2020, COVID had infected President and Mrs. Trump and killed more than a million people worldwide. By the spring of 2022, the pandemic and its side effects had killed an estimated 15 million people globally, some 778,000 of whom were Americans (the Civil War, our deadliest conflict, led to an estimated 650,000 to 750,000 deaths). As people quarantined, social isolation led to a "loneliness epidemic," especially among young adults, and serious health consequences.

Yet, even before COVID, the president's table—which is another way of saying our collective table—was in disarray. Increasingly, Americans were eating apart from each other and less healthily, both literally and metaphorically.

The warning signs were everywhere. Despite ample research showing how beneficial family meals are to children, Harvard researchers found that only 30 percent of families manage to eat together on a regular basis. Though teens can be moody, research shows they enjoy family dinners, and 80 percent of them say that is the time they are most likely to eat well, and talk, laugh, or cry with their parents and siblings. The Harvard researchers found dramatic benefits in communication skills and vocabulary among young children who eat with their families.

But the Bureau of Labor Statistics found that adults spent an average of only thirty-seven minutes a day preparing and consuming a meal at home. Other studies found that students who don't routinely eat with their family are more likely to skip school, and that kids who don't eat with their parents at least twice a week are more likely to become overweight. With a surge in trendy diets, body self-consciousness, food allergies, and religious strictures, "there is a correlation between [increased] food restrictions and [increased] loneliness," observed Ayelet Fishbach, the University of Chicago behavioral scientist. "No one quite knows why," she added, though people adhering to restricted diets "are not part of the group."

The decline of shared family meals does not affect everyone equally. Affluent families have been eating together more frequently in recent decades, while low-income families have been doing so less, the Harvard researchers found. The reasons for this are clear: many people don't have the time or energy to shop, cook, and clean. Others don't have access to healthy foods, or aren't interested in cooking.

At a time when eating at restaurants, buying premade dinners, or ordering takeout are seductively easy options, many people consider home-cooked meals an anachronism, or an expensive indulgence, though premade foods are not always cheaper, and certainly not healthier. Home-cooked meals are higher in fruits, vegetables, proteins, and fiber, and have fewer calories and less fat, sugar, and salt than commercial foodstuffs. *The Atlantic* reported that by 2014 Americans were spending almost as much on fast food as on groceries; a quarter of us eat at least one fast-food meal every day, and the average citizen eats one in five meals in their car. In reality, most of us operate somewhere in the middle of these extremes, bouncing between home-cooked and store-bought foods. But the point is that the combination of social stressors and poor-quality foods has led to a rise in health issues and a decline in sociability.

In Washington, this trend took on a political edge. As the rhetoric sharpened, partisans left the communal table, sealed themselves into ideological fortresses, and rejected cooperation in favor of self-interest. In this atmosphere, questions about the politics of food and the food of politics became divisive, and we pushed our tables further and further away from one another's. Before the pandemic hit, the number of bipartisan events at the White House—which have brought people of all persuasions together since John Adams's opening reception in 1801—was dwindling. The tradition of collegial bargaining and compromise over club sandwiches and quesadillas in the House and Senate dining rooms was increasingly a vestige of the past. Even the District's legendary cocktail parties were in decline, something unthinkable just a few years ago.

As of this writing, it remains an open question whether or not the capital will regain its social-political-gastronomic mojo. There are signs it could. With a pent-up demand after two years of inactivity, Washingtonians flocked to favorite events, such as the Kennedy Center Honors, the Gridiron dinner, and the White House Correspondents' Association bash in 2022. Not surprisingly, more families ate together during the pandemic: a Census report found that some 85 percent of children ate dinner with their parents five or more times per week during the 2020 lockdown, while an American Family Survey revealed that 54 percent of families ate together every day. It would mark a welcome return to common sense if those private habits influenced elected officials to break bread together again on a regular basis. For, as Francine du Plessix Gray wrote: "The family meal is not only the core curriculum in the school of civilized discourse; it is also a set of protocols that curb our natural savagery and our animal greed, and cultivate a capacity for sharing and thoughtfulness. . . . The ritual of nutrition helps to imbue families, and societies at large, with greater empathy and fellowship."

In 1790, Jefferson, Hamilton, and Madison discovered that there is weakness in disunion and strength in breaking bread together, as they brokered their Dinner Table Bargain. And our modest White House dinner in February 2020 demonstrated that good bipartisan conversation over a fine meal is still possible. This is as true at our own table as it is at the president's. Or, to put it another way: if eating together makes us happy and effective, then not eating together makes us unhappy and less effective—as individuals and as a nation.

"People prefer to eat together [rather] than alone," Ayelet Fishbach explained. Her research has found that people, even complete strangers, who eat similar foods are more trusting of one another, work more cooperatively, and are better able to resolve conflicts than those who don't. And, she added, the *way* people share food determines how well they get along. If everyone has their own plate of food, then sharing a meal is simple. But if a group shares, say, a bowl of popcorn, then to ensure harmony everyone should be able to reach the food, take turns helping themselves, and consume equal portions. In other words, Fishbach said, eating together requires "social coordination," which requires people to slow down, take turns, and pay attention to the food and one another.

FOR THIS TO WORK on a national scale the tone must be set at the top. The president is the eater in chief and part of his responsibility is to preside over the nation's table in an active and informed way. "How we produce and consume food has a bigger impact on Americans' well-being than any other human activity," Mark Bittman, Michael Pollan, and other experts have written. "The industry is the largest sector of our economy; food touches everything from our health to the environment, climate change, economic inequality and the federal budget." They recommend creating a national food policy to be administered by a food czar. It's a provocative and timely idea, albeit one that is politically risky.

Some presidents have intuitively understood the symbolic, practical, and political value of food. Jefferson was our greatest epicurean leader in the nineteenth century; the Kennedys set the gold standard for White House entertaining in the twentieth century; and so far, the Obamas have been the most foodie First Couple of the twenty-first century. The Roosevelts were knowledgeable and enthusiastic eaters; Eisenhower and Carter were talented cooks; Lyndon Johnson understood the legislative value of barbecue. Hoover, Wilson, and Nixon treated food as a necessary evil, though their nutritional policies saved millions of lives. By and large, however, these men are outliers: most presidents have failed to recognize the way food connects people and its centrality to the nation's well-being. Instead, they have relied on basic diets and disjointed policies, and not one of them has effectively linked the creation and consumption of the American meal to the impact it has on human and environmental health. The reason for this is clear: food is highly political and big business, and any attempt to change the nation's diet is fraught (as First Lady Michelle Obama discovered when she focused on childhood obesity and planted a vegetable garden, and was roundly criticized by industrial interests).

The United States has had a nominal food policy since 1862, when Lincoln established the Department of Agriculture, and is famously bountiful. In theory, we could provide every citizen with healthy, affordable meals. But in practice we rely on a patchwork system and have never developed a single, coordinated method for the oversight, regulation, and administration of food policy—as Brazil and Mexico have done, for example. As a result, our current system has led to poor nutrition and food deserts in some places and overabundance and waste in others. By subsidizing corn and soybeans, the federal government has created plenty of cheap but unhealthy foods, which contribute to obesity, diabetes, and other diseases. The consolidation of giant farms and meat processors, compounded by lax oversight, has left the country vulnerable to crop blights and health pandemics—as when COVID sickened workers in crowded meatpacking plants and led to supply-chain bottlenecks.

A reliance on fossil fuels and ethanol leads to the pollution of water, soil, and air, which accelerates health and economic disparities. It's a vicious circle built on short-term thinking.

But these are essentially political issues, and they should be resolved by our chief politician, the president. The first thing our leaders can do is to raise the profile of American food and the ranching, farming, and fishing that provide it—including their benefits and costs—so that the public has a better understanding of what's at stake. Once the president convinces voters how central, and dysfunctional, the food system is, it will be harder for industry and its political allies to resist change. Equally important is for our presidents to lead by example—or, as Julia Child wrote, they should raise the nation's "gastronomic image" and empha-size "the good in American cooking." That means First Families should eat well and healthily, but not always expensively, and publicize it. They should spotlight fresh, local ingredients, and regional, historical, and Indigenous cooking traditions more vigorously.

When it comes to formal evenings, First Couples should adhere to tradition but continue to push for the very best, most innovative Ameri-can cuisine. The same goes for the entertainment. The White House is a unique stage, and though state or official dinners should be respectful and serious, to a point, they should also be fun. The intention of these gather-ings is to encourage communication and ensure that 1600 Pennsylvania Avenue remains "a showcase of American art and history," as Jackie Ken-nedy put it. She demonstrated that good food and a little showmanship can reap fantastic political dividends.

At informal events, the eater in chief could experiment with unusual ingredients—"ugly" vegetables (such as bruised tomatoes, which are per-fectly good to eat), "climate conscious" foods (like beans and legumes), plant-based meats, even insects, or invasive species such as lionfish. Hav-ing the president sample such "new" foods will help normalize them and shift the American diet in a more sustainable direction. Those who cringe at the thought might reflect on the fact that humans have been consum-ing brown apples and toasted grasshoppers for centuries; and though pan-fried lionfish is something new, the White House has a long history of serving dishes—such as roasted possum, squirrel stew, and terrapin soup—that are no longer fashionable. The times are a-changing, and we must adapt.

At this moment of turmoil and innovation, seemingly small gestures can take on outsized importance and lead to further change. Take the

Obamas' kitchen garden, for instance. Simultaneously retro and contemporary, it supplied the White House and soup kitchens with fresh produce, taught the First Lady and schoolchildren how to garden, and inspired people to eat healthier, exercise outside, and become self-sustaining. Why not build on that success, expand the garden further, and create a small farm with fruit trees and vines—including wine grapes, in homage to Jefferson, and a grazing cow and sheep, a nod to Taft and Wilson—or perhaps an elephant and a donkey, whose manure could be used for fertilizer, as Michael Pollan once suggested? Outdoor dinners and concerts could be held amid the earthy bounty rather than in the manicured Rose Garden.

In the spirit of modernization, it is high time to elevate the Executive Kitchen, both literally and figuratively. The hearth has always been the center of a home, around which all activity circulates; but at the White House, the small, efficient kitchen is squeezed into a sunless room on the mansion's ground floor. Located far below the State, the President's, and the Family dining rooms, the kitchen requires elevators, stairs, and dumbwaiters to transport its rapidly cooling meals up to hungry guests. This sends the message that the First Kitchen and its staff are an afterthought. That may have once been true, but no longer. Americans are increasingly interested in cooking, and it would be far more efficient, and interesting, to give the White House Kitchen greater pride of place, with plenty of room and sunlight, outfit it with the latest tools and appliances, and allow the public to observe the cooks at work (from a safe distance). As a corollary, the kitchen staff should be better compensated, their work highlighted, and the cooks should be encouraged to spread the good word about the good food at the president's table.

COMMUNAL MEALS HAVE BEEN a launchpad for the American dream for nearly 250 years, and few places on earth rival the White House as a place to eat. The literal president's table—whether it is the grand thirty-foot-long banquet table in the State Dining Room, a small table at a lawn party, or the kitchen counter in the First Family's private quarters—is a practical necessity: it's a place to eat. But the metaphorical president's table encompasses many meanings. It is a symbol of the nation, its bounty, and the many voices and identities of its citizens. As such, it is a political stage, a diplomatic arena, a forum for debate, a cultural showcase. It can be an indicator of our leaders' inner lives, and their administration's priorities. And at the end of the day the president's table is *ours,* the electorate's, for we voters are ultimately responsible for who sits there, what they eat, and why.

Sharing food and drink is an essential means of human connection, but it isn't always easy. We look to our presidents for inspiration, and must hope, or insist, that our leaders pull America's distanced tables close and encourage us all to sit down and break bread, together.

Recipes

George Washington's Striped Bass (Rockfish) Grilled on a Cedar Plank

*This river [the Potomac] is well supplied with various kinds of fish,
at all seasons of the year. . . . [T]he whole shore, in short,
is one entire fishery.*
—George Washington at Mount Vernon, 1793

As the Potomac bent around Washington's eight-thousand-acre Mount Vernon estate, it provided him with a ten-mile-long stretch of shoreline, teeming with shad, herring, bass, carp, perch, sturgeon, and other fish. In spring, gleaming shoals of herring and shad surged up the river to spawn, and the president loved to fish for sport and profit. The season was short, lasting just five or six weeks in April and May, and intense. Slaves and free men worked day and night in shifts, setting seine nets that ran as long as five hundred feet from shore to boats, or from boat to boat, to trap the silver tide. Their haul was remarkable, bringing in tens of thousands of shad and more than a million herring a year. But that was only the first step. Cleaning, preserving the fish in salt, and packing them in barrels for storage or sale was a major production. Nothing went to waste, and the by-products—fish heads, tails, and viscera—were used in the Mount Vernon gardens as fertilizer. Slaves were rewarded for their work in the fishery with a pint of rum a day and given twenty fish per month to eat, an important source of protein.

Washington often served fish at his table, but the majority of his catch was sold to merchants, bartered, or traded. Though he loved farming his land above all else, Washington's three fisheries were consistently his most lucrative business. His fish sold widely, from Philadelphia to Jamaica—where his good name commanded prices twice as high as his neighbors', he was proud to note—and provided an income of up to 250 pounds sterling a year.

To prepare shad or other fish, Washington's cooks used two methods. In the first, they would cut the cleaned, scaled fillets into pieces and add them to water or stock, carrots, potatoes, and parsley, and slow cook the mixture in pots suspended over a fire to make hearty soups or stews. Or, even better, they would nail shad or striped bass (known as rockfish in Virginia) to a plank of wood and roast them before an open fire.

Inspired by the latter preparation, I recalled how fun and delicious it is to cook fish on a cedar plank. (Salmon is most commonly used.) Shad were once the most valuable fish in the Potomac, but have been decimated by overfishing, pollution, and dams, and are difficult to find in markets. In the spirit of George Washington, I suggest you use striped bass as a worthy substitute. Stripers (rockfish) have firm white flesh that is rich and holds its shape well while grilling.

This is a crowd-pleasing recipe for the grill that is far simpler to make than it appears, and tastes even better if you catch the fish yourself. The cedar planks lend the fish a woodsy flavor, enhanced by the use of hardwood charcoal and nicely counterpointed by a simple garnish of fresh herbs and lemon juice.

— TOOLS —

1 cedar plank, soaked in water for an hour (available at cookware and hardware stores, or online; the planks will have burn marks after cooking, but can be reused)

Gas grill or hardwood charcoal

Oven mitts or metal spatula

Baking tray

— INGREDIENTS (FOR TWO PEOPLE) —

Olive oil

1 pound fillet of striped bass

Sea salt and cracked black pepper

Fresh sage

Fresh thyme

Fresh dill

1 lemon

Garnish with a sprinkling of chopped parsley and ½ lemon cut into wedges

— PREPARATION —

Dry the soaked plank and lightly oil one side.

Clean the fish and lay it on the oiled side of the plank, skin-side down.

Salt and pepper the fillet to taste.

Dice the herbs and mix with a dash of olive oil; then carefully apply to the top of the fillet. Squeeze half a lemon over the fish. Cut the remaining lemon into half-moons, and lay them along the fish, spaced evenly. Cover and refrigerate while you prep the grill.

Heat your grill to about 350 degrees. If using hardwood charcoal, set the fire up on one side of the grill so you can move the fish from cool to hot zones.

Place the fish and plank on the grill, and cover. Watching it like a hawk, cook for 8 to 10 minutes, depending on the thickness of the fish (the thinner the fillet, the faster it will cook). If the plank catches fire, spritz it with water. When done, the bass's flesh will be firm to the touch, with a little give when you press your finger on it. If you are unsure, you can cut into the fillet to make sure it is no longer gelatinous inside.

Using oven mitts or a big spatula, carefully remove the plank and cooked fish and place it on the baking tray, which makes it easy to cool and safe to carry. Let it sit under a tent of tinfoil for a few minutes, to allow the juices to flow back into the bass's flesh.

Sprinkle with chopped parsley and serve with lemon wedges on the side.

— TO SERVE —

There are two approaches to presenting this dish. In the first, use a thin spatula to gently separate the bass from its skin, cut the fillet into portions, and serve on plates. In the second, place the baking tray on the table and let people pick at the bass themselves, which is an earthy and fun way to eat.

Washington might have accompanied this dish with wild rice and mushrooms and a green salad, or fresh asparagus in spring. He would likely have paired the meal with a dry white wine, such as a Sauvignon Blanc or Pinot Grigio supplied by Thomas Jefferson.

★ ★ ★

Martha Washington's Preserved Cherries

Food myths have always helped cohere America's immigrant population, and one of the most enduring fables is about a young George Washington chopping down his father's cherry tree with his "little hatchet," then confessing his sin, saying, "I cannot tell a lie." The story was apocryphal and did not appear until the fifth edition of Parson Weems's fanciful biography *The Life of Washington,* in 1806. Despite this caveat, there is no question that Washington was extremely fond of cherries.

Thanks to Martha Washington's recipe books, which she was given as a young bride in 1749 and bequeathed to her granddaughter Eleanor Parke Custis in 1799, we have many of the recipes prepared by the first president's kitchens in New York, Philadelphia, and Mount Vernon, Virginia.

This is a delicious, adaptable recipe for cherry preserves, which can be used as a condiment for savory dishes or in desserts such as cherry cobbler or as a topping for ice cream. It requires only three ingredients: cherries, sugar, and water.

I give two versions of the recipe here: the original version, which calls for two pounds of sugar and two pounds of cherries, drawn from *Martha Washington's Booke of Cookery and Booke of Sweetmeats* (edited by the food historian Karen Hess and published in 1981). Just reading that made my teeth ache, so I updated the recipe for modern eaters.

Martha Washington's Seventeenth-Century Recipe "*To Preserve Cherries*"

Take 2 pound of faire cherries & clip of the stalks in ye midst. then wash them clean, but bruise them not. then take 2 pound of double refined sugar, & set it over ye fire with a quart of faire water in ye broadest preserving pan or silver basen as you can get. let it seeth till it be some what thick, yn put in yr cherries, & let them boyle. keepe allwayes scumming & turning them gently with a silver spoon till they be enough. When they are cold, you may glass them up & keep them all the year.

My Updated Version of the Recipe

— TOOLS —

Colander

Cherry pitter
(optional but recommended)

Medium saucepan

Measuring cup

Long-handled cooking spoon

Bowl or jar to hold your preserves

— INGREDIENTS —

2 pounds fresh cherries

4 cups of water

¼ to ½ cup white sugar
(adjust to personal taste)

— PREPARATION —

Wash the cherries in a colander. Stem and pit them (not necessary, but worthwhile). Boil the water in a medium saucepan; then add the sugar.

When the sugar has dissolved, add the cherries to the pot and boil again. Lower the heat to a simmer. Using a long-handled spoon, stir the cherries occasionally, skimming foam from the surface and discarding it as necessary. When the liquid has been reduced by half and is syrupy, remove the pan from the heat and let the cherries cool.

★ ★ ★

Thomas Jefferson's Salad with Tarragon Vinegar Dressing

Jefferson was a prolific lettuce grower and salad nut (as described in Chapter 3), and his favorite herb was French tarragon, which he used to flavor his salad dressing. The species *Artemisia dracunculus* was found in American gardens before the Revolution (though it may have been Russian tarragon, which is not good to eat), but in 1806 Jefferson ordered a shipment of tarragon roots from a Philadelphia nursery. In France, tarragon is often used in chicken or fish dishes, and in béarnaise sauce. Jefferson steeped his herbs in vinegar for a couple of weeks, and then combined the tarragon vinegar with fine European olive oil to make a snappy vinaigrette. A wormwood, French tarragon is said to stimulate the entire digestive system. This recipe is drawn from *Dining at Monticello*, edited by Damon Lee Fowler, via Monticello.org.

To Make Tarragon Vinegar

— EQUIPMENT —

Medium-large container, such as a jar, jug, or bowl, to steep the vinegar

Screw top or plastic wrap to cover the container

Slim, tall-necked vinegar bottle topped by a screw cap or cork

Label, pen

— INGREDIENTS —

2 cups fresh French (not Russian) tarragon leaves, loosely packed

2 cups white wine or champagne vinegar (not "white vinegar")

Salt and black pepper

1 sprig of fresh tarragon per bottle

— PREPARATION —

Rinse the tarragon under cool, clean water and pat it dry.

On a flat surface, lightly bruise the tarragon leaves to release their flavor. ("Bruising" means to gently press or pound the tarragon leaves to release their aromatic oil. You can use the back of a spoon or other implement.)

Pack about 30 sprigs of tarragon into a medium-large container.

Pour the vinegar over the tarragon in the container.

Cover the jar with the screw top or plastic wrap and let sit in a kitchen window for 2 to 3 weeks, allowing the tarragon flavors to infuse the vinegar.

Add a sprig of fresh tarragon to a slim vinegar bottle.

Strain the vinegar into the bottle, and discard the steeped tarragon.

Seal the bottle with a tight-fitting top.

Label and date the vinegar.

NOTE: The vinegar is shelf stable and will keep for 6 to 8 months.

For the Salad

Serves 6

— INGREDIENTS —

2 tablespoons tarragon vinegar

6 to 8 tablespoons extra-virgin olive oil

6 cups mixed salad greens, such as seasonal lettuce, spinach, endive, radicchio, and watercress

1 small handful of fresh herbs (basil, marjoram, mint, savory), finely chopped

6 small whole scallions, cleaned, with ends trimmed

— PREPARATION —

Pour tarragon vinegar into a salad bowl. Add a small pinch of salt and several grindings of black pepper, and beat with a fork until the salt dissolves.

Slowly add about 6 tablespoons olive oil in a steady, thin stream, until emulsified. Adjust the seasoning and oil to taste.

Add the greens and herbs to the bowl, and lightly toss them with the salad dressing until the leaves are coated. Arrange the scallions around the edge of the bowl.

★ ★ ★

Andrew Jackson's Inaugural Orange Punch

After General Jackson was sworn in as the seventh chief executive on March 4, 1829, he rode his white horse up Pennsylvania Avenue to the President's House. He was trailed by "King Mob," a raucous crowd of thousands of his admirers, who surged into the mansion in search of food and drink. As they guzzled orange punch, a standard drink of the day, furniture was scattered, glassware was smashed, and Jackson was squeezed tightly against a wall, until his associates helped him escape out a window.

"What a scene we did witness! The *Majesty of the People* had disappeared, and a rabble, a mob, of boys, negros, women, children, scrambling fighting, romping. What a pity what a pity! . . . [T]he whole house had been inundated by the rabble mob," the socialite Margaret Bayard Smith reported of the mayhem. "Ladies fainted, men were seen with bloody noses and such a scene of confusion took place as is impossible to describe. . . . But it was the People's day, and the People's President and the People would rule." As the crowd grew rowdier, quick-witted stewards lured them outside with barrels of punch on the lawn.

Recently, the cocktail expert Eric Felten scoured nineteenth-century cookbooks in search of an orange punch recipe for *The Wall Street Journal*. Unimpressed by the overly sweet results—"not anything I'd trample White House furniture to get at"—he tweaked the punch with mulling spices, soda water, and Angostura bitters to make a sprightly rum cocktail.

— INGREDIENTS —

3 parts fresh orange juice	*1 part dark rum*
1 part fresh lemon juice	*1 part cognac*
1 part mulled orange syrup	*2 parts soda water*
(see note below)	*Dash of Angostura bitters*

NOTE: For mulled orange syrup, combine 1 cup sugar with 1 cup water in a pan and bring it to a low boil, stirring to dissolve the sugar. Reduce the heat to a simmer. Add a strip of orange peel and mulling spices—2 cinnamon sticks, a few whole cloves, and a few allspice berries. After simmering for 15 minutes, remove from the heat and let it sit for several hours. Strain and add to the punch.

— PREPARATION —

In a punch bowl, combine the ingredients and cool with a large block of ice. Serve in punch cups with a little crushed ice, and add a dash of Angostura bitters to each glass.

Abraham Lincoln's Gingerbread Men

L incoln adeptly used a childhood story about gingerbread men to win over the crowd during his seven debates with Stephen Douglas in the lead-up to the presidential election of 1860 (see Chapter 5). Though Mary Todd Lincoln did not leave her "receipts" (recipes) behind, it is likely she consulted the most popular cookbook of the day, Eliza Leslie's 1847 opus, *The Lady's Receipt-Book: A Useful Companion for Large or Small Families,* from which this recipe was adapted by Eric Colleary, at the *American Table* blog (www.americantable.org). It is worth noting that even a common recipe like this one carries historical weight: West Indian molasses was readily available on the American frontier because of the slave trade.

Here is Eliza Leslie's original recipe for ginger crackers (Lincoln's mother probably added more flour to her dough to make a firmer gingerbread cookie mix).

Leslie's Original Recipe for Ginger Crackers

Mix together in a deep pan, a pint of West Indian molasses; half a pound of butter; and a quarter of a pound of brown sugar; two large table-spoonfuls of ginger; a teaspoonful of powdered cinnamon; a small tea-spoonful of pearlash or soda, dissolved in a little warm water; and sufficient sifted flour to make a dough just stiff enough to roll out conveniently. Let the whole be well incorporated into a large lump. Knead it till it leaves your hands clean; then beat it hard with a rolling-pin, which will make it crisp when baked. Divide the dough, and roll it out into sheets half an inch thick. Cut it into cakes with a tin cutter about the usual size of a cracker-biscuit, or with the edge of a tea-cup. . . . Lay the cakes at regular distances in square pans slightly buttered. Set them directly into a moderately brisk oven, and bake them well, first pricking them with a fork.

Ginger crackers are excellent on a sea voyage. If made exactly as above they will keep for many weeks.

Eric Colleary's Updated Version

— INGREDIENTS —

1 pint molasses or sorghum

½ pound butter

¼ pound brown sugar

2 tablespoons ginger,
or more to taste

1 teaspoon ground cinnamon

1 teaspoon baking soda,
dissolved in a bit of warm water

3 to 4 cups flour

— PREPARATION —

Preheat the oven to 400 degrees.

Mix the ingredients together, either by hand in a large bowl (as Mrs. Lincoln would have done, using a large wooden spoon) or with a stand mixer (which is much easier).

As the dough comes together into a lump, knead it with clean hands, moving quickly to prevent it from drying. Then beat the lump of dough with a rolling pin.

Divide the dough and roll it into sheets a half-inch thick (be sure to keep them thin, because thick cookies can be hard to eat). Keep the extra dough under a damp cloth. If the dough is too stiff, add extra butter to produce a softer cookie.

Use a tin cookie cutter to cut the sheets of dough into gingerbread men. If your cutter sticks, dip its edges into flour to smooth the way.

Prick the men with a fork, and carefully place them on a baking pan lined with parchment paper, leaving enough space between each man that they can expand while cooking.

Place them in the hot oven for 4 to 6 minutes. Keep an eye on them, and remove them from the oven as soon as they start to brown.

Allow the men to cool before eating.

★ ★ ★

William Howard Taft: Billi Bi (Mussel Soup)

[Billi Bi is] the most elegant and delicious soup ever created.
—Craig Claiborne, food editor of *The New York Times*

When not inhaling steak or possum, President William Howard Taft liked to eat fish and shellfish, and one of his favorite dishes was the creamy mussel soup called Billi Bi (a.k.a. Billy By). Based on rustic seafood soups from the coast of Normandy, the recipe was refined by the chef Louis Barthe at Maxim's in Paris at the turn of the twentieth century. Legend has it that this dish was named after a particularly devoted patron, the millionaire American tinplate tycoon William Brand Leeds Sr.—or perhaps his son, W. B. Leeds Jr.—both known as Billy B. (pronounced "Billy bee").

To save Leeds and his friends the indignity of wrestling with the mussel meat and shells, Maxim's served just the cooking liquor, a silky brew of mussel juice and white wine thickened by heavy cream and egg yolk and made fragrant by aromatics. Billi Bi quickly hopped the Atlantic, where it became trendy enough for President Taft to try and fall hard for. The recipe has gone in and out of fashion since then, and in 1961 Craig Claiborne popularized it in *The New York Times Cook Book*. Further refined by the chef and author Pierre Franey, the dish has been deemed a Times Classic, meaning a "recipe of distinction," which the paper revives every now and then.

Billi Bi is easy to make. As you piece the dish together, the blue-black mussels, purple-white shallots, and green thyme make a beautiful dish; while softly bubbling on the stove, the mussel-wine-cream broth releases heady aromas that get your gastric juices flowing. As a *moule* lover who grew up eating mussels plucked from a granite outcropping in Maine, I feel compelled to add the mussels, and a few of their shells for decoration, back into the broth before serving.

The recipe following is based on a 2015 version in the *Times,* which I slightly altered with less cream, more mussels and wine, and a counterpoint of finely chopped parsley and chives. The result is a beautiful dish that emanates mouthwatering aromas, and is, as Claiborne wrote, "one of the sublime creations on Earth."

— INGREDIENTS —

2 plus pounds mussels

2 peeled shallots, coarsely chopped

2 small white onions,
peeled and quartered

Sea salt and white pepper to taste

Pinch of cayenne pepper

1½ cups dry white wine (such as
Sauvignon Blanc or Pinot Grigio)

2 tablespoons unsalted butter
(or olive oil)

1 bay leaf

2 sprigs of fresh parsley,
plus chopped parsley for garnish

2 sprigs of fresh thyme

Optional: ¼ to ½ cup clam
juice or fish stock to enhance
the mussel brine

2 cups heavy cream

1 egg yolk, lightly beaten

Chopped chives for garnish

— PREPARATION —

Carefully scrub and debeard the mussels.

Place the mussels in a large saucepan or Dutch oven; then add the shallots, onions, salt, pepper, cayenne, wine, butter (or oil), bay leaf, and parsley and thyme sprigs.

Cover the pan. Bring to a boil over medium heat; then reduce the heat and simmer until the mussels open, about 9 minutes. (Discard any mussels that do not open.)

Remove the mussels with a slotted spoon; then strain the broth through a large sieve or colander lined with cheesecloth. Reserve the liquid, which is the base of the soup.

Let the mussels cool; then remove the meat from the shells. Reserve the meat and discard the shells and aromatics.

Place the reserved mussel-wine broth in a saucepan (adding a splash of clam juice or fish stock if you wish), and bring to a low boil. Add the cream and return the liquid almost to a boil. Remove from the heat, and cool slightly; then add beaten egg yolk and stir it into the liquid. Return the saucepan to the stove and, watching like a hawk so the liquid does not boil, reheat enough to thicken the soup.

Remove from the heat and cool slightly; then taste (being careful not to burn your tongue) and adjust the seasoning.

To serve: divide the mussels among soup bowls, spoon the soup over them, then garnish with a small handful of finely chopped parsley and chives.

Feeds four as an appetizer, or two as an entrée. Serve with a warmed baguette, or sliced rustic bread dabbed with olive oil and grilled over a fire.

★ ★ ★

Woodrow Wilson's "Healthy Breakfast"

I n retooling Wilson's breakfast, the navy doctor Cary Grayson insisted the president drink a glass of grape juice with a raw egg, or two, every morning. (See Chapter 8.) While this concoction would certainly jolt the leader of the free world awake, and was believed to be nutritious, Wilson said it tasted as if he were ingesting "an unborn thing."

This morning tonic sounded so unappetizing that I had to try it, for the sake of journalistic integrity. I bought fresh organic eggs and a bottle of Concord grape juice (the recipe can also be made with orange juice), and steeled my gut. Reminding myself that raw eggs are so nutrient dense that people have eaten them for centuries—including Marilyn Monroe, as part of her beauty regimen, and Sylvester Stallone's Rocky, as part of his training regimen—I cracked two eggs with deep yellow yolks into a glass of purple grape juice, then slurped the concoction down. It went easily, the eggs viscous and creamy tasting, and the sweet tang of Concord grape predominating. In short, it was not nearly as odious as I had imagined, and I suffered no gastrointestinal aftereffects. I was relieved by this, and though I enjoyed the experiment, I have not added Wilson's "healthy breakfast" to my morning repertoire.

NOTE: Consumption of raw eggs may increase your risk of food-borne illness such as salmonella.

— TOOLS —

Tall glass
Long-handled spoon or fork for mixing

— INGREDIENTS —

1 bottle of quality grape juice
2 very fresh eggs

— PREPARATION —

Pour enough grape juice that it fills your glass one-half to three-quarters full.

Crack the raw eggs into the glass (crack carefully, so as not to drop eggshell into the juice).

Stir and drink.

★ ★ ★

FDR: *The Reverse Martini*

W hen is a martini not exactly a martini? When it is a reverse martini, which is sometimes called an upside-down martini or wet martini. The recipe for this tempting cocktail reverses the standard ratios by combining one part gin to five parts extra-dry (white) vermouth, garnished with an enlivening twist of lemon. Smooth, sophisticated, and only vaguely alcoholic, the reverse martini is more of a classic aperitif than a bone-dry James Bond thriller.

Franklin D. Roosevelt traveled to global summits with a special martini kit and liked to add olive brine or absinthe to his cocktails. He once served a standard (two parts gin to one part vermouth) martini—garnished with both a lemon twist and an olive—to Joseph Stalin, who described it as "cold on the stomach but not unpleasant." Curtis Roosevelt, a grandson, declared the president's martinis "the worst" tasting, though FDR liked them so much that he was known to have more than one, and burst into college fight songs while Secret Service agents bundled him off to bed.

Julia and Paul Child were also fans of the reverse martini. It was one of their favorite predinner pick-me-ups, which they sipped at all times of the year, though they didn't sing fight songs afterward. Indeed, Julia appreciated the cocktail's light touch, and noted, "The best thing about a reverse martini is you can have two of them."

— INGREDIENTS —

5 parts extra-dry vermouth
1 part gin

Garnish with a strip of lemon rind

— PREPARATION —

Pour the vermouth and gin over ice in a cocktail shaker. Stir well ("40 times," some insist). Strain into a chilled cocktail glass, such as a coupe. Twist a strip of lemon over the drink and drop it into your glass. Take a sip and, as James Beard said, "feel the glow." *À votre santé!*

★ ★ ★

Eisenhower Steak

President Dwight Eisenhower liked to grill three- to four-inch-thick sirloin steaks, which he'd rub with oil and garlic, and then, "as the horrified guests look on, [he] casually flings the steak into the midst of the red and glowing coals," a 1953 article in the *Miami Daily News* reported. I grew up with a friend who cooked steak directly in the coals, but had never tried the technique until I emulated Ike.

Be sure to use lump hardwood charcoal (not chemical-saturated briquettes) and light it with a grilling chimney so that the only thing touching your meat is flame and wood. Use your finger or a thermometer to test the doneness of the meat as it cooks (a meat thermometer should read 120 degrees for rare; 140 degrees for medium; 160 degrees for well done). Have a small spray bottle ready in case of too much flaring. The result will be a really nice piece of steak, charred on the outside with a rosy, juicy interior. I brushed the grit off the steak before slicing; a light dusting of ash didn't bother me at all.

— INGREDIENTS —

1½- to 2-inch-thick boneless ribeye steak (about 14 ounces)

Coarse sea salt and crushed black pepper to taste

Olive oil and a brush

2 garlic cloves, finely minced

Optional: a sprig or two of fresh rosemary to taste

— PREPARATION —

An hour before grilling, season the steak with coarse salt and pepper, and place it uncovered on a plate in the fridge. This will dry the surface of the meat, which will help it form a crust in the fire. Fifteen minutes before grilling, remove the steak from the fridge, and allow it to warm to room temperature.

Mix the oil and garlic, and optional rosemary, in a small bowl, and set aside.

Prepare to grill. Remove the top grate because you will not use it for cooking.

Ignite hardwood charcoal in a chimney, and let it burn until the top turns to gray ash; then distribute it evenly in the bottom of the grill.

Brush the steak with the oil-and-garlic mixture on both sides.

Before cooking the steak, blow softly across the bed of glowing coals to remove loose ash.

Then use tongs or a long-handled fork to nestle the steak directly on top of, or in, the glowing coals.

Cook for about 6 minutes on one side; then turn the steak and cook another 4 to 5 minutes on the other side to achieve a charred exterior and medium-rare interior. (For a ¾-inch steak, cook 3 to 5 minutes on each side; for a 3- or 4-inch steak, cook 8 to 10 minutes per side. For a medium steak, let it cook another 2 or 3 minutes on indirect heat.)

Firmly grasp the charred steak with your tongs, and gently lift it from the embers. Place it on a cutting board, tent it under foil, and let it rest for about 8 to 10 minutes to allow the meat to reabsorb the juices.

Cut into ½-inch slices, or hunks, or serve whole.

★ ★ ★

Lady Bird's Pedernales River Chili

(Created by Zephyr Wright)

After John F. Kennedy was assassinated in November 1963, Lyndon Johnson inherited the presidency, and with it his predecessor's French chef, René Verdon. But the Johnsons didn't like Verdon's fancy cooking, and Verdon didn't like their "homey" tastes for spareribs and garbanzo bean puree, and he quit. Rather than hire another French chef, the Johnsons promoted Zephyr Wright, the Black cook who had worked for the family for twenty-one years. The story did not make headlines, but Sam Johnson, the president's brother, wrote that Wright's food was so good it "made you wish you had two stomachs." Her most celebrated recipe was for Pedernales River Chili, named after the stream running through the Johnsons' ranch. As word spread about the chili, there were so many requests for the recipe that the White House had it printed on postcards that were mailed to the public. The cards identified the dish as "Lady Bird Johnson's Pedernales Chili," though the recipe was Wright's.

Two notes: LBJ reportedly preferred his chili made with venison rather than beef. And I found the postcard recipe less inspiring than its backstory, so I have included a version that makes a smaller helping but, with the addition of garnishings, bumps up the flavor.

— TOOLS —

Dutch oven (a large heavy pot) with a lid

Long-handled cooking spoon

Sharp, medium-sized kitchen knife

Can opener

Measuring cup

Measuring spoons

Zephyr Wright's Original Recipe

Serves 8 to 10

— INGREDIENTS —

4 pounds ground beef

1 large onion, chopped

2 garlic cloves, minced

1 teaspoon dried oregano

1 teaspoon ground cumin

6 teaspoons chili powder (to taste)

2 pounds canned tomatoes, not drained

Salt to taste

2 cups hot water

My Adaptation

Serves 2 to 4

— INGREDIENTS —

1 pound ground beef

1 small onion, chopped

2 garlic cloves, minced

½ teaspoon ground oregano

½ teaspoon ground cumin

2 to 3 teaspoons chili powder, to taste

1 can (14½ ounces) tomatoes, roughly cut into pieces, with tomato liquid

Modest squirt (¼ to ½ teaspoon) of tomato paste

Salt and pepper to taste

½ to ¾ cup hot water

— TO GARNISH —

2 to 4 jots of hot sauce

¼ cup grated sharp cheddar cheese

Handful of finely chopped fresh parsley

Smattering of diced raw onion

— PREPARATION —

Brown the beef, onion, and garlic in a Dutch oven over medium heat, stirring occasionally. Add the oregano, cumin, chili powder, tomatoes, tomato paste, salt and pepper, and hot water. Bring to a boil; then lower the heat and simmer. Skim off the fat, and occasionally stir the chili.

For Mrs. Johnson/Mrs. Wright's recipe, cover and cook for about an hour. They would sometimes add 1 or 2 tablespoons of masa (Mexican corn flour) to thicken the chili and give it depth.

For my adaptation, cook for 8 to 10 minutes uncovered, stirring occasionally. Then cover and simmer on low for another 30 to 35 minutes, making sure the chili doesn't stick to the pan. If too dry, add a splash of water (or tomato juice, stock, beer, or other liquid); if too wet, uncover, raise the heat slightly, and boil off the excess.

Garnish with hot sauce, grated cheese, and parsley to taste. Some like to add a sprinkling of diced raw onion, as in the original recipe.

I like to serve chili with rice or corn bread, as the Johnsons did.

★ ★ ★

Jimmy Carter's Grits

G rits is the first truly American food," wrote Turner Catledge, a native of Mississippi and the first executive editor at *The New York Times.* "On a day in the spring of 1607 when sea-weary members of the London Company came ashore at Jamestown, Va., they were greeted by a band of friendly Indians offering bowls of a steaming hot substance consisting of softened maize seasoned with salt and . . . bear grease. The welcomers called it 'rockahominie.' The settlers liked it so much they adopted it as a part of their own diet. They anglicized the name to 'hominy' and set about devising a milling process by which the large corn grains could be ground into smaller particles. . . . [G]rits became a gastronomic mainstay of the South and symbol of Southern culinary pride. . . . [T]his would be a much happier world if more of its millions had grits."

Carter was a famous devotee of grits, and especially liked it made with cheese and served with bacon and eggs at breakfast. Grits can be made humbly, with just water, butter, and salt, but at the White House the Swiss chef Henry Haller used a fancier recipe that he included in his book, *The White House Family Cookbook.*

— INGREDIENTS —

4 cups chicken bouillon	2 cups grated sharp cheddar cheese
1 cup enriched white hominy	4 egg yolks
1 teaspoon Worcestershire sauce	¼ to ½ cup cold milk
1 stick (½ cup) butter	4 egg whites, at room temperature

— PREPARATION —

Preheat the oven to 350 degrees.

Grease the inside of a 2-quart casserole.

Bring the bouillon to a boil in a 2-quart saucepan; gradually add the grits, stirring with a wire whisk. Reduce heat and continue cooking, stirring vigorously, until mixture thickens. Cover and cook for 15 minutes, stirring often.

Remove from the heat and add the Worcestershire sauce, butter, and 1½ cups of the cheese, stirring until well balanced.

In a small bowl, blend the egg yolks with ¼ cup of milk. Pour into grits and mix thoroughly; add more milk if necessary, thinning to the consistency of Cream of Wheat. In a clean, dry bowl, beat egg whites until stiff. Fold into grits.

Pour the mixture into the prepared baking dish. Sprinkle with the remaining ½ cup of cheese. Bake on middle shelf of preheated oven for 30 minutes or until fluffy and brown. Serve at once.

Acknowledgments

Every book, like every restaurant or political movement, is a collaborative effort, and in this case an exceptional number of people helped bring this book into the world. At heart it is a family project: *Dinner with the President* is dedicated to my parents, Hector and Erica Prud'homme, whose enthusiasms for food, entertaining, politics, and history—usually debated over dinner—set me on a path to consider the presidents and the White House through a gastronomic lens. Speaking of enthusiasms, my indefatigable grandaunt, Julia Child, who helped inspire my interest in this subject with her investigations of presidential food, is a recurring character and presiding intelligence in these pages. And, without a doubt, I could not have undertaken hours of research and written (and rewritten) these words without the amazing support, encouragement, and suggestions of my wife, Sarah, and our children. This book has been a long, sometimes challenging, COVID-delayed, but always fascinating, enlightening, and delicious journey. I am lucky and grateful to have had such a wonderful family sustain me along the way.

Of course there were many others whose generosity, fortitude, and curiosity helped this project. First and foremost, I have benefited from the calm, clear-eyed guidance of my editor, Lexy Bloom, who tweaked my words and tightened my logic to make this a better book. Lexy's able assistant, Morgan Hamilton, kept me on schedule and was helpful in my photo research. I also owe a debt to the copy editor, Ingrid Sterner, who carefully combed through my thicket of words, unsnarled malaprops, and corrected names and dates. And I would also like to thank Sarah New and Sara Eagle, as well as Cassandra Pappas for the book's design, Megan Wilson and John Gall for the jacket design, and Nicole Pedersen and Lorraine Hyland for shepherding the book through production.

I would not have gotten to this estimable crew at Alfred A. Knopf without the sage advice of my agent, Tina Bennett, whom I can always rely on for a wise word, a great pitch, and enthusiastic encouragement.

The presidency is a vast subject, and when it came to researching the food of the White House, I owe special thanks to Constance Carter. The former head of the Science Reference Section at the Library of Congress, she went above and beyond the call of duty to ferret out books, articles, and images—many of which I would never have discovered on my own—and introduce me to people like Betty Monkman, the former chief curator at the White House.

Another wonderful resource were the curators of *Julia Child's Kitchen*, and *FOOD: Transforming the American Table*, the popular exhibits at the Smithsonian's National Museum of American History, in Washington, D.C. I am particularly indebted to Rayna Green, Paula Johnson, Anthea Hartig, and Bethanee Bemis. Apropos of *Julia Child's Kitchen*, I tip my hat to my colleagues at the Julia Child Foundation for Gastronomy and the Culinary Arts, who are stalwart and encouraging.

None of the former presidents or First Ladies I reached out to were willing to talk to me about food. They are busy, of course, and entitled to their privacy; but I wondered if their reticence was due in part to the political nature of the subject, which can be touchy, or because the things we eat can be personally revealing. Nevertheless, I learned a lot about how our leaders lived by visiting their homes—the White House, of course, but also Washington's Mount Vernon; Jefferson's Monticello; and Madison's Montpelier in Virginia; the President Wilson House, in Washington, D.C.; Coolidge's family homestead in Plymouth Notch, Vermont; and Franklin D. Roosevelt's Springwood mansion, in Hyde Park, New York. I had planned further excursions, but COVID shut most historical sites down. I recommend everyone visit these places, even those who assume they are "boring" (they are not), because they bring history alive in a visceral and sometimes unexpected way: you should climb into the oculus atop Monticello to look over the fields once worked by slaves and down onto the University of Virginia campus in Charlottesville; see the fabulous gardens overlooking the Hudson River, the wheelchair ramps, and odd collection of birds that FDR taxidermied as a young man, at Hyde Park; taste the Coolidge family's Plymouth Cheese in Vermont, then visit Silent Cal's simple and dignified grave site nearby, for instance.

I also recommend presidential-adjacent historical sites, such as Valley Forge, Fraunces Tavern, Grant's Tomb, or Yosemite National Park. If you are curious about the subject, there are many museums dedicated to the presidency, or individual presidents, and I had a chance to visit a few of them, including the White House Visitor Center, the White House Historical Association, the Museum of the American Revolution, the Franklin D. Roosevelt Presidential Library and Museum, the John F. Kennedy Presidential Library and Museum, and the William J. Clinton Library and Museum.

As I began my research, I wanted to talk to White House chefs as much as to First Couples, and in that I succeeded beyond my hopes. It did not start well: I could not elicit a response from executive chef Cris Comerford, and by the time I tracked down Henry Haller—who had cooked for five presidents between 1966 and 1987—he had aged and, his wife explained, lost his recall (he died in 2020, at ninety-seven). But I eventually met a half dozen presidential cooks, and each one of them had tales to tell. I began with my old friend Jacques Pépin, who was offered the job as the Kennedys' chef, but declined in order to work for Howard Johnson's restaurant chain. Another Frenchman, the former executive pastry chef Roland Mesnier, was grumpy but amusing. And I had the pleasure of reconnecting with his successor, Bill Yosses, a gem of a human whom I have known since 1987, when we helped build Restaurant Bouley, in New York. I chatted with the Obamas' personal chef and food policy guru, Sam Kass, and got to know the Obamas' favorite Mexican chef, the wonderful Rick Bayless, a recipient of the Julia Child Award in 2016. I had a good time with the former White House sous-chef Frank Ruta, now a successful Washington restaurateur. And I enjoyed a lunch with Anita Lo, the acclaimed New York cook who was the first female guest chef to prepare a state dinner, which she did for Chinese president Xi Jinping in 2015. (Regretfully, Anita's stories, like many others, ended up on the cutting-room floor. But they were good, and maybe I'll return to them one day, or she will.) The most helpful of all was former executive chef John Moeller, who spent thirteen years cooking for presidents Bush Sr., Clinton, and Bush Jr. On President's Day 2020, Moeller whipped up an inspired meal, and shared stories from the First Kitchen, with a group I had gathered for "My Presidential Dinner," as I recount in the conclusion. *Merci*, chefs!

I had a lot of help pulling that presidential dinner together, and for her advice on party logistics, insights on the mores of Washington society, and an establishment Republican's take on the Trump administration, I owe much to George W. Bush's social secretary Lea Berman. She couldn't attend our presidential dinner, sadly. Nor could Jeremy Bernard, an Obama social secretary, and Berman's equally charming coauthor of *Treating People Well: The Extraordinary Power of Civility at Work and in Life*. But I am grateful to them, and to the guests who joined me on a cool, gray February evening for a warm meal and fascinating conversation about what happens behind the scenes at a state dinner.

Along with Chef Moeller, my dining companions that night included: James (Skip) Allen, a former White House usher under five administrations; Lauren Bernstein, a former state department officer and now CEO of the Culinary Diplomacy Project; Lloyd Hand, an attorney, LBJ's chief of protocol, and a gifted conversationalist; Corby Kummer, a James Beard Award–winning food writer and raconteur *extraordinaire;* Theresa McCulla, a food historian and curator at the Smithsonian's National Museum of American History; Betty Monkman, former chief White House curator; Roxanne Roberts, an insightful style reporter and columnist at *The Washington Post;* and Ann Stock, a social secretary for the Clintons and assistant secretary for education under the Obamas. It was a memorable night, and I appreciate their time and anecdotes.

Incidentally, we held "My Presidential Dinner" at the DACOR Bacon House, a historic mansion around the corner from the White House, and the staff there was graciously accommodating—especially the director of operations, Meg Sharley, and the director of communications, Christine Skodon.

As I researched this book, I spoke to a number of thoughtful food writers and restaurateurs, and I am grateful to the following for their time and expertise: Michael Pollan, a teacher, prolific journalist, and author of books such as *The Omnivore's Dilemma;* Alice Waters, the guiding force behind Chez Panisse restaurant and the Edible Schoolyard Project in Berkeley, California, and author; Dan Barber, the acclaimed chef at the two Blue Hill restaurants in New York, and author of *The Third Plate;* Laura Shapiro, a culinary historian and author of *What She Ate;* and Amy Bentley, a professor of nutrition and food studies at New York University, and author of *Inventing Baby Food.*

Speaking of academics, I had read about Dr. Richard Wrangham, a biological anthropologist at Harvard, who has written on the evolutionary importance of cooking with fire. Searching for more information, I stumbled over the *Gastropod* podcast, in which the hosts, Cynthia Graber and Nicola Twilley, interviewed Wrangham, as well as Robin Dunbar, who taught evolutionary psychology at Oxford, Brian Hayden, an archaeologist at Simon Fraser University, and Ayelet Fishbach, a professor of behavioral science at the University of Chicago. These experts revealed the complex underpinnings of human behavior when it comes to cooking, feasting, communal eating, and the way food connects us. Intrigued, I followed up with phone interviews with each of them, for which I am most appreciative.

Many thanks to friends old and new—Jeanne McCulloch, Tanya Steel, Deesha Dyer, Eddie Gehman Kohan, Becky Larimer, Barnet Schecter, and Louisa Spessot. And I am grateful to Hugh Davies and Matthew Levy of Schramsberg Vineyards, and enjoyed a presidential dinner with Victoria Flexner and Jay Reifel of Edible History at the Museum of Food and Drink.

When it came time for me to actually cook a few presidential recipes and mix some White House drinks, I spent wonderful hours leafing through cookbooks, memoirs, magazines, and, in the case of Dwight Eisenhower's "Two Day Vegetable Soup," consulting a facsimile of the hand-typed recipe he gave to the student editors of a Columbia University cookbook. It was a delight to meet Dr. Eric Colleary, who is a curator at the Harry Ransom Center at the University of Texas at Austin, and in his spare time presents historical recipes on his blog, *The American Table*. His experiments informed mine.

There were many friends who kept my spirits up, and offered help and advice along the way. Chief among those was Shaun Donovan, who, as the secretary of housing and urban development in the Obama administration, invited me to lunch in the Navy Mess, then led me on a whirlwind tour of the White House in 2016, an experience that helped seed this book. And Adam Van Doren, a talented painter who illustrated his book, *The House Tells the Story: Homes of the American Presidents,* and generously shared his knowledge and library with me.

Brooklyn, New York
June 2022

Notes

ABBREVIATIONS

GWMV George Washington's Mount Vernon, www.mountvernon.org
  NYT *New York Times,* www.nytimes.com
  TJM Thomas Jefferson's Monticello, www.monticello.org
WHHA White House Historical Association, www.whitehousehistory.org
   WP *Washington Post,* www.washingtonpost.com

INTRODUCTION At the President's Table

xiii On the evening of June 20, 1790: The details of this famous dinner scene are
      largely based on a reconstruction by the historian Charles A. Cerami, who relied
      on Jefferson's notes on the dinner and numerous other sources. Cerami, *Dinner
      at Mr. Jefferson's,* 117–37. Jefferson's account "The Compromise of 1790" appears
      in his introduction to the "Anas" (a compilation of his writing) of February 4,
      1818, excerpted in "Thomas Jefferson on the Compromise of 1790," Bill of Rights
      Institute, billofrightsinstitute.org.
xiv   "two of the most irritating questions": "Thomas Jefferson Residence," AllThings
      Hamilton.com.
xv   served by "dumbwaiters": Cerami, *Dinner at Mr. Jefferson's,* 129–30; "A Greater
      Eye to Convenience," TJM.
xv   "the attendance of servants": Smith, quoted in Cerami, *Dinner at Mr. Jefferson's,*
      126.
xvi   "a bitter pill to Virginia": Cerami, *Dinner at Mr. Jefferson's,* 133.
xvii saving Virginia $13 million: Ibid., 136.
xvii Known as the Dinner Table Bargain: "The Dinner Table Bargain," June 1790,
      American Experience, PBS, www.pbs.org. See also Chernow, *Alexander Hamilton,*
      326–31; Ellis, *Founding Brothers,* 48–76.
xvii "There is no single state paper": Cerami, *Dinner at Mr. Jefferson's,* 137.
xvii "The Room Where It Happens": "The Room Where It Happens," lyrics, Genius
      .com, Broadway Cast Recording, Sept. 25, 2015, genius.com.
xviii "fortress disguised as a home": Obama, *Becoming,* 325.
xviii "an emblem of the American Republic": *Jacqueline Kennedy Entertains: The Art
      of the White House Dinner* exhibit, John F. Kennedy Presidential Library and
      Museum, April 12, 2007–April 3, 2008, www.jfklibrary.org.
xx   the Navy Mess: WHInfo, the White House Mess, whitehouse.gov1.info.
xx   the *Sequoia,* was sold by Jimmy Carter: "Sold for $0: *Sequoia,* the Last US Presi-
      dential Yacht, Is Repossessed," *Guardian,* Nov. 14, 2016.
xx   jambalaya, a fragrant stew: Tipton-Martin, *Jubilee,* 173.

xx   Caesar salad: L. Sasha Gora, "The Surprising Truth About Caesar Salad," BBC Travel, May 22, 2019.

xx   The building stands 168 feet long: "White House Dimensions," WHHA.

xxi   (Chipped and broken pieces are destroyed): "Official White House China: From the 18th to the 21st Centuries," WHHA.

xxi   William Howard Taft (at some 350 pounds): Nora Krug, "An Article Outlines President William Howard Taft's Efforts to Lose Weight," WP, Oct. 14, 2013.

xxii   the White House, which was largely built by slaves: "Did Slaves Build the White House?," WHHA.

xxii   a First Lady descended from slaves: Bonnie Goldstein, "Obama Descended from Slave Ancestor," WP, July 30, 2012.

xxiv   "to show a side of the People's House": Julia and Paul Child Papers, Schlesinger Library, Radcliffe Institute for Advanced Study, Harvard University, quoted in Prud'homme, *French Chef in America,* 13.

xxiv   "She could charm a polecat": Ibid., 57.

xxv   "Many Americans who dislike": Ibid., 18.

xxv   Every minute of the evening: Ibid., 171.

xxv   Haller's menu—one of "the most memorable": Haller, *White House Family Cookbook,* 208.

xxvi   "is responsible for the nation's gastronomic image": Prud'homme, *French Chef in America,* 179.

xxvi   "the good in American cooking": Ibid.

xxvii   the story of Ronald Reagan's jelly beans: See notes for Chapter 16, "Ronald Reagan."

xxvii   The first group of Chinese immigrants arrived: Brad Cohen, "A Brief History of American Chinese Food," *USA Today,* June 14, 2017; Emelyn Rude, "A Very Brief History of Chinese Food in America," *Time,* Feb. 8, 2016.

xxviii   Chinese restaurants in the States: Jennifer 8. Lee, *The Fortune Cookie Chronicles,* March 23, 2009, fortunecookiechronicles.com.

1 · GEORGE WASHINGTON   The First Kitchen

4   spooned a slurry of mutton: Chernow, *Washington,* 328.

4   camp chest: "George Washington's Camp Chest," Smithsonian Institution, National Museum of American History, americanhistory.si.edu.

4   lost all but one of his teeth: "False Teeth," GWMV.

4   stained brown by the dark Madeira wine: "Wooden Teeth Myth," GWMV.

5   "a dreary kind of place": Chernow, *Washington,* 323.

5   Washington's fourteen thousand men: "Valley Forge," GWMV.

5   quartermaster reported: Ibid.

5   "devoured it with as keen an appetite": Martin, *Narrative of a Revolutionary Soldier,* 90.

5   "full of burnt leaves and dirt": Chernow, *Washington,* 325.

5   "fire cakes"—patties of flour and water: Ibid.; Mitchell, *Revolutionary Recipes,* 40–41.

5   three hundred head of cattle: Trumbull, *Jonathan Trumbull,* 226; Mitchell, *Revolutionary Recipes,* 39.

5   "literally naked": Nancy K. Loane, "The ABCs of the Valley Forge Encampment," *Journal of the American Revolution,* Nov. 1, 2016, 7.

5   a third of them had no shoes: Ibid., 10; "Valley Forge," GWMV.

5   bloody streaks in the snow: Chernow, *Washington,* 324.

6   Thirty percent of the army suffered: Ibid., 327.

6   "starve, dissolve, or disperse": Ibid.

6   "Happily, the real condition": Ibid.

6   flogging soldiers caught stealing food: Ibid.

6   "No bread, no soldier!": Ibid., 326.

6   He stood six feet two inches tall: The Presidents of the USA: Heights and Weights, presidenstory.com.

6   he once chased a single fox: Chernow, *Washington,* 125.

7   "avarice and thirst for gain": Ibid., 328–29.

7   "forage the country naked!": McDowell, *Revolutionary War,* 130.

7   filled with bushels of potatoes: Nancy K. Loane, "An Elegant Dinner with General Washington at Valley Forge Headquarters," *Journal of the American Revolution,* June 10, 2014, allthingsliberty.com.

7   "Instead of being blinded": Chernow, *Washington,* 328.

8   Washington's slave cooks, Hannah and Isaac: Loane, "Elegant Dinner with General Washington."

8   an early run of shad: Mitchell, *Revolutionary Recipes,* 41.

8   On May 6, Washington and fifteen hundred men: Chernow, *Washington,* 336; George Washington, "General Orders Headquarters, Valley Forge Sunday, March 1, 1778," Historic Valley Forge, www.ushistory.org.

8   "One might say that the whole revolutionary enterprise": Allgor, *Perfect Union,* 185.

9   in June 1776, Americans sympathetic to the British: Schecter, *Battle for New York,* 96.

9   "bountiful and elegant": Kimball, *Martha Washington Cook Book.*

9   a menu of more than twenty dishes: "George Washington's Last Meal with His Troops," Monday, Nov. 14, 2005, yourlastmealblogspot.

10 "the greatest character of the age": Gillian Brockell, "At the Nation's First Presidential Transfer of Power, George Washington Was 'Radiant,'" *WP,* Jan. 19, 2021.

10 Washington built a 7,600 acre property: "Growth of Mount Vernon," GWMV.

10 In 1775, Washington expanded the kitchen: "Kitchen," GWMV.

11 "swimming in butter and honey": "Hoecakes and Honey," GWMV.

11 "The cook is governed by the clock": Chernow, *Washington,* 580.

11 "Precisely at a quarter before three": G. W. Parke Gustis, *Recollections and Memoirs of Washington,* Lee Family Archive, 1859, leefamilyarchive.org.

11 "an absurd, and truly barbarous practice": "Dinner Etiquette," *Thomas Jefferson Encyclopedia,* TJM.

12 When Senator William Maclay visited: Robert C. Alberts, "The Cantankerous Mr. Maclay," *American Heritage,* Oct. 1974.

12 "entertained in a very handsome style": Ashbel Green, in "The True Story of George Washington: Social Life: As President," by Infoplease Staff, Feb. 28, 2017, www.infoplease.com.

12 "My manner of living is plain": "Keeping an 'Excellent Table' at Mount Vernon," GWMV.

12 "passages of peculiar interest": "Dining at Mount Vernon," GWMV.

12 "The chief part of my happiness": Washington to Warner Lewis, Aug. 14, 1755, Library of Congress, www.loc.gov.

12 On September 14, for instance, he was feted: Steve Hendricks, "The Epic Bender to Celebrate George Washington and the Newly Finished U.S. Constitution," *WP,* Feb. 22, 2018.

14 Martha Washington (who also wore dentures): Chernow, *Washington,* 642.

15 *A Booke of Cookery* and *A Booke of Sweatmeats:* Numerous versions of Mrs. Washington's books are available in print or online, including *Martha Washington Cook Book: A Compendium of Cookery and Reliable Recipes,* ed. E. Neill (Chicago: F. T. Neely, 1892); *Martha Washington's Booke of Cookery; and Booke of Sweetmeats,* ed. Karen Hess (New York: Columbia University Press, 1995).

15 she rarely, if ever, took to the stove: "Life at Mount Vernon Before the Presidency," Martha Washington: A Life, marthawashington.us.

15 three hundred and seventeen men, women, and children: "10 Facts About Washington and Slavery," GWMV.

16 Rachel Lewis, whose "dirty figure": Chernow, *Washington*, 637.

16 Great Cake—a white edifice: "Great Cake," GWMV.

16 slave cook Hercules: "Hercules," GWMV.

17 "a capital cook . . . a celebrated *artiste*": Ibid.

17 "Under his iron discipline": McLeod, *Dining with the Washingtons*, 25.

17 three bottles of rum: Ibid.

17 Hercules was allowed to sell slops: "Hercules," GWMV.

17 a face described as "homely": McLeod, *Dining with the Washingtons*, 25.

17 Richmond, join him in Philadelphia: Ibid.

17 In May 1796, Ona Judge slipped away: Chernow, *Washington*, 759–62.

18 "mortified to the last degree": Tobias Lear to Washington, June 5, 1791, Founders Online, National Archives, founders.archives.gov.

18 "keep them out of idleness and mischief": Craig LaBan, "A Birthday Shock from Washington's Chef," *Philadelphia Inquirer*, Feb. 22, 2010.

18 In early 1797, Hercules was sent outside: Ibid.

18 "appeared like a grove of moving plumes": Ibid.

18 "Are you deeply upset": Ibid.

18 In 1801, Hercules was spotted: Ibid.

19 "We are the only species": Richard Wrangham, *Catching Fire: How Cooking Made Us Human* (New York: Basic Books, 2009); Cynthia Graber and Nicola Twilley, "Shared Plates: How Eating Together Makes Us Human," *Gastropod*, podcast audio and transcript, June 2, 2020, gastropod.com; Wrangham, Zoom interview with author, Dec. 12, 2021.

19 cooking food essentially predigests it: Rachel Carmody, *SciCafe—The Raw Truth About Cooking with Rachel Carmody*, podcast, amnh.org, March 21, 2019; Peter Reuell, "Why Cooking Counts," *Harvard Gazette*, Nov. 7, 2011.

19 "Cooking completely transformed our biology": Wrangham, interview with the author, Dec. 12, 2021.

19 fire was controlled 40,000 years ago, and others saying it was 400,000 years ago: Ibid.; Rachel Moeller Gordon, "Evolving Bigger Brains Through Cooking: A Q&A with Richard Wrangham," *Scientific American*, Dec. 19, 2007.

20 site for the nation's permanent capital: Robert F. Dalzell Jr. and Lee Baldwin Dalzell, "Memory, Architecture, and the Future: George Washington, Mount Vernon, and the White House," in "White House History: George Washington: Houses and Palaces," special issue, *Journal of the White House Historical Association* 6 (Fall 1999): 38–49, issuu.com.

20 In December 1799, he toured Mount Vernon: Chernow, *Washington*, 806–9.

2 · JOHN ADAMS The First Host

23 codfish cakes and potatoes: Cannon and Brooks, *Presidents' Cookbook*, 43.

23 "the most insignificant office": Presidents, John Adams, WhiteHouse.gov, www.whitehouse.gov.

23 Money . . . was a constant worry: Edith B. Gelles, "The Paradox of High Station: Abigail Adams as First Lady," *White House History*, Collection 2, no. 7 (Spring 2000); Whitcomb and Whitcomb, *Real Life at the White House*, 11.

23 lemonade and ice cream: Stewart Mitchell, ed., *New Letters of Abigail Adams, 1788–1801* (Boston: Houghton Mifflin: 1947), 131.

24 due to Abigail's careful management: "Cradle of a Political Dynasty," *NYT*, Oct. 14, 2000.

24 "the most scandalous Drunkenness": Lindsay M. Chervinsky, "The Household of President John Adams," WHHA.

24 "drawing room service": "The President's House—Washington and Adams," theclio.com; Edward Lawler Jr., "The President's House in Philadelphia: A Brief History," Independence Hall Association, May 2010, ushistory.org.

24 In spite of eight years of construction: Jackie Craven, "Building the White House in Washington, D.C.," ThoughtCo., July 3, 2019, www.thoughtco.com.

24 a stolid building 168 feet long: "The White House Building," WhiteHouse.gov, www.whitehouse.gov.

24 Adams found the north door: Paul Brandus, "Nov. 1, 1800: The White House Welcomes Its First President—John Adams," *West Wing Reports,* June 27, 2015, medium.com.

25 "the great castle": "John Adams Moves into White House," This Day in History, Nov. 1, 1800, History.com, www.history.com; Whitcomb and Whitcomb, *Real Life at the White House,* 10.

25 "Even the most trifling articles": Betty C. Monkman, "John and Abigail Adams: A Tradition Begins," WHHA.

25 "I pray Heaven to bestow": Presidents, John Adams, WhiteHouse.gov.

25 He wrote Abigail plaintive letters: Gelles, "Paradox of High Station."

25 She had settled into a rhythm: Ibid.; Harris, *First Ladies Fact Book,* 34, 36.

26 Congress bequeathed the house: Monkman, "John and Abigail Adams."

26 "If we mean to have Heroes": Abigail Adams to John Adams, Aug. 14, 1776, Founders Online, National Archives, founders.archives.gov.

26 Mrs. Adams rolled up her sleeves: Cannon and Brooks, *Presidents' Cookbook,* 39.

26 her husband's $25,000 salary: Ibid., 40.

26 congressmen and "their appendages": Gelles, "Paradox of High Station."

26 "Turtle and every other thing": Cannon and Brooks, *Presidents' Cookbook,* 42.

27 "As we are here": Abigail Adams to Mary Smith Crouch, June 23, 1797, Adams Family Correspondence, vol. 12, Massachusetts Historical Society, www.mass hist.org.

27 Slowed by ill health: Gelles, "Paradox of High Station."

27 restocked her tea service: Monkman, "John and Abigail Adams."

27 citizens' hunger for a presidential housewarming: Graber and Twilley, "Shared Plates"; R. I. M. Dunbar, "Breaking Bread: The Functions of Social Eating," *Adaptive Human Behavior and Physiology,* March 11, 2017; Dunbar, Zoom interview with the author, Jan. 6, 2022.

28 "commensality," a term borrowed from biology: Adam Gopnik, "Sarah Huckabee Sanders and Who Deserves a Place at the Table," *New Yorker,* June 25, 2018; Kerner, Chou, and Warmind, *Commensality,* 1–6.

29 New Year's Day 1801: Cannon and Brooks, *Presidents' Cookbook,* 41.

29 "I held levees once a week": Ibid., 42.

3 · THOMAS JEFFERSON America's Founding Epicure

31 "We are all Republicans, we are all Federalists": "First Inauguration," TJM; Whitcomb and Whitcomb, *Real Life at the White House,* 15.

31 "the lowest and coldest seat": Smith, *First Forty Years of Washington Society,* 12.

31 Standing six feet two and a half inches tall: "Jefferson's Height," TJM.

31 who owned six hundred men, women, and children: Lina Mann, "The Enslaved Household of President Thomas Jefferson," WHHA.

31 "our most illustrious epicure": Hess, quoted in "Thomas Jefferson's Legacy in Farming and Food," TJM.

32 "big enough for two emperors": Frederick Platt, "The Chatter's Back at the Most Visited Home in the World," *NYT,* Jan. 26, 1975.

32   an $83 million debt: National Park Service, Secretary of the Treasury, "The National Debt," www.nps.gov.

32   his Washington "family": "Dining with Congress," TJM.

32   "as great [a] difficulty": Ibid.

33   Lemaire recorded his purchases: Fowler, *Dining at Monticello*, 16.

33   Eventually, Jefferson secured Honoré Julien: "Dining with Congress," TJM.

33   Jefferson's diet was unusual: David Kamp, "The United States of Arugula," *NYT*, Oct. 1, 2006.

34   Jefferson considered "animal food": "Vegetarianism," TJM.

34   "Never before had such dinners been given": "Dining with Congress," TJM.

34   "What he did eat": Whitcomb and Whitcomb, *Real Life at the White House*, 17.

34   began hosting three congressional dinners a week: "Dining with Congress," TJM.

34   "rice soup, round of beef": Ibid.

35   the recipe for vanilla ice cream: "Ice Cream," TJM.

35   "cultivate personal intercourse with the members": "Dining with Congress," TJM.

35   "Neither could he [anywhere else]": Ibid.

35   "Traditional feasts were entertainment": Brian Hayden, "How the Village Feast Paved the Way to Empires and Economics," *Aeon*, Nov. 16, 2016, aeon.co.

36   "make the empire go 'round": Hayden in Graber and Twilley, "Shared Plates."

36   "If you want to build the pyramids": Hayden, interview with the author, Dec. 18, 2021.

36   "Feasts tend to be competitive": Hayden, "How the Village Feast Paved the Way to Empires and Economics."

36   Jefferson used the semiotics: Cannon and Brooks, *Presidents' Cookbook*, 58–59; Graber and Twilley, "Shared Plates"; Hayden, interview with the author, Dec. 18, 2021.

37   "It was the object of Mr. Jefferson": "Dinner Etiquette," TJM.

37   "a great influence on the conversational powers": "Dining with Congress," TJM.

37   "When brought together in society": "Dinner Etiquette," TJM.

37   "she will have to eat her soup": Cannon and Brooks, *Presidents' Cookbook*, 59.

38   "greatest cheese in America": "Mammoth Cheese," TJM.

38   "While I wish to have every thing good": "Dining with Congress," TJM.

38   an annual salary of $25,000: Tom Murse, "Presidential Salaries Through the Years," ThoughtCo., Jan. 19, 2021, www.thoughtco.com.

38   $50 a day on provisions: Drake Baer, "Feasts Kind of Invented Civilization," The Cut, Nov. 22, 2016.

38   the manifest for an 1806 shipment: Fowler, *Dining at Monticello*, 16–17.

38   "Let the price be what it has to be": Tobias Beard, "The Pursuit of Happiness," *C-ville Weekly*, April 8, 2008.

39   "vivacious," "impulsive," and "beautiful": Various sources in "Martha Wayles Skelton," TJM.

39   "song and merriment and laughter": Martha Wayles Skelton Jefferson, George W. Bush White House Archives, georgewbush-whitehouse.archives.gov.

39   "ten years of unchequered happiness": "Our Breakfast Table," TJM.

39   "with cookery book in hand": Fowler, *Dining at Monticello*, 20–21.

39   "A single event wiped away": "Martha Wayles Skelton," TJM.

39   relationship between food and grief: Amelia Nierenberg, "For Many Widows, the Hardest Part Is Mealtime," *NYT*, Oct. 28, 2019.

40   "emerging from the stupor of mind": Thomas Jefferson, Library of Congress, www.loc.gov.

40   "violent burst[s] of grief": E. M. Halliday, *Understanding Thomas Jefferson* (New York: HarperCollins, 2001), 49.

40   "Behold me at length": Betty Goss, "Paris," Nov. 2008, TJM.

40   Mathurin Roze de Chantoiseau's consommé shop: Rebecca L. Spang, "The Invention of the Restaurant," www.rebeccalspang.org.

40   Grande Taverne de Londres: "La Grande Taverne de Londres," *Britannica,* www
      .britannica.com.
41   "run a couple of sacks": Jefferson to Edward Rutledge, July 14, 1787, Founders
      Online, National Archives, founders.archives.gov.
41   "He has abjured his native victuals": Fowler, *Dining at Monticello,* 2.
41   "no apple here to compare": Ibid., 3–4.
41   "for the particular purpose": Ibid., 3.
41   Hemings began his tutorial: "James Hemings," TJM; Edward White, "America's
      First Connoisseur," *Paris Review,* May 21, 2020.
42   Jefferson paid Hemings 24 livres: "James Hemings," TJM.
42   Hemings was made *chef de cuisine:* "The Culinary Legacy of James Hemings,"
      TJM.
42   Paris was home to more than half a million people: "The Life of Sally Hemings,"
      TJM.
42   "this Wide Blot On American . . . Civilisation": "Marquis de Lafayette," TJM.
43   Sally Hemings was trained as their maid: "The Life of Sally Hemings," TJM.
43   "moral and political depravity": "Jefferson's Attitudes Toward Slavery," TJM.
43   his heirs broke up slave families: "Debt," TJM.
43   "as his concubine, one of his own slaves": Thomas Jefferson Papers, 1800–1809,
      Library of Congress, www.loc.gov.
43   In a spate of 2017 media reports: Shaun King, "Thomas Jefferson Was a Horrible
      Man Who Owned 600 Human Beings, Raped Them, and Literally Worked Them
      to Death," New York *Daily News,* July 7, 2017.
43   "Not a victim but an agent of change?": Britni Danielle, "Sally Hemings Wasn't
      Thomas Jefferson's Mistress. She Was His Property," *WP,* July 7, 2017.
44   "the issue is a settled historical matter": "Monticello Affirms Thomas Jefferson
      Fathered Children with Sally Hemings," TJM.
44   John Wayles, had fathered the mixed-race Sally: "John Wayles," TJM.
44   "wasn't Jefferson's mistress; she was his property": Danielle, "Sally Hemings
      Wasn't Thomas Jefferson's Mistress."
44   the word "rape" is linked to appetite: Originally suggested by Helen Rosner,
      "Mario Batali and the Appetites of Men," *New Yorker,* Dec. 13, 2017.
44   spiking the price of bread: Lisa Bramen, "When Food Changed History: The
      French Revolution," *Smithsonian Magazine,* July 14, 2011.
45   Jefferson offered his apartment: "French Revolution," TJM.
45   He brought a few souvenirs: William Short to Jefferson, Nov. 7, 1790, Founders
      Online, National Archives, founders.archives.gov.
45   "The taste of [America was] artificially created": "Wine," TJM.
45   Jefferson waxed poetic about his favorites: Ibid.
45   "disguised in drink": "Memoirs of a Monticello Slave, as Dictated to Charles
      Campbell by Isaac" (1847), wps.prenhall.com.
46   the chef was paid $7 a month: "James Hemings," TJM.
46   "Having been at great expence": Ibid.
46   James was a free man: White, "America's First Connoisseur."
46   "is not given up to drink": Thomas Jefferson to Mary Jefferson, May 25, 1797,
      Founders Online, National Archive, founders.archives.gov.
47   Gordon-Reed speculates: White, "America's First Connoisseur."
47   committed suicide in Baltimore at age thirty-six: "James Hemings," TJM.
47   "There is not a sprig of grass": Jefferson to Martha Jefferson Randolph, Dec. 23,
      1790, Jefferson Quotes and Family Letters," TJM.
47   "Agriculture is our wisest pursuit": Jefferson to George Washington, Aug. 14,
      1787, Jefferson Quotes and Family Letters, TJM.
47   Over sixty years of farming: Nicole Cotroneo Jolly, "Thomas Jefferson's Farming
      Failures," *Modern Farmer,* Oct. 24, 2013.
48   "extremely elegant [meals] cooked": "Edith Hern Fossett," TJM.

48 Frances "Franny" Gillette Hern: "Much to Our Comfort and Satisfaction: Monticello's Enslaved Cooks," TJM.

48 This displaced Peter Hemings: "Peter Hemings," TJM.

48 Jefferson organized his garden: "Attending to My Farm," TJM.

48 "the best wine countries": Ibid.

48 His crops rarely turned a profit: Jolly, "Thomas Jefferson's Farming Failures."

49 Peter Hemings, who was bought: Nick Charles, "Meet James and Peter Hemings, America's First Black Celebrity Chefs," NBC News, Feb. 13, 2020, www.nbcnews.com.

49 Four hundred thousand people tour Monticello: "Monticello and the Big Clean," Jan. 14, 2019, TJM.

49 In 2011, Alice Waters: Laura Moser, "All the President's Produce," *Wall Street Journal,* April 27, 2012; Jane Black, "A Renowned Chef Inspires a Culinary Revolution at Monticello," *NYT,* Sept. 25, 2019.

49 "It's a great improvement": Waters, conversation with the author at Monticello, Sept. 21, 2019, and phone interview, Oct. 28, 2019.

49 The space was equipped: Fowler, *Dining at Monticello,* 25.

49 to wind the clock: Ibid., 19.

50 220-square-foot wine cave: Sandy Hausman, "Thomas Jefferson's Love Affair—with Wine," NPR, Sept. 28, 2008.

50 In 2017 the original hearth: "Uncovering the Stew Stoves in Monticello's First Kitchen," TJM video, March 14, 2017.

50 "I was a big admirer of Jefferson": White, conversation with the author, Monticello Heritage Harvest Festival, Sept. 21, 2019; White, interview with the author, Dec. 16, 2019; Dan Pashman, "When Black Chefs Created Plantation Food," *Sporkful with Dan Pashman,* podcast audio and transcript, Oct. 21, 2019, www.sporkful.com.

4 · JAMES MADISON
To Jemmy's Health, and Dolley's Remorseless Equanimity

52 "Poor Jemmy! He is but a withered little apple-John": Cannon and Brooks, *Presidents' Cookbook,* 80.

52 in a blink, she lost her husband, a son: "Becoming America's First Lady," Montpelier.org, www.montpelier.org.

52 "the great little Madison": Whitcomb and Whitcomb, *Real Life at the White House,* 28.

52 Dolley's aptly named son Payne: Ibid., 30, 34.

53 Montpelier relied on nearly a hundred slaves: "Becoming America's First Lady."

53 claimed to be uninterested in politics ("men's work"): Whitcomb and Whitcomb, *Real Life at the White House,* 28.

53 befriending Elizabeth Merry: "Becoming America's First Lady."

53 "The accomplished Mrs. Madison": Mary Ellen Scofield, "Unraveling the Dolley Myths," WHHA.

53 Dolley's "conciliatory disposition": "Becoming America's First Lady."

54 "a stage from which to convey": Scofield, "Unraveling the Dolley Myths."

54 a veteran French steward, Jean-Pierre . . . Sioussat: Whitcomb and Whitcomb, *Real Life at the White House,* 30.

54 "the trouble of serving guests": Cannon and Brooks, *Presidents' Cookbook,* 82.

54 showcased special or regional dishes: Ibid., 84–95.

54 a Yard of Flannel punch: Ibid., 94.

54 "collection of great and little men": Scofield, "Unraveling the Dolley Myths."

55 "alarm'd [the Federalists] into a return": "Becoming America's First Lady."

55 "a magic influence": Ibid.

55 "perfect security from hostility": Women and the American Story, Resource 4, "Parties and Politics," New-York Historical Society, blog.nyhsdev2.org.

55 "By her deportment in her own house": Allgor, *Perfect Union,* 195.

55 "There is something very fascinating": Scofield, "Unraveling the Dolley Myths."

55 "the worst Congress ever dealt a president": Seale, *The White House Actors and Observers,* 27.

55 accused him of offering to trade sex with Dolley: "Becoming America's First Lady."

55 "the only permanent power in Washington": Henry Schenawolf, "James Madison: Champion of Democracy and Father of Our Constitution," *Revolutionary War Journal,* Jan. 19, 2021, www.revolutionarywarjournal.com.

55 "The superior food, the lovely setting": Allgor, *Perfect Union,* 185.

56 Dolley's "remorseless equanimity": Daniel Fleming, "When Dolley Madison Took Command of the White House," *Smithsonian Magazine,* March 2010.

57 "I set the table myself": Cannon and Brooks, *Presidents' Cookbook,* 83.

57 "a bountiful dinner spread": Ibid.

57 "to 'Jemmy's health'": Fleming, "When Dolley Madison Took Command of the White House."

57 "No one . . . who beheld the radiance of joy": Allgor, *Perfect Union,* 333.

5 · ABRAHAM LINCOLN   Corn, Gingerbread, and Thanksgiving

59 Standing about six feet four inches: David Sim, "In Pictures: Tallest U.S. Presidents in History," *Newsweek,* March 23, 2018.

59 he had weighed a robust 180 pounds: Whitcomb and Whitcomb, *Real Life at the White House,* 130.

59 "seemed unlikely to live": Ibid., 138.

59 Breakfast was one egg . . . Lunch was a biscuit: Mitchell, *Presidential Flavors,* 81–82; Eighmey, *Abraham Lincoln in the Kitchen,* 210.

60 meals featuring his favorite foods: Mitchell, *Presidential Flavors,* 83–84.

60 "Both parties deprecated the war": "Lincoln's Second Inaugural Address," Lincoln Memorial, nps.gov.

60 "eight-dollar plug-hat": Whitcomb and Whitcomb, *Real Life at the White House,* 139.

60 One night, he dreamed that someone: Ibid., 140.

60 "a great public reception": Ibid., 139–40.

61 "The White House looked as if a regiment": Ibid.

61 "I could not help thinking": Amy Henderson, "If Only Hollywood Would Show Us Lincoln's Second Inaugural," *Smithsonian Magazine,* Jan. 15, 2013, www.smithsonianmag.com.

61 Four thousand revelers strolled: Ibid.

61 "Mr. Lincoln was evidently trying": "The Inauguration Ball," *NYT,* March 8, 1865.

62 a 250-foot-long table: "'The Honor of Your Company Is Requested': Lincoln's Second Inaugural Ball at the Patent Office (Teaching with Historic Places)," National Park Service, www.nps.gov.

62 heaped with exquisitely prepared food: "Bill of Fare of the Presidential Inauguration Ball," Library of Congress, www.loc.gov.

62 the confectioner G. A. Balzer: Cannon and Brooks, *Presidents' Cookbook,* 235–36.

62 "ornamental pyramids—nougat, orange, caramel": Ibid.

62 "The onset of the crowd": *Washington Evening Star,* 2nd ed., March 8, 1865, 25, cited in "'Honor of Your Company Is Requested.'"

62 "In less than an hour the table was a wreck": "Inauguration Ball," *NYT.*

63 "some premonition that there would": Whitcomb and Whitcomb, *Real Life at the White House,* 140.

63 "Abe was a moderate eater": Cannon and Brooks, *Presidents' Cookbook,* 237.

63 "Abraham was a good and hearty eater": Eighmey, *Abraham Lincoln in the Kitchen,* 36.

63 "Mr. Lincoln . . . never lost his tastes": Cannon and Brooks, *Presidents' Cookbook,* 236.

64 Despite Kentucky's bounty: McCreary, *Lincoln's Table,* 10; Eighmey, *Abraham Lincoln in the Kitchen,* 38.

64 Apples were a useful fruit: McCreary, *Lincoln's Table,* 12–13.

64 "There is no grain grown in the U.S.": Eighmey, *Abraham Lincoln in the Kitchen,* 10.

65 "eat corn cakes twice as fast": McCreary, *Lincoln's Table,* 3.

65 "Abe . . . [would] put a book inside his shirt": Eighmey, *Abraham Lincoln in the Kitchen,* 10.

65 die of "milk sickness": McCreary, *Lincoln's Table,* 22.

65 Thomas Lincoln married Sarah "Sally" Bush Johnston: Ibid.

65 Sally died in childbirth: Ibid., 30.

65 a muscular 220 pounds: Ibid., ix.

65 "Long Nine": Ibid., 38.

66 "Miss Todd, I wish to dance with you": McCreary, *Lincoln's Table,* 39.

66 Her sisters did not approve: Ibid., 40.

66 She bought eleven pounds of sugar: Eighmey, *Abraham Lincoln in the Kitchen,* 122.

66 Courting Cake: Cannon and Brooks, *Presidents' Cookbook,* 256.

66 "the best cake": Eighmey, *Abraham Lincoln in the Kitchen,* 88–89.

66 "My wife is as handsome": Harris, *First Ladies Fact Book,* 237.

66 Mary Todd Lincoln hired women, or relied on relatives: Temple, *Taste Is in My Mouth a Little,* 33.

66 Eliza Leslie's best-selling *Directions for Cookery:* Ibid., 32.

67 in the 1980s when archaeologists excavated: Eighmey, *Abraham Lincoln in the Kitchen,* 168; Temple, *Taste Is in My Mouth a Little,* 137–41.

67 a Royal Oak #9: Eighmey, *Abraham Lincoln in the Kitchen,* 169.

67 "the original gorilla": Mark Bowden, " 'Idiot,' 'Yahoo,' 'Original Gorilla': How Lincoln Was Dissed in His Day," *Atlantic,* June 2013.

67 "The taste *is* in my mouth a little": Lincoln to Lyman Trumbull, April 29, 1870, in *Collected Works of Abraham Lincoln,* vol. 4, *1809–1865,* quod.lib.umich.edu.

67 "the Hoosier and the Gingerbread Men": Eighmey, *Abraham Lincoln in the Kitchen,* 22–23; McCreary, *Lincoln's Table,* 16; Cannon and Brooks, *Presidents' Cookbook,* 253.

68 "the pleasures of life": "Lincoln's Favorite Foods," everythinglincoln.com.

68 his first encounter with the Democratic senator: Eighmey, *Abraham Lincoln in the Kitchen,* 22–23.

68 "species of humbuggery": Lincoln's rebuttal, 6th Lincoln-Douglas debate, Quincy, Ill., Oct. 13, 1858, www.nps.gov.

68 Mary went to sleep early: McCreary, *Lincoln's Table,* 66.

69 "I have no purpose": Abraham Lincoln, First Inaugural Address (final version), Lincoln Papers, Library of Congress: Series 1, General Correspondence, 1833–1916, www.loc.gov.

69 Willard's Hotel for an inaugural luncheon: McCreary, *Lincoln's Table,* 67; Eighmey, *Abraham Lincoln in the Kitchen,* 205–6.

69 Buchanan was a gourmand fond of duck: Cannon and Brooks, *Presidents' Cookbook,* 225, 230.

69 Cornelia Mitchell: Temple, *Taste Is in My Mouth a Little,* 44–45; Adrian Miller, *President's Kitchen Cabinet,* 44–45; James B. Conroy, "Slavery's Mark on Lincoln's White House," WHHA.

69   Harriet Lane, a blonde woman: Cannon and Brooks, *Presidents' Cookbook,* 220.

70   French chef Charles Gautier: Ibid.

70   Mary spent lavishly on silk brocade dresses: Whitcomb and Whitcomb, *Real Life at the White House,* 132–33.

70   The federal government granted her $20,000: Cannon and Brooks, *Presidents' Cookbook,* 232.

70   "smiling guests [would] pull her to pieces": Ibid., 233.

70   "Gallo-American" menu: Eighmey, *Abraham Lincoln in the Kitchen,* 206.

70   hailed her "exquisite taste": Cannon and Brooks, *Presidents' Cookbook,* 233.

70   lead to a "horrible jam": Ibid., 234.

70   elaborate decorations—a model: Ibid.

71   "Never make any preparation of which alcohol": McCreary, *Lincoln's Table,* 74.

71   "one of the finest displays": Cannon and Brooks, *Presidents' Cookbook,* 233.

71   accused her of outrageous "leniency": McCreary, *Lincoln's Table,* 74.

71   sickened by drinking Washington's water: Whitcomb and Whitcomb, *Real Life at the White House,* 134.

71   "his mother's favorite child": Brady Dennis, "Willie Lincoln's Death: A Private Agony for a President Facing a Nation in Pain," *WP,* Oct. 7, 2011.

72   "a judgment of God upon the Lincolns": Cannon and Brooks, *Presidents' Cookbook,* 235.

72   It was largely due to Sarah Josepha Hale: Ariel Knobel, "For Decades, Southern States Considered Thanksgiving an Act of Northern Aggression," *Gastro Obscura,* Nov. 22, 2018, www.atlasobscura.com.

73   Southerners resented the "repugnant" idea: Ibid.

73   "this theatrical claptrap of Thanksgiving": Ibid.

73   "a day of Thanksgiving and Praise": Transcript for President Abraham Lincoln's Thanksgiving Proclamation from Oct. 3, 1863, obamawhitehouse.archives .gov.

73   Texas refused to declare: Valerie Strauss, "Why We Celebrate Thanksgiving Every Year. It Isn't What You Think," *WP,* Nov. 24, 2016.

73   baking sweet potato pie with bourbon: Knobel, "For Decades, Southern States Considered Thanksgiving an Act of Northern Aggression."

74   the "first Thanksgiving" in America: Rebecca Beatrice Brooks, "History of the First Thanksgiving," *History of Massachusetts Blog,* Aug. 31, 2011, historyof massachusetts.org.

75   the Wampanoags brought five deer and does not mention turkey: Maya Salam, "Everything You Learned About Thanksgiving Is Wrong," *NYT,* Nov. 21, 2017.

75   the "first" Thanksgiving meal between Native Americans and Europeans: Gillian Brockell, "Thanksgiving's Hidden Past: Plymouth in 1621 Wasn't Close to Being the First Celebration," *WP,* Nov. 22, 2017.

75   David Silverman of George Washington University: Claire Bugos, "The Myths of the Thanksgiving Story and the Lasting Damage They Imbue," *Smithsonian Magazine,* Nov. 26, 2019, www.smithsonianmag.com.

75   In 1616, the Wampanoag were devastated by "the Great Dying": Dana Hedgpeth, "This Tribe Helped the Pilgrims Survive for Their First Thanksgiving. They Still Regret It 400 Years Later," *WP,* Nov. 4, 2021.

75   "national day of mourning": "What Does Thanksgiving Mean to Native Americans?," *Native Hope,* blog.nativehope.org.

75   "the next 100 years": Charles M. Blow, "The Horrible History of Thanksgiving," *NYT,* Nov. 27, 2019.

75   In King Philip's War: Áine Cain and Joey Hadden, "The True Story Behind Thanksgiving Is a Bloody One, and Some People Say It's Time to Cancel the Holiday," *Insider,* Nov. 24, 2020, www.insider.com.

75   in 1769, when New Englanders: Bugos, "Myths of the Thanksgiving Story."

76   "the first Thanksgiving, the great festival": Ibid.

77 "he promised to go": Doris Kearns Goodwin, "The Night Abraham Lincoln Was Assassinated," *Smithsonian Magazine,* April 8, 2015, www.smithsonianmag.com.

77 army surgeon, following protocol: Temple, *Taste Is in My Mouth a Little,* 87.

77 "I had an ambition to be Mrs. President": Whitcomb and Whitcomb, *Real Life at the White House,* 141.

6 · ULYSSES S. GRANT
The Drunken Tanner, the Military Genius, and the First State Dinner

79 "we are living at the absolute pinnacle": Cannon and Brooks, *Presidents' Cookbook,* 277–78.

79 hunks of roast beef, turkey: Chernow, *Grant,* 647.

79 Hiram Ulysses Grant (the "S." in his name): Evan Andrews, "10 Things You May Not Know About Ulysses S. Grant," History.net, July 23, 2015, www.history.com.

79 he was nicknamed Useless: Whitcomb and Whitcomb, *Real Life at the White House,* 153.

79 "always aching for a fight": Ibid., 153–54.

79 lost in civilian purgatory: Ibid., 154.

80 "Unconditional Surrender Grant": Ibid.

80 "No, but I do not see": Chernow, *Grant,* 614.

80 Speaking in a soft voice: President Ulysses S. Grant's First Inaugural Address, March 4, 1869, Ulysses S. Grant National Historic Site, National Park Service, www.nps.gov.

80 When he told the organizers: Chernow, *Grant,* 633.

80 several women passed out: Ibid.

81 "Grant's whole character was a mystery": Whitcomb and Whitcomb, *Real Life at the White House,* 159.

81 dubbed "the butcher": Ibid., 154.

81 "practically to charcoal": Cannon and Brooks, *Presidents' Cookbook,* 281.

81 roll bits of bread into spitballs: Ibid., 280–81; Whitcomb and Whitcomb, *Real Life at the White House,* 156.

82 "that tribe of Dents": Jensen, *White House and Its Thirty-Five Families,* 103.

82 War of the Geezers: Ibid., 103.

82 strabismus, or crossed eyes: Whitcomb and Whitcomb, *Real Life at the White House,* 155.

83 With fifty-three thousand citizens: Chernow, *Grant,* 644–45.

83 Washington, D.C., remained a small town: Ibid., 645–46.

83 "damp and unhealthy": Jensen, *White House and Its Thirty-Five Families,* 106.

84 The East Room was done over: Whitcomb and Whitcomb, *Real Life at the White House,* 155.

84 his new billiard room: Chernow, *Grant,* 646; Whitcomb and Whitcomb, *Real Life at the White House,* 159.

84 $20 speeding ticket: Whitcomb and Whitcomb, *Real Life at the White House,* 159.

84 Julia held public receptions: Cannon and Brooks, *Presidents' Cookbook,* 281.

84 "In the Blue Room the President's wife": Jensen, *White House and Its Thirty-Five Families,* 104.

84 inviting the wives of senators and cabinet members: Chernow, *Grant,* 647; "First Lady Biography: Julia Grant," firstladies.org.

84 "The gorgeous costumes of the diplomats": Jensen, *White House and Its Thirty-Five Families,* 105.

84 "brilliant" and "elegant" soirees: Ibid.

85 "pink grenadine, with flounced over-skirt": Ibid., 106.

85 "I'd rather storm a fort!": Cannon and Brooks, *Presidents' Cookbook,* 281.

85 He'd rise at 7:00 a.m. to read: Ibid., 280.

85 Used to spartan rations of cucumbers: Ibid., 281; Kat Kinsman, "Ulysses S. Grant Enjoyed a Morning Cucumber," *Extra Crispy*, MyRecipes, Feb. 13, 2018, www .myrecipes.com.

85 steward named Valentino Melah: "Orphan Becomes White House Steward," WHHA.

85 Known as "the Silver Voiced Italian": McCabe, *Behind the Scenes in Washington*, 376, 381.

85 "aristocratic stew": "Orphan Becomes White House Steward," WHHA; Cannon and Brooks, *Presidents' Cookbook*, 278.

86 One newspaperwoman under Melah's spell: McCabe, *Behind the Scenes in Washington*, 381, 382.

86 a large, flower-draped mirror: Chernow, *Grant*, 647.

86 Grant invited only those he wanted to see: Jensen, *White House and Its Thirty-Five Families*, 104.

86 food bill for Prince Arthur: Cannon and Brooks, *Presidents' Cookbook*, 279; Jensen, *White House and Its Thirty-Five Families*, 106.

86 "I have visited many courts": Chernow, *Grant*, 647.

86 New Year's reception for the public in 1873: Cannon and Brooks, *Presidents' Cookbook*, 279.

87 "Andy ain't a drunkard": Whitcomb and Whitcomb, *Real Life at the White House*, 148–49. This familiar quotation has been disputed; see responses to Jonathan R. Allen, "Andrew Johnson Drunk at Lincoln's Second Inauguration," *The Civil War* (blog), www.nellaware.com.

87 "a drunken tailor": Chernow, *Grant*, 649.

87 "He had very poor brains for drinking": Ibid., 84.

88 He slurred his words "foolishly": Ibid., 80.

88 he'd throw up or suffer the delirium tremens: Ibid., 58.

88 "Liquor seemed a virulent poison to him": Ibid., 80.

88 George B. McClellan, found his lapses: Ibid., 80–81.

88 "Overwhelming evidence suggests that Grant resigned": Ibid., 85–86; "Was Ulysses S. Grant an Alcoholic? An Analysis of Claims Made by Ron Chernow," *Exploring the Past* (blog), Nov. 7, 2018, pastexplore.wordpress.com.

88 "I got in a depressed condition": Chernow, *Grant*, 85.

88 "then Grant was the drunken": Ibid., 649.

89 Grant celebrated his second inauguration: Cannon and Brooks, *Presidents' Cookbook*, 278.

89 Known as the Merrie Monarch: Steve Hendrix, "'Brilliant Beyond All Precedent': The First White House State Dinner for the King of Hawaii," *WP*, April 25, 2018.

90 probably domesticated in prehistoric New Guinea: Tim Denham, "Early Agriculture and Plant Domestication in New Guinea and Island Southeast Asia," *Current Anthropology* 52, no. S4 (Oct. 2011), 379–95.

90 In Hawaii, the first sugar mill: Peter T. Young, "Sugar, the Early Years," *Images of Old Hawaiʻi*, Dec. 3, 2021, imagesofoldhawaii.com.

91 Sugar planters imported workers: "History of Labor in Hawaiʻi," Center for Labor Education & Research, University of Hawaiʻi–West Oʻahu.

91 He was greeted by a full marine battalion: Douglas V. Askman, "Our Royal Guest: American Press Coverage of King Kalākaua's Visit to the United States, 1874–1875," *The Hawaiian Journal of History* 54 (Honolulu: Hawaiian Historical Society, 2020).

91 "no young ladies present": Hendrix, "'Brilliant Beyond All Precedent.'"

92 Sandwich Islanders feasted on up to thirty courses: Cannon and Brooks, *Presidents' Cookbook*, 278; "General Grant's Birthday Dinner," in Ziemann and Gillette, *White House Cook Book*, 504.

92 "No soup, foreign or domestic": McCabe, *Behind the Scenes in Washington,* 381.

92 Kalakaua brought two guards: Cannon and Brooks, *Presidents' Cookbook,* 278.

92 value of exports from Hawaii: Kuykendall, *Kalakaua Dynasty,* 83.

92 The last Hawaiian plantation shut down in 2016: Brittany Lyte, "With Pineapple and Sugar Production Gone, Hawaii Weighs Its Agricultural Future," *WP,* Dec. 17, 2017.

92 the "alcoholic republic": Rorabaugh, *Alcoholic Republic.*

93 "the people of corn": Pollan, *Omnivore's Dilemma,* 23, 101.

93 wedding of their daughter, Nellie: Cannon and Brooks, *Presidents' Cookbook,* 282–83; Chernow, *Grant,* 772–73.

94 Grant led his only daughter: Ibid.; Chernow, *Grant,* 774.

94 Whitman recited his poem: "A Kiss to the Bride," May 21, 1873, Walt Whitman Archive, whitmanarchive.org.

94 soft-shell crab on toast: Cannon and Brooks, *Presidents' Cookbook,* 282.

94 For the grand finale: Ibid., 282–83.

94 As the newlyweds were showered: Chernow, *Grant,* 774.

94 "something rather touching and tragic": Ibid., 774–75.

94 At least forty Grant relatives profited: Salinger, *Encyclopedia of White Collar & Corporate Crime,* vol. 1, 374.

94 Orville Babcock, played a central role: Whitcomb and Whitcomb, *Real Life at the White House,* 160.

95 fifteen-cigar-a-day habit: Geoffrey C. Ward, "A Hero in Spite of Himself," *WSJ,* Oct. 6, 2017.

95 70 percent of net profits: Chernow, *Grant,* 936.

95 earned $450,000: Whitcomb and Whitcomb, *Real Life at the White House,* 162.

95 "never so happy in my life": Ibid.

95 "quite the happiest period of my life": Ibid.

7 · THEODORE ROOSEVELT AND WILLIAM HOWARD TAFT
Two Bears

100 Vice President Theodore Roosevelt: Morris, *The Rise of Theodore Roosevelt,* 780; Brinkley, *Wilderness Warrior,* 394.

100 forty-two years, ten months, and eighteen days old, America's youngest chief executive: Tom Murse, "The Youngest President in American History," ThoughtCo., Oct. 21, 2019, www.thoughtco.com.

100 "I feel as if I should go mad": Jamison, *Exuberance,* 8.

101 the tumor made it painful to eat: "Theodore Roosevelt, Sr.," Theodore Roosevelt Birthplace, National Park Service, nps.gov.

101 a bestiary that included: Whitcomb and Whitcomb, *Real Life at the White House,* 223.

101 "I am of a very buoyant temper": Jamison, *Exuberance,* 8–9.

101 he gained the nickname Teddy: "The Story of the Teddy Bear," Theodore Roosevelt Birthplace, National Park Service, nps.gov.

101 "The light has gone out of my life": Wendy Maloney, "New Online: Theodore Roosevelt Papers," *Library of Congress Blog,* Oct. 17, 2018, blogs.loc.gov.

102 "as calm and imperturbable as a Buddha": Morris, *Theodore Rex,* 449.

102 "Like a shuttle, keeping everything": Cannon and Brooks, *Presidents' Cookbook,* 355.

102 "Whenever I go against her judgment": Whitcomb and Whitcomb, *Real Life at the White House,* 225.

102 Edie miscarried twice: Ibid.

102 "coarse food and plenty of it": Cannon and Brooks, *Presidents' Cookbook,* 352.

102 "stoking up prodigiously": Wagenknecht, *Seven Worlds of Theodore Roosevelt*, 30.

102 fiddlehead ferns that he foraged: Cannon and Brooks, *Presidents' Cookbook*, 359–60.

102 oysters, green turtle soup, crab flake Newburg, quail : "TR's 42nd Birthday Dinner, October 27, 1900 [Courtesy of the Theodore Roosevelt Association]," American Presidents' Food Favorites, foodtimeline.org.

103 At breakfast he would order: Cannon and Brooks, *Presidents' Cookbook*, 352.

103 big bowl of hominy: Ibid., 352–53.

103 black Hu-Kwa from China: Ibid., 353.

103 "the King of Ultima Thule's scepter": Ibid., 354.

103 a temperance group accused Roosevelt: Ibid., 353.

103 "drank two glasses of champagne": Ibid.

103 "in the nature of a bathtub": Ibid., 352.

103 shrewdly spun the press: Whitcomb and Whitcomb, *Real Life at the White House*, 220.

103 "you had to wring the personality out": Jamison, *Exuberance*, 11.

104 "I have seen two tremendous works": Whitcomb and Whitcomb, *Real Life at the White House*, 219.

104 "one of the most useful": Roosevelt, *Winning of the West*, 548.

104 "show some respect to a man": Dewey W. Grantham Jr., "Dinner at the White House: Theodore Roosevelt, Booker T. Washington, and the South," *Tennessee Historical Quarterly* 17, no. 2 (June 1958): 125.

104 "The action of President Roosevelt": Marcia Davis, review of *Guest of Honor*, by Deborah Davis, *WP*, Aug. 17, 2012.

104 "Coon-Faced" and "A Rank Negrophilist": Morris, *Theodore Rex*, 55.

105 " 'Dining' . . . was really a code word for social equality": Deborah Davis, "Teddy Roosevelt's 'Shocking' Dinner with Washington," *Talk of the Nation*, NPR, May 14, 2012.

105 "The president . . . mentioned the inviting": Howe, *George von Lengerke Meyer*, 416.

105 in the racial reckoning of the twenty-first century: Arturo Conde, "Teddy Roosevelt's 'Racist' and 'Progressive' Legacy, Historian Says, Is Part of Monument Debate," NBC News, July 20, 2020, www.nbcnews.com; Rachel Treisman, "New York City's Natural History Museum Has Removed a Theodore Roosevelt Statue," NPR, Jan. 20, 2022.

105 "When I asked Booker T. Washington": John K. Severn, "Theodore Roosevelt Entertains Booker T. Washington: Florida's Reaction to the White House Dinner," *Florida Historical Quarterly* 54, no. 3 (1975): 314.

105 first president to use the mansion's nickname: Whitcomb and Whitcomb, *Real Life at the White House*, 229.

105 Army Corps of Engineers found, "dilapidated": Ibid., 233.

105 "a cross between Neo-Classic": Cannon and Brooks, *Presidents' Cookbook*, 352.

106 A renovation had been rumored: Whitcomb and Whitcomb, *Real Life at the White House*, 233–35.

106 One Thanksgiving meal included: Cannon and Brooks, *Presidents' Cookbook*, 354.

107 "When anyone desires to make": Ibid., 352.

107 "I don't think any family": Ibid., 357.

108 Roosevelt had launched on: Elaine Evans, "The Rough Rider Tours Illinois," Illinois State Historical Society, Oct. 4, 2021, www.historyillinois.org.

108 The two were a contrast in styles: Ralph H. Anderson, "We Will Pitch Camp at Bridalveil!," *Yosemite Nature Notes* 30, no. 5 (May 1951).

108 "poetico-trampo-geologist-bot": Muir to [Robert Underwood] Johnson, Sept. 13, 1889, John Muir Papers, University of the Pacific, scholarlycommons.pacific.edu.

108 "by far the grandest of all": Syd Albright, "History Corner: Yosemite," *Coeur d'Alene/Post Falls Press,* Nov. 21, 2021.

108 "Pres. Roosevelt . . . is cut off": Epting, *Teddy Roosevelt in California,* 78.

108 Grizzly Giant, a sequoia that stands: "The Grizzly Giant: 4 Must-Know Facts About Yosemite's Most Famous Tree," The Redwoods in Yosemite, redwoodsin yosemite.com.

108 three thousand years old: Sequoia Research, National Park Service, nps.gov.

108 "the best kind of steaks": "President Makes Camp at Bridal Veil Falls," *San Francisco Call,* May 18, 1903, 1–2, chroniclingamerica.loc.gov.

109 "An influential man from Washington": Epting, *Teddy Roosevelt in California,* 17.

109 "the sanctum sanctorum of the Sierras": Muir, *Letters to a Friend,* July 26, 1868.

109 "Conservation of natural resources": Christen Duxbury, "The Fundamental Problem," Theodore Roosevelt Conservation Partnership, www.trcp.org.

109 As the guides erected a "shelter half": Constance Carter, "Roosevelt, Muir, and the Camping Trip," *Library of Congress Blog,* Aug. 11, 2016, blogs.loc.gov.

110 "We lay in the open": Epting, *Teddy Roosevelt in California,* 122.

110 thirty-five-mile trek: Ibid., 83.

110 "the greatest view on earth": "President Makes Camp at Bridal Veil Falls."

110 Leidig prepared a second round: "Charlie Leidig's Report of President Roosevelt's Visit in May, 1903," Sierra Club, vault.sierraclub.org.

110 "I stuffed him pretty well": Albright, "History Corner: Yosemite."

110 "The crisp mountain air": "President Leaves Yosemite," *San Francisco Call,* May 19, 1903, 1, chroniclingamerica.loc.gov.

110 Pelican Island, Florida: Whitcomb and Whitcomb, *Real Life at the White House,* 226.

110 He created eighteen national monuments: Elizabeth Kolbert, "Obama the Conservationist," *New Yorker,* Sept. 4, 2016.

111 "the Conservationist President": "Theodore Roosevelt and Conservation," National Park Service, www.nps.gov.

111 "the most consequential camping trip": Kolbert, "Obama the Conservationist."

111 he picked the sausage up like a dead mouse: "The Jungle," Theodore Roosevelt Center, Dickinson State University, www.theodorerooseveltcenter.org.

111 "I aimed at the public's heart": Ibid.

112 shooting the leaders of the Populist Party: Anthony Gaughan, "Harvey Wiley, Theodore Roosevelt, and the Federal Regulation of Food and Drugs," Harvard Law School, Winter 2004, dash.harvard.edu.

112 died from food poisoning: Ibid.

112 "sheer fraud": Ibid.

112 "Uncle Joe" Cannon: Cannon and Brooks, *Presidents' Cookbook.*

112 "the manufacture, sale, or transportation": The Pure Food and Drug Act, History, Art & Archives, U.S. House of Representatives, June 23, 1906, history.house.gov.

113 an annual budget of $5.7 billion: FDA at a Glance, U.S. Food & Drug Administration, Oct. 2019, www.fda.gov.

113 "There is something hanging over his head": Whitcomb and Whitcomb, *Real Life at the White House,* 237.

113 an amiable three-hundred-and-thirty-two-pound legal scholar: Cannon and Brooks, *Presidents' Cookbook,* 370.

113 Nellie Taft, a slim, intense woman: Whitcomb and Whitcomb, *Real Life at the White House,* 238.

114 But at one stop things got weird: Jeffrey Bourdon, " 'Just Call Me Bill': William Taft Brings Spectacle Politics to the Midwest," *Midwestern History* 2, no. 10 (Oct. 2016), scholarworks.gvsu.edu.

114 "inexpressibly happy": Whitcomb and Whitcomb, *Real Life at the White House,* 238, 239.

114 "prison" . . . "loneliest place in the world": Ibid., 239, 248.

114 the first First Lady to smoke cigarettes: Helen "Nellie" Taft, Fascinating Facts, First Ladies Library, www.firstladies.org.

115 built the first Oval Office: Whitcomb and Whitcomb, *Real Life at the White House,* 239.

115 there were rumors of tension: William Manners, "There Was a Storm Outside and a Bit of Frost Within," *American Heritage,* Dec. 1969.

115 weight yo-yoed between 270 and 354 pounds: Krug, "An Article Outlines President William Howard Taft's Efforts to Lose Weight."

115 "liked every sort of food": Jaffray, *Secrets of the White House,* 23.

115 "physical culture man": Kolata, "In Struggle with Weight, Taft Used a Modern Diet."

115 "He wanted a thick, juicy twelve-ounce steak": Jaffray, *Secrets of the White House,* 23.

115 he gorged on grapefruit: Cannon and Brooks, *Presidents' Cookbook,* 370.

115 prodigious quantities of seafood: Ibid., 373.

115 Billy Bi (or Billy By): Sam Sifton, "Craig Claiborne's Classic Billi Bi," *NYT,* March 10, 2015; Ana Kincaid, "The Story of Billi Bi Soup," We Are Chefs, weare chefs.com.

116 "looks as if he actually weighs 400": Jaffray, *Secrets of the White House,* 24.

116 "I tell you, it's a sad state": Cannon and Brooks, *Presidents' Cookbook,* 371.

116 "Somehow, he really didn't take off": Jaffray, *Secrets of the White House,* 25.

116 "While I was talking to him": *As I Knew Them: Memoirs of James Watson* (Indianapolis: Bobbs-Merrill, 1936), 135.

116 "Sleeping Beauty": Whitcomb and Whitcomb, *Real Life at the White House,* 243.

116 "corpulence" was replaced by "obesity": Kolata, "In Struggle with Weight, Taft Used a Modern Diet."

116 Taft wrote to the British diet expert: Krug, "Article Outlines President William Howard Taft's Efforts to Lose Weight"; Andrew M. Seaman, "U.S. President Taft Followed a Weight Loss Program Too," Reuters, Oct. 14, 2013.

117 255 pounds—a loss of 59 pounds: Kolata, "In Struggle with Weight, Taft Used a Modern Diet"; Seaman, "U.S. President Taft Followed a Weight Loss Program Too."

117 ballooned to as much as 354 pounds: Krug, "Article Outlines President William Howard Taft's Efforts to Lose Weight."

117 stuck in a bathtub: Christopher Klein, "Did William Howard Taft Really Get Stuck in a Bathtub?," History.com, Sept. 3, 2018, www.history.com.

117 planted 3,020 cherry trees: Joel D. Treese, "Mrs. Taft and the Cherry Blossoms," WHHA.

117 She replaced the male cooks: Cannon and Brooks, *Presidents' Cookbook,* 374.

117 Nellie had a passion for technology: "Advances in Entertaining," WHHA.

117 "I wanted a woman who could relieve me": Cannon and Brooks, *Presidents' Cookbook,* 374.

117 Nellie kept a gimlet eye: Whitcomb and Whitcomb, *Real Life at the White House,* 247; Cannon and Brooks, *Presidents' Cookbook,* 374.

118 the last bovine to board: WHHA.

118 "butter by the tub": Jaffray, *Secrets of the White House,* 13.

118 hosted a reception for two thousand guests: Cannon and Brooks, *Presidents' Cookbook,* 373.

118 the First Lady collapsed from a stroke: Feather Schwartz Foster, "Nellie Taft's Lonely Dinner," *Presidential History Blog,* June 24, 2013, featherfoster.wordpress .com.

118 "large white possum": Adrienne LaFrance, "President Taft Ate a Lot of Possums," *Atlantic,* Nov. 26, 2015.

118 "it was the reproachful look": "Taft Meets a Possum," *NYT,* Jan. 23, 1909.

118 eighteen-pound "Billy Possum and taters": Lucas Reilly, "Billy Possum: President Taft's Answer to the Teddy Bear," *Mental Floss,* June 10, 2013, www.mentalfloss .com.

118 "Billy Possum" toy: Ibid.; Genevieve Carlton, "Jealous of the Teddy Bear, President Taft Tried to Make Billy Possum Happen," *Ranker,* June 23, 2021, www .ranker.com.

119 not to mention his love of golf: Bourdon, "'Just Call Me Bill.'"

119 "Yes, Taft carried out TR's policies": Manners, "There Was a Storm Outside."

119 Roosevelt began to openly attack Taft: Lewis L. Gould, "1912 Republican Convention: Return of the Rough Rider," *Smithsonian,* Aug. 2008.

120 managed to reconcile in 1918: "Roosevelt Grips the Hand of Taft," *NYT,* May 27, 1918.

120 at 237 pounds, had swelled: "Weight of All U.S. Presidents Elected Between 1789 and 2021," statista.com.

120 a relatively feathery 280 pounds: Kolata, "In Struggle with Weight, Taft Used a Modern Diet."

120 killed 512 large animals: Roosevelt African Expedition Collects for SI, Smithsonian Institution Archives, siarchives.si.edu; Phil Edwards, "All 512 Animals Teddy Roosevelt and His Son Killed on Safari," *Vox,* Feb. 3, 2016, www.vox.com. For total of 23,151 specimens, see "Smithsonian African Expedition (1909)," Smithsonian Institution, www.si.edu.

120 "game butchery": Roosevelt, *African Game Trails,* vol. 1, 15.

120 "I toasted slices of elephant's heart": Morris, *Colonel Roosevelt,* 19.

120 shot a neighbor's dog: Jamison, *Exuberance,* 9.

120 tech bros such as Mark Zuckerberg: Leo Hickman, "Facebook CEO Mark Zuckerberg Only Eats Meat He Kills Himself," *Guardian,* May 27, 2011. Zuckerberg gave up the practice in 2012.

120 showed signs of bipolar disorder: Jonathan R. T. Davidson, Kathryn M. Connor, and Marvin Swartz, "Mental Illness in U.S. Presidents Between 1776 and 1974," *Journal of Nervous and Mental Disease* 194, no. 1 (Jan. 2006): 47–51.

120 Roosevelt was of the latter persuasion: Morris, *Theodore Rex,* 452.

121 "I eat too much": TR to Kermit, in Wagenknecht, *Seven Worlds of Theodore Roosevelt,* 29.

8 · FROM WILSON TO COOLIDGE AND HOOVER
Heartburn, Hard Cheese, and a Hail of Rotten Tomatoes

123 "done up in pajamas": Whitcomb and Whitcomb, *Real Life at the White House,* 259.

123 Wilson broke precedent: Cannon and Brooks, *Presidents' Cookbook,* 385–86.

123 "ball-gown frivolity": Mrs. Josephus Daniels (Adelaide Worth Bagley Daniels), *Recollections of a Cabinet Minister's Wife, 1913–1921* (Raleigh, NC: Mitchell Printing Company, 1945), 7–8.

123 "I am very fond of country hams": Cannon and Brooks, *Presidents' Cookbook,* 387.

123 clear soup, chicken salad, and strawberry ice cream: Ibid., 384–87.

124 fillet of sole, fillet of beef, breast of chicken: Ibid., 384.

124 hostilities broke out in the White House kitchen: Seale, *The President's House,* vol. 2, 69.

124 Wilson's central nervous system: Whitcomb and Whitcomb, *Real Life at the White House,* 256.

124 staring eyes of a moose: Ibid., 259.

125 diagnosed with Bright's disease: Ibid., 257–58.

125   Edith Bolling Galt: Betty Boyd Caroli, "Edith Wilson," *Encyclopaedia Britannica.*

125   "America First": Will-Weber, *Mint Juleps with Teddy Roosevelt,* 219.

125   the president wept in private: Whitcomb and Whitcomb, *Real Life at the White House,* 260.

125   "food will win the war": Suzy Evans, "Woodrow Wilson: 'Foods That Will Win the War,' and Liberty Cabbage," *The History Chef!,* March 27, 2011, lincolnslunch .blogspot.com; Timothy Horning, "Food Will Win the War," *The PhillyHistory Blog,* June 22, 2011, blog.phillyhistory.org.

126   "I did not realize it at the moment": Herbert Hoover Presidential Library and Museum, Museum Exhibit Galleries, The Humanitarian Years, web.archive.org /web/20110109151702/http://hoover.archives.gov/exhibits/Hooverstory/gallery02 /index.html.

126   U.S. soldiers were better fed: "World War I Rations: Full Belly, Fully Ready," Army Heritage Center Foundation, www.armyheritage.org.

126   "Wheatless Mondays and Wednesdays": Together We Win, The Philadelphia Homefront During the First World War, togetherwewin.librarycompany.org; Lauren Young, "The Meatless, Wheatless Meals of World War I America," *Gastro Obscura,* Jan. 10, 2017, www.atlasobscura.com.

127   replace Germanic food names: Evans, "Woodrow Wilson: 'Foods That Will Win the War,' and Liberty Cabbage."

127   "At table I'll not leave a scrap": Kelly Burgess, "The Clean Plate Club: Why Your Family Shouldn't Join," iParenting Media, recipestoday.com.

127   Charles Lathrop Pack: Laura Schumm, "America's Patriotic Victory Gardens," History.com, Aug. 31, 2018, www.history.com; Tomoko Steen and Alison Kelly, "Charles Lathrop Pack: Pioneering the Idea of the 'Victory Garden' in the United States," *Biodiversity Heritage Library* (blog), July 2, 2019, blog.biodiversitylibrary .org; Ruby Scalera, "Not So Secret Gardens," Culture Crush, www.theculture crush.com.

127   most notably Alice Waters: Waters in conversation with the author, Sept. 12, 2019.

127   a flock of sheep: "Why Did President Wilson Keep a Flock of Sheep on the White House Lawn?," WHHA; Whitcomb and Whitcomb, *Real Life at the White House,* 260.

128   Wheat prices spiked dramatically: World War I and Wheat Farmers, Harry S. Truman Library, www.trumanlibrary.gov.

128   a fixed price of $2 a bushel: "Price Control in Wartime," CQ Press Library, library .cqpress.com.

128   in 1918 the administration had to ration sugar: "Food Will Win the War," Together We Win, The Philadelphia Homefront During the First War, together wewin.librarycompany.org.

128   "rather hard game of golf": Whitcomb and Whitcomb, *Real Life at the White House,* 260.

128   "My right eye is like a horse's": Ibid., 258.

128   Grayson's dietary advice: Ibid., 256; Cannon and Brooks, *Presidents' Cookbook,* 387.

129   "a ten-cent pickled mackerel": Whitcomb and Whitcomb, *Real Life at the White House,* 250.

129   "put on his war paint": Woodrow Wilson, AZQuotes.com, www.azquotes.com.

129   "intolerable burden of . . . ignorant Negroes": Becky Little, "How Woodrow Wilson Tried to Reverse Black American Progress," History.com, July 14, 2020.

129   decisions that have tarnished his legacy: Princeton University Office of Communications, "Board of Trustees' Decision on Removing Woodrow Wilson's Name from Public Policy School and Residential College," press release, June 27, 2020.

129   "No man has ever been a success": Whitcomb and Whitcomb, *Real Life at the White House,* 251.

129 "imperious passions": Auchincloss, *Woodrow Wilson*, 22.

129 Mrs. Mary Allen Hulbert Peck: Frances W. Saunders, "Love and Guilt: Woodrow Wilson and Mary Hulbert," *American Heritage*, April/May 1979.

129 "I found him longing": Horst Augustinovic, "Do You Know . . . About Woodrow Wilson's 'Flirtatious Relationship' in Bermuda?," Bermuda.com, www.bermuda .com.

129 Wilson claimed to have told: Molly McCartney, "A President's Secret Letters to Another Woman That He Never Wanted Public," *WP*, Sept. 16, 2018.

130 "poor, mixed, inexplicable nature": Cooper, *Woodrow Wilson*, 100.

130 "Hunger does not breed reform": Woodrow Wilson, "Address to a Joint Session of Congress Concerning the Terms of Armistice Signed by Germany," Nov. 11, 1918, American Presidency Project, University of California, Santa Barbara, www.presidency.ucsb.edu.

130 "there will come some time": Hogan, *Woodrow Wilson's Western Tour*, 159.

130 He accused the hotel staff of being spies: Michael S. Rosenwald, "In 1918, the Flu Infected the White House. Even President Wilson Got Sick," *WP*, Oct. 2, 2020; Auchincloss, *Woodrow Wilson*, 96.

130 "the president is able-minded": Whitcomb and Whitcomb, *Real Life at the White House*, 261.

131 Edith fiercely guarded the door: Anthony Bergen, "Woodrow Wilson's Wives and the Freudian Typo," Dead Presidents, Feb. 4, 2011, deadpresidents.tumblr .com.

131 He was a moderate drinker: Will-Weber, *Mint Juleps with Teddy Roosevelt*, 217–25.

131 considered one of the worst presidents: Jay Tolson, "Worst Presidents: Warren Harding (1921–1923)," *U.S. News & World Report*, Feb. 16, 2007.

131 "the atmosphere was as different": Thomas Mallon, "Less Said," *New Yorker*, March 3, 2013.

132 "silent in five languages": H. W. Brands, "Silent Cal: The Taciturn Coolidge's Term Spoke Volumes About the Modern Presidency," *WP*, Jan. 21, 2007.

132 "I made a bet today": Ibid.

132 "had taught the deaf": Mallon, "Less Said."

132 apple pie . . . pave a road: Cannon and Brooks, *Presidents' Cookbook*, 418.

132 Rebecca (who lived in a tree house): Whitcomb and Whitcomb, *Real Life at the White House*, 283.

132 "Weaned on a pickle": Mallon, "Less Said."

132 pork-apple-pie: Cannon and Brooks, *Presidents' Cookbook*, 415–16.

132 chickens . . . Roosevelt's former mint garden: Ibid., 411.

132 called every meal "supper". . . . nuts: Ibid., 405.

132 roast beef: Ibid., 406.

132 six Virginia hams "seems an awful lot": Cheryl Mullenbach, "White House Secrets Revealed by Iowa Woman in 1920s," IowaWatch.org, Nov. 18, 2017, www.iowa watch.org.

132 his "greatest disappointment": Whitcomb and Whitcomb, *Real Life at the White House*, 276.

132 asked for the recipe: Cannon and Brooks, *Presidents' Cookbook*, 411.

133 The intellectual parts of a dinner: Quan, *To a President's Taste*, 8–17; Daniel L. Wright, "On Food," *The Importance of the Obvious* (blog), July 30, 2013, cracker pilgrim.com.

133 "a chicken in every pot": Whitcomb and Whitcomb, *Real Life at the White House*, 290.

134 contracted malaria, stumbled into a tiger's den: Mayer, *Lou Henry Hoover*, 72, 123; Harris, *First Ladies Fact Book*, 467–77.

134 "If a man hasn't made a million": Whitcomb and Whitcomb, *Real Life at the White House*, 289.

134 "the food regulator of the world": Bertrand M. Patenaude, "Food as a Weapon," *Hoover Digest,* Jan. 30, 2007.

134 "America's Food Czar": Tori Avey, "Discover the History of Meatless Mondays," *The History Kitchen,* PBS, Aug. 16, 2013, www.pbs.org.

134 "The prime objective of the United States": Patenaude, "Food as a Weapon."

134 "Gentlemen, food is a weapon": Ibid.

134 But when five to ten million Russians died: Ibid.

134 "Twenty million people are starving": Herbert Hoover, White House, from Freidel and Sidey, *Presidents of the United States of America,* www.whitehouse.gov.

135 "Medicine Ball Cabinet": Jeffries, *In and Out of the White House,* 331–32.

135 dressed in a formal dinner jacket: Whitcomb and Whitcomb, *Real Life at the White House,* 292.

135 Lou directed her fifty-eight staff members: Ibid., 290.

135 three full-time secretaries: Cannon and Brooks, *Presidents' Cookbook,* 420.

135 they dined alone just once a year: Jeffries, *In and Out of the White House,* 331.

135 "the best" foods: Ibid., 332.

135 they relied on Mary Rattley: Ibid., 335–36.

136 when he burst out of the elevator: Whitcomb and Whitcomb, *Real Life at the White House,* 291.

136 On April 1, 1912, Karl Anderson: John Mundt, "The Historic Penobscot: America's Atlantic Salmon Fishing Legacy," *American Fly Fisher* 22, no. 3 (Summer 1996): 6.

136 "wash one's soul with pure air": Whitcomb and Whitcomb, *Real Life at the White House,* 296.

136 Maine did not vote Democratic: Cannon and Brooks, *Presidents' Cookbook,* 421.

137 The last Presidential Salmon was delivered: Caroline Lester, "The Last Presidential Salmon," *New Yorker,* Aug. 7, 2019.

137 in 2014 only 248 salmon: "Penobscot River Salmon Run Surges for Second Straight Year," NOAA Fisheries, July 28, 2020.

137 only 561 a year later: "Fewer Atlantic Salmon Found in Maine River," Associated Press, Feb. 14, 2022.

137 fifteen generations of Atlantic salmon: John Holyoke, "Maine's Atlantic Salmon Likely to Be on 'Endangered List' Another 75 Years," *Bangor Daily News,* Feb. 13, 2019.

137 "The political machinery [is] unable to cope": Whitcomb and Whitcomb, *Real Life at the White House,* 291–92.

137 Hoover lost thirty-five pounds: Ibid., 297.

137 The staff took bets on how quickly: Cannon and Brooks, *Presidents' Cookbook,* 421; Whitcomb and Whitcomb, *Real Life at the White House,* 296.

137 "minimum actual suffering": Roger Lambert, "Hoover and the Red Cross in the Arkansas Drought of 1930," *Arkansas Historical Quarterly* 29, no. 1 (Spring 1970): 3–19, www.jstor.org; "Drought of 1930–31," *Encyclopedia of Arkansas,* encyclopediaofarkansas.net.

137 The homeless built shanties: "Hoovervilles," History.com, Nov. 2, 2018, www.history.com.

137 "My men are dropping": Whitcomb and Whitcomb, *Real Life at the White House,* 297.

138 "a gibbering idiot": Ibid., 298.

138 "I can't go on with it anymore": Ibid., 297.

9 · FRANKLIN D. ROOSEVELT The Gourmet's Lament

140 private dinner with Wendell Willkie: Roosevelt and Shalett, *Affectionately, F.D.R.,* 324–25; Wendell Willkie (1892–1944), Eleanor Roosevelt Papers Project, George Washington University, erpapers.columbian.gwu.edu.

140 terrapin soup . . . a delicacy made with the flesh: Nesbitt, *White House Diary*, 123.

141 The diamondback terrapin is native: Callum Cleary, "Washington's Lost Food Craze: Terrapin Soup," *Boundary Stones* (blog), WETA, Oct. 19, 2017, boundary stones.weta.org.

141 "white and sweet" terrapin flesh: Ibid.

141 "muddy, dirty, mushy and chewy": Turtle Meat—Boneless, Cajun Grocer, www .cajungrocer.com.

141 By the twentieth century, Heinz: Natasha Frost, "How America Fell into—and out of—Love with Mock Turtle Soup," *Gastro Obscura*, Aug. 3, 2017, www.atlas obscura.com.

141 For the Willkie dinner to succeed: Cannon and Brooks, *Presidents' Cookbook*, 439.

142 Over bowls of the elixir: Fullilove, *Rendezvous with Destiny*.

142 "Great bursts of laughter": Roosevelt and Shalett, *Affectionately, F.D.R.*, 324–25.

142 FDR liked to serve the broth: Nesbitt, *White House Diary*, 307.

142 "These are the bones of rats!": Cannon and Brooks, *Presidents' Cookbook*, 439.

143 kippered herring or creamed chipped beef: Nesbitt, *White House Diary*, 298.

143 He delighted in the "curious food gifts": Ibid., 70–73, 297–98; Roosevelt and Shalett, *Affectionately, F.D.R.*, 238.

143 FDR liked to grind his own coffee: Cannon and Brooks, *Presidents' Cookbook*, 431.

143 "the most delicious thing": Roosevelt and Shalett, *Affectionately, F.D.R.*, 238.

143 "Very few things which I eat": Eleanor Roosevelt, *Mrs. Eleanor Roosevelt's Own Program*, episode 14, June 13, 1940, www2.gwu.edu.

143 "Mother is a wonderful woman": Roosevelt and Shalett, *Affectionately, F.D.R.*, 238.

144 Washington's crab soup: Mitchell, *Presidential Flavors*, 169–70.

144 "Crisis or no crisis, the tension of the country": Laura Shapiro, "The First Kitchen," *New Yorker*, Nov. 22, 2010.

144 "The woman who boils potatoes": Ibid.

144 Milkorno: Elaine Engst and Blaine Friedlander, "Cornell Rewind: The Influence of Eleanor Roosevelt," *Cornell Chronicle*, Dec. 11, 2014.

144 "A loaf of bread sent me": Nesbitt, *White House Diary*, 10.

144 She married Henry Nesbitt: Haber, *From Hardtack to Home Fries*, 116.

145 "kindest face I've ever seen": Nesbitt, *White House Diary*, 9.

145 "Would you mind making up": Ibid., 11–13.

145 "only saloonkeepers are Democrats": Ibid., 14–15.

146 "someone I know": Ibid., 20.

146 "I can't work up any charm for cockroaches": Ibid., 30.

146 Public Works Project No. 634: Ibid., 146; "The White House Kitchen Nightmare," National Women's History Museum, June 28, 2013, www.womenshistory.org.

146 the Roosevelts' first diplomatic dinner: Nesbitt, *White House Diary*, 34–35.

146 Ida Allen, and a rotating cast: Ibid., 118; Nolan Moore, "The Delicious History of the White House Executive Chef," *Mental Floss*, Jan. 23, 2017, www.mentalfloss .com.

147 "economy meals": Nesbitt, *White House Diary*, 42.

147 noodles with chicken scraps: Ibid.; "White House Kitchen Nightmare."

147 gumbo z'herbes: Henrietta Nesbitt's Recipes, Our White House: Looking In, Looking Out, ourwhitehouse.org.

147 "so many meals it all blurred": Nesbitt, *White House Diary*, 40.

147 "I was sick of food": Ibid., 251.

147 "plain foods, plainly prepared": Nelson, *President Is at Camp David*, 16.

147 "My God! Doesn't Mrs. Nesbitt know": Whitcomb and Whitcomb, *Real Life at the White House*, 305.

147   called "Fluffy" behind her back: Haber, *From Hardtack to Home Fries,* 112.

147   "Same Menu Four Days Palls": *NYT,* March 2, 1937.

147   "Do you remember that about a month ago": Roosevelt and Shalett, *Affectionately, F.D.R.,* 238–39.

148   "You ought to get a manager": Nesbitt, *White House Diary,* 50.

148   "did not enjoy a very high reputation": Roosevelt and Shalett, *Affectionately, F.D.R.,* 237.

148   "the worst I've ever eaten": James Atlas, "The Private Hemingway: From His Unpublished Letters, 1918–1961," *New York Times Magazine,* Feb. 15, 1981.

148   "tizzy-wizzies": Nesbitt, *White House Diary,* 263.

148   "When he said 'The vegetables are watery'": Ibid., 185–86.

148   "The responsibility for what she spent": Roosevelt and Shalett, *Affectionately, F.D.R.,* 381–82.

148   he shied from confrontations with his staff: Ibid., 236–37.

148   "it became part of his nature": Ibid., 236.

148   "Pa couldn't even bring himself": Ibid., 237.

149   FDR "liked her cooking": Nesbitt, *White House Diary,* 299.

149   "ostensibly in jest but actually": Roosevelt and Shalett, *Affectionately, F.D.R.,* 237.

149   an ordeal to be borne: Russell Baker, "The Charms of Eleanor," *New York Review of Books,* June 9, 2011.

149   "*deserved* a good time": Allida M. Black, "For FDR, an Enduring Relationship," *WP,* March 1, 1998.

150   "an armed truce that endured": Joseph E. Persico, "FDR's Secret Love," *U.S. News & World Report,* April 18, 2008.

150   "I have the memory of an elephant": Michael Kernan, "Eleanor Roosevelt, Pioneer," *WP,* Sept. 13, 1984.

150   "simple foods that . . . reflected the hard times": Haber, *From Hardtack to Home Fries,* 120–23.

150   Blanche Wiesen Cook: Ibid., 122.

150   "ER's revenge": Shapiro, "First Kitchen."

150   FDR hatched a plan: David Levine, "Franklin Delano Roosevelt: The Picnic That Won the War, the Royal Visit, the Hot Dog Summit of 1939, and Hyde Park on the Hudson Movie," *Hudson Valley Magazine,* Nov. 25, 2012.

151   FDR staged his coup de théâtre: Conradi, *Hot Dogs and Cocktails,* 213–14.

151   The king eyed the hot dog and said, "What should I do?": Doug Mack, "Why American Leaders Relish Hot-Dog Diplomacy," *Gastro Obscura,* June 17, 2022, www.atlasobscura.com.

152   "King Tries Hot Dog and Asks for More": *NYT,* June 11, 1939.

152   "wait for the consequences": Transcript of King George VI's Handwritten Notes for a Memorandum on His Conversation with President Roosevelt on June 10 and 11, 1939, Franklin D. Roosevelt Presidential Library and Museum.

152   "the picnic that won the war": Levine, "Franklin Delano Roosevelt: The Picnic That Won the War."

152   "One p.m. small lunch, about thirty-four": Nesbitt, *White House Diary,* 268–69.

153   nab FDR "by the elevator": Ibid., 264.

153   "'Hush-hush,' 'Confidential,' 'V.I.P.'": Ibid., 271.

153   "We will be having some guests tonight": Author's re-creation, based on Eleanor Roosevelt, "Churchill at the White House," *Atlantic,* March 1965.

153   "going fishing": Nesbitt, *White House Diary,* 266.

153   To cross the Atlantic, Churchill: Stelzer, *Dinner with Churchill,* 66.

154   "looked poor-colored and hungry": Nesbitt, *White House Diary,* 273.

154   "to the Common Cause!": Stelzer, *Dinner with Churchill,* 75.

154   "tummy time": Ibid., 170.

154   He suffered "indy": Ibid., 169, 171.

154 "a hot bath, cold champagne": Edward Helmore, "The Wonderful World of Winnie," *Wall Street Journal,* April 27, 2012.

154 "superannuated drunkard supported": Stelzer, *Dinner with Churchill,* 187.

154 noodle soup; roast beef: Ibid., 79.

154 "new people, new places": Eleanor Roosevelt, "Churchill at the White House."

155 "It was a thrilling experience": Stelzer, *Dinner with Churchill,* 20.

155 "It is fun to be in the same century": Ibid., 41.

155 "Mother would fume and go in and out": Ibid., 79.

155 "two little boys playing soldier": Thomas Maier, "A Wartime White House Christmas with Churchill," *Wall Street Journal,* Dec. 21, 2014.

155 On December 26, 1941: Ibid.

155 "hardboiled egg of a man": Stelzer, *Dinner with Churchill,* 92.

155 in 1942, Stalin had plied Churchill: Ibid., 91–93.

156 Mrs. Nesbitt wrestled with strict rationing: Nesbitt, *White House Diary,* 284–85.

156 "Damn it, I don't want beef!": Ibid., 298.

156 Mrs. Nesbitt noted in her diary: Ibid., 299, 305.

157 The first was held in Tehran: Stelzer, *Dinner with Churchill,* 102.

157 Churchill hosted a party: Ibid., 109–11.

157 "a never-to-be forgotten" event: Ibid., 103.

157 used starvation as a weapon: Shashi Tharoor, "In Winston Churchill, Hollywood Rewards a Mass Murderer," *WP,* March 10, 2018; Shashi Tharoor, "Winston Churchill—War Criminal, Enemy of Humanity & Decency," *Print,* Feb. 16, 2019.

158 The drive to acquire and deny calories: "Food as a Weapon of War," Encyclopedia.com, www.encyclopedia.com.

158 "Hunger Plan": Timothy Snyder, "The Reich's Forgotten Atrocity," *Guardian,* Oct. 21, 2010; Mette Bruaas, "Hitler's Hunger Plan," Nobel Peace Center, May 19, 2021.

158 Vietnamese rice, one to two million people died: Geoffrey Gunn, "The Great Vietnamese Famine," Sciences Po, May 12, 2011.

158 "the stomach governs the world": Stelzer, *Dinner with Churchill,* 169.

158 "tired to the point of an inhuman loneliness": Nesbitt, *White House Diary,* 301.

159 "all went smoothly": Ibid., 309.

159 "A man came in from one of the hotels": Ibid., 306.

10 · HARRY S. TRUMAN
Bourbon, Berlin, and the Comforts of Fried Chicken

161 Truman was tucking into a bourbon: Whitcomb and Whitcomb, *Real Life at the White House,* 319.

161 "Being President is like riding a tiger": "Truman: The First 100 Days," Truman Library Institute, www.trumanlibraryinstitute.org.

161 On May 8, 1945, he celebrated: Peter Grier, "V-E Day: How President Truman Reacted on May 8, 1945," *Christian Science Monitor,* May 8, 2015.

161 "celebrated the winning of the war": *Yank, the Army Weekly,* Sept. 7, 1945.

162 "a dizzy whirl": McCullough, *Truman,* 464.

162 "I just dread moving": Whitcomb and Whitcomb, *Real Life at the White House,* 318.

162 "I'm not the one elected": Ibid., 321.

162 "Although it went unsuspected": West, *Upstairs at the White House,* 63–66.

162 "the Roosevelts' tyrannical housekeeper": Whitcomb and Whitcomb, *Real Life at the White House,* 326–27; Feather Schwartz Foster, "Mrs. Truman and the Housekeeper," *Presidential History Blog,* featherfoster.wordpress.com.

163 "It's time to find a new housekeeper": West, *Upstairs at the White House,* 73–74.

163   "until the Trumans got settled": Nesbitt, *White House Diary*, 312.
163   "We pour whiskey down the guests' throats": West, *Upstairs at the White House*, 73–74.
163   "a meat and potatoes man": Cannon and Brooks, *Presidents' Cookbook*, 450.
163   "no butter, no sugar, no sweets": McCullough, *Truman*, 857–58.
163   "A man in my position": West, *Upstairs at the White House*, 62.
163   "get the engine going": McCullough, *Truman*, 857–58.
163   "emotional separation": Quoted in ibid., 578–79.
164   Vietta Garr: "Miss Vietta Garr," Harry S. Truman National Historic Site, National Park Service, www.nps.gov.
164   "Never so lonesome in my life": Whitcomb and Whitcomb, *Real Life at the White House*, 323–24.
164   "Damn place is haunted": Ibid., 324–25.
164   "sagged and moved like a ship": Michael Beschloss, "Harry Truman's Extreme Home Makeover," *NYT*, May 9, 2015.
165   "skyscraper-strength": Ibid.
165   the building looked almost identical: "Saving the White House: Truman's Extreme Makeover," Truman Library Institute, www.trumanlibraryinstitute.org.
165   "a modern office inside a deserted castle": McCullough, *Truman*, 1043.
165   The 62 rooms, fourteen baths: Russoli and Russoli, *Ike the Cook*, 63.
166   Founding the Citizens Food Committee: Harry S. Truman, Remarks to Members of the Citizens Food Committee, Oct. 1, 1947, American Presidency Project; John W. Ball, "Marshalling America," *WP*, Oct. 6, 1999.
166   Truman launched Operation Vittles: Bob van der Linden, "Supplying a City by Air: The Berlin Airlift," Smithsonian Air and Space Museum, Sept. 14, 2018, airandspace.si.edu; David Kindy, "How the 'Candy Bomber' Left a Lasting Legacy in Cold War Germany," *Smithsonian*, Feb. 24, 2022.
166   At 9:20 on Saturday evening, June 24, 1950: Details from McCullough, *Truman*, 928–31. For background, see Brinkley, *White House Butlers*, 77–78; Debbie Elliott, "On Eve of War, Truman Turned to Comfort Food," NPR, Sept. 30, 2006.
167   At a raucous lunch: James E. Chinn, "Being Home Best, 'Ike' Tells Luncheon," *WP*, June 19, 1945.
167   "simple and homey . . . community supper": Russoli and Russoli, *Ike the Cook*, 32.
167   a spat over protocol: Ibid., 62; Whitcomb and Whitcomb, *Real Life at the White House*, 333.

11 · DWIGHT D. EISENHOWER   The President Who Cooked

170   "Cooking gave me a creative feeling": Russoli and Russoli, *Ike the Cook*, 6–7.
170   Ike grew corn and cucumbers: Ibid., 3.
171   "Food is part of a soldier's pay": Ibid., 7–8.
171   "I was never permitted in the kitchen": Whitcomb and Whitcomb, *Real Life at the White House*, 336.
171   "I was a cooking school dropout": Russoli and Russoli, *Ike the Cook*, back cover.
171   "I've been a mess sergeant": Ibid.
171   the Eisenhowers' marriage was strained: Michael Beschloss, "D-Day Wasn't the First Time Eisenhower Felt as if He Had Lost a Son," *NYT*, June 11, 2014.
171   "hifalutin' gourmet stuff": Russoli and Russoli, *Ike the Cook*, 32.
171   disenchanted with English breakfasts: Ibid., 20, 68.
171   lunch of hot dogs and baked beans: Ibid., 24–25.
172   they subsisted on K rations: Ibid., 28.
172   Ike pictured himself: Ibid., 35.
172   *What's Cooking at Columbia*: Ibid., 39–40.

173   "At last I have a job": Whitcomb and Whitcomb, *Real Life at the White House*, 334.

173   "knife and fork" meetings: Cannon and Brooks, *Presidents' Cookbook*, 466; Russoli and Russoli, *Ike the Cook*, 76.

173   a series of private stag dinners: "What Goes on at Ike's Dinners," *U.S. News & World Report*, Feb. 4, 1955.

174   a stag dinner nearly every week: "More Men Who Came to Dinner," *U.S. News & World Report*, April 8, 1955.

174   invited them to a series of breakfasts: "What Goes on at Ike's Dinners."

174   "In conversation he is not a fencer": Ibid.

174   "hidden weapon . . . presidential charm": "More Men Who Came to Dinner."

174   "Those who have put money and work": "What Goes on at Ike's Dinners."

175   Pink was her signature color: Russoli and Russoli, *Ike the Cook*, 62, 75.

176   "the best career that life": Cannon and Brooks, *Presidents' Cookbook*, 465.

176   Mamie snapped, "What's this?": West, *Upstairs at the White House*, 120–21.

176   "loved quality . . . rich silks and brocades": Melissa Naulin, "'Proud Housewife': Mamie Eisenhower Collects for the White House," WHHA.

176   "terribly disappointed that she couldn't transform": West, *Upstairs at the White House*, 129.

176   complete a project started by First Lady Caroline Harrison: Russoli and Russoli, *Ike the Cook*, 75.

176   "china closet in order": Naulin, "'Proud Housewife.'"

176   "How about lunch, tea & dinner today?": John Kifner, "Eisenhower Letters Hint at Affair with Aide," *NYT*, June 6, 1991.

176   General Omar Bradley said: Merle Miller, *Plain Speaking*, 339–40.

177   "I suppose inevitably, we found ourselves": Kifner, "Eisenhower Letters Hint at Affair with Aide"; Tom Buckley, review of *Past Forgetting*, by Kay Summersby, *NYT*, Feb. 13, 1977.

177   throwing euphoric holiday parties: Cannon and Brooks, *Presidents' Cookbook*, 466; Russoli and Russoli, *Ike the Cook*, 103–4.

177   He was up at 6:00 a.m.: Russoli and Russoli, *Ike the Cook*, 69.

177   Eisenhower's quail hash: Ibid., 77.

177   Mamie steered the cooks: Ibid., 78.

177   "Look, in my house the ladies": Whitcomb and Whitcomb, *Real Life at the White House*, 340.

178   Mamie liked Scrabble and canasta: Russoli and Russoli, *Ike the Cook*, 71.

178   Sun Chop Suey Restaurant: Ibid., 78.

178   "gossips say [the First Family's trays]": Cannon and Brooks, *Presidents' Cookbook*, 466.

178   Ike preferred Westerns: Russoli and Russoli, *Ike the Cook*, 82, 78.

178   "What are those portholes for?": Whitcomb and Whitcomb, *Real Life at the White House*, 340.

178   first real TV president: Russoli and Russoli, *Ike the Cook*, 78–80.

179   "this damnable thing of war": Dwight D. Eisenhower obituary, *Daily Kent Stater*, April 1, 1969.

179   "the military-industrial complex": President Dwight D. Eisenhower's Farewell Address, Jan. 17, 1961, National Archives, www.archives.gov.

179   "You know, farming looks mighty easy": Eisenhower address at Bradley University, Peoria, Ill., Sept. 25, 1956, Dwight D. Eisenhower Presidential Library, Museum & Boyhood Home, National Archives, www.eisenhowerlibrary.gov.

179   189-acre farm near the Gettysburg battlefield: Eisenhower National Historic Site, Virtual Museum Exhibit, National Park Service, www.nps.gov.

179   which he froze and proudly brought: Russoli and Russoli, *Ike the Cook*, 118.

179   Using his position in ways: Whitcomb and Whitcomb, *Real Life at the White House*, 338.

179 cooked for family and friends: Cannon and Brooks, *Presidents' Cookbook,* 467, 471, 479; Russoli and Russoli, *Ike the Cook,* 77, 87, 89; "Eisenhower Steak," Smoke Signals, *WP,* Sept. 17, 2014; Matt Lee and Ted Lee, "For a Better Steak, Cook Directly on Charcoal," *NYT,* June 25, 2015.

180 "hunger and insecurity are the worst enemies": Statement of General Marshall, issued Oct. 1, 1947, noted in Harry S. Truman, "Remarks to Members of the Citizens Food Committee," American Presidency Project.

180 "Food and Fiber as a Force for Freedom": Public Law 480, "Better Than a Bomber," Middle East Research and Information Project.

180 Food for Peace was a way to spread: Russoli and Russoli, *Ike the Cook,* 83.

180 Food for Peace has operated: USAID Office of Food for Peace, www.usaid.gov; Brett D. Schaefer, "Reforming U.S. Food Aid Can Feed Millions More at the Same Cost," *National Review,* May 14, 2018.

180 "food, family, friendship, and freedom": Dwight D. Eisenhower, Remarks at the Opening of the World Agricultural Fair in New Delhi, Dec. 11, 1959.

181 Rysavy brought an unusual global repertoire: Rysavy and Leighton, *Treasury of White House Cooking,* jacket copy and recipes.

181 He preferred steak cooked rare: Harrison Kinney, "Exclusive! White House Chef Reveals President Eisenhower's Special Diet," *McCall's,* Dec. 1957.

181 he and Mamie took a vacation: Russoli and Russoli, *Ike the Cook,* 92; Whitcomb and Whitcomb, *Real Life at the White House,* 344–45.

182 four packs of cigarettes: Whitcomb and Whitcomb, *Real Life at the White House,* 343.

182 "my first serious illness": Eisenhower, *Mandate for Change,* 544–45.

182 suffered through a "lite" diet: Kinney, "Exclusive!"

182 Ike's light diet was as trying: Ibid.

182 Eisenhower must keep his temper: Ambrose, *Eisenhower,* vol. 2, 291.

183 guest list was kept secret: Ibid., 288–89, 571.

184 "Should I run again?": Ibid.

184 "I suspect that Foster's estimate": Ibid., 295.

184 "idleness" for a man of Ike's temperament: Ibid., 571.

184 "What on earth would we talk about?": Whitcomb and Whitcomb, *Real Life at the White House,* 343.

184 "It was years before he asked me": Ibid., 347.

184 On June 7, 1956, President Eisenhower: Ibid., 346; Russoli and Russoli, *Ike the Cook,* 93.

184 "What a bellyache!": Russoli and Russoli, *Ike the Cook,* 93.

184 Rysavy was instructed to make: Kinney, "Exclusive!"

185 That night, David Eisenhower and Julie Nixon: Russoli and Russoli, *Ike the Cook,* 99–101.

185 A year later, the president was confined to bed: Ibid., 102.

185 greeted the Soviet leader Nikita Khrushchev: Cannon and Brooks, *Presidents' Cookbook,* 467.

185 The Soviets reciprocated with dinner: Russoli and Russoli, *Ike the Cook,* 109–110.

186 "nothing short of *awful*": Whitcomb and Whitcomb, *Real Life at the White House,* 340.

186 "I find that self-rising flour": Russoli and Russoli, *Ike the Cook,* 83.

186 "You can't stop the president from cooking": Ibid., 71.

12 · JOHN F. KENNEDY Camelot and Clam Chowder

188 "The food is marvelous": Leonard Bernstein, recorded interview by Nelson Aldrich Jr., July 21, 1965, John F. Kennedy Library Oral History Program.

188 Mrs. Kennedy modeled her soirees: Sally Bedell Smith, "Grace and Power," *NYT*, July 25, 2004.

189 "showcase for great American art and artists": Margaret Leslie Davis, "The Two First Ladies," *Vanity Fair*, Oct. 6, 2008.

189 "Perhaps more than any other President": Baldrige and Verdon, *In the Kennedy Style*, 33.

189 had prepared an exquisite banquet: Ibid., 72.

189 "perhaps the greatest cellist": Ibid., 67.

190 "The moment Senor Casals drew his bow": Ibid., 70.

191 "The French know this": Jacqueline Kennedy Onassis, interviewed by Terry L. Birdwhistell for the University of Kentucky Libraries' John Sherman Cooper Oral History Project, May 13, 1981, transcript in "Jackie Kennedy Talks About the Coopers in 1981 Interview," *Courier Journal*, Nov. 21, 2013.

191 Speaking to the political historian: Sally Bedell Smith, *Grace and Power*, excerpted in *NYT*, July 25, 2004.

192 One night in May 1951: Edward Klein, "Young Love," *Vanity Fair*, Sept. 1996.

193 After defeating Richard M. Nixon: Thomas Reeves, *A Question of Character*, 214–15, as quoted in "Closeness of 1960 Election," Kennedy Library.

193 "took the wine but needed no more": Todd Purdum, "From That Day Forth," *Vanity Fair*, Feb. 2011.

194 "I want a good party": Baldrige and Verdon, *In the Kennedy Style*, 27–28.

194 White House curator: Whitcomb and Whitcomb, *Real Life at the White House*, 352.

194 "Everything in the White House": "Jacqueline Kennedy in the White House," Kennedy Library.

195 The resulting TV documentary: The Reliable Source, "Jackie Kennedy's White House Tour; JFK Library Details Her Role in Restoration," *WP*, Feb. 13, 2012.

195 small round tables: Baldrige, quoted by Maureen Orth, "When Washington Was Fun," *Vanity Fair*, Nov. 5, 2007.

195 she reduced the traditional five-course meals to four: Cannon and Brooks, *Presidents' Cookbook*, 485.

195 "the opposite of what you'd find in a funeral home": Balridge and Verdon, *In the Kennedy Style*, 31–32.

195 Bui Van Han: Henry Voigt, "What Jackie Liked to Eat," *The American Menu* (blog), March 20, 2013, theamericanmenu.com.

195 La Caravelle: Frank DiGiacomo, "La Renaissance de La Caravelle," *Observer*, Jan. 15, 2001; Florence Fabricant, "La Caravelle, a French Legend, Is Closing After 43 Years," *NYT*, May 12, 2004.

196 "I worked at Le Pavillon": Pépin to the author, June 12, 2018.

196 On April 5, 1961, Verdon served a lunch: William Grimes, "René Verdon, French Chef for the Kennedys, Dies at 86," *NYT*, Feb. 5, 2011.

196 "There's nothing like French cooking": Katrina Heron, "Heavy Is the Toque at a State Dinner," *NYT*, Nov. 5, 2009.

196 "I cooked everything fresh": Emma Brown, "Rene Verdon, White House Chef for the Kennedys, Dies at 86," *WP*, Feb. 3, 2011.

196 *la Maison Blanche*: "Jacqueline Kennedy in the White House," Kennedy Library.

197 "how to make average food appetizing": Polan, *Julia Child's* The French Chef, 59.

197 "Nothing is too much trouble": Child with Prud'homme, *My Life in France*, 302.

197 Julius Spessot: Luisa Spessot, phone interview with the author, July 23, 2018.

198 "tastes are distressingly normal": Voigt, "What Jackie Liked to Eat."

198 Joe's Stone Crab: Letitia Baldrige, "A Party in Camelot," *McCall's*, May 1998.

199 "was no less attentive": Voigt, "What Jackie Liked to Eat."

199 Her favorite dinner was cold poached salmon: Voigt, "What Jackie Liked to Eat."

199 Jackie kept her weight at exactly 120 pounds: Sally Bedell Smith, "Private Camelot," *Vanity Fair*, May 2004.

200 "irritating . . . vain . . . impossible to please": Ted Sorensen, in Margaret Leslie Davis, "The Two First Ladies," *Vanity Fair*, Oct. 6, 2008.

200 "I am the man who accompanied": Baldrige and Verdon, *In the Kennedy Style*, 41.

200 The evening "was magic": Ibid., 39.

201 the Pakistanis worried that it would be seen as a snub: Bruce Reidel, "JFK's Forgotten CIA Crisis," *Daily Beast*, Nov. 8, 2015.

201 "a total mastery of detail": Davis, "Two First Ladies."

201 To accommodate 132 guests: Description of Khan state dinner at Mount Vernon in Baldrige and Verdon, *In the Kennedy Style*, 49–50; "Kennedy State Dinner: Four Grand Yachts Transport 140 Guests to a Memorable Feast on the East Lawn," George Washington's Mount Vernon, mountvernon.org.

201 "their own state dinner": "Kennedy State Dinner."

201 "a quiet little phrase of iron": Baldrige and Verdon, *In the Kennedy Style*, 53.

201 Just before the eight o'clock dinner: Reidel, "JFK's Forgotten CIA Crisis."

202 JFK's charm and Jackie's spectacular: Ibid.

202 "As they walked with their escorts": Baldrige and Verdon, *In the Kennedy Style*, 61.

202 Verdon's dinner included crabmeat: Ibid., 62–63; Heron, "Heavy Is the Toque at a State Dinner."

202 Khan as the George Washington of Pakistan: Reidel, "JFK's Forgotten CIA Crisis."

202 "Jackie wanted to do Versailles in America": Davis, "Two First Ladies."

202 "Brains Dinner": Baldrige and Verdon, *In the Kennedy Style*, 88.

203 "Jack and Jackie actually *shimmered*": William Styron, "Havanas in Camelot," *Vanity Fair*, July 1996.

203 Verdon created a seafood mousse: Cannon and Brooks, *Presidents' Cookbook*, 484.

203 "I think this is the most extraordinary": Sally Bedell Smith, "Private Camelot," *Vanity Fair*, May 2004.

204 "intellectual crush": Davis, "Two First Ladies."

204 "Where are the . . . really great Americans": Emery Roe, "Recalibrating Politics: The Kennedy White House Dinner for André Malraux," *When Complex Is as Simple as It Gets*, Dec. 16, 2019, mess-and-reliability.blog.

204 a détente was secretly brokered: Clyde H. Farnsworth, "Where Spies Are . . . or Have Been, or Might Be," *NYT*, Nov. 14, 1985.

204 "Mona Mania" drew more than a million visitors: Davis, "Two First Ladies."

204 golden interlude: Schlesinger, in ibid.

205 "Maybe I'm just dazzled": Lindsey Bever, "Jacqueline Kennedy's Newly Discovered Personal Letters Reveal 14 Years of Secrets," *WP*, May 13, 2014.

205 "No one ever knew John Kennedy": Adam Bernstein, "Charles Bartlett, Pulitzer-Winning Journalist and Kennedy Loyalist, Dies at 95," *WP*, Feb. 18, 2017.

205 His liaisons spanned the gamut: Amy Davidson Sorkin, "Mimi and the President," *New Yorker*, Feb. 10, 2012; Smith, "Private Camelot"; Caitlin Flanagan, "Jackie and the Girls," *Atlantic*, July/Aug. 2012.

205 "like my father in a way": Michael Parsons, "He's Like My Father in a Way—Loves the Chase and Is Bored with the Conquest," *Irish Times*, May 13, 2014; Kate Sheehy, "Jackie Kennedy's Letters to Priest Reveal Loneliness, Suspicion," *New York Post*, May 13, 2014.

205 "Happy biiiirthday, Mis-terr Pres-i-dennt": Marilyn Monroe, "Happy Birthday Mr. President," youtube.com.

205 Jackie arranged for a birthday dinner: Smith, "Private Camelot."

206 "they were doing the twist": Ian Shapira, "JFK's Last Birthday: Gifts, Champagne, and Wandering Hands on the Presidential Yacht," *WP*, May 26, 2017.

206 "never more intense and more complete": Davis, "Two First Ladies."

207 On November 22, JFK had his usual breakfast: Daisy Nichols, "Last Meals of 23 Famous People," The Daily Meal, Aug. 29, 2018, www.thedailymeal.com.

207 "Mr. President, you can't say Dallas": Testimony of Mrs. John Bowden Connally Jr., Warren Commission Hearings, Assassination Archives and Research Center, 147.

207 "No, you certainly can't": Testimony of Mrs. John F. Kennedy, Warren Commission Hearings, Assassination Archives and Research Center, 179.

13 · LYNDON B. JOHNSON
How Barbecue Led to Diplomacy and Chili Led to Civil Rights

209 Ninety-eight minutes: Olivia B. Waxman, "The Story Behind the Photo of LBJ Being Sworn In as President After JFK Died—and the Trailblazing Woman in the Corner," *Time,* Nov. 21, 2018.

209 "An assassin's bullet has thrust upon me": LBJ addresses Congress following JFK's assassination, Address Before a Joint Session of the Congress, Nov. 27, 1963, "Lady Bird Johnson," PBS, 2001, www.pbs.org.

209 by 1962 fifty million Americans: Markku Ruotsila, "Michael Harrington," *Britannica,* www.britannica.com.

209 Even by the U.S. government's conservative estimate: "Poverty in America," *Monthly Labor Review* 87, no. 3 (March 1964), 285–91.

209 For Johnson, the issue was personal: Robert Caro, in "For LBJ, the War on Poverty Was Personal," *Morning Edition,* NPR, Jan. 8, 2014.

209 "No single weapon or strategy": Lyndon Baines Johnson, First State of the Union Address, Jan. 8, 1964, American Rhetoric Online Speech Bank, www.americanrhetoric.com.

209 They called it the Stonewall ranch: Lyndon B. Johnson Ranch House, Park Road 49, Stonewall, Gillespie County, Tex., Library of Congress, loc.gov.

210 On a typical visit: Hal K. Rothman, *"Our Heart's Home": A Historic Resource Study of the Texas White House,* National Park Service Southwest Region, Professional Paper No. 60, 121.

210 a successful radio and TV business: Meathead, "In 1963, a First State Dinner for the Record Books," *HuffPost,* Dec. 6, 2017.

210 Marlboro cigarette ads: Kathleen Salch, "Present at the Creation: Marlboro Man," NPR, Oct. 21, 2002.

210 "began a universalization of the ranch": Rothman, *"Our Heart's Home,"* 73.

211 On December 29, the American and German delegates: Ibid.

211 "left time for relaxation": Max Frankel, "Hopes of U.S. High for Erhard Talks," *NYT,* Dec. 26, 1963.

212 "barbecue diplomacy": Meathead, "In 1963, a First State Dinner for the Record Books."

212 "where no child will go unfed": Lyndon B. Johnson, Remarks in Athens at Ohio University, May 7, 1964, American Presidency Project.

212 "The Great Society rests on abundance": President Lyndon Johnson's "Great Society" Speech, delivered at the University of Michigan, May 22, 1964, Bill of Rights Institute, billofrightsinstitute.org.

212 "A generation ago it would have been": Joshua Zeitz, "What Everyone Gets Wrong About LBJ's Great Society," *Politico,* Jan. 28, 2018.

213 "the central political error": Ibid.

213 "Government is not the solution": Reagan Inaugural Address, Jan. 20, 1981, Reagan Quotes and Speeches, Ronald Reagan Presidential Foundation & Institute.

213 Lady Bird Johnson hired Zephyr Wright: Addie Broyles, "From the Archives: Zephyr Wright's Legacy Lives On Through Famous LBJ Chili Recipe," austin360, Nov. 25, 2015.

213 "almost as popular as the government pamphlet": Rachel Saslow, "Exhibit Shows Government's Role in U.S. Diet; Book Details Drug Firms' Influence," *WP*, June 27, 2011.

213 "Lady Bird Johnson's Pedernales River Chili": Johnson postcard, courtesy of Constance Carter, Library of Congress.

214 "Senator, I'm not going to do it": "Recipes from the President's Kitchen," NPR, Feb. 19, 2008, www.npr.org.

215 "Mrs. Coopersmith . . . is given credit": Brendan Gill, "Barbecue," Talk of the Town, *New Yorker*, Aug. 29, 1964.

215 Johnson-Goldwater donnybrook reached a "fever pitch": "President Johnson's Pedernales River Chili," *UT News*, Feb. 15, 2016.

216 at the end of 1965, Verdon resigned: Brown, "Rene Verdon, White House Chef for the Kennedys, Dies at 86."

216 "I'm here in this country longer": "Versatile Swiss Chef Joins LBJ," *Sarasota Journal*, Jan. 20, 1966.

217 paid $10,000 a year: Henry Haller obituary, *Times* (London), Nov. 28, 2020.

217 "there is no better job": Marian Burros, "White House Chef to Leave in Fall," *NYT*, June 7, 1987.

14 · RICHARD M. NIXON AND GERALD R. FORD
The Unlikeliest Gastro-diplomat and the Instant President

219 "The greatest honor history can bestow": First Inaugural Address of Richard Milhous Nixon, Jan. 20, 1969, Yale Law School, Avalon Project, avalon.law.yale.edu.

219 "I think we could open a grocery store": West, *Upstairs at the White House*, 326.

219 Patricia "Pat" Nixon ordered four steaks: Ibid., 325; Haller, *White House Family Cookbook*, 80–82.

219 "just a bowl of cottage cheese": Haller, *White House Family Cookbook*, 80.

220 "I eat cottage cheese": Whitcomb and Whitcomb, *Real Life at the White House*, 389.

220 "Unless I have a guest": Ibid.

220 "Dick eats everything": Marie Smith, "How Nixon Lives, What He Likes," *WP*, Jan. 17, 1969, in Food Timeline, Richard M. Nixon, www.foodtimeline.org; Haller, *White House Family Cookbook*, 84–85.

220 "I am an introvert in an extrovert's profession": Whitcomb and Whitcomb, *Real Life at the White House*, 384.

220 Richard the Lionheart: Aitken, *Nixon*, 6.

221 "the best potato masher": Michael Rogin and John Lottier, "The Inner History of Richard Milhous Nixon," *Society* 9 (November/December, 1971), 19–28.

221 made enough by gambling on poker: Whitcomb and Whitcomb, *Real Life at the White House*, 387.

221 "If you can't lie": Ibid., 395.

221 "After hooking a limb": Ibid., 391.

221 "If you give me a week": Ibid., 387.

221 concerns about food safety: Theresa Vargas, "Thanksgiving Panic: How a Cranberry Crisis Changed the Way Americans See Food," *WP*, Nov. 20, 2017.

223 Pat Nixon stood just five feet six inches: Whitcomb and Whitcomb, *Real Life at the White House*, 389.

223 "marriage weight" of 175 pounds: Haller, *White House Family Cookbook*, 77.

223 his controlled diet verged on mania: Ibid., 71–72, 78–79, 91.

223 oenophile who collected fine bottles: Whitcomb and Whitcomb, *Real Life at the White House*, 390.

223 The Nixons reserved dessert: Haller, *White House Family Cookbook*, 106–7.

223 Tricia asked Haller for a hot dog: Whitcomb and Whitcomb, *Real Life at the White House,* 389.

224 White House Conference on Food, Nutrition, and Health: "1969 White House Conference," 50th Anniversary of the White House Conference on Food, Nutrition, and Health, Tufts University, 2019, sites.tufts.edu.

224 Marian Wright brought a group of senators: Ellen Meacham, "50 Years Ago, RFK Exposed Hunger in Mississippi Delta," *Clarion Ledger,* April 10, 2017.

224 The media latched on to the story: "Hunger in America," *CBS Reports,* CBS News, peabodyawards.com.

224 "The nation cannot live with its conscience": Walter Cronkite, *CBS Evening News,* Dec. 2, 1969; "White House Conference on Food, Nutrition, and Health," Wikipedia.

225 6.6 million students: Jack Rosenthal, "White House Acts to Provide Meals for More Pupils," *NYT,* Dec. 25, 1969.

225 "as if it had been a major military battle": Whitcomb and Whitcomb, *Real Life at the White House,* 388.

225 "the ineffable boredom of state dinners": Kissinger, *White House Years,* 923–24.

225 "Men don't really like soup": Whitcomb and Whitcomb, *Real Life at the White House,* 389.

226 One afternoon in February 1972: Hugh Davies, interview with the author, June 13, 2018; Maxine Cheshire, "Nixon-Kennedy 'Surprise' Film," *WP,* Feb. 24, 1972.

227 "the week that changed the world": "Nixon in China and the Week That Changed the World," Asia Society: Northern California, asiasociety.org; Allen McDuffee, "How Secret Talks Between the U.S. and China Led to 'the Week That Changed the World,'" timeline.com, Dec. 7, 2017.

227 "If you eat the things of others": Coe, *Chop Suey,* 228.

227 "The Chinese take great pride": Joseph Temple, "Dining for Détente: The Role Food Played During Nixon's Trip to China," International Wine & Food Society, July 18, 2014.

227 Winston Lord, who was married to: Coe, *Chop Suey,* 235.

227 "Banquet food served in [the PRC]": Ibid.

228 in practicing with ivory, wood, and silver chopsticks: Ibid., 232.

228 "Dragon, Tiger, Phoenix" stew: Ibid., 231.

228 "It was very crunchy": Ibid., 232.

228 "What is President Nixon's favorite Chinese food?": Ibid., 233.

228 Haldeman's job was to portray: Ibid., 234, 236.

229 unaware that the chairman was ailing: Ibid., 237.

229 "We had our first taste of food": Ibid., 238.

229 Maotai—a brand of *baijiu:* Ibid., 235.

229 "galley west": Whitcomb and Whitcomb, *Real Life at the White House,* 389.

229 "UNDER NO REPEAT NO CIRCUMSTANCES": Temple, "Dining for Détente."

229 "seize the day, seize the hour": Coe, *Chop Suey,* 239.

230 Meanwhile, platters of food: Ibid., 238–39; Raymond A. Sokolov, "The Menus at Peking Banquet Didn't Do Justice to the Foods," *NYT,* Feb. 26, 1972.

230 "boiled water (cold)": Florence Fabricant, "Nixon in China, the Dinner, Is Recreated," *NYT,* Jan. 25, 2011.

230 Cronkite squeezed his chopsticks: Temple, "Dining for Détente."

230 "The food is vastly more interesting": Sokolov, "Menus at Peking Banquet Didn't Do Justice to the Foods."

231 "Here is a tremendous picture": Ibid., 238.

231 Gallup poll: Temple, "Dining for Détente."

231 gourmet Cantonese cookery flowered: Coe, in Macy Halford, "The Exchange: Chop Suey," *New Yorker,* Oct. 18, 2009; Kate Heyhoe, "Chinese Food Fun," Kate's Global Kitchen, 2009, foodwine.com.

231 One evening in October 1973: Jeanette Smith, "Nixon's Return Visit," *WP,* Oct. 3, 1973.

232 It was one of many cocktails: Greg Morabito, "Remembering Trader Vic's, New York's Favorite Tiki Bar," *Eater New York,* Oct. 30, 2013.

232 "My entire family was very sorry": "Trump to Close a 'Tacky' Trader Vic's," *NYT,* Jan. 25, 1989.

232 "seeing Julie Eisenhower breast-feeding": Roxanne Roberts, "Bye-Bye Mai Tai," *WP,* July 1, 1995.

232 "We decided, 'Why not be young again'": Smith, "Nixon's Return Visit."

233 seventy-five worried Republicans: Martin Tolchin, "One Reaction to Nixon Breakfast," *NYT,* Nov. 15, 1973.

233 In a private meeting with GOP supporters: Don Fulsom, "The Nixon Resignation Quiz," *WP,* Aug. 7, 1994.

233 corned beef hash topped by a poached egg: Haller, *White House Family Cookbook,* 147–48.

233 At 12:03 p.m. on August 9, 1974: Fulsom, "Nixon Resignation Quiz."

233 "We can do it": Richard Norton Smith, "First Lady Betty Ford," *First Ladies,* C-SPAN, Dec. 2, 2013, c-span.org.

233 "Well, it certainly smells better": Fulsom, "Nixon Resignation Quiz."

234 celebrated over lasagna: Cannon, *Gerald R. Ford,* 35.

234 short baby-blue pajamas: Mark Jones, "When the White House Was in Alexandria," *Boundary Stones* (blog), WETA, May 8, 2013, boundarystones.weta.org.

234 fix a breakfast: Haller, *White House Family Cookbook,* 153–55.

234 "You are what you eat": Ibid., 153.

235 "I happen to be the nation's": Gerald Ford, "June 17, 1974—Speech, Grocery Manufacturers' Association, White Sulphur Springs, W. Va.," Gerald R. Ford Vice Presidential Papers, Gerald R. Ford Presidential Library, fordlibrarymuseum .gov.

235 "eating and sleeping are a waste of time": Craig Claiborne, "De Gustibus," *NYT,* Aug. 12, 1975.

235 his lunch, like his predecessor's: Haller, *White House Family Cookbook,* 176–79.

235 "That big Michigan Christmas tree and I": Gerald Ford, "12/17/74—Remarks for the Christmas Ball," President's Speeches and Statements, Reading Copies at the Ford Library.

236 "Great Tamale Incident": "Food Fails: Presidential Edition," *NYT,* July 26, 2016.

236 But when Ford shed fifteen pounds: Haller, *White House Family Cookbook,* 168.

236 Julia Child, a diet skeptic: Prud'homme, *French Chef in America,* 152–56.

236 "do something about improving": Julia Child, "A White House Menu," *New York Times Magazine,* Jan. 16, 1977.

15 · JIMMY CARTER In Search of Grits and Peace

238 "Jimmy isn't mysterious": Whitcomb and Whitcomb, *Real Life at the White House,* 422.

238 a "down-home lunch" in Georgia: Child, "White House Menu."

238 southern staples: catfish, biscuits: Haller, *White House Family Cookbook,* 229–321; Kandy Stroud, "Jimmy Carter, Cheese Buff," *NYT,* Dec. 27, 1976.

239 "Plains Special": Stroud, "Jimmy Carter, Cheese Buff"; "Jimmy Carter's Plains Special Cheese Ring," *Esquire,* Nov. 10, 2008.

239 "the kind of cooking . . . to which [those] who strayed": Haller, *White House Family Cookbook,* 237.

239 "Daddy makes grits": Stroud, "Jimmy Carter, Cheese Buff."

239 "While New Englanders gasped": Haller, *White House Family Cookbook,* 229–31.

239 "That sounds mighty good to me": Child, "White House Menu."

240 "Each family that occupies the White House": Rosalynn Carter, "How We Entertain in the South," *McCall's,* Feb. 1977.

240 the farm made just $187: Charles McFarlane, "7 Presidents Who Farmed: Jimmy Carter," *Modern Farmer*, Feb. 17, 2014.

240 "Jimmy cooked as much as I did": Stroud, "Jimmy Carter, Cheese Buff."

240 "There probably are still people": Carter, "How We Entertain in the South."

241 "If there's any secret to hospitality": Ibid.

241 "The press had painted us": Carter, *First Lady from Plains*, 227.

242 a $600 food bill: Bethany Nagle, "The Inauguration of Jimmy Carter," WHHA.

242 "Hi! C'mon in!": Haller, *White House Family Cookbook*, 234.

242 reading a book at a state dinner: Mary Finch Hoyt, "Now That Carters Have Put Their Stamp on White House Social Life," *U.S. News & World Report*, April 4, 1977.

242 "There was a small accident": Mesnier, *All the Presidents' Pastries*, 107–8.

243 "a friend inside the White House": Chip Heath, "Willie and the Weed Factory," *GQ*, Aug. 31, 2015.

243 "I don't know how I would have managed": Carter, "How We Entertain in the South."

243 "They make me sound like a real prude": Whitcomb and Whitcomb, *Real Life at the White House*, 420.

243 "policy, protocol, the whole image": Hoyt, "Now That Carters Have Put Their Stamp."

244 "Official entertaining can't replace": Carter, "How We Entertain in the South."

244 the morning of July 20, 1978: Carter, "Summit at Camp David," in *First Lady from Plains*, 255–90.

244 "First Egyptian-Jewish peace": Wright, *Thirteen Days in September*, 59.

244 "peace in the Middle East would be": Carter, *First Lady from Plains*, 258.

244 "I slowly became hardened": Ibid., 259.

244 "It was necessary we be completely isolated": Nelson, *The President Is at Camp David*, 112.

244 "It's so beautiful here": Carter, *First Lady from Plains*, 258.

245 Less well known is that burrowed deep beneath: Wright, *Thirteen Days in September*, 63.

245 On September 5, 1978, the three: Carter, *First Lady from Plains*, 256.

246 "Security yes! Land no!": Ibid., 267.

247 "There must be a way": Ibid., 268.

247 Rosalynn had an idea: Ibid., 257, 269.

247 "the Bible says you cannot serve God": Ibid., 270–71.

247 Begin proved less flexible: Ibid., 277.

247 The two relaxed by watching: Ibid., 284.

248 food to feed two hundred: Ibid., 289.

248 toasted to achieving the impossible: Ibid., 288–89.

248 Peace Treaty Dinner for 1,340 people: Haller, *White House Family Cookbook*, 318–20.

249 "The impossible had been made possible": Carter, *First Lady from Plains*, 288.

249 The Carters were frugal, but they did not stint on official entertaining: Carter, *First Lady from Plains*, 232–33, 236.

249 "pigeonholed [Carter] as a hick": Mesnier, *All the Presidents' Pastries*, 291.

250 "There's no doubt about it": Whitcomb and Whitcomb, *Real Life at the White House*, 422.

250 "final supper" at the White House: Mesnier, *All the Presidents' Pastries*, 113.

16 · RONALD REAGAN Jelly Beans, Weight Loss, and Glasnost

252 Reagan celebrated his inauguration: The 49th Presidential Inaugural Luncheon, the Joint Congressional Committee on Inaugural Ceremonies, www.inaugural .senate.gov/49th-inaugural-ceremonies; Reagan, *My Turn*, 235.

252 "With thanks to Almighty God": Bernard Gwertzman, "Reagan Takes Oath as 40th President; Promises an 'Era of National Renewal'—Minutes Later, 52 U.S. Hostages in Iran Fly to Freedom After 444-Day Ordeal," *NYT*, Jan. 21, 1981.

252 At that moment, Jimmy Carter: Terence Smith, "A Weary Carter Returns to Plains," *NYT*, Jan. 21, 1981; Reagan, *My Turn*, 234.

252 At his inauguration: Bob Colacello, "Ronnie & Nancy, Part I," *Vanity Fair*, July 1998.

252 at $16 million, the most expensive: Ibid.

252 Carter's "'people's' inauguration": Bernard Weinraub, "Five-Day 'People's' Inauguration Begins in Capital Tuesday," *NYT*, Jan. 16, 1977.

253 White House staffers "in bare feet": Charles Moore, "Margaret Thatcher's First Visit to Washington of the Reagan Presidency," *HuffPost*, July 21, 2013.

253 "Queen Nancy" Reagan: Colacello, "Ronnie & Nancy, Part I."

253 Reagans' inaugural guests included a dozen: Ibid.

253 "Some folks are jokingly calling it": Pete Earley, "Reagan Inauguration Most Expensive Ever," *WP*, Jan. 16, 1981.

253 Nancy's wardrobe: Colacello, "Ronnie & Nancy, Part I."

253 a man of simple tastes: Haller, *White House Family Cookbook*, 335.

253 "the Iron Butterfly": Colacello, "Ronnie & Nancy, Part I."

253 "scared shitless": Mesnier, *All the Presidents' Pastries*, 118.

254 "Mrs. Reagan, you don't have a chance in hell": Bob Colacello, "The White House's Dinner Theater," *Vanity Fair*, June 2010.

254 "wanted to have people consider her": Ibid.

254 "an amiable dunce": David S. Broder, "Clark Clifford Says Reagan Can Be Beaten," *WP*, Dec. 15, 1983.

254 "a very smart thing": Bob Colacello, "Ronnie & Nancy, Part II," *Vanity Fair*, Aug. 1998.

255 a private, "surprise" black-tie dinner dance: Donnie Radcliffe and Elisabeth Bumiller, "Birthday Bonanza President's Birthday," *WP*, Feb. 7, 1981.

255 Reagan had "nothing there": Geoffrey Wheatcroft, "The Thatcher-Reagan Love Affair Wasn't All Plain Sailing," *Guardian*, Nov. 10, 2014.

255 "This is the century": Colacello, "Ronnie & Nancy Part II."

256 "the relaxed, almost lazy generalist": Moore, "Margaret Thatcher's First Visit to Washington of the Reagan Presidency."

256 "*has* to be fun": Colacello, "White House's Dinner Theater."

256 "How did I do?": White House insider, who wished to remain anonymous, verbally to the author.

256 Haller prepared a classic: Maryse Chevriere, "The Most Elaborate White House State Dinners of All Time," Chowhound.com.

256 "Oh, the anemones": Colacello, "Ronnie & Nancy Part II."

257 "a curious sensation": Larry Clark, "March Madness: The Improbable Making of an American Icon," *Historic America*, March 30, 2021, historicamerica.org.

257 split pea, and hamburger soup: Reagan, *My Turn*, 14.

257 "I thought if he watched the news": Ibid., 15.

257 "the greatest political win": Colacello, "Ronnie & Nancy, Part II."

258 They called the property Rancho del Cielo: Carter Woolly, "Reagan's Ranch in the Heavens," WHHA.

258 twenty-four hundred feet above sea level: Steven R. Weisman, "On Holiday Back at the Reagans' Ranch," *NYT*, Nov. 26, 1981.

258 The house was a simple one-story: Todd Purdum, "Keeping Reagan's Legacy Alive at His Old Ranch," *NYT*, May 24, 1998.

258 Every Thanksgiving, the extended Reagan family: Manuel Roig-Franzia, "At a White House Thanksgiving, Tradition Is a Presidential Thing," *WP*, Nov. 13, 2012.

259 Berkley replaced traditional, sharp: C. K. Hickey, "All the Presidents' Meals," *Foreign Policy*, Feb. 16, 2019; Barbara Gamarekian, "The White House; All the President's Wines," *NYT*, Jan. 15, 1986.

259 "wear my oldest suit": Transcript of "Question-and-Answer Session with Reporters on Foreign and Domestic Policy Issues, April 5, 1982," Ronald Reagan Presidential Library & Museum, reaganlibrary.gov.

259 "world-class worrier": Reagan, *My Turn*, 235.

259 she dropped from a featherweight 114 pounds: Donnie Radcliffe, "First Lady's Weight Loss," *WP*, Sept. 20, 1983.

259 Some worried that Nancy had cancer: "Princess Diana, Nancy Reagan Stay Slim Almost Effortlessly," *South Florida Sun-Sentinel*, Dec. 30, 1985.

259 "The sufferer attempts to take control": Emily T. Troscianko, "Taking, Losing, and Letting Go of Control in Anorexia," *Psychology Today*, Aug. 18, 2015.

259 "People believe that when one occupies": "Princess Diana, Nancy Reagan Stay Slim Almost Effortlessly."

259 "the presidential (or Tecumseh)": Steve Friess, "Bush's Legacy: He Survived!," *Slate*, Jan. 14, 2009.

260 "it was very obvious": Angela D. Blessing, Joyce Wadler, Dirk Mathison, and Margie Bonnett Sellinger, "The President's Astrologers," *People*, May 23, 1988.

260 "the most closely guarded domestic secret": Ibid.

260 "No First Lady need make apologies": Bill McAllister, "The Nancy Reagan Rebuttal," *WP*, June 10, 1988.

260 "Nobody was hurt by it": Mary Kay Linge, "How Ronald Reagan's Wife Nancy Let Her Astrologer Control the Presidency," *New York Post*, Oct. 18, 2021.

260 veal stew and fresh coconut cake: Colacello, "Ronnie & Nancy, Part I."

260 Herman Goelitz Candy Company: "Jelly Belly History," www.jellybelly.com.

261 "Addicts vow" that the candies: "Living: Hill of Beans," *Time*, Feb. 23, 1981.

261 "worldwide company overnight": Kate Kelly, "Ronald Reagan's Jelly Beans," American Presidents & Their Families, America Comes Alive!, americacomesalive.com.

261 three and a half tons: Ibid.

261 "You can tell a lot about a fella's character": "Everything You Need to Know About Jelly Belly Jelly Beans," OldTimeCandy.com, May 12, 2022.

261 "I keep riding younger and younger horses": Haller, *White House Family Cookbook*, 347.

261 "you were the most important person": Schifando and Joseph, *Entertaining at the White House with Nancy Reagan*, 106.

261 "a preternatural affability": Ibid.

261 "role of a lifetime": For example, Roxanne Roberts, "In First Lady, Nancy Reagan Found the Role of a Lifetime," *WP*, March 6, 2016.

261 "You don't just move into the White House": Whitcomb and Whitcomb, *Real Life at the White House*, 432.

262 "the gaze": Richard Zoglin, "The First Lady and the Slasher," *Time*, April 22, 1991.

262 "Ronnie says I should just forget": Whitcomb and Whitcomb, *Real Life at the White House*, 432.

262 A famously picky eater: "Princess Diana, Nancy Reagan Stay Slim Almost Effortlessly."

262 President Reagan's breakfast consisted: Haller, *White House Family Cookbook*, 329.

262 Their "TV dinners" became famous: Eliza Barclay, "Reagan's Unsung Legacy: Frozen Food Day," *The Salt*, NPR, March 7, 2012.

262 "We would have been shot": Mesnier, *All the Presidents' Pastries*, 129–30.

262 "a sophisticated diner. She has an artist's eye": Phyllis Hanes, "Dinner Is Served, Mr. President. Former White House Chef Reminisces About His Tenure at 1600 Pennsylvania Avenue," *Christian Science Monitor*, Jan. 13, 1988.

262 "a tough character": Mesnier, *All the Presidents' Pastries*, 144–45, 152.

263 "I am the only person who decides": Ibid.

263　"Here we see a squirrel eating his nuts": Ibid., 139.

263　"Ketchup Is a Vegetable?": Marion Nestle, "Ketchup Is a Vegetable? Again?," *Food-Politics,* Nov. 15, 2011, foodpolitics.com; and EricT_Culinarylore, "Did Ronald Reagan Say Ketchup Was a Vegetable?," *Culinary Lore,* Nov. 2, 2016, culinarylore.com.

263　"egg on its face": Mary Thornton and Martin Schram, "U.S. Holds the Ketchup in Schools," *WP,* Sept. 26, 1981.

263　$1.44 billion spent on five executive dining rooms: Jonathan Harsh, "Reagan Cuts Eat into School Lunches," *Christian Science Monitor,* Sept. 17, 1981.

263　"That our young people are not as important": Ibid.

263　the president claimed he wasn't aware of the details: Steven R. Weisman, "Reagan Abandons Proposal to Pare School Nutrition," *NYT,* Sept. 26, 1981.

263　a new set of bone china: Helen Thomas, "First Lady Pays $210,000 for New China," UPI, Sept. 12, 1981.

264　"was a symbol of my supposed extravagance": Colacello, "Ronnie & Nancy, Part II."

264　seven kings and three queens: Cook, *Presidential Leadership by Example,* 290.

264　fifty-two state dinners: Hickey, "All the Presidents' Meals."

264　"It was a vital part of our roles": Schifando and Joseph, *Entertaining at the White House with Nancy Reagan,* 165.

265　"The step you are about to take": Elisabeth Bumiller, "A Cozy Little Dinner, Fit for a Prince," *WP,* May 4, 1981.

265　"Nothing short of absolute perfection": Mesnier, *All the Presidents' Pastries,* 141–42.

266　"Would you care to dance?": Kenzie Bryant, "John Travolta Called His Dance with Princess Diana a Highlight of His Life," *Vanity Fair,* Sept. 26, 2016.

266　Diana would famously struggle: Andrew Morton, *Diana: Her True Story* (New York: Simon & Schuster, 1997).

266　Di became "the people's princess": Jane Mendle, "How Princess Diana Changed Lives by Discussing Her Mental Health," *Time,* Aug. 30, 2017.

266　"They thought, 'Those Californians, they don't know anything'": Schifando and Joseph, *Entertaining at the White House with Nancy Reagan,* 121.

267　"Don't you get it?": Colacello, "Ronnie & Nancy, Part II."

267　"Gucci comrade": Nina Martyris, "Cold War, Hot Tea: Nancy Reagan and Raisa Gorbachev's Sipping Summit," NPR, March 8, 2016.

268　the first American-born executive chef: Marian Burros, "White House Said to Pick a Replacement Chef," *NYT,* Aug. 20, 1987; "Chef at White House Quits After 4 Months," Associated Press, Jan. 10, 1988; Moore, "The Delicious History of the White House Executive Chef."

268　a menu that featured American ingredients: "126 VIPs Chosen for Historic White House Dinner During Summit," *Jet,* Dec. 28–Jan. 4, 1988.

17 · GEORGE H. W. BUSH　The Yin and Yang of Broccoli

270　"The principal lesson of WASP cookery": Jonathan Yardley, "Bush's Green Revolution," *WP,* March 26, 1990.

270　"I do not like broccoli": Maureen Dowd, "'I'm President,' So No More Broccoli!," *NYT,* March 23, 1990.

270　"Now, look. . . . There are truckloads": David Hoffman, "Bush the Broccoli Thing," *WP,* March 23, 1990.

271　"You're darn right I do": Tim Carman, "As President, George H. W. Bush Never Wavered from His Hard Line on Broccoli," *WP,* Dec. 5, 2018.

271　"he's no fan of slimy white fish": Peggy Grodinsky, "Dining with Former First Couple Barbara and George Bush," *Houston Chronicle,* Jan. 4, 2006.

271 Bush bought a gallon of milk: Andrew Rosenthal, "Bush Encounters the Super-market, Amazed," *NYT,* Feb. 5, 1992.

271 Her repertoire included: "Recipes by Barbara Bush: Barbecued Chicken; Mush-room Quiche; Zuni Stew," *Classic Celebrity Recipes* (blog), March 12, 2016; "Mexi-can Mound: A Great Bush Favorite," cooks.com.

272 cereal for dinner: Grodinsky, "Dining with Former First Couple."

272 tomato bisque, salad: De Guzman, *Bush Family Cookbook,* 58–59.

272 "it's no exaggeration to say the undecideds could go": Michael S. Rosenwald, "Fragrant Armpits, Napping Aides, Corny Duck Jokes: George H. W. Bush's Wonderful Humor," *WP,* Dec. 4, 2018.

272 long-running affair with Jennifer Fitzgerald: Page, *Matriarch,* cited in Peter Baker, "To Barbara Bush, Donald Trump Represented 'Greed, Selfishness,'" *NYT,* March 27, 2019.

272 When Zachary Taylor died: Michael Marriott, "Verdict In: 12th President Was Not Assassinated," *NYT,* June 27, 1991.

272 "combination of official scandals": Morison, *Oxford History of the American Peo-ple,* as quoted by Andrew Glass, "Zachary Taylor's Body Exhumed, June 17, 1991," *Politico,* June 16, 2011.

273 CNN received a call: Dennis McDougal, "CNN Averts Hoax About Bush's 'Death,'" *Los Angeles Times,* Jan. 10, 1992.

273 "The President is human": Michael Wines, "Bush in Japan; Bush Collapses at State Dinner with the Japanese," *NYT,* Jan. 9, 1992.

273 Chambrin prepared a luscious dinner: Donnie Radcliffe and Roxanne Roberts, "Hail, and Thunder, to the Queen," *WP,* May 15, 1991.

273 Roland Mesnier's dessert: Mesnier, *All the Presidents' Pastries,* 172.

18 · WILLIAM J. CLINTON Torn Between Renunciation and Appetite

278 At his first dinner as president: Marian Burros, "High Calories (and Chef!) Out at White House," *NYT,* March 5, 1994.

278 "We're trying to get a kitchen cabinet": Marian Burros, "Hillary Clinton's New Home: Broccoli's In, Smoking's Out," *NYT,* Feb. 2, 1993.

278 The resulting menu was a sophisticated mix: Ibid.

278 "I can't say I'm very pleased": Burros, "High Calories (and Chef!)."

279 "not hard to please": Ibid.

279 "The president did like unhealthy foods": David S. Martin, "From Omnivore to Vegan: The Dietary Education of Bill Clinton," CNN, Aug. 18, 2011.

279 "Pierre is incapable of doing low fat": Burros, "High Calories (and Chef!)."

279 paid an unprecedented $37,026 settlement: *Boise City News,* May 24, 2013.

279 "Hillary Clinton don't know nothing": Hickey, "All the Presidents' Meals."

279 "The big issue about health": Burros, "High Calories (and Chef!)."

279 "The Clintons, a minority choice": Keith Botsford, "The Clintons Cook Up a Storm," *Independent,* March 26, 1994.

280 "I don't think anyone wants to call that array": Jack Hitt, "Sweetness and Bite," *Slate,* July 23, 1996.

280 "is recognizably different from that": Freedman, *American Cuisine,* 378.

281 The healthy eating trend flowered: Ibid.

281 Food Network, which debuted in 1993: Rachel Sugar, "How Food Network Turned Big-City Chef Culture into Middle-America Pop Culture," Grubstreet .com; Simone Migliori, "The History of the Food Network," WGBH, July 23, 2018.

281 "delicious revolution": "Alice Waters and Her Delicious Revolution," *American Masters,* PBS, March 19, 2003, pbs.org; Freedman, *American Cuisine,* 1.

281 "seasonal, pure foods [and] health": Marian Burros, "First Chef: American, Per-haps?," *NYT,* Dec. 9, 1992.

282 washed each leaf individually: Ruth Reichl, "Hail to the Chef," *Los Angeles Times,* Jan. 7, 1993.

282 served only "perfect" peaches: Alice Waters, "Alice Waters on the Persuasive Power of the Peach," *Vanity Fair,* Nov. 1, 2017.

283 "We chefs . . . believe that good food": Burros, "First Chef."

283 "Just seeing what Clinton eats": Candy Sagon, "Doesn't Clinton Deserve a Break Today?," *WP,* Dec. 16, 1992.

283 "the food police": Laurie Ochoa, "Taking Her Revolution Beyond the Kitchen," *Los Angeles Times,* Aug. 22, 1996.

283 Paul Bocuse declared that nationalism: Burros, "High Calories (and Chef!)."

283 "I would be a hypocrite": Burros, "First Chef."

283 "wouldn't have received such attention": Ochoa, "Taking Her Revolution Beyond the Kitchen."

283 "A decision about the White House chef": Burros, "First Chef."

283 "a breakthrough figure": Burros, "Hillary Clinton's New Home."

284 "I have five kids": David Blum, "The Lives They Lived: Patrick Clark; the Man Who Loved to Cook," *NYT,* Jan. 3, 1999.

284 Hay-Adams paid Clark a princely $170,000: Ibid.

284 received four thousand applications: Scheib and Friedman, *White House Chef,* 12.

284 "We're not going to entertain": Ibid., 15.

284 "a fat band boy": Marian Burros, "A Crusade and Some Diet Advice from That 'Fat Band Boy,'" *NYT,* Oct. 11, 2006.

284 In New Hampshire, he inhaled almost a dozen doughnuts: Martin, "From Omnivore to Vegan."

284 *Saturday Night Live* sketch: Originally aired Dec. 5, 1992: Mike Thomas, "Phil Hartman's Greatest Sketch Ever: Secrets of *SNL*'s Perfect Clinton Parody," *Salon,* Sept. 30, 2014; Don Roy King, "Clinton at McDonald's," *SNL Transcripts Tonight,* snltranscripts.jt.org.

284 Clinton's weight ballooned to 230 pounds: Eric Spitznagel, "America's Fattest Presidents," *Men's Health,* Dec. 13, 2013.

284 "the kind of diet most people his age": Marian Burros, "Bill Clinton and Food: Jack Sprat He's Not," *NYT,* Dec. 23, 1992.

285 "An occasional trip to a fast-food restaurant": Burros, "Hillary Clinton's New Home."

285 "Let's put broccoli in the White House again!": Hillary Reinsberg, "Hillary Clinton Wanted Broccoli in the White House Back in 1992," *BuzzFeed,* July 9, 2013.

285 "I suppose I could have stayed home": Amy Chozick, "Hillary Clinton and the Return of the (Unbaked) Cookies," *NYT,* Nov. 5, 2016.

285 when *Family Circle* asked Mrs. Clinton and Barbara Bush: David A. Graham, "Bill Clinton's Half-Baked Entry in the Presidential Cookie Contest," *Atlantic,* Aug. 18, 2016.

286 "We are trying to move toward healthy": Burros, "Hillary Clinton's New Home."

286 "I'm a lousy cook": Mimi Sheraton, "How Hungry Is Hillary Clinton?," *Slate,* Feb. 20, 2008.

286 "periodically undisciplined about what I eat": Burros, "Bill Clinton and Food."

286 not above the occasional olive burger: Sheraton, "How Hungry Is Hillary Clinton?"

286 became "one of the serious issues": Burros, "Bill Clinton and Food."

286 "a stylish palate": Sheraton, "How Hungry Is Hillary Clinton?"

286 "High Calories (and Chef!) Out at White House": Burros, *NYT,* March 5, 1994.

286 "You should apply for that job": Scheib and Friedman, *White House Chef,* 11.

287 "a backward-looking spectacle": Ibid., 17.

287 "The money might not be as good as you're used to": Ibid., 14.

287 "marks another milestone in the evolution": "White House Sets Healthy Example, Logs Milestone with New Exec Chef," *Nation's Restaurant News,* April 25, 1994.

288 "the Casa Blanca Gang": Scheib and Friedman, *White House Chef,* 58.

288 He quickly learned that the president: Ibid., 38–39, 329.

288 fifteen to twenty thousand mini crab cakes: Ibid., 74.

288 "If you wanted a ripe tomato": Ibid., 43.

288 "Walter, could you please calculate calories?": Ibid., 67.

288 lest the "Clinton diet" become a gossipy distraction: Ibid., 65–66.

289 The South Lawn became a favorite party venue: Ibid., 120–21.

289 "Mrs. Clinton presided over a minor revolution": Mesnier, *All the Presidents' Pastries,* 201.

289 "I was stealing his spotlight": Scheib and Friedman, *White House Chef,* 128.

289 "We were there . . . to bring": Ibid., 56.

290 "an atrocious concoction": Mesnier, *All the Presidents' Pastries,* 207.

290 vegetable garden on the White House roof: Scheib and Friedman, *White House Chef,* 52–54.

290 three standard elements: Ibid., 124.

290 state dinners "are not Escoffier": William Grimes, "Walter Scheib, Innovative Former White House Chef, Is Dead at 61," *NYT,* June 22, 2015.

290 His first state dinner was held: Scheib and Friedman, *White House Chef,* 124–27.

291 the dinner was served "American style": Ibid., 127.

291 "I get to do every day": Grimes, "Walter Scheib."

291 "the Bill and Boris show": "The Bill and Boris Show," *Baltimore Sun,* Oct. 1, 1994.

291 "wanted a taxi to go out for pizza": Becky Little, "When a Russian President Ended Up Drunk and Disrobed Outside the White House," history.com, Aug. 30, 2018.

291 Yeltsin was an alcoholic: Ibid.

292 "That victory is your victory": Martin Weil, "Nelson Mandela Made Many Memorable Trips to Washington," *WP,* Dec. 5, 2013.

292 Mandela state dinner on October 4: Scheib and Friedman, *White House Chef,* 131–37.

292 The Clinton china, which depicts: Ibid., 135.

292 Scheib's kitchen catered 220 dinners: Ibid., 131.

292 The Clintons had invited Patrick Clark: Ibid., 134.

293 "No visiting head of state inspired": Ibid.

293 Chelsea Clinton asked for cooking lessons: Ibid., 82–84.

294 suffered "psychic damage": Todd S. Purdum, "Chelsea Clinton, Still a Closed Book," *NYT,* June 21, 2001.

294 "bore a striking resemblance to cabbages": Mesnier, *All the Presidents' Pastries,* 242.

294 "bent and ugly" coronary artery: "The Last Heart Attack: Dr. Sanjay Gupta Reports," interview with Clinton, CNN, Sept. 3, 2011.

294 "Because of your genetics": Katie Robbins, "Bill Clinton Goes Vegan to Get Healthy," Delish, Aug. 22, 2011.

294 "the way we consume food": Joe Conason, "My Lunch with Bill," *AARP: The Magazine,* Aug.–Sept. 2013.

19 · GEORGE W. BUSH
T-Ball, Freedom Fries, and a Changing of the Guard

297 was as picky an eater: Scheib and Friedman, *White House Chef,* 206–7.

297 Laura Welch Bush, liked food: Ibid., 215–16.

297 "Food wasn't much of a priority": Ibid.

297 Scheib considered his collaboration: Ibid., 205, 216.

298 In those days W. was a charming rake: Lois Romano and George Lardner Jr., "Bush's Life-Changing Year," *WP,* July 25, 1999.

299 In Midland, W. was known for wearing: Amy Herstek, "Black Tie & Boots Gala to Be Bush's Texas-Sized Victory Party," CNN, Jan. 19, 2001; Skip Hollandsworth, "I Had a Ball," *Texas Monthly*, March 2001.

299 the first Little Leaguer in the White House: Scheib and Friedman, *White House Chef*, 241.

299 Sandlot-themed meals: Ibid., 240–53.

299 Bush hosted lunch for Hall of Famers: Ibid., 244–45, 250–53.

300 On May 6, Bush invited two teams of kids: Ibid., 250.

300 Bushes hosted their first state dinner: Ibid., 222–27.

300 The assistant usher Dan Shanks: Ibid., 224.

301 Six days later, Walter Scheib: Ibid., 254–63.

301 "Don't talk to anyone whom you don't know": Ibid., 267.

301 "extreme anxiety": Mesnier, *All the Presidents' Pastries*, 281–82.

302 offered the staff psychological counseling: Scheib and Friedman, *White House Chef*, 265–66.

302 "We could have served [them] ham sandwiches": Ibid., 268.

302 A new protocol created a firewall: Ibid., 266–67.

302 "Right after 9/11 . . . the food changed": Hilary Pollack, "Confessions of a Former White House Chef, Part One," *Vice*, Feb. 5, 2015.

302 Consider the battle over French fries: Timothy Bella, " 'Freedom Never Tasted So Good': How Walter Jones Helped Rename French Fries over the Iraq War," *WP*, Feb. 11, 2019; Sheryl Gay Stolberg, "An Order of Fries, Please, but Do Hold the French," *NYT*, March 12, 2003.

303 The food fight was too delicious: Bella, " 'Freedom Never Tasted So Good.' "

303 "white-wine swillers": Adam Nagourney, "White House Memo; List of Guests Throws Light on the Bush Style," *NYT*, Aug. 19, 2002.

303 "There was no red-state food": Emily Langer, "Walter Scheib, White House Chef Who Served Two Presidents, Dies at 61," *WP*, June 22, 2015; Hilary Pollack, "Confessions of a Former White House Chef, Part Two," *Vice*, Feb. 6, 2015.

304 huevos rancheros for brunch, and bags of Lay's potato chips: Scheib and Friedman, *White House Chef*, 232, 238.

304 fans of barbecue: Pollack, "Confessions of a Former White House Chef, Part One."

304 "You might be considered a presidential assassin": Langer, "Walter Scheib, White House Chef Who Served Two Presidents, Dies at 61."

304 Both were hot sauce aficionados: Pollack, "Confessions of a Former White House Chef, Part One."

304 Yucatan Sunshine Habanero Pepper Sauce: Scheib and Friedman, *White House Chef*, 207.

304 both women favored organic vegetables: Marian Burros, "What's Cooking at the White House? Who's Asking?," *NYT*, Jan. 20, 2009.

305 W. was munching a Hammond pretzel: Moeller, *Dining at the White House*, 206–7; "Bush on Fainting Episode: 'Chew Your Food,' " CNN, Jan. 14, 2002, cnn .com.

305 "like . . . mustard on pretzels": Tim Carman, "White House Memories: Chef John Moeller on Pretzels, Maple Syrup, and Calorie-Counting," *WP*, Feb. 18, 2014.

305 "You're not going to get us to cough up": Elisabeth Bumiller, "D.C. Shocker: The President Snacks Alone," *NYT*, Jan. 20, 2002.

305 "Am I going to be working here": Carman, "White House Memories."

306 Scheib found his role "drastically reduced": Scheib and Friedman, *White House Chef*, 205, 217.

306 "My work had ceased being fun": Ibid., 277.

306 "I was . . . one part private chef": Ibid., 278.

306 "What's your book called": Ibid., 299.

307 Thaddeus DuBois as the new executive pastry chef: Ibid., 308.

307 persuaded Mesnier to rejoin the kitchen: Ibid., 313–15.

307 "I never imagined I'd get *that* call": Yosses in conversation with the author, Aug. 22, 2019.

308 "I don't want the White House to feel like a hotel": Ibid.; Yosses to Andrew Friedman, *Andrew Talks to Chefs,* podcast, episode 68, Dec. 29, 2018.

308 Berman as a coldhearted: Scheib and Friedman, *White House Chef,* 279–87.

309 Those were the last words: Ibid., 291–92.

309 Scheib did not subscribe: Ibid., 292; Marian Burros, "Top White House Chef Is Leaving, an Idea That Wasn't His," *NYT,* Feb. 5, 2005.

309 Scheib was told not to return: Scheib and Friedman, *White House Chef,* 292.

309 "being the most famous anonymous person": Pollack, "Confessions of a Former White House Chef, Part Two."

309 On June 13, 2015, Scheib went for a hike: Grimes, "Walter Scheib"; Edmundo Carrillo, "Former White House Chef Drowned, OMI Reports," *Albuquerque Journal,* June 23, 2015.

310 "intimate secrets that threaten": Mike Jaccarino, "Dark Mysteries Behind Clinton Chef's Drowning," *National Enquirer,* July 2, 2015.

310 flash flood swept him away: Michelle Toh, "Former White House Chef Drowned While Hiking: What to Do in a Flash Flood," *Christian Science Monitor,* June 24, 2015.

310 $80,000 to $100,000: Marian Burros, "First Woman Is Selected as Executive Chef at White House," *NYT,* Aug. 15, 2005.

310 "I look for an open door": Waters, verbally in conversation with the author, July 11, 2019.

310 "Throughout our history": Judith Weinraub, "Group Asks First Lady to Consider Woman for the Top Chef Job," *WP,* March 9, 2005.

311 "sophisticated restaurant food": Candy Sagon, "Toque of the Town: White House Names 1st Female Executive Chef," *WP,* Aug. 15, 2005.

311 quietly offered to Patrick O'Connell: Justin Dickerson, "Way to White House Is Through Its Taste Buds," *Los Angeles Times,* Feb. 27, 2005.

311 "I am delighted": Burros, "First Woman Is Selected."

311 Cristeta Gomez Pasia Comerford: Amanda Cohen, "Lady Chef Stampede: Cristeta Comerford, the White House Chef," Mediaite.com, Oct. 10, 2013; Jose Antonio Vargas, "Hail to the Chef," *WP,* Aug. 22, 2005.

311 "so driven. So ambitious": Vargas, "Hail to the Chef."

312 Moeller . . . bore no grudge: Moeller, *Dining at the White House,* 220–23; Moeller in conversation with the author, Feb. 17, 2020.

312 "That . . . makes a beautiful statement": Burros, "First Woman Is Selected."

312 "a message around the world": Sagon, "Toque of the Town: White House Names 1st Female Executive Chef."

20 · BARACK OBAMA The President with the Global Palate

314 Barack Obama was the son: Barack Obama, *Dreams from My Father,* 10.

314 "The boy should know where his dinner": Ibid., 34–35.

314 decidedly non-American fare: Ibid., 37.

315 his single mother relied on food stamps: Joanne Samuel Goldblum, "Most Powerful Man in the World Grew Up on Food Stamps," *HuffPost,* June 11, 2014.

315 "the main livestock is squirrels": Jason Zengerle, "How Barack Obama Sold Out the Kale Crowd," *New Republic,* April 29, 2014.

316 "insufferable foodie": Rebecca Flint Marx, "What Obama Has Meant for Food," *New Yorker,* Sept. 28, 2016.

316 "President Poupon": Chris Riotta, "Fox News Was Attacking Barack Obama for Using Dijon Mustard at This Point in His Presidency," *Newsweek,* June 9, 2017.

316 He was hailed as "the Food President": David Johnson and Samuel P. Jacobs, "The State of Obama's Plate," *Time,* Jan. 20, 2015.

316 he would scarf down: Morgan Olsen, "Eat Like an Obama at 7 Chicago Restaurants," *Chicago Tribune,* Jan. 9, 2017.

316 "Americans should know": Zengerle, "How Barack Obama Sold Out."

316 "Our entire agricultural system": Joe Klein, "The Full Obama Interview," *Time,* Oct. 23, 2008.

317 "second food revolution": Kim Severson on *The Leonard Lopate Show,* "Obama on Food," WNYC, Jan. 27, 2009, quoted by Melissa Waldron Lehner, "Alice Waters Playing Pol Pot? Ruth Reichl Responds to Inaugural Dinner Bashing," *Civil Eats,* Jan. 29, 2009.

317 "People are so interested in a massive change": Kim Severson, "Is a New Food Policy on Obama's List?," *NYT,* Dec. 25, 2008.

317 Pollan calls Big Food—a $1.5 trillion industry: Michael Pollan, "Big Food Strikes Back," *New York Times Magazine,* Oct. 5, 2016.

317 "paraphrased" Pollan's *Times* article: Ibid.

317 "a one-term president": Glenn Kessler, "When Did Mitch McConnell Say He Wanted to Make Obama a One-Term President?," *WP,* Jan. 11, 2017.

318 "Our nation is at a critical juncture": Kim Severson, "A Pitch to Obama on Food and Farming," *NYT,* Dec. 4, 2008.

318 "Alice is a utopian": A chef, who wished to remain anonymous, to the author.

318 "USDA administrator" is a bland bureaucratic title: Michael Lewis, "Made in the USDA," *Vanity Fair,* Dec. 2017.

319 "an agricultural economy of the future": Michael Grunwald, "Vilsack: Some Hard Choices on Ethanol," *Time,* Dec. 18, 2008.

319 Michael Pollan bristled at this: "Michael Pollan on Vilsack, Agriculture—and Food," *Morning Edition,* NPR, Dec. 18, 2008.

319 "The purity and wholesomeness": Alice Waters, "Alice Waters's Open Letter to the Obamas," *Gourmet,* Jan. 15, 2009.

319 "have a central, core message": Melissa Waldron Lehner, "Alice Waters Playing Pol Pot? Ruth Reichl Responds to Inaugural Dinner Bashing," *Civil Eats,* Jan. 29, 2009.

319 "Pol Pot in a muumuu": "5 Great Chef Disses," *Eater,* Nov. 20, 2009.

319 "When I started writing about food": Lehner, "Alice Waters Playing Pol Pot?"

320 "Nothing is more political than food": John Boone, "Anthony Bourdain on 'Wasted!,' the Politics of Food in the Trump Era and Twitter Trolls (EXCLU-SIVE)", ETonline.com, Oct. 13, 2017.

320 In Chicago, the Obamas reserved Friday nights: Michelle Obama, *Becoming,* 185.

320 "We ordered the same thing": Ibid.

320 This left her with even less time to monitor: Ibid., 238–39.

321 Sam Kass: Ibid., 239.

321 "they both love really good food": Kass in conversation with the author, April 26, 2018.

322 "We eat what we see": Kass, *Eat a Little Better,* 27.

322 But the truth, Obama explained: Michael D. Shear, "Obama Sets the Record Straight on His 7-Almond Habit," *NYT,* July 28, 2016.

322 1.8 million people gathered in Washington: Kass, *Eat a Little Better,* 18.

322 The night before the inauguration: Pollan, "Big Food Strikes Back"; Pollan in conversation with the author, Nov. 13, 2019.

323 celebrated his inauguration with a lunch: Jennifer Treuting, "President Barack Obama's Inaugural Luncheon," *Delish,* Jan. 16, 2009.

323 Jim Robinson was a slave at Friendfield: "Michelle Obama Is Invited to Visit the Grave of Slave Kin," New York *Daily News,* Oct. 14, 2008.

324 "hotly awaited": Darlene Superville, "Obama Mother-in-Law to Join Family in White House," Associated Press, Jan. 9, 2009.

324 "a person with integrity and devotion": Waters, "Alice Waters's Open Letter to the Obamas."

324 "redefine" the position: Tara Parker-Pope, "Alice Waters and Obama's 'Kitchen' Cabinet," *NYT,* Dec. 11, 2008.

324 a "name" chef: Severson, "Is a New Food Policy on Obama's List?"

324 Three candidates who fit that description: Jo Piazza, "Chef Executive: Three Cooks in the Running for Obama's Top White House Kitchen Post," New York *Daily News,* Nov. 8, 2008.

324 "She brings such incredible talent": "Cristeta Comerford to Remain White House Chef," *HuffPost,* Feb. 9, 2009.

324 South Lawn into a vegetable garden: Michelle Obama, *Becoming,* 321.

324 the self-described "mom in chief": Ibid., 329.

324 "will begin to educate their families": Marian Burros, "Obamas to Plant Vegetable Garden at White House," *NYT,* March 19, 2009.

325 "I wanted this garden": Michelle Obama, "Excerpt: *American Grown* by First Lady Michelle Obama," ABC News, May 28, 2012.

325 more optimistically "Victory Gardens": Claudia Swain, "Eleanor and Diana's Victory Garden," *Boundary Stones* (blog), WETA, May 25, 2017, boundarystones.weta.org.

325 Pollan called on George H. W. Bush: Michael Pollan, "Abolish the White House Lawn," *NYT,* May 5, 1991.

326 Scheib grew veggies on the roof: Scheib and Friedman, *White House Chef,* 52–53.

326 "will be able to taste it": Jane Black, "The First Garden Gets Its First Planting," *WP,* April 9, 2009.

327 "phenomenal symbolic value": Zengerle, "How Barack Obama Sold Out."

327 American Council on Science and Health: Michael Pollan, "Big Food Strikes Back: Why Did the Obamas Fail to Take on Corporate Agriculture?," *New York Times Magazine,* Oct. 5, 2016.

327 four biggest meatpacking companies controlled: Zengerle, "How Barack Obama Sold Out."

327 Obama initiated an antitrust investigation: Pollan, "Big Food Strikes Back."

327 "make sure the playing field is level": Ibid.

327 Furious, Big Meat responded: Ibid.

328 "overpromised reforms, underestimated the strength": Zengerle, "How Barack Obama Sold Out."

328 "Let's Move!" campaign: "Let's Move!," blog archive, https://letsmove.obamawhitehouse.archives.gov.

328 "We need you all to step it up": "Remarks by the First Lady at a Grocery Manufacturers Association Conference," White House, March 16, 2010.

328 the First Lady shifted the focus of Let's Move!: Let's Move!, letsmove.obamawhitehouse.archives.gov.

328 "attention to the issue has really helped": Julia Belluz, "How Michelle Obama Quietly Changed What Americans Eat," *Vox,* Oct. 3, 2016.

329 "Little Food": Pollan, "Big Food Strikes Back."

329 "I've seen a shift": Brie Mazurek, "Remembering the Obamas' Food Legacy," KQED, Jan. 20, 2017.

329 "the importance of Michelle's garden": Bayless in conversation with the author, July 2, 2019.

329 "philosophy isn't that different from yours": Ben Rhodes, Director's Cut: "Why

Obama Wanted to Sit Down with Bourdain," *Anthony Bourdain: Parts Unknown,* explorepartsunknown.com.

330 *Anthony Bourdain: Parts Unknown:* "Hanoi," season 8, episode 2, CNN, Sept. 25, 2016, cnn.com.

330 The Vietnamese ambassador to the United States: Rhodes, Director's Cut.

330 Off camera, Bourdain wondered: Anthony Bourdain, "Obama, Bourdain Chew the Fat in Hanoi," CNN Travel, March 21, 2017, cnn.com.

330 "[Tony] taught us about food": Barack Obama (@BarackObama), Twitter, June 8, 2018, 12:01 p.m., twitter.com; Emily Stewart, "Obama Honors Anthony Bourdain: He Made Us 'a Little Less Afraid of the Unknown,'" *Vox,* June 8, 2018.

21 · DONALD TRUMP The Food Fighter

332 When a waiter approached, Trump: Dwight Garner, "Chris Christie Goes Easy on Trump in New Tell-All Book but Hits Out at Steve Bannon," *Independent,* Jan. 29, 2019.

332 "The demand was like Sammy the Bull's": "Comey Book Claims President Trump Sought Loyalty Like Mafia Boss 'Sammy the Bull's' Induction Ceremony," ABC News, April 12, 2018.

333 "I just fired the head of the FBI": Matt Apuzzo, Maggie Haberman, and Matthew Rosenberg, "Trump Told Russians That Firing 'Nut Job' Comey Eased Pressure from Investigation," *NYT,* May 19, 2017.

333 Donald Trump acquired his: Trump, *Too Much and Never Enough,* 95–96.

333 "my mother's meat loaf": Maxine Shen, "Watch President Trump Make Meatloaf on a Vintage Martha Stewart Episode," *Food & Wine,* June 9, 2017.

334 "best meatloaf in America": Donald J. Trump, @realDonaldTrump, Twitter, Dec. 29, 2011.

334 "'There's the menu, you guys order'": Margaret Hartmann, "Chris Christie Brags That Trump Made Him Eat Meatloaf at the White House," *New York,* Feb. 17, 2017.

334 "the person with the power": Trump, *Too Much and Never Enough,* 53.

334 "an amazing peacemaker if he didn't have the problem": Rebecca Kheel, "Trump Helped Draft Will That Excluded His Brother's Children: Report," *Hill,* Jan. 2, 2016.

334 "four major food groups": Michael Kranish, "Trump's Campaign: Big Macs, Screaming Fits, and Constant Rivalries," *WP,* Dec. 2, 2017.

335 "I think fast food's good": Ashley Parker, "Donald Trump's Diet: He'll Have Fries with That," *NYT,* Aug. 8, 2016; Gregory Krieg, "Donald Trump Really Likes Fast Food," CNN Politics, Feb. 19, 2016, cnn.com.

335 "keep the weight down": Nick Carbone, "What the Fork? Trump Explains Why He Used Utensils with His Pizza—Sort Of," *Time,* June 3, 2011.

335 "He would go and work 14 or 16 or 18 hours": Allan Smith, "Trump's Former Campaign Manager Explains His 2,400-Calorie McDonald's Order and Compares Him to 'an Amazing Professional Athlete,'" *Insider,* Dec. 5, 2017.

335 2,630-calorie bomb: C. Brian Smith, "We Ate Trump's Dinner—2 Fish Filets, 2 Big Macs, and a Large Chocolate Shake," *Mel Magazine,* melmagazine.com.

335 "the healthiest individual ever elected": Matt Schudel, "Harold Bornstein, Doctor Who Said Trump Would Be 'the Healthiest Individual Ever Elected' President, Dies at 73," *WP,* Jan. 14, 2021.

335 "blue-collar billionaire": Molly Prince, "Don Jr. Explains Why His Dad Is a 'Blue Collar Billionaire,'" *Daily Wire,* Nov. 11, 2019, dailywire.com.

335 "I have a gut": Philip Rucker, Josh Dawsey, and Damian Paletta, "Trump Slams Fed Chair, Questions Climate Change, and Threatens to Cancel Putin Meeting in Wide-Ranging Interview with the Post," *WP,* Nov. 27, 2018.

335 "I love the Hispanics!": Donald Trump video, in The Hill (@thehill), Twitter, Sept. 13, 2020, 11:34 p.m., twitter.com.

336 "banquet" for the Clemson University Tigers: Maura Judkis, "What It Means That Trump Served Big Macs in the State Dining Room," *WP,* Jan. 15, 2019.

336 "President McDonald Trump": Sacha Baron Cohen, *Borat Subsequent Moviefilm.*

336 it actually cost $2,911.44: Philip Bump, "President Trump's Extravagant, $3,000, 300-sandwich celebration of Clemson University," *WP,* Jan. 15, 2019.

336 "We went out and we ordered": Kaitlan Collins and Liz Stark, "Trump Personally Paying for Clemson's Fast-Food White House Meals," CNN Politics, Jan. 15, 2019.

336 "Our nutritionist must be having a fit": Maura Judkis, "What It Means That Trump Served Big Macs in the State Dining Room," *WP,* Jan. 15, 2019.

337 "the White House into a White Castle": Allyson Chu, "Trump Has Turned the White House into a White Castle: President Roasted for Serving Clemson Fast Food," *WP,* Jan. 15, 2019.

337 "a little bit P. T. Barnum": Megan Garber, "The President's McFeast," *Atlantic,* Jan. 15, 2019.

337 "The media comes across": Annaliese Griffin, "What America Hears When the Press Makes Fun of the Way Trump Eats," *Quartz,* Jan. 19, 2019.

337 "people who eat similar foods": Graber and Twilley, "Shared Plates"; Ayelet Fishbach, interview with the author, Dec. 17, 2021.

337 a dry-aged New York strip: Helen Rosner, "Actually, How Donald Trump Eats His Steak Matters," *Eater,* Feb. 28, 2017.

337 "rocked on the plate": Jason Horwitz, "A King in His Castle: How Donald Trump Lives, from His Longtime Butler," *NYT,* March 15, 2016.

338 "Steaks with even a little bit of red": Rosner, "Actually, How Donald Trump Eats."

338 "Why on earth would someone": Nick Solares, "The Case Against Ketchup," NickSolaris.com.

338 "quintessentially American" foodstuff: Amy Bentley, "Is Ketchup the Perfect Complement to the American Diet?," *Zócalo,* June 4, 2018; Bentley, interview with the author, Jan. 31, 2020.

338 The condiment originated in China: Kat Eschner, "There's Something Fishy About the Ketchup You Put on Your Burgers," *Smithsonian,* June 5, 2017.

338 The secret to Heinz's success: "Is There High-Fructose Corn Syrup in Ketchup?," Knowyourpantry.com.

338 "class leveler": Bentley, interview with the author, Jan. 31, 2020; Bentley, "Is Ketchup the Perfect Complement to the American Diet?"

338 ten billion ounces of ketchup: Casey Seidenberg, "Do You Know How Much Sugar Is in Your Ketchup?," *WP,* June 2, 2015.

339 During a June 2022 House committee hearing: Dana Milbank, "Cassidy Hutchinson Could Read the Ketchup on the Wall," *WP,* June 28, 2022.

339 Food scientists have capitalized on: Michael Moss, "The Extraordinary Science of Addictive Junk Food," *NYT,* Feb. 20, 2013.

339 One tablespoon of HFCS: Melissa Kravitz Hoeffner, "Food Companies Intentionally Make Their Products Addictive, and It's Making Us Sick," *Salon,* March 28, 2019.

339 "Salt is extremely addictive": Ibid.

339 In 2020, just one in five American adults: Jane E. Brody, "How Poor Diet Contributes to Coronavirus Risk," *NYT,* April 20, 2020.

340 "report positive attitudes toward fast food": Mary Kekatos, "Trump's Fast Food Affinity May Be Leading More Americans to Eat Unhealthy Diets, Study Suggests," *Daily Mail,* Jan. 9, 2020.

340 "my every day delicious & healthy breakfast": Christine-Marie Liwag Dixon, "This Is What the First Lady Eats," Mashed, July 10, 2020.

341 turn the garden into a putting green: Anastasia Day, "How the White House Garden Became a Political Football," *WP,* April 3, 2018.

341 Obamas had reinforced it with stone: Helena Bottmiller Evich, "Michelle Obama Sets Her Garden in Stone," *Politico*, Oct. 6, 2016; Burpee Seeds and Plants, "Burpee Funds Permanent White House Kitchen Garden," press release, burpee.com.

341 When Donald Trump arrived in Washington: Carl Abbott, "The Myth That Washington Was a Swamp Will Never Go Away," *Smithsonian*, March 9, 2017; Gillian Brockell, "Is the White House 'a Dump'? A History of Extreme Makeovers at 1600 Pennsylvania Avenue," *WP*, Aug. 7, 2017.

341 "I don't know a chef": Jennifer Steinhauer, "Trump Kicks Away Obama Traditions Even at the Dinner Table," *NYT*, Dec. 14, 2018.

341 "couldn't match the satisfaction": Annie Karni, "Trump's 'Loyal Lieutenant' to Testify on 2013 Russia Visit," *Politico*, Nov. 6, 2017.

341 "We should be eating a hamburger": Tessa Berenson, "Here's Donald Trump's Idea for a Very Unusual State Dinner," *Time*, June 15, 2016.

342 When he hosted China's president: Dan Merica, "Trump, Xi Talked Syria Strike over 'Beautiful' Chocolate Cake," CNN, April 12, 2017.

342 Comerford's menu included seasonal specialties: Chris Fuhrmeister, "Here's the Menu for Trump's Fancy State Dinner with Emmanuel Macron," *Eater*, April 24, 2018.

342 bought the former Kluge estate: Annie Gowen, "Trump Buys Former Kluge-Owned Winery," *WP*, April 7, 2011.

342 meeting was hailed as "le bromance": Nikki Schwab, "Le Bromance Is On!," *Daily Mail*, Feb. 26, 2018.

342 Trump called NATO "obsolete": Cyra Master, "Trump Tells German Paper: NATO Is 'Obsolete,'" *Hill*, Jan. 15, 2017.

342 "some nice ISIS fighters": Quint Forgey, "Macron Confronts Trump on ISIS: 'Let's Be Serious,'" *Politico*, Dec. 3, 2019.

342 Trump's second state dinner: Emily Heil, "On the Menu for the Trumps' Australian State Dinner: A Refined Taste of America," *WP*, Sept. 19, 2019.

343 "a hundred years of mateship": Nina Zafar and Caitlin Moore, "Full Transcript: The Toasts of President Trump and Prime Minister Scott Morrison at the State Dinner for Australia," *WP*, Sept. 20, 2019.

343 In mid-January 2020, an American man: Mike Baker, "A Scramble to Retrace the Steps of the First Wuhan Coronavirus Case in the U.S.," *NYT*, Jan. 22, 2020.

343 By late April 2020, sixty-five hundred workers: Gaby Galvin, "CDC: Nearly 5,000 Meat Processing Workers Infected with COVID-19," *U.S. News & World Report*, May 1, 2020.

344 "It tore me up enough": Alisa Roth, "Pandemic Disruptions Taking a Toll on Farmers' Mental Health," MPRNews, May 28, 2020.

344 "critical infrastructure": Ana Swanson and David Yaffe-Bellany, "Trump Declares Meat Supply 'Critical,' Aiming to Reopen Plants," *NYT*, April 28, 2020.

344 It was an open secret: Joshua Partlow and David A. Fahrenthold, "Trump Organization Fires More Undocumented Workers—a Year After Its Use of Illegal Labor Was Revealed," *WP*, Dec. 31, 2019.

344 Restaurants were particularly hard-hit: Amy McCarthy, "Will the Restaurant Industry Survive Stricter Immigration Screenings?," *Eater*, March 4, 2016.

344 Since the opening of Mathurin Roze de Chantoiseau's Paris consommé shop: Adam Gopnik, foreword to Spang, *Invention of the Restaurant*, xiv.

345 "Do you hear the babies crying?": Meagan Flynn, "Kirstjen Nielsen Heckled by Protesters at Mexican Restaurant. Other Diners Applauded Them," *WP*, June 20, 2018.

345 "the moment in our democracy when people": Avi Selk and Sarah Murray, "The Owner of the Red Hen Explains Why She Asked Sarah Huckabee Sanders to Leave," *WP*, June 25, 2018.

345 "filthy": Madeleine Aggeler, "Trump, Whose Restaurant Has 78 Health-Code Violations, Calls Red Hen 'Filthy,'" The Cut, June 25, 2018.

345 "they're not welcome": John Wagner and Avi Selk, " 'Be Careful What You Wish for Max!': Trump Takes Aim at Waters After She Calls for Public Harassment of His Cabinet," *WP*, June 25, 2018.

345 "Go after her children": Selk and Murray, "Owner of the Red Hen Explains."

345 "should be allowed to eat dinner in peace": "Let the Trump Team Eat in Peace," *WP*, June 24, 2018.

345 "How can a space be open and welcoming": Amy McCarthy, "Trump Officials Don't Deserve Hospitality," *Eater*, June 25, 2018.

346 "Nothing is more fundamental": Adam Gopnik, "Sarah Huckabee Sanders and Who Deserves a Place at the Table," *New Yorker*, June 25, 2018.

346 Lea Berman, George W. Bush's social secretary: Berman and Bernard, *Treating People Well*, xvi.

346 "The personal smooths the professional": Lea Berman and Jeremy Bernard, videotaped discussion of *Treating People Well*, Politics and Prose bookstore, YouTube, Jan. 23, 2018.

346 The ability to "disagree agreeably": Berman in conversation with the author, Nov. 9, 2019.

22 · JOSEPH R. BIDEN We Finish as a Family

349 He gave an inaugural address: Inaugural Address by President Joseph R. Biden Jr., White House: Speeches and Remarks, Jan. 20, 2021.

349 "trust, confidence, and stability": Hanna Flanagan and Gabrielle Chung, "Jill Biden's Inauguration Night Dress Included Subtle Style Nod to All of America," *People*, Jan. 21, 2021.

350 "Everybody knows Joe": Betsy Andrews, " 'Everybody Knows Joe': I Ate at Biden's Favorite Hometown Restaurants," *Food & Wine*, Oct. 30, 2020.

350 "He's pretty much a basic eater": Lauren Barth, "Here's What Jill Biden Typically Eats in a Day," *List*, Jan. 21, 2021, thelist.com.

350 "My name is Joe Biden": Paulina Firozi, "Vice President: 'My Name Is Joe Biden, and I Love Ice Cream,' " *Hill*, May 18, 2016.

350 "ice cream" was his "performance enhancer": Patrick Cooley, "Jeni's Releases Special Flavor for Biden Inauguration," *Columbus Dispatch*, Jan. 19, 2021.

350 White House Chocolate Chip: Ibid.

351 She was an accomplished cook: Alison Ashton, "Jill Biden Shares Her Favorite Foods, What She's Been Reading, and Her Parmesan Chicken Recipe," *Parade*, Jan. 19, 2021.

352 employees had been fired or quit: Merrit Kennedy, "Scientists Desert USDA as Agency Relocates to Kansas City Area," *The Salt* (blog), NPR, July 17, 2019.

352 "Our mission is to provide": Dan Charles, "Biden Plans to Bring Vilsack Back to USDA Despite Criticism from Reformers," *Morning Edition*, NPR, Dec. 9, 2020.

352 "a blatant attack on science": Kennedy, "Scientists Desert USDA."

352 The number of hungry Americans: Christianna Silva, "Food Insecurity in the U.S. by the Numbers," NPR, Sept. 27, 2020; Mireya Villarreal, "More Than 50 Million Americans Facing Hunger in 2020, Projections Show," *CBS Evening News*, Nov. 24, 2020.

353 "It's a tradition I really care about": Mattie Kahn, "What's Cooking, Kamala Harris?," *Glamour*, May 21, 2020.

354 She cooked masala dosas: Monica Chon, "Watch Mindy Kaling and Kamala Harris Cook Indian Food in This Delightful Video," Oprah Daily, Dec. 2, 2019.

354 "onion-cutting goggles": Kahn, "What's Cooking, Kamala Harris?"

354 proper tuna-melt technique: Lydia Greene, "Kamala Harris Shows How to Make a Perfect Tuna Melt Sandwich Recipe," WideOpenEats.com, June 3, 2021.

354   "creased apron": Naomi Lim, "Democratic Women Don Aprons and Pose in Kitchen to Woo 2020 Voters," *Washington Examiner,* May 17, 2019.

355   Recalling the "magic" cilantro rice: Kahn, "What's Cooking, Kamala Harris?"

355   Harris's consistent focus on food: Ibid.

356   "make schmoozing great again": Roxanne Roberts, "Washington's Establishment Hopes a Biden Presidency Will Make Schmoozing Great Again," *WP,* Nov. 23, 2020.

357   "finish with tarallucci and wine": Abigail Napp, "Will Dr. Jill Biden Bring 'Red Sauce' to the White House?," LaCucinaItaliana.com, Nov. 9, 2020.

CONCLUSION   Eating Together

359   "Unfortunately, we're not able to facilitate": Harleth, email to the author, May 24, 2019.

359   John Moeller agreed to prepare: See Moeller, *Dining at the White House;* "Meet Chef John Moeller," Greenfield Restaurant & Bar, www.thegreenfield restaurant.com.

360   "my White House dinner": Author's notes and audiovisual recording from the night of Feb. 17, 2020. For John Moeller's recipes, see Moeller, *Dining at the White House.*

368   COVID had infected President and Mrs. Trump: Tamara Keith, "Trump Takes 'Precautionary' Treatment After He and First Lady Test Positive for Virus," NPR, Oct. 2, 2020.

368   killed an estimated 15 million people globally: "Pandemic Death Toll at End of 2021 May Have Hit 15 Million People, WHO Estimates," Associated Press, May 5, 2022.

368   778,000 of whom were Americans: Jonathan S. Jones, "Covid-19 Has Killed More Americans Than the Civil War. How Do We Remember Them?," *WP,* Dec. 2, 2021.

368   "loneliness epidemic": Colleen Walsh, "Young Adults Hardest Hit by Loneliness During Pandemic," *Harvard Gazette,* Feb. 17, 2021.

368   only 30 percent of families: Jill Anderson, "Harvard EdCast: The Benefit of Family Mealtime," Harvard Graduate School of Education, April 1, 2020, www.gse .harvard.edu.

368   80 percent of them say that is the time: Anderson, "Harvard EdCast: The Benefit of Family Mealtime."

368   The Bureau of Labor Statistics found: Karen Hamrick, "Americans Spend an Average of 37 Minutes a Day Preparing and Serving Food and Cleaning Up," Economic Research Service, USDA, Nov. 7, 2016.

368   studies found that students who: Cody C. Delistraty, "The Importance of Eating Together," *Atlantic,* July 18, 2014.

369   "there is a correlation between [increased]": Fishbach, interview with the author, Dec. 17, 2021.

369   Affluent families have been eating together: Anderson, "Harvard EdCast: The Benefit of Family Mealtime."

369   Americans were spending almost as much on fast food: Delistraty, "The Importance of Eating Together."

369   in the House and Senate dining rooms: Ashley Parker, "On Senate Menu, Bean Soup and a Serving of 'Hyperpartisanship,'" *NYT,* Aug. 19, 2014.

369   Even the District's legendary cocktail parties: Roxanne Roberts, "Buffy Cafritz and Her Lifelong Quest to Bring Washington Together," *WP,* May 7, 2021.

370   a Census report found: Yeris Mayol-Garcia, "Pandemic Brought Parents and Children Closer: More Family Dinners, More Reading to Young Children," Census.gov, Jan. 3, 2022.

370 American Family Survey: Karlyn Bowman, "The Family Dinner Hour: Alive and Well," *Forbes,* Jan. 13, 2020.

370 "The family meal": Francine du Plessix Gray, "Starving Children," *New Yorker,* Oct. 8, 1995.

370 "People prefer to eat together": Fishbach, interview with the author, Dec. 17, 2021.

371 "How we produce and consume food": Mark Bittman, Michael Pollan, Ricardo Salvador, and Olivier De Schutter, "How a National Food Policy Could Save Millions of American Lives," *WP,* Nov. 7, 2014.

371 food czar: Paula Crossfield, "Michael Pollan on Bill Moyers Journal," Civil Eats, Nov. 29, 2008.

371 as Brazil and Mexico have: Bittman and Pollan, "How a National Food Policy Could Save Millions of American Lives."

372 they should raise the nation's "gastronomic image": Child, "A White House Menu."

372 "a showcase of American art and history": National Museum of American History, "Jacqueline Kennedy: Glamour Comes to the White House," https://american history.si.edu.

373 an elephant and a donkey: Michael Pollan, "Abolish the White house Lawn."

Bibliography

Aitkin, Jonathan. *Nixon: A Life.* Washington, D.C.: Regnery History, 1993.

Allgor, Catherine. *A Perfect Union: Dolley Madison and the Creation of the American Nation.* New York: Henry Holt, 2006.

Ambrose, Stephen E. *Eisenhower.* Vol. 2, *The President.* New York: Simon & Schuster, 2014.

Auchincloss, Louis. *Woodrow Wilson.* New York: Penguin Books, 2009.

Baldrige, Letitia, and René Verdon. *In the Kennedy Style.* New York: Doubleday, 1998.

Berman, Lea, and Jeremy Bernard. *Treating People Well.* New York: Scribner, 2018.

Brinkley, Douglas. *The Wilderness Warrior.* New York: Harper, 2009.

Brinkley, Howard. *White House Butlers.* Bookcaps.com, 2013.

Cannon, James. *Gerald R. Ford: An Honorable Life.* Ann Arbor: University of Michigan Press, 2013.

Cannon, Poppy, and Patricia Brooks. *The Presidents' Cookbook.* New York: Funk & Wagnalls, 1968.

Carter, Rosalynn. *First Lady from Plains.* Fayetteville: University of Arkansas Press, 1994.

Cerami, Charles A. *Dinner at Mr. Jefferson's.* Hoboken, N.J.: John Wiley & Sons, 2008.

Chernow, Ron. *Alexander Hamilton.* New York: Penguin Press, 2004.

———. *Grant.* New York: Penguin Press, 2017.

———. *Washington: A Life.* New York: Penguin Press, 2010.

Child, Julia, with Alex Prud'homme. *My Life in France.* New York: Alfred A. Knopf, 2006.

Coe, Andrew. *Chop Suey.* Oxford: Oxford University Press, 2009.

Conradi, Peter. *Hot Dogs and Cocktails.* Surrey, U.K.: Alma Books, 2013.

Cook, Paul David. *Presidential Leadership by Example.* Xlibris, 2001.

Cooper, John Milton. *Woodrow Wilson: A Biography.* New York: Alfred A. Knopf, 2009.

Daniels, Mrs. Josephus (Addie Worth Bagley Daniels). *Recollections of a Cabinet Minister's Wife, 1913–1921.* Raleigh, N.C.: Mitchell Printing Company, 1945.

De Guzman, Ariel. *The Bush Family Cookbook.* New York: Scribner, 2005.

Eighmey, Rae Katherine. *Abraham Lincoln in the Kitchen.* Washington, D.C.: Smithsonian Books, 2013.

Eisenhower, Dwight D. *Mandate for Change, 1953–1956.* Garden City, N.Y.: Doubleday, 1963.

Ellis, Joseph J. *Founding Brothers.* New York: Alfred A. Knopf, 2000.

Epting, Chris. *Teddy Roosevelt in California.* Charleston, S.C.: History Press, 2015.

Fowler, Damon Lee, ed. *Dining at Monticello.* Chapel Hill: University of North Carolina Press, 2005.

Freedman, Paul. *American Cuisine, and How It Got This Way.* New York: Liveright, 2019.

Freidel, Frank, and Hugh Sidey. *The Presidents of the United States of America.* Washington, D.C.: White House Historical Association, 1996.

Fullilove, Michael. *Rendezvous with Destiny.* New York: Penguin Books, 2014.

Haber, Barbara. *From Hardtack to Home Fries.* New York: Free Press, 2002.

Haller, Henry. *The White House Family Cookbook.* With Virginia Aronson. New York: Random House, 1987.

Harris, Bill. *The First Ladies Fact Book.* Revised by Laura Ross. New York: Black Dog & Leventhal Publishers, 2011.

Hogan, J. Michael. *Woodrow Wilson's Western Tour.* College Station: Texas A&M University Press, 2006.

Howe, Mark Antony DeWolfe. *George von Lengerke Meyer.* New York: Dodd, Mead, 1920.

Jaffray, Elizabeth. *Secrets of the White House.* New York: Cosmopolitan, 1927.

Jamison, Kay Redfield. *Exuberance.* New York: Vintage Books, 2003.

Jeffries, Ona Griffin. *In and Out of the White House.* New York: Wilfred Funk, 1960.

Jensen, Amy. *The White House and Its Thirty-Five Families.* New York: McGraw-Hill, 1970.

Kass, Sam. *Eat a Little Better.* New York: Clarkson Potter, 2018.

Kelly, Kitty. *Nancy Reagan: The Unauthorized Biography.* New York: Simon & Schuster, 1991.

Kerner, Susanne, Cynthia Chou, and Morten Warmind, eds. *Commensality: From Everyday Food to Feast.* London: Bloomsbury Academic, 2015.

Kimball, Marie. *The Martha Washington Cook Book.* New York: Coward-McCann, 1940.

Kissinger, Henry. *White House Years.* New York: Simon & Schuster, 2011.

Kuykendall, Ralph S. *The Kalakaua Dynasty, 1874–1893.* Vol. 3 of *The Hawaiian Kingdom.* Honolulu: University of Hawaii Press, 1967.

Martin, Joseph Plumb. *A Narrative of a Revolutionary Soldier.* New York: Signet Classics, 2001.

Mayer, Dale C. *Lou Henry Hoover: A Prototype for First Ladies.* New York: Nova History Publications, 2004.

McCabe, James D. *Behind the Scenes in Washington.* New York: Continental, 1873.

McCreary, Donna D. *Lincoln's Table.* Zionsville, Ind.: Guild Press of Indiana, 2000.

McCullough, David. *Truman.* New York: Simon & Schuster, 1992.

McDowell, Bart, *The Revolutionary War.* Washington, D.C.: The National Geographic Society, 1967.

McLeod, Stephen A., ed. *Dining with the Washingtons.* Mount Vernon, Va.: Mount Vernon Ladies' Association, 2011.

Mesnier, Roland. *All the Presidents' Pastries.* With Christian Malard. Paris: Flammarion, 2007.

Miller, Adrian. *The President's Kitchen Cabinet.* Chapel Hill: University of North Carolina Press, 2017.

Miller, Merle. *Plain Speaking.* London: Victor Gollancz, 1974.

Mitchell, Patricia B. *Presidential Flavors.* Self-published by MitchellsPublications.com, 2015.

———. *Revolutionary Recipes.* Self-published by MitchellsPublications.com, 1991.

Moeller, John. *Dining at the White House.* With Mike Lovell. Lancaster, Pa.: American Lifestyle, 2013.

Morison, Samuel Eliot. *The Oxford History of the American People.* New York: Oxford University Press, 1965.

Morris, Edmund. *Colonel Roosevelt.* New York: Random House, 2010.

———. *The Rise of Theodore Roosevelt.* New York: Random House, 2001.

———. *Theodore Rex.* New York: Random House, 2001.

Muir, John. *Letters to a Friend, Written to Mrs. Ezra S. Carr, 1866–1879.* Boston: Houghton Mifflin, 1915.

Nelson, Dale W. *The President Is at Camp David*. Syracuse, N.Y.: Syracuse University Press, 1995.

Nesbitt, Henrietta. *The Presidential Cookbook*. Garden City, N.Y.: Doubleday, 1951.

———. *White House Diary*. Garden City, N.Y.: Doubleday, 1948.

Obama, Barack. *Dreams from My Father*. New York: Times Books, 1995.

Obama, Michelle. *Becoming*. New York: Crown, 2018.

Page, Susan. *The Matriarch: Barbara Bush and the Making of an American Dynasty*. New York: Hachette Book Group, 2019.

Polan, Dana. *Julia Child's* The French Chef. Durham, N.C.: Duke University Press, 2011.

Pollan, Michael. *The Omnivore's Dilemma*. New York: Penguin Press, 2006.

Prud'homme, Alex. *The French Chef in America*. New York: Alfred A. Knopf, 2016.

Quan, Lee Ping. *To a President's Taste*. With Jim Miller. Emmaus, Pa.: Rodale Press, 1939.

Reagan, Nancy. *My Turn: The Memoirs of Nancy Reagan*. With William Novak. New York: Random House, 1989.

Roosevelt, James, and Sidney Shalett. *Affectionately, F.D.R.: A Son's Story of a Lonely Man*. New York: Harcourt, Brace, 1959.

Roosevelt, Theodore. *African Game Trails*. Vol. 1. New York: Charles Scribner's & Sons, 1910.

———. *The Winning of the West: 3, Men of Action*. New York: Charles Scribner's Sons, 1923.

Rorabaugh, W. J. *The Alcoholic Republic: An American Tradition*. New York: Oxford University Press, 1981.

Russoli, Edward, and Candace Russoli. *Ike the Cook*. Allentown, Pa.: Benedettini Books, 1990.

Rysavy, François, as told to Frances Spatz Leighton. *A Treasury of White House Cooking*. New York: G. P. Putnam's Sons, 1957.

Salinger, Lawrence M. *Encyclopedia of White Collar & Corporate Crime*, vol. 1. Thousand Oaks, Calif.: Sage Publications, Inc., 2005.

Schecter, Barnet. *The Battle for New York*. New York: Penguin Books, 2002.

Scheib, Walter, and Andrew Friedman. *White House Chef*. Hoboken, N.J.: John Wiley & Sons, 2007.

Schifando, Peter, and J. Jonathan Joseph. *Entertaining at the White House with Nancy Reagan*. New York: HarperCollins, 2007.

Seale, William. *The President's House: A History*, 2 vols. Baltimore, Md.: Johns Hopkins University Press White House Historical Association, 1986.

———. *The White House Actors and Observers*. Boston: Northeastern University Press, 2002.

Smith, Margaret Bayard. *The First Forty Years of Washington Society*. Edited by Gaillard Hunt. New York: Frederick Ungar, 1965.

Spang, Rebecca L., *The Invention of the Restaurant: Paris and Modern Gastronomic Culture*. Cambridge, Mass.: Harvard University Press, 2000.

Stelzer, Cita. *Dinner with Churchill*. New York: Pegasus Books, 2012.

Styron, William. *Havanas in Camelot: Personal Essays*. New York: Random House, 2008.

Temple, Wayne C., ed. *The Taste Is in My Mouth a Little*. Mahomet, Ill.: Mayhaven, 2004.

Tipton-Martin, Toni. *Jubilee*. New York: Clarkson Potter, 2019.

Trumbull, Jonathan. *Jonathan Trumbull*. Boston: Little, Brown, 1919.

Trump, Mary L. *Too Much and Never Enough*. New York: Simon & Schuster, 2020.

Wadsworth, Ginger. *Camping with the President*. Illustrated by Karen Dugan. Honesdale, Pa.: Calkins Creek, 2009.

Wagenknecht, Edward. *The Seven Worlds of Theodore Roosevelt*. Guilford, Conn.: Lyons Press, 2010.

West, J. B. *Upstairs at the White House.* New York: Open Road Integrated Media, 2013.
Whitcomb, John, and Claire Whitcomb. *Real Life at the White House.* New York: Routledge, 2000.
Will-Weber, Mark. *Mint Juleps with Teddy Roosevelt.* Washington, D.C.: Regnery, 2014.
Wright, Lawrence. *Thirteen Days in September.* New York: Alfred A. Knopf, 2014.
Ziemann, Hugo, and Mrs. F. L. Gillette. *The White House Cook Book.* New York: Saalfield, 1903. Reprint, Old Greenwich, Conn.: Devin Adair, 1983.

Index

Page numbers in *italics* refer to illustrations.

xiii Courtesy of Texas Christian University Special Collections

xxi Drawing © Fred D. Owen, archt. Mrs. H. S. Owen Collection. Courtesy of the Library of Congress. LC-USZ62-92935.

xxiii Photograph by Paul Child. © Schlesinger Library, Harvard Radcliffe Institute.

3 Painting by William B. T. Trego. Image Courtesy of the Museum of the American Revolution.

22 Painting © Gilbert Stuart, 1800/185. Gift of Mrs. Robert Homans. Courtesy of National Portrait Gallery, Smithsonian Institution.

30 Engraving © David Edwin. Courtesy of National Portrait Gallery, Smithsonian Institution.

51 White House Historical Association (White House Collection)

58 *Abraham Lincoln's Last Reception* © Anton Hohenstein. Courtesy of the Library of Congress, LC-DIG-pga-01590.

78 Mark Miller scanned original newspaper, wood block illustration from unknown artist described in the caption as "OUR SPECIAL ARTIST." Public domain, via Wikimedia Commons.

99 Photograph © Underwood & Underwood, 1903. Courtesy of the Library of Congress, LC-DIG-ppmsca-36413.

122 *President Woodrow Wilson, Seated at Desk with His Wife, Edith Bolling Galt, Standing at His Side.* © Harris & Ewing, 1920. Courtesy of Library of Congress, LC-DIG-ppmsca-13425.

139 Photograph © AP Photo

160 Bettman via Getty Images

169 © Sid Avery/mptvimages.com

187 © Robert Knudsen. Courtesy John F. Kennedy Library (LP-JFK).

208 Stan Wayman/The LIFE Picture Collection/Shutterstock

218 Photograph © Richard Nixon Library. Courtesy of National Archives.

234 Photograph by Trikosko, Marion S. Courtesy of Library of Congress, LC-DIG-ppmsca-08458.

237 Photograph © Jimmy Carter Presidential Library, White House Staff Photographer Collection, Image Number: NLC-WHSPC-07284.10016.

251 Photo by Cynthia Johnson via Getty Images

269 Photograph © AP Photo/Barry Thumma, File

277 Photograph © Clinton Digital Library. Bob McNeely and White House Photograph Office.

296 Greg Mathieson/Mai/The Chronicle Collection via Getty Images

313 Saul Loeb/AFP via Getty Images

331 Photograph © Official White House Photo by Joyce N. Boghosian

348 Photograph © AP Photo/Carolyn Kaster

358 Photograph © the Clinton Library

368 Photograph © Courtesy Barack Obama Presidential Library

COLOR INSERT

A NOTE ABOUT THE AUTHOR

ALEX PRUD'HOMME has been a nonfiction writer for thirty years. As a journalist he covered a wide range of subjects for *The New York Times, The New Yorker, Vanity Fair, Talk,* and *Time.* He has written nine books, on subjects ranging from biotech to terrorism, fresh water, and food. Prud'homme is best known for cowriting Julia Child's memoir *My Life in France,* a best seller that inspired half of the film *Julie & Julia.* He lives in Brooklyn, New York, with his family. For more information, please visit www.alexprudhomme.com.

A NOTE ON THE TYPE

This book was set in Minion, a typeface produced by the Adobe Corporation specifically for the Macintosh personal computer and released
in 1990. Designed by Robert Slimbach, Minion combines the classic
characteristics of old-style faces with the full complement of weights
required for modern typesetting.

Composed by North Market Street Graphics,
Lancaster, Pennsylvania

Printed and bound by Berryville Graphics,
Berryville, Virginia

Designed by Cassandra J. Pappas

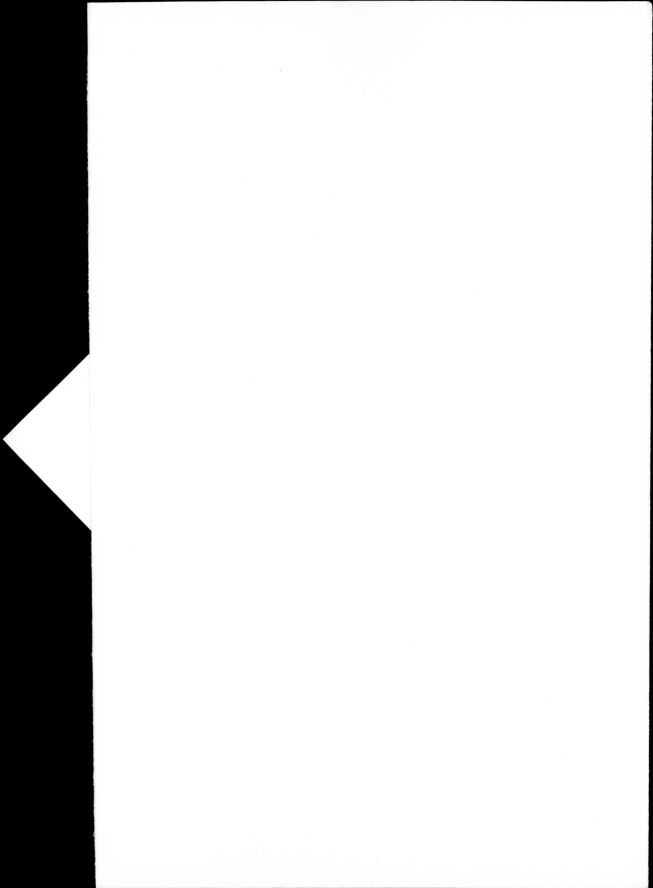

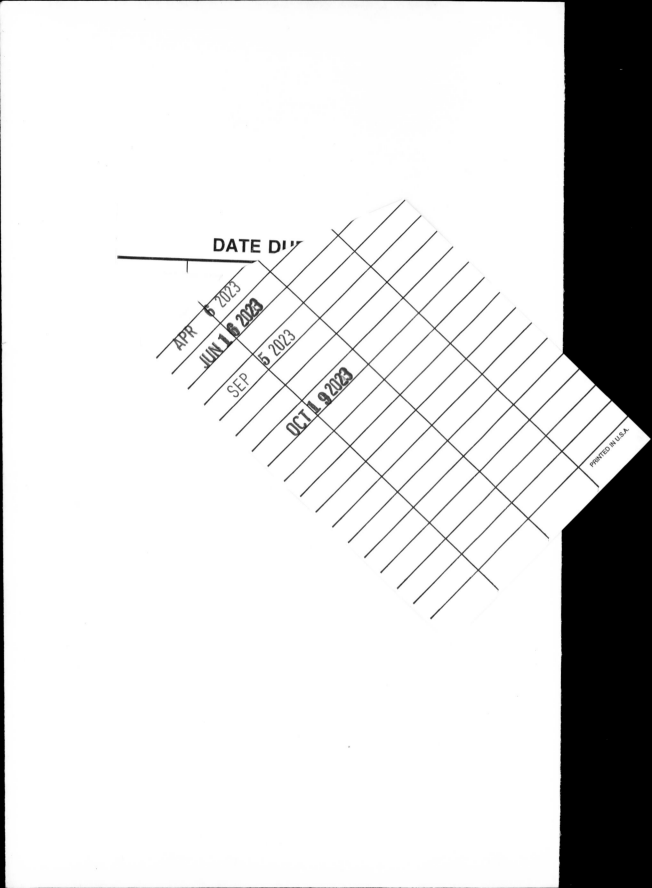

DATE DUE

APR 6 2023

JUN 16 2023

SEP 5 2023

OCT 19 2023

PRINTED IN U.S.A.